ROUTLEDGE HANDI
STRATEGY ANI

This new handbook provides a comprehensive overview of the issues facing naval strategy and security in the twenty-first century.

Featuring contributions from some of the world's premier researchers and practitioners in the field of naval strategy and security, this handbook covers naval security issues in diverse regions of the world, from the Indian Ocean and the Mediterranean to the Arctic and the piracy-prone waters off East Africa's coast. It outlines major policy challenges arising from competing claims, transnational organized crime and maritime terrorism, and details national and alliance reactions to these problems. While this volume provides detailed analyses on operational, judicial, and legislative consequences that contemporary maritime security threats pose, it also places a specific emphasis on naval strategy. With a public very much focused on the softer constabulary roles naval forces play (such as humanitarian assistance, disaster relief, naval diplomacy, maintenance of good order at sea), the overarching hard-power role of navies has been pushed into the background. In fact, navies and seapower have been notably absent from many recent academic discussions and deliberations of maritime security. This handbook provides a much-desired addition to the literature for researchers and analysts in the social sciences on the relationship between security policy and military means on, under, and from the sea. It comprehensively explains the state of naval security in this maritime century and the role of naval forces in it.

This book will be of much interest to students of naval security and naval strategy, security studies and IR, as well as practitioners in the field.

Joachim Krause is Professor of Political Science at the Christian-Albrechts-University of Kiel, Germany, and has published more than 20 books, including, most recently, *Afghanistan, Pakistan and Western Strategy* (Routledge, 2013, co-edited with Charles King Mallory IV).

Sebastian Bruns is Director of the Center for Maritime Strategy and Security at the Institute for Security Policy, University of Kiel (ISPK), Germany.

ROUTLEDGE HANDBOOK OF NAVAL STRATEGY AND SECURITY

Edited by Joachim Krause and Sebastian Bruns

Routledge
Taylor & Francis Group

LONDON AND NEW YORK

First published 2016
by Routledge
2 Park Square, Milton Park, Abingdon, Oxon OX14 4RN

and by Routledge
52 Vanderbilt Avenue, New York, NY 10017

First issued in paperback 2020

Routledge is an imprint of the Taylor & Francis Group, an informa business

British Library Cataloguing in Publication Data
A catalogue record for this book is available from the British Library

Library of Congress Cataloguing in Publication Data
Routledge handbook of naval strategy and security / edited by
Joachim Krause and Sebastian Bruns.
pages cm
Includes bibliographical references and index.
1. Naval strategy–Handbooks, manuals, etc. 2. Sea-power. 3. Naval history, Modern–21st century. I. Krause, Joachim, 1951– editor. II. Bruns, Sebastian, 1982– editor.
V163.R67 2016
359.40973–dc23 2015025489

ISBN 13: 978-0-367-58168-8 (pbk)
ISBN 13: 978-1-138-84093-5 (hbk)

Typeset in Bembo
by Out of House Publishing

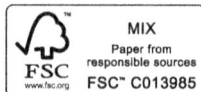

MIX
Paper from
responsible sources
FSC
www.fsc.org   FSC™ C013985

Printed in the United Kingdom
by Henry Ling Limited

CONTENTS

Contents

FIGURES

TABLES

CONTRIBUTORS

Torsten Albrecht, CDR (DEU N), is a professor for maritime defense technology and maritime security at Helmut-Schmidt-University/University of German Armed Forces (Hamburg), as well as assistant Branch Chief for the Security Policy Branch in the Planning Office of the German Armed Forces. He serves in the maritime security section of the Directorate of Politics, MoD, Berlin. Albrecht holds PhDs in maritime and polar atmospheric physics (Freie Universität Berlin/Alfred Wegener Institute for Polar and Marine Research, Department Atmospheric Physics) and in international relations (University of German Armed Forces Munich, Department of International Policy). His academic interests include maritime security policy, maritime operational pictures, and political crises management.

Caitlyn Antrim is Executive Director of the Rule of Law Committee for the Oceans, a committee of experts focused on analysis, education and outreach around issues of the law of the sea. Her speciality is in issues concerning areas of the seas beyond national jurisdiction. Ms Antrim holds the professional degree of Engineer from MIT and is an adjunct professor at the Washington College of Law. In 1982, she served as a Deputy US Representative to the final negotiating session of the UN Conference on the Law of the Sea.

Vasco Becker-Weinberg, Dr. iur. (Hamburg), LL.M (Lisbon), is a professor at the Faculty of Law of the Universidade NOVA de Lisboa and a qualified lawyer at the Portuguese Bar Association. He is the co-coordinator of the LL.M program on "Law and Sea-Economy" and is undertaking post-doctoral studies in public international law at NOVA. He is also a member of CEDIS – Centro de Investigação e Desenvolvimento sobre Direito e Sociedade. He was previously legal advisor to the Portuguese Secretary of the Sea (2013–2015) and a full-time scholar at the International Max Planck Research School for Maritime Affairs at the University of Hamburg (2008–2012). Vasco Becker-Weinberg lectures in several Portuguese and foreign universities and has undertaken extensive research at prominent academic institutions. He has written several works in public international law and the law of the sea and is the author of the recent publications *Joint Development of Offshore Hydrocarbon Deposits in the Law of the Sea* (Springer Verlag: 2014), "Proliferation of weapons of mass destruction and shipping interdiction" (with Guglielmo Verdirame, OUP: 2015), and "Portugal's legal regime on marine spatial planning and management of the national maritime space" (*Marine Policy* vol. 61: 2015).

Tim Benbow is a Senior Lecturer in Defence Studies at King's College London, Joint Services Command and Staff College, UK Defence Academy. He is the Deputy Director of the Corbett Centre for Maritime Policy Studies. His main research areas include maritime strategy; the Royal Navy in the twentieth century; the 'revolution in military affairs' and future warfare; asymmetric warfare; post-1945 warfare; and strategic thought.

Sebastian Bruns recently graduated *magna cum laude* from the University of Kiel with a PhD in Political Science. His dissertation analyses the evolution of US Navy strategy and American sea power 1981–2011. From 2010 to 2011, he was the German Marshall Fund/American Political Science Association Congressional Fellow in Washington, DC, serving Representative Todd Young (Indiana) as military and defence policy aide. His areas of expertise include naval strategy, modern piracy, and German and U.S. foreign policy. He holds an MA in North American Studies (University of Bonn, 2007) and is a member of the German Chief of Navy Staff's expert advisory group on strategy. His most recent projects also include organising the inaugural Kiel Conference (2015), teaching graduate seminars at the University of Kiel (2014–2015), and a steady stream of publications and media appearances.

Brahma Chellaney is Professor of Strategic Studies at the Center for Policy Research, New Delhi. He has held appointments at Harvard University, the Brookings Institution, the Johns Hopkins University's School of Advanced International Studies and the Australian National University. His most recent works include an authoritative study on the profound impact of the growing global freshwater crunch on international peace and security as well as possible ways to mitigate emerging crises.

Anthony H. Cordesman holds the Arleigh A. Burke Chair in Strategy at the Center for Strategic and International Studies, Washington, DC. He has completed a wide variety of studies and books on energy, US strategy and defence plans, lessons of modern war, defence spending and budgeting, NATO modernization, Chinese military power, Middle East security and the recent wars in Iraq and Afghanistan. Cordesman also served in various government positions at the United States Department of State, the Department of Energy and was director of International Staff at NATO.

Ralf Emmers is Associate Dean and Associate Professor at the S. Rajaratnam School of International Studies (RSIS), Nanyang Technological University, Singapore. His main research interests include security studies and IR theory, international institutions in the Asia-Pacific, maritime security and security and international politics of Southeast Asia. He is a graduate of VUB-Vesalius College (Belgium) and earned his MSc and PhD from the London School of Economics.

Lutz Feldt is a retired vice-admiral of the German Navy. His last postings included Inspekteur der Marine (2003–6) and Befehlshaber der Flotte (2000–3). After his retirement, he was President of the German Maritime Institute (2007–12). Since 2013, he has chaired EuroDefense Deutschland and has been involved in several maritime security projects of the European Union since 2009.

Eric Grove is Professor of Naval History and Fellow in Security Studies at Liverpool Hope University. Previously, he was Professor of Naval History and Director of the Centre for International Security and War Studies at the University of Salford and Deputy Head of

Strategic Studies at the Royal Naval College, Dartmouth. Publications include works on British naval policy since World War II, the future of sea power, fleet to fleet encounters and a history of the Royal Navy since 1815. He frequently contributes to radio and television programmes on naval history and the wider security agenda.

Helga Haftendorn is University Professor Emerita at the Free University of Berlin and is currently associated with a number of international Arctic research projects, mainly with Nordic research institutions. Until 2000, she was the director of the Free University's Center for Transnational Foreign and Security Policy.

James R. Holmes is Professor of Strategy at the Naval War College (Newport, Rhode Island). As a former US navy surface warfare officer, he served as an engineering and gunnery officer on board the battleship *Wisconsin* (BB-64) and is a combat veteran of the first Gulf War. He is a graduate of Vanderbilt University (BA, mathematics and German) and earned graduate degrees from the Fletcher School of Law and Diplomacy at Tufts University (MA, LD and PhD, international relations), Providence College (MA, mathematics) and Salve Regina University (MA, international relations).

Xu Hui is a Professor and Deputy Commandant for Academics at the College of Defense Studies, National Defense Studies University of the People's Liberation Army, China. He holds a PhD in Political Science. Academic interests include security aspects of the Asia-Pacific region, Sino-American relations, China's defence and foreign policy and international crisis management. His analysis on Chinese views of international maritime order was supported by **Cao Xianyu**.

Stavros Karlatiras, Commander, Hellenic Navy, is a Staff Officer at the Hellenic Fleet Command (Personnel Branch). From 2011 to 2014, he served as Future Requirements Staff Officer at the Centre of Excellence for Operations in Confined and Shallow Waters (COE CSW) in Kiel, Germany. His previous commands include the Hellenic Fast Patrol Boats Flotilla (Depute Commander), a Fast Patrol Boat (2002) and a Fast Patrol Torpedo Boat (1999) in Greece.

Joachim Krause is Professor for International Relations at the University of Kiel (Germany), a position he has held since 2001. He is also director of the Institute for Security Policy at the University of Kiel (ISPK), the chairman of the German Council on Foreign Relations' scientific council and a member of the executive board at Aspen Institute Germany. Professor Krause previously held positions at the Stiftung Wissenschaft und Politik, the Deutsche Gesellschaft für Auswärtige Politik and the Bologna Center of the Paul H. Nitze School of Advanced International Studies of Johns Hopkins University.

Peter Lehr is Lecturer in Terrorism Studies at the Centre for the Study of Terrorism and Political Violence (CSTPV), University of St Andrews, Scotland/UK. Being a regional specialist on the Indo-Pacific, his teaching and research cover the following areas: maritime safety and security (including piracy and maritime terrorism); political violence and terrorism; and organized crime. He is the editor of *Violence at Sea: Piracy in the Age of Global Terrorism* (New York: Routledge, 2007), and the co-editor (together with Rupert Herbert-Burns and Sam Bateman) of *Lloyd's Maritime Intelligence Unit Handbook of Maritime Security* (Boca Raton: Taylor & Francis, 2009). Currently, he is working on a book manuscript entitled *Like a Parcel of Furies: Piracy from Ancient* *to Modern Times* (Palgrave Macmillan, forthcoming). He earned his PhD (Dr. rer. pol.) from the University of Heidelberg, Germany.

Carlo Masala is Chairholder for International Relations at the University of the German Bundeswehr, Munich and Professor at the Central European University Skalica (Slovakia). He is also a member of the Academic Advisory Board of the NATO Defence College (Rome).

Klaus A. R. Mommsen is a retired captain of the German Navy. A graduate of the German Naval Academy, he became a naval aviator, flying transport aircraft for some ten years. In 1982, he attended the Canadian Forces Command & Staff College (Toronto). His subsequent career saw him mostly employed with military (both naval and joint) intelligence. In 2002, he retired from his final posting as Deputy Chief of Staff (Intelligence) of the German Fleet. As early as 1992, Mommsen started writing for the German naval magazine *MarineForum*, which still lists him as its editor on foreign navies. Subsequently, he has become a renowned German columnist for international naval affairs. He is married and lives in Germany, near Bonn.

Martin N. Murphy is a Senior Research Fellow at the Centre for Foreign Policy Studies at Dalhousie University, Halifax, Canada and Visiting Fellow at the Corbett Centre for Maritime Studies, King's College London. He is the author of several studies of piracy worldwide, in the Gulf of Guinea and off Somalia, including *Contemporary Piracy and Maritime Terrorism, Small Boats, Weak States, Dirty Money* and *Somalia: The New Barbary?* He is currently writing a book on naval warfare in the littorals and engaged in more broadly based research on economic and financial warfare.

Sarandis ('Randy') Papadopoulos is Secretariat Historian of the Department of the Navy. He received his BA in history from the University of Toronto, an MA in military and naval history from the University of Alabama and earned a PhD from the George Washington University (GWU). His publications include articles on the logistics of submarine warfare 1935–45, post-1991 combined naval operations, book reviews, entries in reference works and service as principal co-author of the book *Pentagon 9/11*, published under the auspices of the Historian, Office of the Secretary of Defense. A recipient of the Department of the Navy Superior Civilian Service Award, Papadopoulos is also Region III Coordinator for the Society for Military History.

Diego A. Ruiz Palmer serves on NATO's International Staff, Brussels, Belgium. From 1991 to 2000 and from 2002 to 2012, he held a variety of senior staff positions at NATO Headquarters dealing with armaments planning, crisis management, operations planning and strategic foresight. From 1980 to 1991, he was an analyst conducting research on the NATO–Warsaw Pact balance of forces for the Director of Net Assessment, Office of the Secretary of Defense, US Department of Defense.

Rudolf Roy is currently the Head of the Security Policy Division in the European External Action Service (EEAS), Brussels. In this function he coordinates and manages the EEAS' overall contribution to addressing external security threats to the EU and its partner countries. At the EEAS, he is in charge of the Maritime Security Strategy and the Maritime Security Action Plan. In different functions and positions for over 25 years, Mr Roy was responsible for a wide portfolio of international security-related issues (maritime security, cyber, combating organized crime, police cooperation, counter-terrorism, security research, combating drugs, work with international organizations and third countries).

Alison Lawlor Russell is an assistant professor of Political Science and International Studies at Merrimack College, Massachusetts, and a non-resident research scientist at the Center for Naval Analyses (CNA). She holds a PhD from the Fletcher School of Law and Diplomacy at Tufts University and has been a lecturer at Boston College and Tufts University.

Vijay Sakhuja is Director of National Maritime Foundation, New Delhi. He was previously Director (Research) of the Indian Council of World Affairs, New Delhi. A former naval officer, Sakhuja is author of *Asian Maritime Power in the 21st Century* and has been on the research faculty of a number of think tanks in India.

Nikolaus Scholik studied Political Science at the University of Vienna, Austria. He graduated with the degree of Magister phil. in 2008. His PhD dissertation (2012) covered the geostrategic relevance of maritime choke points. Scholik, who was born in 1945, is a retired colonel (reserve) of the Austrian Army, and his areas of expertise include international politics, security politics and maritime strategy. Before his academic endeavours, he held management positions in international trade from 1967 to 2012.

Peter M. Swartz is a retired US Navy captain and strategist and a principal research scientist at the CNA Corporation (Arlington, Virginia), where he provides research, analyses and recommendations on policy, strategy and operations to US Navy, US Marine Corps and US Coast Guard officials and their staffs. While in the US Navy, he served as an adviser with the Vietnamese Navy during the Vietnam War, as a conceptualizer and drafter of the US Maritime Strategy of the 1980s and as a Special Assistant to the Chairman of the Joint Chiefs of Staff, General Colin Powell, during the Gulf War of 1990–1.

Konstantinos Tsetsos is a research associate at the University of the Bundeswehr, Munich. His research focuses on maritime security, asymmetric conflicts and future studies. He is also lecturer at the University of Central Europe in Skalica and the George C. Marshall Center in Garmisch Partenkirchen.

Brian Wilson, Captain, US Navy (Ret), is the Deputy Director of the Global Maritime Operational Threat Response Coordination Center (US Coast Guard/US Department of Homeland Security) and is a visiting professor at the United States Naval Academy. He previously served in the Pentagon developing maritime security policy, aboard the carrier *Kitty Hawk* (CV-63) and in Antarctica. He also commanded the Region Legal Service Office, Naval District Washington, and was Oceans Policy adviser to the Under Secretary of Defense for Policy.

Toshi Yoshihara holds the John A. van Beuren Chair of Asia-Pacific Studies and is an affiliate member of the China Maritime Studies Institute at the US Naval War College, Newport, Rhode Island. He holds a PhD from the Fletcher School of Law and Diplomacy, Tufts University, an MA from the School of Advanced International Studies, Johns Hopkins University, and a BS from the School of Foreign Service, Georgetown University. He has published widely on China, India and Asian naval strategies.

ACRONYMS AND ABBREVIATIONS

1988 SUA Convention	The 1988 Convention for the Suppression of Unlawful Acts against the Safety of Maritime Navigation and Protocol
3C+I	Communications, Command, Control, and Intelligence
A2/AD	Anti-Access/Area Denial
ABOT	Al Basra Oil Terminal
AC	Arctic Council
AC&W	Aircraft Control and Warning
ACS	Aegis Combat System
ADMM	ASEAN Defence Ministers Meeting
ADF	Australian Defence Force
ADIZ	Air Defence Identification Zone
ADM	Admiral
AEA	Airborne Electronic Attack
AEPS	Arctic Environmental Protection Strategy
AFSB	Afloat Forward Staging Base
AI	Artificial Intelligence
AIP	Air-Independent Propulsion
AIS	Automatic Identification System
AJP	Allied Joint Publication
AMAP	Arctic Monitoring and Assessment Program
AMC	Air Mobility Command
AMISOM	African Union Mission in Somalia
ANWR	Arctic National Wildlife Refuge
AOO	Area of Operations
APEC	Asia-Pacific Economic Cooperation
APS	African Partnership Station
APSC	Asia Pacific Submarine Conference
APT	Advanced Persistent Threat
AQAP	Al Qaeda in the Arabian Peninsula
AQI	Al Qaeda in Iraq

AQIS	Al Qaeda in the Indian Subcontinent
ARF	ASEAN Regional Forum
ARG	Amphibious Ready Group
AS	Submarine Tender
ASB	Air–Sea Battle
ASBM	Anti-Ship Ballistic Missile
ASCEL	Active Strategic Counterattack on Exterior Lines
ASCM	Anti-Ship Cruise Missile
ASEAN	Association of Southeast Asian Nations
ASG	Abu Sayyaf Group
AShM	Anti-Ship Missile
ASUW	Anti-Surface Warfare
ASW	Anti-Submarine Warfare
ATALANTA	European Union Naval Operation (since 2008)
AUSCANZUKUS	Australia, Canada, New Zealand, United Kingdom, United States
AWACS	Airborne Warning and Control System
BAE	British Aerospace/Marconi Electronic Systems
BALTOPS	Baltic Operations
Bbl/d	Barrels per day
BENELUX	Belgium–Netherlands–Luxembourg Military Cooperation
BLUEMASSMED	Blue Maritime Surveillance System Mediterranean
BMD	Ballistic Missile Defence
BMP	Best Management Practices
BOE	Barrels of Oil Equivalent
BRICS	Brazil, Russia, India, China, and South Africa
C2	Command & Control
C4ISR	Command, Control, Communication, Computer, Intelligence, Surveillance, and Reconnaissance
CAFF	Conservation of Arctic Flora and Fauna
CAPT	Captain
CARAT	Cooperation Afloat Readiness and Training (Exercise)
CBM	Confidence-Building Measures
CBO	Congressional Budget Office
CBRN	Chemical, Biological, Radiological, Nuclear Weaponry
CCS	Convention on the Continental Shelf
CDR	Commander
CDRE	Commodore
CDS	Chief of Defence Staff
CEC	Cooperative Engagement Capability
CeCLAD-M	Centre de Coordination de la Lutte Anti-drogue en Méditerranée (Mediterranean area anti-drug enforcement coordination centre)
CENTRIXS	Combined Enterprise Regional Information Exchange System
CEPP	Carrier-Enabled Power Projection
CFSP	Common Foreign Security Policy
CG	Cruiser, Guided Missile
CGPCS	Contact Group on Piracy off the Coast of Somalia
CHENS	Chiefs of the European Navies
CINCHAN	Allied Commander-in-Chief, Channel

CINCSOUTH	Commander-in-Chief, Allied Forces, Southern Europe
CISE	Common Information Sharing Environment
CJTF	Combined Joint Task Force
CLCS	Commission on the Limits of the Continental Shelf
CLF	Combat Logistics Force
CLO	Community Liaison Officer
CMF	Combined Maritime Forces
CNO	Chief of Naval Operations
CNOOC	China National Offshore Oil Corporation
COA	Course(s) of Action
COD	Carrier On-Board Delivery
COIN	Counterinsurgency
CONMAROPS	Concept of Maritime Operations
CONUS	Continental United States
COSMAR	Cape Verde National Maritime Security Operations Center
CPC	Communist Party of China
CRIMARIO	Critical Maritime Routes Indian Ocean
CRIMGO	Critical Maritime Routes Gulf of Guinea
CRS	Congressional Research Service
CS	Continental Shelf
CS21	A Cooperative Strategy for Twenty-First-Century Seapower
CSBA	Center for Strategic and Budgetary Assessments
CSCAP	Council for Security Cooperation in the Asia-Pacific
CSDP	Common Security and Defence Policy
CSG	Carrier Strike Group
CSIS	Center for Strategic and International Studies
CSS	Center for Security Studies
CSW	Confined and Shallow Waters
CTF	Combined (or Coalition) Task Force
CUES	Code for Unplanned Encounters at Sea
CVF	Aircraft Carrier, Future
CVN	Carrier Vessel, Nuclear
CVS	Aircraft Carrier, conventionally powered (ASW)
CVW	Carrier Vessel Air Wing
CWC	Composite Warfare Concept
DC	District of Columbia
DCNS	Direction des Constructions Navales (French armaments group)
DDG	Destroyer, Guided Missile
DDOS	Distributed Denial of Service
DHS	Department of Homeland Security
DNS	Domain Name Server
DOD	Department of Defense (U.S.)
DON	Department of the (U.S.) Navy
DOTMLPFI	Doctrine, Organization, Training, Material, Leadership, Personnel, Facilities, Interoperability
DSG	Defense Strategic Guidance
DTVIA	Drug Trafficking Vessel Interdiction Act
EAS	East-Asia Summit

ECCM	Electronic Counter-Countermeasures
ECM	Electronic Countermeasures
EDA	European Defence Agency
EDF	European Development Fund
EEAS	European External Action Service
EEZ	Exclusive Economic Zone
EIA	Energy Information Administration
ELINT	Electronic Intelligence
EM	Electromagnetic Spectrum
EMCDDA	European Monitoring Centre for Drugs and Drug Addictions
EPAA	European Phased Adaptive Approach
EPPR	Emergency Prevention, Preparedness, and Response
ESG	Expeditionary Strike Group
ESS	European Security Strategy
ESSM	Evolved Sea Sparrow Missile
EU	European Union
EUCAP	European Union's capacity-building effort in the Horn of Africa and the Western Indian Ocean
EUMSS	European Union Maritime Security Strategy
EUNAVFOR	European Union Naval Force
EUROMARFOR	European Maritime Force
EUROSUR	European Border Surveillance System
EUTM	European Union Training Mission
EW	Electronic Warfare
FAO	Food and Agriculture Organization
FCO	Foreign and Commonwealth Office
FFG	Frigate, Guided Missile
FGN	Federal German Navy
FRONTEX	European Union External Borders Agency
FRUKUS	France, Russia, United Kingdom, and United States
FY	Fiscal Year
GAO	Government Accountability Office
GCC	Gulf Cooperation Council
GDP	Gross Domestic Product
GEOINT	Geospatial Intelligence
GIUK	Greenland–Iceland–United Kingdom (gap)
GMCC	Global MOTR Coordination Centre
GO	Governmental Organization
GVS	Geospatial Intelligence Visualization Service
HAWK	Homing All the Way Killer
HDRU	Hazardous Devices Response Unit
HELCOM	Baltic Marine Environment Protection Commission
HUMINT	Human Intelligence
IASSA	International Arctic Science Committee
IBM	International Business Machines Corporation
ICBM	Intercontinental Ballistic Missile
ICEX	Ice Exercise
ICJ	International Court of Justice

IcSP	Instrument contributing to Stability and Peace
IED	Improvised Explosive Device
IEO	International Energy Outlook
IFS	Institutt for Forsvarsstudier
IISS	International Institute for Strategic Studies
ILOMO	International Law of Military Operations
IMB	International Maritime Bureau
IMO	International Maritime Organization
IMP	Integrated Maritime Policy
INCSEA	Incidents at Sea
INTERPOL	International Criminal Police Organization
IO	Information Operations
IRGC	Iranian Revolutionary Guard Corps
IRGCN	Iranian Revolutionary Guard Corps, Navy
IRIAF	Islamic Republic of Iran Air Force
IRIN	Islamic Republic of Iran Navy
IRTC	Internationally Recognized Transit Corridor
IS	Islamic State
ISA	International Seabed Authority
ISAF	International Security Assistance Force
ISMERLO	International Submarine Escape and Rescue Liaison Office
ISPK	Institute for Security Policy University of Kiel
ISPS	International Ship and Port Facilities Security (Code)
ISPSW	Institut für Strategie-, Politik-, Sicherheits- und Wirtschaftsberatung
ISR	Intelligence, Surveillance, and Reconnaissance
ISS	The EU Internal Security Strategy
ISS	International Seapower Symposium
ITLOS	International Tribunal for the Law of the Sea
IUU/IUUF	Illegal, Unreported and Unregulated Fishing
IW	Information Warfare
JCG	Japanese Coast Guard
JCS	Joint Chiefs of Staff
JFACC	Joint Force Air Component Commander
JFQ	*Joint Force Quarterly*
JHSV	Joint High-Speed Vessel
JLOTS	Joint Logistics Over The Shore
JMSDF	Japanese Maritime Self-Defence Force
JOAC	Joint Operational Access Concept
JOE	Joint Operating Environment
JSF	Joint Strike Fighter
JSTARS	Joint Surveillance and Target Attack Radar System
KAAOT	Khor al-Amaya Oil Terminal
LCDR	Lieutenant Commander
LCS	Littoral Combat Ship
LDP	Liberal Democratic Party
LHD	Landing Helicopter Dock (Multi-Purpose Amphibious Assault Ship)
LMSR	Large Medium-Speed Roll-On/Roll-Off Ship
LNG	Liquefied Natural Gas

LoS	Law of the Sea
LPD	Landing Platform, Dock (Amphibious Assault Ship)
LPH	Amphibious Assault Ship, Helicopter
LRID	Long-Range Identification and Tracking
LSD	Landing Ship, Dock
LSL	Landing Ship, Logistic
LTG	Lieutenant General
MAB	Military Advisory Board
MAGTF	Marine Air-Ground Task Force
MAOC	Maritime Analysis and Operations Centre
MAOC-N	Maritime Analysis and Operations Centre – Narcotics
MARCOM	Allied Maritime Command
MARSIC	Enhancing Maritime Security and Safety through Information-Sharing and Capacity-Building
MARSUNO	Maritime Surveillance North
MASE	Maritime Security Program
MCM	Mine Countermeasures
MDA	Maritime Domain Awareness
MEKO	Mehrzweck-Kombination (multipurpose combination)
MERCOSUR	Mercado Comùn del Sur (Southern Common Market)
MERP	Maritime Emergence Response Protocol
MEU	Marine Expeditionary Unit
MHPC	Mine Countermeasures and Hydrography Capability
MILF	Moro Islamic Liberation Front
MIRV	Multiple Independently Targetable Re-entry Vehicle
MLP	Mobile Landing Platform
MMCA	Maritime Military Consultative Agreement
MOC	Maritime Operations Centre
MODU	Mobile Offshore Drilling Unit(s)
MOIS	Ministry of Intelligence and Security (Iran)
MOTR	Maritime Operational Threat Response
MPA	Maritime Patrol Aircraft
MPS	Maritime Prepositioning Ship
MPSA	Maritime Patrol and Surveillance Aircraft
MRV	Multiple/Missile Re-entry Vehicle
MS	Member State
MSA	Maritime Situational Awareness
MSC	Military Sealift Command
MSCHOA	Maritime Security Centre Horn of Africa
MSDF	Maritime Self Defence Force
MSIP	Multi-Stage Improvement Program
MSO	Maritime Security Operations
MSPA	Maritime Security Patrol Area
MSSIS	Maritime Safety and Security Information System
MT	Military Tasks
MTF	Maritime Task Force
MTPY	Metric Tons Per Year
M/V	Motor Vessel *or* Merchant Vessel

NASA	National Aeronautics and Space Administration
NASIC	National Air and Space Intelligence Center
NATO	North Atlantic Treaty Organization
NAVCEN	United States Naval Forces Central Command
NAVEUR	United States Naval Forces Europe
NC	Nordic Council
NCIS	Naval Criminal Investigative Service
NDAA	National Defense Authorization Act
NDP	Naval Doctrine Publication
NDRF	National Defense Reserve Fleet
NDU	National Defense University
NEA	Naval Engagement Activities
NECC	Naval Expeditionary Combat Command
NEO	Non-Combatant Evacuation Operation
NGO	Non-Governmental Organization
NIEM	National Information Exchange Model
nm	nautical mile
NMIOTC	NATO Maritime Interdiction Operational Training Centre
NOAA	National Oceanographic and Atmospheric Administration
NOC	Naval Operations Concept
NSFS	Naval Surface Fire Support
NSW	Northern Seaway
NSWC	Naval Special Warfare Command
NTG	Naval Task Group
NVR	Naval Vessel Register
NWP	Northwest Passage
OAE	Operation Active Endeavour
OCT	Overseas Countries' Territory
OEF	Operation Enduring Freedom
OHQ	Operational Headquarters
OIF	Operation Iraqi Freedom
OPEC	Organization of the Petroleum Exporting Countries
OPSEC	Operations Security
OPV	Offshore Patrol Vessel
OSPAR	The Convention for the Protection of the Marine Environment of the North-East Atlantic
PACOM	United States Pacific Command
PAG	Pirate Action Group
PAME	Protection of the Arctic Marine Environment
PANAMAX	Panama Canal military exercise
PC	Patrol Coastal
PCASP	Privately Contracted Armed Security Personnel
PhD	Doctor of Philosophy
PHIBLEX	US–Philippines Amphibious Landing Exercise
PIJ	Palestinian Islamic Jihad
PLAAF	People's Liberation Army Air Force
PLAG	People's Liberation Army Ground Force
PLAN	People's Liberation Army Navy

PM	Prime Minister
PMSC	Private Military and Security Companies
PNS	Pakistan Navy Ship
PPBE	Planning, Programming, Budgeting, Execution
PRC	People's Republic of China
PSI	Proliferation Security Initiative
PSYOPS	Psychological Operations
RADM	Rear Admiral
RAF	Royal Air Force (UK)
RCN	Royal Canadian Navy
RDML	Rear Admiral (lower half)
Ret	Retired
RFF	Request For Force
RIMPAC	Ring of the Pacific (exercise)
RMB	Renminbi
RMP	Recognized Maritime Picture
RN	Royal Navy (UK)
ROC	Republic of China
ROE	Rules of Engagement
ROK	Republic of Korea
RO/RO	Roll-On/Roll-Off
RPAS	Remotely Piloted Aircraft Systems
RPG	Rocket-Propelled Grenade
RUSI	Royal United Services Institute
SACEUR	Supreme Allied Commander, Europe
SACLANT	Supreme Allied Commander, Atlantic
SAG	Surface Action Group
SAO	Senior Arctic Officials
SAR	Search and Rescue
SDF	Self-Defence Forces (Japan)
SDR	Strategic Defence Review
SDSR	Strategic Defence and Security Review
SDWG	Sustainable Development Working Group
SDV	Swimmer (SEAL) Delivery Vehicle
SEACAT	Southeast Asia Cooperation Against Terrorism (exercise)
SEACOP	Seapower Cooperation Project
SEAL	Sea Air Land (naval special warfare designation)
SEANWFZ	South East Asian Nuclear Weapon Free Zone
SHADE	Shared Awareness and Deconfliction
SIGINT	Signal Intelligence
SILO	Single Integrated Lookout
SIOFA	Southern Indian Ocean Fisheries Agreement
SLBM	Submarine-Launched Ballistic Missile
SLOC	Sea Line(s) of Communication
SMERG	Submarine Escape and Rescue Working Group
SNMCMG	Standing NATO Mine Counter-Measures Group
SNMG	Standing NATO Maritime Group
SOC	Special Operations Craft

SOLAS	Convention on Safety of Life at Sea
SPMAGTF	Special Marine Air Ground Task Force
SPS	Southern Partnership Station
SSBN	Nuclear-Powered Ballistic Missile Submarine
SSC	Small Surface Combatant
SSGN	Nuclear-Powered Cruise Missile Submarine
SSK	Ship Submersible, Killer
SSN	Ship Submersible, Nuclear
STANAVFORLANT	Standing Naval Force, Atlantic
STOL	Short Take-Off and Landing
STOVL	Short Take-Off, Vertical Landing
STRIKFLTLANT	Striking Fleet, Atlantic
STRIKFORNATO	Naval Striking and Support Forces, NATO
SWCC	Special Warfare Combatant Craft
SWP	Stiftung Wissenschaft und Politik
SUA	Convention on the Suppression of Unlawful Acts
SUCBAS	Sea Surveillance Co-Operation Baltic Sea
TAC	Treaty of Amity and Cooperation
T-AKE	Dry Cargo/Ammunition Ship
T-AOE	Fleet Replenishment Oiler
TAR	Tibet Autonomous Region
TFG	Transitional Federal Government
TLAM	Tomahawk Land-Attack Missile
TNT	Trinitrotoluene
TRA	Taiwan Relations Act
TRADE	Training Awareness and Deconfliction
TTP	Thereek e-Taliban Pakistan
UA	University of the Arctic
UAE	United Arab Emirates
UAS	Unmanned Air Systems
UAV	Unmanned Aerial Vehicle
UCAV	Unmanned Combat Aerial Vehicle
UCLASS	Unmanned Carrier-Launched Airborne Surveillance and Strike
UK	United Kingdom (of Great Britain and Northern Ireland)
UKMTO	UK Maritime Trade Organization
UKNLAF	United Kingdom–Netherlands Amphibious Force
UN	United Nations
UNCLOS	United Nations Convention on the Law of the Sea
UNEP	United Nations Environment Programme
UNIFIL	United Nations Interim Force in Lebanon
UNODC	United Nations Office on Drugs and Crime
UNSC	United Nations Security Council
UNSCR	United Nations Security Council Resolution
USA	United States Army
USAF	United States Air Force
USCG	United States Coast Guard
USMC	United States Marine Corps
USN	United States Navy

USS	United States Ship
USSOCOM	United States Special Operations Command
USSR	Union of Soviet Socialist Republics
UUV	Unmanned Underwater Vehicle
VADM	Vice Admiral
VBSS	Visit, Board, Search and Seizure
VPD	Vessel Protection Detachments
WBIED	Water-Borne Improvised Explosive Device
WEU	Western European Union
WFP	World Food Programme
WGA	Whole-of-Government Approach
WHO	World Health Organization
WMD	Weapons of Mass Destruction
WPNS	Western Pacific Naval Symposium
WTO	World Trade Organization

PART I

Context and concepts

1

INTRODUCTION

The changing face of twenty-first-century naval strategy and maritime security

Joachim Krause and Sebastian Bruns

Historically, there are three established uses of the sea for political purposes. The military use of the sea includes power projection and sea control; the diplomatic use includes gunboat diplomacy as well as showing of the flag; the constabulary function, finally, includes peace-keeping and broader maritime security.[1] In the age of globalization, the use of the sea is also of significant economic value. In fact, to guard the very system that is behind globalization, naval strategy and security play a vital role. The relationship of economic prosperity and naval strategy is hardly something new or unique to the twenty-first century.

From Mahan to maritime security order

For more than a century, the theoretical writings of Alfred Thayer Mahan have shaped the strategic thinking about maritime security. His thoughts about naval strategy reflected an Anglo-Saxon understanding of the relevance of maritime power at a time of great strategic uncertainty. His thoughts were developed studying historical developments during the seventeenth and eighteenth centuries with particular reference to Great Britain and the relevance of sea power for its rise to a global power status. He was arguing that sea power was a central strategic asset for any great military power and that controlling the sea was in the long run more important than land warfare.[2] His book has shaped U.S. naval thinking well into the twentieth century. He was already a modern strategic thinker in that he was not only looking at naval military in an isolated fashion. Sea power was for him a precondition for liberal market economies to secure access to overseas markets.[3] Contrary to often-encountered thinking, Mahan has a striking relevance for the twenty-first century as well. After all, sea power continues to be an integral part of many a state's reason – but world politics needs sea control. Mahan's notion that control of sea lines of communication should and could never be absolute, but relative, has lost little of its relevance given the rise of new ambitious maritime powers. Mahan was a navalist, but he also appreciated more differentiated views towards the decisiveness of naval force on the maritime spectrum. In this light, naval forces are considered and employed as inherently flexible, mobile, and scalable – and thus serve to support the ends of security policy in ways that civilian diplomacy, armies, air forces (which Mahan could not fathom at the time of his writings), and other means cannot. However, it is a matter of statecraft to combine these tools accordingly to achieve the best possible outcome, i.e. attain grand strategy objectives. In the twenty-first century, navies do indeed still serve to guard trade, but not exclusively to destroy foreign commerce (save for exceptional circumstances) as Mahan's followers would often emphasize. Mahan's writings came at a time of a changing world, and a search for the United States' place in it. It was a time of technological change, and of the rise of Asia to become a focal point of world politics – much like today, all things considered.

For Mahan, three things were important: (1) a big merchant navy, which was necessary to connect the American market with markets all around the world; (2) an American navy which was able to protect the sea lines of communication by deterring (or if necessary destroying) rival fleets; and (3) a network of naval bases. The U.S. naval strategy of the nineteenth and well into the twentieth century fit this description.[4] Without such a concept and its realization, the globalization of markets and the incredible growth of international economic activities during the past six decades would likely not have happened. By the same token, without U.S. naval supremacy, the globalized and interdependent world of today would never have happened. It is one of the salient features of international politics of the past six decades that under the liberal hegemony of the United States an international liberal order emerged that has no parallels in modern history.[5] This liberal hegemony is built upon a naval supremacy that emerged during World War II, which continued to exist during the Cold War, and which was further developed during the past 25 years. Without it, our world would look totally different.[6]

The use of naval force and broader maritime security policy in the twenty-first century rests on established naval missions (sea control, power projection, maritime presence, and strategic deterrence), and a naval strategic culture which governs the utility of naval force. The multidimensionality of the operating environment, the utter dependence on technology, the physical texture of the world, maritime choke points, geographical position, resources, climate, area, people, and character of a state all play into how maritime power is applied, and which objectives a political ways–ends–means causal relationship for a given state should attain.

Today there is a growing awareness that this liberal hegemony is losing its cohesion and its strength. There are two major developments responsible for this: (1) the global hegemony of the United States is slowly dwindling with the emergence of China and other aspiring powers, which put U.S. leadership in question, be it on land or on the sea; (2) the nature of maritime challenges is changing and, hence, the instruments through which these challenges will have to be addressed. It is the intention of this handbook to provide the reader with an understanding of the nature of these changes and to begin to develop analytical tools upon which policy recommendations can be developed. It has four main parts:

- Part I deals with context and concepts, the maritime order, and the shifting balance of power;
- Part II lists some choke points and strategic areas of interest;
- Part III deals with doctrinal and technological issues on the naval agenda; and finally,
- Part IV provides actor perspectives and policy options.

The global maritime order and the shifting balance of power

The single most important factor shaping the international maritime order, and hence the global order itself, will be the shift in the maritime balance of power. The rise of new great powers and the relative decline of American military and naval power are already taking place. In the theoretical literature the relative decline of U.S. hegemony has been tackled for many years. Surprisingly, very few authors point to the naval dimension, most write about polarity, about historically proven laws regarding the rise and fall of empires, or about the relevance of emerging economic, societal, and technological trends.[7] This book takes up the naval dimension: what is the nature of the shift in naval military balance and from which point on could such a shift translate into tangible political changes that will have consequences for the international order?

For the time being, American naval supremacy is unparalleled in the world; however, there are trends that suggest a weakening of this supremacy:

- The most relevant one is the rise of China as an economic, political, and military power and the subsequent naval build-up.
- There are other rising powers such as India and Brazil, which might also be tempted to invest in a naval military build-up by which U.S. supremacy will be affected. NATO allies and partners (such as Japan and Australia) are equally looking at how to modernize (and in many parts expand) their naval forces to address twenty-first-century security and defense needs.
- Russia and Iran are examples of rentier states ruled by authoritarian political elites, who build their domestic political legitimization upon their declared enmity towards the U.S. as well as the West in general. Both Teheran and Moscow attempt to defy the U.S. in the naval area, either by investing in asymmetric naval warfare (Iran) or in trying to establish naval superiority in the Black Sea and the Baltic Sea.

The most relevant development is the evolving naval military competition between the U.S. and China. This subject has been raised in the scholarly literature during the past few years and there are a growing number of authors who claim that escalation risks are there that cannot be ignored.[8] A similar debate has also been held within the U.S. Department of Defense since the 1990s and has brought about a new doctrinal concept – the air–sea battle.[9]

At the core of this debate is the notion of anti-access/area denial (A2/AD). Anti-access strategies (by China) have the aim of preventing forces of a certain state (the U.S.) from entering into a theatre of operations, be it on land, in air space, or in a maritime area. It is what the Chinese call active strategic counterattack on exterior lines (ASCEL).[10] Area denial operations aim to prevent the freedom of action of (mainly) U.S. forces in the more narrow confines of a land or sea area.[11] Since the late 1990s, the U.S. armed forces have increasingly grown concerned about the emergence of Chinese maritime A2/AD capabilities in East Asia. The A2 threat is mainly brought about by the Chinese deployment of reconnaissance-strike complexes that allow American fixed installations in the region to be put under a threat (and also U.S. naval ships, in particular carrier groups). China has acquired these capabilities by investing in modern satellite as well as anti-satellite and missile technology and by improving its submarine technology. China is meanwhile on the verge of threatening U.S. naval bases and ships within a range of more than 1,500 miles off the Chinese coastline with quite effective kinetic strikes. The AD threat is more of a short-range nature. It involves improved capabilities of the Chinese Air Force to attack naval ships of the U.S. with modern precision ammunition, to use integrated air-defense capabilities, to employ intelligent mines and ship- and submarine-borne missiles to target manoeuvre forces.[12] The Chinese People's Liberation Army (PLA) was able to acquire these capabilities by making huge investments in modern technology, hence emulating the modernization process that U.S. forces started 30 years ago. Meanwhile, the PLA operates in the air, on the water and under water, on land, in outer space, and in cyberspace.

To a certain degree, the modernization of the PLA in its acquisition of A2/AD capabilities reflects a defensive strategy, as China is trying to fend off the presence of (mainly naval) U.S. forces in what China considers its near abroad. However, given the regional context within which this modernization is taking place, its overall strategic direction is offensive as it is part of an attempt towards forceful enlargement of Chinese maritime territory – in the case of the South China Sea this is clearly in violation of the Law of the Sea Convention.

Most of the states that have disputes with China over maritime areas are, in the meanwhile, also undertaking efforts to acquire their own A2/AD capabilities, on a much more limited scale, however.

Most observers point to the fact that the Chinese posture of A2/AD encompasses not only modern aircraft, submarines, ballistic and cruise missiles, fast attack boats, high-tech frigates and corvettes, but that China is placing an extremely high value on cyberspace, information warfare, and anti-satellite warfare.[13] This combination of modernization and force multipliers entails the risk of incentives for first strikes. For the time being, most observers agree that a direct confrontation between the U.S. and China remains unlikely,[14] but this might change. In a not-too-distant future, the Chinese A2/AD capabilities might allow for a decisive blow against the U.S. military presence in East Asia, or at least they could create the perception on the part of the Chinese leadership that this was a real option available to them. Some observers see the possibility that within the next decade the PLA might be able to inflict significant damage to all fixed installations that the U.S. is using to sustain its military forces in the region.[15] It might, by the same token, be in a position to blind the main instruments of strategic intelligence and reconnaissance in the area and sink U.S. naval ships, including aircraft carriers, within a 1,500-mile range off the Chinese coast. Taken together, this might result in some kind of "Pearl Harbor" option, by which the Chinese military might be tempted to destroy most U.S. military assets in the region by a multitude of coordinated strikes.[16]

How realistic this risk actually is, is hard to determine. Primarily, it depends on the overall assessment of the international situation by the Chinese leadership, an equation in which economic interdependence surely plays a crucial role, but where economic aspects could become secondary in nature if the possibility of achieving a major, decisive strategic gain is given (as for instance the possibility to radically shift the balance of forces in East Asia at a stroke). It also depends upon the possibility that China would have a decisive edge in critical technological areas. This is difficult to predict, but in the field of cyber war and information war, major breakthroughs by one side are always a possibility.[17] It also depends on the nature of the Chinese military doctrine. Everything that is known about the Chinese ASCEL doctrine so far points to a preference for striking first, striking deep, and hitting an enemy hard.[18] A doctrine is not a strategy, but strategies often follow doctrinal prescriptions. At the very least, the U.S. will be faced with the choice either to withdraw its military assets from the region China claims as its legitimate defense perimeter, or to stay there and cope with the risk of being subjected to a disarming strike.[19]

But there is also the nuclear element involved, which makes the whole equation more complicated.[20] The United States is currently superior to China in the field of strategic nuclear arms and might consider the use of nuclear weapons as appropriate if China really had the nerve to more or less completely destroy the U.S. military and naval presence within a corridor of 1,500 miles off the Chinese coast within hours. However, the main factor is the perception of the leadership in Beijing with regard to the readiness of the U.S. to respond massively to such a pre-emptive strike. Even the Japanese High Command in 1941 knew that the pre-emptive strike against the U.S. Navy in Pearl Harbor could end in a massive war effort by the U.S. However, they misjudged the American response, because they thought that the U.S. was weak and undecided and on the road towards decline. Nuclear superiority might convince the Chinese leadership at this time that such a strike might backfire, but no one knows how the nuclear equation might have changed ten years from now. If China has a credible strategic nuclear deterrence capability against the U.S., a nuclear response by the U.S. to a non-nuclear Pearl Harbor-like strike might become less likely.

The debate on the Chinese–American naval competition is open and its outcome is hard to predict. In terms of international order, this development is crucial. Its outcome will determine whether the current regional order in East Asia, which is cooperative, based on the sovereignty of states, and by and large peaceful, will be taken over by an order which is more to the liking of the leadership in Beijing, i.e. rather one of different degrees of sovereignty, with most smaller states facing the status of suzerainty.

Of course, this matter is just one facet of strategy, or what many would characterize as the art and science of "control." The questions one needs to answer remain the same in this recent matter as well as in all other perspectives that this book offers in terms of naval strategy and maritime security: What should be controlled? To which end? From when? Until when? And how?

Origin and scope of the book

This book has its roots in an international conference which was held in Berlin October 23–25, 2013. The symposium brought more than 70 experts (among them senior policy-makers, historians, political scientists, active and retired military officers, strategy analysts, policy advisors, and representatives from the defense industry) from three continents to the German capital to discuss current issues of maritime security pertaining to Europe, North America, and Asia. The event, organized by the Aspen Institute Germany under the umbrella of its European Strategy Forum series, was generously supported by the Robert Bosch Foundation (Stuttgart) and arranged in cooperation with the German Maritime Institute (Bonn), the Universität der Bundeswehr (Munich), the Gesellschaft für Sicherheitspolitik und Rüstungskontrolle (Kiel), Lampe & Schwartze Marine Underwriting (Bremen), and Cassidian (Unterschleißheim).

The conference displayed the vast number of maritime security challenges pertaining to national and alliance defense as well as to safeguarding the global commons. Whereas piracy and maritime terrorism had been some of the more high-profile maritime security challenges at the time, the discussions during and between the sessions underscored that failing states, organized maritime crime, aspirations for regional hegemony, naval arms races, quests for marine resources and access to maritime routes and markets, potential for closure of choke points, and new risks in the cyber and space domains could also undermine the maritime security order.

Many of these challenges are hardly new to navies and security policy-makers alike, but many of them go beyond the traditional roles and functions of naval forces as envisaged by naval strategists of the twentieth century. Since the end of the Cold War, a trend to empha-size the softer missions of naval forces, such as humanitarian aid, disaster relief, maritime security operations, and diplomacy, over seemingly harder missions like amphibious land-ings, expeditionary operations, naval gunfire support, or conventional/nuclear deterrence, has shifted the balance for many Western navies. At the same time, states are increasingly looking to their navies to address contemporary risks such as those mentioned above; not least because of the dynamics of globalization, an integrated system of exchanging goods and services which rests decisively on functioning maritime trade and unimpeded con-tainerized shipping by sea. Concurrently, naval forces – given reliable doctrine and a reser-voir of functioning maritime strategic thought and resources – have an increasing political and military value in international security: Given the geographic, legalistic, geopolitical, technological, and operational opportunities of naval force in the global environment, they truly can be the "Swiss Army knife" for states willing to invest in and utilize naval assets for anything from diplomacy and show-of-force at the low end to extended deterrence, expeditionary operations, amphibious operations, and naval fire support at the high end. In Europe and North America, where a growing uneasiness towards extended nation-building or counterinsurgency campaigns involving tens of thousands (and often more) of soldiers can be observed, this proves to be interesting given the sustained trends of shrinking defense budgets and declining ship numbers.

As we set out to edit the papers presented at the 2013 conference as a book, we realized that there was much more to be said with regard to naval strategy and security than could be covered in a three-day conference. We strongly felt that there is a marked absence of written analyses on naval matters. Thus, we decided to complement the proceedings of the conference with essays by more authors covering additional fields of interest.

While the rise of piracy off the Horn of Africa had generated enormous interest in the policy and academic worlds, few analyses covered broader geopolitical and naval strategic aspects of our age. Geoff Till's excellent standard work *Seapower: A Guide for the 21st Century*, now in its third edition (2013), remains one of the few lighthouse projects that explained the opportunities and limitations of contemporary naval power and the subsequent implications for strategic thinkers and practitioners. Therefore, we developed the idea of a producing a comprehensive handbook to reflect the current state of research, offer guidance on contexts and concepts, and present selected choke points and key maritime focus areas. In addition, this volume also looks at doctrinal and technological issues on the naval agenda, and for the first time brings together actor perspectives and policy options. The book should thus provide thought-provoking impulses for everyone interested in aspects of contemporary naval strategy and security. We also hope that it informs and motivates younger colleagues to take up the study and analysis of naval strategic matters, which both the policy and the academic world so desperately need.

Little did we anticipate the events around the Russian–Ukraine war and the rise of the self-titled Islamic State in Syria and Iraq from 2014, which are but two landmark geopolitical developments that have upended many of the convictions some of us have held dear for very long. While these events have partially informed the design and orchestration of the manuscript, a handbook dealing with very recent developments can only go so far. It should thus not be construed as a cover-it-all work with unchangeable truths, but rather as a one-stop resource designed to display the vast spectrum of naval issues on the current international security agenda in the second decade of the twenty-first century.

We cordially invite you to use these chapters for opinion-forming, teaching, dissemination, policy prescriptions, and analysis. By all means, we look forward to your criticism about issues contained in – or even omitted from – this book. Here at the Institute for Security Policy at the University of Kiel (ISPK), we will remain committed to continuing to research and analyze maritime strategic issues, as we have done for a few years now with conferences, various publications, doctoral dissertations, and seminars. We look forward to your continuing cooperation.

Acknowledgements

We would like to thank Routledge (in particular Ms. Hannah Ferguson and Mr. Andrew Humphrys) for their enduring patience, help, and support in producing this volume. We are also thankful to Mr. Emre Küçükkaraca for assisting with the articles from authors whose native language is not English. Heartfelt thanks go out to all of the authors who have shared their insights and perspectives for this book. None of what they have written should be construed to represent the views of the agency or institution which they represent, or that of the editors for that matter.

Notes

1 Ken Booth, *Navies and Foreign Policy* (New York: Holmes & Meier, 1979); Eric Grove, *The Future of Sea Power* (London: Routledge, 1990).

2 Alfred Thayer Mahan, *The Influence of Sea Power upon History, 1660–1783* (Boston: Little, Brown & Co., 1890); Mahan, *The Influence of Sea Power upon the French Revolution and Empire, 1793–1812*, 2 vols. (Boston: Little, Brown & Co., 1892); Mahan, *The Interest of America in Sea Power, Present and Future* (London: Sampson Low, Marston & Company, 1897); Mahan, *Sea Power in Relation to the War of 1812*, 2 vols. (Boston: Little, Brown & Co., 1905); Mahan, *Naval Strategy Compared and Contrasted with the Principles and Practice of Military Operations on Land: Lectures Delivered at U.S. Naval War College, Newport, R.I., between the Years 1887 and 1911* (Boston: Little, Brown & Co., 1911); John B. Hattendorf (ed.), *Mahan on Naval Strategy: Selections from the Writings of Rear Admiral Alfred Thayer Mahan* (Annapolis, MD: Naval Institute Press, 1991).

3 Philip A. Crowl, "Alfred Thayer Mahan: The Naval Historian," in Peter Paret, Gordon A. Craig, and Felix Gilbert, eds. *Makers of Modern Strategy from Machiavelli to the Nuclear Age* (Princeton, NJ: Princeton University Press, 1986), pp. 444–77; William Livezey, *Mahan on Sea Power* (Norman, OK: University of Oklahoma Press, 1981); Ronald B. St John, "European Naval Expansion and Mahan, 1889–1906," *Naval War College Review* 23, 7 (1971), pp 74–83; Mark Russell Shulman,. "The Influence of Mahan upon Sea Power," *Reviews in American History* 19, 4 (1991), pp. 522–7.

4 Harold and Margaret Sprout, *The Rise of American Naval Power, 1776–1918* (Princeton, NJ: Princeton University Press, 1939); Harold and Margaret Sprout, *Toward a New Order of Sea Power. American Naval Policy and the World Scene, 1918–1922* (Princeton, NJ: Princeton University Press, 1943); Bernard Brodie, *A Guide to Naval Strategy*, rev. edn (Princeton, NJ: Princeton University Press, 1944).

5 Mackenzie Eaglen and Bryan McGrath, *Thinking about a Day without Sea Power: Implications for U.S. Defense Policy* (Washington, DC: Heritage Foundation, Backgrounder 2555; May 16, 2011).

6 G. John Ikenberry, *After Victory. Institutions, Strategic Restraint, and the Rebuilding of Order after Major Wars* (Princeton, NJ: Princeton University Press, 2001); G. John Ikenberry, *Liberal Leviathan. The Origins, Crisis, and Transformation of the American World Order* (Princeton, NJ: Princeton University Press, 2011); Ian Clark, *Hegemony in International Society* (Oxford: Oxford University Press, 2011); Torbjørn L. Knutsen, *The Rise and Fall of World Orders* (Manchester: Manchester University Press, 1999), ch. 7; Philip Bobbitt, *The Shield of Achilles. War, Peace, and the Course of History* (New York: Anchor Books, 2002), ch. 27.

7 See for instance I. William Zartmann (ed.), *Imbalance of Power. US Hegemony and International Order* (Boulder, CO and London: Lynne Rienner, 2009); Fareed Zakaria, *The Post-American World* (New York and London: W. W. Norton, 2009); Neil Ferguson, *Colossus: The Rise and Fall of the American Empire* (New York: Penguin Books, 2004); Amy Chua, *Day of Empire. How Hyperpowers Rise to Global Dominance, and Why They Fall* (New York: Doubleday, 2007), chs. 9 and 11; Barry Buzan, *The United States and Great Powers. World Politics in the Twenty-First Century* (Cambridge: Polity Press, 2004); Parag Khanna, *The Second World. Empires and Influences in the New Global Order* (New York: Random House, 2008).

8 See Geoffrey Till, *Asia's Naval Expansion. An Arms Race in the Making?* (Abingdon: Routledge for IISS, 2012).

9 Department of the Army, Department of the Navy, Department of the Navy – Marine Corps, Department of the Air Force, *Air–Sea Battle. Service Collaboration to Address Anti-Access and Area Denial Challenges* (Washington, DC: Department of Defense, May 2013).

10 Aaron L. Friedberg, *Beyond Air–Sea Battle. The Debate over US Military Strategy in Asia* (Abingdon: Routledge for IISS, 2014), p. 25; Evan Braden Montgomery, "Contested Primacy in the Western Pacific. China's Rise and the Future of U.S. Power Projection," *International Security* 38, 4 (Spring 2014), pp. 115–49 (pp. 129–39).

11 See Andrew Krepinevich, Barry Watts, and Robert Work, *Meeting the Anti-Access and Area-Denial Challenge* (Washington, DC; Center for Strategic and Budgetary Assessment, 2003), p. 15.

12 Christian Le Mière, "The Spectre of an Asian Arms Race," *Survival* 56, 1 (February/March 2014), pp. 139–56 (p. 141).

13 Roger Cliff, Mark Burles, Michael S. Chase, Derek Eaton, and Kevin L. Pollpeter, *Entering the Dragon's Lair: The Implications of Chinese Anti-Access Strategies* (Santa Monica, CA: RAND Corporation, 2007); David Shambough, *Modernizing China's Military: Progress, Problems and Prospects* (Berkeley, CA: University of California Press, 2002).

14 Montgomery, "Contested Primacy in the Western Pacific," p. 131.

15 Friedberg, *Beyond Air–Sea Battle*, p. 82. Hugh White, *The China Choice: Why America Should Share Power* (Collingwood, VIC: Black Inc., 2012), p. 74.

16 Jan van Tol, with Mark Gunzinger, Andrew Krepinevich, and Jim Thomas, *Air–Sea Battle. A Point-of-Departure Operational Concept* (Washington, DC: Center for Strategic and Budgetary Assessments, 2010), pp. 20–1.

17 See David C. Gompert and Martin Libicki, "Cyber Warfare and Sino-American Instability," *Survival* 56, 4 (August/September 2014), pp. 7–21.

18 Friedberg, *Beyond Air–Sea Battle*, p. 25.

19 Montgomery, "Contested Primacy in the Western Pacific," p. 139.

20 See Stephen J. Cimbala, "Anticipatory Attacks: Nuclear Crisis Stability in Future Asia," *Comparative Strategy* 27, 1 (2008), pp. 113–32.

2

THE COMPLEX NATURE OF TODAY'S MARITIME SECURITY ISSUES

A European perspective

Lutz Feldt

The maritime domain is one of the four domains of the global commons, and it has a long history, which has been understood and acknowledged for centuries. But since we began to exploit airspace, outer space, and especially cyberspace, the notion of "well understood and acknowledged" no longer applies: the nature of the maritime domain is different today – it is no longer well understood nor generally acknowledged.

History shows that a geography-centric view of the maritime world is neither promising nor sustainable: a Euro-centric view, a U.S.-centric or a China-centric view is a danger for the maritime domain. The problem with all of these perspectives is that they support two dangerous developments. First, the belief that a regional perspective can be transferred to other regions as well and that many regional solutions do not accept the principle "Think globally, but act regionally and locally." What we need is a mentality to understand both aspects: the global and the regional dimensions of the maritime domain. Second, possessing its own ancient customs and traditions of self-reliance and autonomy, the maritime world has remained largely self-governing, with shipping seen as operating over the horizon, out of sight and out of mind, gaining visibility only when a disaster has occurred.

This issue becomes more and more troubling because the mitigation of risks and challenges at sea are beyond the capabilities of a single nation in the twenty-first century. When we attempt to achieve better maritime awareness, we must argue with facts and figures. We should talk about "sea lines of communication," and we frequently raise the point that 90 percent of all goods currently travel from port to port, from state to state, and from continent to continent: but what does this mean to a normal member of our society, to the man or woman on the street? Whereas the big accidents which occurred at sea, from *Deep Water Horizon* to *Amoco Cadiz*, are in our common memory, the question remains: what is the positive impact and the consequences for an enduring maritime domain awareness?[1] What is missing? Or better: what is the problem?

The root problem is "sea blindness" – a failure to appreciate the essential maritime component in most human activities. The sea is out of sight and out of mind to a virtually connected population that travels by land and air and thinks of the sea only as vacation destination. The great majority of our leaders and citizenry are landsmen with no maritime experience at all.

They are familiar with air travel, as large portions of the population have traveled at least once by airplane. They know from movies and television that aircraft, airports, and the skies are monitored by radar operators, and that aircraft off course or in trouble can be quickly identified and assisted. Because few people have any experience with maritime transportation, they unconsciously assume and expect that the kind of orderliness, safety, and security as well as traffic management they see in aviation also exists at seaports and on the ocean. When they discover that this is not the case, they are disappointed and often wonder why the maritime community has not entered the modern age.[2]

Sea blindness suits a secretive industry, which does not relish scrutiny and transparency. But it also suits governmental organizations, in particular those that are reluctant to share information and whose mind-set is not solution-oriented. This underlines the most important challenge: the need for a change of mindsets. Two conclusions can be drawn from this. First, we need a narrative about the oceans and seas which catches the attention of our leadership and citizens. Second, we have to overcome the culture of secrecy and acknowledge that today security lies in transparency. When dealing with such a subject as complex as "maritime security," it is essential to understand the context. Before dealing with maritime security issues, it is necessary to look in depth at what is implied by "security" and to define the terms "safety" and "defense" as both are part of the spectrum of security and directly affect maritime security issues. There is a general consensus about the definition of "safety," for which responsibility lies with the International Maritime Organization (IMO) and a common understanding that "defense" is the responsibility of states to protect their citizens and their interests. But there is no common definition or comparable consensus yet about the term "maritime security." For example, the IMO has, for convenience, amended Chapter XI of the "International Convention for Safety of Life at Sea" (SOLAS) with a subordinate chapter, XI-2, dealing with maritime security.[3] This pragmatic decision, promptly taken, was widely appreciated, since an open discussion on maritime security in the United Nations (UN) environment would have been very sensitive and therefore become a protracted process with no guarantee of agreement at the end.

The most important outcome of this process was the International Ship and Port Facility Security (ISPS) code, which offers one perception of maritime security. This view remains a rather narrow one deserving further consideration and development. What maritime security needs most is informed awareness of its importance; described as Maritime Domain Awareness (MDA) or Maritime Situational Awareness (MSA). It is necessary to understand the difference between the terms: Maritime Situational Awareness is the much broader term and includes the situation ashore as well. If this awareness is absent and the complexity of maritime issues results in a lack of knowledge as well, and one then adds the common tendency of states and individuals to ignore new challenges for as long as possible, then some serious thinking is required to confront the issues. As is often the case, the issue of security attracts popular attention only once the lack of it becomes apparent: as long as all goes well, there is no incentive to acquire the assets or undertake the necessary measures to preserve it. When circumstances change, however, the collective initial reaction is to complain that policy and military leaders did not take the necessary initiatives in time. In the past, most substantive initiatives have been driven by particular events (accidents, natural disasters, or terrorist attacks): the ISPS code itself stems from the terrorist attacks on the United States in September 2001.

When popular concern is limited, policy-makers are often tempted to restrict funding for important issues if they do not seem urgent. Very often it is an event which drives politicians to certain reactions rather than acting in response to analysis and assessment.

The corollary to this introduction is asking the question about whether "Maritime Security Issues" would be better recast as "Maritime Insecurity Issues."

To complicate matters further, there is a perception that security is not so much a definable condition, but an essential diffuse feeling, which could be far from realistic, as it deals with apparent risks, something that might happen, rather than an existential danger.

The term "security" is increasingly used nowadays in the domain of international relations, especially since it has become the official aim of many collective and regional security organizations such as NATO and the European Union. By the skilful use of "security" as a byword, NATO was able to ensure its survival beyond the Cold War. Security is also the justifying rationale for most, if not all, of the military endeavors undertaken by the West in recent decades. This leads one to a second significant aspect of the term "security." It is likely to imply very different requirements and increasingly significant implications, depending on the different conditions prevailing in a particular country. The requirements for "security" frequently widen and increase: the wealthier you are, the higher your security needs, whether on a personal or governmental level. If one compares what politicians meant by the term in the 1970s to what they mean today, it can be seen that it now hides a much more ambitious and comprehensive "shopping list" than in the past. Last, but not least, "security" has another dire effect. In the search for perfect security, nations often spread instability around themselves, much as when the owner of a mansion keeps unleashed dogs roaming in his garden to protect himself from burglars. Sooner or later the dogs will jump over the fence to kill a chicken or even severely injure a passer-by. When judging security, we should be aware of the need to accept a certain degree of risk, which cannot be removed, but which needs to be managed in an appropriate manner.

As already mentioned, the term "security" encompasses two other terms: "safety" and "defense." To explain the complex nature of maritime security, one has to start with definitions. In the maritime domain, responsibilities can be distributed among several maritime agencies using a variety of descriptions, both military and civilian. This stems from and leads to the variety and ambiguity in defining the terms "security" and "safety" and how they apply in the maritime domain. Another source of confusion is the terms of interpretation: sometimes viewed as an activity, sometimes as an aim or a condition. In particular, the military tends to consider "security" as a condition, rather than an activity, implying that no action is required unless the condition or status quo has been disrupted. On the other hand, if "security" is defined as an activity, it requires constant attention and effort, not just in the face of hostile action, but when confronted by all types of illegal, illicit, and criminal actions, which occur continually in peacetime. In the context of this analysis it is more appropriate to adopt the "activity" interpretation. It is also important to differentiate between security and safety. As one definition states, "Maritime Security is the combination of preventive and responsive measures to protect the maritime domain against threats and intentional unlawful acts."[4]

By including both preventive and responsive measures, such definitions aim to cover both law enforcement (i.e. civilian and military) and defense operations. Both constabulary and defense agencies have distinct and direct responsibilities with regard to maritime security.

On the other hand, "Maritime Safety is the combination of preventive and responsive measures intended to protect the maritime domain against, and to limit the effect of, accidental or natural danger, harm, and damage to the environment, risk, or loss."[5] Maritime safety, by the use of the inclusive term "maritime domain," is understood to refer to dangers to the ship, its crew and passengers and/or cargo, and to navigation. It also covers the prevention of pollution by ships and includes sanctioning illicit pollution and intervention to limit the damage of an incident. The number of agencies with maritime safety responsibilities is large, including constabulary, traffic control, fishery protection, customs, and environmental protection, as well as search and rescue agencies. National defense ministries, despite their extensive capabilities, should normally be seen as having a supporting or subsidiary responsibility, rather than primary responsibility.

To take a second approach in explaining the complexity of maritime security, it is appropriate to talk about the assessment of risk in the maritime domain. It is helpful to divide these kinds of situations in the maritime domain into challenges, risks, threats, and vulnerabilities.

Challenges are tasks or situations that test existing abilities. In the security context, challenges relate to internal or structural factors that must be overcome by adopting the right approach or changing the present mindset. One of the most challenging tasks is to achieve a change of mind in the field of information sharing in the maritime domain between the different agencies with maritime responsibilities, which often act in isolation from each other.

In principle, we can divide the main risks and threats into three categories. First, those emanating from the sea that directly affect a nation's territory and citizens; second, those affecting global/common maritime interests; and third, those affecting global resources at, in, or under the sea.

Risks are situations likely to result in danger or an unwelcome outcome if certain events turn out in undesired ways. Risks of unintended accidents or natural catastrophes include tsunamis in the Mediterranean or the combination of extreme tidal ranges with low pressure systems in the North Sea. European maritime interests are affected when the flow of energy or other strategically important commodities along major trade routes are at risk. The security of underwater pipelines and submarine cables is vital: they carry a high percentage of gas and oil resources and 90 percent of all internet traffic is transmitted by submarine cables with a potentially drastic impact if damaged. Risks affect Europe's own resources at sea, such as fisheries, oil, gas and mineral deposits within member states' Exclusive Economic Zones (EEZ), or wind farms, tidal, and offshore power hubs. Long-term factors must be considered as well: risks to biodiversity, the import of alien species or diseases; marine accidents, collisions, groundings, and wrecks posing risks to ships, ports, and coasts; poor safety regulation of wind, wave, and tidal energy farms given that the very limited experience available to date may render them prone to new and potentially serious kinds of accidents.

Threats are man-made activities, adversely affecting the EU and its population. They can be understood as:

- *Terrorism*, using the sea as either a base or a conduit for attacks ashore, e.g. through infiltration of terrorists, or the use of explosives and even weapons of mass destruction (WMD). Enough evidence exists to confirm that the sea has also been used by terrorism as a line of communication to infiltrate operatives, explosives, and weapons into target countries, often taking advantage of the implicit covertness and large cargo capacity of ships. The limited protection of EU ports from an attack by sea makes the prospect of a ship exploding inside a harbor perhaps the most worrying threat.
- *Illegal immigration*, including human trafficking, which can endanger the internal stability of EU countries.
- *Narcotics and arms trafficking*, which can destabilize foreign countries and, in turn, create damaging effects within Europe.
- *Threats that affect European maritime interests along all major trade routes*, especially at geographical choke points, must also be considered.
- *Piracy*, which not only affects trade routes but also fishing activities in certain fishing grounds; *local wars* or regional terrorism in the vicinity of choke points can pose serious threats. Besides the direct damage to state finances and legitimate business, an established network can launder money and engage in more profitable drug or weapon smuggling as well as other goods and contraband.
- *Territorial water claims and claims related to the EEZ* can affect Europe's maritime interests and are a potential area of conflict whose probability is increasing. Finally, the environmental

degradation resulting from the dumping of toxic waste at sea as well as illegal, unreported, and unregulated (IUU) fishing endangers European interests.

Apart from the challenges, risks, and threats considered above, Europe also has significant vulnerabilities in the maritime domain. The most serious is that all European member states, even the landlocked ones, depend on the seas, as they all benefit from maritime trade through European ports. The logistic supply chain has to be considered from a company's point of production to the most distant customer: the product or component parts have to be transported by land, sea, and air. For most goods, the sea-based element of transport is usually the longest and most difficult from the loading port to the discharge port. Consideration of maritime safety and security has to apply throughout the whole chain, from port to sea to port, as optimizing only one part will not safeguard the commodities. This also holds true for passenger travel: the rapid rise in large cruise ship operations makes an already challenging task even more complex and daunting.

As the essential commodities are shipped along global trade routes, which connect different continents, notably Asia, the Americas, and Africa, they are exposed to attacks at any point, especially when far from Europe. Any interruption in these supplies could have a significant impact on the quality of life for the people of Europe. A further European vulnerability lies in the large number of Europeans living and working overseas in international trade, working for European industries and commercial enterprises operating abroad or as members of non-governmental organizations (NGO). Tourists are similarly vulnerable, as they are increasingly attracted by eco- and adventure tourism in exotic destinations where risks are an inherent part of the attraction. They not only represent potential hostages, but can also be subject to accidents far from search and rescue assets, e.g. in Arctic or Antarctic waters.

Emergency evacuations have been carried out recently by some EU member states, whose air and naval units have rescued citizens of European and non-European states, as in Libya, or in other countries all over the world. Some European countries, which are members of NATO and/or the EU, maintain a permanent naval presence in certain conflict areas in addition to coast guards and other maritime services, in order to be able to react rapidly in the case of necessity. Article 222 of the Lisbon Treaty of the European Union, the "Solidarity Clause," could, through its European External Action Service (EEAS), lead the EU to establish a more permanent set of mutual support arrangements and contingency plans in this regard. The "Permanent Structured Cooperation"[6] could be used to facilitate this approach. In comparison with airports, EU sea ports have a lower degree of security and handle large quantities of containers and a high number of people, cruise ships, and especially ferries, at any one time. One of the challenges is to overcome the reluctance of the maritime community to accept a better security regime and to avoid the temptation to ignore risks and threats, as they did with piracy for a long period. The appropriate and affordable balance between security and commercial interests is difficult to achieve but, if done in concert with the major insurance companies, would seem well worthwhile. Two other aspects have to be considered when trying to explain the complexity of maritime security today: the geography of the seas around Europe, and the complexity of Europe's internal organization. In the European Atlas of the Seas, examining the eight sea basins of Europe, we find the following introduction:

> Europe is surrounded by oceans and seas. The EU has some 70,000 km of coastline. Almost half of all EU citizens live within 50 km of the sea. Almost 40% of the EU's GDP is generated in the maritime regions, and a staggering 90% of the EU's foreign

trade is conducted by sea. To raise awareness of Europe's oceans and seas the European Commission has developed a European Atlas of the Seas for anyone interested in the maritime world and our common maritime heritage.[7]

There are fact sheets for eight sea basins: the Baltic Sea, the North Sea, the Celtic Sea, Biscay/Iberia, the Black Sea, the Mediterranean Sea, the Arctic Ocean, and the more comprehensive and general overseas areas. These defined basins offer a valuable insight into the European Commission's view of the maritime domain: the Celtic Sea and Biscay/Iberian Sea are seen as separate seas, the Arctic Sea is also included as well as the overseas territories of member states. This has a significant influence on the further development of maritime security issues. The peninsular geography of Europe creates another, well-known vulnerability, in offering non-European countries easy access to all ports, while being able to "complicate" the global freedom of navigation, including access to strategic key regions in overseas territories. Relations with these overseas countries' territories (OCT) are focused on safety and a few specific security aspects. Defense challenges remain the responsibility of member states. But some of their military assets, mostly naval submarine, surface, and air assets, are permanently deployed to certain OCT. The OCT – numbering 26 countries and territories – have constitutional ties with Denmark, France, the Netherlands, and the United Kingdom. Although their nationals are in principle EU citizens, the territories are not part of the EU or directly subject to EU law. A special "associate" status with the EU is designed to help OCT economic and social development. Many are small islands and face particular challenges: remoteness, vulnerability to economic shocks and climate change, and difficulties in building and maintaining infrastructure or sustainable energy supply.[8]

Access to the global maritime domain is a core interest of all nations, which have acknowledged the importance of the maritime domain for the well-being of their citizens and the security of their interests. The development of anti-access and area denial (A2AD)[9] policies is a crucial part of the complex maritime domain. Both strategies will increase in importance. They already represent a threat in the South China Sea today and will remain on the list of potential maritime conflicts in the future.

The EU also has to deal with the vast number of different authorities acting in the maritime domain. The basic function for all maritime-related activities in Europe and globally is maritime surveillance and a maritime picture of the situation, locally, regionally, and globally. To achieve this, one can identify six functions, which are related to maritime safety and security in member states:

- border control;
- customs;
- fishery control;
- defense;
- law enforcement; and
- marine environmental protection.

These six functions are carried out, nationally and regionally, using more than 60 different maritime surveillance-related initiatives working in relative isolation from each other. One result is often fragmented and incomplete information and knowledge of occurrences in the seven sea basins and beyond. The European Union's maritime activities are based on the "Integrated Maritime Policy,"[10] a document, covering a wide range of maritime tasks and challenges. It has three policy pillars: social, environmental, and economic. It does not integrate any security responsibilities, which lie outside the original competence of the European Commission before the Lisbon Treaty was agreed. The level of integration achieved so far is nonetheless significant and the eight chapters spell out encouraging progress in both regional and functional approaches, offering a window of opportunity for improved maritime surveillance.[11]

Therefore, the main challenges to progress are:

- for authorities to achieve a mentality shift from working in relative isolation towards working in networks;
- to overcome legal barriers to appropriate information exchange as national, EU, sectoral, and horizontal legislation needs to be respected and, potentially where necessary, amended; and
- to spell out the technological choices to be made to enable connectivity between existing systems and networks to provide a seamless and cost effective flow of maritime information.

The response from the European Commission to deal with these challenges is an initiative called the "Common Information Sharing Environment" (CISE) for cooperative surveillance in the European maritime domain together with the Council and the member states.[12] It is worth having a closer look at how this roadmap uses another approach to meet the ambition of explaining the complexity of maritime security. The roadmap identifies six fundamental steps to be carried out before establishing a CISE. Its approach is attractive from a global point of view as it can be used as a blueprint for other regions. The six steps are:

- identifying all the user communities, i.e. those that use and provide maritime related information, including port authorities, keeping in mind the ISPS code, mentioned above;
- mapping the data sets and conducting gap analysis, observing what information is available, but not shared with all the other user communities;
- identifying common data classification levels;
- developing the technical support framework for CISE. It is important to realize that CISE is not a new or centralized system; CISE is a network of existing systems, properly interconnected;
- establishing appropriate access rights; and
- ensuring that legal provisions are respected.

Work on all six steps is important, but for the purposes of this discussion, "user communities" are more relevant. They differ from region to region in number and competence, but one finds at least five to seven different user communities in all littoral states: coast guard and navy, customs, fishery protection, and environmental protection. There can be a significant difference in the role of a coast guard, responsible for law enforcement and border control, and its position in the national safety and security organization. For historical reasons, European states have very different structures, which is part of the complexity of today's maritime security issues. Coast guards may come under the Ministries of the Interior as well as Ministries of Defense. The European Union prefers to use the term "coast guard function," which leaves it open as to how the member states organize themselves.

"Maritime Surveillance" and the "Six steps of CISE" are one way to overcome these differences in an acceptable and progressive way. It has already been shown that an agreed base-line start position is essential to ensure progress through the later stages of the process. The initiative to accompany the process with two pilot projects in the European maritime domain was a brilliant idea. Both projects, "MARSUNO"[13] in Northern Europe and "BLUEMASSMED"[14] in the Mediterranean Sea, proved the idea in principle and showed in detail the improvements and possible synergies of a "Common Information Sharing Environment." Other informal initiatives have also been established to facilitate "Maritime Domain Awareness." One of these informal initiatives is the "North Atlantic Coast Guard Forum."[15] This brings together 17 European coast guard representatives with Russian, Canadian, and United States authorities. Countries without a coast guard, like Germany, participate with representatives from different ministries, which is irritating for most of the other nations. The "Mediterranean Coast Guard Functions Forum" and the idea of a "Greater Middle East Coast Guard Forum" all have a similar goal: to bring neighboring littoral coast guards and their governments together in order to become more effective.

The European Parliament has proposed the formation of a European coast guard. This initiative produces very diverse reactions and would have a very different impact in various member states. In principle, the development of a European coast guard is very much in line with the informal studies undertaken by the Coast Guard Forum. The vision of a European Navy is a topic that has been carefully discussed in the Chiefs of the European Navies Meeting, given the sensibilities over sovereignty. The principal idea of all these meetings has spread globally[16] and regionally[17] and they are, on the one hand, very important facilitators in the field of safety and security, but, on the other hand, also limited to a specific group of maritime stakeholders. Their influence in the political arena is thus difficult to assess and to leverage.

Another informal organization is the annual meeting of the Chiefs of the European Navies (CHENS).[18] Since 2002, they have met with the aim of developing solutions to current problems and challenges. Three working groups have been established, dealing with "Maritime Strategies Dialogue," "Maritime Security Operations," and "Maritime Cooperation with Africa." The published documents are an important contribution to bringing the different aspects of the complex maritime security agenda together. The studies are open for joint and combined initiatives, on the one hand, and for civilian–military cooperation, on the other. Both approaches represent a very encouraging attempt to generate acceptance for what policy officials and experts usually call the "comprehensive approach."

"CHENS Maritime Security Best Practice Guidelines" is a document which attempts to simplify the issue. It states that "Maritime Security is to be considered the combination of Maritime Security Operations and Maritime Situational Awareness. Maritime Security implies information analysis and action at sea, and both complement each other."[19] The real value of this approach is that it shows the interdependency between both. Maritime Security Operations (MSO) are based on information analysis conducted in the maritime domain, and information obtained in MSO will be a valuable input to Maritime Situational Awareness (MSA).

Examining this issue further, there is another possible approach to explain the complexity of the maritime domain. From the user community's perspective, one can take another view and divide the utility of the global maritime domain into four areas. The global maritime domain can be used for transport, as a resource, as a habitat, and as a means to project power. This analytical framework provides the opportunity to look more deeply into the vital importance of the maritime domain. In doing so, it should be remembered that the maritime domain is one of four domains altogether, which are all interconnected: the maritime, which includes surface and subsurface, airspace, outer space, and cyberspace. The "subsurface domain" deserves particular attention in the future and will substantially increase the complexity of maritime security issues. This is due to the fact that submarines, be they civilian or military, have become assets which can be employed on all levels: tactical, operational, and strategic in military terms and as research, control, and maintenance assets for civilian tasks. The ownership of submarines is now no longer exclusively bound to governments but increasingly to NGOs, enterprises, and commercial companies.

On the surface, developments are equally complex: Approximately 90 percent of all raw commodities and merchandise are transported by sea. Three-quarters of that cargo passes through international choke points. The relevant topics for maritime transport are therefore economic development, trade barriers, regulation, and maritime infrastructure. For decades, the shipments of crude oil, gas, and petroleum products have dominated sea-borne trade in volume terms. Today, the container industry is one of the driving factors together with the installation of maritime infrastructure such as wind farms and sea-bed exploitation in dangerous maritime environments including the Arctic region. This might reduce the importance of choke points, but they are still maritime areas with a great potential for all kinds of risks, threats, and vulnerabilities. Thus, it is necessary to look at those choke points with the potential of becoming areas of concern for the international community.[20]

Emphasizing the significance of choke points does not imply that certain regions are not of similar significance to the aforementioned strategic bottlenecks. One such region is the Arctic. From the maritime transport aspect, both seaways, the Northern Sea Route and the North-West Passage, deserve attention: opportunities, risks, and challenges have to be balanced. Disputes about legal issues, about the Exclusive Economic Zones, and the influence of non-Arctic states will be quite high on the political agenda. Policy-makers will be forced to comprehend and explain the complex nature of maritime security and how to accommodate their national Arctic strategies to a region where extreme weather conditions and uncharted passages are daily fare.

Most of the choke points mentioned above are not close to Europe, but they are nonetheless of vital importance for the continent: energy resources, ports, inland waterways, and the entire global supply chain depends on the safety and security of maritime transport and unfettered access to all the ports in the global maritime domain. Asian ports already play a key role in this global transport system and it is in the interest of all member states that its peaceful development continues. In addition to transport, the maritime domain is also used as a resource. Fishing is one of Europe's major enterprises. Consequently, fishery protection is one of the services required by the user communities mentioned above. Today around 50 percent of the world's fish stocks have been fully depleted and more than 30 percent have been overexploited. Climate change has created new problems, and illegal and unreported fishing represents a double threat – to fish stocks and to legitimate fishermen.

Offshore reserves become increasingly important. Europe's offshore reserves are declining, but new reserves are being exploited in other areas. The Arctic region will become an area of interest and the Arctic Council has opened its membership to a number of non-Arctic area countries as permanent observers. From a maritime safety view, and especially under security aspects, the Arctic region deserves much more attention than is now being paid to it by the European Union and non-Arctic member states.

The European Union has not achieved, as anticipated, the status of a permanent observer, but it is already engaged in the Arctic in scientific research both directly and through three of its member states. Norway is also playing a very supportive role towards the EU in the Arctic region.

Another underappreciated topic is the global network of submarine cables which connects the continents. The "Submarine Cable Map,"[21] based on information from the Global Bandwidth Research Service, is an impressive figure which provides an inside look into the management of the world's intercontinental digital traffic. Before adding another perspective, it seems appropriate to come to a brief interim conclusion.

As a first step, the complexity of maritime security issues can be solved, at least in part, by agreeing on a set of definitions. To improve our level of understanding we need to decide whether maritime security is a condition requiring a response when the status quo has been disrupted or whether it is an activity requiring continuous attention and effort. The next step could be to deal with the vulnerabilities, risks, threats, and challenges of the maritime domain. In this context, the European sea basins require different approaches for cultural and historical reasons, which cannot be ignored.

The geography of Europe and its sea basins have to be considered, and it is worth having a deeper look into the influence of geography not only in European seas but worldwide. Robert Kaplan's recent book *The Revenge of Geography: What the Map Tells Us about Coming Conflicts and the Battle against Fate* incorporates old but nevertheless valid knowledge including the important role of geopolitics. Another relevant book is *Monsoon: The Indian Ocean and the Future of American Power*.[22] When geography is different, weather conditions and neighborhoods differ as well.

CISE, together with the step-by-step approach and the successful pilot projects, has started off a process: there are already changes afoot in the current fragmented state of maritime awareness and maritime services working in isolation from each other. This constitutes a huge success for the CISE initiative. Looking at the maritime domain from four different perspectives is useful and improves understanding: using the maritime domain for transport, as a resource, as a habitat, and for power projection helps to clarify some of the complexity of security issues.

NATO and the EU are both important actors in security matters and the fact that their approaches have been remarkably different deserves analysis. Before doing so, however, a brief look at the global stakeholders seems appropriate:

- The United Nations, through its International Maritime Organization, the IMO, is the international guardian for safety and security regulations, agreements, and standards, but it tends to be a reactive administration whose leadership ambitions are limited. The first UN-led maritime operation is the United Nations Interim Force in Lebanon (UNIFIL), specifically the Maritime Task Force (MTF) tasked with Maritime Surveillance and Maritime Capacity Building (which includes the education and training of the Lebanese Navy and Coast Guard).[23] In the legal realm, things are different: The UN does not possess actual capabilities for the enforcement of its Convention on the Law of the Sea (UNCLOS).
- The United States Navy, Coast Guard, and Marine Corps have a common "Maritime Strategy"[24] and the U.S. government supports the IMO (although the U.S. is not a signatory to the UNCLOS). The U.S. Navy is the only global stakeholder with the capacity to act at all three levels: strategic, operational, and tactical. The U.S. Navy, together with the Coast Guard and the Marine Corps, have a Maritime Security Operations Concept which is currently executed through three Combined Maritime Forces.
- The North Atlantic Treaty Organization, through its many navies, has the capability to act on all three levels as well. It has an Alliance Maritime Strategy and a Maritime Security Operations Concept. NATO commands four standing naval maritime/mine counter-measure groups (SNMG/SNMCMG) with a broad variety of capabilities. Its Partnership for Peace Programme, in place since the early 1990s, has provided education and training to a great number of navies worldwide and achieves better interoperability and mutual understanding.
- The European Union delivers some effect through the Commission, the Military Staff, and the European Defence Agency, but the EU has limited military experience to date and its maritime aims remain fragmented from a security perspective. In June 2014, the European Union published a "European Maritime Security Strategy."[25]
- The African Union's ambition is to have an own Maritime Security Strategy for the whole of Africa. The implementation process of the strategy needs a business plan. The process is

supported by the EEAS and the European Commission, through different, but not always coordinated, projects.

- Countries such as Brazil, Russia, India, and China have their own individual naval and broader maritime ambitions. Strong support for their navies stems from both traditional and modern strategic thinking, which should be acknowledged and accepted.

Europe's security ambitions are based on the "European Security Strategy: A Secure Europe in a Better World,"[26] first published in 2003 and amended in 2008 by a "Report on the Implementation of the European Security Strategy: Providing Security in a Changing World."[27] Both documents paid scant attention to the maritime domain; the 2008 report briefly acknowledges piracy, but Maritime Situational Awareness is not mentioned. The European Security Strategy (ESS) establishes three strategic objectives: addressing the threat, building security in our neighborhood, and achieving an international order based on effective multilateralism.

Crises can develop far from Europe but still seriously affect European countries, if not properly addressed. Thus, two approaches are offered: The first line of defense will often be abroad; the traditional term for this concept is protection in depth. The EU must be ready to act in advance of a crisis occurring: prevention should be a high priority. The threats are not exclusively of a military nature nor can they be tackled by purely military means. Such approaches call for a synergistic set of actions and require a maritime surveillance system, situational awareness being a pre-requisite for prevention.

To achieve more stability in the neighborhood, it is not enough to act in the Balkans, in the Southern Caucasus, in the Mediterranean, or in Northern Africa or to contribute to resolving the Arab–Israeli conflict by acting only on land. The Mediterranean and Black Sea must become more stable environments, which, in principle, requires a maritime point of view and policy approach. Any attempt to undermine legal and peaceful trade, to carry out hostile and illegal actions, or overexploit resources should be identified and countered promptly. Illegal immigration is a great challenge and risk for all the neighboring countries. Internal crisis and civil war in some countries on the North African coast pose an ongoing threat to all member states; the maritime dimension of these risks and threats must be assessed and countered. In more practical terms, the EU must ensure that Turkey's role is taken into account in the two sea basins of the Mediterranean and Black Sea. The enduring bilateral conflict between Greece and Turkey is an obstacle to achieving "Security in our Neighborhood." It must certainly be possible to start a dialogue, moderated by the EU, with the aim of stopping the present practice of blocking each other's initiatives without even discussing and evaluating them. The present lack of security in the Eastern Mediterranean Sea is a strong argument for starting such a process and maritime security can provide a starting point for this engagement. It is a matter of concern for both the EU and NATO. A prerequisite for any collaboration and subsequent response is effective and cooperative surveillance and enforcement systems capable of ensuring a minimum degree of good governance in this part of the European maritime domain. Much has already been achieved in this respect. NATO's operation "Active Endeavour"[28] represents one answer to the risks and threats; another answer is provided by the virtual regional traffic center in Rome[29] and the use of the Maritime Safety and Security Information System.[30]

Collaboration with third parties in building maritime situational awareness and monitoring the sea is paramount in achieving international order based on multilateralism. It relies on mutual trust and confidence being established. This applies in particular to the shared sea basins, where information exchange is critical for the common good, such as the Arctic, the Baltic Sea, the Black Sea, and the Mediterranean Sea basins.

As late as 2013, the EEAS started to draft a document addressing European maritime security with the aim of contributing to an open, safe, and secure global maritime domain.[31] The EU undoubtedly has strategic interests around the globe and needs to be able to safeguard these interests adequately and efficiently. Here, the challenge is to link existing policies with a broader approach to security that includes all aspects of this complex issue.

Maritime security is a broad concept covering many policy sectors, and tends to mean different things to different actors. Logically, initiating and developing a strategy must be founded on operational and strategic needs rather than legal ones. The necessary legal framework must follow the political decisions. Such legal modifications are possible, if the draft takes a holistic, cross-sector approach. Europe's difficulties in finding a definition of maritime security that can be agreed upon between member states and avoids sector-specific definitions, which do not reflect collective purposes, are evident.

It makes sense to have a brief look into NATO's ambitions and how far both the EU and NATO complement each other pragmatically. But this review into NATO is limited to the Alliance's maritime ambitions and policies. NATO's perspective is based on its Strategic Concept[32] from 2010, the so-called "Active Engagement in Modern Defence." The three objectives are deterrence and collective defense, crisis management, and cooperative security. In comparison to the three objectives of the European Security Strategy (addressing the threats, building security in our neighborhood, and achieving an international order based on effective multilateralism), NATO's objectives are more concrete and more easily understood. The ESS is open to different interpretations; how the objectives are actually met depends on the respective political will at the time and the political leadership of the member states. This can be either an advantage or an excuse for doing nothing.

NATO and the EU are both important actors from a regional and global perspective, so it is worth examining their relative ambitions more closely. NATO and the EU are superficially similar with similar membership and a similar area of responsibility and both are, to a degree, political organizations. But a closer examination shows important differences, even as they share a recent growing interest in all maritime issues. NATO is a political organization able to draw on well-established security relationships and networks to contribute to its aim of cooperative security and particularly maritime security. It is already a global stakeholder, not just in its core tasks of collective defense and deterrence, but also in its crisis management, cooperative security, and maritime security tasks. Operational experience and military capabilities are provided to the alliance by member states following a national decision. Members of NATO are sovereign states. The North Atlantic Council provides political guidance, but the political level of ambition differs between nations and this has an impact on the alliance's cohesion. Agreement can be reached at the strategic level, but the sovereign nations retain their right to make national decisions.

NATO's most important feature is its very successful command structure, which has achieved considerable coherence through more than 60 years of common training, exercises, and operations, together with common policies and procedures and a high degree of technical standardization.

In contrast to the EU, which is primarily an economic and political union, NATO is a political organization without a mandate of its own. This explains why NATO is sometimes characterized as a military alliance (under the Washington Treaty it is in fact both political and military).[33] The European Naval Operation "Atalanta" and its successes could be seen as a facilitator to achieve and improve the maritime footprint of the Union. One consequence is the

European Union Maritime Security Strategy (EUMSS). The Maritime Security Strategy covers both the internal and external aspects of the Union's maritime security. It serves as a comprehensive framework, contributing to a stable and secure global maritime domain, in accordance with the ESS, while ensuring coherence with EU policies, in particular the Integrated Maritime Policy (IMP) and the Internal Security Strategy (ISS).[34] The ambition is to cover the global maritime domain and a pragmatic approach is based upon four guiding principles and eleven objectives.

The "cross-sectoral approach" is aimed at linking all partners from civilian and military authorities, respecting each other's national and internal organization. "Functional integrity" ensures that the strategy does not affect the respective competences of the Union and its member states and reflects the sovereign rights and the binding role of international law, especially the UNCLOS. This is underlined in the principle "Respect for rules and principles" and reinforced by the last principle, "Maritime multilateralism," which particularly mentions the United Nations and NATO. The objectives are a logical implication of the guiding principles: good governance at sea, promoting enhanced common situational awareness and better sharing of information, and stressing the "need to share" as a consequence of the cross-sectoral approach. The ambition to enhance the role of the EU as a global actor and security provider is one of the objectives which reaches beyond the regional European sea basins.

Europe is linked through history, geography, and culture to the Middle East, Africa, Latin America, and Asia. These relationships are important assets which need to be built upon. In addition, ASEAN, MERCOSUR, and the African Union are mentioned as important contributors in the development of future security structures. Developing strategic partnerships with these countries and alliances is particularly crucial. This is the political ambition. Unfortunately, the EU still lacks a strategic concept or practical plan for its engagement in Asia. The ambitions that have been stated need to be implemented and Europe needs a higher political profile in Asia.

Europe is a political actor in its own right, but in contrast to NATO it is primarily a civilian actor. Such an approach could be complementary, but to work it would need a high degree of common understanding and intensive permanent coordination. Neither NATO nor the EU is in a position to achieve this yet.

The European Common Security and Defence Policy, CSDP,[35] is an agreed policy for mainly security and defense diplomacy and operations. It is understood as part of the Union's foreign policy, which is much more focused on trade and commercial and environmental protection issues. The European Maritime Security Strategy will form part of the CSDP, clarifying Europe's maritime interests and ambitions and contributing to better coordination with NATO.

From here towards the drafting of a European Union Maritime Security Strategy is only a short step, recalling the path from the European Security Strategy, which did not touch maritime aspects at all, towards the Integrated Maritime Policy, which in turn deals with all maritime aspects beyond security and defense. Thus, the European Union Maritime Security Strategy is another but critically important step to a better understanding of the complexity and comprehensiveness of the maritime domain. Currently, the European Union's operation "Atalanta" is deterring piracy off the coast of Somalia and far beyond, and can be considered a wide success. The EU provided substantial assistance ashore and at sea and, so to speak, a unique first-ever experience in "maritime capacity-building" which is still ongoing today. EUNAVFOR's success facilitated and deeply affected the thinking about the value of a Maritime Security Strategy, endorsed by the European Council in June 2014.

Keeping the "step-by-step" approach, this has been a significant achievement. The objectives of the new strategy are as follows:

1 internal and external aspects of the union's maritime security;
2 the strategy must be coherent and inclusive and cost-efficient;
3 a coordinated approach will enhance the growth and business potential of the seas;
4 safe use of the seas and security of the maritime borders;
5 cross-border and cross-sectoral cooperation among all maritime stakeholders, supporting the United Nations Convention on the Law of the Seas, UNCLOS, and its further development; and
6 multilateralism as a key principle, together with enhancing solidarity among member states. The definition of maritime security interests aims to achieve a better common understanding and to establish a reliable framework for Maritime Security Operations.

The protection of the EU against maritime security threats is considered instrumental for the Union. Measures include safeguarding the energy supply by sea, the protection of critical maritime infrastructure (wind farms, ports, terminals, off-shore installations, underwater cables, and pipelines), the protection of all economic activities at sea, and the promotion of scientific maritime research.

As a key aspect, the EU emphasizes the protection of its member states' economic interests, the sustainable exploitation of natural and marine resources in the different maritime zones in Europe and beyond, and the prevention of illegal, unregulated, and unreported fishing. Such comprehensive maritime domain awareness beyond purely technological assets mandates intellectual and financial investments which will soon pay off.

The "complex nature of today's maritime security issues" is thus a consequence of three factors: the transition from the industrial to the information age, globalization, and climate change. The urgent need for "maritime domain and situational awareness" is a precondition to achieve "good governance at sea." The three factors have wrought changes in the maritime domain in recent decades and attempts to comprehend this should follow three principles:

- Think globally, but act regionally and locally, opt for a step-by-step approach.
- Tell the maritime story: a narrative about the maritime domain as a global common good needs more than just maritime experts: it needs other advocates – artists, writers, and philosophers together with scientists and researchers.
- Explain climate change as a huge challenge with many opportunities and some serious risks: keep an open mind for the opportunities in the maritime domain.

Notes

1 *Deepwater Horizon* was a semi-submersible offshore drilling rig. On April 20, 2010, the rig (while positioned in the Gulf of Mexico) suffered an explosion that killed 11 people. The resulting fire could not be extinguished and the rig sank two days later. The seabed oil well was left gushing and caused the largest offshore oil spill in U.S. history. VLCC *Amoco Cadiz* was a Liberian-flagged crude carrier which ran aground off the coast of Brittany (France) on March 16, 1978. The tanker subsequently broke into three pieces and spilled its complete cargo of more than 1.6 million barrels of crude oil and 4,000 tons of fuel oil, wasting the fragile marine ecosystem. It remains one of the largest tanker disasters in history.
2 Dana A. Goward, "Maritime Domain Awareness: The Key to Maritime Security," in Myron H. Nordquist, Rüdiger Wolfrum, John Norton Moore, and Ronán Long, eds., *Legal Challenges in Maritime Security* (Center for Oceans Law and Policy) (Leiden and Boston: Martinus Nijhoff Publishers, 2008), pp. 513–25.

3 Chris Trelawny, "IMO Maritime Security Policy." Background paper. www.unece.org/fileadmin/DAM/trans/doc/2008/ac11/4th_ppt01e.pdf, accessed August 28, 2015.

4 *Martime Surveillance in Support of CSDP. The Wise Pen Team Report to EDA Steering Board*, Brussels, March 15, 2010, p. 45.

5 *Ibid.*, p. 46.

6 Sven Biscop, *Permanent Structured Cooperation and the Future of ESDP* (Egmont Paper 20). www.egmontinstitute.be/paperegm/ep20.pdf, accessed August 28, 2015.

7 Eight Sea Basins, in European Atlas of the Seas. http://ec.europa.eu/fisheries/sea_basins/index_en.htm, accessed August 28, 2015.

8 Sea Basins, Outermost Regions. http://ec.europa.eu/maritimeaffairs/atlas/seabasins/outermostregions/long/index_en.htm, accessed August 28, 2015.

9 Nathan Freier, "The Emerging Anti-Access/Area-Denial Challenge." http://csis.org/publication/emerging-anti-accessarea-denial-challenge, accessed August 28, 2015.

10 Progress Report on the EU's Integrated Maritime Policy, Brussels, October 15, 2009. http://ec.europa.eu/maritimeaffairs/policy/, accessed August 28, 2015.

11 A Common Information Sharing Environment (CISE). http://ec.europa.eu/maritimeaffairs/policy/integrated_maritime_surveillance/index_en.htm, accessed August 28, 2015.

12 Draft Progress Report on the Roadmap to Establishing CISE for the Surveillance of the European Maritime Domain. No date, the author holds a copy.

13 Maritime Surveillance in the Northern Sea Basins, a Pilot Project. www.marsuno.eu/, accessed August 28, 2015.

14 See www.bluemassmed.net/, accessed August 28, 2015. The Bluemassmed project is aimed at increasing the cooperation for maritime surveillance in the Mediterranean Sea and its Atlantic Approaches.

15 See http://arcticportal.org/features/703-north-atlantic-coast-guard-forum-meeting-in-iceland, accessed August 28, 2015. The North Atlantic Coast Guard Forum is an informal cooperation between 17 European Countries and Russia, the United States, and Canada.

16 See www.ccg-gcc.gc.ca/e0007869, accessed August 28, 2015. The North Pacific Coast Guard Forum was established in 2000, following the good experience of the NACGF, by Japan, Korea, Russia, and the United States. Canada and China have joined NPCGF.

17 See http://ec.europa.eu/information_society/newsroom/cf/mare/itemdetail.cfm?item_id=11178, accessed August 28, 2015. The Mediterranean Coast Guard Functions Forum is another informal meeting with focus on safety and security scenarios in the Mediterranean.

18 See www.chens.eu/SitePages/History.aspx, accessed August 28, 2015. Chiefs of European Navies meetings dealing with security and defence matters.

19 The document drafted by the Chiefs of the European Navies about Maritime Security Best Practice Guidelines is available at http://dev.chens.eu/Products/MSO%20BEST%20PRACTICE%20GUIDELINES.pdf, accessed August 28, 2015.

20 The most important internationally recognized bottlenecks include the following. The Strait of Malacca between Indonesia, Malaysia, and Singapore links the Pacific with the Indian Ocean and the South China Sea. Apart from the natural navigational hazards, risks and threats from piracy and armed robbery and disputes over maritime boundaries present a potential risk of interstate conflict. The Strait of Bab el-Mandeb lies between Somalia, Djibouti, Yemen, and Eritrea, linking the Indian Ocean with the Red Sea. This is an area of enduring local conflict between Djibouti and Eritrea over maritime borders, as well as an area renowned for piracy. The Suez Canal links the Red Sea with the Mediterranean Sea through Egypt. This choke point is permanently at risk due to domestic unrest and territorial disputes in the region. In this region, the Mediterranean Coast Guard Functions Forum can be used to lower tensions. The Strait of Gibraltar, connecting the Atlantic Ocean with the Mediterranean Sea, is one of the vital sea routes. The Strait of Gibraltar was threatened by terrorists in 2003. The North Atlantic Council decided to extend the ongoing Operation Active Endeavour to escorting non-military ships traveling through the strait. The Straits of Hormuz, located between the United Arab Emirates, Oman, and Iran, links the Persian Gulf with the Arabian Sea. The straits experience continual tensions due to sovereignty disputes over several islands and the aggressive attitude of Iran towards neighboring states. The Taiwan Straits, separating China from Taiwan, connect the South China Sea with the East China Sea. Political tensions and risks persist, principally due to political differences and disputes about demarcation of maritime borders. Three major crises have occurred in the past between China and Taiwan due to China's irredentist "one China" policy. China's ambition to become the dominant power in the region poses an existential risk to some states and a potential risk

to others if the "nine-dashed line" approach to her maritime borders is actively pursued. The Korea Strait, located between South Korea and the Japanese islands of Kyushu and Shikodo, links the East China Sea with the Sea of Japan. Despite long-standing disputes between South Korea and Japan, no significant change is to be expected to current peaceful development. The ambitious and aggressive attitude of China's non-military maritime services in the region could facilitate agreements between both countries.

21 See www.submarinecablemap.com/, accessed August 28, 2015. The Submarine Cable Map is a free resource from TeleGeography. It offers a surprising inside look at the huge number of submarine cables and their importance for global communication.

22 Robert Kaplan, *The Revenge of Geography: What the Map Tells Us about Coming Conflicts and the Battle against Fate* (New York: Random House, 2012) and *Monsoon: The Indian Ocean and the Future of American Power* (New York: Random House, 2010).

23 UNIFIL's MTF has been operational since 2006. For a review from the German perspective, see Sebastian Bruns, "UNIFIL's Maritime Task Force and Germany's Contribution," in Bernhard Chiari (ed.), *Auftrag Auslandseinsatz. Neueste Militärgeschichte an der Schnittstelle von Geschichtswissenschaft, Politik, Öffentlichkeit und Streitkräften. Neueste Militärgeschichte, Analysen und Studien* (Band 1) (Freiburg i.Br./ Berlin/Vienna: Rombach, 2012), pp. 151–9.

24 www.navy.mil/local/maritime/150227-CS21R-Final.pdf, accessed August 28, 2015. *A Cooperative Strategy for 21st Century Seapower* represents a historic first: the first formal U.S. maritime strategic document which features the signatures of the US Navy, US Coast Guard, and US Marine Corps.

25 Council of the European Union, "European Union Maritime Security Strategy," Brussels, June 24, 2014. http://register.consilium.europa.eu/doc/srv?l=EN&f=ST%2011205%202014%20INIT, accessed August 28, 2015.

26 "A Secure Europe in a Better World, European Security Strategy," Brussels, December 12, 2003. www. consilium.europa.eu/uedocs/cmsUpload/78367.pdf, accessed August 28, 2015.

27 "Report on the Implementation of the European Security Strategy: Providing Security in a Changing World," Brussels, December 11, 2008. www.consilium.europa.eu/ueDocs/cms_Data/docs/pressdata/ EN/reports/104630.pdf, accessed August 28, 2015.

28 See www.mc.nato.int/ops/Pages/OAE.aspx, accessed August 28, 2015. Under operation Active Endeavour, NATO ships are patrolling the Mediterranean and monitoring sipping to help detect, deter, and protect against terrorist activity. The operation has changed from an asset-based operation to a network-based operation by experience.

29 See www.5plus5defence.org/sites/EN/PagesEN/V-RMTC.aspx, accessed August 28, 2015. The Virtual Regional Traffic Centre consists of a virtual network that links the operational centers of the participating navies.

30 See https://mssis.volpe.dot.gov/Main/, accessed August 28, 2015. The Maritime Safety and Security System (MSSIS) is a freely shared, unclassified, near real-time data collection and distribution network, maintained by the Volpe Centre in Boston, USA.

31 In April 2010, the European Council called for a European Maritime Security Strategy building on the European Security Strategy's three objectives. Outline drafting was started, but was delayed by the fact that the Lisbon Treaty and the Solidarity Clause, Article 222, together with the Mutual Defence Clause, Article 42.7, had not yet been implemented. These documents describe very well the situation in the EU together with its opportunities and challenges.

32 See www.nato.int/cps/en/natolive/topics_56626.htm, accessed August 28, 2015. The Strategic Concept is an official document that outlines NATO's enduring purpose and nature and its funda-mental security tasks. It provides guidelines for the adaptation of its military forces.

33 Still, NATO and the EU – as currently demonstrated off the Horn of Africa – may work in parallel and in conjunction as they field naval task forces which can be complemented by nationally commanded task groups and units (such as the U.S. Navy's assets in the Western Indian Ocean and the Combined Maritime Forces in that area). It has to be recognized that some European nations choose to contribute to one or the other operation.

34 Council of the European Union, "European Union Maritime Security Strategy," p. 2.

35 See www.eeas.europa.eu/csdp/structures-instruments-agencies/, accessed August 28, 2015. In order to enable the European Union to fully assume its responsibility for crisis management, the European Council decided to establish permanent political and military structures.

3

THE FUTURE OF NAVAL CONFLICT AND LESSONS FROM HISTORY

Tim Benbow

This chapter considers how naval conflict might develop through to the middle of the twenty-first century.[1] It outlines some of the broad factors that will influence it, in particular the international strategic context, and then explores the impact of technology in the form of new and emerging capabilities. This second section in particular draws on history to explore previous examples of debates about the impact of new technologies on navies; this is not to claim that history provides either objective 'lessons' or even exact parallels. It does, however, offer a useful guide that clarifies to some extent the questions that must be asked as well as the answers that might be offered. It is not realistic to put forward detailed predictions of how the future might unfold over a decade, let alone over 30 or 40 years; yet, it is possible and even useful to look forward and to think about how events might develop in outline, if not in great detail.

When considering the future, there are two opposite pitfalls to be avoided. The first is in assuming continuity or linear development of the present. There is always the possibility of a major shock in international politics that fundamentally affects what happens thereafter; the end of the Cold War would be one example and the attacks on the United States of 9/11 would be another. Looking forward, there could well be an event – or several – that might have a similarly seismic impact, whether that would be the US turning decisively to isolationism, China fragmenting, the Euro collapsing with the consequent impact on the European Union, or the international economic order moving from free trade to protectionism. None of these is particularly far-fetched and any of them would have enormous consequences for international affairs as a whole and for naval conflict specifically. The second pitfall is focusing exclusively on change and consequently underestimating continuity. This has frequently been a vice of those trying to interpret the impact of a new military technology. Armed conflict, as well as the international system more broadly, is adaptive but also has greater resilience than is sometimes attributed to it. The challenge is to achieve a sensible balance between emphasising continuity and change, while also remaining open to the possibility of more significant turning points.

The strategic context

The context for naval conflict is established by the character of the international system. There have occasionally been idealistic predictions that the era of great power war was over, or that history (albeit defined in a rather narrow sense) had ended. Alternatively, some commentators have given in to the temptation to perceive what they wish to see, hence announcing the unusability of armed force or even the demise of the state. Any of these major transformations in the international system would have great impact on naval conflict, yet they are vanishingly unlikely. The state has proved remarkably resilient as the bedrock of the international system. It is not the only significant actor on the world stage, but many of the others (including most international organisations and many terrorist and insurgent groups) are important as agents of a state – though that is not to deny that some companies, international organisations, non-governmental organisations or terrorist groups can have an important role in world affairs in their own right. The state will continue to form the basis of world politics. These states will also continue to have competing interests that they will see as justifying the use of force. While the resort to military means will be constrained to varying degrees, the restraints are mainly self-imposed and will therefore apply more to some states (such as the United States and the UK) than others (such as Russia or China).

The contemporary world order involves a range of rising powers – not only the obvious examples such as China and India but also many regional powers. These states are increasingly able to afford advanced weapons and there is lively competition to supply them. The result is that there is a growing number of states with advanced military capabilities, which they can use to defend their perceived interests. Advanced weapons systems can lead to a rather shallow military capability without wider competences that are more difficult and time-consuming to acquire, but this has not in the past prevented states from attempting to use them.

It is difficult to foresee any decline in the causes of disputes which can lead to the use of force. The classic sources of conflict have not gone away, such as access to resources, which could well broaden to include water and agricultural land, as well as new resources which hitherto could not be exploited, such as in the Arctic or on the sea bed. There is no shortage of disputes over territory, while ideology (with religion as a subset) remains a potent source of conflict. A range of widely acknowledged pressures on economies, societies and states – such as climate change, mass migration and unstable political structures – can easily lead to internal conflict that spreads into neighbouring states or otherwise affects the international system. It would not be difficult to add many more potential causes of armed conflict to the list but these suffice to justify an assumption that armed conflict will continue to be a significant factor in international politics. Such conflict may remain confined within a single state but can also spread more widely or, alternatively, a regional or extra-regional power (of which, as argued above, there is an increasing number) could determine that its interests are threatened to an extent that demands intervention.

The use of force by states will therefore continue to be a prominent feature of world politics. This applies particularly at sea. There is always a competition to find a catchy label for an emerging period in history; the current century is variously predicted to be a 'Chinese century', an 'Asian century' or a 'Pacific century'. Each of these is sufficiently vague to have some plausibility while also being incomplete and even a little intellectually lazy, as such headline terms often are. A more plausible candidate could be offered: the twenty-first century will be a *maritime* century. The sea has always played a central, although often surprisingly overlooked role in international affairs. It was enormously important in the nineteenth century in peacetime, conflict and war, and even more so in the twentieth century. It is difficult to see the use of the sea being any less significant over the rest of the current century.

There are many reasons for this prediction. First, there is a growing concentration of population centres and economic activity close to the sea, while its commercial use is continuing to increase as world trade expands. Second, many of the causes of conflict referred to above apply particularly at sea, whether in the form of disputed maritime boundaries, access to fisheries, minerals and other resources, or even challenges to the rights of passage and access enshrined in international law. The UK Ministry of Defence paper *The Future Character of Conflict* concluded with convenient alliteration that the future battlespace will be 'congested, cluttered, contested, connected and constrained'.[2] It might well have added a sixth adjective in the form of 'coastal'. Third, the major existing powers such as the US, UK, France and Japan all place considerable importance on their use of the sea for economic, diplomatic and political purposes. While they might be in relative decline to some degree, this does not mean – as some of the more excitable headlines suggest – that they will not continue to be important actors. The same can be said of many medium powers for which the sea is, if anything, of growing importance, such as Australia or Canada. Moreover, the rising powers (which are joining the existing powers rather than usurping them), such as China and India as well as various other key regional powers in Asia and Latin America, all look to the sea. The states that are likely to be the most significant players in international politics in the future – both established and rising – share the important characteristic of a heavy dependence on the sea for economic purposes, as well as an established or growing awareness of its benefits for military purposes.

UK maritime doctrine lists several attributes of the sea that make it appealing for the use of force, such as the legitimate access and presence that it allows, as well as the mobility and flexibility that it provides to military forces.[3] These characteristics have long made naval forces the option of choice for many states when intervening beyond their borders, not least because they permit deployment without the need to seek permission to station troops or aircraft on the territory of other states, with all the diplomatic complications, political compromises and military disadvantages that this often entails. Clearly not every military operation can be conducted from the sea and there will remain some aims that can only be achieved by committing large numbers of troops on the ground – though there might well be an increasing wariness about taking on such costly and demanding commitments. Further, naval capabilities are expensive to acquire and difficult to master; yet on the other hand, a large number of states evidently see the effort as well worth it.

The argument from this first section is that the state will continue to form the foundation of the international system and that the use of force will be no less prominent a feature of the next 50 years than it has been over the past 50. Further, the nature of future conflict, the orientation of the principal world and regional powers and the advantages of naval power for a range of objectives mean that the sea is likely to be at least as important as an avenue for state activity as it has been to date. Armed conflict will continue to be central to international politics, and much of this will continue to be naval conflict.

The challenge of new technology

The principal reason why some would disagree with this argument would be the impact of technology – specifically emerging weapons systems that are interpreted as challenging naval power. According to this argument, the increasing range, accuracy and striking power of submarines, land-based aircraft and anti-ship missiles pose an ever greater challenge to the major surface warships that are at the heart of the naval capabilities of the great powers. As a result, the argument continues, the ability of these fleets to act against significant opposition is ever more curtailed and their value greatly reduced; the sea might well be used for military purposes but surface warships will have less of a role.

There are many weapons that threaten large surface warships. As a result of the globalisation of the international arms trade, advanced weapons are widely available. This supply side of the equation is matched by a strong demand: the reliance of the major Western powers on large warships for influence and intervention is evident, giving those states hostile to such activities ample incentive to seek ways to prevent them or at least to raise their cost and complexity. While relatively few states possess nuclear-powered submarines, developments in their more widely available diesel-electric cousins have made them quieter and faster, and improved their range; they can also deploy sophisticated torpedoes or even anti-ship missiles. Similarly, ever more states possess land-based aircraft which again can carry sophisticated anti-ship weapons while also being equipped or upgraded with advanced targeting or electronic warfare systems. Land-based anti-ship missiles, whether cruise or ballistic, are ever more widely available; the former are becoming faster, stealthier and harder to counter, while the latter would be extremely difficult to defend against and could potentially threaten warships well out to sea. Further ahead, hypersonic weapons (those travelling at over five times the speed of sound) offer the potential of rapid and responsive strikes, though the technical problems that remain to be solved are considerable.[4] The effectiveness of these offensive capabilities is increased by longer range (notably over-the-horizon) or space-based surveillance and targeting systems, electronic and cyber warfare capabilities and, for the most sophisticated opponents, anti-satellite weapons. It is easy to overlook the more basic sea denial weapons in the form of the naval mine, which is more affordable than most of the alternatives and is steadily advancing in sophistication; at the very least it can cause complications for and impose delays on any intervening navy. Any assessment of threats to naval forces must also take into account weapons that do not target the warships themselves, but rather the aircraft on which they depend for so much of their potential in power projection. Modern air defence systems pose a considerable threat to non-stealthy aircraft (and stealth could become less of an advantage as intensive efforts to counter it begin to pay off) and even to land-attack missiles.

Even assuming only linear development of such weapons systems (that is, not factoring in any sudden leap forward in capability or a dramatic new invention), it is easy to understand the view that the threats to intervening navies are becoming ever more lethal, perhaps even reaching a level that makes these fleets unusable against any but the smallest powers. So, is the onwards march of technology inevitably bringing about the eclipse of naval power?

The dynamics of technological change

There is something in such arguments but perhaps less than meets the eye, or so previous experience of attempts to discern the impact of technological change would suggest. There are plenty of famous cases where new technologies have been initially underestimated, with their actual impact only becoming clear after painful and costly lessons on the battlefield. However, the list of technological innovations and new weapons systems that have been *exaggerated*, with equally damaging results, is just as great, though oddly less well known. For every thinker who dismissed the impact of air power, for example, there was one (or actually rather more) who greatly overstated its impact[5] – with the latter group, of course, still existing. This tendency has been particularly prevalent concerning naval power; a whole series of developments have led to the demise of the surface warship being prematurely hailed. In the late nineteenth century, torpedo boats were going to make capital ships obsolete; in the early twentieth century it was the submarine, then land-based aircraft, nuclear weapons, anti-ship missiles, swarm tactics, asymmetric attacks and cyber warfare. All too often, the argument has begun with the observation that a novel weapon poses a threat to large warships … and then leapt directly to the conclusion that the latter are therefore obsolete.

The flaws in these claims are interesting to note, not least because of the number of times that they have been – and continue to be – repeated.[6] First, they exaggerate the vulnerability of warships due to a focus on the final stages of an engagement (for example, a bomb or a missile hitting a ship) without considering what is required to make that engagement occur successfully. The ship has to be located (which, for example, proved remarkably difficult for land-based aircraft throughout the Second World War), a weapon-carrying aircraft or vessel has to get within attacking range, it has to launch a successful attack and the attack has to cause significant damage to the target. Each of these steps is more difficult to accomplish than its usual portrayal suggests, because of the second flaw in the argument: it understates the ability of warships and navies to adapt and to counter the threats that face them. This adaptation might be technological (such as giving battleships quick-firing guns capable of engaging small, fast torpedo boats), or tactical (such as accompanying capital ships with 'torpedo-boat destroyers', or later, anti-submarine escorts), or operational (relating to the ways in which task forces and fleets deploy and fight) – or, more likely, all three. Third, such claims overlook the ways in which new technologies do not only threaten navies but can also be adopted by them, incorporated and used either to counter various threats, to conduct existing roles more effectively or to add new roles to what navies can do. Weapons systems that can be used in sea denial can also be used by intervening navies, for a tactical defensive in one area, or as part of their overall operational design. Other innovations, such as Directed Energy Weapons, would be well suited to deployment on warships, potentially greatly increasing their capacity to engage aircraft, missiles or small attacking craft. Fourth, at the wider strategic level, such arguments neglect the fact that while sea denial may be all that some states require or the most to which they can aspire, many states need not merely prevent others from using the sea but also to use it positively themselves. They have therefore invested in countering the various threats to surface warships.

This argument should not be misconstrued. Of course warships can be sunk. Yet so too can infantry be killed, tanks destroyed, aircraft shot down and their bases destroyed. The central issue is whether the level of risk prevents them from conducting their assigned roles, or whether the cost of adapting them becomes prohibitive for a particular state. The effect of technological advance is not simply to make particular weapons systems obsolete through vulnerability. The battleship, for example, did not disappear from modern fleets because it was vulnerable – with its armour, it was clearly less vulnerable than the aircraft carrier that replaced it as the centrepiece of the modern fleet; further, battleships had long been vulnerable to the guns of other battleships, as well as to more recent threats such as torpedoes. The reason for the demise of the battleship was rather that other platforms and systems (notably nuclear-powered submarines, anti-ship missiles and naval aircraft) could more effectively perform its roles while offering other capabilities besides.

The impact on navies of changing technology has been enormous in fostering adaptation and change in the appearance of warships, the systems they carry, the balance of task forces and fleets, their tactics and strategies. However, it has not removed the fundamental need of the majority of states to use the sea, including for military purposes. It has increased the range of options available for asymmetric approaches of sea denial (of which more below) and it has raised the cost of the highest-end naval capabilities above the level that many states are prepared to pay. That this impact is fundamental and far-reaching is undeniable; yet this is not the outcome that has been predicted by many thinkers who exaggerate and misunderstand the process of technological change.

Developing technology and modern navies

This argument is important because it has considerable relevance for future naval conflict – not least in suggesting that there are grounds for scepticism about some of the claims made on behalf of new weapons systems. Throughout the twentieth century, a succession of new technologies were interpreted as spelling the end for major surface warships. Yet in the middle of the second decade of the twenty-first century, the navies of the major powers continue to be centred on large warships, notably aircraft carriers and large amphibious ships. Far from being in decline, ever more states are acquiring both categories of warships, including China, India, Japan and Russia as well as the more traditional users of these capabilities such as the US and Britain. These ships will be in service for many decades, so it is already clear that naval conflict will be dominated by major surface warships until at least the middle of the twenty-first century.

A number of caveats need to be added to this statement. First, these classes of warships have long been one part of a wider force structure that integrates a range of different ships, aircraft and other systems; this tendency is likely to continue and to widen to include a greater range of assets and capabilities. Second, the ever wider availability of weapons systems such as those referred to above will not render large surface warships obsolete but will rather push them to adapt further and will alter, and to some degree constrain, the way in which they operate.

A good example here is the increasing use of unmanned air systems (UAS).[7] These are sometimes portrayed as being a threat to the longevity of manned aircraft, given their greater survivability and the greater willingness to risk their loss. Why risk an expensive aircraft with its expensively trained aircrew when a cheaper UAS can do the job instead? One response to this question, of course, is that sometimes the UAS *cannot* do the job; despite the steep curve of their improving capability, there are still some roles of manned aircraft that UAS cannot perform, not least those requiring the judgement of someone on the spot. There is, of course, the further concern that the use of UAS depends on a high degree of mastery of the electromagnetic spectrum, which might not always be enjoyed against a sophisticated opponent, potentially leaving valuable capabilities open to interference. Once again, it is worth turning to history for guidance. When surface-to-air missiles (SAMs) were first introduced, some thinkers and decision-makers predicted that they would make both manned fighters and anti-aircraft guns obsolete. What actually emerged was a mixed system, involving a combination of manned fighters, SAMs and guns. Similarly, long-range missiles suitable for attacking targets on the ground have not replaced strike aircraft but have rather been added to the inventory to be used alongside them and, indeed, to be delivered by aircraft. So far, UAS have been used in addition to manned aircraft rather than instead of them, and while their use is likely to expand in the future, this basic pattern will remain the same. Much like manned aircraft before them, UAS are well suited to use from warships, whose capabilities they greatly enhance. They increase the effective range of warships, allowing them to gather information, counter threats and strike targets at greater range. Moreover, while some UAS are small, the more capable models offering long range, long endurance and heavy payload, tend to need a large deck from which to operate, such as that of an aircraft carrier or a large amphibious ship. As with other innovations before, UAS will be added to the increasingly diverse naval force, helping it to counter other threats and improving its ability to conduct its assigned roles. (The role of unmanned surface and sub-surface systems is also likely to increase greatly, though like their aerial counterparts, the effect is likely to be to join existing platforms – even to be deployed from them – rather than to replace them.)

The long-running process that has seen naval task forces become broader and more diverse is accelerating. They already include surface warships, organic naval aircraft (including helicopters as well as fixed-wing aircraft, and now UAS too), submarines and land-based aircraft. These naval task forces, moreover, operate in a context that is increasingly combined (i.e. with allies) and joint (i.e. with other services) – the latter in particular altering how navies operate. Their activities are now often closely integrated with land-based aircraft or with land forces, and also, crucially, with national 'enablers' such as strategic intelligence support, and various systems in the new domains of space and cyber, which have been added to the familiar sea, air and land. It is perhaps becoming ever more misleading to refer to 'naval conflict' given this increasing level of integration with other services and capabilities. In some ways, this is nothing new; Julian Corbett, the great naval theorist, frequently emphasised the crucial importance of conceiving of naval strategy and operations within their proper, broader context.[8] It has, however, become ever wider and more closely inter-twined with other capabilities to a degree undreamt of in Corbett's time.

Dilemma: quality or quantity?

The onwards march of technology and the emergence of new capabilities present dilemmas for the leading military powers. One hardy perennial debate mainly affects the hard-pressed medium military powers, though also having some relevance to the larger powers; that is, the balance between quality and quantity. Put simply, high-end warfighting demands increasingly sophisticated and therefore expensive capabilities; yet designing a fleet around these tends to result in fewer and fewer platforms, raising questions about the capacity of the navy concerned to fulfil all the roles that national policy might require of it (let alone its ability to withstand losses in a conflict, raising the concern that its highly capable warships become too precious to risk). Peacetime and low-level conflict roles tend to require larger numbers of platforms, which need not necessarily possess the highest level of warfighting capability. Yet focusing too much on these lower-cost, lower-capability platforms runs the risk of reducing flexibility and having ships on station that would not be capable of participating in the more demanding missions should this become necessary.

To give a concrete example, the Royal Navy has built a class of six highly sophisticated air defence destroyers, the Type 45.[9] The rationale for such capable warships is that they are required for the most demanding warfighting tasks in a national or, more likely, a coalition operation, which remains a fundamental driver for British policy. Critics, however, suggest that the high cost of these ships reduces the number of platforms available too far, with the result that there are fewer available for maritime security operations, or for routine presence around the world. They argue that it is inefficient to have such an expensive warship conducting anti-piracy patrols in the Indian Ocean; the Naval Staff would respond that the Type 45 can do this and then at short notice move a couple of hundred miles north and take part in high-intensity warfighting operations, which a cheaper patrol corvette would be unable to do. This case is merely the latest example of a long debate over how to achieve a balance between numbers and capability. During the Cold War, there were enough warships to do both; the US Navy referred to the 'high-tech/ low-tech mix', while the Royal Navy (using one of those cricketing terms that foreigners so appreciate) referred to the 'first eleven and second eleven'. The principle was that older ships would provide the lower-capability end – you do not build less capable ships. At times proposals were aired suggesting that, say, rather than build two expensive vessels, it would be preferable to build three cheaper ones to provide more hulls. Such ideas tended to founder on the concern that financial considerations would distort the decision-making process, with any suggestion that less capable warships were acceptable likely to be seized on by the money men, with the end result being not three but rather only two of the less capable ships.

This dilemma existed during the Cold War but has become sharper more recently with emerging technologies. On the one hand, these raise the cost of warships capable of the highest-end operations; yet on the other hand, they could also present some possible solutions. One of the big debates around the turn of the century concerned the existence and implications of a 'revolution in military affairs'.[10] The most relevant concept for naval conflict to emerge from this debate was that of 'network-centric warfare', that is, where the elements of a military force operate not as individuals but as distributed parts of a connected whole, also referred to as a 'system of systems'. This concept first emerged in the naval sphere, with the 'cooperative engagement capability' devised by the US Navy to counter the high-end threat from the USSR. Indeed, naval warfare has long featured a fluid balance between dispersion and concentration; one of the best descriptions of network-centric warfare can be found when Corbett writes that concentration should not be understood as 'huddled together like a drove of sheep, but distributed with regard to a common purpose, and linked together by the effectual energy of a single will'.[11] The further development of the capabilities associated with this concept has presented some interesting ideas for the future structure of navies – not least in reigniting the issue of the balance within the fleet and raising the question of whether the increased diversification and dispersion of naval forces has reached a threshold that effectively means a shift to a new model.

One such idea was laid out in a 2012 doctrine note from the UK Development, Concepts and Doctrine Centre advocating the 'Black Swan sloop' concept.[12] This paper (conceived as a contribution to the debate over the future shape and balance of the fleet) suggested a new approach to the issue of quality versus quantity. It acknowledged the need for greater numbers of platforms but rejected the argument that large surface warships represent 'quality':

> There is no doubt that the current and future surface combatants will be capable of conducting a wide range of tasks across the full spectrum of maritime operations. However, these large combatants will be too few, too costly, too mission essential and most importantly too vulnerable to be risked in a contested littoral.[13]

The envisaged warship, given the historically resonant label of 'sloop of war', would act in groups, as the core of an integrated network of manned and unmanned platforms. Its own fit of sensors, weapons and unmanned systems would be modular and would vary depending on the tasks to which the ship was committed, giving a degree of flexibility. The 'Black Swan' vessels would focus on the roles of securing sea control (including maritime security and global presence, though also having a role in warfighting operations) and would therefore complement the larger, more sophisticated vessels designed for force projection. This concept is a relatively ambitious one: although it does not envisage the end of aircraft carriers or large amphibious vessels, it does advocate a major change to the familiar model of destroyers and frigates. It is not simply a suggestion of large numbers of cheap corvettes but rather a radically different approach that acknowledges emerging threats and seeks to counter them, while also meeting Britain's needs at sea, by the use of emerging technologies and novel concepts. Such ideas are bound to become more prevalent in future debates over force structures.

Asymmetric approaches

Naval forces, especially the larger surface platforms, are expensive and technologically demanding to acquire and to operate. There are heavy penalties in attempting to play the conventional naval game with inferior forces, as losses occur disproportionately. It is therefore not surprising that many actors that perceive a need either to use the sea or to disrupt or prevent another's use of it have adopted an asymmetric approach. This term means fighting an opponent with forces, tactics or strategies that are dissimilar to his, with the aim of exploiting an advantage of one's own or a weakness of the opponent.[14]

Some actors that confront states are inherently asymmetric. Much attention has been devoted to the role in international affairs of non-state actors, such as terrorist or insurgent groups. Some such groups do use force and some of them have sought to use the sea, either for transportation, for strikes against shipping (merchant ships or even warships) or to launch attacks against the shore.[15] Some of the capabilities used are fairly rudimentary, there have been few successful attacks and many more that have been frustrated or defeated. Nevertheless, some insurgent groups, particularly those acting as clients of states, have been able to acquire advanced weapons, and the high value and visibility of merchant shipping and, in particular, warships (whose prestige value is high) makes them tempting targets. Countering non-state asymmetric actors will be a major role for many navies, and a minor though still significant role for the leading ones.

It would be misleading to assume that 'asymmetric' is synonymous with 'non-state'. There is a long history of states adopting asymmetric approaches, arguably even more at sea than on land. Even in the sailing era, for example, France and then the young United States did not seek to contest command of the seas with the Royal Navy but rather to inflict economic losses by raiding commerce. From the mid-nineteenth century onwards the industrial revolution began to provide further options for those who wished to avoid taking on the leading naval powers at their own game. In the late nineteenth century, for example, there arose in France the 'jeune école', which argued that rather than build a battlefleet to counter that of the Royal Navy, a better approach would be to focus on large numbers of small, agile torpedo boats which would overwhelm the powerful but ponderous British battleships.[16] This idea never took hold in official policy partly because of the process outlined above, which saw successful adaptation, but also because France needed to use the sea herself and could not simply rely on sea denial. Other states made effective use of new weapons that provided an asymmetric advantage, not least Japan which opened the 1904–5 war against Russia with a torpedo boat attack against the latter's fleet in harbour, much as it would do again in 1941 with a carrier strike against the US fleet in Pearl Harbor. Germany in the First World War initially sought a traditional, Mahanian fleet-against-fleet struggle for supremacy against the Royal Navy. Yet when this strategy was defeated, an asymmetric approach ensued of using submarines not against warships, as had been widely anticipated, but against merchant shipping; while ultimately unsuccessful, this campaign forced Britain and its allies to expend disproportionate resources compared to those invested in the U-boat fleet.

Throughout the post-1945 period, the evident difficulty of countering the fleets of the major powers in a symmetric fashion made asymmetric weapons and approaches (notably the use of submarines, land-based aircraft, anti-ship missiles and mines) highly attractive. It is a useful corrective to the occasional tendency to overrate the success of asymmetric warfare to note that these were largely unsuccessful, at best imposing minor delays on operations. Countering these strategies and tactics was possible but, as explained above, increasingly expensive. As weapons technology continues to advance and proliferate, however, a modern asymmetric approach could raise the risk and cost above what many would-be intervening navies would be willing to pay.

A modern example of an asymmetric approach is Iran, which has made extensive preparations for a campaign in and around the Strait of Hormuz, aiming to disrupt shipping and complicate the activities of a US naval force. Iran's objective is to deter the US from launching offensive action and also to coerce Washington's regional allies to deny access to bases. This strategy is a broad one, taking in many elements; it includes naval and maritime options such as the relatively familiar submarines, mines, fast attack craft, land-based aircraft and anti-ship missiles. It also extends to more asymmetric means such as use of swarms of small craft in suicide attacks, threats of ballistic missile attack against US facilities in the region and the threat of proxies such as Hezbollah launching terror attacks against the interests of the US and its allies. Further off, the apparent goal of acquiring a nuclear capability also fits into an asymmetric approach to preventing US military action.

Such an approach for Iran is far more promising than seeking to build larger surface warships, a lesson painfully learned during the 'tanker wars' phase of the Iran–Iraq conflict, when the surface forces of the Iranian Navy were rapidly defeated. The attention devoted to the capability of Iran to 'close the straits', disrupt international shipping or even inflict potentially prohibitive losses on an intervening US force suggests that the threat is taken seriously. However, it is not guaranteed to succeed, given the resources and capabilities of the US and its allies. One problem for those who exaggerate the effectiveness of asymmetric approaches is that, to paraphrase the famous expression, 'it takes two to be asymmetric'; those who convince themselves that asymmetric means offer a low-cost option against a great power risk a severe shock when their opponent escalates, retaliating in a devastating, albeit conventional, fashion against their military or governmental infrastructure. Iran, for example, has a range of potential vulnerabilities not least its own fuel exports. Asymmetric warfare conducted by non-state actors or, even more, by states is undoubtedly a major nuisance to the leading powers, and can cause significant damage; it is not necessarily a game changer. However, this conclusion might need to be revised should an emerging superpower make effective use of an approach which might broadly be seen as asymmetric.

'A2/AD' versus 'air–sea battle'

One of the most important relationships for the twenty-first century is that between the US and China. This pivotal relationship has particular significance for future naval conflict because the possibility – however slight – of an armed clash between the two defines the high end of future conventional warfare. Further, the two leading powers of the twenty-first century have devoted considerable thought to how a future conflict between them might unfold.

China stepped up its precautions against US naval power projection as a result of a chastening experience in 1996. Clumsy Chinese military pressure against Taiwan, intended to influence the elections there, resulted in the US reacting with the deployment of two carrier groups to the Taiwan Straits as a very visible show of support. Opinion in the West was divided over whether this had a deterrent effect on China, but the latter's subsequent policy suggests that the potential influence of the US carriers was taken very seriously indeed. There is an evident aim in Chinese strategy to develop force structures and doctrine to induce the US Navy to pull back from the areas that China considers as most central to its vital interests at sea.

The panoply of modern military capabilities opposing navies have been given the label of 'Anti-Access and Area Denial', or 'A2/AD'. This approach – exemplified but by no means confined to China – aims to complicate an opponent's entry into a particular region and then to hinder its movement and operations within it. It thereby aims to frustrate the access and mobility that are the great advantages provided to intervening powers by the use of the sea, for example compelling the US to operate from bases at greater distances from the theatre of operations (thus reducing the effectiveness of its forces) and at higher levels of risk.[17] While the main focus in discussions of A2/AD is China, which represents the most developed and powerful form of the approach, it is also one that others could well seek to emulate.

In the case of China the strategy involves a range of systems both naval, such as a rapidly expanding submarine force and surface warships, and land-based, including aircraft and, in particular, large numbers of increasingly sophisticated cruise and ballistic missiles. (The best publicised anti-carrier system is the DF-21, a conversion of a ballistic missile originally designed to carry a nuclear weapon but now with a conventional warhead; its speed of approach would greatly complicate any attempt to engage it with defensive weapons.)[18] These military capabilities are backed by a huge supporting infrastructure of land–, air–, sea– and space-based intelligence-gathering systems, long-range surveillance and targeting systems, as well as by electronic warfare, operations against the space systems on which the American way of war is so dependent and cyber warfare. This network would be used to threaten and attack deployed US naval forces as well as their bases and supporting infrastructure. The threat to US warships, particularly the aircraft carriers, is designed to hold them at a distance from the areas of concern to China, while the threat to bases aims to erode the willingness of host states to place themselves at risk by granting such facilities to the US as well as to make them less effective for support in time of war.

Some accounts of Chinese anti-access capabilities run ahead of reality. There are formidable technical problems associated with attempting to strike a moving target such as an aircraft carrier with a ballistic missile, not least the difficulties of identifying and acquiring the target and also terminal guidance at enormously high speeds. They would be a greater threat against fixed facilities.[19] Even if their use against carriers were technically feasible, there would be political constraints on their use. A successful attack against a US carrier would itself be highly escalatory in any situation short of full-scale war and the US has ample means of retaliation. Similar problems apply to the use of other Chinese capabilities such as anti-satellite weapons or cyber warfare. While it is always important to guard against complacency or underestimating a potential opponent, there is also the danger of exaggerating its capabilities – not least of conflating current capabilities with future aspirations.[20] Moreover, while China's military capabilities will no doubt improve, so too will those of the US, particularly when directed specifically against A2/AD networks.

Regardless of the reality of the Chinese threat, the US has clearly taken it seriously, both in terms of grand strategy – in the form of the 'pivot' (or 'rebalance') towards Asia – and also in terms of defence planning. Inevitably, the spectre of A2/AD has driven a response in the US, in the form of 'Air–Sea Battle' (ASB).[21] This concept is driven by cooperation between the US Navy and the US Air Force (a cynic might suggest that getting these two notoriously uneasy bedfellows to work together is quite an achievement by China) but also envisages an important role for land forces. It involves US forces continuing to move beyond mere deconfliction and cooperation to integration, including maritime, air, land, space and cyber forces. It envisages drawing on the whole breadth of existing and planned capabilities, including cyber attack, information operations and electronic warfare, as well as manned and unmanned platforms on and under the sea, in the air and in space, with the aim of 'Networked, Integrated Attack-in-Depth'.[22] Some assets such as aircraft carriers would initially be held at distance, while submarines, small surface warships (such as destroyers and littoral combat ships) and unmanned systems operate inside the enemy's core areas, with land-based aircraft operating from more distant air bases, to unravel and defeat the enemy defensive system. This initiative is at a very early stage and the individual programmes that comprise it are vulnerable to reductions in the defence budget. Nevertheless, the Air–Sea Battle concept provides an indication of the form that high-end naval conflict might take. As noted above, the initiative is not solely directed against China and would have utility against any other state that seeks to disrupt or deter US intervention at or from the sea, including the asymmetric approaches of a potential challenger such as Iran.

In some ways, of course, it is stretching the term 'asymmetric' to apply it to China's strategy for naval conflict. The capabilities envisaged are by any standards highly sophisticated and enormously expensive, albeit sharply different from those of the US. Further, China shows increasingly clear signs of becoming a conventional naval power itself. During the Cold War, depictions of the USSR as solely a continental power were increasingly confounded as its navy steadily developed in capabilities, in the roles it undertook and the regions to which it was deployed. This process was in part the result of reflection on the Western use of naval power in limited war, crisis and unstable peace, as set out by the long-time commander-in-chief of the Soviet Navy, Admiral Sergei Gorshkov.[23] While some analysts inside China as well as outside have portrayed the country as overwhelmingly continental in orientation, it should not be a surprise that as its economy has developed and its power increased, it has looked increasingly to naval power. In economic terms, China is enormously dependent on the sea to import raw materials and to export industrial goods. For China, an approach confined to sea denial alone is not an option. It is therefore to be expected that the Chinese Navy will become an increasingly familiar presence at steadily growing distances from home. Moreover, China's own dependence on the sea and on the globalised international economy more broadly provides not only a strong reason to avoid armed conflict with the US, but also incentives to look to cooperation at sea. The Chinese deployment for anti-piracy patrols off East Africa is significant in this respect.

There are signs that China is developing the types of capabilities that would give it a more traditional fleet for operations further from home – in addition to rather than instead of an A2/AD approach to a confrontation with the US. Interestingly, there is an awareness in Chinese writing about anti-ship ballistic missiles that they cannot replace traditional naval assets such as aircraft carriers and submarines, and that they cannot provide sea control.[24] China has accelerated work on a former Soviet aircraft carrier, with the apparent intention to use it to ascend the formidable learning curve involved in operating fixed-wing aircraft from carriers. It is also building up other capabilities that would permit force projection at greater range, building larger amphibious ships including LPDs ('Landing Platform Dock', or amphibious assault ships capable of landing forces by helicopter as well as by using traditional landing craft) with plans for larger and more capable LHDs (helicopter assault ships).[25]

The future of the aircraft carrier

Perhaps the principal debate relating to naval capabilities, certainly the longest in duration, concerns the continuing centrality of the aircraft carrier. No other naval asset, no other military platform has been the subject of more premature obituaries. It is easy to understand institutional antipathy carriers. For air forces, they represent the heresy of air power outside their control (which, embarrassingly, has repeatedly proved its value and versatility relative to land-based aircraft as recently as in operations against Islamic State in Iraq and Syria). For armies and for politicians, they are capital-intensive assets which mean less to spend on other defence or non-defence priorities.

In view of the criticism directed against them, which ranges from the informed to the merely vitriolic, their survival is rather surprising – and this cannot simply be ascribed to institutional inertia from navies, since they have been opposed by many equally powerful and no less inert institutions. Ever since the Second World War, these vessels have been at the heart of the major fleets. Despite their demise being repeatedly hailed, they have successfully adapted and retained their position in navies, fending off threats both conceptual and military from land-based aircraft and from various weapons systems proclaimed to have made them obsolete. As explained above, this process has involved the adaptation of the task force more widely, taking in a wider range of assets, and has also benefited from improvements in the capabilities of the aircraft operating from the ships. The accusation of vulnerability so repeatedly hurled against them has never quite stuck; partly because all military systems are 'vulnerable' but also because empirical evidence contradicts it: despite being involved in a huge number and variety of conflicts and despite the efforts made by opponents, not a single carrier has been hit by an enemy, let alone sunk, since the later stages of the Second World War. Moreover, no aircraft has been lost to enemy action, on the deck of a carrier in this period, either. It is salutary to compare these statistics with the number of air bases knocked out or overrun and the number of aircraft destroyed on the ground by a range of threats from missile strikes to insurgent attack.

Indeed, the carrier seems to be enjoying something of a resurgence. The US is continuing to build large-deck carriers, which play a central role in its envisaged response from high-end conventional warfare such as ASB to countering asymmetric approaches.[26] Britain is currently building two carriers, which will be the largest warships ever put into service by the Royal Navy. France, India, Italy, Russia, Spain and Thailand all deploy carriers. The Japanese Maritime Self-Defence Force has commissioned a 'destroyer', which at 19,000 tons displacement and with a full through-flight deck might well have been labelled a carrier in another navy.[27] As noted above, for all the effort devoted to countering the US Navy's carriers, China also realises their immense utility for sea control and force projection beyond the range at which land-based aircraft can support naval operations. As one Chinese admiral wrote:

> Aircraft carriers symbolize a country's overall strength. They are also the core of the navy's combined-arms sea operations. Building carriers has all along been a matter of concern for the Chinese people. To modernize our national defense and build a perfect weaponry and equipment system, we have to consider the development of carriers.

The article that cites this quotation explains that the Chinese intention for carriers is not to go toe-to-toe with their US Navy counterparts in a repeat of the Pacific War, but rather to support naval operations (both sea control and power projection) at a greater distance than is currently possible for the Chinese Navy.[28] Far from being in decline, aircraft carriers are being deployed in an increasing number of navies.

The reason for this is their evident utility, demonstrated on many occasions, in naval operations both at and from the sea, at all levels from regional war to limited intervention and naval diplomacy.[29] Given the argument at the outset of the chapter, predicting that conflict at and adjacent to the sea will become increasingly prevalent, it is not surprising that more states are seeking the advantages that the capability offers.

This is not, of course, to argue that carriers will remain unchanged or that their roles and uses will be the same as in previous decades. Several states have commissioned helicopter carriers – particularly for anti-submarine warfare or amphibious operations – either in addition to or instead of conventional fixed-wing carriers on the conventional model (including the US, UK, France, Soviet Union, Brazil, Spain, Italy and Australia). The current intention for the British *Queen Elizabeth*-class carriers is that they should be able to combine the roles of carrier strike and amphibious warfare in an ambitious concept known as 'Carrier Enabled Power Projection'. Carriers will continue to evolve. They will deploy unmanned aircraft alongside their existing complement. They will operate in a closely integrated fashion with other surface, sub-surface, air (both naval and land-based) and space systems. This will include novel platforms, such as smaller, networked surface combatants or warships and submarines optimised for strike against land,[30] and within a context of new capabilities, notably cyber warfare. They will continue to have considerable utility in high-end conventional warfare – albeit being constrained in the very highest-threat environments, perhaps operating at greater distances than hitherto in the early stage of a conflict. They will be more central in the far more likely scenarios at the lower and middle range of conflict intensity.[31] Carriers have been in service for nearly 100 years; they will continue to be a central feature of naval conflict for many decades to come.

Lower-intensity roles

Much of this chapter has focused on warfighting operations by naval forces, as these tend to receive the most attention. However, much of what navies do on a routine basis, day by day, is quite different, as well as being far less influenced by changing technology. The roles of naval forces in the future will continue to be varied, across a wide spectrum of types and intensities of conflict. This broad range of activities is peculiar to navies, with no exact parallel among land or air forces, and once again finds ample precedents in history:

> The function of the fleet, the object for which it was always employed, has been three-fold: firstly, to support or obstruct diplomatic effort; secondly, to protect or destroy commerce; and thirdly, to further or hinder military operations ashore.[32]

As now, more states will tend to focus on the more limited end of the scale than aspire to the most demanding operations – though it is likely that the number of states in the latter category will increase rather than diminish.

At the least ambitious end of the scale lie constabulary and humanitarian operations. These include policing national waters, countering crime at sea (such as smuggling or illegal fishing), or responding to humanitarian emergencies. Every navy, even the smallest, conducts these operations.

Moving up a level lie maritime security operations. These include the protection of shipping against harassment or interference, or operations against more developed threats such as piracy or maritime terrorism. Some of these activities are conducted within a state's own territorial waters; the more capable navies will contribute to such operations in more distant waters – the multinational operations in the Gulf of Aden and the Indian Ocean being a good case in point. Closely linked to this sort of activity is the often overlooked diplomatic role of navies,[33] gathering situational awareness and building relationships, supporting and reassuring friends, deterring potential enemies and providing a presence that permits rapid response in a crisis, ideally to prevent or contain it. While much attention is devoted to power projection, this broader, longer-term activity that might be termed 'influence projection' will continue to be hugely significant in the international system, as the major powers use it to interact with each other and to maintain a military presence in their key regions of interest.

Conclusion

The variety of naval operations and the range of naval conflict will remain as broad as before, ranging from constabulary and presence activities, through maritime security, to limited intervention, regional conflict and up to high-end conventional war. There will still be a combination of operations at sea and operations from the sea. The former will include maritime security operations and counter-terrorism but also protection of shipping and assertion of rights of navigation or disputed waters. The latter will include strikes against shore targets as well as amphibious raids and Special Forces operations, on a scale varying widely from small, brief interventions – which are likely to be particularly prominent and conducted by a wider range of states – to longer campaigns.

A bigger change might be expected in who is conducting naval operations. The traditional naval powers (notably the US, UK, France, arguably Russia) will continue to be prominent but they will increasingly be joined by the rising powers such as China and India both within and outside their own regions, as well as by a host of medium navies in their own regions. The advance of technology will increasingly stretch the spectrum of fully capable, to limited global, to local navies. Operations will often be conducted by a multinational force, either drawing on formal alliances or on a more *ad hoc* basis. One interesting possibility is the increasing role of non-state actors in naval conflict, whether in the shape of terrorist groups conducting attacks at or from the sea, or private security companies protecting shipping against pirate attack.

Developing technology has long been a principal driver of changes in naval conflict and this will remain the case. Some new technologies threaten warships and navies, some assist and enhance them, most do both. Any suggestion that large warships are becoming obsolete should be treated with extreme caution, not least because of the previous collapse of so many claims along these lines. While other options can provide some capability in sea denial, for the many states and roles that require the positive use of the sea, surface warships remain essential. They will, however, continue to adapt and will increasingly operate in the context of diverse and integrated force structures that involve land, air, space and cyber systems – and a combination of manned and unmanned platforms – in addition to the traditional naval platforms, surface, subsurface and air. The result of the continuing to-and-fro cycle of technological advance will leave some states by the wayside and will reduce the roles and capabilities to which some other states aspire; but these laggards will be replaced by emerging world and regional powers who are keen to make use of the sea.

The strategic environment and the threats and opportunities presented by emerging technology establish the questions for the future of naval conflict. The key factor in the outcomes of the process, and the main area where answers must be sought, lies in politics. How far will the US reorient its forces towards maritime capabilities as it seeks to balance against China in the context of a diminishing economic and technological lead? To what extent will the UK and other European powers devote the required resources to defence policy in general and to naval forces in particular? As regards Europe, will there be effective cooperation or 'burden sharing', or will its navies simply shrink in isolation? Will Russia collapse or revive, and how far will it look to its navy to support its overseas interests? How far will the rising powers continue the trajectory of their naval development by acquiring the capabilities for power projection at distance from their home territory? What regional powers will emerge as key players and what roles will they seek to conduct at sea? It is in these issues that the key developments framing future naval conflict will unfold.

Notes

1 The analysis, opinions and conclusions expressed or implied in this chapter are those of the author and do not necessarily represent the views of the Joint Services Command and Staff College, the UK Ministry of Defence or any other government agency.
2 Ministry of Defence, *Strategic Trends Programme: Future Character of Conflict* (Development, Concepts and Doctrine Centre, February 2010), especially pp. 20–5. Available at: www.gov.uk/government/uploads/system/uploads/attachment_data/file/33685/FCOCReadactedFinalWeb.pdf, accessed 1 February 2015.
3 Ministry of Defence, *Joint Doctrine Publication 0–10: British Maritime Doctrine* (Development, Concepts and Doctrine Centre, August 2011), especially section 2-1, which list the attributes of maritime power as access, mobility, lift capacity, sustained reach, versatility, poise and resilience, which combine to provide leverage. Available at: www.gov.uk/government/uploads/system/uploads/attachment_data/file/33699/20110816JDP0_10_BMD.pdf, accessed 1 February 2015.
4 See, for example, 'Speed Is the New Stealth', *Economist*, 1 June 2013, which argues that such a weapon system could replace stealth capabilities, which other states will increasingly be able to counter.
5 For an entertaining example that blends a little insight with a lot of exaggeration, see Alexander P. de Seversky, *Victory through Air Power* (New York: Simon & Schuster, 1942), or his 1943 Walt Disney film of the same name.

6 This argument is developed at greater length in Tim Benbow, 'Navies and the Challenge of Technological Change', *Defence Studies* 8, 2 (June 2008), 207–26.

7 They are also referred to as 'unmanned aerial vehicles', or UAVs; when armed, they are referred to as 'unmanned combat aerial vehicles', or UCAVs.

8 See in particular, Julian S. Corbett, *Some Principles of Maritime Strategy* (London: Longmans, 1911).

9 The original plan was for 12 but this was scaled back due to reductions in the defence budget and expenditure on the prolonged campaigns in Iraq and Afghanistan.

10 For a more detailed exposition of my views on this subject, see Tim Benbow, *The Magic Bullet? Understanding the 'Revolution in Military Affairs'* (London: Brassey's, 2004). Essentially, I argue that an RMA comparable with previous cases that were widely recognised as such was indeed underway – but that the implications of an RMA were not what some of its more excitable adherents hoped; its effect are undermined by friction and chance – which will not be eliminated – and by the adaptation of opponents (both symmetric and asymmetric). In particular, it does not offer an easy military solution to complex strategic problems.

11 Corbett, *Some Principles of Maritime Strategy*, p. 131. He was paraphrasing approvingly the words of Alfred T. Mahan.

12 Joint Concept Note 1/12, *Future 'Black Swan' Class Sloop-of-War: A Group System* (Development, Concepts and Doctrine Centre, May 2012). Available at: www.gov.uk/government/uploads/system/uploads/attachment_data/file/33686/20120503JCN112_Black_SwanU.pdf, accessed 1 February 2015.

13 *Future 'Black Swan' Class Sloop-of-War*, pp. 1–13.

14 For more on asymmetric warfare, see Benbow, *The Magic Bullet?*, ch. 7; also Tim Benbow, 'Irresistible Force or Immoveable Object? The Revolution in Military Affairs and Asymmetric Warfare', *Defense and Security Analysis* 25, 1 (March 2009), 21–36.

15 See Martin Murphy, 'The Blue, Green and Brown: Insurgency and Counter-insurgency on the Water', in Tim Benbow and Rod Thornton (eds), *Dimensions of Counter-insurgency: Applying Experience to Practice* (London: Routledge, 2008), 57–73.

16 Theodore Ropp, 'Continental Doctrines of Sea Power' in Edward M. Earle, *Makers of Modern Strategy: Military Thought from Machiavelli to Hitler* (Princeton, NJ: Princeton University Press, 1943), 447–54.

17 For an interesting account of anti-access strategies, which shows that they are far from new, see Sam J. Tangredi, *Anti-Access Warfare: Countering A2/AD Strategies* (Annapolis, MD: Naval Institute Press, 2013).

18 For considerable detail about how the Chinese armed forces envisage using anti-ship ballistic missiles, see Andrew S. Erickson and David D. Yang, 'Using the Land to Control the Sea? Chinese Analysts Consider the Antiship Ballistic Missile', *Naval War College Review* 62 4 (Autumn 2009), 53–86.

19 For an analysis of the threat posed by Chinese ballistic missiles to US carriers and also air bases, as well as the US response, see Marshall Hoyler, 'China's "Antiaccess" Ballistic Missiles and US Active Defense', *Naval War College Review* 63 4 (Autumn 2010), 84–105.

20 Robert S. Ross argues that China 'is still unable to challenge US dominance at sea or upend the balance of power in the region'; Robert S. Ross, 'The Problem with the Pivot', *Foreign Affairs* 91, 6 (November–December 2012), p. 73. His analysis suggests that China's recent assertiveness stems not from confidence but rather from a perception of insecurity.

21 See Aaron L. Friedberg, *Beyond Air–Sea Battle: The Debate over US Military Strategy in Asia* (London: Routledge/IISS, 2014).

22 See Jan Van Tol, Mark Gunzinger, Andrew F. Krepinevich and Jim Thomas, *AirSea Battle: A Point-of-Departure Operational Concept* (Washington, DC: Center for Strategic and Budgetary Assessments, 2010); Air–Sea Battle Office unclassified briefing, 'Air–Sea Battle: Concept and Implementation', 12 October 2102. Also General Norton A. Schwartz, USAF and Admiral Jonathan W. Greenert, USN, 'Air–Sea Battle: Promoting Stability in an Era of Uncertainty', *American Interest*, 20 February 2012. The authors (respectively the Chief of Staff of the USAF and the Chief of Naval Operations) draw the parallel with cooperation between the US Army and US Air Force to defeat Soviet bloc land forces with concepts such as 'Follow-on Forces Attack' and 'AirLand Battle'. Interestingly, they suggest that Air–Sea Battle would be relevant against non-state as well as state opponents.

23 See Sergei Gorshkov (Fleet Admiral, Soviet Navy), *The Sea Power of the State* (Oxford: Pergamon, 1979).

24 Erickson and Yang, 'Using the Land to Control the Sea?', p. 68. Again, comparison with the writings of Gorshkov – in which he argued that the USSR needed a surface fleet as well as the submarines on which some of his compatriots were content to rely – is instructive.

25 Daniel J. Kostecka, 'From the Sea: PLA Doctrine and the Employment of Sea-Based Airpower', *Naval War College Review* 64, 3 (Summer 2011), 11–31. He argues that China sees the amphibious platforms as primarily useful for assaults in the South China Sea but also for wider roles such as counter-piracy, humanitarian relief or non-combatant evacuation.

26 For contrasting approaches in the US debate, see Captain Henry J. Hendrix, US Navy, and Lieutenant-Colonel J. Noel Williams, US Marine Corps (Ret), 'Twilight of the $UPERflous Carrier', *Proceedings of the US Naval Institute* 137, 5/1,299 (May 2011); and Scott C. Truver, 'Now Hear This – "Semper CVN!", *Proceedings of the US Naval Institute* 139, 9/1,327 (September 2013).

27 Vice-Admiral Yoji Koda, 'A New Carrier Race? Strategy, Force Planning and JS *Hyuga*', *Naval War College Review* 64, 3 (Summer 2011), 31–60.

28 Kostecka, 'From the Sea'; quotation cited p. 11.

29 An account and analysis of the use since 1945 of carriers (and also amphibious ships) by the Royal Navy can be found in Tim Benbow, *British Uses of Aircraft Carriers and Amphibious Ships 1945–2010*, Corbett Paper 9 (Corbett Centre for Maritime Policy Studies, March 2012). Available at: www.kcl.ac.uk/sspp/departments/dsd/research/researchgroups/corbett/corbettpaper9.pdf, accessed 1 February 2015.

30 The US has for some time operated cruisers, destroyers and nuclear submarines with land-attack missiles in addition to their other weapons systems. It has also deployed dedicated missile battery ships in the form of four 'SSGNs', Ohio-class former ballistic nuclear missile submarines converted to carry as many as 154 Tomahawk land-attack missiles, as well as being able to deploy special forces.

31 One analyst sees the roles of the carrier changing and its utility narrowing, with greater emphasis on providing the eyes of the fleet (possibly acting in support of submarines) and less on hit-and-run raids, though acknowledging that they will retain a role in 'scenarios short of high-end missile combat'; Robert C. Rubel, 'The Future of Aircraft Carriers', *Naval War College Review* 64, 4 (Autumn 2011), p. 23.

32 Julian Corbett, *England in the Seven Years' War: A Study in Combined Strategy*, vol. 1 (Cambridge: Cambridge University Press, 2010) (reprint of the original Longmans, Green, and Co. 1907 edition), p. 6. I am indebted to Dr James Bosbotinis for this quotation.

33 The classic text on this important field of activity is James Cable, *Gunboat Diplomacy 1919–1991: Political Applications of Limited Naval Force* (London: Macmillan/IISS, 1994).

PART II

Choke points and strategic areas

4

THE EAST CHINA SEA DISPUTE

Ralf Emmers

Introduction[1]

The sovereignty dispute over the Senkaku/Diaoyu Islands in the East China Sea is arguably the most contentious maritime security flashpoint in East Asia. Japan, the People's Republic of China (PRC), and the Republic of China (ROC)/Taiwan have each laid similar claims to the Senkaku/Diaoyu Islands. The conflict has periodically hampered China–Japan relations since the resurgence of the issue in the early 1970s. Beijing and Tokyo were able to shelve the debate to normalize their relations in 1972. Yet the hope of former Chinese leader Deng Xiaoping that a future generation would be able to resolve the matter has been left unrealized. Historical grievances combined with rising nationalism and energy interests has led one analyst to argue that "if there is a flashpoint to ignite a third Sino-Japanese War, it will be the ownership of the Diaoyu Islands in the East China Sea."[2]

The Senkaku/Diaoyu conflict revolves around a series of small unoccupied islands. The island cluster is approximately 120 nautical miles northeast of Taiwan, 200 nautical miles east of China, and 200 nautical miles southwest of Okinawa. Five are considered islets while three are identified as barren rocks. In total, their land amounts to just 7 square kilometers. The Senkaku/Diaoyus are considered valuable, however, as they are strategically located near vital sea lanes of communication and the surrounding seabed is suspected to be rich in hydrocarbon resources. The strategic, economic, and territorial importance of the islands is matched by their symbolic significance to China, Japan, and Taiwan. Furthermore, the fate of this dispute bears importance for other territorial claims held by the contenders. As a result, none of the claimants has so far been willing to make concessions with regard to their territorial claims and the impasse remains a formidable stumbling block toward any form of long-term and peaceful resolution of the disputes.

Recurrent skirmishes have occurred between the disputants and the situation in the East China Sea has continued therefore to be characterized by volatility and uncertainty. While a sustained military clash in the East China Sea remains an unlikely scenario, risks of miscalculations or accidents that could lead to limited confrontation still exist and need to be kept in mind. In contrast to the situation in the South China Sea or the Sea of Japan, the East China Sea is particularly dangerous as it involves the world's second and third largest economies. With large military budgets, their modern navies and air forces face each other in a small geographical area surrounding the Senkaku/Diaoyu Islands. This implies that the strategic and financial consequences of a short-term military clash would be felt both regionally and globally.

This chapter starts by reviewing the history and geostrategic importance of the dispute before examining its main driving forces discussed in terms of nationalism, energy considerations, and shifts in the power balance. It then reviews various attempts at conflict management before examining the escalation of the East China Sea dispute since 2010. It notes that the escalation of tension needs to be viewed in the wider context of a rising China and power competition in East Asia. Finally, the chapter compares the East China Sea to other territorial disputes in East Asia including the situation in the South China Sea and the conflict over the Dokdo/Takeshima Islands in the Sea of Japan. While driven by similar factors, the chapter argues, the Senkaku/Diaoyu issue is more volatile and dangerous due to the geopolitical considerations involved and a higher level of militarization.

The history of the conflict

Japan has been in physical control of the Senkaku/Diaoyu Islands since 1972. This followed the conclusion of the Okinawa Reversion Treaty in 1971. In the agreement, control of the islands and neighboring Okinawa was returned to Japan after being administered by the United States since the end of World War Two. However, controversy over the circumstances both at the time of Japan's incorporation and reversion of the islands has left the dispute open to Chinese claims.[3]

China contends that the islands were ceded to Japan, as part of Taiwan, under the Treaty of Shimonoseki that followed the end of the 1895 China–Japan War. When the San Francisco Peace Treaty was signed in 1951, Japan renounced all claims over Taiwan but the Senkaku/Diaoyu Islands remained in U.S. control. At issue therefore is whether the Treaty of Shimonoseki should be interpreted as inclusive of the Senkaku/Diaoyu Islands. As Taiwan is so near to the contested islands, China concludes that the treaty was referring to the Senkaku/Diaoyus when including Taiwan's "appertaining islands."

China's own case relies on the principles of historical discovery and usage, dating back to the Ming Dynasty.[4] Beijing contends that traveling Chinese fishermen first discovered the Senkaku/Diaoyu Islands and that it has been known since the sixteenth century that the islets were part of China's coastal defense system.[5] In 1893, Qing Dynasty Empress Dowager Tsu Hsi issued an imperial edict related to the use of the islands. Their discovery combined with this official act constitutes the thrust of China's historical claim to sovereignty today.[6] In contrast, Tokyo asserts that the Senkaku/Diaoyu Islands were incorporated into Japanese territory at the end of the nineteenth century, through a Cabinet decision unrelated to the China–Japan War and the Shimonoseki Treaty, after surveying the islands and considering them *terra nullius*.[7] From the 1950s, the islands were leased to the U.S. and then returned to Japan under the Okinawa Reversion Treaty.

China's formal protests contesting Japanese sovereignty over the Senkaku/Diaoyu Islands were filed following a 1968 United Nations geological survey that estimated that a large quantity of oil and gas was present in the surrounding area. Not until 1970 did both the PRC and the ROC claim the Senkaku/Diaoyu Islands as part of Chinese territory. Likewise, Japan had not paid much attention to the islands until then. Tensions later subsided as Beijing and Tokyo worked to normalize relations in 1972. The larger advantages provided by the Peace and Friendship Treaty led to the deferral of the issue in favor of increased bilateral trade and cooperation.[8] Deng Xiaoping reiterated the policy shared by China and Japan of shelving the issue, noting that the "next generation will certainly be wiser. They will find a solution acceptable to all."[9]

Nevertheless, neither China nor Japan has backed down on its claims to sovereignty since the normalization of bilateral relations. There has been no concession over the fundamental question of rightful ownership. While China has settled 17 of its 23 territorial disputes since 1949, Beijing has offered no compromise on the Senkaku/Diaoyu Islands. On its part, Japan is hesitant to admit that the islands are in fact disputed by China. As neither China nor Japan is open to negotiation on the issue, the entire sovereignty dispute remains at an impasse.

Geostrategic importance

The geostrategic importance of the Senkaku/Diaoyu Islands and the wider maritime area surrounding the islands should not be overlooked. While more attention and focus has sometimes been placed on the disputes in the South China Sea, the East China Sea region is, arguably, the more dangerous maritime flashpoint in East Asia given that the issue directly involves the great powers and that the economic and political consequences stemming from a military confrontation in this area would likely be more severe.

Should open conflict break out in the region, the U.S. may be forced to intervene owing to its treaty obligations to assist Japan. Moreover, unlike the situation in the South China Sea, the East China Sea is "not surrounded by smaller, weaker nations that Beijing can attempt to influence."[10] This suggests that the level of naval capabilities would play a central role in a confrontation. This has already been evidenced by the constant build-up of military capabilities by Beijing and Tokyo as well as by the strong U.S. military presence in the region.

The islands are also close to vital shipping lanes. The disruption of commercial navigation in a case of open conflict would have worldwide repercussions. The three major economies in the region (China, Japan, and South Korea) would be hardest hit. Russia is also likely to be significantly affected as it has increasingly used the East China Sea to export its natural resources.[11] Finally, the dispute in the region presents itself as an avenue for competition between the U.S. and China for power and primacy in the wider East Asian region.

Driving forces

Various driving forces have transformed the Senkaku/Diaoyu dispute into a volatile maritime flashpoint in East Asia. The conflict has been driven by nationalistic sentiments, energy considerations, and threat perceptions as well as the growing importance of such issues in China–Japan relations. Still, it should be noted that the dispute over the contested islands has so far remained generally peaceful. The leadership in China and Japan, while not conceding any ground on the issue of sovereignty, has sought to avoid a military confrontation in the East China Sea.

The disputed territory has evoked strong nationalistic sentiments in the claimant states partly because Chinese and Japanese officials have relied on nationalist rhetoric to gain domestic support. In China, the invocation of nationalism has offered Chinese officials an easy way to divert blame for the failure of their own policies and to bolster regime legitimacy.[12] Historical claims and resentment toward Japan enable the Chinese government to unify its people.[13] Yet such nationalism is tightly monitored by the government and primarily aimed at a domestic audience. It thus serves as a political tool to increase support for the leadership and create a sense of domestic unity.[14] In Japan, politicians must cater to the demands of their constituencies. This allows nationalist interests to gain a larger voice. For example, visits to the Yasukuni War Memorial in Tokyo are meant to appease the conservative wing of the Liberal Democratic Party (LDP). Mark J. Valencia writes that "in Japan, numerically small but well-organized and funded rightists make 'surrender,' or even concession on sovereignty claims, politically difficult if not impossible."[15]

Beyond the immediate leadership in Beijing and Tokyo, the conflict in the East China Sea is driven by deep popular mutual antipathy. Denny Roy reminds us that a barrier to "a substantially improved bilateral relationship is grassroots ill will. Undercurrents of mutual unfriendliness persist in both societies."[16] In China, the dispute over the Senkaku/Diaoyu Islands evokes memories of the Pacific War and the Japanese occupation of Chinese territory until the Japanese surrender in August 1945. The contested territory is therefore regarded as a national symbol and the ongoing conflict with Tokyo as an illustration of Japan's failure to confront its colonial history. Moreover, contentious history textbooks published in Japan that minimize war crimes as well as visits by top officials to the Yasukuni Shrine exacerbate such nationalistic feelings in China.

The Senkaku/Diaoyu dispute has also been influenced by the possible access to gas and oil deposits as well as by the exploitation of fisheries. The sovereignty dispute is therefore in part a dispute over control of offshore resources. Japanese, Chinese, and Taiwanese fishing vessels are particularly active in the East China Sea and demand for fishery resources is growing rapidly. Oil present in the East China Sea has been projected to be between 10 and 100 billion barrels' worth.[17] Other estimates have referred more specifically to a capacity of 80 to 100 billion barrels of oil reserves.[18] Likewise, the amount of natural gas believed to be at stake varies greatly. For instance, in the case of the Chunxiao/Shirakaba field, it varies from Japan's estimate of 200 billion cubic meters to China's estimate of 20 million.[19]

Finally, in terms of the military balance, Japan is in physical control of the disputed islands and has at this point superior defense capabilities and equipment relative to China. Japan has the advantage of being a treaty ally of the United States and the bilateral security treaty would oblige Washington to defend the Senkaku/Diaoyus as Japanese territory in case of a military engagement with China. The U.S. Pacific Command is in charge of fulfilling the mutual defense treaty. Even without American support, the Self-Defense Forces (SDF) have superior air and naval capabilities to China despite Japan being officially "disarmed" under Article 9 of its constitution since the end of World War Two. Beyond the SDF, Tokyo can also rely on the Japanese Coast Guard (JCG),[20] which has in recent years responded to Chinese naval activities in the East China Sea by increasing its presence around the contested islands.

Nevertheless, the naval power balance is shifting toward growing regional competition, as China continues to make advancements in strengthening its naval capabilities (see Table 4.1 for a comparison of Chinese and Japanese naval capabilities). Despite the PRC's traditional lag in military capability, the country has been a rising strategic concern for Japan since the end of the Cold War. Beijing has sought to substantially strengthen its military power in recent years, as its double-digit increases in military spending have resulted in large defense budgets. For example, China's defense budget for 2014 was US-$132 billion, up 12.2 percent over 2013.[21] Japan's defense budget has traditionally been less than 1 percent of the country's gross domestic product (GDP) and it is unlikely that Tokyo will be able to commit more than 1 percent of its GDP to national defense in the future due to domestic constraints. Large parts of the Chinese military budget have been committed to building up a blue-water navy capable of competing with Japan and to a lesser extent the United States. Indeed, acquiring a blue-water navy is also meant to help the PRC extend its defense perimeter into the Western Pacific, a maritime area that has been dominated by the U.S. Navy since 1945. As a result, the East China Sea dispute has in recent years been affected by the Chinese naval build-up and its wider strategic aspirations in the Pacific.[22]

Table 4.1 Naval capabilities of China and Japan

China[a]	Japan
Navy	*Maritime Self-Defense Force*
Submarines 70	Submarines 18
Principal surface combatants 70	Principal surface combatants 47
Patrol and coastal combatants 216+	Patrol and coastal combatants 6
Mine warfare 53	Mine warfare 36
Principal amphibious vessels 3	Landing ships 4
Landing ships 85	Landing craft 20
Landing craft 152	*Naval aviation*
Naval aviation	Aircraft 78 combat capable
Aircraft 332 combat capable	Helicopters 134
Helicopters 103+	*Coast guard*
Coast guard	Patrol and coastal combatants 389+
Patrol and coastal combatants 70+	Aircraft 25
	Helicopters 46

Source
Data adapted from International Institute for Strategic Studies, *The Military Balance 2014*, pp. 230–40, 250–4.

Note
[a] Excludes assets held by Taiwan.

Conflict management

A number of conflict-management measures have been proposed by analysts to ease tensions in the East China Sea. These have mostly concentrated on engaging in confidence-building measures, specifically military exchanges.[23] Better communication and closer relations between the United States, Chinese, and Japanese militaries could, for example, prevent misunderstandings from escalating to the point of military conflict. International arrangements have also been cited as a possible means to bring China and Japan closer together. Tensions may be reduced, for instance, by creating a code of conduct requiring all parties to refrain from actions that could worsen the situation on the ground, such as the building of new facilities on the disputed islets.[24]

Yet, the East China Sea issue is complicated by the absence of regional institutions in Northeast Asia. The sub-region lacks inter-state bodies to diffuse tensions through conflict-management mechanisms. The Northeast Asian states have not established their own security dialogue despite being members of various Asian-wide institutions led by the Association of Southeast Asian Nations (ASEAN) such as the ASEAN Regional Forum, the ASEAN Plus Three, and the East Asia Summit. Established in December 2008, the Japan–China–South Korea Trilateral Summit has lost momentum over the deterioration of China–Japan relations and it has not moved ahead in defusing sources of regional conflict. Moreover, the Six-Party Talks, that brings together the two Koreas, China, Japan, Russia, and the United States to prevent nuclear proliferation on the Korean peninsula, have been suspended. China and Japan are therefore likely in the short to medium term to continue relying on bilateralism and, in the case of Tokyo, on defense ties with the United States to preserve stability in Northeast Asia.

Likewise, a scenario involving the legalization of the dispute through the use of international arbitration remains equally unlikely in the years to come. For a start, Japan does not recognize that the Senkaku/Diaoyu Islands are disputed by China although both parties agreed to disagree on the issue in November 2014. Japan is therefore unlikely to agree to bring the case before the International Court of Justice (ICJ) in The Hague or the International Tribunal for the Law of the Sea in Hamburg.[25] Moreover, Taiwan is not a member of the United Nations and thus in no position to submit its claims to the ICJ or the International Tribunal. Even if China and Japan agreed to rely on international arbitration, it is important to note that the United Nations Convention on the Law of the Sea (UNCLOS) does not specify how to resolve maritime territorial disputes.

Rather than a legalistic approach, analysts have in recent years envisioned some form of joint exploration and development agreement as the most feasible way forward.[26] China and Japan made progress on joint fisheries management when they settled on a bilateral fisheries agreement in 1997 that later came into force in 2000. Significantly, the fisheries agreement did not undermine the Chinese and Japanese exclusive economic zone (EEZ) and continental shelf claims, nor did it question their sovereign rights to the disputed islands.[27] Less success has been achieved in the joint management of hydrocarbon resources. China and Japan reached in June 2008 an "in-principle consensus" on joint development of gas deposits in the East China Sea, starting with an initial block in the Chunxiao/Shirakaba field.[28] The deal was part of an effort to transform the East China Sea into an area of "peace, cooperation and friendship" benefiting the interests of the two nations.[29] Taiwan was once again not a party to the agreement. The consensus did not address the continuing dispute over boundary demarcation, as China and Japan stressed that they maintained their sovereignty claims over the disputed territory. For example, then–Chinese Foreign Minister Yang Jiechi announced that the consensus did not mean that the dispute over boundary demarcations, sovereignty, and EEZs had been resolved.[30]

Nevertheless, disagreements quickly appeared due to different interpretations of what had been agreed upon. Tokyo claimed that both parties were supposed to carry out joint development in the Chunxiao/Shirakaba field while Beijing argued that it had only agreed to capital participation and that Japan had recognized China's sovereign rights over the field.[31] The 2008 agreement has so far not been implemented. China and Japan have also failed to reach similar agreements applicable to other disputed areas in the East China Sea. Instead, cases of unilateral survey drilling have continued to cause diplomatic tensions. Moreover, the consequences of repeated crises since 2010 have made the implementation of the in-principle consensus unlikely.

Escalation of tension

Standoffs involving fishermen and coast guards have been recurrent in the disputed waters of the East China Sea. A fisheries incident in 2010 illustrated the poor relationship between China and Japan as well as the nationalistic sentiments invoked by the sovereignty dispute. On September 7, 2010, a Chinese fishing vessel operating in the disputed waters collided with patrol boats of the JCG.[32] The subsequent detention of the Chinese skipper led to a major diplomatic incident between Beijing and Tokyo, including the cancellation by China of the planned summit with then-Japanese Prime Minister Naoto Kan. The Japanese authorities eventually released the Chinese captain on September 24, 2010, although this appeasing gesture did not prevent Beijing from asking for an apology and compensation from Tokyo the next day. Following the 2010 crisis, the JCG seized a Chinese fishing vessel accused of illegally harvesting corals near the Senkaku/Diaoyu Islands in December 2011. The Japanese authorities arrested the Chinese captain and crew members, which threatened to once again escalate bilateral relations. Yet, in contrast to the events of 2010, the Chinese Foreign Ministry only called on Tokyo to respect the rights of the arrested fishermen.[33]

A new cycle of escalation started in mid-2012 when the Japanese government announced its intention to buy the Senkaku/Diaoyu Islands. While Japan has administrated the islands since 1972, its government still leased them at the time from a private owner with the exception of the islet of Taisho, which was already state-owned. The announcement by then-Prime Minister Yoshihiko Noda was in response to a proposal by Tokyo's Governor Shintaro Ishihara to purchase the Senkaku/Diaoyus under the Tokyo regional government for commercial development. Noda wanted the disputed territory to remain undeveloped so as to prevent an escalation of the sovereignty dispute with China.[34] Beijing still condemned Noda's plan, stating that the islands were Chinese territory and could therefore not "be bought or sold."[35]

These events were followed by Chinese patrol vessels sailing in waters near the disputed Senkaku/Diaoyu Islands further raising friction between China and Japan. Tokyo responded by calling back its ambassador to China for consultation. Japanese authorities also arrested Chinese activists in August 2012 after some of them set foot on one of the disputed islands. Japan eventually nationalized the Senkaku/Diaoyus on September 11, 2012. In response, anti-Japanese protests erupted in several Chinese cities and at least a dozen Chinese surveillance ships as well as numerous fishing vessels sailed into the territorial waters of the disputed islands. Days of popular anti-Japan demonstrations peaked on the anniversary of the "Mukden Incident" that occurred on September 18, 1931 and became the pretext for the Japanese invasion of China. In addition, Beijing cancelled the celebrations marking 40 years of diplomatic relations with Tokyo. As many as 40 Taiwanese fishing boats and 12 Taiwanese patrol vessels also entered the contested waters near the Senkaku/Diaoyus in late September 2012 in response to the nationalization of the contested islands by Japan.

The victory of Shinzo Abe and of his center-right political party, the LDP, in the Japanese national elections in December 2012 further complicated bilateral relations with Beijing. Since his election, Abe has adopted a more nationalistic foreign policy and has called for a revision of the Japanese constitution and the removal of restrictions on the activities and capabilities of the SDF. Abe also visited the Yasukuni Shrine in December 2013, further worsening relations with China. On the one hand, Abe has strong nationalist and conservative views, which antagonize relations with Beijing. On the other hand, Chinese President Xi Jinping uses the territorial dispute with Japan to respond to nationalistic sentiments and domestic frustrations in China. The Chinese incursions in the disputed waters of the East China Sea have mostly continued since the nationalization of the Senkaku/Diaoyu Islands in 2012. The repeated incursions are meant to test through non-military means the will of Japan to administer the Senkaku/Diaoyus and to push Tokyo to acknowledge that the islands are indeed disputed by China. Bilateral relations remained frozen from 2012 until 2014. Chinese President Xi Jinping refused to meet Prime Minister Abe until November 2014, when both leaders met on the sidelines of the Asia-Pacific Economic Cooperation (APEC) forum held in Beijing. The first bilateral meeting since the two leaders came to power was made possible by a prior agreement to agree to disagree on the East China Sea situation.

A high level of tension had previously been reached when China announced an Air Defense Identification Zone (ADIZ) over the East China Sea in November 2013 that covers a large part of the semi-enclosed sea. The establishment of such a zone is by itself neither controversial nor a source of escalation. The United States, Japan, and the Republic of Korea (ROK) have, for example, relied on similar identification zones since the Cold War period.[36] Over 20 states have established ADIZs around their territories to provide them with early notification of foreign civilian aircrafts entering their national airspace.[37] It should also be noted that an ADIZ is not a territorial claim and that it has no basis in international law. Still, China was criticized for its lack of consultation with Japan and South Korea, whose existing ADIZs overlap with the

Chinese one, and for the fact that the Chinese ADIZ covers the contested Senkaku/Diaoyu Islands. Moreover, China's ADIZ has been controversial as it requires all civilian aircraft to identify themselves "even if they are only passing through the zone and have no intention of entering Chinese airspace" and demands that military aircraft "must also identify themselves, or else face 'defensive emergency measures' by Chinese armed forces."[38] In response, the United States Air Force sent two B-52 bombers into the Chinese ADIZ without notifying the Chinese authorities, while Tokyo went a step further and advised its commercial airlines to ignore the identification zone when only passing through it. The U.S. military and the Japanese SDF have also agreed to ignore the Chinese ADIZ when it comes to the conduct of their military operations in the East China Sea.[39]

The United States has played an indirect but significant role in the Senkaku/Diaoyu dispute. As mentioned above, it administered the islands from the end of World War Two until the conclusion of the Okinawa Reversion Treaty with Japan in 1971. While Washington has not taken a position on the sovereignty dispute, the Senkaku/Diaoyu Islands have been included in the U.S.–Japan Treaty of Mutual Cooperation and Security, signed during the San Francisco Conference in 1951. Then-U.S. Secretary of State Hillary Clinton repeated the U.S. position in 2010 when she declared that the islands fell under Article 5 of the bilateral treaty, implying that Washington would support Tokyo in case of a military conflict with Beijing over the disputed territory. Standing next to Prime Minister Abe, President Barack Obama confirmed the U.S. position during a state visit to Japan in April 2014 when he stated that the bilateral security treaty covers the disputed islands in the East China Sea.[40] The United States has, however, preserved its neutrality over the sovereignty dispute by taking no sides on the legal validity of the respective territorial claims. Obama's statement in Tokyo still angered Beijing and fuelled the regional security dilemma. Teo explains that "Japan views the inclusion of the Senkaku/Diaoyu islands in the US–Japan security treaty as a US commitment to regional peace and stability. China is likely to view it as destabilising."[41] It is too soon to say whether the U.S. strategic commitment to the disputed islands will ultimately maintain the status quo by deterring China from using its armed forces to press its territorial claims in the East China Sea or instead further escalate the situation and in a worst-case scenario lead to an open conflict involving China, Japan, and the United States.[42]

Other territorial disputes in East Asia

The East China Sea dispute is often compared to the South China Sea conflict, which also plays a destabilizing role in East Asia. Like the East China Sea, the South China Sea issue is driven by nationalism, the exploitation of hydrocarbon resources and fisheries, as well as by the rise of China. The United States is also indirectly involved in the South China Sea in light of its security treaty with the Philippines and its interest in the preservation of the freedom of navigation principle. Washington has not taken sides in the sovereignty dispute, as in the case of the Senkaku/Diaoyus. The disputed islets in the South China Sea are particularly small but they could enable the claimants to gain jurisdictional rights over the surrounding waters and seabed. None of the claimants is again willing to make concessions on sovereignty, leaving the territorial issue at an impasse. Yet, in contrast to the East China Sea, the debates over the Spratly and Paracel Islands in the South China Sea are affected by the complexity of the overlapping claims and the multilateral nature of the disputes. The claimants involved are Brunei, China, Malaysia, the Philippines, Taiwan, Vietnam, and possibly Indonesia.

The Senkaku/Diaoyu dispute can also be compared to the bilateral dispute over the Dokdo or Takeshima Islands, as they are respectively known in South Korea and Japan. The Dokdo/

Takeshima Islands are a group of small islets in the Sea of Japan or the East Sea, as it is called in Korea. The islets are considered uninhabitable, and the ROK Coast Guard is patrolling the waters around the islets to reinforce Korea's control of the disputed islands and to dissuade Japanese vessels from approaching. The Dokdo/Takeshima issue has remained an irritant in bilateral relations, preventing a deepening of diplomatic ties between Japan and Korea despite a high level of economic interdependence. The poor relationship is the result of the historical animosity stemming from the Japanese occupation of Korea from 1910 until 1945. The Koreans deeply resent past Japanese actions and such sentiments take on a physical manifestation over the disputed Dokdo/Takeshima Islands.[43] Anti-Japanese nationalism is frequently used by Korean political elites to rally popular domestic support.[44] The Dokdo/Takeshima issue also resonates with nationalist and revisionist groups in Japan. In addition, beyond nationalism, the Dokdo/Takeshima Islands have been important to Japan and Korea due to the living natural resources at stake. The waters around the islands are rich in fishery resources and both countries have large commercial fishing capabilities active in the Sea of Japan.

The Dokdo/Takeshima dispute has escalated in recent years as a spoiler in Japan–South Korea relations. In March 2010, the Japanese education ministry approved elementary school social studies textbooks describing the disputed islets as Japanese territory, provoking an immediate Korean diplomatic response and demonstrations held in front of the Japanese Embassy in Seoul. In July 2011, three Japanese lawmakers from the LDP were denied entry upon arrival in Seoul. The LDP politicians were planning to visit the Dokdo/Takeshima Islands to restate Japan's claims to the disputed islands. In August 2012, President Lee Myung Bak was the first Korean head of state to visit the Dokdo/Takeshima Islands. The visit provoked an immediate diplomatic response from Tokyo, including the calling back of the Japanese ambassador to Korea for consultation. This was followed by popular protests in both countries and a significant worsening in bilateral ties. The current South Korean President Park Geun Hye has so far refused to meet Japanese Prime Minister Shinzo Abe bilaterally due to his nationalistic rhetoric and visit to the Yasukuni Shrine in December 2013.

As with the East China Sea dispute, the prospect for conflict resolution in the Sea of Japan is limited. International arbitration does not constitute a likely scenario to resolve the conflict. Japan is keen to present the overlapping claims to the ICJ but South Korea has refused, as it does not recognize the dispute and considers the Dokdo/Takeshima Islands to be Korean territory. This is therefore the opposite of the East China Sea situation, where Japan controls the Senkaku/Diaoyus and refuses to acknowledge that they are disputed by China.

In short, the East China Sea and Sea of Japan disputes are both driven by nationalistic sentiments and to a lesser extent by the quest for natural resources, while the prospect for resolution remains unlikely in both cases. Still, despite these similarities, the two disputes must be differentiated in terms of the risks involved. The East China Sea issue has been transformed by rising competition between China, Japan, and the United States. The resulting escalation of the territorial conflict makes the Senkaku/Diaoyu dispute a significant flashpoint in East Asia. In contrast, the Dokdo/Takeshima question involves two treaty allies of the United States and physical engagement between their respective navies and coast guards has been rare. The Dokdo/Takeshima issue has therefore not been militarized to the same extent and the risk of conflict over the islands has remained marginal.

Conclusion

The situation in the East China Sea has echoed the worsening of China–Japan relations since 2010. Despite strong economic ties, the bilateral relationship has continued to be undermined by mistrust and popular mutual antipathy. The dispute over sovereignty has caused repeated diplomatic rows as well as tensions and incidents at sea. It has also evoked popular nationalistic sentiments in the claimant states, as it continues to resonate with wider historical grievances and popular animosities. Access to living and non-living natural resources has also influenced the territorial dispute over the Senkaku/Diaoyus. Finally, the dispute has been influenced by the Chinese naval build-up and aspirations in the Western Pacific as well as by power competition with Japan and the United States. Japan is in physical control of the disputed islands and has superior defense capabilities relative to China. Yet, the power balance is shifting as China builds up its naval strength. The United States is also involved through its commitment to defend Japan in case of an open conflict over the Senkaku/Diaoyu Islands. Ultimately, managing the dispute is dependent on increasing trust between Beijing and Tokyo. Beyond the immediate economic interests, historical grievances and nationalism are the primary reasons the territorial dispute has escalated in recent years. If both could become less of an issue in the future, the dispute over the Senkaku/Diaoyu Islands may be calmed, if not eventually resolved.

Notes

1 This chapter builds on Ralf Emmers, *Geopolitics and Maritime Territorial Disputes in East Asia* (London: Routledge, 2010).
2 Unryu Suganuma, *Sovereign Rights and Territorial Space in Sino-Japanese Relations: Irredentism and the Diaoyu/Senkaku Islands* (Honolulu: University of Hawaii Press, 2000), p. 151.
3 China is understood to be inclusive of both the PRC and the ROC, as their claims are the same and are generally considered as one.
4 Erica Strecker Downs and Phillip C. Saunders, "Legitimacy and the Limits of Nationalism: China and the Diaoyu Islands," in *The Rise of China: An International Security Reader*, ed. Michael E. Brown, Owen R. Cote, Jr., Sean M. Lynn-Jones, and Steven. E. Miller (Cambridge, MA: MIT Press, 2000), p. 52.
5 Tao Cheng, "The Sino-Japanese Dispute over the Tiao-yu-tai (Senkaku) Islands and the Law of Territorial Acquisition," *Virginia Journal of International Law* 14, 2 (1974), p. 256; Mark J. Valencia, "The East China Sea Dispute: Context, Claims, Issues, and Possible Solutions," *Asian Perspective* 31, 1 (2007), p. 153.
6 Guoxing Ji, "Maritime Jurisdiction in the three China Seas," Institute on Global Conflict and Cooperation, Policy Paper 19 (San Diego, CA: University of California, October 1995), p. 11.
7 Cheng, "The Sino-Japanese Dispute," p. 244.
8 Min Gyo Koo, "Liberal Peace Theory and the Disputes over the Dokdo/Takeshima, Senkaku/Diaoyu, and Paracel and Spratly Islands" (paper presented at the Conference on Northeast Asia's Economic and Security Regionalism: Old Constraints and New Prospects, Center for International Studies, University of Southern California, March 2006), p. 13.
9 Statement by Deng Xiaopeng, as cited in Zhongqi Pan, "Sino-Japanese Dispute over the Diaoyu/Senkaku Islands: The Pending Controversy from the Chinese Perspective," *Journal of Chinese Political Science* 12, 1 (2007), p. 74.
10 Michael Auslin, "Don't Forget about the East China Sea," in *East and South China Seas Bulletin 2* (Washington, DC: Centre for a New American Security, May 3, 2012), p. 3.
11 *Ibid.*
12 See Suisheng Zhao, "China's Pragmatic Nationalism: Is It Manageable?" *Washington Quarterly* 29, 1 (2005), p. 132.
13 Suganuma, *Sovereign Rights and Territorial Space*, p. 14.
14 Caroline Rose, "'Patriotism Is Not Taboo': Nationalism in China and Japan and Implications for Sino-Japanese Relations," *Japan Forum* 12, 2 (2000), p. 170.
15 Mark J. Valencia, "Domestic Politics Fuels Northeast Asian Maritime Disputes," *AsiaPacific Issues* 43 (Washington, DC: East–West Center, 2000), p. 4.
16 Denny Roy, "The Sources and Limits of Sino-Japanese Tensions," *Survival* 47, 2 (2005), p. 201.
17 Downs and Saunders, "Legitimacy and the Limits of Nationalism," p. 51.

18 Joshy M. Paul, "Territorial Dispute in the East China Sea and Its Effects on China-Japan Relations," *Maritime Affairs* 4, 1 (Summer 2008), p. 116.

19 Valencia, "The East China Sea Dispute," p. 132.

20 See Richard J. Samuels, "'New Fighting Power!' Japan's Growing Maritime Capabilities and East Asian Security," *International Security* 32, 3 (Winter 2007/8): 84–112.

21 The Editorial Board, "China's Disturbing Defense Budget," *International New York Times*, March 9, 2014. www.nytimes.com/2014/03/10/opinion/chinas-disturbing-defense-budget.html, accessed August 28, 2015.

22 See Kamlesh K. Agnihotri, "Naval Power Dynamics in the Western Pacific Ocean: Impact on the Maritime Situation in East and South China Seas," *Maritime Affairs* 9, 2 (Winter 2013): 4–19.

23 International Crisis Group, "Northeast Asia's Undercurrents of conflict," *Asia Report No. 108*, December 15, 2005.

24 *Ibid.*, p. 26, see also Peter Kien-hong Yu, "Solving and Resolving the East China Sea Dispute: Beijing's Options," *Korean Journal of Defense Analysis* 17, 3 (Winter 2005), p. 127.

25 Suganuma, *Sovereign Rights and Territorial Space*, p. 161.

26 See Mark J. Valencia, "The East China Sea Dispute: Prognosis and Ways Forward," *Pacnet 47A* (Honolulu, HA: Pacific Forum CSIS, September 15, 2006).

27 Mark J. Valencia, "Maritime Confidence and Security Building in Asia: Recent Progress and Problems" (paper presented at the 12th Meeting of the CSCAP Maritime Cooperation Working Group, Singapore, December 2002), p. 5.

28 "China, Japan and Taiwan," *The Economist*, June 21, 2008, p. 40.

29 Embassy of the People's Republic of China in Liberia, "Chinese Foreign Minister Q&A on East China Sea," June 24, 2008. http://lr.chineseembassy.org/eng/majorevents/t468646.htm, accessed August 28, 2015.

30 *Ibid.*

31 Tara Davenport, Ian Townsend-Gault, Robert Beckman, Clive Schofield, David Ong, Vasco Becker-Weinberg, and Leonardo Bernard, "Conference Report" (Conference on Joint Development and the South China Sea, Organized by the Centre for International Law, June 2011, Singapore), p. 21.

32 See Yves Tiberghien, "The Diaoyu Crisis of 2010: Domestic Games and Diplomatic Conflict," *Harvard Asia Quarterly* 12, 3/4 (Winter 2010): 70–8.

33 Yoko Wakatsuki, "Japan Arrests Chinese Fishermen after 7-Hour Chase," CNN, December 20, 2011. http://edition.cnn.com/2011/12/20/world/asia/japan-china-fisherman/index.html, accessed August 28, 2015.

34 "Save the Senkaku from Jingoism," *Financial Times*, July 9, 2012, p. 8.

35 Cited in Michael Wei, "Japan Plan to Buy Disputed Islands Draws China's Condemnation," *BloombergBusiness*, July 8, 2012.

36 See David A. Welch, "What's an ADIZ? Why the United States, Japan, and China Get It Wrong," *Foreign Affairs*, December 9, 2013. www.foreignaffairs.com/articles/east-asia/2013-12-09/whats-adiz, accessed August 28, 2015.

37 Richard Bitzinger, "China's ADIZ: South China Sea Next?" *RSIS Commentaries* (Singapore: S. Rajaratnam School of International Studies, December 2, 2013), p. 1.

38 *Ibid.*

39 "Japan, U.S. Reaffirm Plans to Militarily Ignore China ADIZ," *Japan Times*, February 3, 2014. www.japantimes.co.jp/news/2014/02/03/national/politics-diplomacy/japan-u-s-reaffirm-plans-to-militarily-ignore-china-adiz/, accessed August 28, 2015.

40 Juliet Eilperin, "Obama says U.S. Will Stand By Treaty Obligations to Japan," *Washington Post*, April 24, 2014. www.washingtonpost.com/world/president-obama-affirms-us-will-stand-by-treaty-obligations-to-japan/2014/04/24/425dd9c8-cb62-11e3-93eb-6c0037dde2ad_story.html, accessed August 28, 2015.

41 Sarah Teo, "US Presence in the Asia Pacific: Messages from Obama's East Asia Tour," *RSIS Commentaries* (Singapore: S. Rajaratnam School of International Studies, April 30, 2014), p. 2.

42 Hugh White, "Bold Move on US Pivot Promise," *Straits Times*, May 3, 2014, p. A38.

43 See Victor D. Cha, "Hate, Power, and Identity in Japan–Korea Security: Towards a Synthetic Material–Ideational Analytical Framework," *Australian Journal of International Affairs* 54, 3 (2000): 309–23.

44 See Min Gyo Koo, "Economic Dependence and the Dokdo/Takeshima Dispute between South Korea and Japan," *Harvard Asia Quarterly* 9, 4 (2005): 365–78.

5

IMPROVING MARITIME SAFETY AND SECURITY IN THE SOUTH CHINA SEA

Vasco Becker-Weinberg

Introduction

Over the years, as a result of overlapping claims, disputes in the South China Sea regarding the exercise of rights of sovereignty and jurisdiction have increased, particularly with respect to the exploration and exploitation of non-living marine natural resources. The ongoing disputes have not prevented coastal States from undertaking seabed activities in these maritime areas, often without regard for the protection and preservation of the marine environment, or for the potential impacts that these activities might have on international navigation. Other unilateral actions have included the occupation by military force of many islands and features in order to hypothetically strengthen States' claims to the adjacent maritime areas.

This phenomenon is not exclusive of the South China Sea but has particular significance here due to the fact that this is a region heavily dependent on maritime transportation and transit, principally because much of the world's international trade goes through the Straits of Malacca and Singapore. The South China Sea is also the most important loading and unloading area in the world.[1] Therefore maintaining security and stability in the region is both of regional and global concern.

In addition to unlawful and competitive seabed activities, the South China Sea also faces criminality and terrorism at sea, which further enhances the global importance of ensuring maritime security in this part of the world. These threats are only efficiently and successfully addressed through an integrated and transnational approach, at a regional and global level. Notwithstanding, recent practice has seen an increase of outsourcing of security services to private entities that also operate in disputed areas of the South China Sea. Despite the impressive results achieved by such private entities, their accountability and the liability of States in these cases is not a straightforward matter, and one that must be considered also in the context of the maritime disputes of the South China Sea.

Although it will not be the subject of examination, another relevant menace that demands international cooperation in the South China Sea is illegal, unreported and unregulated fishing (IUU/IUUF). The Asia-Pacific region as a whole includes valuable and interrelated marine ecosystems that together have some of the richest marine biological diversity in the world. The fisheries that this abundant marine biological diversity supports are an important source of protein and livelihood for a large part of the world's population and coastal communities.[2] As a result, IUUF also constitutes a serious threat to the stability of the region.

Another aspect that must not be disregarded is the fact that the geopolitics of the South China Sea is not limited to the interaction between coastal States. Despite the fact that there are examples of cooperation between these and States outside of the South China Sea region with respect to combating criminality and terrorism at sea,[3] there have been situations where tensions have run high. This was the case, for example, of the incidents with the USNS *Bowditch* (T-AGS-62) and the USNS *Impeccable* (T-AGOS-23), which took place in China's claimed exclusive economic zone (EEZ).[4] These and other similar situations also contribute to the growing militarization and escalation of disputes in the South China Sea, and provide an excuse for the increase of military capabilities of coastal States.

Maritime jurisdiction in the South China Sea

Recent developments in the South China Sea have considerably shrunk the prospects for the delimitation of boundaries in disputed maritime areas, either by agreement or compulsory settlement mechanisms.[5] Traditionally, States prefer to settle maritime boundaries by agreement, partly due to the uncertainty of the outcome of compulsory mechanisms. Consequently, in the absence of an agreement, deadlock situations are susceptible of continuing for generations without any progress. In some instances they become instrumental for promoting nationalistic rhetoric that may inevitably result in conflict, creating regional and global instability. Moreover, the entrenchment behind nationalism makes it very difficult for States to initiate or resume negotiations, since any attempt would create a sense of capitulation at the national level. It is therefore essential that coastal States refrain from provoking and encouraging a nationalistic discourse at home and from adopting hostile actions. Neither is beneficial or susceptible of resulting in an advantageous legal outcome for the States concerned.

In the present deadlock situation, the only possible way for coastal States to move forward would be through functional cooperation, allowing the *managing* of the disputes and the adoption of measures for the protection and preservation of the marine environment from pollution by seabed activities, as well as securing international navigation and safeguarding other activities and uses of the sea. These measures could include, for example, the adoption of contingency plans for pollution control and prevention, reinforcement of national authorities' efficiency, sharing of information, or development of capabilities.

One possible model for functional cooperation could be achieved through the implementation of provisional arrangements, such as joint development agreements, that could allow the undertaking of seabed activities in disputed maritime areas, without hindering sovereignty claims.[6] However, reaching an understanding on provisional arrangements has not been easily attainable. The main impediment has been the lack of clarification by certain coastal States of what they consider and identify as being the disputed maritime area and the legal title upon which they establish their claims. Both elements are essential, seeing that the rights of coastal States to undertake seabed activities in disputed maritime areas and to enforce jurisdiction, including on matters of maritime safety and security, are intrinsically connected with the legal entitlement upon which they found their claims.[7] In order to determine the existence and extent of a conflict between two or more States regarding opposing or overlapping maritime claims, States are required to make their claims known and to substantiate them with respect to their respective legal title and the identification of the relevant maritime area. In what concerns specifically the exercise of jurisdiction over oil rigs located in disputed maritime areas, this too is established on the basis of the legal entitlement to grant the right to develop the resources of the seabed and subsoil. This form of entitlement includes the right to consent, authorize and regulate the construction, operation, use and decommission of oil rigs and other installations.[8]

Seabed activities in disputed maritime areas

The fact that disputed maritime areas are not subject to the sovereignty or jurisdiction of a singular coastal State does not mean that seabed activities in these areas are not subject to an international binding legal regime, or that coastal States cannot be made responsible. Although the United Nations Convention on the Law of the Sea (UNCLOS)[9] does not include specific rules dealing with the management of disputed maritime areas, international law does provide that States are subject to procedural duties. These include exchanging information and consultation, and States' not exercising their rights within their territory in such a manner as to cause harm or damage to neighboring States.[10]

The interrelation or "functional link" between procedural and substantial obligations is not always evident, particularly when international courts or tribunals recognized compliance with substantial obligations, despite the fact that procedural obligations had been breached. This is the case, for example, if a claimant State would not notify a neighboring State of its intent to develop offshore hydrocarbon deposits located in a disputed maritime area close to the boundary line of that State, thus not creating "the conditions for successful co-operation between the parties," but acting, nonetheless, with "due diligence in respect of all activities which take place under the jurisdiction and control," adopting "appropriate rules and measures" and "also a certain level of vigilance in their enforcement and the exercise of administrative control applicable to public and private operators, such as the monitoring of activities undertaken by such operators, to safeguard the rights of the other party."[11]

In the *Pulp Mills on the River Uruguay* case, the International Court of Justice (ICJ) took into consideration the distinction between procedural and substantial duties in its evaluation of States' compliance with the duty of information, particularly regarding the obligation of one State to provide the other with the results of environmental impact assessments of activities that have trans-boundary effects and the adoption of measures to protect and preserve the environment.[12] In this case, the Court considered that the relevant State had breached its procedural obligations to inform the other State, seeing that providing information on the environmental impact assessment on any plan that was liable to cause significant trans-boundary harm to another State would be required before any decision on the environmental viability of that plan could be reached.[13]

In cases such as the South China Sea where there are maritime areas of overlapping claims, coastal States are required to inform all other claimant States of their intention to undertake seabed activities in these areas, including the identification and location of mineral resources. No exploitation or exploration activities may be undertaken without the previous consent of all claimant States with respect to the disputed maritime area where those resources are found. The lack of self-restraint jeopardizes the delimitation of maritime boundaries and may inevitably lead to competitive drilling and potential waste of resources, in addition to causing a considerable threat to regional stability, as well as to the marine environment.

In what concerns specifically the protection and preservation of the marine environment, Article 192 of UNCLOS recognizes that *all* States, including those that are landlocked, have a general obligation to protect and preserve the marine environment, without distinguishing between maritime areas that are subject to coastal States' sovereignty and jurisdiction, or that are beyond national jurisdiction, or even those that are disputed. This general obligation can be best understood as States being required to undertake all measures to ensure that seabed activities and installations under their jurisdiction or control are carried out and operate in a manner that does not cause damage or pollution, without unjustifiably interfering with the activities of other States.[14] States must, as a result, monitor the risks and effects of the activities occurring under their control and inform other States of these risks and effects and of possible consequences that such activities might have, as well as determine the appropriate means to deal with them.[15] Should damage or pollution occur, the relevant coastal States must ensure that it does not spread beyond the maritime areas where they exercise sovereign rights, in order to mitigate or limit the damage sustained.[16]

Consequently, coastal States in the South China Sea may be made responsible for failing to adopt the necessary measures to prevent or mitigate damages, or for not informing a neighboring State of the existence of a risk of trans-boundary harm or damage, without prejudice to the liability of States for damages resulting from internationally wrongful acts, or which might result from establishing a link between the non-fulfillment of the previously mentioned obligations and the extent of damages.[17] This is particularly worrying when one takes into consideration that there is a general lack of information on pollution from seabed activities in the South China Sea and where several installations are rapidly reaching the end of their service.[18] The lack of information on the number and location of offshore installations in operation or that are no longer in use and failure to fully apply international rules and standards creates a less demanding legal regime, thus endangering even further the marine environment, as well as the safety of navigation and other uses of the sea.

Despite valuable efforts by the Association of Southeast Asian Nations (ASEAN) to promote regional stability in the greater Asia-Pacific region, and important initiatives regarding the protection and preservation of the marine environment,[19] interesting regional developments are taking place in other parts of the world that could serve as valuable case studies for the South China Sea.

At the level of the European Union (EU), Member States have taken to cooperate on the adoption of common standards, without hindering or in any way affecting their sovereignty and jurisdiction over their respective national maritime areas. Cooperation has increased partly as a result of the *Deepwater Horizon* catastrophe in the Gulf of Mexico.[20] Although it is not possible to generalize on the economic costs of offshore accidents, those resulting from the *Deepwater Horizon* catastrophe in the Gulf of Mexico are colossal,[21] prompting concerns in the EU regarding the financial consequences should a similar incident occur in maritime areas adjacent to coastal Member States.

The EU has placed at the top of its agenda the reduction of occurrence of major accidents related to offshore oil and gas activities and to limit their consequences in order to increase the protection of the marine environment and of coastal communities.[22] It has envisaged, for the very first time, comprehensive EU legislation on oil platforms aimed at ensuring the highest safety standards in the world. The EU has emphasized the importance of sharing and exchanging experience, identifying best practices among regulatory authorities and industry, as well as improving implementation measures.

The EU essentially strives to level all Member States to a common denominator and encourages the adoption of prevention and preparedness regimes at the highest possible level. In this respect, the EU has also set up the European Union Offshore Oil and Gas Authorities with the overall task to serve primarily as a forum for the exchange of experiences and expertise between national authorities and the EU Commission. Other relevant legislation applicable to oil spills are the Environmental Liability Directive[23] and also the Waste Framework Directive, particularly with respect to oil escaping from an offshore installation or structure and may result in imposing the obligation on the polluter of cleaning up, regardless of fault of the producer of waste.[24]

Another example of regional efforts may be seen in the Northeast Atlantic Ocean, where there are a significant number of oil and gas offshore installations. The Convention for the Protection of the Marine Environment of the North-East Atlantic (OSPAR) provides that States shall take all possible steps to prevent and eliminate pollution from offshore sources.[25] It also establishes the prohibition of dumping of wastes or other matter from offshore installations, as well as the dumping, and the prohibition of leaving wholly or partly in place, of disused offshore installations.[26] OSPAR also monitors the development of offshore installations and maintains an updated inventory of all oil and gas offshore installations in the OSPAR maritime area. This database includes the name and identification number, location, operator, water depth, production start date, current status, category and function of the installations. In this regard, we should also mention the international standards for the removal of abandoned and disused installations and structures prepared by the International Maritime Organization (IMO) to ensure the safety of navigation and prevent potential adverse effects on the marine environment.[27]

Piracy, armed robbery and proliferation of WMDs

There has been an increase in the number of reported incidents of piracy and armed robbery against ships in the South China Sea, particularly in the Straits of Malacca and Singapore, and also in Indonesia.[28] In recent years, the increasing *professionalism* of pirates and of other criminals and their access to material and financial resources has made criminality at sea extremely rewarding and difficult to combat.

Proliferation of weapons of mass destruction (WMDs) is also of great concern, not only for the South China Sea, but also globally. In 2002, as a result of the interception and boarding by the Spanish Navy of the cargo vessel *So San*, a ship suspected of carrying suspicious material from North Korea to Yemen, the United States of America launched the Proliferation Security Initiative (PSI) to combat the proliferation of WMDs.[29] PSI participants currently number more than a hundred States, including from the South China Sea.[30] Yet, despite PSI having celebrated more than a decade in existence, the arrest in 2013 by the authorities of Panama of the North Korean ship *Chong Chon Gang* shows that the threat remains real.[31]

The existing legal framework to combat piracy, armed robbery and proliferation of WMDs is not without its shortcomings. In the case of piracy,[32] although there is recognition of universal jurisdiction in the high seas or in any other place outside the jurisdiction of any State there is no obligation to secure jurisdiction or to prosecute and punish pirates. There is also no obligation to pass legislation or to secure criminal jurisdiction.[33] On the other hand, armed robbery[34] does not give rise to universal jurisdiction and PSI does not create a legally binding regime,[35] thus safeguarding the principles of freedom of navigation and flag State jurisdiction.[36] Notwithstanding, PSI provides a platform for bilateral agreements allowing interception and boarding operations,[37] including with littoral States of the South China Sea.[38]

Much of the State and multilateral practice in recent decades has been in response to two events: the hijacking of the *Achille Lauro*[39] and the terrorist attacks of September 11, 2001.[40] These events shaped the work of the IMO on maritime security.[41] It was precisely as a result of these events that, respectively, the 1988 Convention for the Suppression of Unlawful Acts against the Safety of Maritime Navigation and Protocol (1988 SUA Convention)[42] and the 2005 Protocol to the 1988 SUA Convention were adopted.[43] However, one of the main concerns in the drafting of the 2005 Protocol to the 1988 SUA Convention was that the freedom of navigation and the principle of flag State jurisdiction should not be hampered.[44] Indeed, although interception and boarding operations offer the clearest response available against proliferation of seaborne WMDs, and despite many flag States being unable to exercise jurisdiction effectively over ships flying their flag, flag States are reluctant to allow interception and boarding by foreign ships.[45] These operations are only possible with the consent of the respective flag States and within certain safeguards.[46] Indeed, despite such multilateral efforts and even much earlier ones,[47] States have not achieved a comprehensive legal framework for combating terrorism or criminality at sea, and effectively guaranteeing maritime security.[48]

The ASEAN Plus Three Cooperation Work Plan 2013–17 recognizes the importance of States pursuing joint actions and measures and capacity-building activities concerning security cooperation, based on mutual understanding, confidence and solidarity, and strengthening peace and stability cooperation in the region, including measures on non-proliferation of WMDs, as well as combating transnational crime and enhancing maritime cooperation, namely, with respect to fighting against piracy and armed robbery. Already the First ASEAN Defence Ministers' Meeting-Plus, held in Ha Noi, on October 12, 2010, reinforced the importance of this forum as "a key component of a robust, effective, open, and inclusive regional security architecture," recognizing the existence of "complex and transnational security challenges that are beyond the scope of any country to handle alone, such as … maritime security, terrorism, proliferation of [WMDs] … transnational crime." The meeting noted the importance of sharing information and concrete cooperation in areas of common interest.[49]

UNCLOS does not include rules on maritime security that can be invoked to justify any general right of interdiction. Security concerns are mentioned in the context of the right of innocent passage through the territorial sea and archipelagic waters without being intercepted on condition that passage is innocent, i.e. that passage is not prejudicial to the peace, good order or security of the coastal State and that the ship does not engage in any threat or use of force against its sovereignty, territorial integrity or political independence, or in any other manner in violation of the principles of international law embodied in the United Nations Charter.[50] Elsewhere, UNCLOS provides that the high seas, the Area, the exclusive economic zone (EEZ) and the continental shelf up to 200 nautical miles are reserved for peaceful purposes, and that marine scientific research and the use of research installations shall be exclusively for peaceful purposes,[51] while military uses are not within the scope of the Convention.[52] The use of armed personnel and of weapons on board ships is also not regulated in the law of the sea. These matters are subject to the law of the relevant flag State and port and coastal States may adopt legislation to that effect with respect to the access to ports and to the territorial sea.[53] In what concerns the exercise of States' rights and the performance of their duties under the law of the sea, these are subject to the general obligation of settling international disputes by peaceful means and to the prohibition on the threat or use of force.[54] In turn, the use of force is limited by the general criteria of necessity and reasonableness, i.e. the State may be entitled to use reasonable force in light of the refusal to comply with the arrest if there are no other practicable means to board, search, seize and bring into port the suspected ship.[55]

The exercise of self-protection by the shipping industry

Traditional enforcement mechanisms recognized under international law have not been able to provide a wide-ranging response to the exercise of jurisdiction and law enforcement against criminality at sea, partly due to the legal, economic and political challenges that are difficult to fully overcome. This prompted the shipping industry to fully undertake the right and responsibility to exercise self-protection,[56] namely through a combination of preventive and protective measures[57] and the placing of armed personnel on board ships. Nonetheless, the IMO recognizes that measures of avoidance, evasion, deterrence and delay remain the best practices of self-protection against piracy.[58] Other factors that often contribute to such inability is the lack of information-sharing and capacity-building or the effective implementation of international legal instruments and the adoption of measures under domestic law.

It is currently acknowledged that the use of private and military security companies (PMSCs) is extremely efficient in dealing with threats such as piracy and armed robbery.[59] However, the hiring of these companies and of their services raises important legal questions concerning the use of force at sea and of armed personnel on board ships with respect to the exercise of flag, port and coastal State jurisdiction. It is mostly when incidents occur that international law is really put to the test.[60] This was the case, for example, of the 2012 incident involving the Italian oil-tanker *Enrica Lexie* when privately contracted Italian Navy marines on board killed Indian fishermen off the coast of Kerala, mistaking them for pirates.[61] Although the matter concerned the use of military on board ships, the IMO had already in 2009 referred to the importance of flag States providing clarity regarding their policy on the use of military or law enforcement officers on board ships flying their flag.[62]

Although international law considers the use of force a last resort and, in most cases, it deals with incidents where States intervene and in relation to the interdiction of foreign vessels and not the use of force at sea,[63] PMSCs and the rendering of military and security services on board ships have been the subject of several guidelines and recommendations. These guidelines and recommendations were developed by States, the IMO and other organizations[64] and have received significant support from the PMSCs community.[65] They address a wide variety of issues, including on the appropriate use of force and the carriage of firearms and ammunition on board ships. Although there is presently some fragmentation of these soft-law instruments, they strive to set a common denominator for the regulation of the activities of PMSCs and of armed personnel on board ships.

Nonetheless, the efficiency of such recommendations and guidelines depends on flag States but also on port and coastal States. Without States adopting the necessary legislative and enforcement measures at national level, it is not possible to ensure that PMSCs and armed personnel on board ships comply at all times with the rules applicable to the protection of human rights. States must lay the legal foundations for the effective exercise and enforcement of criminal jurisdiction at sea, in addition to coordinating the implementation of measures to avoid creating the conditions for abuses and violations of human rights to occur. States should therefore strive to achieve legal harmonization on the use of force by PMSCs and armed personnel, as well as the treatment under national law of abuses or violations of human rights, namely through the enactment of legislation on liability of PMSCs and armed personnel on board. Meaningful cooperation between States' judicial and judiciary bodies on the enforcement of common standards is indispensable to bridge the governance gap which creates "the permissive environment for wrongful acts by companies of all kinds without adequate sanctioning and reparation."[66]

States must ultimately make sure that PMSCs and armed personnel are accountable and susceptible of being prosecuted for human rights abuses or violations resulting from actions or omissions, at least those committed on board ships flying their flag. A different question altogether is if States may allow for action to be brought in their national courts for such actions or omissions when they take place on board foreign ships.

The fact that States do not adopt all necessary measures under domestic law to regulate PMSCs and the services they provide, or enact legislation on the use of force at sea in compliance with international law to prevent human rights abuses by PMSCs personnel, or that States allow PMSCs to operate without any supervision by national authorities, does not mean that there is a legal void or that PMSCs and their personnel may not be accountable, including in disputed maritime areas.

Flag States may not exempt themselves from complying with international law and enforcing the relevant rules on board ships flying their flags. Likewise, PMSCs and their personnel may not act on board ships as if there is no law.[67] They are subject to the control and the law of the flag State when they operate on board flying its flag. This control concerns the protection of national interests when they render their services but also before PMSCs establish themselves in that State's jurisdiction, either directly or through local partnerships.[68] Also, when flag States make a decision to allow the presence and use of armed personnel on board ships, they ought to establish the rules for the assessment of PMSCs, namely their human rights track record and the aptitude of their personnel. These are also procedural duties, which, in this case, are connected with the general obligation of all States to protect human rights. Indeed, seeing that the obligation to protect human rights is an obligation of means rather than of result and that the most efficient and immediate legal system for ensuring compliance is that of the flag State, it would ultimately fall to the latter to adopt the necessary measures to protect those rights and/or to put an end to the situation of wrongfulness. States remain therefore responsible for the lack of due diligence and for allowing a permissive environment for human rights abuses to occur.[69]

Correspondingly, national courts of flag States must exercise jurisdiction, adjudicating and enforcing claims against PMSCs and their personnel for human rights abuses or violations on board ships. Flag States must safeguard the right of victims to obtain reparation through civil litigation and take appropriate measures to investigate and offer effective remedies for wrongful conduct of PMSCs and their personnel. Flag States must also recognize that the serious violation of a particular human right and the gross or systematic failure by the company to comply is actionable directly in the national courts on the grounds of breach of international law.[70]

Persistent failure by flag States to comply with these obligations is generally attributed to the lack of means to conduct investigations and for effective adjudication, irrespective of States overwhelmingly recognizing that the applicable international legal framework to the protection of human rights has a high degree of legitimacy. States are often reluctant to enforce the law and to act against corporate-related abuses or when business and human rights are at loggerheads.[71] Indeed, States may grant PMSCs and their personnel immunity from prosecution or other similar procedural impediments such as guaranteeing non-extradition in the case of foreign entities. Such limitations restrict the effective protection of human rights, underlining the complexities resulting from PMSCs and their personnel not being accountable for their actions.[72] It is in this regard that unsuccessful attempts have been made to recognize the existence of corporate responsibility to respect human rights in all situations and independently of States' duties or capabilities.[73] Seeing that flag States cannot justify the violation of certain international human rights or their failure to protect them based on the fact that these are not recognized in their national law, they are ultimately responsible for their protection, even when means are not in place to do so,[74] or if the perpetrators are of different nationality.[75]

The foundation of the responsibility to protect lies in obligations inherent to the concept of sovereignty, which in turn embraces the responsibilities to prevent and to react. Indeed, the concept of sovereignty must be viewed both as control and responsibility and taken into account in the context of international accountability.[76] For example, the ICJ, in the *DRC/Uganda* case, found that States' duty to protect from violence extends to a positive obligation to protect people from violence at the hands of that State's military or of non-State actors, even abroad. In this case, the violence was committed by rebel groups acting in the territory of the Democratic

Republic of Congo occupied by Uganda.[77] It is altogether a different question if home States have extraterritorial obligations.[78]

This means that in the case of flag States allowing the *externalization* of military and security services they retain their obligations under international law and are responsible for violations of rules of international law committed by PMSCs and their personnel when such violations are attributable to the State. In this respect, the Draft Articles on Responsibility of States for Internationally Wrongful Acts[79] provide in Article 5 that the conduct of persons or entities that are legally empowered by the law of the State (i.e. the flag State) to exercise elements of the governmental authority (i.e. security on board ships) shall be considered an act of that State under international law. It also refers in Article 8 to the actions of persons and entities that take place under the control of the State.

Furthermore, although one may not refer directly to complicity between flag States and PMSCs (complicity is not a concept that exists in the current terminology of the law of international responsibility or one that would be applicable between States and non-State actors[80]), any State, by its actions or omissions, may in fact assist or aid such corporations to violate human rights, both within and outside its own territory. On the other hand, it has been argued that if prosecution against a State that violates human rights in its territory may not be possible (such as on board a ship flying its flag), perhaps it is possible against non-State actors that are complicit in direct human rights violations or collaborate with or profit from such violations.[81]

The IMO has expressly recognized the responsibility of flag Sates to ensure that ships flying their flags implement measures to protect themselves and the conditions in which they can do so, including with respect to the carriage and use of firearms and ammunition and the presence of armed personnel.[82] The IMO has developed recommendations for flag States regarding PMSCs, although it has also "strongly discouraged" the use of firearms by seafarers for personal protection or for the protection of a ship and has underlined that it "may pose an even greater danger if the ship is carrying flammable cargo or similar types of dangerous goods."[83] The IMO further clarified that if armed security personnel are allowed on board ships, the master, ship owner, operator and company should take into account the possible escalation of violence and other risks.[84]

The IMO has also underlined the importance of complying with both port and coastal States' law on the carriage and use of firearms on board. The IMO recalls that ships in the territorial sea and ports are subject to port and coastal States' legislation, including with respect to the presence of firearms and ammunition on board ships and the use of force for self-defense, and that, therefore, masters, ship owners, operators and companies should seek clarification of the applicable national regulations. Consequently, port and coastal States must make their national policy known regarding the embarkation, disembarkation and carriage of armed personnel, firearms and ammunitions and security-related equipment.[85]

The IMO has provided interim guidance to PMSCs on placing personnel on board ships in high-risk areas[86] and has called upon States to adopt the Best Management Practices.[87] Despite the fact that the said interim guidance is not legally binding, the motivation was essentially to provide a sort of minimum denominator recommendations on the competencies and abilities of PMSCs' personnel, as well as to assist in the development of an international standards and certification process for PMSCs.[88]

These recommendations followed a questionnaire issued by the IMO, which underlined this organization's understanding that "the carriage of armed personnel was a matter to be decided by the ship owner within the framework of the national legislation and policies of the flag State concerned, that there was an urgent need for a consistent approach to the issue and the avoidance of an escalation of violence due to the inappropriate use of force."[89] The questionnaire further emphasized the importance of the shipping industry and PMSCs knowing the conditions and requirements regarding privately contracted armed security personnel on board, firearms and security-related equipment. Moreover, States should adopt the legislation, policies and procedures relating to the carriage, embarkation and disembarkation of firearms and security-related equipment through their territory and the movement of such armed personnel.[90] States must also amend weapons legislation and provide for efficient sanctions and compliance procedures that also serve as a reasonable deterrent for abuses and violations to occur. Germany and the United Kingdom are two of the countries that have taken significant steps to regulate maritime security providers, including companies and individuals.[91]

Companies and ship owners seeking to hire PMSCs must also exercise their own due diligence.[92] This could be legally required and reflected in key aspects, such as determining the necessary insurance coverage for PMSCs and their personnel. Such coverage would take into account the security threats affecting ships and port facilities, personal accident, medical care and hospitalization and repatriation of injured persons. This insurance coverage should also cover loss or damage as a result of criminal activity, similar to insurance against acts of piracy, war (which may also include piracy) and strike risks.[93] In particular, it should provide for damages caused by the actions of armed personnel on board ships, including death. In these cases, assessment is necessary of the actions or omissions of the person or those at their command and the compliance with rules of command and control,[94] including on the use of force, and the contribution of such actions and omissions towards the damage or risk and of potential concurrent causes. In the case of piracy, for example, the subject matters which insurance is intended to protect are the ship and its cargo.[95]

Therefore, in the case of the use of armed personnel on board ships the relevant subject matters should be substantially broader and as a result the respective insurance coverage would most likely be higher. For example, recalling the outline of the *Enrica Lexie* incident, if armed personnel on board a ship decided to sink a vessel suspected of imminent piratical attack and killed those on board as a result, regardless of the lawfulness of their actions (the sinking of a suspect pirate vessel violates international law), the costs associated with such an insurance coverage would be potentially exorbitant. These and other similar costs will inevitably have an impact on shipping and maritime trade.[96]

The disputes in the South China Sea do not exempt flag, port and coastal States from acting in accordance with the aforementioned obligations. Yet, despite certain joint efforts to improve port State control,[97] States have not fully implemented the necessary measures in that respect.[98] It remains the case that in disputed maritime areas, claimant coastal States hold responsibility.

Conclusion

The speculative role played by the *oil factor* in the South China Sea disputes is unlikely to drop as claimant States compete to secure exclusive access to maritime areas considered to have great mineral resource potential. Neither is it likely that coastal States will withdraw from occupied islands and features that they consider strengthen their claims to the respective adjacent maritime areas.[99] This makes maritime delimitation, presently, unachievable. Consequently, as an alternative to unblock the existing situation, coastal States could defer their disputes in order to pursue the joint development of resources and the undertaking of other economic activities in disputed maritime areas, without hindering their national claims. Yet, regardless of the implementation of similar provisional arrangements, coastal States of the South China Sea must cooperate, at both regional and global level, to ensure maritime safety and security, namely, through concrete actions that can significantly improve the existing situation.

Notes

1 United Nations Conference on Trade and Development, *Review of Maritime Transport 2013*, Report by the UNCTAD Secretariat, p. 9, http://unctad.org/en/PublicationsLibrary/rmt2013_en.pdf, accessed March 2015.
2 United Nations, Asia Development Bank, *Green Growth, Resources and Resilience. Environmental Sustainability in Asia and the Pacific*, ed. UN-ESCAP/ADB/UNEP (Bangkok: United Nations, Asia Development Bank, 2012), p. 12, www.unep.org/dewa/Portals/67/pdf/G2R2_web.pdf, accessed March 2015.
3 Yann-huei Song, "Security in the Strait of Malacca and the Regional Maritime Security Initiative: Responses to the US Proposal," in *Global Legal Challenges: Command of the Commons, Strategic Communications, and Natural Disasters*, ed. Michael D. Cartsen (International Law Studies 83) (Newport, RI: Naval War College, 2007), pp. 97–156.
4 Raul Pedrozo, "Close Encounters at Sea: The USNS *Impeccable* Incident," *Naval War College Review* 62, 3 (Summer 2009): 101–11.
5 On the disputes in the Asia-Pacific region and prospects for delimitation of maritime boundaries, see Vasco Becker-Weinberg, *Joint Development of Hydrocarbon Deposits in the Law of the Sea* (Heidelberg, New York, Dordrecht, London: Springer-Verlag, 2014), pp. 144–65.
6 Articles 74(3) and 83(3) of UNCLOS.
7 Becker-Weinberg, *Joint Development*, pp. 73–100.
8 See *S.S. Lotus (France v. Turkey), 1927 P.C.I.J., Series A – No. 10*, pp. 18–9; *Award between the United States and the United Kingdom relating to the rights of jurisdiction of United States in the Bering's sea and the preservation of fur seals, decision of 15 August 1893*, in Reports of International Arbitral Awards (New York: United Nations), vol. XXVIII, pp. 263–76. Also see Hossein Esmaeili, *The Legal Regime of Offshore Oil Rigs in International Law* (Aldershot, Burlington, VA, Singapore, Sydney: Dartmouth/Ashgate, 2001), p. 88.
9 Adopted in Montego Bay, Jamaica, on December 10, 1982, and entered into force on November 16, 1994 (1982 UNTS 1833, 397).
10 International Law Association, *Report of the International Committee on the Legal Aspects of the Conservation of the Environment*, by Professor Dietrich Rauschning (Manila Conference, 1978), pp. 390–411 and (Belgrade 1980), pp. 548–50. See Brian D. Smith, *State Responsibility and the Marine Environment: the Rules of Decision* (Oxford: Clarendon Press, 1988), pp. 83–5.
11 *Pulp Mills on the River Uruguay (Argentina v. Uruguay), Judgment, I.C.J. Reports 2010*, paras. 113, 197. Also see Joint Dissenting Opinion of Judges Al-Khasawneh and Simma, *ibid.*, paras. 26–7.
12 *Ibid.*, paras. 113, 115.
13 *Ibid.*, paras. 119, 120, 158 Also see *Gabčikovo-Nagymaros Project (Hungary/Slovakia), Judgment, I.C.J. Reports 1997*, 78; ITLOS, *Request for Advisory Opinion submitted to the Seabed Disputes Chamber*, paras. 145–9. The Seabed Disputes Chamber considered that carrying out an environmental impact assessment was a direct obligation under UNCLOS and a general obligation under customary international law and consequently "should be included in the system of consultations and prior notifications set out in article 142."
14 Article 194(2) and (4) of UNCLOS. Also see *Legality of the Threat or Use of Nuclear Weapons, Advisory Opinion, I.C.J. Reports 1996*, para. 29.
15 *The MOX Plant Case (Ireland v. United Kingdom), Request for provisional measures*, ITLOS No. 10, 2001, paras. 82, 84, 89(1). Also see *Lac Lac Lanoux Arbitration (France v. Spain), 24 I.L.R. 1957*, p. 133; *Corfu Channel Case, Judgment of April 9, 1949, I.C.J. Reports 1949*, p. 18.
16 Article 194(2), (3)(c) and (4) of UNCLOS. Also see *Gabčikovo-Nagymaros Project*, para. 80.
17 It should also be noted that certain legal regimes are applicable as a result of States being party to the same or because such regimes are part of customary international law also applicable to the protection and preservation of the marine environment. Furthermore, States may adopt laws and regulations to prevent, reduce and control pollution of the marine environment from installations and structures under their jurisdiction and activities in the seabed. For an overview of international binding legal regimes applicable in the South China Sea, see Vasco Becker-Weinberg, "Seabed Activities and the Protection and Preservation of the Marine Environment in Disputed Maritime Areas of the Asia-Pacific Region," in *Securing the Ocean for the Next Generation*, ed. Harry N. Scheiber and Moon Sang Kwon (Berkeley: University of California, 2013), pp. 253–99. Also see articles 56(1)b)(iii)(3), 193 and 194(3)c) of UNCLOS.

18 GESAMP (IMO/FAO/UNESCO-IOC/UNIDO/WMO/IAEA/UN/UNEP Joint Group of Experts on the Scientific Aspects of Marine Environmental Protection), 2007. Estimates of Oil Entering the Marine Environment from Sea-Based Activities. Rep. Stud. GESAMP no. 75, pp. 24–6, 43, 47, 63, www.gesamp.org/data/gesamp/files/media/Publications/Reports_and_studies_75/gallery_1042/object_1042_large.pdf, accessed March 2015.

19 Becker-Weinberg, "Seabed Activities."

20 Commission Staff Working Paper, Impact Assessment, Annex I, Proposal for a Regulation of The European Parliament and of the Council, on safety of offshore oil and gas prospection, exploration and production activities [SEC(2011) 1292, 27.10.2011], p. 7. For purpose of comparison, the largest oil spill in Europe, the *Ekofisk Bravo* platform in Norway, resulted in about 2 percent of the *Deepwater Horizon* spill. The EU legislation excludes from its scope mobile offshore drilling units (MODUs) and equipment installed thereon, which might lead to fragmentation of applicable legislation to equipment installed and used on MODUs.

21 This accident claimed the lives of 11 persons and injured 16 others and poured hydrocarbons into the Gulf of Mexico for 87 days, causing the largest oil spill in history of the United States of America (almost 5 million barrels of oil were discharged from the Macondo well into the Gulf of Mexico) and significant environmental damage, affecting the lives of hundreds of thousands of people living in coastal communities. See U.S. Coast Guard, *Report of Investigation into the Circumstances Surrounding the Explosion, Fire, Sinking and Loss of Eleven Crew Members aboard the Mobile Offshore Drilling Unit Deepwater Horizon in the Gulf of Mexico, April 20–22, 2010*, vol. 1, *Systems and Responsibilities within U.S. Coast Guard Purview under the U.S. Coast Guard-Minerals Management Service Memorandum of Agreement dated 27 March 2009*, MISLE Activity Number: 3721503.

22 Commission Decision of January 19, 2012 on setting up of the European Union Offshore Oil and Gas Authorities Group (2012/C 18/07). Also see Communication "Facing the Challenge of the Safety of Offshore Oil and Gas Activities," October 12, 2010 [COM(2010)560].

23 Directive 2004/35/EC of the European Parliament and of the Council of April 21, 2004 on environmental liability with regard to the prevention and remedying of environmental damage.

24 Directive 2008/98/EC of the European Parliament and the Council of November 19, 2008 on waste and repealing certain Directives. The applicability of this Directives to maritime oil spills is not explicit in the EU legislation and is based on the jurisprudence from the Court of Justice of the European Union, see ECJ case C-188/07 (*Commune de Mesquer v. Total France SA and Total International Ltd.*).

25 Convention for the Protection of the Marine Environment of the North-East Atlantic, made in Paris on September 22, 1992 and entered into force on March 25, 1998. See John Paterson, "Decommissioning of Offshore Installations," in *Oil and Gas Law: Current Practice and Emerging Trends*, ed. Greg Gordon, John Paterson, and Emre Üşenmez (Dundee: Dundee University Press, 2007), pp. 149–85; Alexander Proelß, *Meeresschutz im Völker- und Europarecht. Das Beispiel des Nordostatlantiks* (Berlin: Duncker & Humblot, 2004), pp. 215–21; Morakinyo Adedayo Ayoade, *Disused Offshore Installations and Pipelines. Towards "Sustainable Decommissioning"* (The Hague, London, New York: Kluwer Law International, 2002), pp. 47–77.

26 Article 5 of OSPAR and articles 3(1) and 5 of Annex III of OSPAR. Also see Section 2 of OSPAR Decision 98/3 on the Disposal of Disused Offshore Installations, Ministerial Meeting of the OSPAR Commission, adopted in Sintra on July 22–23, 1998, and entered into force on February 9, 1999.

27 IMO resolution A.672(16), *Guidelines and Standards for the Removal of Offshore Installations and Structures on the Continental Shelf and in the Exclusive Economic Zone*, adopted on October 19, 1989; IMO resolution A.671(16), *Safety Zones and Safety of Navigation around Offshore Installations and Structures*, adopted on October 19, 1989. Also see Article 60 of UNCLOS.

28 ReCAAP, *Regional Cooperation Agreement on Combating Piracy and Armed Robbery Against Ships in Asia, Information Sharing Centre, Quarterly Report*, January 1–September 30, 2014: *Piracy and Armed Robbery against Ships in Asia*, pp. 11, 13, 16, 17. According to this report: "A total of 129 incidents of piracy and armed robbery against ships reported in Asia during January-September 2014, of which the bulk … were petty theft incidents." In addition to the South China Sea, other important shipping routes in the Indian Ocean and the Gulf of Guinea have been the setting for piracy and armed robbery. Although in the last decade there has been an resurgence of these incidents, it should be pointed out that the IMO has been addressing the matter for many years, e.g. IMO Resolution A.545(13), adopted on November 17, 1983, *Measures to Prevent Acts of Piracy and Armed Robbery against Ships*; IMO Resolution A.686(17), adopted on November 6, 1991, *Prevention and Suppression of Acts of Piracy and Armed Robbery against*

Ships; IMO Resolution A.738(18), adopted on November 4, 1993, *Measures to Prevent and Suppress Piracy and Armed Robbery against Ships.*

29 Proliferation Security Initiative, www.state.gov/t/isn/c10390.htm, accessed March 2015; and Statement of Interdiction Principles, www.state.gov/t/isn/c27726.htm, accessed March 2015. Also see "Remarks by the President to the People of Poland, May 31, 2003," http://georgewbush-whitehouse. archives.gov/news/releases/2003/05/20030531-3.html, accessed March 2015. On the *So San* incident and PSI, see Natalie Klein, *Maritime Security and the Law of the Sea* (Oxford: Oxford University Press, 2011), pp. 107–8, 193–208; Yann-Huei Song, "The U.S.-Led Proliferation Security Initiative and UNCLOS: Legality, Implementation, and an Assessment," *Ocean Development and International Law* 38 (2007), pp. 101–10, 119–22; Daniel H. Joyner, "The Proliferation Security Initiative: Nonproliferation, Counterproliferation, and International Law," *Yale Journal of International Law* 30 (2005), p. 507; Michael A. Becker, "The Shifting Public Order of the Oceans: Freedom of Navigation and the Interception of Ships at Sea," *Harvard International Law Journal* 46 (2005), pp. 131, 147–67; Douglas Guilfoyle, "The Proliferation Security Initiative: Interdicting Vessels in International Waters to Prevent the Spread of Weapons of Mass Destruction?" *Melbourne University Law Review* 29 (2005), pp. 735–6, 740–1; Michael Byers, "Policing the High Seas: The Proliferation Security Initiative," *American Journal of International Law* 98 (2004): 526–45.

30 List of Proliferation Security Initiative Participants, www.state.gov/t/isn/c27732.htm, accessed March 2015.

31 *Statement of the Permanent Mission of Panama to the United Nations, in relation to the North Korean ship MV Chong Chon Gang, 19 July 2013*, www.panama-un.org/Noticias/330-Statement-of-the-Perm anent-Mission-of-Panama-to-the-United-Nations,-in-relation-to-the-North-Korean-ship-MV- Chong-Chon-Gang.html, accessed November 2014; *Statement by the Ministry of Foreign Affairs [Cuba] about the North Korean ship Chong Chon Gang seized in the Panama Canal, 16 July 2013*, www.cubamin- rex.cu/en/statement-ministry-foreign-affairs-6, accessed March 2015. The United Nations Security Council established a Committee pursuant to UN Resolutions (Security Council) n. 1718 (2006), October 14, 2006, imposing certain measures relating to North Korea, e.g. an arms embargo and a nuclear ballistic missiles and other WMD programmes-related embargo, www.un.org/sc/commit- tees/1718/index.shtml, accessed March 2015. Also see UN Resolution (Security Council) n. 1874 (2009), June 12, 2009.

32 Article 101 of UNCLOS: "Piracy consists of any of the following acts: (a) any illegal acts of violence or detention, or any act of depredation, committed for private ends by the crew or the passengers of a private ship or a private aircraft, and directed: (i) on the high seas, against another ship or aircraft, or against persons or property on board such ship or aircraft; (ii) against a ship, aircraft, persons or property in a place outside the jurisdiction of any State; (b) any act of voluntary participation in the operation of a ship or of an aircraft with knowledge of facts making it a pirate ship or aircraft; (c) any act of inciting or of intentionally facilitating an act described in subparagraph (a) or (b)."

33 On the shortcomings of the piracy regime under UNCLOS, see José Luis Jesus, "Protection of Foreign Ships against Piracy and Terrorism at Sea: Legal Aspects," *International Journal of Marine and Coastal Law* 18 (2003), pp. 380–1.

34 Armed robbery against ships has been identified by the IMO as "any illegal act of violence or deten- tion or any act of depredation, or threat thereof, other than an act of piracy, committed for private ends and directed against a ship or against persons or property on board such a ship, within a State's internal waters, archipelagic waters and territorial sea;" or "any act of inciting or of intentionally facilitating an act described above." Section 2.2 of the Code of Practice for the Investigation of Crimes of Piracy and Armed Robbery against Ships, approved by IMO Resolution A.1205(26), adopted on December 2, 2009. Also see IMO Resolution A.1044(27), adopted on November 30, 2011, *Piracy and Armed Robbery against Ships in Waters off the Coastal of Somalia*; IMO MSC.1/Circ. 1333, June 26, 2009, *Recommendations to Governments for Preventing and Suppressing Piracy and Armed Robbery against Ships.*

35 Anthony Aust, *Modern Treaty Law and Practice* (Cambridge: Cambridge University Press, 2007), p. 17; Richard Gardiner, *Treaty Interpretation* (Oxford: Oxford University Press, 2008), p. 20. Also see Ted L. McDorman, "From the Desk of the Editor-in-Chief," *Ocean Development and International Law* 36 (2005), pp. 381–2; Stuart Kaye, "Freedom of Navigation in a post-9/11 World: Security and Creeping Jurisdiction," in *The Law of the Sea*, ed. David Freestone, Richard Barnes, and David Ong (Oxford: Oxford University Press, 2006), pp. 347, 357.

36 Becker argues that "behind a façade of multilateral cooperation, the PSI is ultimately a loose instrument by which to facilitate more effective unilateral action by individual states to make possible and lawful

the claims of one state upon vessels of another." See Michael A. Becker, "The Shifting Public Order of the Oceans: Freedom of Navigation and the Interdiction of Ships at Sea," *Harvard International Law Journal* 46 (2005), p. 221. Also see Guilfoyle, "The Proliferation," p. 740.

37 Article 110(1) of UNCLOS provides that a State may grant its consent by treaty to another State for the purpose of intercepting and boarding in the high seas ships flying its flag.

38 List of Proliferation Security Initiative Ship Boarding Agreements, www.state.gov/t/isn/c27733.htm, accessed March 2015.

39 The *Achille Lauro* incident has in occasion been wrongfully defined by some States as piracy, even though it did not fulfill the relevant requirements. See Jesus, "Protection," pp. 388–9. Also see L. C. Green, "The *Santa Maria*: Rebels or Pirates," *British Year Book of International Law* 37 (1961): 496–505; Larry A. McCullough, "International and Domestic Criminal Law Issues in the *Achille Lauro* Incident: A Functional Analysis," *Naval Law Review* 36 (1986): 53–108.

40 See Christopher C. Joyner, "Suppression of Terrorism on the High Seas: the 1988 IMO Convention on the Safety of Maritime Navigation," *Israel Yearbook on Human Rights* 19 (1989), p. 348; Klein, *Maritime Security*, pp. 147–51; Kaye, "Maritime Security in the post-9/11 World," pp. 327–48.

41 IMO resolution A.584(1X), *Measures to Prevent Unlawful Acts which Threaten the Safety of Ships and the Security of their Passengers and Crews*; MSC/Circ. 443, *Measures to Prevent Unlawful Acts against Passengers and Crew on Board Ships*; IMO resolution A.924(22), of November 20, 2001, *Review of Measures and Procedures to Prevent Acts of Terrorism which Threaten the Security of Passengers and Crews and the Safety of Ships*. The aim was to revise international legal and technical measures to prevent and suppress terrorist acts against ships at sea and in port, as well as to improve security on board ships and on port. The legal framework for maritime security was also further developed with the amendments to the 1974 Safety of Life at Sea Convention and in particular of Chapter XI, which introduced the International Ship and Port Facility Security Code (ISPS Code). The objectives of the ISPS Code included the establishment of an international legal framework to detect threats and take preventive measures against security incidents affecting ships or port facilities used in international trade (Article 1.2.1). The ISPS Code does not allow the boarding of vessels at sea by non-flag States. See Malvina Halberstam, "Terrorism on the High Seas: The *Achille Lauro*, Piracy and the IMO Convention on Maritime Safety," *American Journal of International Law* 82 (1988), pp. 291–2; Hartmut G. Hesse, "Maritime Security in a Multilateral Context: IMO Activities to Enhance Maritime Security," *International Journal of Marine and Coastal Law* 18 (2003): 327–40.

42 Adopted in Rome on March 10, 1988 and entered into force on March 1, 1992, published at 1678 UNTS 221. The 1988 SUA Convention and the 1988 Protocol for the Suppression of Unlawful Acts against the Safety of Fixed Platforms Located on the Continental Shelf had the purpose of ensuring that appropriate action was taken against persons committing unlawful acts against ships and fixed platforms on the continental shelf, namely the seizure of ships by force, acts of violence against persons on board ships and the placing of devices on board a ship to destroy or damage it. The 1988 SUA Convention followed the models of the Convention for the Suppression of Unlawful Seizure of Aircraft, adopted in The Hague on December 16, 1970 and entered into force on October 14, 1971, published at 860 UNTS 105, and the Convention for the Suppression of Unlawful Acts against the Safety of Civil Aviation, adopted in Montreal on September 23, 1971 and entered into force on January 26, 1973, published at 974 UNTS 178.

43 Adopted in London on October 14, 2005 and entered into force on July 28, 2010, IMO Doc. LEG/CONF.15/21.

44 Robert C. Beckman, "The 1988 SUA Convention and 2005 SUA Protocol: Tools to Combat Piracy, Armed Robbery, and Maritime Terrorism," in *Lloyd's MIU Handbook of Maritime Security*, ed. Rupert Herbert-Bruns, Sam Bateman, and Peter Lehr (Boca Raton, London, New York: CRC Press, 2009), pp. 194–6.

45 Vasco Becker-Weinberg and Guglielmo Verdirame, "Proliferation of Weapons of Mass Destruction and Shipping Interdiction," in *The Oxford Handbook of the Use of Force in International Law*, ed. Marc Weller (Oxford: Oxford University Press, 2015), pp. 1019–25.

46 Article 8bis(10).

47 Convention for the Prevention and Punishment of Terrorism, on November 16, 1937, League of Nations Doc. C.546M.383 (1937), not in force. On the historical evolution of the concept of international terrorism, see Reuven Young, "Defining Terrorism: The Evolution of Terrorism as a Legal Concept in International Law and its Influence on Definitions in Domestic Legislation," *Boston College International and Comparative Law Review* 29 (2006): 23–68. Also see United Nations, *A More Secure*

World: Our Shared Responsibility. Report of the Secretary-General's High-level Panel on Threats, Challenges and Change (New York: United Nations, 2004), pp. 51–2, paras. 157–64.

48 Jesus, "Protection," p. 387.

49 Also see *2011 Joint Declaration of the ASEAN Defence Ministers on Strengthening Defence Cooperation of ASEAN in the Global Community to Face New Challenges, Jakarta, 19 May 2011*, www.asean.org/news/item/joint-declaration-of-the-asean-defence-ministers-on-strengthening-defence-cooperation-of-asean-in-the-global-community-to-face-new-challenges-jakarta-19-may-2011, accessed March 2015; and *2011 Joint Communiqué of the 44th ASEAN Foreign Ministers Meeting, Bali, 19 July 2011*, www.asean.org/images/archive/documents/44thAMM-PMC-18thARF/44thAMM-JC.pdf, accessed March 2015.

50 Adopted in San Francisco, on June 26, 1945, http://treaties.un.org/doc/Publication/CTC/uncharter.pdf, accessed March 2015. See Articles 17, 18, 19(1), (2) lit. (a), 24(1), 25(3), 52(1) and 54 of UNCLOS. Similarly, all ships enjoy the right of transit passage in straits used for international navigation, see Articles 38, 39 and 45 of UNCLOS. On the sovereign immunity of warships and government vessels and the exercise of coastal State jurisdiction, see articles 29 to 32 of UNCLOS. On the definition of innocent passage, see R. R. Churchill and A. V. Lowe, *The Law of the Sea* (Manchester: Manchester University Press, 1999), pp. 82–5.

51 Articles 58(2), 88 and 141 of UNCLOS deal, respectively, with the EEZ, the high seas and the Area. Articles 239, 240 lit. (a), 242(1), 246(3) and 258 of UNCLOS with marine scientific research. On the concept of "peaceful purposes" and its applicability to UNCLOS, see B. A. Boczek, "Peaceful Purposes Provisions of the United Nations Convention on the Law of the Sea," *Ocean Development and International Law* 20 (1989), pp. 364, 368–81.

52 Donald R. Rothwell and Natalie Klein, "Maritime Security and the Law of the Sea," in *Maritime Security: International Law and Policy Perspectives from Australia and New Zealand*, ed. Natalie Klein, Joanna Mossop, and Donald R. Rothwell (London, New York: Routledge, 2010), pp. 28–9.

53 PMSCs have been known to use practices to avoid potential violation of the laws and regulations of port and coastal States, such as dumping their weapons at sea or using offshore platforms as deposit. See Anna Petrig, "The Use of Force and Firearms by Private Maritime Security Companies against Suspected Pirates," *International and Comparative Law Quarterly* 62 (2013), pp. 686–7.

54 Article 301 of UNCLOS and 2(3) and (4) of the United Nations Charter. See E. D. Brown, *The International Law of the Sea*, vol. 1, *Introductory Manual* (Aldershot, Brookfield, WI, Singapore, Sydney: Dartmouth/Ashgate, 1994), pp. 161–207; Churchill and Lowe, *The Law*, p. 183; Donald Rothwell and Tim Stephens, *The International Law of the Sea* (Portland, OR, Oxford: Hart, 2010), p. 397; Yoshifumi Tanaka, *The International Law of the Sea* (Cambridge: Cambridge University Press, 2012), p. 186; Malcolm D. Evans, "Maritime Boundary Delimitation: Where Do We Go from Here?" in *The Law of the Sea: Progress and Prospects*, ed. David Freestone, Richard Barnes, and David Ong (Oxford: Oxford University Press, 2006), pp. 137–60.

55 Articles 107(1), 110(1), (2) and (3), and 111(5) and (8), 224 and 304 of UNCLOS. The International Tribunal for the Law of the Sea (ITLOS) underlined in the *Saiga* case the importance of a graduated response in trying to stop a suspected ship. Other conditions identified by international jurisprudence include the arrest of the ship by a warship or government ship, and the adoption of measures that do not exceed the legitimate use of force, such as the deliberate sinking of an unarmed ship, or the endangering of human life. The assessment of the necessity and reasonableness of the use of force will depend on the circumstances of each case, taking into account the alleged offence and the conduct of the ship. The State will be liable for any use of unjustified force. See ITLOS, *The M/V "Saiga" (No. 2) Case (Saint Vincent and the Grenadines v. Guinea), 1 July 1999*, paras. 155–6; *S.S. "I'm Alone" (Canada v. United States), Joint Final Report of the Commissioners in the Case of the "I'm Alone," dated January 5, 1935, and filed with the Secretary of State at Washington and the Minister of External Affairs for Canada at Ottawa, January 9, 1935, 3 United Nations Reports of International Arbitral Awards 1609*, pp. 1617, 1618; *The Red Crusader (Commission of Enquiry, Denmark–United Kingdom) (1962) 35 ILR 485*.

56 Douglas Guilfoyle, "Piracy off Somalia and Counter-Piracy Efforts," in *Modern Piracy: Legal Challenges and Responses*, ed. Douglas Guilfoyle (Cheltenham, UK, Northampton, MA: Edward Elgar, 2013), pp. 49–58.

57 See *Best Management Practices for Protection against Somalia Based Piracy: Suggested Planning and Operational Practices for Ship Operators, and Masters of Ships Transiting the High Risk Area, version 4* (Edinburgh: Witherby Publishing Group, 2011); Annex 2 to IMO MSC31/Circ. 1339, 14 September 2011, *Piracy and Armed Robbery against Ships in Waters off the Coast of Somalia: Best Management Practices for Protection against Somalia-Based Piracy*; IMO MSC.1/Circ. 1334, June 23, 2009, *Piracy and Armed Robbery against*

Ships: Guidance to Shipowners and Ship Operators, Shipmasters and Crews on Preventing and Suppressing Acts of Piracy and Armed Robbery against Ships; IMO MSC.1/Circ. 1332, June 16, 2009, *Piracy and Armed Robbery against Ships in Waters off the Coast of Somalia, Annex 1 (Suggested Planning and Operational Practices for Owners, Operators, Managers and Masters of Ships Transiting the Gulf of Aden and off the Coastal of Somalia)*.

58 IMO Resolution MSC.324(89), adopted on May 20, 2011, *Implementation of Best Management Practice Guidance*; The European Parliament also underlined that the use of armed personnel could not "substitute the necessary comprehensive solution to the multifaceted threat from piracy," calling upon the European Commission and Council "to work towards shaping an EU approach to the use of certified armed personnel on board in order to ensure proper implementation of the IMO guidelines in this regard." See European Parliament resolution of May 10, 2012 on maritime piracy (2011/2962(RSP)), 2013/C 261 E/06, Official Journal of the European Union, C 261E/34, 10.9.2013, para. 29.

59 James Kraska emphasizes the fact that there has not been a successful hijacking of any ship with armed security on board. See James Kraska, "International and Comparative Regulation of Private Maritime Security Companies Employed in Counter-Piracy," in *Modern Piracy: Legal Challenges and Responses*, ed. Douglas Guilfoyle (Cheltenham, UK, Northampton, MA: Edward Elgar, 2013), p. 249. For a recent analysis of the effectiveness of PMSCs' actions, see Achilles Skordas, "The Dark Side of Counter-Piracy Policies," in *The Law and Practice of Piracy at Sea: European and International Perspectives*, ed. Panos Koutrakos and Achilles Skordas (Oxford and Portland, OR: Hart, 2014), pp. 320–2.

60 On the use of force in operations at sea, see Tulio Treves, "Piracy and the International Law of the Sea," in *Modern Piracy: Legal Challenges and Responses*, ed. Douglas Guilfoyle (Cheltenham, UK, Northampton, MA: Edward Elgar, 2013), pp. 142–5; Andrew Murdoch and Douglas Guilfoyle, "Capture and Disruption Operations: The Use of Force in Counter-Piracy off Somalia," in *Modern Piracy: Legal Challenges and Responses*, ed. Douglas Guilfoyle (Cheltenham, UK, Northampton, MA: Edward Elgar, 2013), pp. 150–3, 166–9; Alexander Proelss, "Piracy and the Use of Force," in *The Law and Practice of Piracy at Sea: European and International Perspectives*, ed. Panos Koutrakos and Achilles Skordas (Oxford and Portland, OR: Hart, 2014), pp. 53–66.

61 The incident sparked serious diplomatic controversy between Italy and India but also the EU. The officers where arrested and charged with murder and are still pending trial. Italy claims to have exclusive jurisdiction. On the *Enrica Lexie* incident, see Noah Black, "Criminal Jurisdiction over Maritime Security in the Indian Ocean," *Cornell International Law Journal Online* 1: 77–82, http:// cornellilj.org/wp-content/uploads/2013/11/Black-Criminal-Jurisdiction-Martime-Security-final. pdf, accessed March 2015. On June 26, 2015, Italy instituted arbitral proceedings under Annex VII to UNCLOS against India, subsequently submitting on July 21, 2015, a Request to ITLOS for the prescription of provisional measures. On August 24, 2015, ITLOS delivered its Order in the "Enrica Lexie" Incident (Italy v. India), Provisional Measures case, prescribing that both countries should suspend all court proceedings and should refrain from initiating new ones that could aggravate or extend the dispute submitted to the arbitral tribunal, or might jeopardize or prejudice the carrying out of any decision which the arbitral tribunal may render, https://www.itlos.org/fileadmin/itlos/documents/ cases/case_no.24_prov_meas/C24_Order_24.08.2015_orig_Eng.pdf, accessed 25 August 2015.

62 IMO MSC.1/Circ. 1333, June 26, 2009, para. 8. Also see IMO MSC.1/Circ. 1334.

63 See Douglas Guilfoyle, *Shipping Interdiction and the Law of the Sea* (Cambridge: Cambridge University Press, 2009), pp. 271–94.

64 See International Organization for Standardization, Standards for Guidelines and the Certification of Private Maritime Security Companies: ISO/PAS 28007:2012, *Ships and Marine Technology – Guidelines for Private Maritime Security Companies (PMSC) Providing Privately Contracted Armed Security Personnel (PCASP) On Board Ships (and pro forma contract)*.

65 For example, see Security Association for the Maritime Industry, www.seasecurity.org, accessed March 2015.

66 United Nations, "Promotion and protection of all human rights, civil, political, economic, social and cultural rights, including the right to development. Protect, respect and remedy: a framework for business and human rights," Report of the Special Representative of the Secretary-General on the issue of human rights and transnational corporations and other business enterprises, John Ruggie, UN Doc. A/ HRC/8/5, April 7, 2008, para. 3. Also see International Law Association, Report of 74th Conference, The Hague Conference, August 15–19, 2010, "Non State Actors," by Professor Malgosia Fitzmaurice and Dr. Cedric Ryngaert, p. 634.

67 Andrew Clapham, *Human Rights Obligations of Non-State Actors* (Oxford: Oxford University Press, 2006), p. 31.

68 M. Sornarajah, *The International Law on Foreign Investment* (Cambridge: Cambridge University Press, 2004), p. 117.

69 Chia Lehnardt, "Private Military Companies and State Responsibility," in *From Mercenaries to Market: The Rise and Regulation of Private Military Companies*, ed. Simon Chesterman and Chia Lehnardt (Oxford: Oxford University Press, 2007), p. 155. Similarly, see Robert McCorquodale and Penelope Simons, "Responsibility beyond Borders: State Responsibility for Extraterritorial Violations by Corporations of International Human Rights Law," *Modern Law Review* 70 (2007), pp. 619–20. Also see August Reinisch, "The Changing International Legal Framework for Dealing with Non-State Actors," in *Non-State Actors and Human Rights*, ed. P. Alston (Oxford: Oxford University Press, 2005), p. 81: "The policy rationale underlying such 'vicarious' or 'subsidiary' liability is clear: to increase pressure on states by continuing to hold them responsible for 'out-sourced' or 'delegated' activity in order to make sure that they have a direct interest in regulating the behavior of non-state actors to whom they have transferred state tasks."

70 See UN Resolution (General Assembly) no. 60/147, March 21, 2006, *Basic Principles and Guidelines on the Rights to a Remedy and Reparation for Victims of Gross Violations of International Human Rights Law and Serious Violations of International Humanitarian Law*. This resolution emphasizes that the Basic Principles and Guidelines do not entail new international or domestic legal obligations but identify mechanisms, modalities, procedures and methods for the implementation of existing legal obligations under international human rights law and international humanitarian law, which the resolution recognizes are complementary though different as to their norms.

71 United Nations, "Promotion and protection of all human rights, civil, political, economic, social and cultural rights, including the right to development. Business and human rights: further steps towards the operationalization of the 'protect, respect and remedy' framework." Report of the Special Representative of the Secretary-General on the issue of human rights and transnational corporations and other business enterprises, John Ruggie, UN Doc. A/HRC/14/27, April 9, 2010, para. 18. Also see "Report of the High Commissioner for Human Rights on her Office's consultation on operationalizing the framework for business and human rights," Human Rights Council, 14th Session, UN Doc. A/HRC/14/29, April 16, 2010; and "Report of the United Nations Commissioner on Human Rights on the sector consultation entitled 'Human rights and the financial sector', February 16, 2007," Human Rights Council, 4th Session, UN Doc. A/HRC/4/99, March 6, 2007.

72 Yäel Ronen underlines that, although there is nothing in human rights theory that precludes the imposition of legal obligations on actors other than States, these are under international law the exclusive holders of human rights obligation. This is turn, Ronen concludes, is an inadequate system of guarantee of human rights. Non-State actors that exercise powers similar to those of States often remain unaccountable for their abuse of that power because their conduct does not amount to international crimes and is not related to an armed conflict. Ronen also draws attention to the fact that States might be willing to recognize the applicability of human rights obligations in situations where such applicability would exempt States themselves from responsibility, thus evading their responsibility for failure to prevent conduct which amounts to human rights violations by non-State actors over which they exercise some control. See Yäel Ronen, "Human Rights Obligations of Territorial Non-State Actors," *Cornell International Law Journal* 46 (2013): 21–50.

73 See United Nations, *The Corporate Responsibility to Respect Human Rights: An Interpretive Guide* (New York: United Nations, 2012).

74 *Barcelona Traction, Light and Power Company, Limited, Judgment, I.C.J. Reports 1970*, para. 33.

75 *The M/V "Saiga" (No. 2) Case*, para. 106: "The provisions referred to in the preceding paragraph indicate that the Convention considers a ship as a unit, as regards the obligations of the flag State with respect to the ship and the right of a flag State to seek reparation for loss or damage caused to the ship by acts of other States and to institute proceedings under article 292 of the Convention. Thus the ship, every thing on it, and every person involved or interested in its operations are treated as an entity linked to the flag State. The nationalities of these persons are not relevant."

76 ICISS, *The Responsibility to Protect: Report of the International Commission in Intervention and State Sovereignty* (Ottawa: International Development Research Centre, 2011), p. 12.

77 *Case concerning Armed Activities on the Territory of Congo (Democratic Republic of Congo v. Uganda), Judgment I.C.J., 19 December 2005*, paras. 178–80.

78 McCorquodale and Simons, "Responsibility," p. 605.

79 International Law Commission, "Draft Articles on Responsibility of States for Internationally Wrongful Acts, Report of the International Law Commission on the work of its fifty-third session," in *Yearbook of the International Law Commission* (New York, Geneva: United Nations, 2006), part 2, vol. 2, p. 26.

80 See Vaughn Lowe, "Corporations as International Actors and International Law Makers," *Italian Yearbook of International Law* 13 (2004), p. 31. The ICJ considered that complicity included the provision of means to enable or facilitate the commission of the crime; see *Application of the Convention on the Prevention and Punishment of the Crime of Genocide (Bosnia and Herzegovina v. Serbia and Montenegro), Judgment, I.C.J. Reports 2007*, p. 217, para. 419. Also, Article 16 of the Draft Articles on Responsibility of States for Internationally Wrongful Acts, reads that: "[a] State which aids or assists another State in the commission of an internationally wrongful act by the latter is internationally responsible for doing so if: a) [t]he State does so with knowledge of the circumstances of the internationally wrongful act; and b) [t]he act would be internationally wrongful if committed by that State." The Commentary to this article states in para. 5 that it will be sufficient if the aid or assistance contributed significantly to the act. In the case of PMSCs, if a corporation assists a States to commit an international crime, it will be responsible as an accomplice under international criminal law if it supports the crime or had knowledge that its actions would assist the commission of the crime; whereas, if a corporation assists a State in violating customary international law without committing an international crime, it be found liable for breach of its own obligations. Differently, see McCorquodale and Simons, "Responsibility," pp. 613–15.

81 Reinisch, "The Changing," p. 65, underlines that corporate complicity is a complex issue and one should differentiate between various degrees of involvement and culpability.

82 IMO Resolution MSC.324(89). Also see IMO MSC.1/Circ. 1046/Rev. 2, May 25, 2012, *Revised Interim Recommendations for Flag States Regarding the Use of Privately Contracted Armed Security Personnel On Board Ships in the High Risk Area*; IMO Resolution A.1044(27), para. 8.

83 IMO MSC.1/Circ. 1334, paras. 59 to 61: "Seafarers are civilians and the use of firearms requires special training and aptitudes and the risk of accidents with firearms carried on board ship is great. Carriage of arms on board ship may encourage attackers to carry firearms or even more dangerous weapons, thereby escalating an already dangerous situation. Any firearm on board may itself become an attractive target for an attacker. It should also be borne in mind that shooting at suspected pirates may impose a legal risk for the master, shipowner or company, such as collateral damages." Also see IMO MSC.1/Circ. 1333, June 26, 2009, paras. 5–7. The EU has too made recommendations on these matters, see Commission Recommendation of March 11, 2010 on measures for self-protection and the prevention of piracy and armed robbery against ships, 2010/159/EU, Official Journal of the European Union, L 67/13, 17.3.2010. These recommendations are intended to complement the guidance provided by IMO MSC.1/Circ. 1334.

84 IMO MSC.1/Circ. 1046/Rev. 2.

85 IMO Resolution A.1044(27), para. 8(d). Also see IMO MSC.1/Circ. 1408/Rev. 1, May 25, 2012, *Revised Interim Recommendations for Port and Coastal States Regarding the Use of Privately Contracted Armed Security Personnel On Board Ships in the High Risk Area.*

86 IMO MSC.1/Circ. 1443. "High Risk Area" is defined in IMO MSC.31/Circ. 1339, para. 2.4, section 2, 4: "The High Risk Area defines itself by where pirate activity and/or attacks have taken place. For the purpose of BMP the High Risk Area is an area bounded by Suez and the Strait of Hormuz to the North, 10°S and 78°E. unless otherwise defined by the flag-State." Also see IMO MSC.1/Circ. 1405/ Rev. 2, May 25, 2012, *Revised Interim Guidance to Shipowners, Ship Operators and Shipmasters on the Use of Privately Contracted Armed Security Personnel On Board Ships in the High Risk Area.* The IMO has also issued recommendations in the event of hijacking, see IMO MSC.1/Circ. 1390, December 9, 2010, *Guidance for Company Security Officers (CSOs) – Preparation of a Company and Crew for the Contingency of Hijack by Pirates in the Western Indian Ocean and the Gulf of Aden.*

87 Circular Letter No. 3164, 14 February 2011, *Responding to the Scourge of Piracy.* For an overview of the regulation of PMSCs and the position of States, the IMO and the shipping industry regarding the use of private contracted armed security personnel onboard ships, see Kraska, "International," pp. 219–49.

88 IMO MSC.1/Circ. 1443, paras. 1.5 and 2.3.

89 IMO MSC-FAL.1/Circ. 2, September 22, 2011, "Questionnaire on information on port and coastal State requirements related to privately contracted armed security personnel on board ships."

90 *Ibid.*, paras. 6 and 7.

91 On the United Kingdom's change in policy to allow the use of privately contracted armed guards on board ships flying its flag, see Andrew Murdoch, "Piracy and the UK," in *The Law and Practice of Piracy at Sea: European and International Perspectives*, ed. Panos Koutrakos and Achilles Skordas (Oxford and Portland, OR: Hart, 2014), pp. 218–20. On the German law applicable to maritime security providers, see Doris König and Tim René Salmon, "Fighting Piracy: The German Perspective," in *The Law and*

Practice of Piracy at Sea: European and International Perspectives, ed. Panos Koutrakos and Achilles Skordas (Oxford and Portland, OR: Hart, 2014), pp. 241–7. For a comparative study of different jurisdictions, see International Chamber of Shipping, *Comparison of Flag State Laws on Armed Guards and Arms on Board (16 January 2013)*, www.ics-shipping.org/docs/default-source/Piracy-Docs/comparison-of-flag-state-laws-on-armed-guards-and-arms-on-board3F9814DED68F.pdf, accessed March 2015.

92 Kraska, "International," p. 237.

93 Keith Michel, "Piracy and Carriage of Goods by Sea," in *Modern Piracy: Legal Challenges and Responses*, ed. Douglas Guilfoyle (Cheltenham, UK, Northampton, MA: Edward Elgar, 2013), p. 313.

94 Clear rules for command and control, particularly involving the use of force, should be included in the contract, see Kraska, "International," p. 237. On the implications of the use of armed personnel for the command-and-control procedures, see Petrig, "The Use," pp. 695–7.

95 Peter MacDonald Eggers, "Insurance Protection against Piracy," in *Modern Piracy: Legal Challenges and Responses*, ed. Douglas Guilfoyle (Cheltenham, UK, Northampton, MA: Edward Elgar, 2013), p. 269.

96 On the potential economic impact of terrorist attacks on maritime trade, see Philipp Wendel, *State Responsibility for Interferences with the Freedom of Navigation in Public International Law* (Berlin, Heidelberg, New York: Springer Verlag, 2007), pp. 28–9.

97 For example, the Memorandum of Understanding of 1994 on Port State Control in the Asia-Pacific Region, and the Code of Good Practice for Port State Control Officers, www.tokyo-mou.org/, accessed March 2015.

98 For an overview, see Song, "Security," pp. 119–21.

99 Clive Schofield, "What's at Stake in the South China Sea? Geographical and Geopolitical Considerations," in *Beyond Territorial Disputes in the South China Sea: Legal Frameworks for the Joint Development of Hydrocarbon Resources*, ed. Robert Beckman, Ian Townsend-Gault, Clive Schofield, Tara Davenport, and Leonardo Bernard (Cheltenham, UK, Northampton, MA: Edward Elgar, 2013), p. 42.

6

STRATEGIC FEATURES OF THE INDIAN OCEAN REGION

James R. Holmes

The primary purpose in this chapter is to supply readers with an analytical template for gauging the worth of potential naval stations, and of narrow seas that provide access to and from waters such as the Indian Ocean region. The chapter relies mainly on the writings of sea-power theorist Alfred Thayer Mahan, and in particular on his survey of the strategic features of the Gulf of Mexico and Caribbean Sea. As it turns out, Mahanian geostrategic analysis is a tool useful for appraising maritime theaters far beyond the Americas. The chapter reviews how Mahan sized up candidate positions for naval bases before moving on to his analysis of straits and other narrow seas. It then surveys the Indian Ocean region in general terms before examining the Strait of Malacca, Strait of Hormuz, and Bab el-Mandeb Strait. With any luck, this method of assessing oceans and littoral zones will help seafaring powers with a stake in South Asia devise sound strategy.

Judging strategic features

Look back to look ahead. By consulting Alfred Thayer Mahan's works on American geopolitics, observers can glean some idea of what he would say about strategic competition in South Asia were he alive today. That naval historian compared the Caribbean Sea and Gulf of Mexico to the Mediterranean Sea in hopes of deriving insights into strategic effectiveness in semi-enclosed expanses. He saw "a very marked analogy in many respects" between the Mediterranean and Caribbean seas – "an analogy which will be still closer if a Panama canal-route ever be completed," allowing east–west transit and shortening communications between the Atlantic and Pacific oceans by thousands of miles.[1] The logic Mahan articulated for America's Mediterranean holds for any aspiring sea power that possesses the economic vitality, military strength, and political resolve – the lineaments of great power – to make use of important strategic features in or adjoining the Indian Ocean or Persian Gulf.[2] (He held forth on the Persian Gulf in one of his essays, long before the discovery of oil and natural gas afforded the region its current geopolitical prominence.[3]) Even small marine states can deploy artful strategy to deny geographic assets to stronger rivals or to exploit these assets themselves. Indeed, strategic guile is all the more important for the weak, who cannot afford to throw resources at problems.

An expansive view of such matters came naturally to Mahan, a philosopher of sea power as well as a naval strategist.[4] Geography molded any contest for access. For Mahan, studying the particular geographic surroundings is a prerequisite for competitive enterprises. He proclaims that "geography underlies strategy."[5] Mahan delights in quoting or paraphrasing Napoleon's maxim that "war is a business of positions," doing so four times in *Naval Strategy* (1911), his last major work. Consequently geographic analysis comes first, at sea as on land.

When pondering whether to open an oceanic theater, affirms Mahan, makers of strategy must begin by surveying its physical characteristics. To design and prosecute strategy, they must evaluate geographic features, determine which are critical and which are secondary, and integrate important features into their plans along with maritime forces able to shape events. "In considering any theater of actual or possible war, or of a prospective battlefield," Mahan insists, "the first and most essential thing is to determine what position, or chain of positions, by their natural and inherent advantages affect control of the greatest part of it."[6] Where to station forces to assert – or deny – control of key positions constitutes "a matter of prime importance" for any power that covets access to faraway expanses.[7]

Geography, then, constitutes the fixed setting within which maritime strategy – a dynamic, intensely interactive human enterprise – unfolds. Interestingly, his most influential work, *The Influence of Sea Power upon History, 1660–1883*, contains the *least* geographic content, beyond the general axiom that the extent and conformation of territory are two of the six inescapable determinants of maritime might. That few readers venture beyond *The Influence of Sea Power upon History* may help explain strategists' habit of overlooking the geopolitical dimension of his writings.

Where do likely theaters of competition and conflict lie? Mahan casts this question in terms of purpose and power. Wealth coupled with weakness, he says, invites extraregional powers to intervene. Certain regions, "rich by nature and important both commercially and politically, but politically insecure, compel the attention and excite the jealousies of more powerful nations."[8] Regions combining abundant natural resources and vibrant trade and commerce with governments too frail to withstand great-power encroachment beguile acquisitive foreign powers.

How did Mahan estimate the strategic value of geographic positions? As noted before, he considered overseas naval stations to be, collectively, one of three pillars of sea power. External powers must be choosy about the sites they select, lest they disperse forces too thinly while exposing their navies to piecemeal defeat in wartime. Mahan proposes that "the strategic value of any position, be it body of land large or small, or a seaport, or a strait, depends, 1, upon situation (with reference chiefly to communications), 2, upon its strength (inherent or acquired), and, 3, upon its resources (natural or stored)."[9] It would be fitting to make relations with prospective host governments a *de facto* fourth determinant, or enabler, of a site's value. Absent of decent working relations, a port will remain off-limits, negating its geostrategic leverage.

Thus amended, Mahan's simple construct retains its analytical power today. Consider its elements in turn. First, in maritime strategy as in real estate, location ranks atop the priorities list. To be worth occupying, prospective bases must lie along "strategic lines." Otherwise, innate strength and resources matter little. Harbors near heavily trafficked sea lines of communication (SLOCs) are ideal, positioning the fleet close to its sphere of action. Proximity to friendly seaports is another advantage. It allows fleet detachments to combine for defensive or offensive action in wartime, rendering mutual support. Proximity to hostile naval stations allows squadrons to watch or interdict enemy movements.

Isolation, on the other hand, detracts from a position's value. Even Gibraltar would be worthless as a naval station, despite its unsurpassed natural defenses, if situated alongside waters devoid of merchant and naval traffic.[10] A fleet based there would be immune to assault but would find little to do. Stout defenses would be moot. Nor can a sea power do much about ill-positioned features. "Strength and resources," observes Mahan, "may be artificially supplied or increased, but it passes the power of man to move a port which lies outside the limits of strategic effect."[11] Natural defenses can be augmented to a degree, while resources can be shipped in overland or oversea. Position is eternal.

Second, a seaport needs military strength, or defensibility, in order to fend off maritime or landward assault while projecting naval force outward. A squadron stationed at a base capable of protecting itself can prowl the seas independently, executing its missions confident that its landward refuge will be there when it returns. Rugged natural defenses are desirable. Cliffs overlooking seaward approaches, for instance, render amphibious assault unpalatable while letting defenders rain gunfire on an enemy fleet. Defenders can emplace guns on both sides of a narrow harbor mouth, creating overlapping fields of fire. Hence Lord Nelson's quip that a ship's a fool to fight a fort. If a base lacks inherent protection against attack, naval engineers must fortify it – or look elsewhere for a more defensible site. Defensibility is especially complex in this age of missile warfare. Hardening infrastructure against missile strikes from the sea demands expensive, labor-intensive measures. The proliferation of inexpensive antiship weaponry, on the other hand, can augment the striking power of bases. Truck-launched antiship missiles can be positioned at the base itself, along nearby coasts, or well inland, converting the littoral zone into a *de facto* fortress.[12] How the offense–defense balance is likely to play out is a question worth asking when appraising a seaport's defensibility.

Third, "resources" refers to shipyards to refit merchantmen and ships of war, provisions to restock visiting ships, and goods to supply the residents of the port. Foodstuffs, fuel, spare parts, and ammunition are only some of the items a base needs. Self-supporting ports are ideal. Large islands and coastal harbors boasting ample backcountry can provide for many of their needs. Sites not so endowed must ship in cargoes of critical goods. Dependence on external supplies exposes the port and fleet to a naval quarantine. Observes Mahan, resource-poor Gibraltar would wilt without seaborne supplies – its peerless strategic position and defenses notwithstanding.[13] Its relationship with the Royal Navy was symbiotic: warships based there could control access to the Mediterranean Sea, but ship crews and the inhabitants of the fortress would starve unless the fleet ruled the waves, assuring regular shipments.

Judging narrow seas

Mahan expands in *Naval Strategy* on his position/strength/resources template, applying it to straits and other confined waterways as well as to islands and coastal sites. He adds three metrics peculiar to narrow seas. "The military importance of such passages or defiles," he says, "depends not only upon the geographical position, but also upon their width, length, and difficulty." More specifically, a strait is a "strategic point" whose value depends on its "situation" on the nautical chart; on its "strength, which may be defined to consist in the obstacles it puts in the way of an assailant and the consequent advantages to the holder"; and on "resources or advantages, such as the facility it gives the possessor for reaching a certain point." A well-placed passage shortens the distance from place to place for the belligerent who holds it.[14] Denying an enemy fleet passage forces it to follow longer, more roundabout, and probably more debilitating and costly routes to its destination.

As in his analysis of bases, Mahan cautions against evaluating narrow seas without accounting for their larger geographic contexts. When "fixing the value of any passage," it is crucial to calculate the number and availability of nearby alternatives. "If so situated that a long circuit is imposed upon the belligerent who is deprived of its use, its value is enhanced." Scarcity magnifies a waterway's importance. Its value rises if it constitutes "the only close link between two bodies of water, or two naval stations." Finally, he urges strategists to consider the underwater topography of narrow seas. There is a vertical dimension to Mahan's analysis, then, even though he was concerned mainly with surface shipping. The presence of convoluted channels, shallow water, or shoal water helps determine a passage's offensive and defensive potential.[15] A hard-to-navigate passage represents an asset to the defender, a bane to opponents unfamiliar with its intricacies and quirks.

Finally, Mahan notes in passing that "a certain regard must be had to political conditions, which may be said to a great extent to neutralize some positions." Social or political upheaval in the surrounding country, for example, can work against or even negate a site's value, under-cutting its defensibility or impoverishing even a wealth of resources. Mahan dismissed Haiti as a base for just that reason. The island's constant revolutionary upheaval, or sociopolitical "noth-ingness," rendered it "an inert obstacle" to nineteenth-century U.S. maritime strategy.[16]

Such comments about social, cultural, and political context have the feel of an afterthought for Mahan. Nevertheless, he does acknowledge that there are diplomatic indices of geostra-tegic merit. Position, strength, and resources are not everything for a base. Learning the cultural terrain can be just as crucial. Alliance relations, then, belongs in the Mahanian framework as an additional metric.

Today, strong nations no longer wrest choice pieces of territory from their owners to use as bases. It is imperative, consequently, to take account of prospective host nations' interests and views – lest their governments restrict or refuse access in stressful times. The best-situated, most defensible, most lavishly supplied seaport in the world holds little value if it remains off-limits when needed most. Alliance management represents an enabler for any forward-leaning mari-time strategy, letting a seagoing state tap bases' physical potential.

Underwater terrain

The undersea dimension seems like an afterthought in Mahan's analysis of narrow seas, pre-sumably because Mahan conducted his analysis before submarines had fulfilled their potential. For him the primary concern was that seamounts, reefs, and other obstructions can narrow the choice of courses for ships cruising on the surface. Careless piloting could leave a surface vessel aground. Such perils persist. In 2012, for example, the U.S. Navy minesweeper *Guardian* (MCM-5) foundered on a reef in the Sulu Sea and had to be broken up.[17]

Yet underwater topography is at least as crucial for submarines cruising the depths. A pas-sage's underwater conformation may differ markedly from that on the surface, meaning that submarines may have to trace a somewhat different route to make their way through. They also might have to traverse channels in shallow water, exposing themselves to detection and tracking. This is an uncomfortable prospect for submarine crews, who thrive on concealment. In Mahanian parlance, then, a passage's width, length, and difficulty may be different for subma-rines than for surface craft. Submarines resemble ground forces in that the terrain beneath them matters – in shallow zones, at any rate.

Not just physical features, furthermore, but a host of variables relating to seawater itself – temperature and salinity, to name two – influence sound propagation, which is central to sub-marine and antisubmarine operations. Acoustics and kindred subjects are absent from Mahan's works yet shape undersea warfare to a striking degree. It would be worth undertaking a close study of South Asian subsurface topography and hydrography, compiling an undersea coun-terpart to his analysis of features with which surface navies must contend. Understanding the undersea topography is essential for transiting or operating near narrow seas – warranting an addition to the Mahanian template of width, length, and difficulty.

Mahan surveys South Asia

Now turn to South Asia. Mahan cruised the Indian Ocean in 1867, en route to ports of call in East Asia. This was before he commenced his career as an author. He evidently viewed it as a thoroughfare by which shipping reached the Far East, rather than as a maritime theater in its own right. His attitude may have foreshadowed the U.S. military's "I-95" syndrome. American mariners are reportedly in the habit of speeding through South Asian waters and skies on their way to other destinations while paying scant heed to the surroundings – much as motorists hurtle along interstate highways such as Interstate 95, the main north–south artery on the U.S. East Coast. Mahan chronicled religious and cultural curiosities in such ports of call as Muscat and Bombay, yet made little mention of these seaports' strategic characteristics.[18]

One needs to rectify this oversight. As Mahan notes, the more plentiful the supply of nautical passages, the less value any given passage holds. At first blush it may seem as though individual straits should command less importance in the Indian Ocean region than in expanses like the Mediterranean Sea, given the Mediterranean's dearth of outlets to the open sea. Substitutes are available should any Indian Ocean narrow sea be closed to shipping. After all, the Indian Ocean is scarcely an enclosed sea. In this sense it resembles the Caribbean, whose southeastern fringe amounts to open sea. The Lesser Antilles do little to obstruct the sea lanes.

As Indian thinker K. M. Panikkar notes, the Indian Ocean is unique in that the Eurasian landmass constitutes a "roof" overhead, preventing northward movement by sea except through a few choke points. But the ocean is open to the bottom. Africa forms its western wall, the Malay Peninsula, Indonesian archipelago, and Australia its eastern wall.[19] Antarctica bounds the ocean far to the south. It would verge on impossible for any hostile power to deny outsiders access to a waterspace so vast and empty. Nor are there many islands where military forces could ensconce themselves. The U.S. military has used the British territory of Diego Garcia as a platform to wage war in the Middle East and Central Asia. But Diego Garcia and other islands such as Mauritius and the Maldives, with their small size and poor resource endowments, are deficient by the Mahanian standards of strength and resources. Much like Jamaica in Mahan's day, a symbiotic relationship between the fleet and the seaport would prevail. Only a dominant sea power could put such Indian Ocean outposts to effective use, since they would depend on sea- and airborne cargoes to support naval or air forces in times of strife. And in the extreme case – in the event that all passages were closed to the north – vessels could simply skirt around the Cape of Good Hope or scud along the southern Australian shoreline.

As in the Caribbean, however, pressing interests summon attention away from the easiest passages. The most difficult passages are the best placed, and thus the most valuable for merchant and naval shipping. In Mahan's day and in our own, both transatlantic shipping and coastwise shipping bound for eastern North American ports gravitated toward the shortest routes, such as through the Strait of Florida or the Anegada Passage, east of Puerto Rico. Similarly, circuitous routes to and from the Indian Ocean and Persian Gulf regions would impose heavy costs on merchant fleets, measured not just in fuel but in the time consumed on longer voyages and in wear-and-tear on hulls, machinery, and crews. Small wonder shipping routes crisscross the northern reaches of the Indian Ocean, passing the Indian subcontinent en route to Malacca, Hormuz, or Bab el-Mandeb. A smaller proportion of Atlantic-bound shipping rounds the Cape of Good Hope.

Staging military operations along the southern rimland of Eurasia would prove trying should these passages be barred. Expeditionary forces would have to traverse vast distances simply to reach likely scenes of action – and the geography along the way would be congested and potentially contested. Yet important strategic imperatives beckon seagoing states' attention. The Strait of Hormuz ranks high on the list. By Mahanian logic, Hormuz commands almost unlimited value for Persian Gulf states, and for seafaring states that ply the Gulf for commercial or military reasons. Oil and gas supplies concentrate minds.

But larger geopolitical imperatives are at work as well. Spykman would describe the Bay of Bengal and Arabian Sea as part of the "girdle of marginal seas" from which sea services can radiate power into the Eurasian rimlands and thence into the vast interior.[20] He attributed the Royal Navy's dominance, and in turn the British Empire's longevity, in large measure to its dominance of such waters. In all likelihood – he perished in 1943 – he would say the same of U.S. maritime supremacy since 1945. Like Mahan, he preached the gospel of commercial, political, and military access to important theaters.[21] Detouring around such expanses could amount to relinquishing American primacy along the southern tier of Eurasia.

Commercial and naval shipping that does hug the northern reaches of the Indian Ocean, moreover, must transit maritime anterooms to the east or west. This makes a marked difference with the Mediterranean and Caribbean. Shipping reaches the high seas once it clears Gibraltar or one of the exits from the Caribbean. Not so in maritime South Asia. Geography compels strategists to concern themselves with strategic conditions not just in the Indian Ocean but in the adjacent South China Sea and the Red Sea, both potentially hazardous bodies of water. They must pay attention not just to Malacca or Bab el-Mandeb but to the Lombok, Sunda, Luzon, and Taiwan straits and the Suez Canal. That the South China Sea is hotly disputed between China and neighboring claimants to Southeast Asian waters, islands, and atolls hardly needs belaboring. Unrest in Egypt or piracy in the Gulf of Aden could threaten access to the western Indian Ocean, whether by raising insurance costs off Somalia or by closing the Suez Canal.

Mahan would call attention to India's peculiar geography. It is at once a massive peninsula jutting out into regional waters, bestowing influence on forces based along the eastern and western coasts, and a half-island appended to continental Eurasia. The Himalayas and Hindu Kush form formidable natural ramparts to India's north, helping isolate the subcontinent from the rest of continental Eurasia. In effect the mountain ranges comprise part of the region's oceanic geography. In these senses India resembles the Italian peninsula, from which strong forces could regulate the Mediterranean sea lanes. (The Mediterranean, admittedly, is far narrower to the south of the Italian boot than is the Indian Ocean south of India. The vastness of the Indian Ocean grants shipping the option of bypassing India at greater distances, whereas the solid Italian and North African landmasses compress the shipping lanes transiting the Mediterranean into a relatively predictable, easily monitored thoroughfare.) While the "stopping power of mountains" is no more impenetrable a shield than the "stopping power of water" in this air and missile age, natural defenses against overland invasion prime New Delhi to think of the Indian Ocean as a zone of special interest – a sphere where its interests should prevail.[22]

Strategists cannot simplify the geometry of Indian Ocean maritime strategy as neatly as Mahan simplified that of the Caribbean basin. Lesser South Asian countries with strong allies are better positioned and equipped to influence their neighborhoods than were weak American states during the *fin de siècle* era. Mahan was able to inscribe a triangle on his map enclosing all important geostrategic features found in the inland seas. A line connecting New Orleans (Louisiana) with Colón formed one side. A second side originated at Pensacola (Florida) and runs through, and somewhat beyond, St. Thomas. The final leg started at Colón and ran through Cartagena and Curaçao, intersecting with the Pensacola–St. Thomas leg east of Martinique.

Everything outside the triangle could be safely excluded from consideration. Mahan cited two reasons why. One, applying his position/strength/resources paradigm revealed that there was no seaport of consequence along the desolate coastline stretching westward from New Orleans, along the Texan and Mexican coasts, through the northern tip of the Yucatan Peninsula.

Two, Mexico was politically stable and deployed no serious navy. It presented no threat, actual or latent. Strategists, then, could disregard the shores west of the Mississippi Delta because it was inert from a sea-power standpoint. By default, all significant features lay within the Mahanian triangle.[23]

Geostrategists today cannot discount the potential of minor South Asian states as blithely as Mahan discounted Mexico's a century ago. Mahan might classify the African coast as he did the Mexican and Guatemalan coasts, with few useful seaports and no navies capable of mounting a threat. To the north, however, Pakistan boasts a capable navy and a loose alliance with China. To the east, Australia and Indonesia field credible navies of their own and are committed to upgrading them to world-class standards in quality, if not in numbers of hulls. The northern reaches of the Indian Ocean should rank uppermost in the minds of strategists, in short, but the waters to the southeast and southwest cannot be discounted from the sea-power calculus.

And finally, no survey of the Indian Ocean region would be complete without pointing out how technological progress influences the Mahanian template for strategic features. Mahan correctly called attention to the relationship between fleets and naval stations, noting that the base might depend on the fleet for defense and external supplies as much as the fleet depended on the base as a place of refuge and resupply. The world's armed services, however, may be witnessing a shift in the offense–defense balance as land-based antiship weaponry comes to boast greater range, precision, and destructive power.

For example, the Pentagon estimates that the Chinese People's Liberation Army's (PLA) antiship ballistic missile (ASBM) can strike throughout the South China Sea and most of the Bay of Bengal from mobile launchers on Chinese territory. Should the ASBM live up to its hype, new operational vistas will open up for Beijing and its partners in South Asia, both to defend any PLA forces operating there from afar or to hold adversaries' forces at risk. Maritime strategists, consequently, may find themselves forced to revise how they measure a site's defensibility in the coming decades. No longer are fleets the sole arbiter of sea power.

Access points to the Indian Ocean and Persian Gulf

Having established why the northern Indian Ocean concentrates minds, we now turn to specific entryways to and exits from the region. Mahanian methods – both his three metrics of width, length, and difficulty, and the one added here, underwater terrain for submarine operations – make an excellent way to foresee the demands of operating in and around narrow passages such as the Malacca, Hormuz, and Bab el-Mandeb straits.

Strait of Malacca

Together the Singapore Strait and Malacca Strait comprise the waterway commonly known as the Strait of Malacca. The Singapore Strait is the eastern entry point from the South China Sea. Bordered by Singapore to the north and the Riau and Lingga archipelagos to the south, the strait is about 60 nautical miles long altogether. It is about 20 nautical miles wide at its eastern entrance, and 10 miles wide to the west, where it joins the Strait of Malacca. It is only about 1.7 miles wide at its narrowest point, at Phillips Channel due south of Singapore.[24] Together the straits are some 448 nautical miles long. The western entryway opens to 173 nautical miles wide at the northwestern terminus separating Sumatra from Thailand.[25]

The best alternative to Malacca is the Lombok–Makassar Strait, which pierces the Indonesian archipelago to the south yet adds some 972 nautical miles to journeys from East to South Asia.

Farther to the east is Sunda Strait, used mainly by vessels conducting local trade between Java and southern Sumatra.[26] Westbound shipping must pass through the Andaman and Nicobar islands, Indian-held archipelagos athwart the western approaches to Malacca, to reach the open sea.

In Mahanian parlance, then, the Strait of Malacca is an extraordinarily long passage, narrow in places, that – owing to shallow water, shifting seabed, and tempestuous weather – can be difficult to traverse. Its funnel shape constricts shipping into a fairly narrow channel off Singapore, while it is impassable to submerged submarines for part of its length. Its complex geography engages many states' politics in and around the seaway. From a military standpoint, it would be possible for the U.S. Navy or some other force to assert control of the passage. As a political matter, it would verge on impossible except in the most extreme circumstances. Few political leaders could justify such an undertaking.

As noted before, the Andamans and Nicobars belong to India. The Indian armed forces thus are well positioned to assert a measure of influence over the strait's western approaches. For instance, antiship missiles poised on the islands could create overlapping fields of fire, granting New Delhi the option of shutting the passages between the islands in wartime. Submarines poised to the west of the island chain could reinforce an Indian decision to cordon off traffic bound to or from the strait. Here again, the situation would have to be truly dire for the Indian leadership to take such an action, with all the sweeping and long-lasting economic and political repercussions it would entail. India nonetheless occupies the strongest position to influence the shipping lanes, since it can do so from sovereign territory.

No comparable island barrier lies to the east of the strait. Indeed, the southern reaches of the South China Sea are largely vacant of islands or coastal sites that are suitable for bases, or where host nations would grant basing rights. The capacity of any remote sea power to exert the degree of influence in the South China Sea that India wields to the west is doubtful at best. Nearby ports such as Cam Ranh Bay, in Vietnam, or Laem Chabang, a container port in Thailand, flank the routes leading to Malacca and could conceivably play host to naval task forces. That Hanoi or Bangkok would permit foreign navies to use their soil in this manner appears far-fetched. Assuming that Singapore would refuse to permit a navy intent on staging some sort of quarantine to use its port facility at Changi – a safe assumption, and one that would also hold for Indonesia and Malaysia – outsiders would depend on expeditionary forces able to sustain themselves at sea for long intervals to keep watch over the eastern approaches. Few fleets are up to such a challenge. In light of such difficulties, many specialists question not just the politics but the practicality of mounting a naval blockade at Malacca.[27] Others call on the United States to do just that in case of war with China.[28] The jury remains out on whether such an option would be operationally feasible or strategically effective.

Bab el-Mandeb Strait

The Bab el-Mandeb Strait joins the western Indian Ocean to the Red Sea, and thence to the Mediterranean Sea via the Suez Canal. The strait is just over 16 nautical miles wide. The island of Perim, located to the east, divides it up into two channels: Bab Iskender, which is approximately 1.6 nautical miles wide (and too shallow for submarines to transit underwater), and Dact-el-Mayun, which is about 13.5 nautical miles wide and is navigable by undersea as well as surface craft.[29] (A long, straight fairway unfolds northwesterly from the Strait into the Red Sea proper.) By Mahanian standards, the western passage of Bab el-Mandeb is short, wide, and easy to traverse.

The political and strategic setting, furthermore, is more permissive than the surroundings at Malacca, where oil and other shipping interests beckon the attention of powers both great and small. As noted before, Africa is largely devoid of countries that entertain serious maritime ambitions that might infringe on maritime security. And of those, none boast the naval means to make good on such ambitions. The same might be said of the Arabian Peninsula to the east. Nor do governments in the Horn of Africa or the Arabian Peninsula possess much in the way of land-based antiship weaponry. Nor does any great marine state have any obvious stake in asserting control over the Strait or its approaches. These are seemingly benign surroundings.

Under these conditions, the major challenges to maritime security in the western Indian Ocean are the ones that make headlines, namely piracy in the Gulf of Aden, which has elicited multinational counterpiracy patrols over the past four-plus years, and unrest in Egypt, which could prompt the government or its adversaries to attempt to close the Suez Canal. The Strait of Malacca is hardly free of piracy. Still, the proportion between constabulary challenges and power politics clearly skews toward power politics in Southeast Asia, whereas constabulary duty predominates to the west. The narrow seas resemble each other outwardly. In strategic terms, the settings could scarcely be more different.

Strait of Hormuz

The Strait of Hormuz commands surpassing value in Mahanian parlance, by virtue of its being the only nautical gateway to the Persian Gulf region. For inhabitants of the Gulf or external powers with vital interests there, this seaway's importance resembles that of Gibraltar before 1869, when the Suez Canal opened. It is the lone outlet from the open ocean to a fully enclosed sea (and, in the case of Gibraltar, to another fully enclosed sea, the Black Sea, via the Dardanelles and Bosporus). Nor is any manmade construction project likely to change that. Strategists have mused about digging an alternative to the Malacca Strait across Thailand's narrow Kra Isthmus, or circumventing the Panama Canal through Nicaragua. There are no obvious sites where the Strait of Hormuz could be bypassed.

If great-power maritime competition appears prevalent around Malacca, and constabulary work predominates off the Horn of Africa, irregular maritime warfare poses the most headaches in and around the Strait of Hormuz. The passage ranges from 17.8 to 51.3 nautical miles wide. It is deep enough to permit underwater transit. At the northernmost point of the transit, however, the shipping routes are only about 1.6 nautical miles wide, in large part because the passage is too shallow at some points to permit deep-draft vessels to make the transit safely. Nor can shipping take a straight course through, as it does through the Bab el-Mandeb Strait. Ships take a northerly course, then make a sharp port turn toward the southwest off the northern tip of Oman (where the traffic separation scheme mentioned above is located), before making a slight starboard turn to due west.[30]

In Mahanian terms, then, the Strait of Hormuz demands a fairly long transit through seas comparable in width to Phillips Channel, the narrowest point in the Malacca Strait. Ships must make a sharp maneuver along the way. These topographical challenges are more than manageable under routine circumstances. But the political and strategic dynamics are far less permissive at Hormuz than at Bab el-Mandeb or Malacca. This transit takes place entirely within reach of Iranian shore-based antiship weaponry such as cruise missiles or tactical aircraft, as well as the host of small surface combatants fielded by the Iranian Revolutionary Guard Corps. The Islamic Republic's modest fleets of submarines and minelayers further complicate matters.

Such weaponry is challenging enough on the high seas. It is even more menacing in confined waters, where ships have little room to maneuver for defensive or offensive purposes. To reach the Gulf proper, finally, inbound vessels must pass within easy reach of Abu Musa and the Tunb Islands, which are claimed both by Iran and the United Arab Emirates but are under

Iranian military control. This is a setting where an inferior local power can hope to mount an effective access- or area-denial strategy – deterring entry into the Persian Gulf in wartime or exacting a high price for operating there. This is a theater posing distinct operational challenges. Millennium Challenge 2002, an exercise in which U.S. Marine general Paul Van Riper pummeled a U.S. Navy task force while commanding a "Red" (read Iranian) force made up of speedboats and other small craft, underlines the dilemmas facing American commanders even when pitted against a seemingly outmatched foe in the Gulf.

A Mahanian prognosis

What might Alfred Thayer Mahan say about this strategic landscape? This cursory survey of the Indian Ocean basin suggests a few preliminary takeaways for contemporary strategists. First, although these straits appear superficially similar – they are focal points through which shipping travels hither and yon – they are quite different when taken in tandem with the larger strategic setting. Great-power competition appears most prevalent in and around the Strait of Malacca, asymmetric international competition at Hormuz, police duty at Bab el-Mandeb. Sizing up geographic features in isolation from politics is a grievous mistake. Geostrategic analysis suggests how to apportion finite resources. If lawlessness is the strategic problem in the Gulf of Aden, coast-guard-like capabilities may be the best tool for the job. Forcible-access capabilities appear most appropriate for the Persian Gulf. Traditional naval capabilities may deliver the greatest returns on the investment at Malacca. Elastic force deployments, by which heavy naval forces shift from side to side on the map, backing up on-scene forces as conditions warrant, may represent the best overall approach.

Second, varying geopolitical conditions could give rise to cooperation or competition in these theaters, even if the same cast of characters is present in each. For example, juxtapose U.S.–China relations in the South China Sea with U.S.–China relations in the Gulf of Aden. Things are tense between Washington (and its allies) and Beijing in Southeast Asia, where precious national interests are at stake for all coastal Asian states. Few such interests are in jeopardy in the western Indian Ocean, where only the common interest in unencumbered navigation prevails. By most accounts, the seagoing states patrolling the Gulf of Aden have worked together amicably – no matter how much they may be at odds elsewhere on the map. It remains to be seen how strategic interactions will shape up around Hormuz should China, India, and other naval newcomers establish presences there.

And third, it is hard to escape the conclusion that the Strait of Hormuz is the most important of the three narrow seas examined here, as well as the thorniest and most immediate military problem. Absent safe passage to and from the Persian Gulf, the Bab el-Mandeb and Malacca straits lose much – though of course not all – of their value as outlets to East Asia and the Atlantic world. Facing down the Iranian military, then, probably represents the best use of U.S. maritime resources if Washington is compelled to choose among theaters. Allies and friends can manage the relatively permissive surroundings in the Gulf of Aden and the Strait of Malacca. (All bets are off if China tries to enforce its claims to "indisputable sovereignty" in the South China Sea, infringing on freedom of the seas there.[31]) If Europeans, Indians, and Southeast Asians can police their own extended neighborhoods, so much the better.

Notes

1 Alfred Thayer Mahan, *The Influence of Sea Power upon History, 1660–1783* (1890; repr. New York: Dover, 1987), p. 33.

2 Geostrategist Nicholas Spykman makes the Caribbean–Mediterranean analogy even more explicit than did Mahan. See Nicholas Spykman, *America's Strategy in World Politics: The United States and the Balance of Power* (New York: Harcourt, Brace, 1942), pp. 46–9.

3 See Alfred Thayer Mahan, "The Persian Gulf and International Relations," in Alfred Thayer Mahan, *Retrospect & Prospect: Studies in International Relations, Naval and Political* (Boston: Little, Brown, 1902), pp. 209–54.

4 Harold Sprout and Margaret Tuttle Sprout, *The Rise of American Naval Power, 1776–1998* (Princeton, NJ: Princeton University Press, 1944), p. 236.

5 John B. Hattendorf (ed.), *Mahan on Naval Strategy. Selections of the Writings of Rear Admiral Alfred Thayer Mahan* (Annapolis, MD: Naval Institute Press, 2015), p. 319.

6 *Ibid.*, p. 22.

7 *Ibid.*, pp. 235–6.

8 *Ibid.*, p. 306.

9 Alfred Thayer Mahan, *The Interest of America in Sea Power, Present and Future* (London: Sampson Low, Marston & Company, 1897), p. 283.

10 Mahan, *Naval Strategy*, p. 132.

11 Mahan, *Interest of America in Sea Power*, p. 283.

12 See James R. Holmes, "A 'Fortress Fleet' for China," *Whitehead Journal of Diplomacy and International Relations* 11, 2 (Summer/Fall 2010), pp. 115–28, http://blogs.shu.edu/diplomacy/files/2012/05/009_Holmes_Layout-1a.pdf, accessed August 28, 2015.

13 Mahan, *Naval Strategy*, pp. 132–3.

14 *Ibid.*, pp. 309–10.

15 *Ibid.*

16 *Ibid.*, p. 346.

17 U.S. Pacific Fleet Public Affairs, "USS Guardian Grounding Investigation Results Released," U.S. Navy Website, June 20, 2013, www.navy.mil/submit/display.asp?story_id=74930, accessed August 28, 2015.

18 Alfred Thayer Mahan, *From Sail to Steam* (New York: Harper & Brothers, 1907), pp. 198, 217–28.

19 K. M. Panikkar, *India and the Indian Ocean: An Essay on the Influence of Sea Power on Indian History* (New York: Macmillan, 1945), p. 19.

20 Nicholas J. Spykman, *The Geography of the Peace*, ed. Helen R. Nicholl, intro. Frederick Sherwood Dunn (New York: Harcourt, Brace, 1943), pp. 24–5.

21 Mahan, *Retrospect & Prospect*, p. 246.

22 John J. Mearsheimer, *The Tragedy of Great Power Politics* (New York: W. W. Norton, 2001).

23 *Ibid.*, pp. 311–13.

24 National Geospatial-Intelligence Agency, *Sailing Directions (Enroute): Strait of Malacca and Sumatera*, Pub. 174, 11th edn (Bethesda, MD: U.S. National Geospatial-Intelligence Agency, 2010), p. 117.

25 Donald B. Freeman, *The Straits of Malacca: Gateway or Gauntlet?* (Montreal and Kingston: McGill-Queen's University Press, 2003), pp. 6–9.

26 *Ibid.*, pp. 6–9.

27 See for instance Gabriel B. Collins, Andrew S. Erickson, Lyle J. Goldstein, and William S. Murray, *China's Energy Strategy: The Impact on Beijing's Maritime Policies* (Annapolis, MD: Naval Institute Press, 2008), pp. 299–410.

28 See, for example, T. X. Hammes, "Offshore Control: A Proposed Strategy for an Unlikely Conflict," *INSS Strategic Forum*, June 2012, www.dtic.mil/dtic/tr/fulltext/u2/a577602.pdf, accessed August 28, 2015.

29 U.S. National Geospatial-Intelligence Agency, NGA Chart 62100, Jazirat al Hanish as Saghir to Bab el Mandeb, October 2004.

30 U.S. National Geospatial-Intelligence Agency, NGA Chart 62480, Strait of Hormuz to Qatar, 2nd edn., March 2003.

31 John Pomfret, "Beijing Claims 'Indisputable Sovereignty' over South China Sea," *Washington Post*, July 31, 2010, www.washingtonpost.com/wp-dyn/content/article/2010/07/30/AR2010073005664.html, accessed August 28, 2015.

7

INDIAN OCEAN SECURITY

Developments in ocean law, trade, and resources

Caitlyn Antrim

In the years since World War Two, major advances in offshore technology, increases in maritime trade, and the growing economic value of offshore energy, mineral, and living resources have led to a breakdown of the centuries-old division of the ocean between three-mile territorial seas under coastal state authority and the high seas, where freedom of navigation and exploitation typically reigned. Following a period of expanding coastal state claims over the seas and their resources, the 1982 United Nations Convention on the Law of the Sea established a new order of the oceans that promised the stability needed to protect sovereignty, provide for national security, promote trade and development, and safeguard the marine environment. This is particularly important in the Indian Ocean, where intense use, overlapping claims of sovereignty, and dysfunctional governments are putting the international legal regime under great stress and increasing the danger of conflict.

Maritime zones in the Indian Ocean

The Law of the Sea Convention defines ocean zones and the rights and obligations of states within those zones (see Box 7.1). It establishes organizations to carry out collective responsibilities for defining the boundaries of national jurisdiction and managing mineral resources beyond those limits. It also promotes peaceful settlement of disputes through alternative processes for conflict resolution, with some issues subject to mandatory settlement of disputes.

The Indian Ocean encompasses a wide range of geographical, geological, and biological features. The region includes several of the most heavily travelled international straits, major fisheries, and areas with high potential for discovery of energy and mineral resources. The nations bordering the region range from the most developed of the developing world to some of the world's poorest and most dysfunctional states.

The coastal and island states of the Indian Ocean region likewise demonstrate a wide range of interests. International law, primarily the Law of the Sea Convention, plays a pivotal role in peaceful resolution of such conflicts. Regional legal and policy initiatives have further mitigated international tension through diplomatic processes, but political, economic, and environmental issues could still lead to disputes and conflict.

Box 7.1 Ocean zones: rights and responsibilities

Under the Law of the Sea Convention, the ocean is classified into eight zones:

Territorial Sea: the coastal seas extending as far as 12 miles from shore, in which the coastal state has sovereign authority, subject to the recognition of the right of innocent passage for ships on their way from one location to another.

Contiguous Zone: an area extending 12 miles beyond the territorial sea, in which the coastal state may enforce fiscal, immigration, sanitary, and customs laws.

Exclusive Economic Zone (EEZ): the seas beyond the territorial sea extending to 200 nautical miles, in which a coastal state has the sovereign right to manage, exploit, and protect mineral and living resources, subject to providing access to unused portions of what the coastal state determines to be the maximum allowable catch of the living resources. Other states are guaranteed high-seas navigation rights and the right to lay and maintain cables and pipelines, with the need for coastal and maritime states to accommodate one another's rights.

Continental Shelf: both the seabed of the EEZ and the areas of the seabed beyond the EEZ that meet geological requirements specified in the LoS Convention. The coastal state manages the resources of the continental shelf and shares revenues of exploitation of mineral resources of the shelf beyond the EEZ with the international community

High Seas: the waters beyond the EEZ in which activities are under the authority of the flag state, and subject to only a limited number of international prohibitions, such as piracy and slave trade.

The Area: the portion of the ocean floor beyond the limits of national jurisdiction. Mineral resources of the Area are managed by the International Seabed Authority established by the LOS Convention.

International Straits: straits that are used in international navigation regardless of whether they are sufficiently narrow to otherwise be considered territorial seas subject to innocent passage. International straits are subject to the regime of Transit Passage in which ships and aircraft may pass through or over international straits in their "normal mode" without the restrictions imposed on innocent passage.

Archipelagic Waters: those waters within boundary lines drawn to encompass the islands of archipelagic states. Passage through archipelagic waters is subject to conditions similar to Transit Passage in designated sea lanes and innocent passage in other areas of the waters.

Source: Caitlyn Antrim, "International Law and Order: The Indian Ocean and South China Sea," in David Michel and Russell Strictlor, eds, *Indian Ocean Rising: Maritime Security and Policy Challenges*, Washington DC: Stimson Center, 2012, p. 66. www.stimson.org/images/uploads/research-pdfs/Book_IOR_2.pdf, accessed March 26, 2015. Reproduced with permission.

Current issues and disputes

In some cases, the LoS Convention provides detailed prescriptions of rights and obligations at sea. In others, general guidance is provided for later definition, leaving issues of jurisdiction to be resolved as they arise. This has led to a number of current or potential disputes in the four areas of concern listed below.

Maritime boundaries, sovereignty, and resource jurisdiction

Determination of areas of sovereignty and national jurisdiction is progressing in a generally satisfactory direction with only a few, but significant, problem areas.

Resolving competing claims to maritime space

Maritime boundaries are primarily based on sovereignty over land territory, according to rules expressed in the LoS Convention and in customary international law, legal precedents regarding breadth of maritime zones, and principles of equidistance and equity in determining boundaries between adjacent or opposing states. States bordering on the Indian Ocean have turned to the dispute resolution processes of the LoS Convention to address competing claims.

Claims to the continental shelf beyond the EEZ

The Indian Ocean generally has a narrow geological continental shelf, but in many locations coastal states are endowed with a broad continental margin, which is defined in the LoS Convention as the juridical continental shelf. A coastal state may propose an outer boundary of the continental shelf when it extends beyond the EEZ in accordance with rules laid out in the LoS Convention. The boundary is to be submitted to the Commission on the Limits of the Continental Shelf for a recommendation on finalization of the claim or guidance as to how it should be revised. The Commission, established by the LoS Convention, is composed of experts in geology, geophysics, or hydrography. It provides assurance to the parties to the LoS Convention that the coastal state has conformed to the rules of the Convention in establishing its boundary for the extended continental shelf.

Australia submitted the first claim to an extended continental shelf in the Indian Ocean in 2004. Mauritius and the Seychelles submitted their first claim to an extended continental shelf in 2008, making the submission jointly with the intent to negotiate a division of the shelf between the two countries at a later date. To date, 17 countries in the Indian Ocean region have submitted 21 claims to the Commission on the Limits of the Continental Shelf seeking recommendations that proposed boundaries be accepted as final.[1]

Shifting coastlines and disappearing islands

Areas of coastal state jurisdiction are measured from baselines drawn along coasts and around archipelagos. The LoS Convention was written with only limited consideration of possible shifts in the geography of the coastline. Coastal states are to submit their baselines to the United Nations, but only in the case of river deltas is there guidance as to the revision of baselines to reflect changes of the physical coastline. In this case, the coastal state need not revise its baselines in the face of shifting coastlines.

There are three additional cases in which baselines, and the maritime jurisdiction they bring, might be reconsidered based on changes of geography. One is the removal of physical material in a way that changes the basis for baselines. A decade ago Malaysia expressed concern that Singapore's use of sand to extend land beyond its previous boundaries could change the median line in the waters between Singapore and Malaysia to Malaysia's disadvantage.[2] A second case is the modification of a coastline due to natural disaster, such as the subsidence of territory in an earthquake or massive coastal erosion due to events such as tsunamis or hurricanes. The third is the case of sea level rise that submerges some or all of the territory of an island nation. Would a state, or at least its claim to maritime jurisdiction, disappear if its land territory no longer qualified as having an EEZ under the LoS Convention? This issue could arise in the case of the Maldives, where future sea level rise could submerge the land of the archipelago and force migration of the population. If claims to EEZs and continental shelves could be retained in spite of loss of the islands on which claims were made, the resources of the EEZ and continental shelf might provide financial support for the population wherever it might relocate. Another question is whether artificial enhancement of islands before they are lost could exempt the territory from the lack of recognition of maritime zones accorded to artificially created islands.

Archipelagic baselines and sea lanes

As archipelagic states, Indonesia and the Maldives are able to draw baselines that enclose their islands and from which the territorial sea and EEZ may be determined. Self-interest and domestic pressure encourage archipelagic states to interpret the rules in establishing these baselines broadly, sometimes exceeding the provisions of the LoS Convention. The zones of authority may encroach on jurisdictional claims of nearby states or the freedom of navigation of maritime nations.

Similarly, the establishment of sea lanes through archipelagos could become a source of friction or conflict if they are established or revised without due consideration of the interests of maritime nations in shipping and aviation routes and paths for undersea cables.

Coastal state threats to maritime freedoms

The Law of the Sea Convention is a comprehensive document in terms of the issues it addresses, but it does not spell out every detail of how it is to be implemented. States party to the Convention are expected to implement its provisions in good faith and to respect the rights of other parties. This is particularly true in the EEZ, where coastal states may establish laws and regulations pertaining to exploration and exploitation of natural resources, marine scientific research and protection of the marine environment while taking into account rights of other states to exercise high seas freedoms. Warships and ships on government service are exempt from the provisions related to the protection of the marine environment, but are expected to honor the intent of regulations as much as possible.

Innocent passage

The right of innocent passage through the territorial sea is long-standing and the LoS Convention simply provides greater clarity and limits discretion by the coastal state over passage. Innocent passage never included a requirement for prior notification in customary law or previous agreements and was not added by the 1982 Convention. In spite of this, a number of states in the region now claim that foreign flag vessels, especially nuclear-powered ships and submarines, must give prior notification before exercising the right, among them are India and Pakistan.[3] These claims are challenged periodically under the U.S. Navy's "Freedom of Navigation" program.

Transit passage

The right of transit passage derives from pre-Convention rights to pass through straits used in international navigation with additional navigational freedoms defined in the Convention. Some straits states have claimed that the right of transit passage is available only to parties to the Convention and that non-parties only have the right to innocent passage through international straits.

As traffic through straits increases, the financial and regulatory burdens on states bordering the straits have risen, as have the risks of catastrophic accidents and acts of piracy and armed robbery at sea. The LoS regime leaves straits states responsible for providing for safety of navigation but does not provide mechanisms for covering the costs of providing an international service. These costs can be quite high for a developing state so international arrangements that provide for necessary services while respecting the sovereignty of the straits states and freedom of navigation for maritime states will be needed in the future.

The right of transit passage through the Strait of Hormuz by states not party to the LoS Convention has been challenged in statements from the Iranian government and by Oman. Having not ratified the LoS Convention itself, Iran is in a position to deny recognition of the more lenient Transit Passage regime of the Convention, but it still is bound by customary law, reinforced by the decision of the International Court of Justice, that provides a non-interruptible right of innocent passage through straits used in international commerce. While innocent passage may suffice for commercial vessels, it is not sufficient for warships and it does not apply to aircraft.

Limits on navigational freedoms in the EEZ

In spite of provisions of the Convention that protect high seas navigation rights in the EEZ, and specifically protect rights of government ships (including warships), some states have sought to limit military activities within their EEZ. Most notable are the actions by China to challenge and harass military aircraft and government-owned ships engaged in survey and observation activities beyond the territorial sea. The mid-air collision of a Chinese fighter and a U.S. Navy EP3 reconnaissance aircraft in 2001 (with the loss of the life of the Chinese pilot) demonstrated the seriousness of attempts to expand coastal state jurisdiction at sea. Within the Indian Ocean region, India claims the right to require prior consent for foreign military activities in the EEZ, and 24-hour advance notice for vessels entering the EEZ with cargoes containing "dangerous goods and chemicals, oil, noxious liquid and harmful substances and radioactive material."[4] Myanmar, Bangladesh, Pakistan, Saudi Arabia, and Yemen have made similar rights to require prior notice of passage in circumstances not covered by the LoS Convention. These claims have all been protested by the United States as unjustified restrictions on navigation rights. India made a declaration upon ratifying the Convention that claimed limits on foreign military activities in the EEZ, with similar declarations being made by several other Indian Ocean states.[5] To date, these declarations have not been put into practice.

Advance notice of cable and pipeline maintenance in the EEZ

The right to lay and maintain cables and pipelines across the seabed of the EEZ is explicitly protected in the LoS Convention. In spite of undersea cables providing the international communications infrastructure of the region, some countries in the Indian Ocean have claimed the right to impose permitting and advance notification of cable maintenance activities in their EEZs that undermine the Convention's intent.

Monitoring, regulation, and enforcement

Parties to the LoS Convention have the right to manage resource development, marine scientific research, and environmental protection in their EEZs and the duty to combat piracy on the high seas. Without the capability to monitor activities and to enforce regulations at sea, coastal states lose the ability to fulfill their responsibilities to combat illegal activities. Without ships and shore facilities to monitor activities and enforce laws and regulations, both coastal and shipping states may suffer loss and damage.

Management of the EEZ

The LoS Convention established that the resources of the EEZ fall under the sovereign jurisdiction of the coastal state as far as 200 nautical miles (nm) from shore. This leaves it to the state to establish management policies governing resource exploitation, dumping of waste and other exploitation and environmental activities, to monitor activities in the EEZ, and to inspect vessels and enforce regulations. This requires a substantial investment that many developing states are unable to make.

Somalia is a case in point regarding the loss of a national resource due to a lack of capacity for offshore management and regulation. While it would be an exaggeration to blame the rise of Somalia-based piracy solely on the decimation of its offshore fisheries and the displacement of fishermen to other activities, the failure to protect and utilize its once-rich offshore fisheries is a major economic loss that undermines the development of a national government capable of regulating activities in its own EEZ.[6]

Piracy

The points of confluence of the heavily travelled, high-value sea routes in the Indian Ocean have become attractive hunting grounds for pirates. Small-scale piracy, based on the capture of ships and cargo for booty that occasionally rose to serious levels in the western Indian Ocean near the Horn of Africa and the Strait of Malacca, has been supplanted by capture and ransom activities against lightly crewed vessels with high-value cargoes traveling from the Persian Gulf and the Suez Canal, even as piracy in the eastern Indian Ocean has declined.

In 2011, as of September 27 of that year, there were 194 incidents off Somalia resulting in 24 hijackings, 400 hostages, and 15 hostage deaths in 2011. In the same period in 2013, there were only 13 incidents in that region reported to the International Maritime Bureau: two suspicious vessels, four vessels fired upon, two hijackings (a dhow and a fishing boat), and five attempted attacks.[7] While incidents and attacks dropped over two years, due to a combination of naval intervention, more cautious routing and watch standing on ships, and the introduction of private security guards on ships in the Gulf of Aden and the Persian Gulf, piracy, robbery, and other crimes against vessels remained high along the Indonesian coast and the Straits of Malacca and Singapore.

Piracy is an international crime to which all maritime nations must respond, but many states were slow in enacting domestic legal authority to act against pirates. Some states participating in anti-piracy patrols in the Arabian Sea lacked legislative authority to try and punish pirates and eventually had to turn them loose. In other cases, local actions against Somalia-based pirates were impeded by the lack of a capable national government to act against pirates within national waters. Action against shipping by foreign states within a coastal state's territorial sea is normally a violation of international law. Maritime states had to seek a resolution of the UN Security Council to authorize the pursuit and capture of pirates within Somalia's territorial sea. Between 2008 and 2013, the Security Council adopted ten resolutions dealing with piracy, armed robbery at sea, and control of the flow of arms. It also endorsed operations of Combined Task Force 151 and other forces combating piracy off the shores of Somalia.

Public guards and private military security firms

When naval forces in the Arabian Sea were able to reduce pirate attacks on commercial vessels, the placement of private security personnel on commercial vessels in the region was cautiously evaluated and slowly implemented. The presence of armed guards has been given credit by some observers for the sharp reduction in attacks, but further analysis is needed to determine the relative contributions of the naval and coast guard ships at sea and the private guards on ships.

The introduction of private military personnel and armed guard vessels and armory ships raises issues not contemplated in the LoS Convention. The Convention identifies only the militaries of states as having authority to conduct boardings and use force against ships of other states. The authorization of private vessels to act with deadly force has largely fallen into disuse since the Paris Declaration Respecting Maritime Law of April 16, 1856 in which, among its provisions, privateering was abolished among the signatories. Even the United States, which did not sign the declaration, has abided by its provisions since the U.S. civil war 150 years ago

The February 15, 2013 fatal shooting of two Indian fishermen in the Indian contiguous zone by Italian marine guards detailed to the private ship MT *Enrica Lexie* elevated the uncertain role of security guards on private vessels to a legal issue as Indian authorities charged the guards with murder and proceeded with court action.

The issue of private security forces arose again in October, 2013 when India impounded the U.S.-owned, Sierra Leone-flagged, Ukrainian- and Indian-crewed MV *Seaman Guard Ohio* for illegal activities in India's territorial sea and contiguous zone.

While the private military security industry has developed a voluntary industry code of conduct and best practices, the legal status of the industry, and the guards and vessels, remains uncertain. If the industry continues to grow, the legal status, and the rights and obligations of the industry, must be clarified or else incidents are likely to grow in number.

Illegal, unreported, and unregulated fishing on the high seas

The increasing sophistication of fishing systems has allowed modern fishing vessels and fleets to enter a fishery and quickly harvest the resource before moving on to other grounds. Poor developing states with limited resources to invest in coast guards capable of patrolling their EEZ and enforcing fishery regulations have left their offshore resources vulnerable to illegal, unreported, and unregulated (IUU) fishing, with major economic losses both to the state and to local fishing industries. IUU fishing has proven even more problematic for fisheries that straddle the EEZ and the high seas, or fisheries that migrate across national and international zones.

Increased demand for fish for domestic consumption and international trade will put increased pressure on high seas and straddling fish stocks. If coastal state and flag state capacity to monitor fishing in the EEZ and on the high seas is unable to track fishing activities and enforcement on the sea and in port is not able to enforce regulations, then there will be an increase in IUU fishing to the detriment of coastal state fishing interests and of consumers.

All of the coastal states bordering the Indian Ocean belong to one or more regional fishery bodies and most belong to a regional seas program. Increasingly, they may turn to inter-governmental and non-governmental organizations for assistance in developing management plans for their EEZs.

Protection of the marine environment

The Law of the Sea Convention establishes that states are responsible for enacting and enforcing laws to prevent pollution of the marine environment, but assigning responsibility, by itself, is not sufficient. The Convention encourages the development of regional and global agreements that lay out specific rules to address pollution from land or continental shelf activities that may be subject to binding dispute settlement, either through the Convention or through other processes specified in the regional agreement.

Ship breaking

Dismantling ships to salvage equipment and recycle metals is a labor-intensive activity. The ship dismantling industry has moved to India and other nations with large, low-cost labor forces. Ships are constructed with large amounts of hazardous materials and over their working life they may accrue quantities of petroleum products. Breaking ships down releases these materials. Rather than dismantle vessels in an enclosed dock that could contain hazardous materials, ships are often simply run up on shore, where they are dismantled and harmful materials may be washed to sea to the detriment of the environment, marine ecosystems, and coastal population.

Climate change and sea level rise

Projections of rising sea levels due to global climate change have serious implications for coastal cities and infrastructure. They also have implications for maritime jurisdiction if rising sea levels move maritime baselines inward, taking with them the territorial seas and EEZs that are drawn from those baselines. More critical is the threat to the very existence of small island nations, where land territory may rise only meters above current ocean levels. Rising sea levels could eventually eliminate an island state's land territory and with it all of their claims to EEZs and continental shelves.

Sea level rise-induced migration has already occurred with the submergence of Bangladesh's Bhola Island in 1995. However, the loss of Bhola Island, which was located inside the coastal baselines, had no effect on the country's maritime jurisdiction.[8] Looking forward, the Maldives (where 80 percent of the country's territory has an elevation of 1 meter or less above sea level) faces prospects of being submerged by rising sea levels. This would force the migration of the population off the archipelago, and eliminate the Maldives' EEZ, with parts of its continental shelf likely being transferred to India and the British Indian Ocean Territories.

Proposal for a marine protected area in the British Indian Ocean Territories

A decision by the United Kingdom to establish a marine protected area in the Indian Ocean in the region of the British Indian Ocean Territories provoked opposition in that it would prevent indigenous people from returning to the territories from which they were removed fifty years ago when the U.K. began preparations for the establishment of the U.S. naval base in Diego Garcia. Supporters of the U.K. proposal for a marine protected area in these waters include the British government and some major international environmental NGOs. Opponents, who claim the designation of the marine protected area is a ploy to make it impossible for the displaced people to return to productive occupations in their former home, include human rights organizations, other environmental organizations, and some neighboring island states where people displaced by the British have migrated. Efforts to resolve the issue by financial compensation have thus far been rejected by the U.K.

In March of 2015, the Permanent Court of Arbitration ruled for Mauritius and against the United Kingdom. It found that the U.K. had improperly declared a marine protected area without consultation with Mauritius. It found the MPA invalid and ordered that the U.K. and Mauritius engage in negotiations regarding the terms of any future marine protected area. It also made any expansion of the base at Diego Garcia contingent on agreement of the government of Mauritius.[9]

State capacity for monitoring and enforcement

The expansion of national sovereignty over living, mineral, and energy resources 200 nautical miles or more from shore was viewed as a boon to coastal states by the negotiators at the Third UN Conference on the Law of the Sea. But the extension of national jurisdiction brought with it the task of monitoring and regulating activities in this vast area and that, in turn, requires an investment in maritime constabulary capability. Such forces can constitute a substantial cost for small and underdeveloped coastal states.

The functions of maritime forces are illustrated by the mission statement of the Maldives Coast Guard:

- defending the nation and its territorial integrity;
- protecting the territorial waters and securing the resources of the EEZ;
- safeguarding the marine environment and coastal area;
- enforcing the maritime law;
- assisting the people and conducting search and rescue missions;
- responding to national emergencies and crises;
- providing support and mobility to other services.[10]

For nations with substantial commitment to naval forces that include frigates and destroyers, missions may include tasks such as anti-piracy patrols, patrolling sea lanes or escorting vessels or engaging in interdiction of vessels carrying interdicted articles such as weapons of mass destruction under the Proliferation Security Initiative.

Multilateral agreements and organizations

The Indian Ocean is an area of intense multinational activity. All but one of the nations bordering the Indian Ocean are parties to the Law of the Sea Convention. Iran has signed but not yet ratified the Convention. All are members of the International Maritime Organization and of at least one regional fisheries organization, and most are members of a regional seas program as well.

The Law of the Sea Convention serves as a framework agreement upon which more specialized treaties, organizations, and activities are established. These agreements, organizations, and activities include a framework convention governing fish stocks on the high seas, the operation of the International Seabed Authority in managing minerals beyond national jurisdiction, safety, security and environmental agreements negotiated under the International Maritime Organization, and security partnerships such as the Proliferation Security Initiative.

International fishing agreements

Fisheries and fish stocks that exist wholly or partially outside national jurisdictions pose a special problem for fishery management. Fishing on the high seas is a freedom for all states, and the lack of effective enforcement of sustainable fishing policies permits highly mobile fishing fleets to over-exploit a resource and move on, leaving once-rich resources depleted and damaged.

The UN "Fish Stocks Agreement" was opened for signature in 1995 and came into force in 2001.[11] The agreement provides the framework for the establishment and operation of regional agreements to manage high seas and straddling fish stocks in accordance with the LoS Convention. The Southern Indian Ocean Fisheries Agreement (SIOFA) is a regional agreement negotiated under the Fish Stocks Agreement to address high seas fisheries in the southern Indian Ocean region.

As the UN agency responsible for international fishery issues, the Food and Agriculture Organization (FAO) plays a key role in promoting sustainable fishing in regions around the world, both in national waters and on the high seas. Under FAO, four regional fishery commissions have been established in the Indian Ocean and South East Asian region: the Asia Pacific Fishery Commission, Bay of Bengal Programme Inter-Governmental Organization, Indian Ocean Tuna Commission, and South West Indian Ocean Fisheries Commission.

Seabed minerals beyond national jurisdiction

All parties to the LoS Convention are also members of the International Seabed Authority (ISA), the agency that manages the mineral resources of the seabed beyond the limits of national jurisdiction. There are three known categories of hard minerals on the world's deep seabed: polymetallic nodules of manganese and iron oxides enriched in nickel, copper, cobalt, and rare earth elements on the abyssal floor of the deep seas; cobalt crusts consisting of iron and manganese oxides enriched in cobalt, nickel and, on occasion, platinum group metals found on the slopes of seamounts; and polymetallic sulfides of copper and zinc, sometimes enriched with gold found near spreading centers and subduction zones.

Over the first decade of the twenty-first century, rising demand for metals contained in deep seabed minerals, particularly in China, drove metal prices upward and increased commercial interest in seabed mineral deposits. India, China, South Korea, and Germany have each sponsored national applicants for ISA recognition of exclusive rights to explore mineral sites in the Indian Ocean. India's first claim was approved in 2001 for a deposit of polymetallic nodules. As of 2014, claims by China, the Republic of Korea, India, and Germany for deposits of polymetallic sulfides along the Southwest and Central Indian Ocean ridges have been approved.

Maritime safety and security agreements

All of the coastal states of the Indian Ocean are members of the International Maritime Organization. The IMO is the source of international rules and guidelines governing shipping operations that coastal states apply to international shipping in order to protect against vessel-source marine pollution through a uniform set of international regulations. The IMO also works with straits and archipelagic states to gain agreement on the designation of sea lanes in international straits.

Several key maritime safety and security conventions have been negotiated under the auspices of the IMO. With regard to shipping, two of the most important are the Convention on

Safety of Life at Sea (SOLAS) and the Convention on the Suppression of Unlawful Acts (SUA). Both of these agreements have been supplemented and modified through subsequent protocols. Most recently, protocols to the SUA have been negotiated to address acts of international terrorism.

The IMO also supports regional efforts to promote maritime security. In 2009, the IMO convened a meeting in which East African nations adopted the "Code of Conduct Concerning the Repression of Piracy and Armed Robbery against Ships in the Western Indian Ocean and the Gulf of Aden."[12] The signatories requested that IMO and other international organizations provide support in implementing the Code of Conduct, particularly in building national capacity to effectively implement the code.

The United Nations Security Council has the authority to intervene in matters affecting peace and security in the oceans. The threat of piracy emanating from Somalia led the Security Council to issue a series of resolutions encouraging a maritime response and authorizing actions that would otherwise exceed national authority as recognized by the LOS Convention.

The recent addition of private military security companies to the anti-piracy campaign in the Gulf of Aden and the Arabian Sea pose new issues not contemplated under the Law of the Sea Convention.

Regional environmental programs

There are regional environmental organizations that, while not law-making bodies, have significant policy roles in the Indian Ocean region.

The UN Environment Programme (UNEP) supports two "Regional Seas" programs in the Indian Ocean. The first, which is administered by UNEP, is the East Africa Regional Seas program, with members spanning the coast and islands from South Africa to Somalia. The principal legal framework is the "Nairobi Convention," which coordinates programs meant to strengthen capacity to protect, manage, and develop the coastal and marine environment.

The second regional seas program is the South Asia Cooperative Environment Programme. This body, which includes Pakistan, India, Bangladesh, Maldives, and Sri Lanka, oversees implementation of the South Asian Seas Action Plan, which addresses integrated coastal zone management, oil spill contingency planning, human development, and environmental impacts of land-based activities.

International dispute settlement bodies

As parties to the LoS Convention, regional coastal states (except for non-parties Iran and Cambodia) have recourse to the dispute-settlement mechanisms created by the Convention: the International Tribunal on the Law of the Sea or the Arbitration and Special Arbitration panels provided by the Convention (they also have recourse to the International Court of Justice). While there is a strong preference for diplomatic processes over judicial approaches to resolve boundary disputes the Convention's dispute-resolution system has been used on several occasions to resolve maritime boundary disputes in the Indian Ocean.

Peaceful settlement of maritime disputes

Claims to maritime zones are guided by principles in the Law of the Sea Convention, but other principles, including equity and historic use, can require further negotiation, conciliation, or binding settlement to resolve overlapping claims. While resolution of disputes over sovereign control or resources or territory can lead to armed conflict, coastal nations in the Indian Ocean have resolved, or are in the process of seeking peaceful resolution of, a number of boundary disputes. For example, India and Sri Lanka have a negotiated maritime boundary and other states have turned to the LoS Convention's dispute-settlement provisions for assistance in resolving border and boundary disputes.

An encouraging note is seen in the use of the dispute-settlement provisions of the Law of the Sea Convention to resolve maritime boundary disputes in the Bay of Bengal. Bangladesh and Myanmar took a dispute over the division of authority over the EEZ between the two states in the Bay of Bengal to the International Tribunal for the Law of the Sea. The Tribunal reached a decision on March 14, 2012 that resolved the dispute within the EEZ.[13] Bangladesh and India subsequently resolved their dispute through the Permanent Court of Arbitration,[14] leaving only a claim by Sri Lanka over part of the Bay of Bengal that overlaps other claims to be resolved.

China and Indian Ocean security

The Indian Ocean provides China with access to the oil of the Persian Gulf and the minerals of Africa that are essential to China's economic security and growth. It also provides a route to expand trade to and through the Indian Ocean region. In recent years China has invested in the development of ports and bases along the coast. Developments in Myanmar, Sri Lanka, and Pakistan gave rise to concerns of Chinese militarization of the Indian Ocean that were expressed by Western analysts as a "string of pearls" strategy by China to establish bases around the ocean's periphery.

China has continued to expand its investment in maritime facilities in the Indian Ocean region, but has emphasized its economic interests. In explaining this program, China described it as a new "Maritime Silk Road," which evokes the ancient land and sea trading routes between China, central Asia, and the Mediterranean. China's economic commitment to the development of the Indian Ocean region is vast in scope, extending beyond the Indian Ocean to West Africa and to the Mediterranean Sea. The economic commitment is also large, running into tens of billions of dollars. If fully implemented, the Maritime Silk Road would increase China's access to oil and minerals and open markets for its products in one of the most populous regions of the world.

China has coordinated anti-piracy activities with other states in the past. It should be anticipated that as Chinese trade along the Maritime Silk Road increases, its own naval forces will operate to protect shipping there and will take advantage of regional ports and bases to support the activities of its forces. This, in turn, will increase interaction with the two other major naval powers in the region: India and United States.

The United States and the Indian Ocean

The sea lanes of the Indian Ocean are critical to the economic and security interests of the United States. It is important for the United States to protect its navigation rights in the region, maintain respect for U.S. power and influence, and prevent local jurisdictional disputes from growing into maritime conflicts. In this, the United States gains from the use of international law to avoid the need to threaten to use force against any Indian Ocean state.

As a non-party to the LoS Convention, the U.S. may not be able to utilize international legal mechanisms to their full extent. Instead, it could be forced to incur political costs of visible challenges to regional states by the U.S. Navy to demonstrate support for the navigational freedoms important to the United States. Such challenges will have to be weighed against potential costs to regional support for international partnerships, such as the multinational anti-piracy task force and the proliferation security initiative. The leverage of the United States in keeping the practice of law of the sea consistent with the intent of the LoS Convention is significantly weakened by its failure to become party to the LoS Convention. The policy of challenging what it views as excessive claims can only be a stopgap measure until the peaceful mechanisms to challenge claims become available through membership in the Convention.

Role of international law in the Indian Ocean

With the Indian Ocean as home to the navies of the region, to Chinese naval activities, and to the U.S. Navy in its bases on Diego Garcia and in the Persian Gulf, there is no regional maritime hegemon to set or enforce rules and behavior at sea on its own. Instead, the Indian Ocean is governed by a regime based on rules of codified and customary law of the sea that builds on the framework of the UN Convention on the Law of the Sea and other international maritime agreements and domestic laws and regulations of coastal states in their territorial sea, EEZ, and continental shelf.

The strengths of international law in promoting peace and sustainability in the Indian Ocean include rules and processes for determining maritime boundaries that defuse conflict by focusing on implementation of agreed-upon principles and providing increased clarity of national rights and obligations in ocean zones for both coastal and distant water states reduces chances for serious disputes. Mechanisms for settlement of maritime disputes under the LoS Convention have gained increasing respect and wide application. Regional recognition of the Law of the Sea Convention and membership in the IMO provide a common basis for establishing international ocean policy and addressing disputes among nations.

There are some significant weaknesses of international law as a basis for regional peace. Implementation of principles and general provisions depends on both the good faith obligations of sovereign states to implement provisions of the Convention and their technical and financial capacity to do so. Additional agreements are necessary to create rules and regulations for protection of the high seas fisheries and the marine environment. Without means to monitor offshore activities and enforce rules at sea, less-developed coastal states cannot protect the resources of their own EEZ. Long-term stability of international law requires adherence by major ocean powers. Failure of a state to join the LoS Convention undermines its influence in promoting strict adherence to the Convention.

Opportunities to improve peace and stability through application of international law include the use of existing intergovernmental organizations to address multinational and trans-boundary issues. Regional organizations can promote the development of binding multilateral agreements to protect the marine environment. Formal review of claims to continental shelves beyond the 200-mile EEZ is underway, and dispute resolution processes are available to assist in resolving overlapping claims. Partnerships with the United States and other advanced maritime states can give access to monitoring capability and to training of coast guards in monitoring systems and enforcement capacity. The International Tribunal for the Law of the Sea and related arbitral panels have gained a reputation for dispute resolution in the region that can provide an alternative to recourse to threats and use of force.

Threats to international law, peace, and stability include unilateral declarations of authority over the seas and seabed in excess of the provisions of the LoS Convention that could lead to disputes and demonstrations involving coastal and maritime states. Without clear and binding agreements on the status of private military security companies at sea, the legal vacuum could lead to armed conflict. Failed states and states that lack the capability to monitor their waters and enforce their laws can lose control of the resources of their own EEZ and continental shelf. Retreat of coastal baselines due to rising sea level or natural disaster could raise uncertainty about control of maritime space and resources off shore. The non-party status of the U.S. weakens its ability to hold other states to the intent of the terms of the LoS Convention. At the extreme, states party to the Convention could decide to leave the Convention to expand their claims or work with likeminded states to amend the Convention more to their benefit.

Conclusions

The Indian Ocean hosts major trade routes deposits of energy and minerals and large fish stocks. New investment in the region as part of China's Maritime Silk Road program will increase activity on the Indian Ocean even more. As activity increases, so will the potential for conflict. Serious conflict is not inevitable. Countries of the region have already demonstrated a commitment to peaceful dispute resolution practices, but there are issues that should be addressed at the regional level to ensure that peace continues to prevail.

When security in the Indian Ocean is threatened, it is likely to be the result of failure of legal, diplomatic, and constabulary functions at the state and international levels. The Law of the Sea Convention and related agreements and organizations have established a structure for peaceful use of the seas. Nations should reinforce their commitment by rejecting interpretations that conflict with the text of the Convention and by encouraging both the United States and Iran to join other Indian Ocean coastal states by acceding to the Convention.

Increased exploitation of resources within national EEZs will require increased investment in national maritime monitoring and constabulary capacity. Resources beyond national jurisdiction must be managed and the management of high seas and straddling stocks are still in need of a multilateral solution.

The rise of piracy led to the introduction of private maritime forces. The need to provide security for operations on the high seas, far from shore and with potentially confusing connections to national governments, raises questions as to whether private security companies should provide services and what government or organization will be responsible for their actions. This issue needs to be addressed in a regional or global approach.

Increased activity of regional maritime constabulary forces and the navies of India, the United States, China and other navies could increase the frequency of international incidents at sea. Coordination and cooperation among these forces is essential if accidents and mistaken intentions are to be dealt with short of conflict. One approach would be to establish an "Indian Ocean Coast Guard and Naval Forum" based on the regional coast guard forums recently established in the northern Pacific and Atlantic oceans. Such a forum could promote familiarity with local maritime activities, cultural practices and understanding of regional languages, facilitate cooperation, improve communications, collaborate in Maritime Domain Awareness, and promote shared missions among the armed forces to provide safety, security, and cooperation in the region.

Notes

1 UNEP Shelf Programme at http://continentalshelf.org/onestopdatashop/4204.aspx, accessed March 28, 2015.
2 Permanent Court of Arbitration, Case Concerning Land Reclamation by Singapore in and Around the Straits of Johori, September 2005, www.pca-cpa.org/showpage.asp?pag_id=1154, accessed March 26, 2015.

3 Government of the Sultanate of Oman, *Declaration upon Ratification of the 1982 UN Convention on the Law of the Sea*, Declaration #1 by Oman, August 17, 1989. See also the understandings filed by Yemen, Saudi Arabia, Pakistan, and India on their ratification or accession to the LoS Convention, www.un.org/depts/los/convention_agreements/convention_declarations.htm#Algeria%20Upon%20ratification, accessed March 28, 2014.

4 U.S. Department of Defense DoD 2005.1-M, *Maritime Claims Reference Manual 441* (2005), p. 263. Claim made by India in January 1998.

5 Government of the Republic of India, *Declaration on Ratification of the 1982 UN Convention on the Law of the Sea*, Paragraph b, June 29, 1995, states "The Government of the Republic of India understands that the provisions of the Convention do not authorize other States to carry out in the exclusive economic zone and on the continental shelf military exercises or maneuvers, in particular those involving the use of weapons or explosives without the consent of the coastal State," www.un.org/depts/los/convention_agreements/convention_declarations.htm#India%20 Declaration%20made%20upon%20ratification, accessed October 22, 2013. Similar declarations regarding military activities in the EEZ were made by Bangladesh and Pakistan upon their ratification of the Convention.

6 Jasmine Hughes, "The Piracy-Illegal Fishing Nexus in the Western Indian Ocean." *Strategic Analysis Paper: Future Directions International (Australia)*, February 10, 2011, http://somfin.org/files/0/9/6/4/8/293199-284690/Piracy_IUU_relation.pdf, accessed September 28, 2011.

7 International Chamber of Commerce International Maritime Bureau website: www.icc-ccs.org/piracy-reporting-centre/live-piracy-map, accessed October 20, 2013.

8 Emily Wax, "In Flood-Prone Bangladesh, a Future That Floats." *Washington Post*, September 27, 2007, www.washingtonpost.com/wp-dyn/content/article/2007/09/26/AR2007092602582.html, accessed October 8, 2011.

9 Permanent Court of Arbitration, "Reasoned Decision," Chagos Marine Protected Area Arbitration (*Mauritius v. United Kingdom*), www.pca-cpa.org/showfile.asp?fil_id=1782, accessed March 26, 2015.

10 Maldivian Coast Guard, Wikipedia, http://en.wikipedia.org/wiki/Maldivian_Coast_Guard, accessed October 21, 2013.

11 The United Nations Agreement for the Implementation of the Provisions of the United Nations Convention on the Law of the Sea of 10 December 1982 relating to the Conservation and Management of Straddling Fish Stocks and Highly Migratory Fish Stocks, U.N. Document A/CONF.164/37 of September 8, 1995 entered into force on December 11, 2001.

12 A summary of the Djibouti Code of Conduct with links to downloadable PDF files of the code is available on the IMO website at www.imo.org/OurWork/Security/PIU/Pages/DCoC.aspx, accessed October 22, 2013.

13 International Tribunal on the Law of the Sea, Judgement in the case of the Dispute concerning Delimitation of the Maritime Boundary between Bangladesh and Myanmar in the Bay of Bengal, March 14, 2012, www.itlos.org/fileadmin/itlos/documents/cases/case_no_16/C16_Judgment_14_03_2012_rev.pdf, accessed August 28, 2015.

14 Permanent Court of Arbitration, Decision of July 7, 2014 in the case of the "Bay of Bengal Maritime Boundary Arbitration between Bangladesh and India," www.pca-cpa.org/showpage.asp?pag_id=1376, accessed March 27, 2015.

8

THE GULF

How dangerous is Iran to international maritime security?

Anthony H. Cordesman

The role of energy exports in determining the importance of the Iranian threat

Iran has steadily built up its capabilities for asymmetric warfare in the Gulf since its defeat by the U.S. Navy and Air Force during the "tanker war" phase of the Iran–Iraq War in 1987–8.[1] It has focused on modernizing and improving its mix of missile, air, and naval warfare capabilities in ways that allow it to fight an unconventional or asymmetric war that try to compensate for its aging and limited conventional warfare capabilities and offset the superior forces the U.S., Britain, France, and the Gulf Cooperation Council states now deploy in the region. In doing so, it has tried to respond to the lessons of the first Gulf War in 1990–1 and the invasion of Iraq in 2003, and demonstrate its potential ability to "close the Gulf" both to give it leverage over neighboring states and deter an attack on Iran.

The resulting build-up of Iran's naval, air, and missile capability is steadily increasing its ability to pose a wide range of threats to maritime traffic into and outside of the Gulf. Its forces now include a wide range of land-based surface-to-surface and anti-ship missiles, submarines and miniature submarines, minelaying vessels and smart mines, air-launched missiles, and small, easily dispersed missile patrol boasts. One potential target of this threat is the steady increase in bulk cargo shipments into the Gulf, Arabian Sea/Gulf of Oman, and Red Sea – shipments that are of steadily growing strategic importance to the Gulf states.

It is the threat Iran poses to Gulf energy exports, however, that poses the most critical danger to the economies and stability of the other Gulf states, and is the key hazard to both international maritime security and the global economy. There is no question that the secure flow of maritime traffic from the Gulf is critical to the global economy and every developed nation. The United States Government's Energy Information Agency reports that:

> The Strait of Hormuz is the world's most important oil chokepoint due to its daily oil flow of about 17 million bbl/d in 2013, up from between 15.7–15.9 million bbl/d in 2009–2010. Flows through the Strait in 2013 were roughly 30 percent of all seaborne traded oil, or almost 20 percent of oil traded worldwide. More than 85 percent of these crude oil exports went to Asian markets, with Japan, India, South Korea, and China representing the largest destinations. In addition, Qatar exports about 2 trillion cubic feet

per year of liquefied natural gas (LNG) through the Strait of Hormuz, accounting for almost 20 percent of global LNG trade. Furthermore, Kuwait imports LNG volumes that travel northward through the Strait of Hormuz.[2]

The International Energy Agency (IEA), Organization of the Petroleum Exporting Countries (OPEC), and the U.S. Department of Energy all project a steady increase in Gulf production over time. The Energy Information Administration (EIA) estimates that Gulf producers will make up some 36 percent to 40 percent of total global energy liquids production through 2040, and production will rise by some 8 to 10 million barrels a day by 2040.[3] Such estimates are uncertain both in terms of alternative fuels, new sources of production, and the politics and stability of key producers in the region. Gas exports are also an increasingly important part of maritime traffic through the Gulf. The EIA summarizes the present and future role of the key Gulf gas producing states as follows:

> Four major natural gas producers in the Middle East – Qatar, Iran, Saudi Arabia, and the United Arab Emirates – together accounted for 85 percent of the natural gas produced in the Middle East in 2010. With more than 40 percent of the world's proved natural gas reserves, the Middle East accounts for 21 percent of the total increase in world natural gas production in the *IEO2013* Reference case, growing from 15.9 trillion cubic feet in 2010 to 31.5 trillion cubic feet in 2040.[4]

The EIA notes that there are very limited alternatives to exporting through of the Strait of Hormuz. It notes that:

> At its narrowest point, the Strait is 21 miles wide, but the width of the shipping lane in either direction is only two miles, separated by a two-mile buffer zone. The Strait is deep and wide enough to handle the world's largest crude oil tankers, with about two-thirds of oil shipments....
>
> Most potential options to bypass Hormuz are currently not operational. Only Iraq, Saudi Arabia, and the United Arab Emirates (UAE) presently have pipelines able to ship crude oil outside of the Gulf, and only the latter two countries currently have additional pipeline capacity to circumvent Hormuz.[5]

The Strait of Hormuz may be the most vulnerable point for attack, but Iran can carry out military attacks anywhere in the Gulf, and has steadily increasing capability in the Gulf of Oman, Arabian Sea, Indian Ocean, and Red Sea. Oil and gas pipelines will reduce dependence on maritime traffic through the Strait of Hormuz over time, but shifting tanker loading to ports in Oman and the UAE will not eliminate the risk of Iranian military action, and as Libya once showed, a nation like Iran could also carry out covert mine warfare or submarine attacks in the Red Sea.

The potential scale of the Iranian maritime threat

There is no clear way to predict what kind of threat air–sea–missile Iran may pose if it ever does chose to use force against the maritime traffic, but it is important to note that Iran is as dependent on the stable flow of maritime traffic and energy exports as its neighbors. It is one thing for Iran to use the threat of attacking such traffic or ports and offshore facilities in the Gulf, Arabian Peninsula, and Red Sea – or limited asymmetric attacks that do not escalate to a major conflict – to intimidate or pressure other Gulf state and outside powers. It is quite another to actually escalate to a level of conflict that does critical damage to regional and global strategic interest and can trigger a massive or all-out military response.

The strengths and weaknesses of Iran's naval forces

The regular Iranian Navy (IRIN) has serious limitations, both because it has not been able to fully modernize since the fall of the Shah in 1979, and because of losses during the Iran–Iraq War. It had some 18,000 men in 2012. According to IISS, this total included two marine brigades of some 2,600 men and a 2,000-man naval aviation force. It had bases at Abu Musa, Bandar Abbas, Bandar Anzali, Bander-e Khomeini, Bander-e Mahshahar, Bushehr, Chah Bahar, Farsi, Jask, Kharg Island, and Siri, while the IRGC's naval branch (IRGCN) operates from Abu Musa, Bandar Abbas, Farsi, Halileh, Khorramshahr, and Larak.

Iranian sea–air threats

Iran learned during the "Tanker War" in 1987–8 that it cannot compete with the U.S. in conventional naval warfare, and now faces an added threat from far more serious southern Gulf naval forces. Iran's naval forces are, however, still an important part of its capabilities to fight an air–sea battle in the Gulf, if they are made part of a broader campaign of naval asymmetric warfare. As the following sections of this chapter show, Iran has built up substantial capabilities for asymmetric warfare in the Gulf and the Arabian Sea, including submarines and submersibles, mine warfare capabilities, anti-ship missiles, marines and special forces, and a wide variety of smaller craft that can be used to swarm targets in the Gulf or in a battle of attrition.

Military and intelligence experts see a variety of Iranian air–sea threats in the Gulf – many of which go beyond the capabilities of the Iranian Navy *per se* and involve the Naval Branch of the IRGC. These "stacked threats" include:

- A mine warfare threat with Iranian stocks of 6,000-plus mines, pre-staged mine deployments that can be rapidly dispersed, a wide range of platforms and the ability to deploy a low-cost, low-tech, high-impact forces that could be anonymous if mines were laid covertly or using commercial ships and small craft.
- An expanding inventory of coastal defense anti-ship missiles like the C-802 with steadily improving capabilities and ranges. Examples include the *Hendijan* PGG with C-802s and *Peykapp III* WPTG with C-704s – possibly supported by F-4Es with some variant of the C-700 or C-800 series – and Iran's new domestically produced *Khalij Fars*, stacked to overwhelm anti-missile systems.
- Submarines, with three *Kilo*-class conventional submarines, and *Yono*-class midget submarines.
- A wide range of fast attack with a wide range of platforms, some with modern Chinese anti-ship missiles and wake homing torpedoes, steadily improving weaponry.
- New very high-speed (70 knot), low-observable boats like the *Bladerunner* 35 that carry high payloads of explosives and are designed for suicide missions.
- Groups or "clusters" of such smaller surface ships that can be quickly dispersed throughout the Iranian coast and can be used in groups to attack military or commercial surface vessels.
- Special forces, marines, and naval guards units that can be used to attack or raid offshore facilities and coastal targets, although Iran's set of 13 landing ships restricts its amphibious reach.

- Covert forces like the Al Quds force that can be used to develop local forces and extremists for sabotage attacks on naval or other facilities.
- Efforts to develop rockets and ballistic missiles capable of homing in on ships at much longer ranges like the *Khalij Fars*.
- Lack of over-the-horizon and general-purpose sensors, reducing range of fast-attack craft to visual range strikes coordinated by weakly networked land-based C⁴ISR, compensated for by new domestically produced radars and expanding HUMINT network within the Gulf.

Although Iran's mix of corvettes, missile boats, and diesel-electric submarines is large enough to present a challenge during the initial phase of any major clash, Iran's conventional fleet and air force are better suited to supporting its IRGC forces in asymmetric warfare. Iran probably does have some weapons systems or tactics the USN is not expecting, but its ability to surprise U.S. forces is hindered by pervasive intelligence efforts.

Iran has also developed a different type of naval rearmament encompassing midget submarines and patrol boats suited to hit-and-run raids to frigates and other major combatants. The smaller ships appear designed for an unconventional campaign against the U.S. Navy; the larger vessels, however, are better suited for intimidating Gulf neighbors and projecting Iranian influence against the comparatively weak GCC navies.

Submarines

Iran has three *Kilo*-class submarines it bought from Russia in the 1990s, and is building two small submarines on its own. Its *Kilo*-class submarines can fire long-range homing torpedoes and lay smart and conventional mines. It acquired its first *Ghadir*-class 120–50-ton midget submarine in 2007 and now has up to 17. It also has at least one 90-ton midget submarine, and eight small submersibles for inserting Special Forces and minelaying.

Iran's three *Kilo*-class submarines and other smaller submarines offset some of the weaknesses of its major surface forces. The *Kilo* is a relatively modern and quiet submarine that first became operational in 1980. Iran has completed a refit of one of its *Kilo*s, and will likely begin modernizing the second if it believes the submarine will not be needed in the near future.

Each *Kilo* has six 530 mm torpedo tubes, including two wire-guided torpedo tubes. The *Kilo* can carry a mix of 18 homing and wire-guided torpedoes or 24 mines. Russian torpedoes have guidance systems including active sonar homing, passive homing, and wire guidance, but experts believe Iran may only have shorter range, wake-homing torpedoes. Some reports indicate that Iran bought over 1,000 modern Soviet mines along with the *Kilo*s and that the mines were equipped with modern magnetic, acoustic, and pressure sensors.

Iran has, however, had serious problems in maintaining its submarines much less refit them, and it has not provided realistic training. Its submarines rarely submerge in training or exercises, and many of Iran's drill claims are little more than propaganda. This leads some experts to feel that they would only pose a relatively limited and short-lived threat if they were actually deployed and used in combat.

Iranian midget submarines provide another threat. The *Ghadir*s and other Iranian midget submarines do drill more regularly than its *Kilo*s and submerge more often in exercises. Iranian midget submarines possess both torpedo-firing and mine-laying capabilities, and their small size may enable them to operate more effectively in the Strait or the Gulf. However, the capabilities of these boats are still unknown; much depends on their sensors and ability to hide from dedicated ASW platforms. If they are unable to mask propulsion noises, even the cluttered environment of the Gulf will not protect them from Western or even Gulf ASW assets. They might be effective in a prolonged war of attrition against both commercial and military vessels. While their smaller weapons load would probably restrict them to one attack per sortie, they would be able to use torpedoes or lay mines unpredictably across major tanker routes, target civilian vessels without sonar, and potentially threaten sonar-equipped warships in unfamiliar waters. In coordination with packs of fast-attack craft, surface-to-surface missiles, or other surface threats – although it is unclear if Iran has practiced such maneuvers – the midget submarines represent an effective component of Iran's broader overall asymmetric naval strategy.

Corvettes and major surface ships

Iran still has a large navy by the standards of the developing world. Sources differ over how many of Iran's older Western-supplied ships like its one *Damavand*-class and two *Babr*-class destroyers should be still be counted as active, and how other Iranian ships should be classed.

Iran still has two *Bayandor* (PF103)-class corvettes launched in 1963 and commissioned in 1964.[6] Their weapons control, search/track radars, and sonars have not been fully modernized since the mid-1960s, although some aspects of the electronic warfare capabilities, communications, and battle management systems in the *Bayandor* seem to have been upgraded during 2001–13.[7] Iran reportedly began modernizing these vessels with 76 mm deck guns, C-802C-803 missiles, and torpedo tubes in 2007. The C-802 is a sea-skimming missile with a range of 120 kilometers, a 165-kilogram warhead, and a maximum speed of Mach 0.9. While they must still be far below the quality of American frigates or corvettes, their weapons systems (if not sensors and electronic warfare systems) may now approach southern Gulf standards.[8]

The IISS and Jane's also differ over the number and status of Iran's other ships and boats. The IISS estimate in the 2014 edition of its *Military Balance* was that Iran had six active corvettes. These include one 1,500-ton Iranian-built *Jamaran*- or *Moudge*-class missile corvette (or light frigate) launched in 2010 with one undergoing sea trials and another under construction at Bandar Abbas, completing construction in 2014 or 2015.[9] (Other sources indicate one version called the *Moudge* entered service as early as 2005, and a second called the *Damavand* is already operating in the Caspian.) These are armed with CSS-N-4 or C-802 anti-ship missiles, *Fajr* missiles (reverse engineered SM-1 air defense missiles), regular and long-range homing torpedoes, and Sikorsky SH-3 Sea King ASW helicopters. According to other sources, a 2,000-ton corvette or frigate called the *Sahan* is near completion.

Iran has three more modern operational *Alvand*- (Vosper Mark 5) class frigates: the *Alvand*, the *Alborz*, and the *Sabalan*. They were launched during 1967–8 and commissioned during 1968–9. Two have been upgraded to carry four Chinese C-802 anti-ship missiles each on twin launchers.[10] The C-802 is a sea-skimming missile with a range of 120 kilometers, a 165-kilogram warhead, and a maximum speed of Mach 0.9. Iran has also indigenously produced three frigates modeled on the *Alvand* – *Jamaran*, *Damavand*, and *Sahand* – armed with C-802 missiles and surface-to-air missiles, as well as deck guns. The *Jamaran* has undertaken limited open-water activities, while the *Sahand* is still in dry dock awaiting completion. The *Damavand* has been assigned to the Caspian Sea. The sonar, radar, electronic warfare, and weapons-guidance systems of these ships are still unknown.[11]

Missile patrol boats

The Iranian Navy still has three British-supplied Vosper Mark 5 class corvettes it first received in 1971 and calls them the *Alvand* class. These are 1,540-ton ships that have been refitted with C-802 anti-ship missiles. Iran also has two US-supplied 1,130-ton *Bayandor*-class frigates, one of which was being refitted and re-entered service in June 2013.[12] These date back to 1964, but have been refitted with C-802 anti-ship missiles and a 76 mm gun. Iran also has a small, US-supplied 580-ton corvette (missile patrol boat) refitted with C-802 missiles.

There also seems to be agreement that Iran has 14 active 275-ton *Kaman-* (*Combattante II*) class coastal armed missile patrol boats which date back to the late 1970s and early 1980s, but have been refitted with two to four C-802 missiles, and three of which have been heavily updated (sometimes called the *Sina* class).

Other patrol boats and smaller vessels

The Iranian Navy has an estimated four 70-ton *Zafar* patrol boats armed with either MLRS rocket launchers or C-701 anti-ship missiles, and nine Chinese Cat-14 20-ton missile patrol boats armed with C-701 anti-ship missiles.[13] In addition, the IISS estimates that Iran had 16 *Kashdom*, 3 *Kayvan*, 6 MkII, and 10 MkIII and 3 *Parvin* patrol boats ranging from 13 to 80 tons and armed with a mix of torpedoes, guns, and MLRS systems.[14]

The IISS reports that Iran's Navy had three *Kajami* semi-submersible patrol boats, 14 aging hovercraft dating back to the Shah's time (some not operational), and 25 *Peykapp* fast-attack boats.[15]

Mine warfare

The Iranian Navy has adapted two *Hejaz*-class LSTs for minelaying. It has two *Riazi*-class mine countermeasures boats, one *Shahrokh*-class minesweeper as a training ship in the Caspian, and two aging US-supplied MS-292-class minesweepers. Iran can, however, use virtually any surface ship for minelaying, including the dhows that cross the Gulf as trading vessels.[16]

Iran can use its regular navy, naval guards, and any civilian ship to lay a variety of mines. It has invested in both its own mine development and Chinese mines, with an estimated stockpile of over 3,000 devices.[17] Its older mines are effective systems and at some $6,000 a mine, are easy to disperse in large numbers with potentially devastating effective consequences for far more costly combat and commercial ships. According to various experts it has also acquired, reverse engineered, developed, and improved a range of "smart mines," including bottom mines. It is preparing to lay them on both sides of the Strait, creating safe passages close to Iran's shoreline through which its own and neutral (i.e. any Gulf state Iran chooses not to antagonize) tankers could sail.

Naval aviation

The Iran Navy's 2,600-man naval aviation branch is one of the few air elements in any Gulf navy, with three Orion PF-3 maritime patrol aircraft (one possibly non-operational plus a possible fourth of uncertain status; Jane's mentions only two Orions), some 16 light transport aircraft, and an inventory of 13 armed helicopters (10 SH-3D and 6 RH-53D), although their operational status is uncertain.[18] Its war plans include using the SH-3Ds for anti-submarine warfare missions – although experts feel Iran only exercises and uses helicopters in resupply and logistic missions to areas like its offshore and island ISR facilities.

Anti-ship missile forces

Iran's anti-ship missile (AShM) arsenal represents a key part of its asymmetric anti-access/area denial (A2/AD) strategy. An A2/AD strategy is particularly effective in the Persian Gulf, Straits of Hormuz, and Gulf of Oman because of the relatively confined spaces of these bodies of water. The wide variety of platforms from which Iran can launch AShMs presents a "360 degree threat."[19] In addition to coastal, ship, and fixed-wing platforms, Iran recently integrated AShMs onto helicopters and aims to develop submarine-launched missiles.

Surface vessels that can fire AShMs are a crucial part of Iran's asymmetric strategy. Part of this strategy calls for swarms of small vessels to attack larger enemy vessels. Although it is difficult to ascertain the current operational readiness of Iran's surface fleet, a 2009 report by the U.S. Office of Naval Intelligence stated that approximately half of the IRIN's missile-armed surface combatants were in "very poor material condition, limiting their readiness and operational endurance."[20] To make up for this, coast-launched AShMs can be used in conjunction with small-boat swarm attacks in order to saturate enemy vessel defenses. AShMs based on coastal platforms are small, mobile, and can be disguised as civilian vehicles, making destruction of these platforms difficult.[21]

Iran's AShMs can be put into three broad categories, short range, mid-range, and long range. Short-range AShMs, like the C-801, *Kowsar*, and *Nasr*, are generally rocket-powered and are commonly found on small fast-attack craft. The Chinese C-701 and C-704 missiles were used to develop the *Kowsar* and *Nasr*, respectively. In September 2013, Iran claimed to have produced a helicopter-launched version of the *Nasr* missile and planned to produce a version that could be launched from fighter aircraft. A picture showing a Bell 206 with a modified *Nasr* missile attached to it was released alongside this statement.[22]

The C-801 was also imported from China in 1987–8 and is in Iranian service as the *Tondar*. Mid-range AShMs, which include the C-802, *Noor*, and *Qader*, feature small air-breathing engines, making these missiles anti-ship cruise missiles (ASCMs). *Noor* and *Qader* are both based on the C-802, which was imported from China. These missiles are found on Iran's frigates, corvettes, and fixed-wing aircraft. The *Qader* was claimed to have been integrated onto helicopters at the same time the same claim was made with *Nasr*. While the Mi-17 was specified as the platform for the *Noor*, no specific helicopter was given as the platform for the *Qader*.[23] Considering that the *Qader* is slightly larger than the *Noor* but similar in the sense that it is also a C-802 derivative, the Mi-17 is likely the helicopter platform for the *Qader*. Long-range AShMs, including *Ra'ad* and *Khalij Fars*, are currently only found on land-based platforms.

The *Ra'ad* is a modified HY-2, while the *Khalij Fars* is an anti-ship ballistic missile variant of the *Fateh*-110 ballistic missile. All of these missiles can be launched from land and coastal platforms. Moreover, "systems mounted on truck trailers could be easily disguised as civilian vehicles and relocated to make them harder to find and destroy during a conflict."[24]

Iran depends heavily on its coastal, island, and ship-borne anti-ship missile forces to make up for its lack of airpower and modern major surface vessels. Iran's Western-supplied missiles are now all beyond their shelf life, and their operational status is uncertain. Iranian forces are now equipped largely with land-based Chinese- or Iranian-made anti-ship missiles like the *Ra'ad* coastal defense missiles – some deployed near the Strait of Hormuz and some which Iran claims have terminal home capability or could be directed against naval targets by forward deployed aircraft or drones.

Iranian ships made heavy use of the anti-ship missiles Iran bought from the People's Republic of China (PRC), or now produces indigenously. They have replaced most Western-supplied missiles with Chinese designs. For example, the Iranian Navy's missile patrol boats include 13 operational 275-ton French-made Combattante II (*Kaman*-class) fast-attack boats, with four currently under construction. These boats are reported to be armed with two to four C-802 Sardine anti-ship missiles, one 76 mm gun, and to have maximum speeds of 37.5 knots.

According to *Jane's Naval Guide*, nine of these are from the original French shipment during the early 1980s, while Iran has constructed another four with comparable equipment.[25]

The *Kaman*-class fast-attack boats were originally armed with four U.S. Harpoon missiles, but their Harpoons may no longer be operational. At least five had been successfully converted to launchers carrying two to four C-801/C-802s. Iran supplied the C-802s that Hezbollah successfully used against one of Israel's most modern *Sa'ar* class-5 missile ships during the fighting in 2006.

Iran has sought to buy more advanced anti-ship missiles and anti-ship missile production facilities from Russia, North Korea, and China, and possibly has even attempted to obtain Chinese-made missile armed frigates. Some sources have claimed that Iran has bought eight Soviet-made SS-N-22 "Sunburn" or "Sunburst" anti-ship missile launch units from Ukraine and has deployed them near the Strait of Hormuz. However, U.S. experts have not seen evidence of such a purchase and doubt that Iran has operational holdings of such systems. The "SS-N-22" is also a title that actually applies to two different modern long-range supersonic sea-skimming systems – the P-270 *Moskit* (also called the 3M80) and the P80, or P-100 *Zubr/Oniks*.

Iran regularly announces that it has deployed new anti-ship missiles or is developing them. For example, it claims to have successfully developed over-the-horizon missile-targeting capabilities, building variants of the *Fateh*-110 and *Shahab* with homing guidance systems for use in anti-ship warfare. This claim appears to be borne out to some extent by the development of by *Khalij Fars* – an upgraded *Fateh*-110 with a rudimentary seeking and steering mechanism for targeting ships. While its real-world capabilities are unknown, it would represent a valuable layer of Iran's anti-ship "stack." However, Iran makes so many claims for so many systems, it is impossible to distinguish propaganda from reality.

Naval guards, marines, special forces, and marines

The naval branch of the IRGC – or IRGCN– continues to grow, and the IISS estimates that it had 18,000 men, including some 2,600 marines in 2014.[26] These figures do not include elements of the Army's Special Forces, which have one Special Forces Brigade, a Commando Division with three brigades, and six independent commando brigades as well as an air borne brigade.

Elements of these Army forces have shown they could play an active combat role in the Gulf during the Iran–Iraq War, and sometimes play a role in exercises involving naval forces or simulated targets in the Gulf. They also do not include the Iranian Al Quds Forces – a separate force within the IRGC – which along with the MOIS could infiltrate maritime and port targets or indoctrinate and train native saboteurs. It should be stressed that maritime conflict does not have to involve maritime targets. It can involve raids on islands, offshore facilities, and ship seizures using small craft.

As for the IRGCN, it is organized to present asymmetric threats that include capabilities that can support a battle of attrition, and focused, limited clashes throughout the Gulf that would not cripple Iran's own sea lines of communication (SLOCs) or necessarily provoke major U.S. reprisals

Structure and organization

The IRGCN is operational in the Gulf and the Gulf of Oman (with most of its forces in the former[27]), and could operate elsewhere if given suitable sealift or facilities. It has five different commands within the Gulf, including a new fifth naval command designed to cover Abu Musa and the Tunbs – the three islands it took from the UAE and which have become the center of several recent air and sea confrontations between Iranian and UAE forces.[28]

The IRGC's naval branch has bases in the Gulf, many near key shipping channels and some near the Strait of Hormuz. These include a wide variety of facilities at Al-Farsiyah, Halul (an oil platform), Sirri, Abu Musa, Bandar-e Abbas, Khorramshahr, and Larak. It also controls Iran's coastal defense forces, including naval guns. It used to deploy HY-2 Seersucker land-based anti-ship missile unit deployed in five to seven sites along the Gulf coast, but these seem to either be in the process of being replaced by C-700 or C-800 series missiles and different coastal-surveillance radars.

As of 2011, Iran's Navy has sent warships into the Mediterranean and claimed intentions of sending ships into the Atlantic, but any real operational capability is doubtful.[29] Iran's larger ships are worn and aging, they have limited endurance at sea, and they cannot fight effectively against modern ships with the kind of air support that other navies will have.

Mohammad Ali Jafari, the Commander of the IRGC, inaugurated the fifth naval command zone of the IRGC in early November 2012. He stated that the IRGC was "increasing, expanding, and improving the expert capabilities in the naval defense" in all five zones and that "The fifth zone of the Guards; naval force is one of the naval defense chains which is in particular responsible for the defense of the Iranian islands in the Gulf."[30]

Ships and small craft

The IRGC naval forces have at least 40 light patrol boats, 10 *Houdong* guided missile patrol boats armed with C-802 anti-ship missiles, a battery of HY-2 Seersucker land-based anti-ship missiles, up to 20 mini submarines, and swimmer delivery vehicles (SDVs). Some of these systems could be modified to carry a small CBRN weapon, but are hardly optimal delivery platforms because of their limited-range payload and sensor/guidance platforms that are unsuited for delivering such sensitive devices.

Various sources indicate that in 2014, the IRGCN had 10 171-ton Chinese-built *Houdong*-class missile patrol craft with four C-802s each, which were delivered in the mid-1990s, and three support ships. It had large numbers of additional coastal and inshore patrol craft. Some estimates credited the IRGCN with 5 *China Cats*, 10 *Thondor* with two twin C-802 launchers, 25 *Peykaap II* with two single C-701 launchers, 15 *Peykaap I* fast-attack boats potentially armed with twin torpedo tubes, 10 *Tir*-class fast patrol boats with twin torpedo tubes and a machine gun, 10 *Pashe* fast patrol boats with twin 23mm ZSU-23 cannon and search radar, and roughly 20 *Ghaem* patrol boats with small arms and an extended duration deployment capability.

Jane's estimates that the IRGCN had 37 coastal patrol boats – 17 *Peykaap I*, 10 *Pashe*, and 10 *Ghaem* – along with 150 inshore patrol craft – 30 *Murce* (one MLR system and machine gun), 100 *Ashura I* (small vessel with one machine gun, center space for a mine or rocket launcher, and small arms), and 20 *Boghammar* (one machine gun and MLR system normally, but a wide range of customized units are now believed to be in use.[31]

The *Kayvian, Parvin*, MkII, MkIII, and *Ghaem* patrol boats are thought to be inshore boats, lacking both missiles and the ability to operate independently. Most of these craft are operational and can be effective in patrol missions. They lack sophisticated weapon systems or air defenses, other than machine guns and SA-7s and SA-14s. The IRGCN also seems to have four landing ships. The IISS estimates it has 2 *Hejaz* with mine-laying capacity and 2 MIG-S-5000s.

Probable effectiveness

Unlike IRGC ground forces, which have seen limited deployment in Iraq and Afghanistan, IRGCN has not had significant combat experience with asymmetric warfare since the late 1980s, except for efforts limited to the occasional harassment of British and American naval vessels in the Gulf. The IRGCN does, however, carry out large-scale exercises and demonstrates capabilities that it might be able to deliver conventional weapons, bombs, mines, and CBRN weapons into ports and other logistics centers as well as critical infrastructure including oil and desalination facilities. The IRGCN has also stressed its mine warfare capability. The IRGC's naval branch can carry out extensive raids against Gulf shipping, amphibious assaults with the land branch of the IRGC against objectives like the islands in the Gulf, and raids against Saudi Arabia or other countries on the southern Gulf coast. They give Iran a major capability for asymmetric warfare. The Guards appear to be represented unofficially in some embassies, Iranian businesses and purchasing offices, and other foreign fronts as part of the broader Iranian intelligence network, as well as for their own military intelligence and purchasing needs.

The broader shift to asymmetric warfare

This complex mix of shifts in the forces of Iran's Navy and Naval Guards explains why Iranian naval doctrine and exercises now emphasize asymmetric tactics. Iran emphasizes a mix of smaller systems that can target either expensive, vulnerable merchant traffic – essentially an improved version of the 1984–8 Tanker War – or conventional U.S. naval vessels attempting to operate in the Strait of Hormuz or the Gulf.

Iran learned in 1987–8, and in years of exercises that followed, that it cannot concentrate large numbers of small forces for "swarming" and exercise effective command and control. It must be able to disperse them as much as possible, and may have to keep larger conventional naval surface forces in port or outside any combat action to avoid having them destroyed.

Recent accounts suggest Iran has encountered difficulties coordinating more than ten boats at a time. These packs would be capable of targeting tankers or isolated military vessels, or harassing multiple warships in hit-and-run strikes. By focusing on smaller fleets, Iran is able both to preserve its forces for a war of attrition and retain the command and control necessary to target individual ships, potentially avoiding the random strikes that led the Tanker War to escalate.

Since the end of the Iran–Iraq War, Iran has attempted to compensate for the weaknesses of its surface fleet by obtaining new anti-ship missiles and missile patrol craft from China, and developing its own long-range anti-ship missiles and a ballistic missile with anti-ship capabilities. It acquired and then cloned midget submarines from North Korea, and bought three *Kilo*-class submarines from Russia. It bought and reverse-engineered more modern "smart" mines, and also purchased wake-homing torpedoes.

Iran has simultaneously expanded the capabilities of the naval branch of the IRGC, developed its fast attack craft, and upgraded some of its older surface ships. Iran's exercises have also included a growing number of joint and combined arms exercises with the land forces and the air force – although such joint exercises are limited and Iran still has problems in coordinating the elements of its individual services.

Iran has improved its ports and strengthened its air defenses, while obtaining some logistic and technical support from nations like India and Pakistan. It has attempted to participate in joint exercises, joining the Indian Navy and Pakistani Navy for small-scale training. The IRIN has also deployed off the coast of Africa for anti-piracy operations, giving the Navy experience with extended blue-water deployments.[32] Furthermore, it has engaged in supporting Russian deployments to Bandar Abbas and port visits as far afield as Sri Lanka.[33]

The Iranian Air Force: a weak and aging force

The most likely forms of asymmetric and conventional maritime conflict in the Gulf and nearby waters in the Indian Ocean and Red Sea– and the key measures of containment and deterrence – are determined largely by the mix of air, missiles, and naval power on each side. The air balance decisively favors the U.S. and southern Gulf states. While southern Gulf air forces have limits, the Iranian Air Force (IRIAF) still lags far behind the capabilities of the GCC air forces and even further behind the combined capabilities of the GCC and U.S. air forces. Iran lags badly behind the Gulf states in modernizing its air forces. Iran's most advanced fighters consist of a small number of export versions of the Su-24 and MiG-29, whose avionics lag far behind their Russian counterparts and date back to the early 1990s.

The IISS Military Balance for 2014 indicates that Iran has a total of 334 combat aircraft in inventory.[34] These include more than 75 F-5s and F-5IIs, 43 F-14s, 65 F-4D/Es, more than 6 RF-F-E, and 5 P-3MP Orions. This is a total of at least 194 aging U.S. aircraft supplied more than 30 years ago when the Shah was still in power – some 58 percent of Iran's air force. Iran has 24 low-quality F-7Ms and 10 Mirage F-1Es it got from Iraq in 1991. This raises the total of aging, obsolete aircraft to 228 or 68 percent. Iran's combat aircraft imports since the fall of the Shah consist of 36 early export versions of the MiG-29 fighter, 30 early export versions of the SU-24MK, and 7 Su-25 anti-tank attack aircraft. None compare to first-line U.S., British, or French combat aircraft. None compare to Saudi holdings like 81 F-15C/Ds, 71 F-15S, 80 Tornados, and 24 Typhoons – a total of 256 more capable aircraft than any in the Iranian inventory. None compare to a smaller Gulf air force like the UAE, which has 139 modern fighters: 54 F-16E Block 60, 25 F-16F Block 60, 16 Mirage 2000-9DAD; 44 Mirage 2000-9EAD, and 7 Mirage 2000 RAD.

Iran has sought more modern fighters from Russia, but past reports of sales have never materialized. As a result, Iran has sought to develop its own fighters, the most notable of which are the *Saeqeh* ("Thunderbolt") and the *Azarakhsh* ("Lightning"), both of which are based on the Northrop F-5. Iran has also made many claims to have modernized its fighters and their systems and munitions, although many such claims are clearly exaggerated: Iran's air units suffer from limited access to required spare parts and upgrades, reducing Iran's effective airpower to roughly 60 percent of its existing planes; furthermore, while information on training is classified, Iran has made public far fewer air force exercises than missile and naval drills.

Iran is producing its own aircraft but so far has only deployed small numbers of its *Azarakhsh* (a design that seems to have been derived by reverse engineering the U.S. fighters in Iranian service), and up to six *Saegheh* Iranian-made fighters (a design Iran claims is superior to the F-18 but seems to be an upgraded version of the F-5F).

These limits to Iran's air force are particularly important as Iran has air bases that are only a few minutes' flight time from critical targets in the Gulf and the coastal areas of the southern Gulf states. As for its structure and strength, the IRIAF is divided into three commands – Eastern, Southern, and Western, with the latter having the majority of active squadrons – with most of the advanced aircraft home-based in the interior of the country. Air command is split between the Iranian air force and the IRGC air force, with the former primarily controlling aircraft and the latter the caretakers of the strategic missile forces.

The uncertainties affecting Iran's aircraft and modernization

Taken at face value, much of Iran's air force is something of a military museum. It is a tribute to Iran that it can keep so many of its U.S.-supplied and older Russian and Chinese aircraft flying, but none of the Western-supplied aircraft in Iran's inventory have been modernized by the U.S. since the fall of the Shah. Military and intelligence experts suggest, however, that Iran has been relatively successful in maintenance, material, and management – enabling the IRIAF to continue flying despite an almost complete blockade on new parts.

Maintenance has been aided by the fact that Iran developed extensive illegal purchasing networks during the Iran–Iraq War and has maintained them ever since. It has kept many of its aircraft flying, although it is unclear that it can fly more than 60 percent of its 297–312 remaining combat aircraft at any given time.[35] It does seem likely that its sortie generation rate over time would be a fraction of the rate that the U.S. and better southern Gulf air forces could generate. A combination of cannibalization and re-engineered similar parts also enables Iran to maintain its systems. These efforts have been particularly successful with the F-4 and C-130, while the F-14 – which proved to be a maintenance problem for the U.S. as well – remains far below operational capacity. Iran has been trying to get the SU-22, -24, and -25s that it obtained from Iraq in 1991 to full effectiveness.

Military and intelligence experts also feel that Iran has proven unable to reverse engineer the more advanced elements of American and Soviet aircraft, although Iran's reverse engineering skills have improved. Iran has made efforts to update many of its aircraft, but the need to reverse engineer and improvise is a critical shortcoming since their U.S.-flown counterparts – especially the 44 F-14s and 65 F-4D aircraft still in Iranian service – went through a series of U.S. Multi-Stage Improvement Programs (MSIPs) that corrected design problems, improved flight performance and sortie generation capability, and modernized their avionics and radars for air-to-air and air-to-ground/sea operations after 1979. More broadly, however, Iran only has limited airborne AC&W, ISR, and maritime surveillance capability in peacetime, although it has an extensive network of land-based radars and an increasing number of short-to-long-range unmanned aerial vehicles to provide airborne targeting, surveillance, and attack capability against maritime targets. It lacks the level of AC&W and ISR capability it needs to sustain and protect its systems in the event of a significant attack. Iran claims to have created electronic warfare aircraft by upgrading Ukrainian Antonov AN-140s and to have modernized the avionics on its three PF-3 Orion maritime patrol aircraft in its naval aviation forces. If Iran has been successful, its aging AN-140s could function as mini-AWACs in a crisis, and provide airborne radar for one coast. If Iran also made use of the relatively advanced radar in its F-14s, it could provide limited but functional airborne radar coverage in peacetime. Iran also has improved its land-based radar coverage, and claims to have a mix of unmanned combat aerial vehicles (UCAVs and UAVs) it can use to make up for some of the limitation in its aircraft – likely visual surveillance and reconnaissance. The success of its AN-140 upgrade program is in doubt, however, after the 2006 crash of an Iran-140 that killed the Ukrainian and Russian scientists on board, along with the Iranian managers who ran the program. Combined with Iran's ongoing difficulties in producing its own engines, this event also raised questions about Iran's indigenous airplane manufacturing capability.

Iran's naval aviation branch

As noted above, Iran still has significant naval aviation forces, although their readiness and operational capabilities are limited by the age of many of its systems. As of 2013, three ASW-capable

P-3F Orion MPA form the core of the Iranian naval air arm. Its fixed-wing transport assets included five Do-228; four F-27 Friendship; four Turbo and Commander 680. It had three Falcon 20 ELINT aircraft. Its helicopter assets included ten SH-3D Sea King ASW aircraft; three RH-53D Sea Stallion mine warfare aircraft; and a large mix of transport aircraft that included five Bell 205A (AB-205A); two Bell 206 Jet Ranger (AB-206); and two Bell 212 (AB-212).

Iran's strengths and weaknesses in fighting a maritime air war

Given this background, it should be clear why it is easier to analyze Iran's order of battle than its warfighting capabilities. There are few meaningful data on IRIAF's real-world warfighting capabilities. Like all the elements of the IRGC and other Iranian military forces, the Iranian air force does seem heavily dependent on conscripts and short-service personnel, and to have encountered problems in terms of its military politics and leadership. Current Iranian exercises, command and control, technology, and vulnerabilities to outside attack or suppression do indicate Iran might have critical problems in managing large air operations. Iran's lack of modern technology for integrating operations and creating the most advanced situational awareness possible could be critical. Iran's newer defense concept – relying on decentralized forces that are relatively unaffected by command and control strikes – is likely to be far less effective in aerial warfare, where small forces have a much harder time hiding and launching irregular attacks without warning. Iran's air force also conducts few joint exercises with its Army, IRGC, or Navy and those it does conduct are fixed set-piece exercises with guaranteed success – a form of exercise training that can do more harm than good.

Summarizing the air balance: the U.S., the southern Gulf problem, and Iran's capability for air combat

While Iran's air force does have the range to strike maritime traffic, ports, offshore facilities, and petroleum export targets in the Gulf, its offensive capability is unlikely to survive in any protracted air battle. The Iranian air force will also be limited by its inexperience with large-scale operations and the actual use of many of its upgrades and munitions in combat. Iran will also be limited by aircraft ranges in penetrating deep into Saudi Arabia. Iran is unable to strike targets all across the Gulf without secure refueling, while all of Iran is vulnerable to tanker-supported Arab or U.S. strike aircraft. While Iranian air forces could conceivably benefit by launching a surprise attack or the elimination of Arab radar by their own missile forces, advanced radar systems and long-range missiles (HAWK and Patriots) would still probably seriously degrade any Iranian operation.

These limits to Iran's capabilities must, however, be kept in perspective. Although Iran's air assets fall far short in quality relative to those of its steadily modernizing Gulf neighbors, the southern Gulf states do have some special vulnerabilities which could be exploited if the U.S. does not provide overall battle management and ISR capability. The southern Gulf states have talked for years about interoperability and integrated air operations and air defense systems, but made far too little progress. There are many areas where their systems and stocks are not interoperable, readiness and training levels vary sharply by country, and so do preparedness and reliability.

Moreover, Iran also has short- and medium-range rockets and missiles, and dealing with Iran's longer-range missile systems and air and naval power cannot be separated from missile power. Iran's longer-range missile forces are limited today in terms of range, payload lethality, and accuracy. They are more useful in terms of posing political threats and as tools of intimidation than as effective warfighting forces.

Even today, however, Iran can volley enough shorter-range systems on ports and petroleum facilities to have a serious potential impact on Iraq's and Kuwait's export and maritime shipping capacity, and Iran's capabilities to volley continue to grow. Its capabilities will also change vastly in the future if it can deploy nuclear-armed medium- to long-range missiles or even missiles with conventional precision and terminal homing warheads. Iran is seeking such systems and this not only affects the balance or airpower but balance in terms of surface-to-air and missile defenses.

Summing up: maritime threats and asymmetric forces

In short, Iran has developed a mix of *conventional* and *asymmetric* land, air, and naval capabilities that can threaten its neighbors' maritime traffic, challenge the U.S., and affect other parts of the Middle East and Asia. Iran may also be able to use state and non-state actors as proxies to threaten and manipulate a range of neighboring states, including Afghanistan, Iraq, and Israel. Its forces are intended to offset superior military technology through sheer numbers, stealth, and high mobility. Iran understands that it cannot reasonably win a fight against the U.S. in a conventional war or direct frontal confrontation, and these assets are designed to strike at vulnerable targets and critical infrastructure, such as Gulf shipping, oil tankers, oil platforms, and coastal desalination facilities. Iran has also proven its capability to use such forces effectively. Iran's past actions have shown this threat is all too real:

- Iranian tanker war with Iraq;
- oil spills and floating mines in the Gulf;
- use of Al Quds Force in Iraq;
- Iranian use of UAVs;
- border and coastal "incidents";
- arms transfers, in cooperation with Syria, to Hezbollah;
- pilgrimage "incidents" in Mecca;
- missile and space tests; expanding range of missile programs (future nuclear test?);
- naval guards' seizure of British boat, confrontation with U.S. Navy, exercises in the Gulf;
- development of limited "close the Gulf" capability;
- Hamas/PIJ arms transfer and their rocket attacks on Eilat, Aqaba in August 2010;
- Iran regularly practices "swarming" targets in the Gulf with large numbers of small craft, shore-based anti-ship missiles, missile-armed aircraft, and increasing support from UAVs/UCAVs;
- increasingly arming and supporting insurgents in Afghanistan.

These are all reasons to stress that the limits to the maritime threat posed by Iran's conventional forces need to be kept in careful perspective. Iran has spent two decades building up capabilities for asymmetric and irregular warfare. The end result is still a mix of Iranian forces the U.S. can counter relatively quickly with the large-scale use of its own forces, combined with a strong ability to escalate against targets within Iran. Still, any such escalation means a major war, and a full-scale use of force by the U.S. would dramatically raise tensions in the Gulf and further poison long-term relations with Iran.

Notes

1 For a description of this fighting in 1987–8, see Anthony H. Cordesman, *The Lessons of Modern War*, vol. 2, *The Iran–Iraq War* (Boulder, CO: Westview, 1990), pp. 271–353.

2 U.S. Department of Energy, Energy Information Administration, *World Oil Transit Chokepoints* (Washington, DC: GPO, 2012), www.eia.gov/countries/analysisbriefs/World_Oil_Transit_Chokepoints/wotc.pdf, pp. 1–2 (accessed February 2, 2015).

3 U.S. Department of Energy, Energy Information Administration, *International Energy Outlook 2013* (Washington, DC: GPO), July 2013, www.eia.gov/forecasts/ieo/pdf/0484(2013).pdf, pp. 28–33, 177–257 (accessed July 2013).

4 *Ibid.*, pp. 52–3.

5 U.S. Department of Energy, *World Oil Transit Chokepoints*, pp. 7–8.

6 "Middle East and North Africa," *Military Balance* 114, 1 (2014), pp. 297–354; p. 320.

7 Stephen Saunders, *Jane's Fighting Ships 2005–2006* (London: Jane's Information Group, 2005), pp. 336–43.

8 "Iran," in *Jane's World Navies: 2011*, ed. Alexander von Rosenbach (London: Jane's Information Group, 2011).

9 "Middle East and North Africa," *Military Balance*, p. 320.

10 *Ibid.*

11 "Islamic Republic of Iran Navy, IRIN; Iranian Revolutionary Guard Corps (IRGC) Navy," *Global Security*, www.globalsecurity.org/military/world/iran/navy.htm (accessed February 2, 2015).

12 "Iranian Navy Re-launches Upgraded Bayandor Ship," Naval-technology.com, June 12, 2013, www.naval-technology.com/news/newsiranian-navy-re-launches-upgraded-bayandor-ship (accessed February 2, 2015).

13 "Middle East and North Africa," *Military Balance*, p. 320.

14 *Ibid.*

15 *Ibid.*

16 *Ibid.*

17 "Iran," *Jane's World Navies: 2011*.

18 "Middle East and North Africa," *Military Balance*, p. 320.

19 "Navy, Iran," in *Jane's Sentinel Security Assessment: The Gulf States* (Alexandria, VA and Coulsdon, UK: Jane's Information Group, 2013), 18-2.

20 *Ibid.*, 17-4.

21 *Ibid.*, 17-2.

22 "IRGC Navy Choppers Equipped with Indigenous Cruise Missiles," Tasnim News Agency, February 28, 2014, www.tasnimnews.com/english/Home/Single/297863 (accessed August 28, 2015).

23 "Exclusive: IRGC's MIL17 Helicopters Equipped with Anti-Ship Cruise Missiles," Fars News Agency, April 7, 2014, http://english.farsnews.com/newstext.aspx?nn=13930118000857 (accessed August 28, 2015).

24 "Navy, Iran," *Jane's Sentinel*, 17-6.

25 *Ibid.*

26 "Middle East and North Africa," *Military Balance*, p. 320.

27 "Iran," *Jane's World Navies: 2011*.

28 "Iran to Strengthen Naval Presence in Gulf," *Gulf Daily News*, November 5, 2012, p. 2.

29 Ernesto Londoño and Thomas Erdbring, "Iran Hails Warships' Mission in Mediterranean," *Washington Post*, February 22, 2011.

30 "Iran to Strengthen Naval Presence in Gulf," p. 2.

31 Note that other sources give different numbers of both IRGC and IRIN vessels. The above list is not exhaustive, and given the nature of many of these craft – machine guns, MLR system, mine-laying capacity – Iran could convert dual-use pleasure and commercial craft in times of war.

32 "Iran," *Jane's World Navies: 2011*.

33 Christopher Harmer, *Iranian Naval and Maritime Strategy* (Washington, DC: Institute for the Study of War, 2013), p. 27.

34 "Middle East and North Africa," *Military Balance*, p. 321.

35 "But 40 percent to 60 percent have limited or no mission capability at any given time, and many are so old or poorly supported that they cannot sustain a high sortie rate." Iran Primer, *The Conventional Military*, http://iranprimer.usip.org/resource/conventional-military (accessed August 28, 2015).

9

MARITIME SECURITY IN THE MEDITERRANEAN

Europe's fragile underbelly

Thorsten Albrecht, Carlo Masala and Konstantinos Tsetsos

Introduction

The Mediterranean area represents a pivotal geostrategic region for the security of the European Union (EU). It serves both as a natural geographic border between the European, African, and Asian continents as well as a political and cultural frontier between Occident and Orient. Furthermore, due to its importance as a primary maritime trade route from Asia to Europe and its potentially vast deposits of natural resources it constitutes a vital source for future European political and economic development. The Mediterranean is the largest mostly enclosed sea of the world, at approximately 2.5 million km². It is connected to the Atlantic through the Strait of Gibraltar and to the Red Sea through the Suez Canal. Through the Dardanelles and the Bosporus Straits it is also connected to the Black Sea. Traditionally, the Mediterranean Sea has been a transit route for inner-European trade as well as imports from Africa and Asia (especially since the opening of the Suez Canal in 1869). Due to its geographical proximity to North Africa and the Middle East as well as to the recent regional political crises in the course of the Arab rebellion and the Syrian Civil War, the Mediterranean once again highlights its historical, political, and economic importance for the maritime security of the EU.[1]

In contrast to its political significance for European security and economic prosperity, Europe's decision-makers seem to have so far neglected its importance by displaying a sea-blindness that jeopardizes maritime security in the Mediterranean. In times of economic crisis, conflicts in the Middle East, the refugee crisis, and the deterioration of the EU–Russian relationship, various conflicts and security-related issues remain unsolved and receive only secondary attention in day-to-day politics. This chapter addresses these political, military, economic, societal, and environmental security issues associated with maritime security in the Mediterranean and intends to highlight the necessity for intensive political engagement in order to reduce risks and vulnerabilities that originate from Europe's soft security/political underbelly. Whilst the possibility of classic symmetric inter-state conflict with direct political and economic consequences for the EU cannot be excluded entirely, disputes concerning territorial, border, and exclusive economic zone (EEZ) issues still pose a direct threat to European security. Maritime security considers security and defense risks along with economic, energy policy, and ecological developments. Since the terrorist attacks of 9/11, international maritime terrorism as well as pirate attacks (e.g. in the Gulf of Aden) have become major asymmetric threats in the maritime domain in the

	Carriers	Amphibious ships	Sub marines	Destroyers, frigates	Corvettes	Amphibious craft	Coast guard
2008	5	23	45	97	13	167	326
2012	4	23	43	81	13	125	459

Figure 9.1 European Mediterranean naval platforms

Source
Based on Michael Codner, "The Security of the Mediterranean Sea," in *Strategy for Southern Europe*,
IDEAS Reports 17 (London School of Economics, 2013), pp. 29–35; p. 34.

Note
In addition to European platforms, the U.S. 6th Fleet, headquartered in Naples, Italy, is permanently
stationed in the Mediterranean.

twenty-first century. While conventional naval capabilities are still the main focus, as Figure 9.1
shows, in light of recent security developments in the Mediterranean area, a trend of transformation that shifts the emphasis of Mediterranean naval platforms from expeditionary navies to
more constabulary capabilities has emerged from 2008 to 2012.

A small reduction of conventional maritime platforms is met with a radical increase of constabulary vessels to meet those threats and security risks situated below war levels.

In addition, regional, political, economic, ethnic, and religious sub-state conflicts in the
vicinity of maritime choke points (e.g. the Suez Canal) endanger economic sea lines of communication (SLOC). While illegal migration, weapons or drug trafficking, and organized crime
are direct maritime threats that threaten Europe's security, environmental pollution, reductions
in biodiversity, illegal fishing, and maritime disasters are notable indirect threats. Together with
these direct and indirect threats, EU member states are confronted with maritime vulnerabilities. Modern industrial and service societies depend on open SLOC, the security of critical
infrastructure at sea, as well as safeguarding sea-based natural resources. European businesses
involved in maritime commerce as well as millions of tourists in the Mediterranean represent
additional vulnerabilities for states. These soft targets can be an objective for hostage-taking
and terrorist attacks in order to blackmail states. Thus, the protection of European civilians and
businesses can be considered a duty and responsibility of EU states within the framework of the
new maritime security environment.[2]

Inter-state conflicts

Although inter-state conflicts in Europe are considered a thing of the past, they cannot be
excluded in their entirety. As the Yugoslavian Wars in the 1990s proved, post-Second World
War Europe is not entirely free from the perils of inter-state conflict. In addition, extra- and
intra-state wars in the vicinity of the Mediterranean, such as the Lebanon War in 2006 or the
ongoing Syrian Civil War, illuminate state fragility and indicate existing risks and potential
security policy-related spill-overs. The Arab Spring has contributed significantly to governmental instability and societal radicalization in North Africa. Several inter-state disputes exist in
the Mediterranean that can transform the region into a crisis hotspot that threatens the maritime security of Europe. Alongside the Syrian Civil War that has the potential to spread further
in the region, political instability of some North African Mediterranean littoral as well as the

Israeli–Palestine and Israeli–Iranian conflicts can lead to inter-state and regional conflicts. In the Western Mediterranean, the conflict between Morocco and Spain over the EEZ implications of Ceuta and Melilla and their offshore islet as well as the British–Spanish low-level conflict over the sovereignty of Gibraltar represent the most pressing issues. In the Central Mediterranean, for want of militarized antagonism, divergent Italian and French EEZ interests highlight that even EU member states have difficulties in delimitating their respective national maritime claims. Lastly, in the Eastern Mediterranean, the still unresolved division of Cyprus, territorial and border disputes between Greece and Turkey in the Aegean, as well as diverse interpretations and recognitions of national EEZs (Greece, Turkey, Israel, Cyprus, Lebanon, Gaza) create additional potential for conflicts.

Aegean dispute

The complex sovereignty dispute over maritime economic zones, namely EEZ and continental shelf (CS), in the Aegean burdens bilateral relations between Greece and Turkey since the 1970s, with tensions escalating short of war in 1987 (Sismik crisis) and 1996 (Imia/Kardak crisis). While several diplomatic initiatives were introduced in the course of the 1999 Helsinki summit in support of paving the way for Turkey's EU accession, the issue remains unresolved. The main reason is its complexity; the Aegean dispute consists of various overlapping territorial, airspace, and maritime disputes. Greece, as party to both international treaties, argues on the basis of the Convention on the Continental Shelf (CCS) 1958 and the United Nations Convention on the Law of the Seas (UNCLOS)[3] 1982 that all its islands are eligible areas for territorial waters, a CS, and an EEZ, seeks to extend the territorial waters from the coastline and its islands to 12 nm and considers the principle of equidistance/median line for the demarcation of EEZs and CS as supported by international law.[4] Furthermore, it intends to implement a 10 nm national airspace and denies Turkish claims about so-called "grey zones" (areas that include disputed islets, some inhabited, and not covered by the Treaty of Lausanne of 1923 or the Paris Treaty of 1947). The Turkish position concentrates rather on a political solution of the dispute and emphasizes bilateral agreements with respect to CS delimitation, such as the Bern Agreement of 1978. Though Turkey is not party to either the CCS or UNCLOS and rejects the jurisdiction of the International Court of Justice (ICJ), the Turkish position on CS delimitation rests on the CCS by referring to special circumstances in deviation from the median line as well as recent ICJ rulings that apply that rule. Turkey argues that Greek islands are located on the Turkish CS and therefore should not be considered in the delimitation of the Greek and Turkish EEZ and CS in the Aegean. The EEZ and CS should therefore be created by ignoring the Greek islands and based on the mainland coastal baselines along the 25th median in the center of the Aegean. Turkey also claims that the island of Kastelorizo (some 150 km east of Rhodes) should be excluded from the delimitation, because it would connect the Greek EEZ with a potential Cypriot EEZ and block Turkish access to the Eastern Mediterranean. Furthermore, the intended extension of Greek territorial waters from 6 nm to 12 nm on the basis of the UNCLOS[5] is considered by Turkey a *casus belli*.[6] This would create a Greek Aegean encompassing 71.5 percent and grant Turkey a mere 8.8 percent, with 19.7 percent being high seas.[7] For Turkey, several small islets along the Turkish coast and south of Crete are to be considered "grey zones," because sovereignty was not officially transferred to Greece in 1923 and 1947. As Figure 9.2 shows, based on a strict interpretation of the UNCLOS, a potential Greek and Cypriot EEZ would limit a Turkish EEZ in the Mediterranean significantly and expand the EU's EEZ from Gibraltar to Israel.

Figure 9.2 EEZs in the Mediterranean based on UNCLOS equidistance principle

Source
Map created by the authors.

Note
EU member states (light grey), non–EU states bordering the Mediterranean (grey).

The tensions between the two countries are highlighted by daily mock dogfights between fighter-jets, overflights of disputed and non-disputed islands by Turkish jets,[8] collisions of coast guard vessels, and occasional harassment of FRONTEX helicopters on border patrol duty by Turkish radar. This militarized inter-state dispute has various implications for maritime security in the Eastern Mediterranean. First of all, in failing to overcome their differences, both countries could embark into a limited war due to an incident involving the sinking of ships or the downing of a fighter aircraft. Second, this territorial conflict between two NATO member states exemplifies a core problem of the Western defensive alliance: the lack of a suitable mechanism provided by the NATO Charta to deal with conflicts between members and the signal this ongoing internal dispute projects to the rest of the world. Third, although Greece has become one of the main campaigners for Turkey's EU accession, Turkey is "frustrated by the Greek tendency to seek gains in the Aegean by leveraging its EU membership against Turkey."[9] In addition, the dispute has further implications regarding Greek–Turkish rivalry over Cyprus and potential natural resource exploitation, while the linkage of the Aegean dispute with the Cyprus problem further intensifies the political deadlock. In addition, the dispute hampers cooperative border control efforts between the two countries in various other security-related policy fields and to a certain degree that enables organized crime bodies to expand their human trafficking and drug trafficking activities in the Aegean border region. Lastly, the inability of the EU to broker a deal favorable to one of its members with a candidate country highlights the neglect of European leaders to address an enlargement of the EU's EEZ and the economic potential it holds for the Union.

Levant basin and Cyprus dispute

In 2009, offshore exploration in Israel led to the discovery of natural gas and oil reserves with an estimated volume of 3.5 billion cubic meters of natural gas and 1.7 billion barrels of oil in the Levant basin.[10] This find in the Leviathan prospect represents a serious alternative to minimize

European dependence on Middle Eastern and Russian energy supplies.[11] Upon this discovery, Cyprus and Israel intensified their economic cooperation and demarcated their respective EEZ borders. The cooperation goal is to create an energy hub to process natural gas and to export it via pipelines through Greece to the European continent. Cyprus has issued licenses to the U.S.-based Noble Energy Inc. in order to explore neighboring prospects (Block 12) and demarcated its EEZ borders with Egypt (2003) and Lebanon (2007).[12] Israel's attempt to demarcate its EEZ border with Lebanon led to a dispute over an area of 854 km². A further issue of conflict that arises is a potential EEZ of the Gaza Strip, which is to this day not demarcated. The missing political solution to the continued Greek–Turkish conflict over Cyprus and its linkage to the Aegean dispute, the non-recognition of the EU member Cyprus by Turkey, the intensified cooperation between Cyprus and Israel as well as the exploration of its EEZ by Cyprus lead to tensions in Greek–Turkish and Turkish–Israeli relations. Turkey demands a suspension of the sea drilling and recognizes it as *casus belli*, as long as the Cyprus issue remains unresolved, for it fears the economic disadvantage of the Turkish Cypriot population. As Turkey is not a signatory to the UNCLOS, it does not recognize the treaties between Cyprus, Israel, and other Mediterranean states nor Israel's and Cyprus's right to a 200-mile EEZ. In the case of Cyprus, it dismisses the UNCLOS standard that even inhabited islands have the right to a CS or EEZ,[13] while Turkey recognizes the CS of Northern Cyprus and supports Turkish Cypriot claims for a disproportionately large part of Cyprus's CS and EEZ. As Figure 9.3 shows, this is a highly implausible claim for Northern Cyprus and is manifestly a tactical move to question Cyprus's own EEZ maritime boundaries with Israel and Egypt. It is as if Northern Cyprus was allocating itself the continental shelf of almost the entire island of Cyprus, except for its western offshore zone, which Turkey claims to be part of its own continental shelf.[14]

The EEZ dispute led to recent alliance and power shifts between Greece, Israel, and Cyprus on the one side, and Turkey on the other, and it offers a potential inter-state conflict scenario. The enhancement of Israeli–Cypriot and Israeli–Greek political, military, and economic cooperation signals that Turkish aspirations for a larger EEZ in the Eastern Mediterranean will be met, if necessary even militarily, by all three countries. Naval standoffs, harassing of research vessels, and guerrilla exploration operations in disputed EEZs have increased significantly in the region. In contrast to Greece and Cyprus, which are rather cautious in threatening Turkey directly, Israeli government officials made it clear that any interference in economic exploitation efforts by Turkish vessels and aircraft will be met with all necessary means. With the Turkish government considering Israel a "terrorist state,"[15] the threat of war or militarized incident is significant. The main goals of the EU should prioritize solving the Cyprus issue. It is crucial for both the Aegean dispute and in finding an equitable solution to the EEZ dispute in the region. In the absence of a long-term solution, the potential for war, involving one or more member states of the EU, is considerable. Even if Cyprus reverts to a more passive role, Israeli exploitation efforts and Turkish responses could spark a regional crisis that has the potential to drag both Cyprus and Greece and ultimately the EU into the conflict.

Ceuta, Melilla, Perejil Island, and Gibraltar disputes

Morocco, which established an EEZ in the Mediterranean basin in 1981,[16] is in dispute with Spain over the sovereignty of the Perejil Islands near the Gibraltar Straits. The Kingdom also does not recognize the Spanish exclaves Ceuta and Melilla (as well as other Spanish possessions on the African continent) and considers those areas as remnants of Spanish colonialism. In July 2002, Morocco established a small garrison on the uninhabited island of Perejil (some 8 km West of Ceuta) in order to monitor illegal migration and smuggling. Since the rocks are

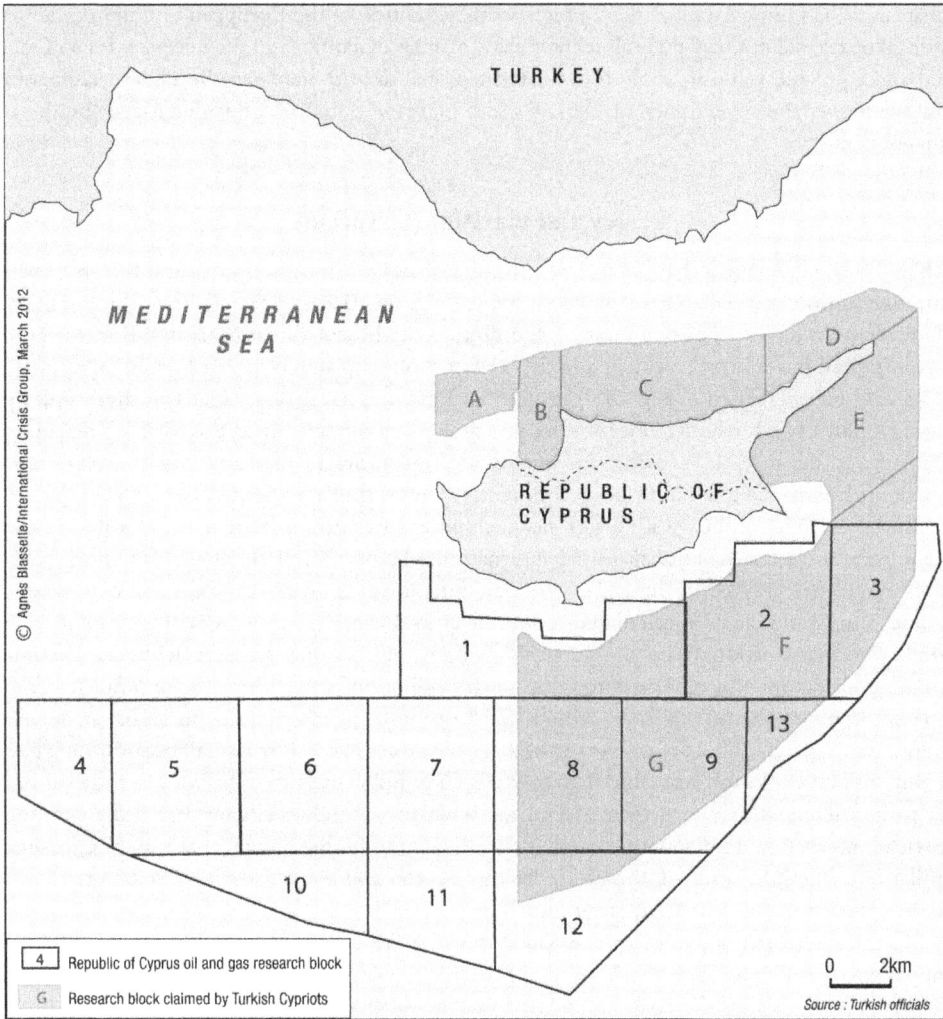

Figure 9.3 The Turkish Cypriots' claimed hydrocarbon research blocks

Source
International Crisis Group, "Aphrodite's Gift: Can Cypriot Gas Power a New Dialogue?" Europe Report No. 216-2, April 2012.

disputed by both countries and Spanish protests were ignored, Spanish commandos recaptured the island a week later. Although reclaimed by Spain without the use of violence and returned to *status quo ex ante* in the same year, this incident highlights the divergent claims of both countries regarding the sovereignty of various rocks and islets off the Moroccan coast. These differences are very material. The Spanish exclaves limit Moroccan EEZ in the Mediterranean. Furthermore, the Ceuta exclave allows Spain to extend its territorial waters and EEZ across the Straits of Gibraltar. Due to the lack of treaties internationalizing the straits, passing this maritime choke point with military vessels requires informing the Spanish authorities. Although conflict remains on a low level, due to its proximity to the strategically important Strait of Gibraltar, its reach into the Western Mediterranean and the Spanish–Moroccan disputes over the Western

Sahara as well as some Atlantic islets, it requires the attention of the European Union in order to settle all territorial disputes by diplomatic means. Similar dynamics and the necessity for a mediated and equitable solution apply to a related regional dispute between the United Kingdom and Spain over the sovereignty of Gibraltar, although the potential of a militarized dispute is non-existent.

Piracy and maritime terrorism

While the Mediterranean has been a hub for pirate activity since antiquity and featured even state-like entities specializing in pirate activities (e.g. the Barbary States), the contemporary Mediterranean region is free of piracy. According to the International Maritime Bureau,[17] the last attempted pirate attack occurred in 2011, with none registered in 2012 or 2013. In 2014, in a single piracy-related event ISIS captured an Egyptian naval vessel that was then sunk by the Egyptian navy. In the Mediterranean, piracy is more likely to take the form of maritime terrorism. In the post-9/11 world, the exploitation of means of maritime public transport as a weapon by malevolent actors poses a potentially high threat. A September 11 event at sea cannot be excluded either. With a significant number of critical infrastructures located in the Mediterranean, a terrorist attack on an international harbor, oil platforms, or off-shore wind parks would seriously harm the EU's economic fundaments as well as import and export capabilities and would create incalculable economic costs. If ships are used as platforms for operations or even as weapons, they can seriously hamper international trade. A deliberate sinking, ramming, or detonation of a captured ship in the vicinity of a maritime choke point (e.g. the Turkish Straits or the Suez Canal) would lead to months of interference in global trade and energy transport. In 2002, the oil tanker MV *Limburg* was attacked by a small boat off the coast of Yemen. The explosion not only damaged the ship and caused the spilling of crude oil but led to interferences in international maritime trade for several weeks by practically shutting down all international trade with Yemen. If coordinated to hit the Suez Canal and/or Gibraltar, similar attacks might landlock the entire Mediterranean and cut off maritime access to global markets due to the lack of alternate routes.

Maritime terrorist activities in the Mediterranean are no novel phenomena as two well-known incidents show. The 1985 hijacking of the Italian cruise ship MS *Achille Lauro* by Palestinian terrorists off the coast of Egypt led to the death of a U.S. passenger of Jewish heritage. The terrorists demanded the release of imprisoned Palestinians and sought to blackmail Israel and the U.S. to give in to their demands. Besides hostage-taking, terrorists may use maritime vessels to move weapons and explosives. The seizure of the *Baltic Sky* by Greek commandos in the Ionian Sea in 2003, which was loaded with TNT and detonators and bound for Sudan, highlights how terror organizations increasingly seek to utilize maritime routes for resupply.[18]

Further maritime terror activities are to be expected, as plans found with an Al-Qaida terrorist of Austrian descent who was arrested in Berlin in early 2012 show. A data drive in his possession was encrypted and contained hundreds of Al-Qaida documents. The evaluation of the documents made clear that Al-Qaida plans attacks against maritime targets, primarily cruise and merchant ships, in order to harm Western states.[19] Although experts expect the next large-scale maritime terrorism attack to target East African ports,[20] the Mediterranean is equally vulnerable with an important share of the global cruise ship market. The Al-Qaida documents point towards large-scale hostage-taking on cruise ships and their media exploitation for propaganda purposes. Maritime terrorism is very cost-effective for terrorists. The attack on the American guided-missile destroyer *Cole* (DDG-67) in 2000 cost Al-Qaida approximately $5,000, while this sum was enough to disable a warship worth about $1 billion.

A similar cost-effectiveness ratio can be expected if terrorist organizations seek to hijack passenger ships, misuse cargo ships, or attack critical infrastructure installations by ramming them with hijacked vessels.

Thus, maritime stakeholders in the Mediterranean will have to address the rising threat of maritime terror by international, national, and private cooperation that enhances mechanisms of prevention as well as counter-terrorism responses. Such prevention mechanisms may include intelligence operations outside the EU in order to assess risk levels and anticipate terrorist activities before malevolent actors choose to act.[21] Furthermore, in light of increased digitization of maritime commerce and navigation, maritime cyber security will have to be dramatically increased to protect maritime assets as well as critical infrastructure dependent on maritime trade.[22]

Illegal migration

Political turmoil in the wake of the Arab Spring and ongoing conflicts in Afghanistan, Iraq, and Syria led to a significant influx of refugees and asylum seekers to Europe through the Mediterranean. In addition to conflict refugees, asylum seekers attempt to enter the EU as economic migrants in order to overcome the general economic situation, overpopulation, and political instability in their home countries. The majority of such migration is illegal, because asylum is granted only in cases of political prosecution, while economic migration is legal only in cases in which it was preceded by recruitment. The number of illegal migrants registered, arrested, and deported in the EU amounts to approximately 500,000 yearly.[23] Regarding the total number of illegal immigrants in the EU, only estimates exist and those vary from 4 to 8 million.[24] The security relevance of illegal migration can be derived from the annual number of registered illegal immigrants at the EU borders. While over 106,000 (48,000 over sea) illegal border crossings were registered in 2009,[25] there were 104,000 (24,000 over sea) in 2010[26] and 141,000 (71,000 over sea) in 2011.[27] A slight decrease to 107,000 (60,000 over sea) illegal border crossings in 2013[28] can be attributed to a stabilization of post-Arab Spring states as well as several joint maritime operations. Although the increase of illegal migration since 2010 coincided with the political revolutions in Northern Africa, a general trend is still indicative, pointing to a higher influx in the future. Crises such as the downfall of North African governments in 2011 can lead to migration waves (see Figure 9.4), and show that the European maritime capabilities are insufficient to cope with migration waves, while the limited capacities of reception centers can lead to a humanitarian state of emergency. With the majority of migrants choosing the way over land (through the border triangle Greece, Bulgaria, Turkey and the eastern border of the EU), intensified FRONTEX operations on land have led to an increase of maritime migration. However, despite a slight decrease in overall illegal border crossings in 2013, a long-term trend of increasing illegal migration by sea is identifiable. Due to the geographical circumstances, a broad border protection and comprehensive control of all EU sea borders is close to impossible. In Ceuta and Melilla and at some locations in the Aegean, the distance between the EU's border and third states is less than 1,000 meters. This allows migrants to enter EU territory even without a craft. There are now over 19,500 migrants who died while attempting to enter EU territory (13,000 of those drowned) for the period from 1988–2011[29]. Due to the high death ratio of illegal migrants crossing the sea, minimizing human suffering is one of the core goals of the European external border surveillance system. The economic follow-up costs accruing from the necessary border protection, humanitarian aid for and black labor by illegal migrants cannot be estimated.

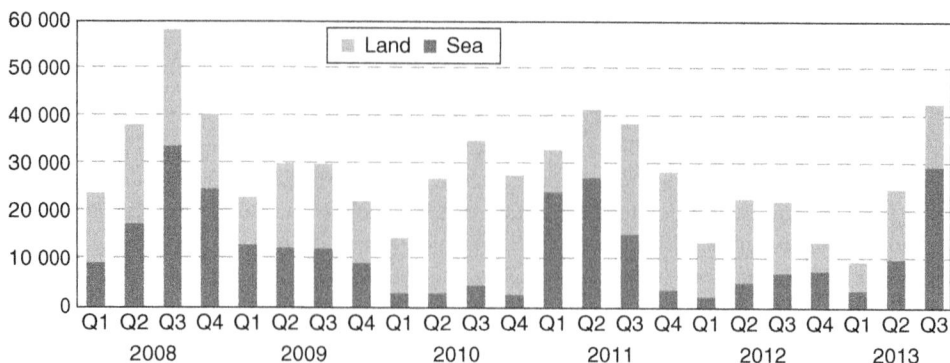

Figure 9.4 Total quarterly detections of illegal border-crossings

Source
European Agency for the Management of Operational Cooperation at the External Borders of
the Member States of the European Union, *FRAN Quarterly* (Third Quarter, 2013), p. 12, http://
frontex.europa.eu/assets/Publications/Risk_Analysis/FRAN_Q3_2013.pdf, accessed April 30, 2014.
Reproduced with permission.

As Figure 9.4 shows, FRONTEX is recording wave-like migration spikes that coincide with
political crisis in Europe's vicinity (e.g. the Libyan crisis in 2011 or Syrian crisis in 2013) as well
as seasonal differences. While the first and fourth quarter of each calendar year display a decrease,
spikes are likely to occur in the second and third quarter due to meteorological conditions.
What stands out is the constant increase of sea-borne illegal border-crossing attempts over time.
In Q3 2013 alone, more than half of all border crossings were made by sea, a trend that will
intensify due to Bulgarian and Greek efforts at increased land-border surveillance and patrol.
With current UNHCR estimates ranging from 7 to 10 million migrants at the EU's borders
hoping for a chance to enter Europe, the number of illegal crossing and asylum applications is
expected to rise exponentially.[30]

According to the Dublin II Regulation, EU states cannot refuse the entry of migrants or
rapidly repatriate them. As soon as migrants successfully enter the EU, the host country has to
initiate an application of asylum that may take up to one year to complete (Dublin II Regulation
2003, article 10). This humanitarian side of illegal migration, although not posing a direct security
threat, has implications for border security authorities, because focusing on illegal migration may
reduce the capability of the police and coast guard to adequately concentrate on weapon- and
drug-trafficking or other crime-related activities.[31] Further security relevant problems that arise
directly from illegal migration include border violations, corruption of officials, and organized
crime activity, especially human trafficking and human rights violations. Moreover, the import
of religious, ethnic, and political conflicts into the EU poses a potential threat, as do scenarios
of sleeper cells of terrorist organizations entering the EU under the disguise of political asylum.

Possible preventive actions needed to reduce illegal migration and associated activities
of international organized crime call for a common European coast guard, an expansion of
FRONTEX personnel and operations, better legal coordination of EU member states by reducing policy and legal discrepancies, as well as extensive bilateral agreements with non-EU states
in the Mediterranean and beyond to enhance border security. Furthermore, businesses and
private actors should be included in a holistic approach that reduces demand (e.g. prostitution)
and consumption (e.g. drugs) which encourage illegal migration and human trafficking thus
substantially decreasing profits of international crime organizations.[32]

Maritime choke points, sea lines of communication, and environmental risks

As a largely enclosed sea, the Mediterranean is prone to disruption of lines of communication at maritime choke points, by accidents, terrorist attacks, and environmental maritime risks that endanger the free passage of ships, cargo, and trade. While the Strait of Gibraltar is geographically less prone to disruptions due to its size, both the Suez Canal and the Turkish Straits, with their limited space for maneuver, are extremely vulnerable. The Suez Canal (opened in 1869), for instance, is only 200 meters wide in some sections and can be crossed only in one direction at a time, while the Turkish Straits with a width of 1.3 to 6 km allow multidirectional shipping. While the Suez Canal is internationalized and allows free passage "in time of war as in time of peace, by every vessel of commerce or of war, without distinction of flag" (Article 1) since the Convention of Constantinople of 1888, the Turkish Straits, as the Montreux Convention Regarding the Regime of the Straits of 1936 clarifies, allows free passage only to merchant ships and restricted passage to military vessels in times of peace (Article 2-15), whereas in times of war passage is dictated by the discretion of the Turkish government (Article 20). Both straits feature historical incidents that illuminate their importance for maritime security and global trade. During the so-called "Turkish Straits Crisis" from 1946 to 1953, the Soviet Union contested the Montreux Regime and accused Turkey of mismanaging the administration of the Straits in favor of the Western allies, while the Suez Crisis of 1956 as well as the Six Day War in 1967 and the Yom Kippur War of 1973 led to a closing of the Suez Canal for international commerce. Today, various threats, risks, and vulnerabilities exist again in association with these maritime choke points that endanger Europe's security and economic prosperity.

The Suez Canal, although of less importance for Europe's oil imports than in previous decades,[33] is still the primary gateway for European imports and exports to Asian and African markets. While similar disruptions for European productivity as caused by the oil crisis 1973 could be mitigated by heavier reliance on non-fossil-fuel-based energy sources, alternative routes, and pipelines, the impact of a blockade of the Suez Canal for European trade would be more severe. The economic harm associated with a total closure of the Suez Canal for European and global trade is incalculable, but would likely amount to billions of euros per week. In the absence of military conflicts in the region, the limited navigational space of the Suez Canal makes it extremely vulnerable to terrorist attacks. The sinking of a ship to block the canal or a large-scale oil spill in the waterway would impair global trade for months. The easy accessibility of the canal waters along its 200 km stretch as well as increased terrorist activity in the Sinai since the Arab Spring highlight the vulnerability and risk of a deliberate attack interfering with global maritime trade. Although in 2013 the Egyptian military and security forces foiled several terrorist attacks that attempted to sink or capture ships in the canal and tightened security measures in the Sinai, the risk for future attacks remains unchanged.[34] This vulnerability of ships passing the canal is further enhanced by the low speed of ships, a precautionary measure dictated by the canal authorities to minimize the risk of erosion of the Suez banks, the creation of tsunamis in the canal, and the danger of ships going aground.

In the Turkish Straits that connect the Mediterranean with the Black Sea, with over 50,000 vessels passing through the Bosporus and Dardanelles annually coupled with the unique attribute of being surrounded by one of Europe's largest megacities, is one of the most dangerous waterways worldwide. About 20 percent of the vessels that pass the straits carry dangerous cargo,[35] so that the risk and impact of an environmental disaster would be higher than that of a terrorist attack. The first major accident occurred in 1960 when the Greek-flagged M/T *World Harmony* collided with the Yugoslavian-flagged M/T *Peter Zoranic*. Twenty crew members, including both shipmasters, died; the resulting oil pollution and fires lasted several weeks, suspending traffic in the strait.[36] In the twenty-first century, although no grave accident has yet been recorded, the number of accidents increased in relationship to increases in traffic.[37] With the discovery of more Caspian oil and gas fields, the straits will witness a boost in traffic as well as an increase in dangerous good transports. Although at first glance an aspect of maritime safety, the security-relevant risks associated with an environmental disaster in the Turkish Straits are evident. The population of a megacity such as Istanbul can be severely endangered by oil spillage, ship accidents involving chemicals, oil fires, as well as environmental pollution originating from accidents in the straits. Furthermore, the high risk of a blockade of the Bosporus, which like the Suez Canal is narrow, could practically lead to a cessation of trade between the Mediterranean and the Black Sea.

As shown, both choke points are not only vital to European maritime trade and access to global markets, but highly vulnerable to disruptions and blockades by either malicious actors or human error. Therefore, both national and international efforts are necessary to secure free passage and increase the safety and security of these maritime European lifelines in the Mediterranean.

Conclusion

This chapter has addressed the most pressing security risks and associated vulnerabilities that exist or may develop in the Mediterranean in the near future. Apart from North America, Europe is arguably the safest and most secure continent. As we have shown, the Mediterranean is its Achilles' heel, a potential source for various conflicts originating from a variety of different policy fields, from inter-state disputes to environmental issues. Maritime security is a guarantee for economic prosperity in the EU and a cornerstone of the future economic development of its leading economies. Nevertheless, many of the maritime stakeholders, such as governments, institutions, public authorities, as well as the general public, suffer from sea-blindness as observed in the limited attention directed towards maritime security.[38] The significance of the maritime domain within European security, defense, and economic policy is supposed to be well known, but due to the numerous actors, institutions, and agents involved as well as the complex institutional division of labor within the EU and between the respective maritime states, it lacks a clear common strategic vision. Harmonization and expansion of national and European strategies as well as the efficient and effective integration and development of existing national and international measures are necessary in order to provide maritime security in the Mediterranean and beyond. Such measures in the area of maritime patrols, common armaments and research goals, as well as a European coast guard and international cooperation can considerably reduce the threats of inter-state conflicts, the risks of illegal migration and maritime terrorism, as well as the dangers of environmental hazards.

Disregarding the outlined potential security developments in Europe's soft underbelly and directing only limited attention to them is perilous, since it endangers the security of EU member states and its citizens as well as their present and future economic prosperity.

Notes

1 Carlo Masala and Konstantinos Tsetsos, "The Maritime Dimension of the European Union's and Germany's Security and Defense Policy in the 21st Century." ISPSW Strategy Series: Focus on Defense and International Security 229, May 2013, International Relations and Security Network (ISN), Berlin, www.isn.ethz.ch/isn/Digital-Library/Publications/Detail/?id=164132, accessed April 30, 2014.
2 *Ibid.*, p. 7.

3 Greece bases its position on Article 6(1) and 6(2) of the CCS and Article 3, 15, 55–8, 76–85 and 121(2) of the UNCLOS.

4 Petros Siousiouras and Georgios Chrysochou, "The Aegean Dispute in the Context of Contemporary Judicial Decisions on Maritime Delimitation." *Laws* 3 (2014).

5 Turkey applies the UNCLOS 12 nm criteria and median EEZ demarcation in the Black Sea.

6 M. N. Schmitt, "Aegean Angst: A Historical and Legal Analysis of the Greek–Turkish Dispute." *University Law Review* 2 (1996).

7 Turkish Ministry of Foreign Affairs, "Background Note on Aegean Disputes," 2014, www.mfa.gov.tr/background-note-on-aegean-disputes.en.mfa, accessed April 30, 2014.

8 International Crisis Group, "Turkey and Greece: Time to Settle the Aegean Dispute." *Europe Briefing* 64 (2011), p. 9, www.crisisgroup.org/~/media/files/europe/turkey-cyprus/turkey/b64-%20turkey%20and%20greece-%20time%20to%20settle%20the%20aegean%20dispute.pdf, accessed April 30, 2014.

9 *Ibid.*, p. 16.

10 United States Geological Survey, "Assessment of Undiscovered Oil and Gas Resources of the Levant Basin Province, Eastern Mediterranean," 2010, p. 1, http://pubs.usgs.gov/fs/2010/3014/pdf/FS10-3014.pdf, accessed April 30, 2014.

11 Niklas Anzinger, "Will the Eastern Mediterranean Become the Next Persian Gulf?" *American Enterprise Institute for Public Policy Research* 3 (2013), p. 3, www.aei.org/wp-content/uploads/2013/07/-will-the-eastern-mediterrranean-become-the-next-persian-gulf_091536411207.pdf, accessed April 30, 2014.

12 The Lebanese parliament has yet to ratify this treaty due to the Israeli–Lebanese disputes over their EEZ. Ayla Gürel, Fiona Mullen, and Harry Tzimitras, "The Cyprus Hydrocarbons Issue: Context, Positions and Future Scenarios," PCC Report 1 (2013), p. 5, http://file.prio.no/publication_files/Cyprus/Report%202013-1%20Hydrocarbons.pdf, accessed April 30, 2014.

13 Michael Emerson, "Fishing for Gas and More in Cypriot Waters." *Insight Turkey* 1 (2013), p. 170.

14 *Ibid.*

15 Ece Toksabay, "Turkey's Erdoğan calls Israel a 'Terrorist State'," *Reuters*, November 19, 2012, www.reuters.com/article/2012/11/19/us-palestinians-israel-turkey-idUSBRE8AI0FH20121119, accessed April 30, 2014.

16 Thomas Dux, *Specially Protected Marine Areas in the Exclusive Economic Zone (EEZ): The Regime for the Protection of Specific areas of the EEZ for Environmental reasons under International Law* (Berlin: LIT, 2011), p. 331.

17 ICC International Maritime Bureau, "Piracy and Armed Robbery against Ships. Report for the Period 1 January–31 December 2013," 2014, p. 6, www.ship.sh/attachment/files/2013_Annual_IMB_Piracy_Report.pdf, accessed April 30, 2014.

18 Helena Smith, "Nato 'Terror' Tipoff on Explosives Ship Sailing to Sudan," *Guardian*, June 24, 2003, www.theguardian.com/world/2003/jun/24/alqaida.terrorism, accessed April 30, 2014.

19 Nic Robertson, Paul Cruickshank, and Tim Lister, "Documents Reveal al Qaeda's plans for Seizing Cruise Ships, Carnage in Europe," CNN, May 1, 2012, http://edition.cnn.com/2012/04/30/world/al-qaeda-documents-future/index.html, accessed April 30, 2014.

20 Ryan M. Barnett, "The Next Terrorist Attack: Al Qaeda's Maritime History and Ambitions," Consultancy Africa Intelligence, September 5, 2013, www.consultancyafrica.com/index.php?option=com_content&view=article&id=1341:the-next-terrorist-attack-a-detailed-look-at-al-qaedas-maritime-history-and-ambitions&catid=60:conflict-terrorism-discussion-papers&Itemid=265, accessed April 30, 2014.

21 Gilles de Kerchove, "EU Counter-Terrorism Policy in the Mediterranean – Ready and Waiting?" in *Maritime security in the Mediterranean: Challenges and Policy Responses*, ed. Giles Merritt (Brussels: SDA, 2011), p. 33.

22 European Network and Information Security Agency, "Analysis of Cyber Security Aspects in the Maritime Sector," 2011, www.enisa.europa.eu/activities/Resilience-and-CIIP/critical-infrastructure-and-services/dependencies-of-maritime-transport-to-icts/cyber-security-aspects-in-the-maritime-sector-1/at_download/fullReport, accessed April 30, 2014.

23 Masala and Tsetsos, "Maritime Dimension," p. 9.

24 CLANDESTINO, "Clandestino Project Final Report," 2009, p. 7, http://clandestino.eliamep.gr/wp-content/uploads/2010/03/clandestino-final-report_-november-20091.pdf, accessed April 30, 2014.

25 European Agency for the Management of Operational Cooperation at the External Borders of the Member States of the European Union, *FRAN Quarterly* (Second Quarter, 2010), p. 23, www.frontex.europa.eu/assets/Publications/Risk_Analysis/FRAN_Q2_2010.pdf, accessed April 30, 2014.

26 European Agency for the Management of Operational Cooperation at the External Borders of the Member States of the European Union, *FRAN Quarterly* (First Quarter, 2011), p. 29, www.frontex. europa.eu/assets/Publications/Risk_Analysis/FRAN_Q1_2011.pdf, accessed April 30, 2014.

27 European Agency for the Management of Operational Cooperation at the External Borders of the Member States of the European Union, *FRAN Quarterly* (Second Quarter, 2012), p. 40, http://frontex. europa.eu/assets/Publications/Risk_Analysis/FRAN_Q2_2012.pdf, accessed April 30, 2014.

28 European Agency for the Management of Operational Cooperation at the External Borders of the Member States of the European Union, *FRAN Quarterly* (Third Quarter, 2013), p. 13, http://frontex. europa.eu/assets/Publications/Risk_Analysis/FRAN_Q3_2013.pdf, accessed April 30, 2014.

29 Gabriele Del Grande, "La Strage," Fortress Europe Blog, http://fortresseurope.blogspot.co.uk/p/ la-strage.html, accessed April 30, 2014.

30 United Nations High Commissioner for Refugees, "Global Trends 2011," 2012, www.unhcr.de/file-admin/user_upload/dokumente/06_service/zahlen_und_statistik/GlobalTrends_2011.pdf, accessed April 30, 2014.

31 Louise Shelley, *Human Smuggling and Trafficking into Europe: A Comparative Perspective* (Washington, DC: Migration Policy Institute, 2014), p. 3.

32 *Ibid.*, p. 16.

33 William Komiss and Lavar Huntzinger, "The Economic Implications of Disruptions to Maritime Oil Chokepoints," CNA, 2011, p. 18, www.cna.org/sites/default/files/research/The%20 Economic%20Implications%20of%20Disruptions%20to%20Maritime%20Oil%20Chokepoints%20 D0024669%20A1.pdf, accessed April 30, 2014.

34 Steve Wilson, "Failed 'Terrorist' Attack on Suez Canal Ship," *Telegraph*, September 1, 2013, www.tele-graph.co.uk/news/worldnews/africaandindianocean/egypt/10278671/Failed-terrorist-attack-on-Suez-Canal-ship.html, accessed April 30, 2014.

35 Özgecan S. Uluscçu, Birnur Özba, Tayfur Altıok, and İlhan Or, "Risk Analysis of the Transit Vessel Traffic in the Strait of Istanbul," Laboratory for Port Security at Rutgers University, 2008, p. ii, http://dimacs.rutgers.edu/port_security_lab/Report%20on%20Risk%20Analysis%20of%20the%20 Maritime%20Traffic%20in%20the%20Strait%20of%20Istanbul.pdf, accessed April 30, 2014.

36 *Ibid.*, p. 14.

37 Bayram Oztürk, Özkan Poyraz, and Elif Özgür, "Turkish Straits: Some Considerations, Threats and Future," in *The Turkish Straits: Maritime Safety, Legal and Environmental Aspects*, ed. Nilüfer Oral and Bayram Oztürk (Istanbul: Turkish Marine Research Foundation, Publication 25, 2006), p. 126.

38 Masala and Tsetsos, "Maritime Dimension," p. 30.

Bibliography

Anzinger, Niklas. "Will the Eastern Mediterranean Become the Next Persian Gulf?" *American Enterprise Institute for Public Policy Research* 3 (2013). www.aei.org/wp-content/uploads/2013/07/-will-the-easte rn-mediterrranean-become-the-next-persian-gulf_091536411207.pdf. Accessed April 30, 2014.

Barnett, Ryan M. "The Next Terrorist Attack: Al Qaeda's Maritime History and Ambitions." Consultancy Africa Intelligence, September 5, 2013. www.consultancyafrica.com/index.php?option=com_con tent&view=article&id=1341:the-next-terrorist-attack-a-detailed-look-at-al-qaedas-maritime-history-and-ambitions&catid=60:conflict-terrorism-discussion-papers&Itemid=265. Accessed April 30, 2014.

Clandestino. "Clandestino Project Final Report," 2009. http://clandestino.eliamep.gr/wp-content/ uploads/2010/03/clandestino-final-report_-november-20091.pdf. Accessed April 30, 2014.

Codner, Michael. "The Security of the Mediterranean Sea." In *Strategy for Southern Europe*, IDEAS Reports 17. London School of Economics, 2013, pp. 29–35.

Convention between Great Britain, Germany, Austria-Hungary, Spain, France, Italy, The Netherlands, Russia and Turkey. "Constantinople Convention," 1888. www-rohan.sdsu.edu/dept/polsciwb/brianl/ docs/1888ConstantinopleConventionon.pdf. Accessed April 30, 2014.

de Kerchove, Gilles. "EU Counter-terrorism Policy in the Mediterranean – Ready and Waiting?" In *Maritime Security in the Mediterranean: Challenges and Policy Responses*, ed. Giles Merritt. Brussels: SDA, 2011, pp. 33–34.

Dublin II Regulation. "Council Regulation (EC) No 343/2003 of 18 February 2003 Establishing the Criteria and Mechanisms for Determining the Member State Responsible for Examining an Asylum

Application Lodged in One of the Member States by a Third-Country National," 2003. http://eur-lex. europa.eu/legal-content/EN/ALL/?uri=CELEX:32003R0343. Accessed April 30, 2014.

Dux, Thomas. *Specially Protected Marine Areas in the Exclusive Economic Zone (EEZ): The Regime for the Protection of Specific Areas of the EEZ for Environmental Reasons under International Law*. Berlin: LIT, 2011.

Emerson, Michael "Fishing for Gas and More in Cypriot Waters" *Insight Turkey* 1 (2013): 165–81.

European Agency for the Management of Operational Cooperation at the External Borders of the Member States of the European Union. *FRAN Quarterly* (Second Quarter, 2010). www.frontex.europa.eu/assets/Publications/Risk_Analysis/FRAN_Q2_2010.pdf. Accessed April 30, 2014.

European Agency for the Management of Operational Cooperation at the External Borders of the Member States of the European Union. *FRAN Quarterly* (First Quarter, 2011). www.frontex.europa.eu/assets/Publications/Risk_Analysis/FRAN_Q1_2011.pdf. Accessed April 30, 2014.

European Agency for the Management of Operational Cooperation at the External Borders of the Member States of the European Union. *FRAN Quarterly* (Second Quarter, 2012). http://frontex.europa.eu/assets/Publications/Risk_Analysis/FRAN_Q2_2012.pdf. Accessed April 30, 2014.

European Agency for the Management of Operational Cooperation at the External Borders of the Member States of the European Union. *FRAN Quarterly* (Third Quarter, 2013). http://frontex.europa.eu/assets/Publications/Risk_Analysis/FRAN_Q3_2013.pdf. Accessed April 30, 2014.

European Network and Information Security Agency. "Analysis of Cyber Security Aspects in the Maritime Sector," 2011. www.enisa.europa.eu/activities/Resilience-and-CIIP/critical-infrastructure-and-services/dependencies-of-maritime-transport-to-icts/cyber-security-aspects-in-the-maritime-sector-1/at_download/fullReport. Accessed April 30, 2014.

Fortress Europe Blog. http://fortresseurope.blogspot.co.uk/p/la-strage.html. Accessed April 30, 2014.

Gürel, Ayla, Mullen, Fiona, and Tzimitras, Harry. "The Cyprus Hydrocarbons Issue: Context, Positions and Future Scenarios," PCC Report 1 (2013). http://file.prio.no/publication_files/Cyprus/Report%20 2013-1%20Hydrocarbons.pdf. Accessed April 30, 2014.

ICC International Maritime Bureau. "Piracy and Armed Robbery against Ships. Report for the Period 1 January–31 December 2013," 2014. www.ship.sh/attachment/files/2013_Annual_IMB_Piracy_Report.pdf. Accessed April 30, 2014.

International Crisis Group. "Aphrodite's Gift: Can Cypriot Gas Power a New Dialogue?" Europe Report No. 216–2, April 2012.

International Crisis Group. "Turkey and Greece: Time to Settle the Aegean Dispute." *Europe Briefing* 64 (2011) www.crisisgroup.org/~/media/files/europe/turkey-cyprus/turkey/b64-%20turkey%20and% 20greece-%20time%20to%20settle%20the%20aegean%20dispute.pdf. Accessed April 30, 2014.

Komiss, William, and Huntzinger, Lavar. "The Economic Implications of Disruptions to Maritime Oil Chokepoints." CNA, 2011. www.cna.org/sites/default/files/research/The%20Economic%20 Implications%20of%20Disruptions%20to%20Maritime%20Oil%20Chokepoints%20 D0024669%20A1.pdf. Accessed April 30, 2014.

League of Nations. "Montreux Convention Regarding the Regime of the Straits," 1936. http://sam.baskent.edu.tr/belge/Montreux_ENG.pdf. Accessed April 30, 2014.

Masala, Carlo, and Tsetsos, Konstantinos. "The Maritime Dimension of the European Union's and Germany's Security and Defense Policy in the 21st Century." ISPSW Strategy Series: Focus on Defense and International Security 229, May 2013, International Relations and Security Network (ISN), Berlin. www.isn.ethz.ch/isn/Digital-Library/Publications/Detail/?id=164132. Accessed April 30, 2014.

Oztürk, Bayram, Poyraz, Özkan, and Özgür, Elif. "Turkish Straits Some Considerations, Threats and Future." In *The Turkish Straits: Maritime Safety, Legal and Environmental Aspects*, ed. Nilüfer Oral and Bayram Oztürk. Istanbul: Turkish Marine Research Foundation, 2006, pp. 116–34.

Robertson, Nic, Cruickshank, Paul, and Lister, Tim. "Documents Reveal Al Qaeda's Plans for Seizing Cruise Ships, Carnage in Europe." CNN, May 1, 2012. http://edition.cnn.com/2012/04/30/world/al-qaeda-documents-future/index.html. Accessed April 30, 2014.

Schmitt, M. N. "Aegean Angst: A Historical and Legal Analysis of the Greek–Turkish Dispute." *University Law Review* 2 (1996): 15–56.

Shelley, Louise. *Human Smuggling and Trafficking into Europe: A Comparative Perspective*. Washington, DC: Migration Policy Institute, 2014.

Siousiouras, Petros, and Chrysochou, Georgios. "The Aegean Dispute in the Context of Contemporary Judicial Decisions on Maritime Delimitation." *Laws* 3 (2014): 12–49.

Smith, Helena. "Nato 'Terror' Tipoff on Explosives Ship Sailing to Sudan." *Guardian*, June 24, 2003. www.theguardian.com/world/2003/jun/24/alqaida.terrorism. Accessed April 30, 2014.

Toksabay, Ece. "Turkey's Erdoğan calls Israel a 'Terrorist State'." *Reuters*, November 19, 2012. www.reuters.com/article/2012/11/19/us-palestinians-israel-turkey-idUSBRE8AI0FH20121119. Accessed April 30, 2014.

Turkish Ministry of Foreign Affairs. "Background Note on Aegean Disputes," 2014. www.mfa.gov.tr/background-note-on-aegean-disputes.en.mfa. Accessed April 30, 2014.

Uluscçu, Özgecan S., Özba, Birnur, Altıok, Tayfur, and Or, İlhan. "Risk Analysis of the Transit vessel Traffic in the Strait of Istanbul." Laboratory for Port Security at Rutgers University, 2008. http://dimacs.rutgers.edu/port_security_lab/Report%20on%20Risk%20Analysis%20of%20the%20Maritime%20Traffic%20in%20the%20Strait%20of%20Istanbul.pdf. Accessed April 30, 2014.

United Nations. "Convention on the Continental Shelf," 1958. http://legal.un.org/ilc/texts/instruments/english/conventions/8_1_1958_continental_shelf.pdf. Accessed April 30, 2014.

United Nations. "United Nations Convention on the Law of the Seas," 1982. www.un.org/depts/los/convention_agreements/texts/unclos/unclos_e.pdf. Accessed April 30, 2014.

United Nations High Commissioner for Refugees. "Global Trends 2011," 2012. www.unhcr.de/fileadmin/user_upload/dokumente/06_service/zahlen_und_statistik/GlobalTrends_2011.pdf. Accessed April 30, 2014.

United States Geological Survey. "Assessment of Undiscovered Oil and Gas Resources of the Levant Basin Province, Eastern Mediterranean," 2010. http://pubs.usgs.gov/fs/2010/3014/pdf/FS10-3014.pdf. Accessed April 30, 2014.

Wilson, Steve. "Failed 'Terrorist' Attack on Suez Canal Ship." *Telegraph*, September 1, 2013. www.telegraph.co.uk/news/worldnews/africaandindianocean/egypt/10278671/Failed-terrorist-attack-on-Suez-Canal-ship.html. Accessed April 30, 2014.

10

ARCTIC SECURITY

New challenges in a diverse region

Helga Haftendorn

While the Arctic Ocean during the Cold War had been a central theater of bipolar confrontation, today it is an area of peaceful cooperation devoid of acute military threats. In 2008 the five Arctic Ocean states – Canada, Denmark with Greenland and the Faroe Islands, Norway, Russia, and the USA – explicitly reaffirmed their sovereign rights over their Arctic lands and asserted their will to solve conflicts in accordance with the 1982 UN Law of the Sea Convention. This chapter surveys the remaining problems in the area and whether it will be possible to solve them peacefully. In some areas, sea boundaries have not yet been finally delimitated, and thus can provide for tensions. Strong disagreements also exist concerning the use of Arctic marine passages such as the Northern Sea Route along the Siberian coast and the North West Passage through the Canadian Archipelago. As a result of climate change, new challenges have come up in relation to the prospecting of natural resources; besides oil and gas the Arctic holds large deposits of special metals and rare earths. Resource extraction causes deep concerns about a degradation of a largely pristine environment and damages to human and animal habitats. Tensions also exist between the indigenous peoples and prospectors from industrialized countries. A regional governance system centered on the Arctic Council has been put into place but still lacks effectiveness.

The puzzle

In 2007–8 two events served as wake-up calls that brought the Arctic region[1] to the attention of the world. One was Russia's flag-planting demonstration on the ocean floor beneath the North Pole in August 2007 with which Moscow underlined its interest in the Arctic; Russia symbolically staked out its claim to billions of dollars' worth of oil and gas reserves.[2] The second event was a report from the U.S. Geographical Service on estimates of identified or suspected oil and gas reserves in the circumpolar region as totalling more than 90 billion barrels of crude oil (or corresponding gas equivalents, BOE).[3] These two events sent contradictory messages to the public. On the one hand they insinuated a "battle for the Pole" to reap the region's wealth that could lead to military conflict,[4] and on the other they held the promise of rich Arctic natural resources. The latter produced a sense of euphoria about the prospect of an energy boom comparable to the nineteenth-century California gold rush. But the euphoria about easily recoverable Arctic hydrocarbons soon died down when the Arctic states started calculating their returns in view of an adverse Polar climate, deficient logistics, and a lack of substantial financial resources. The concern that Arctic states might be fighting for influence and resources has also abated. They realized that they had more to gain from cooperation and observation of legal rules than from conflict.

Why are the Arctic countries, among them two superpowers who are regional competitors for resources and influence, not engaging in open conflict? So far they have been respecting the existing legal systems such as the UN Law of the Sea Convention (UNCLOS)[5] and have settled their disagreements by negotiation and by striving for compromise solutions. This includes the Russian Federation. There are two explanations for the dichotomy between an expectation of violent conflict due to competition for scarce resources and the existence of a basically peaceful situation in the Arctic region. One is that the Arctic states are realizing that they have more to gain from cooperation than from confrontation. The other answer refers to the tremendous pressure of the impact of climate change that forces them to close ranks to fight the emanating risks.

National strategies of Arctic countries

In contrast to the Antarctic, the Arctic region is not governed by an international treaty. At their meeting in Ilulissat, Greenland, in May 2008 the five Arctic Ocean states explicitly reaffirmed their sovereign rights over their Arctic lands and stated that their interests will not be served by an international treaty.[6] The eight Arctic countries – Finland, Iceland, and Sweden in addition to the five coastal states – are trying to find solutions for the parallel challenges of developing their northern territories and reaping the economic returns from Arctic resources while at the same time working for regional stability. The Arctic Council (AC), created by the eight in 1996, is not a supranational institution but provides a forum where sovereign states can coordinate their Arctic policies; national Arctic strategies are thus decisive.

Climate change confronts the Arctic countries with various challenges. When they developed their Arctic strategies, they responded to different climate effects, diverging geostrategic positions, historical experiences, size and population, economic and military power. At the outset they devised their own national Arctic strategies. These were designed to safeguard their sovereignty and security, and to create positive conditions to exploit the natural resources of the region for the benefit of their economies.[7] A stable environment and harmonizing priorities necessitated additional multilateral strategies parallel to their national concepts.

Among the first countries to devise an Arctic strategy was Norway. Based on a 2004–5 report to the Storting and for the purpose of further developing the northern part of the country, in 2006 the Norwegian Government issued a new High North Strategy.[8] Because of its country's dependence on the Arctic's rich natural resources – in particular fish and hydrocarbons – Norway has long practiced sustainable resource management in the North. The idea is that all human activity, such as fishing, transport, and oil and gas production, must be managed in a way that ecosystems are not harmed. Though the major focus of the High North Strategy has been domestic, its implementation has taken place in the context of the Barents region. In 1993 Norway took the initiative to establish various fora for collaboration in the region.[9] In its strategy document Oslo emphasized that it wants to build friendly relations with Russia and strengthen cooperation with Moscow on various levels. One fruit was the 2010 bilateral treaty on the delimitation of the Barents Sea boundary.

Norway values the work of both the Arctic Council (AC) and the Nordic Council (NC) because it shares a short land and a long sea border with Russia. Because Russia is a member of the Arctic Council, Oslo prefers the AC to the NC. When Norway assumed the chair of the

Arctic Council for the period 2006–8, it announced that during its chairmanship it would give high priority to the sustainable use of the Arctic's natural resources. Norway further wants to make the Arctic a leading region for reducing greenhouse gases.

Besides Norway, one of the most active countries in the region is Canada. It sees itself as an Arctic country par excellence because about 40 percent of Canada's territory is situated north of the Arctic Circle. The provinces Yukon, Northwest Territories, and Nunavut, however, have only a population of about 110,000 inhabitants – of whom 52.8 percent are indigenous people – compared to a population of about 35 million in the rest of Canada. New finds of mineral resources, a rise in Arctic tourism, and a growing concern about Canada's national integrity and security have caused the government of Prime Minister Stephen Harper to emphasize that "Canada has a choice when it comes to defending our sovereignty in the Arctic; either we use it or we lose it."[10] In order to avoid losing it, Canada in the past two decades has been quite active in Arctic affairs. The Canadian government follows a rather self-sufficient Arctic policy, making the region a key priority, but it does not prioritize international over national considerations.

After a lively though mainly academic domestic debate in 2009 the government released "Canada's Northern Strategy: Our North, Our Heritage, Our Future."[11] The document elaborated Canada's priority areas: exercising Arctic sovereignty, promoting social and economic development, protecting the North's environmental heritage, and improving Northern governance so that the Northerners have a greater say in their own destiny. In 2010 a "Statement on Canada's Arctic Foreign Policy" followed.[12] While the first document was directed at the peoples of the North, the second added a foreign policy dimension aimed at creating a favorable international environment. Specifically mentioned is Canada's strategic engagement with its premier partner in the Arctic: the United States. Canada's Minister of Health and the Arctic Council, Leona Aglukkaq, announced that her government's priority was to create conditions for a dynamic economic growth in the North, vibrant communities, and healthy ecosystems. Mrs. Aglukkaq is the first person with an Inuit background to represent one of the member states at the Arctic Council. Her program also involves responsible resource development, accountable and safe Arctic shipping, and the creation of sustainable circumpolar communities.[13]

Denmark's Strategy for the Arctic has been modeled after the Norwegian example of emphasizing cooperation among Northern states and does not follow Canada's emphasis on national sovereignty. A joint Greenlandic–Danish draft was published in May 2008 and served to embed Greenland in Denmark's Arctic Strategy and to clarify its representation in international relations. The final document aimed at positioning the Kingdom of Denmark, including Denmark, Greenland, and the Faroe Islands, as an active player in the Arctic. The government affirmed its commitment to work for "a peaceful, secure and safe Arctic; with sustainable growth and development; with respect for the Arctic's fragile environment and nature; and in close cooperation with our international partners."[14]

Denmark's program emphasized attention to the peoples of the Arctic, mega trends in the region, climate change, biodiversity, integrated resource management, and operational cooperation. From its multilateral orientation, Copenhagen deplored the Arctic Council's limitations and inability to fulfill its mandate as a sustainable Arctic organization. The Danish Government has therefore advocated the enlargement of its agenda and the extension of its mandate. When it invited Canada, Norway, Russia, and the U.S. to a meeting of the Arctic Ocean coastal states at Ilulissat, Greenland – much to the anger of those Council members that were left out – it wanted to overcome the limitations of the AC's mandate and enable the five directly affected countries to agree on an agenda of political recommendations. Insisting on their sovereign rights over their Northern lands, waters, shelves, and their living as well as material resources, in the Ilulissat declaration the five Arctic littoral states pledged to settle any conflicts in accordance with international law, above all the UN Convention on the Law of the Sea.[15]

In September 2008 then-President Dimitri Medvedev signed a new Russian Arctic strategy that should be seen in connection with several other strategy texts: on Russian Maritime Doctrine (2001), Foreign Policy (2008), National Security (2009), and Energy (2010). In these documents Moscow underlined its claim to use the Arctic region as a strategic resource base able to provide solutions for Russia's social and economic problems.[16] Its Arctic strategies should also serve to protect Russia's economic interests in the region. Following up on former Soviet President Mikhail Gorbachev's 1987 Murmansk speech,[17] the region was to be maintained as a zone of peace and cooperation. In contrast to Russia's 2007 flag-planting demonstration and the resulting Western concerns, the Arctic strategy paper was a well-balanced policy statement emphasizing cooperation, not confrontation. The importance of mutually advantageous bilateral and multilateral cooperation was outlined and has commended for this purpose the Arctic Council and the Barents Regional institutions.

After the re-election of President Vladimir Putin in 2012 Moscow intensified its activities in the Arctic. In 2013 the President signed a new version of Russia's Arctic strategy which focused on the development of the Arctic regions of the Russian Federation.[18] Already a few years earlier Russia had resumed patrols of its nuclear submarines in Polar waters and ordered overflights over Norway's and Canada's coastal areas. Russia also accelerated its programs for building a fleet of new nuclear submarines and of nuclear- and diesel-powered large icebreakers. They are to reinforce the interplay of petro-economic interests and the struggle for political-military superiority.[19] Putin's "pet project" was gaining control over the underwater Lomonossov and Mendeleyev ridges in the Arctic Ocean.[20] As these ridges are also linked to the North American land mass, Russia can only succeed with the agreement of its neighbors in the North. Along with domestic and financial constraints, this ambition will put a brake on military sabre-rattling. Moscow has further underlined its resolve to accept UNCLOS as binding law.

Since Secretary of State William H. Seward in 1867 bought Alaska from Tsarist Russia, the United States has also been an Arctic country. In contrast to Canada and Russia, however, the Arctic region has for a long time not been at the centre of U.S. attention. During his very last days as President, George W. Bush signed a fairly uncontroversial Arctic strategy document which has since remained in place. Its top policy goal is meeting national security and homeland security needs relating to the Arctic region.[21] Only when the Arab Spring put into doubt a sustained secure supply of oil from the Gulf region did the Arctic's hydrocarbon resources come under closer U.S. scrutiny. In February 2013 the White House announced a new plan setting priority areas for the next five years of federally sponsored research on and for the Arctic region. With the dramatically falling price of oil and gas, mainly due to the use of new technologies such as fracking, this inflated interest in Polar hydrogens abated. On May 10, 2013 President Barack Obama signed a new Arctic strategy that commits the U.S. to "exercise responsible stewardship … with the aim of promoting healthy, sustainable, and resilient ecosystems over the long term."[22] In preparation for assuming the Arctic Council's chair in May 2015, the Administration also released an Implementation Plan for its Arctic Strategy.[23]

A display of a stronger U.S. political presence in the Polar region is encumbered by the fact that Washington – because of opposition in the U.S. Senate – has not yet ratified the Law of the Sea Convention. Yet the first Obama Administration, and in particular then-Secretary of State Hillary Clinton, has at several instances called for its urgent ratification. The U.S. is also hampered in showing a strong Arctic maritime force. For constabulary and research purposes the U.S. Coast Guard has only one medium icebreaker, the *Healey*; an older one, the *Polar Star*, is being retrofitted. There are plans for constructing – or possibly leasing – a new heavy polar icebreaker, but realization will take time and require substantial funds. While Russia can rely on many and different types of icebreakers for marking its Arctic presence, the U.S. instead has to draw on its large fleet of nuclear submarines. Nevertheless, the U.S. Navy and the Coast Guard have developed operational plans for the Arctic.[24] On the political level the U.S. participates in many bilateral and multilateral fora for promoting its interests in the region. One is the Arctic Council, which Washington values highly but does not wish to see transformed into an international organization or its mandate substantially enlarged.

Less obvious but not less important is the role of the non-coastal Arctic states. Iceland, except for a small island off its north coast, is situated south of the Polar Circle but regards itself as "coastal" in terms of fishery rights, and is included in some of the broader (climatic and societal) definitions of the Arctic. The country faces many of the same challenges as do the Arctic coastal states, but because of its small size it is less self-supporting than they are. Sweden, though the last Northern country to develop an Arctic strategy, has forcefully chaired the Arctic Council in the period 2011–13 and contributed much to strengthening its procedures. The Swedish Arctic Strategy was developed in preparation of its assumption of the chair; it focuses on the far-reaching changes in the Arctic region and the new opportunities provided.[25] Plans included a joint AC communication strategy, an agreement on oil-spill preparedness and response, and consideration of establishing a joint response task force.[26] Finland, squeezed in between its two Scandinavian neighbors to the West and Russia to the East, has lost its access to the Arctic Ocean (in the Petsamo/Petchenga area) as a result of World War II. For historical and geographical reasons the Finnish Government follows a balanced approach between containment and cooperation with Russia.[27]

This short overview over Northern states' Arctic strategies shows that in all countries national and multilateral approaches are closely intertwined though the mixture varies. Sharing common interests in regional stability and protection of the Arctic environment as well as following similar economic and ecologic agendas has, however, drawn the Arctic states closer together. But it has not led to an agreed common vision for the future of the Arctic.

Political disputes among Arctic states

The Arctic is currently a peaceful region in military terms though one should not rule out the possibility of future violent conflicts, e.g. on status and control over the Lomonossov Ridge. Except regarding the status of Hans Island,[28] the most obvious disagreements are on sea borders; there are no territorial disputes on land. A hopeful sign has been the settlement of the long-term dispute between Norway and Russia on their maritime boundary in the Barents Sea in 2010 after 40 years of negotiations. The Norwegian–Russian border treaty was quickly ratified by both the Russian Duma and the Norwegian Storting.[29] In another case, the U.S. and the Soviet Union back in 1990 had reached an agreement on their Bering Sea border, settling on a compromise between a median and a sector line; but Russia refused to submit it to the Duma for ratification.[30] It sticks to the position that Russia no longer need feel bound to the agreement signed by former Soviet Foreign Minister Edvard Shevardnadze. Moreover, it claims that Russia's boundaries have essentially been determined by a decree of April 15, 1926 in which the Soviet Union claimed all lands and islands in an Arctic Ocean sector between 32° 34' and 168° 4' west. Still, as long as there are no new hydrocarbon finds in the Bering region, the issue is neither on Washington's nor Moscow's political screen.

In the Beaufort Sea Canada and the U.S. disagree over the extension of the maritime boundary between Alaska and Yukon through their EEZs; at the core of the disagreement are the rights over a triangular-shaped area of about 6.250 nm². Canada takes the position that this boundary had been settled in an 1825 Convention between Great Britain and Tsarist Russia that defined the border line between Alaska and Yukon as following the 141° W meridian "as far as the frozen ocean."[31] The U.S., however, argues that no maritime border has yet been legally defined; if it were set, according to UNCLOS it should follow the median line between the two coastlines – which would give to the U.S. at Canada's expense a large area with potentially rich natural resources. Because of the close and friendly relations between both countries, Ottawa and Washington will eventually find a compromise solution. Since 2010 Canadian and U.S. scientists have jointly mapped the sea floor. Their governments consider making a joint submission under UNCLOS regulations to the Commission on the Limits of Continental Shelf (CLCS) – though to be a party to such a submission, the U.S. first would have to accede to the UN Convention.

Much more concrete are two other disagreements. One concerns the Svalbard Archipelago and the interpretation of the 1920 Spitsbergen/Svalbard Treaty. This agreement prohibits any use of the island for warlike purposes and guarantees an equal treatment of their nationals and ships in regard to fishing, hunting, and other commercial activities on land and in the territorial waters (4 nm in 1920, currently 12 nm) to all parties. Controversial is whether Svalbord sits on the Norwegian coastal shelf – as Norway claims – or has a shelf of its own. According to its interpretation, Oslo denies that the treaty's privileges apply to the areas beyond the territorial waters of Svalbord, over which Norway claims full jurisdiction.[32] This view is contested by Russia and a number of other states who demand access to the archipelago's living and material resources. This conflict could become more acute if new deposits of oil and gas or valuable minerals were discovered in the area.

A greater potential for serious conflict is Russia's claim to the Lomonossov Ridge as part of its extended coastal shelf. Based on available public evidence, it is quite likely that the CLCS will recognize this mid-ocean ridge as the common shelf of Russia, Canada, and Danish Greenland and call on all three countries to negotiate for an equitable solution. For their preparation Canada and Denmark are closely cooperating and jointly mapping the sea floor; in 2014 both countries submitted provisional requests to the CLCS for judgement. As Moscow's dramatic 2007 flag-planting demonstration at the North Pole indicates, its claim to the Lomonossov Ridge and the North Pole are matters of Russian national prestige; a negative outcome could aggravate tensions among the Arctic Ocean coastal states.

Russia has since embarked on a number of submarine missions for further data collection; most remarkably in September 2012 with a deep-sea expedition down to 3,000 meters at the Mendeleyev Ridge with its new and top-secret titanium nuclear submarine *Losharik* to collect materials for proving its claim to the Arctic Ocean ridges.

Though until now Russia has strictly observed the UNCLOS convention and considers it to be to the best of its national interests, many observers fear that Moscow's underpinning of its great power ambitions with intensified military activities may contribute to a new arms race in the Arctic.[33] Another source of anxiety is the high concentration of nuclear-powered ships and the huge amount of nuclear debris resting in the region. Approximately 100 decommissioned nuclear submarines are moored or have been sunk in the Barents Sea. Some still have their nuclear fuel on board, posing a deadly risk to the population of the area. All along the coast (and in the country itself) legacies of Soviet military activity are threatening the environment. For about ten years, Norway together with a number of other nations has cooperated with Russia on reducing the risks of nuclear contamination in the Northwest and helped with the disposal of the huge amounts of nuclear waste and scrap on the Kola Peninsula.

Russian sabre-rattling has raised concerns and stimulated corresponding actions in several countries. For example, Canadian PM Harper has announced plans to develop his country's military presence in the Arctic to reassert Canadian sovereignty in the High North, though this announcement was also intended for domestic purposes.[34] Norway has also enhanced the presence of its armed forces in northern Norway and intensified maritime surveillance. It has moved its military headquarters from the Stavanger area to Reitan outside of Bodø. Oslo is further investing in the construction of new ice-strengthened frigates and offshore patrol vessels.[35] In 2009 the Danish Folketing, too, approved a new defense program for the period 2010–14 which staked out guidelines for Denmark's security in the Arctic and its plans to increase its military activities.[36] A joint Arctic command comprising both the Faroes and Greenland has been formed and a mobile Arctic intervention force discussed. For strengthening aerial and maritime policing, navy and air force will get new capabilities including Arctic-capable helicopters and ice-resistant patrol boats. But Denmark and Norway wish to avoid any militarization of the Arctic and seek to balance defense awareness and increased cooperation with Russia on various levels.[37]

Another international issue for which a permanent solution has yet to be found is the right of passage through the Arctic straits. According to UNCLOS each state has the right of innocent passage through international straits as defined in Articles 17–26. The problem is how to define in concrete terms an international strait. Canada and Russia have drawn straight borderlines around their territorial waters in a way that includes all major islands; they consider Arctic passages such as the Northwest Passage (NWP) and the Northern Seaway (NSW) as internal waterways, and they request advance travel authorization for other nations' ships. But most other countries insist that these straits are international waters. In view of the closeness of Canadian–American relations, Ottawa has agreed to presume that permission for passage has been granted to U.S. research icebreakers, though Canada continues to hold on to its former legal interpretation. But this "agreement to disagree" does not extend to other kinds of vessels or those of other nations. With the melting of Arctic sea ice and the opening up of the seaways, Canada's position will certainly be challenged by other nations as well. Some experts have proposed setting up a multilateral straits management authority for navigation in the Arctic passages (comparable to that on the St. Lawrence Waterway). This suggestion has, however, been opposed by the Canadian Government.

Russia's drawing of straight borderlines around its large Siberian peninsulas and islands is even more debatable. In practice it is respected by most shipping nations. Skippers, however, complain about bureaucratic and time-consuming authorization procedures, high fees, and mandatory ice-breaker escort. In September 2011 the Russian Duma approved new legislation with detailed and somewhat modified rules for passage through the NSW. Neither Canada nor Russia distinguishes between traffic to local destinations and transit traffic. Arctic navigation would be much facilitated if an international agreement was reached that respected Arctic Ocean states' legal positions but provided pragmatic rules for innocent passage. With receding ice cover, the Northern Seaway along the Siberian Coast will more and more enable access to resource sites and facilitate the shipping of the Arctic's resources to customers in Asia and Europe – at least during the summer months from mid-July to mid-September – though existing facilities need to be upgraded.

NATO has no formal role in the Arctic, due to Canadian opposition.[38] For military action it has to rely on its members' forces. Its military potential is very limited; the only NATO-owned military asset is its fleet of Airborne Warning and Control System planes (AWACS) based at Geilenkirchen, Germany. Air surveillance patrols over Iceland and the Baltic states are organized by NATO but performed by member states on a rotational basis. If need arises, the alliance can field additional aircraft tasked for a reconnaissance role from the USA, the U.K., Norway, and Denmark. Though NATO has no active role in the Arctic region, because of U.S. membership the alliance is nevertheless seen as the most credible element of reassurance. For some years there has been widespread cooperation of navies and coast and border guards among Arctic states. As a reaction to Russia's annexation of the Crimean Peninsula and its meddling in the Ukrainian conflict, in the spring of 2015 Canada and Norway cancelled all joint military exercises.

However, new Arctic military challenges will be different from those during the Cold War; they will stem from fundamentally changed interests and ambitions.[39] According to Norway's former Chief of Defense, General Sverre Diesen, they might arise from greater accessibility to raw materials and the opening of new lines of communication; other sources might be strategic competition, miscalculation, or an accident caused by military forces. To meet these potential risks the Arctic states need non-military competences suitable to cope with them. Hard capabilities are also essential for power projection, strategic deterrence, and marking presence. Maritime security relies on aerial and naval reconnaissance, satellite communications, strategic lift, and defense support, and search-and-rescue missions. Soft capabilities should help countries to address climate change, disaster response, and humanitarian assistance. When national actions replace joint activities, the Arctic states need capabilities to coordinate their policies and bundle their potentials.

Another gold rush? New finds of oil and gas deposits

When in the spring of 2008 the news spread that north of the Polar Circle large deposits of oil, gas, and special metals existed and could be exploited with existing technologies, this changed the world's political geography. The question surfaced of who will be extracting the more than 50 billion barrels of crude oil or its equivalents in gas (barrels of oil equivalents, BOEs). The UNCLOS Treaty was not very specific on this issue; it gave the littoral states a right to extend their EEZs to 200 nm and even further if they could prove that their coastal shelves extended that far out into the ocean and if the CLCS concurred. At a few places the coastal shelves overlap and require negotiation between competitors. The Arctic nations are concerned that if a state happens to come first, it could control the resources in not-yet-delimited areas. Thus the five Arctic Ocean coastal states in the Ilulissat declaration laid claim to all living and material resources on their coastal shelves and the adjoining sea. Russia's submarine mission to the North Pole and the placement of its flag in the summer of 2007, thus marking its claims, had set the alarm clocks ringing.

Climate change has made the area more accessible for prospectors and developers of its rich resources that for centuries were hidden under a thick blanket of seemingly eternal ice. On the Arctic Ocean's coastal shelves large deposits of oil and gas have been prospected. In North America oil and gas drilling has so far focused on Alaska's North Slope, Prudhoe Bay, and the (Canadian) Mackenzie Delta. Oil has been drilled in Alaska since 1896. The Prudhoe Bay field is the largest oil field so far discovered in North America. Its oil is transported through the 800-mile-long Trans-Alaska Pipeline to Valdez, where it is shipped to consumers in the south. Because of concern about oil spills and a degradation of the very fragile Arctic environment the exploration of new sites – especially in the area of the Arctic National Wildlife Refuge (ANWR) – is heavily resisted by conservationists and local people. Much to their discontent, U.S. Interior Secretary Ken Salazar in December 2012 has announced plans to allow oil and gas drilling in the National Petroleum Reserve on Alaska's North Slope.[40] Large hydrocarbon deposits are suspected in the Beaufort Sea area, though before they can be exploited on a large scale, an American–Canadian sea border agreement has to be reached.

In contrast to Greenland's western sea basin that has so far not yielded any commercially exploitable returns, the Barents Sea has turned out to be a treasure trove for new gas and oil discoveries.[41] The Norwegian part of the Barents Sea holds rich deposits of oil and gas. So far Snøhvit is the most developed field; it came on stream in 2007. The gas from Snøhvit is transported by pipeline to Melkøya and further processed and liquefied to LNG, which is transported by special tankers to markets. In 2012 a set of new deposits was discovered north of the Snøhvit field. The discoveries of Skurgård and Havis have been estimated at between 400 million and 600 million BOE. The Goliat field further to the east is also being developed, with production starting late in 2014/15.

Since the ratification of the Norwegian–Russian treaty on their Barents Sea border,[42] oil and gas exploitation in the Barents Sea has surged. The formerly disputed area holds several promising prospects including Centralnoye and Severo Kildinsky just east of the mid-line. A third gas discovery further east, Shtokman, was first announced in 1989 and promised to be one of the largest gas fields in the world; but because of high investment costs its exploitation was put on hold. Very large discoveries have also been made in the Kara Sea further east. In another region of the Russian North, in the Tilman-Pechora Basin of Siberia, large deposits were discovered, also at the north margin of the West Siberian Basin and on the Laptev Sea Shelf. The development of these resources has been, however, very slow due to the daunting costs of developing the technologies and the extensive infrastructure required.[43] Russia's Siberian deposits contain sufficient oil and natural gas to supply about 70 percent of the oil and 90 percent of the gas production needed for Russia.[44]

Other Arctic riches: special metals and rare earths

Besides hydrocarbons the Arctic region holds many of the richest deposits of mineral resources such as in various kinds of special metals and rare earths, though their profitability varies. The latter are essential for "green industries" but are scarce and costly; industries will thus take an extra effort to exploit them even in an inhospitable climate. North American deposits are well researched; copper, gold, lead, and zinc are extracted. In limited quantities titanium and diamonds are found. The value of resources in Alaska in the period 1995–2000 has amounted to more than 1 billion U.S. dollars annually.[45]

Greenland is also considered very rich in natural resources. At the beginning of this century the extraction of copper, lead, tin, and gold was temporarily suspended; in view of their high costs extraction was not considered profitable. Next to China, Greenland has the largest deposits of rare earths. In southern Greenland the Kvanefjeld mine is well known for its prolific resources of rare earth elements, uranium, and zinc. Most are, however, blended with uranium oxide, the extraction of which had been outlawed by the Greenland authorities. After self-government in 2010, in order to regain control over their resource development, the authorities bought back licences from the Australian enterprise that had planned its mining.

The Greenland parliamentary election in 2013 brought the country's resource problem to the fore. Should this resource-rich country prioritize earnings from extraction and export of special metals and rare earths, or should it try to prevent any acts by which their pristine habitat could be degraded and traditional community life disrupted? While the previous left-leaning Inuit Ataqatigit Party had supported careful resource exploitation with, however, zero-tolerance for uranium mining and selling, the incoming social democrat Siumut Party wants to use the island's mineral resources more extensively. It wishes to develop Greenland's mining industry in order to reduce its dependency on subsidies from Denmark, even if this requires shelving the ban on uranium mining.

Since 2011 gold has been mined at Nalunaq in southern Greenland and shipped from the close-by harbour of Nanortalik. Its special feature is that the crude gold is processed in a subterranean mine using local kyanite (aluminium silicate) in order to minimize damage to the environment. The operator of the mine plans an annual production of about 24,000 ounces of pure gold. The commercial exploitation of extractable mineral resources such as gold, lead, zinc and of industrial minerals such as feldspar, kryolit, magnetite, and quartz in west and north Greenland is, however, hampered by difficult climatic conditions, the lack of an efficient infrastructure, and the tough preconditions for granting extraction licenses in order to circumscribe damages to the very sensitive Arctic habitat.

In contrast to the conditions in Greenland and in the Canadian Arctic, in Scandinavia mining companies can draw on a well-developed infrastructure. The rich iron ore deposits in Bjørnevatn in Finmark, north Norway, are transported by the firm's railway to the ice-free harbor of Kirkenes. Quartz, feldspar, and nepheline are also mined. Several occurrences of aluminum, gold, copper, platinum, titanium, and zirconium have been prospected; they are studied to find out whether they will merit commercial mining. In Mosjøn, close to Mo i Rana in Norland, unwrought aluminum is extracted and processed by the U.S. multi Alcoa.

The Swedish deposits of iron, copper, and other metals are also substantial. Especially rich finds of iron oxide, copper, and gold are extracted in Norbotten, the Kiruna region, in Malmberget, Altik, Lakselv, and Rönnskär, and additionally in the Finnish Kolari district. There is also substantial extraction and smelting of zinc, copper, lead, as well as gold and silver. From Kiruna, the products are shipped by rail to the ice-free Norwegian port of Narvik and from there to consumers in the south.

Iceland has few extractable mineral resources. Its most important resource is hot thermal water, which is used at many places by industry. Iceland's oldest aluminum plant is in Straumsvik, on the Reykjavik–Keflavik highway, and produces annually about 189,000 tonnes of aluminum. On the Arkanes Peninsula is another big aluminum plant that has a capacity of about 260,000 mtpy (metric tonnes per year). Still bigger at 346,000 mtpy is the output of Fjarðaál Aluminium Works in eastern Iceland that operates together with a hydroelectric power station in Káranjúkar. Because of the rich supply of geothermal power these plants can be operated profitably – though not sustainably, as the raw material has to be imported and the end product transported to its customers abroad. Iceland's aluminum plants are therefore conveniently situated at ice-free fjords and have their own loading facilities. The construction of an additional aluminum plant at Bakki, close to Husavik in northern Iceland, has been shelved because of the government's serious environmental concerns; it has also not approved the recruitment of Chinese workers. Without cheap labor, the management fears that the plant cannot be operated profitably and has therefore suspended the project.

The Arctic regions of Russia also hold large deposits of mineral resources, above all cobalt, nickel, lead, tin, zinc, mercury, and uranium, most of which are already processed. The geomorphological structure of the Kola Peninsula is very conducive for a variety of rare earths. Among the other minerals that also abound in this region are titanium sodium silicates; also carbonates, oxides, and phosphates. Most remarkable are the unusually high concentrates of titanium, zirconium, phosphors, manganese, strontium, zinc, lead, barium, and uranium to be found. The industrial development of the Kola Peninsula started in the 1930s; it was intensified in the Stalin period. In the 1960s so-called "mono cities" were built. These are settlements that were built directly on top of or very near to the mines and the smelters. A haunting example is the town of Nickel on the Murmansk–Kirkenes road. The exhausts of the nickel smelter cover the prefabricated apartment buildings and their inhabitants, the roads, and the countryside with a thick grey layer. Criticism is repudiated with the argument that Western "environmental hooey" was used to hurt the Russian economy.

Prospecting in all Arctic regions is hindered by the long polar nights' darkness, the exhausting cold and stormy weather, and the distance from processing sites. Transportation is seriously hampered by the lack of an effective infrastructure. In many parts of the Arctic region there are hardly any railroads and few overland highways. Only a small number of deep-water harbors and few modern airports exist. Special risk factors in Arctic waters are ice flows. Any large-scale extraction of natural resources will thus take time and a careful calculation of costs and benefits. It will depend on an evaluation of world market prices, before any commercial extraction and processing of the Arctic's resources can be considered profitable.

The evolution of the Arctic Council

Safeguarding of the environment is important for all Arctic states – now even for Putin's Russia.[46] In the last two decades the Arctic countries have strengthened cooperation on protecting their fragile habitats. At the invitation of the Finnish Government, in 1989 officials from the eight Arctic countries, including the Soviet Union, gathered in Rovaniemi to discuss cooperative actions for protecting the Arctic environment. Gorbachev's Murmansk speech, in which he called for improved cooperation in the region, had set the tone.[47] Two years later the eight nations adopted an Arctic Environmental Protection Strategy (AEPS) and a joint action plan. The strategy concentrates on cooperation in scientific research, sharing of data about pollution, and assessing the environmental impact of economic development.[48] The AEPS was unique in bridging the Cold War divide and including representatives from the Arctic region's indigenous peoples in the operation of the strategy. One of its major objectives has been recognizing and, to the extent possible, seeking accommodation of traditional and cultural needs, values, and practices of Arctic indigenous peoples as determined by them.

From the AEPS a more comprehensive institution evolved: the Arctic Council (AC). On a Canadian initiative, the Council was established in 1996 with a resolution adopted by the officials of the eight Arctic states – i.e. not in the form of a treaty. In the Ottawa Declaration the eight set up a high-level intergovernmental forum to address various kinds of Arctic challenges, recognizing among other things that these demanded scientific answers to help policy-makers devise appropriate solutions.[49] For this purpose five working groups were set up for dealing with an Arctic monitoring and assessment program (AMAP), conservation of Arctic flora and fauna (CAFF), emergency prevention, preparedness, and response (EPPR), protection of the Arctic marine environment (PAME), and sustainable development (SDWG). Most important was the *Report on Impacts of a Warming Arctic: Arctic Climate Impact Assessment* (2004) which provided a benchmark for their environmental protection strategies.[50] For specific issues the AC also set up specialized task forces. In these groups scientific expertise is developed which the members then translate into non-binding resolutions, recommendations, and/or treaties.

In 2011 the AC member states concluded the first internationally binding treaty – the Agreement on Cooperation on Aeronautical and Maritime Search and Rescue.[51] Several recent accidents in the Arctic had underlined the urgency of building effective emergency management systems. In the case of an aircraft crash near Resolute in 2011, survivors were helped by hundreds of military personnel that were already in the region taking part in Operation Nanook, the Canadian military's annual northern training exercise. When the Canadian clipper *Adventurer* struck an uncharted rock in the waters of western Nunavut, however, the CCG icebreaker *Amundsen* had to travel 500 miles over two days to start rescue operations. Passengers were only saved because of good weather and calm seas.[52]

To protect the delicate Arctic environment against the negative effects of shipping, in 2013 the AC member states also reached consensus on the prevention of marine oil pollution.[53] At the Kiruna Ministerial meeting in May 2013 an agreement on Cooperation on Marine Oil Pollution Preparedness was adopted.[54] It has also been suggested that the Arctic states should agree on linking resource extraction to ecological standards.

In a slow evolutionary process the AC took up several other issues relevant to the region. Arctic states value knowledge and science as "currencies of influence."[55] The University of the Arctic (UA) serves as a focal point to link Arctic scientific research centers and teaching institutions across the region; the International Arctic Science Committee (IASSA) provides a supranational scientific hub. At the political level, it has been proposed that AC members should endorse a common vision on the future of the Arctic that could facilitate future agreements. A joint perspective on the Polar region and its problems might take the form of an Agreement on Basic Principles, a device that in the past has been used to bridge the East–West divide for joint action on arms control arrangements.

Today, the Arctic Council is the very lynchpin of Arctic governance. There are several reasons why it has become such a relevant institution. Besides the Western Arctic states, the AC includes Russia, which still remembered as an aggressive power, "even more so after its annexation of Crimea." Further, it brings together representatives from the eight member countries with delegates of the indigenous peoples' groups and of a number of interested non-Arctic states and organizations as observers. Its main function has been to ensure an effective implementation of the Arctic Environmental Protection Strategy, though it has taken up other issues as well. But the AC remains a decision-preparing rather than a decision-taking institution.[56] The signing of the S&R Treaty has, however, stimulated hopes that the AC could become a platform for negotiating additional legally binding agreements on Arctic issues.

In order to strengthen the AC, the Senior Arctic Officials (SAO) have recommended several measures that were approved by the Ministers at their 2011 Nuuk meeting – such as the establishment of a permanent AC secretariat in Tromsø, the approval of a joint communication strategy, and an agreement on criteria for the role and admission of observers.[57] The new secretariat is funded by a common budget of up to $US 1 million to which each member and observer state contributes. Hitherto all expenses had been covered according to the principle that costs lie where they fall, and by voluntary contributions from member and observer countries. The Canadian chair (2012–14) was instructed to prioritize the search for more secure funding of AC activities. It was hoped that a data bank for storing the results of the AC's scientific programs could also be build. To make the Arctic voice heard in the world, in May 2012 the AC adopted an Arctic Communication Strategy.[58] These steps have reinforced Arctic governance structures without circumscribing members' sovereignty.

When Sweden took over the chair in May 2011, Foreign Minister Carl Bildt outlined several key areas for further work of the Arctic Council. First, the AC should not only analyze challenges but also do something about them. Bildt referred to a very common reaction of Arctic countries: outlining a problem, urging resolution, and then camouflaging their disagreement by creating new institutions or by delegating the problem to a subgroup for further study. He also advocated making mandatory the "Polar Code" for navigation in Arctic waters.[59] Second, the AC should improve communication, e.g. telling the public of the important work that is going on in the Council and its working groups. The Arctic voice should be heard in the world. With the adoption of an AC Communication Strategy in May 2012 it has created a suitable instrument. However, the AC shies away from establishing formal links with other institutions or forming an "Arctic Caucus" within them. Bildt's third focus was on the human dimension. In order to be legitimate, the AC must achieve sustainable development for the people living in the region.[60] There is still a long way to go in this matter, especially in relation to indigenous peoples' livelihood and their participation in common Arctic affairs. In 2014, an updated version of the Arctic Human Development Report II was published.[61]

It has often been asked whether the AC should not take on a more active role in the emerging security environment of the Arctic. A tentative effort in this direction was the meeting of the Arctic states' chiefs of defense in 2012. The AC could also serve as a hub for networks of inter-/multinational agreements, institutions, and organizations in the region and coordinate the whole gamut of circumpolar activities with security relevance, such as implied when the S&R and emergency response protocols were negotiated.[62] So far it has been quite difficult to convince members that the AC should also deal with hard security issues, even if many military issues are closely linked to economic and ecological matters. Some Arctic states have been very reserved, usually for domestic and other non-security reasons, about any new and overt NATO involvement in the region.[63] Apprehension about including security in the Arctic agenda has often been fed by a fear that this could – perhaps involuntarily – contribute to making military issues more important. If the AC wants to avoid a militarization of the Polar region, however, it should seek to adopt confidence-building measures and look at improved information exchange about military matters such as deployments and exercises. The Council should also devise arms control activities that will enhance regional stability.

Conclusions

The Arctic is a region subject to rapid change which involves a broad set of interacting developments difficult to control: political, economic, and ecological. Climate change has made the region more amenable to human habitation, more accessible for resource extraction, and more open for destination and transit traffic in the Arctic Ocean and the Polar passages. New species of animals and plants are showing up, while the survival of others is threatened. With melting glaciers, a receding ice cover, and increasing human penetration risks have multiplied that a pristine land is irreversibly degraded and much of the original habitat destroyed. Though there are efforts and strategies to arrest this fateful development, the national strategies and multilateral conventions so far adopted are inadequate; the Arctic Council still lacks competences for serving as an efficient governing institution.

Why then are the Arctic countries, among them two superpowers that are regional competitors for resources and influence, not engaging in open conflict? So far all states have respected the existing legal systems such as UNCLOS, IMO, and various other conventions. They have settled their disagreements by negotiation and by striving for compromise solutions. The region's environmental challenges can only be controlled and the preservation of a sustainable human habitat safeguarded by joint or at least coordinated multinational efforts. The remarkably cooperative Russian approach to a large degree results from its leadership's awareness that the country needs international partners for both the development and the exploitation of its rich natural resources, and for the removal of the military debris and the rotting nuclear submarines of the late Soviet Union in the Barents Sea. While the U.S. and Canada assume that they can cope nationally with most of the Arctic challenges, the smaller Nordic states and Finland prefer multilateral approaches. For Arctic countries big and small, the AC has served as a clearing house and as a confidence-building framework as well. The Arctic states in general see more gains in cooperation than they do in confrontation.

This analysis provides an answer to the puzzle why in the absence of effective governance and in spite of the Arctic countries' competition for resources and influence the result has not been anarchy and open conflict. The explanation is that the Arctic states instead prefer adherence to the legal stipulations of UNCLOS, and the settling of their disagreements by negotiation. The Arctic states have realized that they can gain more from cooperation than from confrontation. The Ukrainian crisis has thus left only a fairly small dent in this network of cooperation. The tremendous pressure of climate change and its impact force them to close ranks and jointly fight the challenges of a changing macroclimate. In the foreseeable future no violent conflicts are very likely because Arctic states will continue to feel bound by the Law of the Sea Convention and the regulations they have agreed upon in the Arctic Council. They will continue to cooperate in fighting the risks of climate change. As a result, no Arctic war is currently lingering on the horizon.

Acknowledgments

I wish to thank the Fritz-Thyssen-Stiftung, Cologne, for financial support for Arctic travel; it provided me with a first-hand view of the beauty and the problems of the Arctic region. Further thanks go to Alyson Bailes and her colleagues at the University of Iceland in Reykjavik for providing a stimulating environment for discussing Arctic issues.

Notes

1 The Arctic is defined as the region north of the Arctic Circle at 66° 33′. Other definitions delineate the Arctic as the area north of the 10° C isotherm for July.
2 Tom Parfitt, "Russia plants flag on North Pole seabed," *Guardian*, August 2, 2007, www.guardian.co.uk/world/2007/aug/02/russia.arctic, accessed August 28, 2015.
3 Kenneth J. Bird, Ronald R. Charpentier, Donald L. Gautier *et. al.*, "Circum-Arctic Resource Appraisal: Estimates of Undiscovered Oil and Gas North of the Arctic Circle," U.S. Geological Survey Fact Sheet 2008-3049, Version 1.0, July 23, 2008, http://pubs.usgs.gov/fs/2008/3049/…, accessed August 28, 2015.
4 Scott Borgerson, "Arctic Meltdown: The Economic and Security Implications of Global Warming." *Foreign Affairs* 87, 2 (March/April 2008), pp. 63–77; Margaret Blunden, "The New Problem of Arctic Stability." *Survival* 51, 5 (October/November 2009), pp. 121–42.
5 United Nations, Declarations and Statements Regarding the Convention on the Law of the Sea, www.un.org/Depts/los/convention_agreements/convention_declarations/Russian%20Federation%20Upon%20signature, accessed August 28, 2015.
6 The Ilulissat Declaration, Arctic Ocean Conference, Ilulissat, Greenland, May 27–29, 2008, www.oceanlaw.org/downloads/arctic/Ilulissat_Declaration.pdf, accessed August 28, 2015.
7 Alyson J. K. Bailes and Lassi Heininen, *Strategy Papers on the Arctic or High North: A Comparative Study and Analysis*. Reykjavik: Institute of International Affairs, University of Iceland, 2012; Lassi Heininen, "The State of Arctic Strategies and Policies – A Summary." In Lassi Heininen (ed.), *Arctic Yearbook 2012*. Akureyri: Northern Research Forum and University of the Arctic, 2012, pp. 2–46.
8 *Opportunities and Challenges in the North: Report No. 30 (2004–2005) to the Storting*, ed. Norwegian Ministry of Foreign Affairs, 2005; Norwegian Ministry of Foreign Affairs, *The Norwegian Government's High North Strategy, 2006*, www.regjeringen.no/upload/UD/Vedlegg/strategien.pdf, accessed August 28, 2015; the 2009 follow-up document mainly focused on the socio-economic development of the North: *New Building Blocs in the North: The Next Steps in the Government's High North Strategy, 2009*, www.regjeringen.no/upload/UD/Vedlegg/Nordområdene/new_building_blocks_in_the_north.pdf, accessed August 28, 2015. Oslo uses the term "High North" to describe policies directed at the Norwegian North, Bear Island and the Svalbard Archipelago, and the Barents region.
9 BEAC members are Norway, Denmark, Finland, Iceland, Russia, and Sweden (plus observers and a representative from the EU Commission); it meets at Foreign Minister level and works on a number of projects benefiting the peoples of the Barents region; www.beac.st/in_English/Barents_Euro-Arctic_Council.iw3, accessed August 28, 2015.
10 "PM Harper on Arctic: 'Use it or lose it'," *Times Colonist* (Victoria), July 10, 2007, www.canada.com/topics/news/story.html?id=7ca93d97-3b26-4dd1-8d92-8568f9b7cc2a, accessed August 28, 2015.

11 Canadian International Council, *Foreign Policy for Canada's Tomorrow*, nos. 1, 3, and 4, July 2009, www. canadianinternationalcoiuncil.org, accessed August 28, 2015.

12 Department of National Defence, *Canada First Defence Strategy*, May 2008, www.forces.gc.ca/site/ pri/first-premier/June18_0910_CFDS_english_low-res.pdf, accessed August 28, 2015; Department of Foreign Affairs and International Trade, Canada, *The Northern Dimension of Canada's Foreign Policy*, 2008, www.international.gc.ca/polar-polaire/ndfp-vnpe2.aspx?view=d, accessed August 28, 2015; Minister of Indian Affairs and Northern Development and Federal Interlocutor for Métis and Non-Status Indians, *Canada's Northern Strategy. Our North, Our Heritage, Our Future*, 2009, www. northernstrategy.ca, accessed August 28, 2015; Government of Canada, *Statement on Canada's Arctic Foreign Policy: Exercising Sovereignty and Promoting Canada's Northern Strategy Abroad*, www.international. gc.ca/arctic-arctique/assets/pdfs/canada_arctic_foreign_policy-eng.pdf, accessed August 28, 2015; "Statement on Canada's Arctic Policy," August 20, 2010, www.international.gc.ca/polar-polaire/assets/ pdfs/CAFP_booklet-PECA_livret-eng.pdf, accessed August 28, 2015.

13 "Canada's Second Chairmanship of the Arctic Council," Address by Minister Leona Aglukkaq at Arctic Frontiers Conference, January 21, 2013, Tromsø, Norway, www.international.gc.ca/ media/arctic-arctique/speeches-discours/2013/01/23a.aspx?lang=eng&view=d, accessed August 28, 2015.

14 Danish Ministry of Foreign Affairs, *Arktis i en brydningstid. Forslag til strategi for aktiviteter i det arktiske område* (The Arctic at a time of change. Proposals for a strategy for Arctic activities), May 2008. http://arcticportal.org/images/stories/pdf/DANSK_ARKTISK_STRATEGI.pdf, accessed August 28, 2015; Kingdom of Denmark, *Strategy for the Arctic 2011–2020*, 2011, http://um.dk/en/~/media/ UM/English-site/Documents/Politics-and-diplomacy/Greenland-and-The-Faroe-Islands/Arctic%20 strategy.pdf, accessed August 28, 2015.

15 Ilulissat Declaration.

16 Russian Federation, *The Foundations of the Russian Federation Policy in the Arctic until 2020 and Beyond*, September 18, 2008, www.securityaffairs.org/issues/2010/18/russia%27s_new_arctic_strategy.pdf, accessed August 28, 2015; see also Katarzyna Zysk, "Russia's Arctic Strategy." *JFQ* 57 (2nd Quarter 2010), pp. 103–10, www.ndu.edu/press/lib/images/jfq-57/zysk.pdf, accessed August 28, 2015.

17 "Gorbachev Calls for Peace, Cooperation in the Arctic," AP News Archive, October 1 1987, www. apnewsarchive.com/1987/Gorbachev-Calls-For-Peace-Cooperation-in-Arctic/id-…, accessed August 28, 2015.

18 "Russian Strategy of the Development of the Arctic Zone and the Provision of National Security until 2020." In Lassi Heininen (ed.), *ArcticYearbook 2013*. Akureyri: Northern Research Forum and University of the Arctic, 2013, www.arcticyearbook.com/index.php/commentaries-2013/74-russian-strategy-of-the-development-of-the-arctic-zone-and-the-provision-of-national-security-until-2020-adopted-by-the-president-of-the-russian-federation-on-february-8-2013-pr-232.

19 "Russia Launches Program on Arctic Development to 2020," *Barents Observer*, February 2013, http:// barentsobserver.com/en/arctic/2013/02/russia-launches-pro…, accessed August 28, 2015.

20 In a 2001 submission to the CLCS, Russia requested the recognition of large areas in the Arctic Ocean, extending to the North Pole, the Lomonossow and the Mendelevich Ridge, as extensions of the Russian coastal shelf and EEZ. This demand was turned down by the CLCS; it requested further documentation to prove Moscow's claims.

21 "National Security Presidential Directive and Homeland Security Presidential Directive," No. 66, January 9, 2009, www.fas.org/irp/offdocs/nspd/nspd-66.htm, accessed August 28, 2015.

22 The President of the United States, "National Strategy for the Arctic Region, May 2013," www.white-house.gov/sites/default/files/docs/nat_arctic_strategy.pdf, accessed August 28, 2015.

23 U.S. Government, "Implementation Plan for the National Strategy for the Arctic Region, January 2014," www.whitehouse.gov/sites/default/files/docs/implementation_plan_for_the_national_stratgy_ for_the…, accessed August 28, 2015.

24 U.S. Navy Arctic Roadmap, 2009, www.navy.mil/navydata/documents/USN_artic_roadmap.pdf; U.S. Department of Defence, *Report to Congress on Arctic Operations and the Northwest Passage*. Washington, DC: Department of Defense. May 2011, www.defense.gov/pubs/pdfs/Tab_A_Arctic_Report_Public. pdf, accessed August 28, 2015.

25 *Sweden's Strategy for the Arctic Region*, www.government.se/content/1/c6/16/78/59/3baa039d.pdf, accessed August 28, 2015; Sweden's Chairmanship Programme for the Arctic Council 2011–2013, www.government.se/content/1/c6/16/79/98/537a42bf.pdf, accessed August 28, 2015; "Arctic Challenges and the Future Perspectives of Arctic Cooperation," Speech by Carl Bildt, Swedish Minister

of Foreign Affairs, at Carlton University, May 17, 2012, www.government.se/sb/d/15783/a/193302, accessed August 28, 2015.

26 Arctic Council Task Force on Arctic Marine Pollution Preparedness and Response, www.arctic-council. org/index.php/en/about-us/task-forces/280-oil-spill-task-force, accessed August 28, 2015.

27 Government of Finland, Government Resolution, "Russia Action Plan," April 16, 2009; formin. finland.fi/public/download.aspx?ID=42535&GUID..., accessed August 28, 2015; see also *Finland's Strategy for the Arctic Region*, Prime Minister's Office Publication, 6/2010, formin.finland.fi/public/ download.aspx?ID=63216&GUID..., accessed August 28, 2015.

28 The sea border between Canada and Greenland in the Nares and Lincoln Straits has been delimited but the nationality of the small and rocky Hans Island that sits right on it has been left open. It has been the site of a tug-of-war with all the aspects of comedy. Canada and Denmark feel that it is not worth a show of force and search for a pragmatic solution, such as some kind of joint management and control.

29 Treaty between the Kingdom of Norway and the Russian Federation concerning Maritime Delimitation and Cooperation in the Barents Sea and the Arctic Ocean, Murmansk, September 15, 2010, www. regjeringen.no/upload/SMK/Vedlegg/2010/avtale_engelsk.pdf, accessed August 28, 2015.

30 Agreement between the United States of America and the Union of Soviet Socialist Republics on the maritime boundary, June 1, 1990, in *United Nations, Delimitation Treaties InfoBase*, DOALOS/OLA (= national legislation of coastal states, as made available throughout the years to the United Nations).

31 Convention between Great Britain and Russia (Petersburg Treaty, February 16, 1825), http://explor-enorth.com/library/history/bl-ruseng1825.htm, accessed August 28, 2015. In 1867, Tsarist Russia sold Alaska to the U.S.

32 [Norwegian] Minister of Foreign Affairs, "Svalbord and the Surrounding Maritime Areas – Background and Legal Issues," www.regjeringen.no/en/dep/ud/selected-topics/civil-rights/..., accessed August 28, 2015.

33 See Siemon T. Wezeman, "Military Capabilities in the Arctic." SIPRI Background Paper, March 2012. For further information about the Arctic countries' military capabilities deployed in the Polar region, see also the annual *Military Balance*, published by the International Institute for Strategic Studies (IISS).

34 "PM Harper on Arctic."

35 Øynstein Bø [Deputy Permanent Representative Permanent Delegation of Norway to NATO], "Security in the High North – Perceptions and Misperceptions." Bergen, October 8, 2009, www. norway-nato.org/en/news/Security-in-the-High-North–Perceptions-and-misperceptions, accessed August 28, 2015.

36 *Arktis i en brydningstid. Forslag til strategi for aktiviteter I det arktiske område* (The Arctic in times of transi-tion), Udenriksministriet and Grønlands Hjemmestyre, May 2008. English version of the defence pro-posal submitted to the Storting in June 2009: *Danish Defence Agreement, 2010–2014*, merln.ndu.edu/ whitepapers/Denmark2010-2014English.pdf, accessed August 28, 2015.

37 Christian Le Mière and Jeffrey Mazo, *Arctic Opening: Insecurity and Opportunity*. London: Routledge for IISS, 2013.

38 Helga Haftendorn, "NATO and the Arctic: Is the Atlantic Alliance a Cold War Relic in a Peaceful Region Now Faced with Non-Military Challenges?" *European Security* 20, 3 (September 2011), pp. 337–62.

39 General Sverre Diesen, "Security and the Northern Region." In Rose Gottemoeller and Rolf Tamnes (eds.), *High North: High Stakes. Security, Energy Transport, Environment*. Oslo: Fagbokforlaget, 2008, p. 47.

40 Arthur C. Banet, Jr., "Oil and Gas Development on Alaska's North Slope: Past Results and Future Prospects," U. S. Department of the Interior, Bureau of Land Management, 1991, www.blm.gov/ pgdata/etc/medialib/blm/ak/aktest/ofr.Par.49987.File.dat/OFR_34.pdf, accessed August 28, 2015; Resource Development Council, "Alaska's Oil & Gas Industry," www.akrdc.org/issues/oilgas/over-view.html, accessed August 28, 2015.

41 Norwegian Ministry of Petroleum and Energy/Norwegian Petroleum Directorate, "Facts – The Norwegian Petroleum Sector," www.npd.no/en/Publications/Facts/, accessed August 28, 2015.

42 Treaty between the Kingdom of Norway and the Russian Federation concerning Maritime Delimitation and Cooperation in the Barents Sea and the Arctic Ocean.

43 See Nadezhda Nikolaevna Filimonova, "Regionality of the Arctic and North: Management, Economy, Sozium, Culture." *Arctic and the North* 12 (2013), pp. 4–13.

44 U.S. Energy Information Administration, "Oil and Gas Resources of the West Siberian Basin, Russia," November 1997, ftp.eia.doe.gov/petroleum/0617.pdf, accessed August 28, 2015.

45 U.S. Geological Survey, "Alaska Resource Data File," *Minerals Yearbook*, 2007, http://ardf.wr.usgs. gov/ardf_data/1225.pdf, accessed August 28, 2015; Canadian Natural Resources, *Canadian Minerals Yearbook 2010*, www.nrcan.gc.ca/minerals-metals/business-market/canadian-minerals-yearbook /4334, accessed August 28, 2015. DERA, "Das mineralische Rohstoffpotential der nordameri-kanischen Arktis," January 2014, www.deutsche-rohstoffagentur.de/DE/Gemeinsame/Produkte/ Downloads/DERA_Rohstoffinformationen…02.pdf, accessed August 28, 2015.

46 "Putin Tells Governors to Prioritize Environment," RIANOVSTI, April 10, 2012, http://en.rian.ru/ Environment/20120410/172729746.html, accessed August 28, 2015.

47 "Gorbachev calls for Peace."

48 Arctic Environmental Protection Strategy (AEPS), Rovaniemi, Finland, June 1991, www.arctic-council. org/index.php/en/about/documents/file/53-aeps, accessed August 28, 2015; Rovaniemi Declaration on the Protection of the Arctic Environment, June 14, 1991, http://arcticcircle.uconn.edu/ NatResources/Policy/rovaniemi.html, accessed August 28, 2015.

49 Declaration on the Establishment of the Arctic Council, and Joint Communiqué of the Governments of the Arctic Countries on the Establishment of the Arctic Council, September 19, 1996, www. arctic-council.org/index…/5-declarations?…ottawa-declaration, accessed August 28, 2015.

50 Arctic Council, *Report on Impacts of a Warming Arctic: Arctic Climate Impact Assessment*, 2004, www.acia. uaf.edu/pages/overview.html, accessed August 28, 2015.

51 Arctic Council, *Agreement on Cooperation on Aeronautical and Maritime Search and Rescue*, May 2011, www.ifrc.org/docs/idrl/N813EN.pdf, accessed August 28, 2015.

52 "Canadian Rescue Capacity Questioned in Wake of Arctic Ship Grounding," www.canada.com./ news/Canadian+rescue+capacity+questioned+wake+Arctic+ship+grounding/3457291/story.html, accessed August 28, 2015.

53 Emergency Prevention Preparedness and Response, Arctic Council, *Summary Report and Recommendations on the Prevention of Arctic Marine Oil Pollution in the Arctic*, 2013, http://eppr.arctic-council.org/…pdf, accessed August 28, 2015.

54 Emergency Prevention Preparedness and Response, Arctic Council, *Agreement on Cooperation on Marine Oil Pollution Preparedness and Response in the Arctic*, www.arctic-council.org/eppr/agreement-on-cooperation-on-marine-oil-pollution-preparedness-and-response-in-the-arctic/, accessed August 28, 2015.

55 Jennifer Rhemann, "Looking within and outside the Arctic to Increase the Governance Capacity of the Arctic Council." In Tom Axworthy, Timo Koivurova, and Waliul Hasanat (eds.), *The Arctic Council: Its Place in the Future of Arctic Governance*. Toronto: Munk-Gordon Arctic Security Program, 2012, p. 42, gordonfoundation.ca/sites/default/files/publications/The%20Arctic%20Council_FULL_1.pdf, accessed August 28, 2015.

56 Senior Arctic Officials (SAO) Report to Ministers, Nuuk, Greenland, May 2011, p. 75, SAO_ Report_to_Ministers_-_Nuuk_Ministerial_Meeting_May 2011.pdf, accessed August 28, 2015.

57 Nuuk Declaration, Arctic Council Nuuk Ministerial Meeting, May 2011, www.arctic-council.org/ index…/5-declarations?…nuuk-declaration, accessed August 28, 2015.

58 *A Communications Strategy for the Arctic Council*. Stockholm, May 2012, www.arctic-council.org/… /118-deputy-ministers…, accessed August 28, 2015.

59 IMO Polar Code, November 2014, www.imo.org/MediaCentre/HotTopics/polar/Pages/default.aspx, accessed August 28, 2015.

60 Bildt, "Arctic Challenges."

61 Arctic Council, *Arctic Human Development Report*, 2004. http://hdr.undp.org/en/reports/regional-reports/other/arctic_2004_en.pdf, accessed August 28, 2015; *Arctic Human Development Report II*, 2014, www.google.de/url?sa=t&rct=j&q=&esrc=s&source=web&cd=6&ved=0CEsQFjAF&url=http%3A %2F%2Fold.uarctic.org%2FAHDR, accessed August 28, 2015.

62 Piotr Graczyk, "The Arctic Council Inclusive of Non-Arctic Perspectives. Seeking a New Balance." In Tom Axworthy, Timo Koivurova, and Waliul Hasanat (eds.), *The Arctic Council: Its Place in the Future of Arctic Governance*. Toronto: Munk-Gordon Arctic Security Program, 2012, pp. 281–5, gordonfoun-dation.ca/sites/default/files/publications/The%20Arctic%20Council_FULL_1.pdf, accessed August 28, 2015.

63 Haftendorn, "NATO and the Arctic."

PART III

Doctrinal and technological issues on the naval agenda

11

THE COMPLEX NATURE OF TODAY'S MARITIME SECURITY ISSUES

Why whole-of-government frameworks matter

Brian Wilson

This chapter focuses on the substantive elements of whole-of-government frameworks that integrate land and maritime agencies within a government, particularly in the response to piracy, drug trafficking, and illegal migration. The complex nature of contemporary maritime security threats underscores the need to share information expeditiously across multiple agencies within a government as well as align response efforts.

The interagency is both a process and community that involves multiple national-level agencies and departments. The interagency has also been referred to as the operating space below a head of state and above departments.[1] Countries with whole-of-government[2] frameworks or centers for the response to maritime threats/events, or which have head of state direction, include, among others, Australia (Australian Maritime Information Fusion Cell/Border Protection Command), Canada (Maritime Event Response Protocol), Cape Verde (National Maritime Security Operations Center [COSMAR]), India (Cabinet Committee on Security, including inter-ministerial groups), Japan (Crisis Management Center/Cabinet Information Center), Philippines (Executive Order 57), Singapore (National Maritime Sense-Making Group), Sweden (Swedish Civil Contingencies Agency and a crisis coordination secretariat located in the Prime Minister's office), the United Kingdom (National Maritime Integration Centre), and the United States (Maritime Operational Threat Response Plan).

These processes recognize the complexity of maritime threats and involvement of both civil and military agencies. The challenge today, along with effective at-sea capabilities, is effectively leveraging all governmental – and at times, non-governmental – resources that are now involved. More agencies are involved, in part, because the expertise required to address catastrophic fuel spills, biohazards, energy disruption, pandemics, terrorism, and piracy is often distributed throughout a government. Along with high-profile threats, governments respond to migrant smuggling, drug trafficking, and illegal fishing on a daily basis.[3]

If a vessel is suspected of transporting cocaine on the high seas, for example, a Coast Guard operational asset, along with land-based representatives from the Ministries of Justice and Foreign Affairs, could be involved. Further, if the vessel of interest is not registered, or flagged, by the State conducting the interdiction, diplomatic engagement will be necessary to confirm registry, obtain approval to stop, board, and search, along with, potentially, obtaining a waiver of jurisdiction.[4] Even with a waiver, in most States, Ministry of Justice officials will have the final word on whether the interdicting State prosecutes.

The governance challenge is ensuring the existence of a process to acquire and validate information and align efforts across multiple agencies – or even nations.[5] Effectively counter-ing transnational criminal activities on the high seas imposes a greater demand for integration. Governments, however, are generally aligned in a vertical manner, whereas the response to maritime threats[6] is often horizontal, involving military, law enforcement/judicial, and diplo-matic agencies (with separate chains of command).

Further compounding the response challenge is the inherent tension of balancing maritime security[7] considerations with the expeditious movement of legitimate cargo. For instance, a foreign-flagged cargo ship en route to a port in the United States disclosed that it was carrying liquid urea, a legitimate fertilizer that could also be used as an explosive.[8] U.S. officials then received information that the ship was in poor material condition, had not made a port call in North America in more than a decade, and intended to dock in an area with critical infrastruc-ture. Later reports identified potential links between the vessel's owner and a terrorist organiza-tion. Even with this data, it was not clear whether the ship represented a threat or was simply transporting legitimate, though hazardous cargo. A whole-of-government process guided assess-ments, discussions, and decisions.

More than 90 percent of global trade moves on the oceans, carried by 50,000 merchant ships flagged in approximately 150 nations. One million seafarers transport 120 million con-tainers and other cargo annually. Maritime trade frequently involves cargo moving across mul-tiple countries with a multinational crew, ownership in one country and registry in another. Uncertainties also exist in the maritime space: It may be difficult for one agency to determine, for instance, whether an explosion in a container occurred because of damaged cargo or signals the first in a series of attacks; whether an offshore oil platform leak is a temporary setback or the beginning of a catastrophic event; or whether an undocumented passenger represents a clerical oversight or a security threat.

Some national-level processes and interagency centers operate with command and control constructs, others unity of effort, and yet a separate band operate with just operational maritime law enforcement agencies. To effectively bridge the intersection of civil and military agencies, discussions in whole-of-government frameworks could include:

- the authority to board;
- evidence collection;
- disposal of prohibited weapons and materials;
- procedural rights to be afforded to potential defendants and material witnesses;
- delivery of evidence;
- transportation of defendants and witnesses to another State exercising jurisdiction;
- disposition of legitimate cargo; and
- environmental considerations (weather, difficulty in returning to port, distance from port).

The existence of a structured process to guide, document, and resolve these discussions – in advance of the threat – is tremendously beneficial. In the absence of a process that mandates coordination, information stovepipes, miscommunication and redundancy are possible, and decisions affecting a nation may be made without a complete situational picture. Moreover, national-level coordination isn't consistently effective on an *ad hoc* basis.

More than 40 years ago, a Lithuanian sailor desperate to defect to the United States leapt from the deck of a Soviet ship onto a U.S. Coast Guard cutter.[9] Informal discussions between U.S. Government departments were unproductive, as there was not a formal process to guide coordination. In the absence of whole-of-government-developed courses of action, a Coast Guard commander gave an order to return the 40-year-old sailor to the Soviets. Simas Kudirka did not go easily, though; several Soviets had to beat him into submission, all while aboard a U.S. military vessel in the U.S. territorial sea off Martha's Vineyard, Massachusetts.[10]

Widespread media coverage, including condemnation, followed. A *New York Times* editorial wrote that the forcible removal of Kudirka is "surely one of the most disgraceful incidents ever to occur on a ship flying the American flag." The *Washington Post* asserted, "No more sickening and humiliating an episode in international relations has taken place within memory."

Presidential briefings and Congressional hearings thoroughly examined the event.[11] Bad decisions contributed to the outcome, but the lack of coordination among federal departments contributed as well. Kudirka's mishandled asylum request sparked high-level interest in a bureaucratically obscure, but vitally important aspect of governance: How to ensure the timely alignment of federal agencies. Following Kudirka, a process was created in the United States to align the response to migrants, fishing violations, and maritime drug trafficking that could adversely affect U.S. foreign affairs.

The U.S. process created in 1978, however, addressed only nonmilitary incidents. That changed in 2005 when an interim MOTR Plan was approved (the final MOTR plan was signed in 2006) directing whole-of-government coordination to maritime threats. The responses to two unrelated incidents, M/V *Palermo Senator* and CSAV *Rio Pueblo*, that occurred after September 11, 2001, but before the approval of the MOTR Plan, highlight the need for a documented, consistent, and repeatable process.

In September 2002, the *Palermo Senator* tested positive for radiation during an inspection at the Port of Newark. "Noises in the containers raised concerns that stowaways might be on board. In verifying that there were none, inspectors noted low-level radiation from the cargo holds." The Liberian-flagged, German-owned ship was then designated a "high threat vessel" and ordered to leave port and anchor in a security zone several miles off the coast.[12]

Personnel from the FBI's Hazardous Devices Response Unit (HDRU), the Department of Energy's Radiological Assistance Program, U.S. Navy Special Forces, and U.S. Coast Guard inspected *Palermo Senator* and its 655 containers. The inspections revealed that the positive readings came from, "naturally occurring radiation in the ceramic tiles" in *Palermo Senator*'s cargo.[13]

After three days at anchorage, the 708-foot ship was cleared to enter port. *Palermo Senator* provided lessons in interagency operational collaboration and technical challenges. An FBI audit conducted by the Office of the Inspector General in March 2006, concluded:

Nuclear detection equipment has limitations. The HDRU cannot detect every type of nuclear device that could be placed within a ship's cargo hold. HDRU officials said the most likely method for conducting a search (of every container in *Palermo Senator*) would involve using a crane to remove the containers and individually searching them. This method is time consuming, likely taking weeks to complete, and presents additional challenges. For example, officials are unlikely to want to keep a ship in port that is suspected of having a WMD aboard. It would take a second ship and special equipment to perform this kind of search at sea.[14]

In 2004, exhaustive inspections occurred off the port of Newark of a container ship suspected of transporting biological contaminated cargo. Information was forwarded to the U.S. Department of Agriculture asserting that lemons from Argentina aboard CSAV *Rio Pueblo* were intentionally contaminated.[15] Six days of inspections, tests, and fumigation yielded no evidence that the 1 million lemons, valued at $70,000, were biologically spiked. The cache of lemons was nevertheless destroyed.[16] While the response in *Rio Pueblo* has scathingly been called "Lemon-Gate,"[17] similar to *Palermo Senator*, it highlights the need for a documented, consistent, and repeatable process.

A head of state, or as authorized, a Cabinet-level committee, may direct a coordinated response to a threat. In those cases, determining the desired national outcome is typically not an issue. However, it is not realistic to expect a head of state – or even a Cabinet-level committee – to be involved in every maritime security issue, ranging from whether to board a foreign flagged vessel, the method of transporting detainees captured on water, the text of a press statement, or what to do with seized cargo (all of which could occur daily).

The challenge isn't necessarily about leadership or ensuring personnel are trained. The speed with which data is passed has changed operations and governance: preliminary information that was previously evaluated at the tactical level and reviewed by multiple levels now can be immediately forwarded to senior officials. Tactical- or field-level personnel may not even know with whom to share their information in other agencies, nor necessarily be empowered to do so.

Where there is not a command and control process, horizontal coordinating mechanisms are based on unity of effort. Horizontal frameworks similarly do not operate to prevent an agency from acting in self-defense or taking action in accordance with their procedures (also referred to as "functional integrity" by the European Commission [EC]). In 2014, the EC issued a joint communication to the European Parliament and the Council regarding "elements for a European Union maritime security strategy." In discussing the key elements of coordination and alignment, the EC paper identified four essential elements (emphasis in original):

> (1) *A cross-sectoral approach:* all partners from civilian and military authorities (law enforcement, border control, customs, and fisheries inspection, environmental authorities, shipping supervision, research and innovation, navies) to industry (shipping, private security, communication technology, capability support, social partners) need to cooperate better.
>
> (2) *Functional integrity:* there should be no change of mandate, responsibilities or competences for each stakeholder. The focus should be instead on which specific functions or tasks can better be achieved by working together with other stakeholders.
>
> (3) *Maritime multilateralism:* a key principle when dealing with complex issues requiring an international response and cooperation in the maritime domain is multilateralism. The EU is stronger, and its interests are best protected, when speaking with one voice to international partners.
>
> (4) *Respect for rules and principles:* the EU promotes respect for international law, human rights and democracy, and full compliance with UNCLOS and the goals enshrined therein as the key elements for rules-based good governance at sea.

An insightful article authored by Helena Lindberg and Bengt Sundelius examined Swedish "whole-of-society" disaster resilience.[18] In part, they concluded:

- How groups (agencies) deal with information varies greatly, from safety officials who are open, to military, who aren't;
- A key element [to an aligned, effective response] is forging trusted relationships;
- The reality of trans-boundary risks is increasingly pushing European member states to deepen their cooperation and tighten the web of resilience across the Union; and
- EU capacity for managing risks and crises has been considerably boosted over the past few years, but is still marked by a lack of overall coherence.[19]

Details of whole-of-government processes are instructive regarding the coordinated response to migrants, drug smugglers, illicit fishing violations, as well as maritime terrorism and piracy. The MOTR process, for example, brings together national-level representatives designated by their agency and, at times, those at the tactical/operational level.

The response to a threat could be resolved in one coordination activity or could span several discussions. MOTR coordination activities may include a summary of the threat along with legal,[20] operational, and policy issues. Those involved in MOTR coordination activities are generally commanders and captains and their civilian equivalents, though more senior officials can be involved, including ambassadors, generals, and admirals. MOTR coordination identifies a lead federal agency, courses of action, and a desired national outcome. Each coordination activity seeks to generate agreement on the facts and identify uncertainties and ambiguities, assigning their resolution to participants. Coordination is required and the plan is used almost daily, but frequent use is not the only contributing factor to its effectiveness.

Explicitly articulating actions that are required and designating the agencies responsible for their accomplishment removes ambiguity and supports whole-of-government action. Of course, without command and control, disputes are inevitable. Higher-level involvement, however, to resolve disputes is infrequently required. Tension between agencies is not necessarily a negative element. Officials with different perspectives, training, and backgrounds often forge greater responses to an issue than from only one agency. However, without a process to ensure the timely flow of information and decision-making, that productive tension cannot happen.

That being said, a process will have to overcome cultural differences between agencies. Even within the same government, words may have different meanings. The U.S. Defense Department's almost 500-page dictionary of terms defines some words differently than other departments and many do not even have a dictionary.[21]

Even with agreement, there are tremendous logistics challenges in the maritime environment. In one instance, the U.S. Coast Guard interdicted the FV *Bangun Perkasa* in 2011 for high seas drift-net activity where nets, some as long as 60 miles, are dropped into the ocean, indiscriminately destroying maritime life. The Coast Guard seizure in waters near Japan prompted a 2,600-mile transit to Dutch Harbor, Alaska, vessel in tow, which took weeks. Discussions on courses of action, diplomatic engagements, and judicial options occurred through the MOTR process. Decisions reached under MOTR may also address disposition, some of which have considerable financial implications for the government. The "total cost of seizing the vessel, keeping it tied up … for the better part of two years, and then scrapping it is estimated at $1.1 million."[22]

As a horizontal coordinating mechanism, those involved in MOTR have no authority to direct or compel another agency to take (or not take) action, regardless of who is designated lead. The Department of Justice could not direct the Navy to use a specific ship to rescue a pirated vessel, and conversely, the Navy couldn't direct the Department of Justice to prosecute. MOTR is used when another process, plan, or order does not exist to address the threat. In this regard, MOTR fills a vacuum and does not replace or supplant existing structures. There is no set model in this regard, though, as some national-level processes have primacy in all maritime threat or event responses.

As noted above, timely information flow and effectively assessing data are critical, but often elusive, enablers of a response. An examination of crisis management noted, "Because of large organizations and ingrained bureaucracies … information gets filtered, watered down, distorted, polished, or squeezed under the table for reasons wholly unrelated to the situation at hand."[23] National-level processes are most effective when they eliminate those concerns by compelling information sharing at the earliest possible opportunity and including tactical-level personnel, if possible, on coordination activities.

With dozens of information fusion and command centers in the United States, for example, ensuring timely and accurate information flow is a continual challenge. A number of capabilities and programs support "integrating and sharing information, including intelligence, to better inform decisions affecting … security, safety, [the] economy, and environment" including, among others, Long Range Identification and Tracking (LRIT) system; National Information Exchange Model (NIEM); Maritime Safety and Security Information System (MSSIS); Single Integrated Lookout (SILO) List; and Geospatial Intelligence (GEOINT) Visualization Service (GVS).[24]

The recent and tragic Ebola virus disease highlighted the imperative of expeditious medical treatment, education, information sharing, and coordinated responses. Though the vast majority of issues related to Ebola occurred on land, the maritime sector was involved in several issues. Considerations in future responses to a significant infectious disease, pandemic or potential pandemic in the maritime sector include evaluating:[25]

- What is the disease and how many passengers/crew members have it?
- How contagious is the disease?
- Who is in charge of the disease control effort – and how are efforts being coordinated with responsible agencies?
- What is the plan for disease control?
- What kind of medical care is available to those infected and those at risk?
- Can the disease be treated?
- Is the disease airborne? Waterborne?
- How will vaccines and antiviral medicines be distributed?
- What is the risk to the population? Could it be fatal?
- Is there a contingency plan if current control measures fail? What does the contingency plan say and what is the worst case?
- Will infected people be isolated or quarantined? If so, how long will the quarantine and isolation last?
- If there is a quarantine and/or isolation, what is the legal basis?
- How effective is the quarantine and isolation in preventing the spread of the disease?
- What are the legal rights of a person who is quarantined or isolated?

It is not expected that officials will initially have answers to every question, but discussing those issues in advance of an event will better position a response in a potentially chaotic and confusing environment. Dr. Randy Hyer and Dr. Vincent Covello of the World Health Organization developed the above inquiries in their seminal examination of responding to public health emergencies.[26]

A whole-of-government process must drive representatives toward a *national* outcome, as opposed to an *agency* position. If pirates, for example, are detained on board a military platform, the navy or coast guard objective may be to clear the decks as soon as possible. Investigative or diplomatic issues may take days or weeks, during which time those detained could possibly have to remain aboard the warship. The warship may not be fully capable of conducting other missions with those detainees on board. Reconciling competing agency priorities requires a structured process.

"It appears that few organizations – public or private – have these mechanisms for collective sense making in place. As a consequence, policy-makers may get bogged down in internal warfare over the nature and scope of the impending threat, thus creating an image of paralysis and ineffectiveness."[27] The importance of alignment is generally recognized, though without a structured, mandated, and exercised process, there is no consistency.

A study of crisis management concluded

[T]he main problem, borne out by historical and laboratory studies alike, is that individuals in groups do not share and use information effectively in advising leaders or reaching collective decisions ….With a crisis, there is a high degree of uncertainty – what is happening, how did it happen, what's next, how bad will it be; what can we do? Essential information is often unavailable – a uniform picture of events rarely emerges in a crisis.[28]

The existence of a crisis management process enables civil and military agencies to address and prepare for, in advance of an event, difficult legal, policy, resource and operational questions.

A European Council on Security and Defense report released on October 15, 2013 by the High Representative/Head of the EDA on the Common Security and Defense Policy recommended that Union security must, "allow for the deployment of the right assets, timely and effectively on the whole spectrum of crisis management operations."[29] The report continued, "Over the past few months a broad consensus has emerged on the need to further improve the planning, conduct and support of civilian CSDP (Common Security and Defense Policy) missions, and in particular to expedite their deployment." Areas being considered include exercises and "improving advanced planning on the most likely crisis scenarios requiring the use of an EU rapid response."

The development of an agency contact matrix has also proved essential to timely and effective interagency coordination. Though it sounds simple, in departments with thousands of personnel, it is not always readily known who has responsibility for specific threats, such as a fishing incursion or drug trafficking case. If there are legal issues, for example, who should be consulted and does the location of the threat or flag state of the vessel involved require yet others to be consulted? And separately, is the representative authorized to provide a formal departmental position?

Another governance challenge is creating a process by which departments that are not co-located or under the same Cabinet Secretary come together for discussions, courses of action development, and decisions. In this regard, whole-of-government frameworks must be uniquely tailored for a State's organization, priorities, and head of state direction. Where there is not a command and control process, a unity of effort framework can bring together multiple agencies. A unity of effort framework would typically not prevent an agency from taking required action in accordance with their procedures. A European Union policy paper recognized, "an integrated governance framework for maritime affairs requires horizontal planning tools that cut across sea-related sectoral policies and support joined up policy making."[30]

The rank (or pay-grade) of participants is yet another key consideration in national-level coordination frameworks. Processes benefit from the inclusion of relatively senior-level officials that are subject matter experts. For example, commanders/captains (0–5/0–6), and at times admirals/generals, and their civilian equivalents, are often representatives to whole-of-government coordination frameworks. Subject matter experts that have the ability to communicate with senior levels of their organization ensure that the whole-of-government process has representatives capable of devoting time, resources, expertise, and focus to issues that may frequently arise.

The successful response to the *Maersk Alabama* hijacking in 2009 (portrayed in the film *Captain Phillips*) led to the creation of an office dedicated to supporting the MOTR process. The Global MOTR Coordination Center (GMCC), a Department of Homeland Security Office within the U.S. Coast Guard, was established in February 2010 to support United States interagency response and to serve as a national MOTR coordinator and its executive secretariat. While the MOTR process has existed since 2005, the GMCC, a small office of three civilians and two active duty military officers, provides a number of support functions including providing trained and dedicated facilitators, institutionalizing MOTR structure and processes, maintaining MOTR protocols, assisting with annual war games and exercises, and capturing lessons learned and best practices.

The response to drug submarines is emblematic of interagency, legal, and operational challenges in maritime law enforcement. Prior to the enactment of the Drug Trafficking Vessel Interdiction Act (DTVIA) of 2008,[31] when the United States Coast Guard approached crudely constructed, aqua-blue vessels, known as semi-submersibles, or drug subs, crews were generally aware that they could avoid criminal prosecution if they destroyed evidence of their drug trafficking before law enforcement officials arrived. In one case, as the USCG boarding team neared the semi-submersible, the crew opened the scuttling valves to sink their fiber-glassed submersible. The status of the four crewmen was quickly changing from captured cocaine smugglers to search and rescue survivors. Because the crewmembers were unable to scuttle the 11 bales of cocaine, valued at more than $350 million, before the boarding team arrived, there would be a prosecution. Discussions with representatives from the Departments of Homeland Security, Justice, and State unfolded through the MOTR process.[32] Though the DTVIA closed the legal gap, whole-of-government coordination remains an essential element of the response to drug traffickers aboard semi-submersibles.

A promising new development is coordination frameworks to bridge national-level processes, such as between the United States and Canada.[33] Under the MERP (Maritime Event Response Protocol)–MOTR Strategic Protocol (developed in 2012), representatives from the MOTR process share information and discuss maritime threats with Canadian colleagues from MERP. Some of the exchanges have included representatives from more than a dozen agencies. Nothing in the MERP–MOTR Strategic Protocol supplants or replaces existing relationships between the military, law enforcement, diplomatic, or customs officials. Rather, the Strategic Protocol provides a connective thread for varied agencies to have improved awareness and to better position a response.

As originally established, the American MOTR and Canadian MERP processes have different initiation thresholds, did not interface and did not include participation of members from the other country inevitably leading to non-synchronized understanding and actions. Given that maritime threats do not always respect geographic boundaries, a means of effective and rapid communication and coordination between Canada and the United States would best position both nations to respond successfully to maritime threats to North America. The MERP/MOTR Strategic Integration Protocol ... provide(s) guidance for enhanced coordination of bi-national efforts, including strengthened parallel planning and aligned efforts, supporting a perimeter approach to improve the efficiency and effectiveness of the maritime security response capabilities of both nations.[34]

Multiple benefits, including safety of life, mission accomplishment, and efficiency flow from an effective collaborative construct.[35] A study by U.S. Congressional Research Service noted that additional benefits from a collaborative framework include: ending or reducing policy fragmentation, making agencies aware of different perspectives and orientations, mitigating conflict among agencies, increasing agency productivity, enhancing efficiency, reducing redundancy and cutting costs, heightening the attention to and priorities for cross-cutting programs, changing organizational cultures, and changing bureaucratic and administrative cultures.[36]

Improvements in technology have dramatically enhanced tracking and monitoring capabilities along with the speed with which data is passed. Possessing more information doesn't necessarily ensure a better response, nor does it guarantee that a threat will be identified in a timely manner. Overcoming potential breakdowns in information flow is crucial, particularly with so much data. For example, media coverage of a 2013 maritime seizure in Jamaica highlighted the perils of rapid information dissemination prior to its validation. Articles reported that Jamaican port authorities stated that they had seized 3,300 *missile warheads*, which would represent one of the greatest maritime seizures ever. Multiple media outlets around the globe carried the story. It would take several hours to clarify that the seizure wasn't missile warheads, but rather, *warheads for bullets*, all of which could fit into four shoeboxes. In an environment where there is an expectation of near immediate information flow, coverage of the warheads seizure represents a cautionary tale regarding data validation.

"Authorities often cannot provide correct information right away. They struggle with mountains of raw data (reports, rumors, pictures) that quickly amass when something extraordinary happens. Getting ... actionable information requires a major communications effort,"[37] as well as a keen ability to understand what information is important and what information is lacking as data flows. Moreover, a recurring concern in responses is that by, "applying the 'right' response to the wrong problem ... operators continued to exacerbate the problem."[38]

Awareness of key questions that must be asked, authorities, policy guidance, and the inclusion of subject matter experts represent essential elements of an effective coordination process, which in turn better positions the response in a time-sensitive and potentially confusing environment.[39] In some situations, the most difficult issue may be the one that senior officials first raise: What is happening?[40] Equally challenging questions and policy decisions include: What agency or department is responsible for responding, what is being done, if more than one agency is involved, what is being done to coordinate actions, who is affected, why did it happen, and where did it happen?[41]

A Chatham House study concluded that, "there cannot be adequate planning for all eventualities ... but governments ... must identify robust, but not necessarily threat-specific processes to mitigate [the events]."[42] National-level coordination frameworks represent such a process. The study further noted:

Robust but adaptable structures for coordinated decision-making are crucial because when stakeholders make different judgments about risk during a crisis public confidence can be rapidly eroded. Sharing best practices and where relevant, capacity, especially across sectors, and red-teaming [high-impact, low-probability] scenarios with key decision-makers – focusing in particular on critical sectors such as transport and communications will be essential to enhance preparedness in coping with the unexpected.[43]

Another examination regarding the importance, and challenges, of alignment was released in 2013 by IBM.[44] Even though the study focused on land operations, it confirmed why several countries have recently developed maritime collaborative frameworks. "Few agencies have the funding, expertise, or influence to achieve their goals single-handedly. Moreover, complex problems require interdisciplinary – and hence interagency – solutions …. Coordination, however, is easier said than done. Agencies differ in their goals, priorities, and cultures."[45] Recommendations of the IBM study include ensuring "regular, structured opportunities for information sharing and joint analysis and planning," the designation of experienced facilitators, and articulating "shared goals and priorities."[46]

Another key enabler of an effective whole-of-government process is documenting lessons learned. "The crisis experience offers a reservoir of potential lessons for contingency planning and training for future crises. We would expect all those involved to study these lessons and feed them back into organizational practices, policies and laws."[47] However, without a structured process, it is difficult to secure consensus on the lessons learned as well as which agency should lead/document those efforts. If not addressed, there is a greater likelihood of mistakes being repeated, or gaps continuing.

Frameworks that have recently surfaced across the globe recognize that the maritime domain uniquely requires collaboration.[48] The mere existence of a plan or interagency center, however, doesn't ensure information will be shared or that meaningful coordination will occur. Transparency is a key enabler; actions that are documented and distributed best position an effective whole-of-government response. Awareness, familiarity, civility, and training also contribute to the effectiveness of interagency coordination. Whole-of-government mechanisms, which now exist in more than ten countries, will continue to flourish if they remain adaptive and inclusive.

Note: The views expressed are those of the author and do not reflect the official policy or position of the U.S. Navy, U.S. Coast Guard or Department of Homeland Security.

Notes

1 Project on National Security Reform, "Forging a New Shield," November 2008; available at: http://0183896.netsolhost.com/site/wp-content/uploads/2011/12/pnsr_forging_a_new_shield_report.pdf, accessed August 28, 2015.
2 Andrea Baumann, Center for Security Studies (CSS), "Whole of Government: Integration and Demarcation," CSS Analysis in Security Policy, No. 129, March 2013, Center for Security Studies, Zurich, available at: www.css.ethz.ch/publications/DetailansichtPubDB_EN?rec_id=2441, accessed August 28, 2015. "There is as yet no internationally agreed standard model for WGAs (whole of government approaches). One would search in vain for a uniform definition of such integrated approaches. In principle, WGAs aim to improve coordination within a given government. In addition, however, states sometimes also aspire to coordinate their activities with those of other state or non-state actors, as a coherent overall strategy at the governmental level is often seen as being necessary, but not sufficient. This is generally referred to as a 'Whole of System approach'."
3 See "Preparing the December 2013 European Council on Security and Defense," Final Report by the High Representative/Head of the EDA on the Common Security and Defense Policy, Brussels, October 15, 2015. Available at: http://eeas.europa.eu/statements/docs/2013/131015_02_en.pdf, accessed August 28, 2015: "The EU has strategic maritime security interests around the globe and needs to be

able to safeguard them against significant maritime risks and threats – ranging from illegal migration, drug trafficking, smuggling of goods and illegal fishing to terrorism maritime piracy and armed robbery at sea as well as territorial maritime disputes and acts of aggression or armed conflict between states."

4 See U.N. Convention against Illicit Trafficking in Narcotic Drugs and Psychotropic Substances [The Vienna Drug Convention], December 20, 1988, 28 ILM 493, which includes, among other things, a requirement that States Parties designate a competent authority. Article 17 provides, "At the time of becoming a Party to this Convention, each Party shall designate an authority or, when necessary, authorities to receive and respond to such requests. Such designation shall be notified through the Secretary-General to all other Parties within one month of the designation." Article 17 further provides that "[p]arties shall co-operate to the fullest extent possible to suppress illicit traffic by sea, in conformity with the international law of the sea."

5 This chapter focuses primarily on national-level coordinating mechanisms. That said, maritime threats are not confined to one geographic area and routinely cross jurisdictional boundaries and maritime zones. Bi-national, regional, and international collaboration remains essential to effective maritime security. For example, an array of states, nongovernmental organizations, and the shipping industry impressively collaborated to repress Somali piracy. The combined task forces, judicial support, and multinational contact groups, among others, that were developed share similar traits regarding the value of collaboration. There is not one nation, command, or unit in charge of operational efforts in the Horn of Africa, for example, but a unity of effort exists against Somali piracy. Counter-drug efforts have also sparked considerable collaboration.

6 The U.S. National Security Strategy (February 2015): "An array of terrorist threats has gained traction in areas of instability, limited opportunity, and broken governance. Our adversaries are not confined to a distinct country or region.… No threat poses as grave a danger to our security and well-being as the potential use of nuclear weapons and materials by irresponsible states or terrorists." Available at: www.whitehouse.gov/the-press-office/2015/02/06/fact-sheet-2015-national-security-strategy, accessed August 28, 2015.

7 Christian Bueger, "What Is Maritime Security," *Marine Policy* 53, 1 (2015): 159–63, available at: http://dx.doi.org/10.1016/j.marpol.2014.12.005, accessed August 28, 2015; "Maritime security is a buzzword. It has no definite meaning. It achieves its meaning by actors relating the concept to others, by attempts to fill it with different issues and by acting in the name of it.… If the precise phrasing differs across agencies, the 2008 UN Secretary General's Report on *Oceans and the Law of the Sea* provides an outline of the threats commonly included …: (1) Piracy and armed robbery, (2) terrorist acts, (3) the illicit trafficking in arms and weapons of mass destruction, (4) the illicit trafficking in narcotics, (5) smuggling and trafficking of persons by sea, (6) illegal, unreported and unregulated fishing and (7) international and unlawful damage to the marine environment." The UNGA Report is document A/63/63, March 10, 2008.

8 Gary L. Tomasulo, Jr., "Evolution of Interagency Cooperation in the United States Government: The Maritime Operational Threat Response Plan, June 2010," pp. 52–5, available at: http://dspace.mit.edu/bitstream/handle/1721.1/59157/659552377.pdf?sequence=1, accessed August 28, 2015.

9 Committee on Foreign Affairs, Hearings before the Subcommittee on State Department Organization and Foreign Operations of the Committee on Foreign Affairs, House of Representatives; Attempted Defection by Lithuanian Seaman Simas Kudirka. 91st Congress, Second Session, December 3, 7, 8, 9, 14, 17, 18 and 29, 1970. See also, Secretary of Transportation John A. Volpe, Memorandum for the President, Subject: Attempted Defection by a Crew Member of the *Sovetskaya Litva*, December 2, 1970.

10 Algis Ruksenas, *Day of Shame: The Truth about the Murderous Happenings Aboard the Cutter Vigilant during the Russian–American Confrontation off Martha's Vineyard* (Philadelphia, PA: David McKay Company, Inc., 1973), pp. 247–8.

11 *Ibid.*, pp. 268–72.

12 Ronald Smothers, "Ship's Radiation Is Traced to Harmless Tiles," *New York Times*, September 14, 2002.

13 *Ibid.*

14 FBI Office of the Inspector General Audit Report 06-26 of March 2006, "Efforts to Protect the Nation's Seaports" (Redacted and Unclassified), available at: www.justice.gov/oig/FBI/a0626/findings2.htm, accessed August 28, 2015.

15 "An Anonymous E-Mail Alleged That (The Lemons) were Laced with a Biological Agent." Paul Blustein and Brian Byrnes, "Lemons Caught in a Squeeze," *Washington Post*, September 10, 2004.

16 *Ibid.* A Coast Guard spokesman, Lieutenant Commander Benjamin Benson, stated, "Although all these tests were coming back negative, there was always this lingering concern that may there's something in there."

17 *Ibid.*

18 Helena Lindberg and Bengt Sundelius, "Whole-of-Society Disaster Resilience: The Swedish Way," in David Kamien (ed.), *McGraw-Hill Homeland Security Handbook* (New York: McGraw-Hill, 2012), pp. 1295–319.

19 *Ibid.* Further: "Instead of one group that coordinates, Sweden has 'coordination areas'; during coordination, assigned responsibilities of an agency doesn't change; Sweden is in a 'flow society' environment [and as such, is …] dependent on multinational collaboration; and achieving a whole of society approach requires fostering a culture of horizontal coordination and networking across jurisdictional borders."

20 Legal authorities set the parameters on how a State or States may respond to a particular threat. But legal authority is only one element of an effective response. See, e.g., Jonathan G. Odom, "Leveraging Federal Law to Support Decision Making in Homeland Defense Operations," *PHALANX – The Bulletin of Military Operations Research* 39, 1 (March 2006), available at http://papers.ssrn.com/sol3/papers.cfm?abstract_id=1877305, accessed August 28, 2015. ("In short, we must always remember that, in the equation of military operations, the law is merely a factor. It is not the answer to the equation itself. … Conceptually, tell me what you want to do to accomplish our assigned mission, and I will tell you if and how we can legally do it. To be sure, the law is a factor in operations. However, the law should not drive strategy, plans, and operations.")

21 *Department of Defense Dictionary of Military and Associated Terms,* Joint Staff Publication 1-028, November 2010 (as amended through January 15, 2015), available at: www.dtic.mil/doctrine/new_pubs/jp1_02.pdf, accessed August 28, 2015.

22 Stephanie Joyce, "F/V *Bangun Perkasa* Finished Long Journey to Scrapyard," APRN, July 5, 2013, available at: www.alaskapublic.org/2013/07/05/fv-bangun-perkasa-finished-long-journey-to-scrapyard/, accessed August 28, 2015.

23 Arjen Boin, Paul 't Hart, Eric Stern, and Bengt Sundelius, *The Politics of Crisis Management: Public Leadership under Pressure* (Cambridge: Cambridge University Press, 2005).

24 See the United States National Maritime Domain Awareness Plan for the National Strategy for Maritime Security (December 2013); released by the White House, available at: www.whitehouse.gov/sites/default/files/docs/national_maritime_domain_awareness_plan.pdf, accessed August 28, 2015. See also, U.S. Department of Transportation's Volpe Center website at: https://mssis.volpe.dot.gov/Main/, accessed August 28, 2015.

25 Randall N. Hyer and Vincent T. Covello, *Effective Media Communication during Public Health Emergencies: A World Health Organization Handbook* (Geneva: WHO, 2007).

26 *Ibid.*

27 Boin *et al., The Politics of Crisis Management.*

28 *Ibid.*

29 "Preparing the December 2013 European Council on Security and Defense."

30 "Communication from the Commission to the European Parliament, The Council, The European Economic and Social Committee and the Committee of the Regions, An Integrated Maritime Policy for the European Union," Commission of the European Communities, Brussels, October 10, 2007, COM (2007) 575-final, available at: http://eur-lex.europa.eu/legal-content/EN/TXT/?uri=CELEX:52007DC0575, accessed August 28, 2015.

31 Interdictions of drug subs prior to 2008, such as the one discussed above, highlighted that drug smugglers could skirt prosecution if law enforcement officials failed to recover evidence, and, second, highlighted the existing enforcement structure did not account for the national security danger that the new maritime vehicle presents. The United States passed the Drug Trafficking Vessel Interdiction Act (DTVIA): Drug Trafficking Vessel Interdiction Act of 2008, Pub. L. No. 110-407, 122 Stat. 4296 (2008) (codified at 18 USCA § 2285 (West 2010)), to close this legal gap. This federal statute criminalized the operation of fully submersible or semi-submersible vessels that are without nationality, navigating or having navigated outside of a nation's territorial sea with the intent to evade detection. Essentially, the conveyance was outlawed regardless of its contents.

32 *Ibid.*

33 NMIO Technical Bulletin, "NORAD and Maritime Domain Awareness," National Maritime Intelligence-Integration (NMIO) Office, April 2012, vol. 2, available at: http://nmio.ise.gov/docs/NMIO_QuarterlyVOL2.pdf, accessed August 28, 2015.

34 *Ibid.*

35 Frederick M. Kaiser, "Interagency Collaborative Arrangements and Activities: Types, Rationales, Considerations," Congressional Research Service, May 31, 2011, available at: www.fas.org/sgp/crs/misc/R41803.pdf, accessed August 28, 2015.

36 *Ibid.*

37 *Ibid.*

38 *Ibid.*

39 *Ibid.*

40 *Ibid.*

41 *Ibid.*

42 Bernice Lee and Felix Preston, with Gemma Green, *Preparing for High-Impact, Low-Probability Events, Lessons from Eyjafjallajokull*, Chatham House Report, January 2012, available at: www.chathamhouse.org/sites/default/files/public/Research/Energy,%20Environment%20and%20Development/r0112_highimpact.pdf, accessed August 28, 2015.

43 *Ibid.*

44 Andrea Strimling Yodsampa, *Coordinating for Results: Lessons from a Case Study of Interagency Coordination in Afghanistan*, IBM Center for the Business of Government, Collaborating across Boundaries Series (Washington, DC: IBM Center for the Business of Government, 2013), available at: www.businessofgovernment.org/sites/default/files/Coordinating%20for%20Results.pdf, accessed August 28, 2015.

45 *Ibid.* The study noted that challenges include: "competing goals and priorities; cultural differences; power disparities; competition; different assumptions and expectations; and lack of line authority over other agencies."

46 *Ibid.*

47 Boin *et al.*, *The Politics of Crisis Management*.

48 A former Judge Advocate General of the U.S. Coast Guard, Rear Admiral Bill Baumgartner, remarked that the interagency space is the new operating environment: "The Coast Guard lives completely in a partner world. There are only very few of our missions that we can actually do without either inter-agency, joint-service, or private industry partners. We consider that one of our core competencies. There is something to be said for growing up with the reality that you don't have everything you need to get done, get your job done so you learn how to influence people, you learn how to be what one of my bosses told me once is you don't have to be in command to be in control. I think we've got a lot of our officers that have taken that to an art form. I tell my judge advocates I expect them to be something I call a fearless integrator. I expect them to integrate across missions in the Coast Guard, integrate across agencies, and lead their clients in that effort." *The Reporter* 36, 4 (2009), "Year in Review," p. 162, U.S. Air Force's Judge Advocate General's Corps, available at: www.afjag.af.mil/shared/media/document/AFD-100510-067.pdf, accessed August 28, 2015.

12

THE CHANGING NATURE OF NAVAL CONFLICTS IN CONFINED AND SHALLOW WATERS (CSW)

Stavros Karlatiras

Historical outline

When mankind first began to sail the seas, for many millennia the maritime operational space was limited to the CSW environment. Only a few centuries ago, after the exploration of the high seas, the maritime operational field of action expanded to cover the entire water space. Additionally, it should also be noted that CSW remain of critical importance despite a shifting focus to deeper waters, not only for the military but also for the political, economic, and scientific fields.

Tracing back in history, numerous famous and decisive naval engagements have been fought in coastal areas as well as narrow and shallow waters. A well-known example is the Battle of Salamis in 480 B.C., during which the fleet of the Greek city-states alliance defeated an overwhelmingly superior Persian fleet. Other excellent examples are the naval battles of the seventeenth to early nineteenth centuries, often referred to as the "Golden Age of Sail." The Anglo-Dutch Wars, the struggle for the American and West Indian Colonies, and the period of the Revolutionary and Napoleonic Wars lend credence to and illustrate our claim.

A majority of the naval engagements during World War I were fought in or near coastal waters. Specific examples include battles in the North Sea, the English Channel, the Mediterranean Sea, the Black Sea, and the Baltic Sea. Control of narrow seas and especially choke points was of critical importance to the Entente as well as to the Central Powers.

In World War II, most of the world's coastal areas and marginal seas including all seas adjacent to Europe, the Caribbean, and the Southern Pacific formed the battlespace for numerous, not just naval but increasingly joint, encounters. It wasn't until after the outbreak of war that army commanders realized the importance of controlling the narrow seas while campaigning ashore.

When NATO was established in 1949 one of its fundamental roles was to act as a powerful deterrent against military aggression. In this role, NATO's success was reflected in the fact that throughout the entire period of the Cold War, NATO forces were never involved in any military engagements. For much of the latter half of the twentieth century, NATO remained vigilant and prepared by aligning its naval forces in accordance with the threat it was facing. NATO also maintained a set of naval forces capable of war-fighting both in the open oceans and the littorals.

Confined and shallow waters: a vital interface

Suggesting that the future security environment is getting more complex than former periods is not trivializing the complexity of the past. In effect, it simply clarifies the influence of globalization – expanding connectivity, complexity, and uncertainty – on international relations in a more multipolar and increasingly demanding world system.

The security environment of today and tomorrow may be characterized by several accelerating trends. It encompasses a plethora of potential threats, adversaries, and actors with divergent motivations. In terms of the maritime domain, about 70 percent of the earth's surface is covered with water; approximately 80 percent of the world population lives within 500 km of a sea shore, 90 percent of international trade in goods are transported via sea lines of communications and 75 percent of that trade passes through a few narrow and thus vulnerable straits. Hence the maritime environment includes sea lines of communication (SLOCs), choke points, ports, and other infrastructure such as pipelines, oil and natural gas platforms or trans-oceanic telecommunications cables.[1]

Based on the global, regional, and local operations of international, national, commercial, and institutional stakeholders acting in the region, CSW are priority areas of interest linking the high seas with the coasts and its hinterland. Seaports are the hubs of global transportation routes where all merchant shipping operations start and end. Even trans-oceanic traffic is partially conducted through narrow straits and passages leading to seaports.

As it stands, special importance is to be attached to the vital interface of many legal, organizational, economic, technological, governmental personnel, and/or civilian spheres of responsibility and their interdependencies: these are what make the confined and shallow waters unique.

The maritime environment of today is experiencing a wide range of challenges (national as well as local, regional, and global) which require both a comprehensive approach and collective efforts to address.[2] Maritime security is a basic prerequisite for smooth functioning of the global economy. Hence ensuring maritime security is a huge challenge facing many entities worldwide from public and private sectors, specifically pointing at:

- preserving navigational freedom;
- facilitating commerce; and
- maintaining good governance at sea.

The military significance of CSW

Maritime power, both in an authoritative and physical sense, is substantiated by the ability of an actor to gain control over sea areas of his interest (surface, subsurface, airspace) associated to the freedom of movement as well as action within these areas, and concurrently to exert diplomatic, economic, and military influence at a time and place of his choice. Maritime power has traditionally been employed globally to maintain the freedom of navigation as an essential foundation for the economic prosperity and overall welfare of states; conversely it has been regularly used to disrupt the SLOCs of an opponent. In this regard, maritime forces offer their utility across the entire spectrum of war-fighting: first at an early stage to deter an opponent and/or to prepare the operational environment, then to secure access and establish sea control, followed by power projection – often in a joint campaign or by forces ashore (through strike, amphibi-ous, and/or joint fires operations). Lastly, they are used to secure the withdrawal of own forces.

In order to fulfill such tasks and missions a naval force should be able to successfully operate within the littorals and consequently also within the CSW, as part of the littorals. This conver-gence zone between the high seas and the coast varies in its extension on both sides of the shoreline. Its limits depend on geographical and operational factors. Apart from mere geograph-ical and military factors, further aspects – namely political and economic interests – are also to be taken into account when defining this specific littoral zone.

The area of CSW (being part of the littorals) does not necessarily extend as far offshore or as far inshore as the littoral zone. However, fjord-like environments, deltas, and streams, even vast inland waters, can be regarded as CSW although they might extend deep beyond the beaches adjacent to the shoreline.

The littorals, especially CSW, offer more natural and geographic challenges to both attack-ers and defenders than open and deep waters. In these waters for instance there are greater opportunities for surprise and disguise. The effects of oceanography and meteorology are more distinctive in CSW and significantly complicate operations compared to open ocean. Water depth clearly limits not just the movements of vessels with deeper drafts but also influences the consistency of the element 'water' itself, just as its temperature, the salinity, the condition of the seabed, or the character and the shape of the coast do. All of these factors affect, for instance, the performance of underwater sensors. Similarly, air temperature, wave height, wind speed, humidity, precipitation, cloud amount, or the presence of fog affect radar, infrared sensors, and radio communications, while haze and other forms of visual distortion affect the performance of optical devices. Furthermore, radio and radar signals can also be distorted by nearby land masses.[3] All of these factors significantly influence military assets both in their employment and performance. In summary, no other maritime area is more directly affected by environmental features than CSW.

CSW challenge military operations and planners with a multifaceted and confusing envir-onment. The increased risks must be thoroughly assessed and countered as quickly and effect-ively as possible because maneuvering space is restricted and reaction time is significantly reduced. In CSW, naval forces are extremely vulnerable to a variety of both conventional and non-conventional threats that emerge simultaneously or in close succession. Specifically, hybrid threats[4] that attempt to exploit naval vulnerabilities through a variety of asymmetric approaches (e.g. IEDs, suicide assets) pose a lethal danger to naval forces, regardless of whether they are state or non-state actors. In addition, cyber attacks are undoubtedly extremely critical in CSW as they may jam or deceive technical navigation and weapon guidance as well as surveillance and communication systems (e.g. Global Positioning System [GPS], Recognized Maritime Picture [RMP], or data and voice communication). It is more than obvious that a navy's ability to operate in CSW under unpredictable competitive pressure whilst at the same time maintaining accurate and timely threat assessment proves to be increasingly challenging.

Additionally, layered anti-access/area denial (A2/AD)[5] capabilities are to be faced. They are mainly oriented to increase the degree of friction, to expand a naval zone of influence, and to enhance risks to naval forces operating in CSW. The intensity of the respective sustained multi-dimensional threats raises fundamental questions about the survivability as well as the necessity of naval forces to operate in this most heavily congested environment. Basically having access to the technologies and comparable means utilized by NATO forces, the Alliance has to assume that any opponent may conduct extensive A2/AD missions and along with that could pose a credible threat in CSW. Information technology, precision-guided munitions, stealth tech-nology, unmanned or autonomous vehicle systems, cruise missiles, and use of satellite bandwidth are only some of the already available technologies and means. Furthermore, the supplier's willingness to share technologies, the trend to reduced costs by using commercial products, and increasingly eased access to international arms markets contribute to this ongoing proliferation.

The inevitable presence of people further adds to this complexity. The masses that actually make their living or commute on inshore waterways exceed their numbers on the open oceans by multiples. This effect is gaining even more significance as most of the world's mega-cities are located on or close to the coast.[6] Hence, the CSW environment also reflects urban warfare issues. The assumption that most of the civilians are going to leave or avoid the area when this operational space is transformed into battle-space may prove to be incorrect. People in many parts of the world are dependent on the unhampered use of the coastal waters and will therefore take what others may consider to be insane risks. Unless an area becomes a theater for major conflict, commercial trade and fishing is very likely to continue, because any impediments would cause dire consequences to those individuals whose livelihood depends on those means.[7]

In crisis and conflict the presence of neutrals and uninvolved individuals is not just a challenge with regard to avoiding collateral damage; they may also deliberately be exploited to disguise intentions of an opponent, to impede maritime situational awareness (MSA), and may even be used as human shields. The expectation must therefore be that the volume of maritime traffic is likely to remain at normal or near-normal level despite the dangers. Identifying targets of interest within the mass of normal traffic will, in many cases, be achieved only by approaching, interrogating, and occasionally boarding suspicious craft.[8]

The CSW operational environment encompasses the maritime, air, land, space, and cyber domains as well as the information space and in that regard, also all associated opposing, friendly, and neutral systems (political, military, economic, social, informational, infrastructure, legal, and others). Understanding this complex environment has always required a perception broader than just an adversary's military force and combat capabilities. The specific requirements for and the particular types of operations in CSW demand a comprehensive understanding of such systems and capabilities that are relevant for a successful conduct of missions and tasks in this environment.

Furthermore, CSW should be also regarded as an adjacent maritime area to the high seas and an essential part of the operations area (e.g. for amphibious or reinforcement operations). In this vein, by attaining (local) sea control in CSW, smooth and possibly unhindered movement of naval forces approaching from the high seas could be also attained. CSW should also be considered from the aspect of its landward areas, which influence greatly action at sea (e.g. weapon and sensor employments from land, logistics, etc.). Bearing all this in mind, CSW are areas of exceptional relevance for military operations. Needless to say, CSW pose a significant challenge to military planners and commanders; easily summarized in the phrase "think big in a confined space."

Rising complexity in the CSW battle-space

As part of the transition zone interfacing land and sea, CSW are at the very heart of that sphere where all military domains interrelate: the military theater with the largest share in 'jointness.' In other words: CSW are an essential battlefield of increasing importance, while also facing the challenges that arise from growing complexity. Without question the geographical environment of CSW is very challenging, which creates manifold natural and manmade obstacles for military, in particular maritime operations. Already, and expected to be even more so in future, CSW are heavily trafficked areas. Besides the commercial traffic on main global maritime routes intersecting the littorals as well as the regional and local coastal transportation, a broad spectrum of further marine traffic is noticeable – of course regionally varying. This increasingly dense traffic provides favorable conditions for illegal trafficking. In addition to the confusing terrain and the multitude of contacts, artificial islands and critical superstructures such as gas and oil rigs, wind energy generators, and other exploration platforms will increasingly exert a tremendous influence on operations in CSW and consequently further enhance the already challenging complexity of this battle-space.

In principle, rapid technological progress (notably within the past two decades and especially in the sphere of electronic media) has facilitated the acceleration of information technology as a key player in today's operational area. This has in turn made cyberspace (examined in more detail later) an increasingly crucial aspect of the battle-space. Consequently, new notions about conduct of warfare (e.g. cyber warfare through sabotage of critical infrastructure that is con-nected to and dependent on the internet) and protagonists (e.g. non-state and hybrid actors) have recently come to the foreground and are expected to continue to evolve into significant factors in the future. Areas of specific impact will include congested and cramped environments, like CSW, where many possible threats appear simultaneously.

Adding this additional factor will increase the level of complexity and ambiguity in the operational space, affecting especially MSA. If this vast amount of information (a variety and high number of threats hidden amongst the even larger amount of contacts and available infor-mation) is not interpreted, processed, and maintained in such a restricted space as CSW, vessels could easily fall victim to information overflow resulting in a kind of 'sea blindness.' From an attacker's point of view, these multi-dimensional/asymmetric threats, in concert with 'surprise' (an inherent characteristic of CSW environment), generate a formidable combination of possi-bilities. The impact of such possibilities is increased exponentially by the unique characteristics of this environment.

In connection with 'surprise,' CSW are also characterized by 'speed': speed of data exchange and picture compilation, speed of command and control, speed of (re-) action. In order to be faster than an adversary and also to maintain the initiative, 'speed' must remain a key require-ment in future military campaigns, particularly those involving CSW. This will be achieved through knowledge, decision, and technological superiority (e.g. Artificial Intelligence [AI]). In the near future, AI will likely continue to be context-specific, restricted to certain types of problems. Expansion to a broader context or stepping outside the frame of a particular problem will still require a human interface. However, as machine intelligence advances the functional comprehension and decision competence of AI will progress, being increasingly able to operate in complex and cramped environments.[9] Their importance and gravity in shaping the outcome of a campaign will steadily increase over the upcoming years.

As previously stated, the battle-space in CSW is heavily influenced by the adjacent densely urbanized areas. These are melting pots where social, economic, and political interests easily come into conflict, being superimposed by the overarching technological progress. Coastal mega-cities will especially complicate and greatly challenge combat missions as well as the political, social, and economic landscape in the future. The tendency for people to cluster in that sphere of gravity in concert with intensified connectivity among them will further increase this complexity. As such, military action ashore will affect significantly the maritime environment and vice versa. And, in having also the interdependencies of the strategic, oper-ational, or tactical level in mind, any reduction of discrete distances among these levels as well as among combatants and non-combatants enhances the demand for changing the character of military activity (which implies changes to military mindset governing the current status), as well as sound judgment, especially an enhanced ability to distinguish abnormalities in a blurred environment.

Returning to cyberspace, this is the latest aspect of the modern battle-space undoubtedly transforming communication in the information age. NATO defines four domains as global commons: air, maritime, space, and cyberspace. It is important to identify and clarify the interests in each of these domains as well as to understand the implications and complexity of an increasingly inter-connected world, to grasp the nature of threats to those interests, and to allocate resources as efficiently as possible to counter threats and reduce related risks. 'Cyberspace' is basically related to 'Information and Data Flow' whilst 'Maritime' is primarily related to 'Security,' also for instance involving commerce, trade and critical infrastructure, both being vital for an unhampered flow of cargo and values. But how do data flow and the flow of cargo or values inter-relate?

Actors from around the world, whether they are individuals or threat networks, may easily impede operations in CSW by misusing cyberspace. This should be considered in direct conjunction with the dissemination of modern technologies, openly available at very small cost, and ready for use. Partial non-availability of information technology as a result of cyber attacks will affect companies that are either directly or indirectly related to sea-trade, sea-touristic, or any other kind of maritime commerce. This may cause significantly negative effects to social, organizational, and governmental structures as well as the financial markets. The list of imaginable hazards must be extended to include not only individual losses, like ships or life, but also the massive after-effects following in the wake of events such as deliberately provoked environmental catastrophes or major disasters (e.g. a maximum credible accident in a nuclear power plant, very often located at or very close to the shoreline).

Thus, enhancing cyber resilience[10] is tantamount to increasing security in the maritime domain, which is in turn basically nothing else but an improvement of cyberspace security. An interactive maritime cyber response process is an appropriate way to prevent, detect, assess, and respond to cyber challenges in the maritime domain. Such a coordinated process expands cyber domain awareness and provides a constant military assessment of both compliant and non-compliant actors – necessary to be conducted on all command levels.

On the bottom line, the maritime and in particular the CSW environment should be recognized as a highly complex battle-space where a network of innumerable stakeholders and individuals is active in manifold specific realms and levels, sharing obvious as well as hidden dependencies of various intensity. This requires a concerted, effective interface analysis approach for efficient cyberspace security as well as an established 'cyber situational awareness' on all command levels.

Diversity of actors in CSW

A broad variety of heterogeneous 'players' is active in CSW, most of whom use CSW in a peaceful way, while potentially creating implications for military operations. Some actors operating in CSW environments, however, may be connected to threat networks or be pursuing other malicious intents calling for governance up to the employment of military power. This spectrum relevant for operations in CSW ranges from:

- ill-equipped – however, very determined – individuals (e.g. criminals or insurgents), to sophisticated and capable paramilitary groups (e.g. terrorists or militia), up to well-organized, -equipped, and -trained military forces (multi-capable, including increased A2/AD, hybrid, cyber);
- state actors (e.g. military forces, coast guards, or police) and governmental organizations (GOs) (e.g. hydrographic services), to non-state actors such as commercial actors (e.g. shipping companies or fishery), as well as non-governmental organizations (NGOs) (e.g. humanitarian aid organizations or private maritime security companies [PMSC]);

- democratic states with separation of power and rule of law over totalitarian states up to rogue nations;
- recognizable soldiers on the battlefield, up to invisible cyber warriors fighting in front of their personal computer, free from battle stress – and enjoying the anonymity provided by the cyber domain.

In general, a partial reversal of the military modes of action along with a diversification in basic policies is to be expected. State actors are likely to develop capabilities for the conduct of asymmetric approaches[11] and bring them back to bear (e.g. in avoiding extensive force-on-force engagements by waging long-term insurgencies designed to exhaust the opponent), whilst at the same time non-state actors are likely to embrace conventional forms of war (e.g. in copying specific methods of attack or in taking advantage of the technology diffusion by utilizing high-tech armament such as high-end sensors, guided weapons, space and cyberspace systems).[12]

Actors using the cyber domain to pose threats or carry out belligerent acts will become a more important factor to be considered in future operations. Information networks may be utilized for more than just waging a propaganda war; they may rather be exploited – not just by cyber warriors – as the primary means of communication and information exchange in order to synchronize and coordinate combat action.[13] Actors will no longer have to operate only in a geographically restricted environment such as CSW, but may be externally positioned anywhere in the world using information technologies, with relatively little immediate risk, to generate effects 'inside' an Area of Operations (AOO). Growing cyber and hybrid threats from non-conventional forces and means will make the conduct of operations in CSW increasingly demanding and challenge the *modus operandi* of the Alliance even more in future. As such, advanced capabilities will be required and evolved rules of engagement (ROE) should be considered to deal with threat networks, especially when not acting inside a defined AOO.

The emergence of armed private security actors such as PMSC on board merchant ships is also to be noted. Such actors may provide enhanced protection to threatened vessels and therefore make an important contribution to maritime security. However, they operate outside any military chain of command or governmental control and thus may not (necessarily) pay regard to established ROE. Further expansion of the private security sector is very likely; for instance, future employments of PMSC to secure offshore critical infrastructure or even execute coast guard tasks are quite probable. Hence, PMSC can evolve to partly relieve regular military forces. In this context, opportunities for cooperation with the private security sector in order to address and tackle common threats should be further investigated and necessary arrangements fixed (e.g. legal status or widely acknowledged policies and procedures).

The aforementioned variety of actors in such a complex and unique environment like CSW, where operations are challenged not just by very specific geological and physical conditions, but also by difficult command and control conditions such as coping with potentially degraded and blurred information, will render the distinction between combatants and non-parties extremely difficult. The increasing public and private involvement in future conflicts demands enhanced discrimination and threat assessment capabilities. On the other side, there may also be beneficial cross-domain synergies between military forces and other agencies, such as NGOs or PMSCs.

Main parameters for prospective operations in CSW

Direct engagements between the major powers cannot be precluded, but they remain not very likely, especially due to the nuclear stalemate. As long as the overall supremacy of the Alliance is indisputable, the risk of a major conflict may be reduced. In any case we are not living in a world of comprehensive peace. Incompatible political, social, and cultural (including religious convictions) systems as well as a mutual desire for conquering economic interests bear an inherent and enduring potential for conflicts involving force of arms. In this context, maritime operations being carried out in the future in a large-scale scenario are not foreseen, but rather in the manner of recent events. Thus, local or at worst regional conventional conflicts are to be expected because of the struggle of some states for hegemony and rising nations, rogue states, or transnational groups of terrorists attempting to expand their sphere of influence by carrying out belligerent acts, including executing limited wars. Although the Alliance must retain its genuine defense capacity for large-scale conflicts, it has to prepare for smaller-scale conflicts that are virtually always linked to operations in CSW.

Future conflicts in CSW will be characterized by short notice, rapid escalation, limited duration, and high intensity leading to increased mortality as well as danger of collateral damages; all this taking place simultaneously or consecutively and being conducted in the way of 'conventional' war-fighting. Operations below the threshold of war, for instance constabulary and humanitarian missions aiming at supporting stability in concert with civilian organizations and entities, should also be expected to be conducted in CSW. These operations will be multi-faceted and generally conducted without the use of weapons. However, elements of high-intensity combat may not be completely ruled out, for instance, in policing missions. The Alliance is well advised to provide capacities for the entire range of potential tasks, in other words, to have appropriate capabilities at hand that are optimized for operations in CSW.

The age of global economy inevitably implies the emergence of related risks and threats. Prospective targets in CSW are likely to be maritime trade, critical maritime offshore and coastal infrastructure (facilities/installations such as wind-power plants, oil rigs, sea-cables, or ports), and other technological equipment (e.g. automatic identification, navigation or logistic supply systems, business and government IT, or communication networks). Undoubtedly all these constitute high-value targets for probable cyber attacks.

Such challenges are of general public interest and hence significant for the entire human community. Consequently, maritime forces must be well prepared to support their security. Any stake of the Alliance in this matter spins off into enhanced maritime security especially in the challenging CSW environment. Generally, as world trade will be more than ever dependent on unhampered seaways, SLOCs constitute potential targets vulnerable to assaults.

In mirroring these basic characteristics of future conflicts towards the previous findings, they will have following dire consequences for CSW:

- even further rising complexity (enhanced variety and number of actors, threats and risks in a congested and contested environment);
- more inscrutability (heterogeneous mixture of numerous actors that are increasingly interconnected and not necessarily physically present, often hiding amongst uninvolved third parties and hence difficult to distinguish);
- increasingly also extensively unmanned and autonomous systems (in a strategic role, reducing the crew risks and being very cost-efficient);
- decline of 'symmetry' in warfare (unequal opponents by definition but equal by technology as well as more and more by tactics);
- growing importance of cyber domain (advances in cyber technology increase the importance of controlling cyberspace and concurrently denying its use by opponents);
- increasing speed – high operational tempo (crisis response on short notice, more frequent and drastic changes to the tactical as well as operational situation with little or no warning on the battlefield);

- incremental lethality (rapidly staggered attacks of short duration, carried out with high vehemence and sophisticated weapons);
- overload of information, commercial or military;
- increasingly dense and contested operational environment (due to urbanization, development of trade, exploitation of natural resources, etc.);
- fading distinctions between military–civilian and public–private perceptions as well as perceptions of sovereignty (e.g. PMSCs more and more acting in maritime security).

As such, prospective operations in CSW will pursue the following general objectives:

- Unlimited access to:
  - the maritime portion of the global commons;
  - the AOO;
  - key coastal strips/infrastructure ashore (in case of joint operations).
- Freedom of:
  - action/operational maneuver (gaining/maintaining the initiative);
  - navigation.
- Protection of:
  - maritime trade and SLOCs;
  - high-value assets;
  - critical infrastructure, both sea-borne (like platforms, ships) and ashore on the coastline (power plants, harbor facilities) in all domains;
  - computer networks and technologies sensitive for military operations.
- Ability to:
  - deploy world-wide and at the same time to prevail in a hostile CSW environment;
  - establish (local) sea control;
  - perform effective MSA;
  - carry out enduring operations;
  - respond in a scaled but decisive way (having capabilities at one's command to counter insurgency and terrorist actions up to conventional force-on-force combat).
- Enforcement of:
  - governance;
  - the rule of international law;
  - maritime security.
- Support to actions ashore/interaction with forces ashore.

Of course these characteristics will differ from operation to operation in their attributes and specifications, with numerous combinations possible. However, the objectives will keep us busy in the future – definitely with regard to the maritime domain.

To clarify once more: In no way do all these aspects mean that conventional areas of maritime warfare are to be neglected. To this end, the capability to prevail in operations against sophisticated opponents is always to be regarded as a core capability. The traditional symmetric threat will thus remain as a fundamental and integral part of future capability evaluations. However, the portfolio of required capabilities must be expanded to counter asymmetric as well as hybrid and cyber threats which, in the future, are likely to be the main maritime forces employed in CSW.

Bearing all that in mind, future naval forces need to be well organized, well equipped, and well trained[14] to conduct all types of joint and combined operations in CSW ranging from humanitarian aid and disaster relief over small-scale contingencies up to major war-fighting conflicts, be they regular- or irregular-oriented. In that regard, consequent and realistic training (war-gaming, synthetic training, and live exercises) incorporating CSW characteristics should also be considered.

Epilogue

Confined and shallow waters is a challenging environment with a broad spectrum of particularities that contribute to its unique complexity and significance. The latter is deduced from the fact that CSW are the very focal point of the littoral transition zone that not only connects the high seas with land masses, but furthermore involves all dimensions relevant for mankind. Therefore, this environment will play an even more vital role in future conflicts and subsequent military operations. Not only due to its contested and cramped character (both at sea as well as ashore) but also owing to the very specific operational conditions (a variety of actors involving a broad scope of warfare areas), CSW constitute an extremely challenging environment for military commanders planning and conducting joint and combined operations in the AOO.

The overall significance of the littorals for humankind has not changed throughout history; it may rather have increased and will most likely continue in that direction within the upcoming decades. Likewise, the military relevance of CSW – being part of the littorals – has always remained enormous. This did not change when technological progress half a millennium ago allowed the use of the high seas. It may be disputed amongst historians whether there have been shifts in the main focus, but CSW have doubtless always been and will remain in future a prominent battle-space at the intersection of all military domains.

Notes

1 NATO Allied Maritime Strategy, II: The Maritime Security Environment, March 18, 2011.
2 Lutz Feldt, Peter Roell, and Ralph D. Thiele, *Maritime Security: Perspectives for a Comprehensive Approach*, ISPSW Strategy Series, Focus on Defence and International Security 222 (Berlin: ISPSW, 2013), p. 2.
3 Milan Vego, *Naval Strategy and Operations in Narrow Seas* (London: Frank Cass Publishers, 2003), pp. 33–40.
4 "Those posed by adversaries, with the ability to simultaneously employ conventional and non-conventional means adaptively in pursuit of their objectives." NATO, "Hybrid Threats Description: BI-SC Input for a New Capstone Concept for the Military Contribution to Countering Hybrid Threats" (2010), para. 7.
5 Anti-access (A2): Action intended to slow deployment of friendly forces into a theater or cause forces to operate from distances farther from the locus of conflict than they would otherwise prefer. A2 affects movement to a theater. Area-denial (AD): Action intended to impede friendly operations within areas where an adversary cannot or will not prevent access. AD affects maneuver within a theater.
6 David Kilcullen, *Out of the Mountains: The Coming Age of the Urban Guerrilla* (New York: Oxford University Press, 2013), p. 32.
7 The continuation of tanker traffic during the 1984–8 "Tanker War" in the Persian/Arabian Gulf may serve as an exemplary proof of this thesis.
8 Martin Murphy, *Littoral Combat Ship: An Examination of its Possible Concepts of Operation* (Washington, DC: CSBA, 2010), pp. 13–14.
9 Robert O. Work and Shawn Brimley: *Preparing for War in the Robotic Age* (Washington, DC: Center for a New American Security, 2014), p. 25.
10 "To achieve this, systems are to be developed that will have enhanced self-monitoring capabilities, such as self-diagnosis/self-adaptive/ healing platforms and networks. (A) Self-protecting: To anticipate, detect, identify and protect against attacks from anywhere. Self-protecting components can detect hostile behaviors as they occur and take corrective actions to make themselves less vulnerable. The hostile behaviors can include unauthorized access and use, virus infection and proliferation, and

denial-of-service attacks. (B) Intelligent agents and remote (self) management features." HQ Supreme Allied Commander Transformation, Long Term Requirements Branch, *Technology Trend Survey: Future Emerging Technology Trends. A Food-for-Thought Paper to Support the NATO Defence Planning Process* (September 2011), pp. 67–8.

11 "It would be utterly misleading to assume that 'asymmetric' is synonymous with 'non-state'. There is a long history of states taking advantage of asymmetric approaches, arguably even more at sea than on land. Even in the sailing era of war between the great powers, for example, France and then the young United States did not seek to context command of the seas with the Royal Navy but rather to inflict economic losses by raiding commerce. From the mid-nineteenth century onwards the industrial revolution began to provide further options for those who wished to avoid taking on the leading naval powers at their own game. In the late nineteenth century, for example, there arose in France the 'jeune école', which argued that rather than build a battle-fleet to counter that of the Royal Navy, a better approach would be to focus on large numbers of small, agile torpedo boats which would overwhelm the powerful but ponderous British battle-fleet." Theodore Ropp, "Continental Doctrines of Sea Power," in Edward M. Earle (ed.), *Makers of Modern Strategy: Military Thought from Machiavelli to Hitler* (Princeton, NJ: Princeton University Press, 1943), pp. 447–54.

12 For example, the increase in autonomous systems, even usable by small groups or single persons, can be ascribed to that diffusion.

13 For example, individual fighters sailing with appropriately shaped and equipped jet skis could disseminate data in real time globally resulting in an uncontrolled information environment.

14 Covering all aspects of DOTMLPFI (Doctrine, Organization, Training, Material, Leadership, Personnel, Facilities, Interoperability).

13

POWER-PROJECTION VS. ANTI-ACCESS/AREA-DENIAL (A2/AD)

The operational concepts of the U.S. Navy (USN) and the People's Liberation Army Navy (PLAN) in the Indo-Pacific region

Nikolaus Scholik

With a particular focus on the situation in the Indo-Pacific region, there are only two remaining major players on the global maritime 'chessboard' today, the United States and the People's Republic of China. While lessons can be drawn regarding the importance of sea power by examining strategic considerations and goals at a theoretical level – Mahan[1] and Corbett[2] and all of the more modern points of view – the operational feasibility of all strategic requirements, as seen below, poses quite different demands on the political, military, arms industry and technological capabilities of any particular state.

Nowadays, maritime strategy is, more so than ever before, subject to factors of political intent, rapid technological progress and economic potential, as well as all the other related parameters. Furthermore, there is the proven and recognized supremacy of the United States through the USN. This naval supremacy coerces all states also pursuing global ambitions as part of their (overall) strategy, together with the United States itself, to embark on a new, comprehensive arms race. Comprehensive because, in contrast to earlier times when maritime armament primarily meant combat capability via water, ship or fleet against ship or fleet, the scope of maritime warfare has continually expanded since the middle of the last century. It now includes warfare under, on and over the water, in near space, the area of electronic combat and battle management, cyber war[3] (data security and the fight to control it) and the corresponding and increasing requirements for training and leadership. In addition, there is economic uncertainty throughout the world to the extent that there is no state or system of states, no local or regional economy nor politico-economic system that is not affected.

Globalization and the interconnection of all economic trade, with consequences that reach deep into national systems, lead to political unrest that, in turn, is additionally challenged by global terror and organized crime, and is increasingly difficult to resolve peacefully.

Strategic requirements

Given these external difficulties, current power relations in the maritime sphere – those of course that are operationally feasible – have remained relatively unchanged for several decades. It is a constant for all maritime powers to recognize the USN as being the only navy to possess global military projection capabilities and consequently the global capacity for military intervention at any time. Let us briefly remind ourselves of the United States' strategic maritime objectives:

- limiting regional conflicts;
- preventing wars between [major] powers – deterrence;
- winning war(s), once engaged;
- promoting international partnerships;
- preventing local disturbances;
- achieving supremacy through a position of absolute maritime strength; and
- maintaining a world-wide power-projection capacity.

After an unsuccessful attempt by the Soviet Union to create a capable blue-water navy during the Cold War,[4] only China, since the political changes under Deng Xiaoping from 1979 on, has developed an increasing emphasis on maritime power, that could, from a United States point of view, jeopardize American supremacy in the mid- to long term. The mutual inter-dependence that has existed and has been built upon for some decades, particularly at an economic level,[5] has not led to any substantial rapprochement in the area of security.

The powerful role of the United States as the security partner of several important states in the Asian-Pacific region contradicts China's long-term objectives to acquire political dominance which is on par with its economic dominance; first regionally and then globally. China's strategic maritime objectives are fundamentally different, bearing in mind its evident weaknesses and insufficient capabilities:

- winning time plus regional/global deterrence;
- arming with pursuing the long-term objective of power projection;
- coastal capabilities and "string of pearls"[6] in preference to blue-water navy[7] (operational deep-sea fleet); and
- reaching a position of regional power up to the second string of islands in the short-term.

While American objectives are clearly defined and the necessary hard- and software are both available and under constant development, we should look more closely at China's requirements in order to better evaluate its operational capacity.

The PLAN's operational potential is deployed in accordance with the strategic requirements and allocated to theaters of action. The most sensitive regions are the East and South China Sea and the continuation of the main route in the Indian Ocean through the Straits of Malacca. This is where China's key maritime security issues are concentrated – North Korea, Taiwan, territorial differences with Japan, Vietnam, Malaysia and the Philippines and also the substantial difficulties of protecting Chinese sea routes for imports (raw materials) and essential exports. Bearing in mind its recognized weaknesses, in particular versus the USN, the leaders of the PLAN have closely studied the strategic and operational principles of Mahan and Corbett. A further medium-term aspect of strategic maritime planning is the increase in maritime strength in the area of projection capability; at all times, however, achieving reunification with Taiwan (if necessary, and as a last resort, with military means) remains a major political objective.

The PLAN's operational concept

Here, one should briefly return to Mahan in order to explain his operational theories, which the PLAN has studied closely. In his principal work, Mahan concerns himself with this very problem: a weak navy facing a potentially stronger opponent; in connection with this concept he coined the expression "fortress fleet." This may be understood as naval forces (a fleet as it was previously called), which almost exclusively operate under the fire protection of coastal batteries. There have, of course, been huge technical changes since Mahan's reflections on the subject and consequently entirely new requirements have emerged. However, as we shall see, the fundamental idea remains valid. The second concept that should, at this point, be mentioned is the "fleet in being." This can be construed as naval forces which (almost) never leave safe harbor. Their very existence, however, compels the opponent to maintain forces at the ready. It appears that a "fleet in being" represents part of a doctrine of access denial and not an instrument of power projection or control/security of sea routes.

Before analyzing the PLAN's operational rationale in relation to the strengths of the USN, further terms should be clearly defined: first, the term "power projection," which is the USN's principle strategic objective. This can be understood as the deployment of some or all elements of national power in order to move effective forces to and from various locations with the purpose of responding to crises, providing deterrence and underpinning stability. The response to power projection that has already been used in the title of this chapter, i.e. the abbreviation A2/AD, is defined in the following way: A2, or anti-access, means that action can be taken or capabilities employed, even over greater distances, in order to prevent opposing forces from accessing an area of operation (deterrence). AD, or area-denial, defines action and capabilities, normally over shorter distances, that do not deny the opponent access to a theater of operation but are intended to limit his scope of activity in that space.

It is no surprise that the PLAN's strategies are exactly geared to the operational application of their concept to deal with power projection. In the face of the USN's operative strength and PLAN's weakness in this area, A2/AD measures are most likely to be successful as long as the strategic objectives remain more defensive than offensive. Taiwan – a conflict that the United States is obliged to and much rather wants to avoid (for political reasons) – could be an important exception in this scenario.

A2/AD

The anti-access/area-denial concept is understood as an integrated part of China's defense. In this sense, we can speak of a joint[8] concept, similar to the one promoted in the United States. However, in the same way as in the United States, where "military branch thinking" also continues to prevail, it is unclear what the general staff understands by "joint" and what successful operations would be. The fundamental concept of A2/AD certainly envisages the deployment of all three branches of combat forces, e.g. the movement of PLAAF (People's Liberation Army Air Force) and PLAG (People's Liberation Army Ground Forces)[9] to the coast; AD, in terms of a military branch (underwater and on the surface), would tend to be one of the PLAN's tasks. First of all, however, let us look at the conceptual aspect: the theater (combat area of some magnitude)[10] that stretches from China's territory to that of the opponent (in our analysis, that of the United States, i.e. to the opposite Pacific coast) is a vast area.[11] Since Chinese defense fundamentally incorporates all means, including strategic nuclear weapons, the application of the A2/AD doctrine is to be seen as applicable within the area up to the second chain of islands – the line through the main Japanese

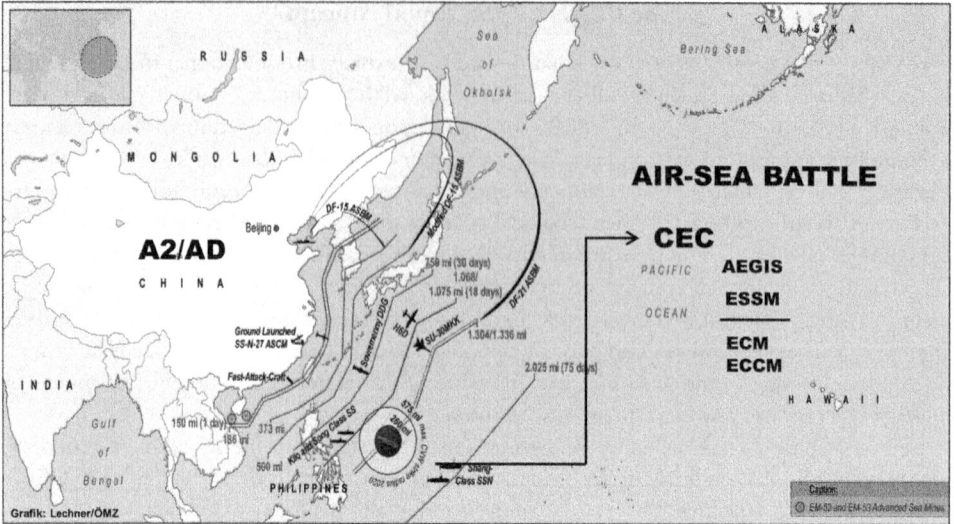

Figure 13.1   Maritime operative concepts of the Chinese Navy

island, Honshu, above the northern Marianas, Guam, Micronesia, Palau and from there following a vertical line south (approx. 1,300 nautical miles parallel to the Chinese Pacific coast). Beyond this point and in the sense of a "fortress fleet," only strategic submarines, long-distance bombers and various (ballistic) types of rocket would be effective. Electronic reconnaissance and cyber warfare are of course effective outside of these areas, *de facto* universally, if the necessary technology is available.

Figure 13.1 shows the systems based on this concept and the rationale for their deployment with reference both to separation and deployment distances and the supply intervals which have to be assigned to each system. In general, the alignment is intended to impede the access of opposing maritime forces (CSG/NTG: carrier strike group/naval task group)[12] and limit their radius of operation to areas near the coast. In the most favorable instance, strong A2/AD capacities would thus prevent the access of these forces up to a distance where their moveable systems (CVW: carrier air wing)[13] cannot be deployed with full effect. At the present time, a USN CVW can cover an operational radius of approximately 260 nautical miles; with the successive supersession of the Nimitz-class aircraft carriers by the Ford-class aircraft carriers (CVN 78 ff. from 2015 on) and the planned replacement of the present principal USN fighter plane, the F-18 Super Hornet, with the new multi-purpose fighter plane, JSF F 35-C (joint strike fighter), the operational radius will increase to 575 nautical miles. This means that all Chinese A2/AD measures, according to PLAN, are designed, in the first instance, to keep USN carriers away from areas beyond the second island chain, and/or to limit their effectiveness the nearer they approach the Chinese coast. This is achieved as shown in Table 13.1.

If we consider the U.S. CSG concept in this theater, we should evaluate the opponent's likely response. It may be construed as an anecdote, but in answer to the question, "which threat from the opponent is most alarming," an American carrier commander is supposed to have answered: "submarines." An operational and comprehensively equipped A2/AD model (joint) with proven coordination of forces and full network and electronic integration (3C+I: communication, command, control + intelligence/military intelligence) would represent a new dimension

Table 13.1 Range of Chinese anti-access/area-denial measures, and principal military branch to employ them

Coastal area	up to 150 NM	sea mines	PLAN
		fighter/ground attack aircraft	PLAN/PLAAF
	up to 186 NM	ASCM SS-N-27[a]	PLAG
Medium range	up to 373 NM	ASBM DF-15[b]	PLAN
	up to 500 NM	ASBM DF-15 mod.	PLAN
	up to 750 NM	DDG *Sovremenny*-class guided-missile destroyers[c]	PLAN
		Kilo-/Song-class hunter/killer submarines[d]	PLAN
Long range	up to 1075 NM	H6D reconnaissance aircraft[e]	PLAAF
	up to 1304 NM	long-distance bomber SU-30MKK[f]	PLAAF
	up to 1336 NM	ASBM DF-21[g]	PLAG

Notes

a ASCM: Anti-Ship Cruise Missile/Cruise Missile.

b ASBM: Anti-Ship Ballistic Missile.

c Soviet/Russian destroyer class, 4 PLAN-units.

d *KILO*-class: SS (Ship Submersible) diesel hunter-killer submarines of Soviet origin. *SONG*-class: SS Chinese diesel-electric hunter-killer submarines.

e Chinese manufactured under licence of the Soviet TU-16, originally a medium- to long-range bomber; the HS/version D serves marine long-distance reconnaissance and as ECM-guidance system.

f Suchoi built more than 70 modified versions (-MKK) of the SU-30 for the PLAAF.

g ASBM DF-21A: mobile ballistic anti-ship missile, nuclear or conventional warhead.

of deterrence which would need to be monitored, in relation to power projection, by American politics (alliances in the region, Taiwan, South Korea, Japan, the Philippines and Australia) and the USN. This is, of course, happening: American think tanks, the USN, their training centers and the JCS (Joint Chiefs of Staff) have examined this challenge in detail, remembering that the announcement of a strategic or operational concept by no means equates to its perfect deployment. Correspondingly, we must also evaluate China's approach to the announcement of new weapon systems and armament. As an example, let us look more closely at the presentation of the first Chinese aircraft carrier that the world saw in November 2012. In reality, the *Liaoning* was the former Soviet carrier, *Varyag*, of the *Kusnezov*-class, which was laid up in Ukraine in 1988.[14] The hull was sold to China in 1998, while the *Liaoning*'s construction was only "finished" at the Chinese Dalian wharf with its commission in September 2012 as a training and exercise ship. It cannot be compared to deployable carriers other nations field – it lacks all essential elements of a deployable CSG; as part of a group with 3C, it has no functional AEGIS[15] combat management system nor any trained and proven interaction capacity. Furthermore, when referring to operational capability (if required politically and/or militarily), one carrier actually requires two carriers due to rotational deployments. The ASBM D-21A Dongfeng and the Chinese stealth bomber Chengdu J-20 were presented in a similar way in the last two years.

Nevertheless, Chinese efforts in the maritime sphere are taken absolutely seriously by the Americans; not least they can be used as a lever to obtain further funds when presenting new requirements in Congress. As there is little change to be expected in terms of superiority, it should not be confused with invulnerability in the upcoming decade. The USN takes the Chinese A2/AD concept very seriously and has taken counter-measures that are discussed in the section on air–sea battle. Finally, it should be taken into consideration that any open attack on an American carrier in international waters, i.e. more than 12 nautical miles beyond the coast, would most likely be interpreted as a *casus belli* by the Americans and would be answered correspondingly. Here, one faces an old and unresolved point of conflict between the United States and China: on principle, China refuses other countries' warships the "right of innocent passage" within the 200 nautical mile EEZ (Exclusive Economic Zone)[16] – this, however, without any military and legal backing. In times of high tension, this policy could very well lead to a confrontation with an uncertain outcome.[17]

Both sides have the option of nuclear-strategic deterrence, although it must be acknowledged that, currently, the United States has a substantial advantage in terms of quantity, quality and design in virtually all areas. From this point of view, A2/AD and the American counter-model are, in principle, fully comparable with the stalemate position between the United States and the Soviet Union during the Cold War (with the difference that, politically and militarily, the underlying relations between China and the United States are quite different). However, any war, and the attack on a carrier (the Japanese attack on Pearl Harbor in December 1941, designed as a preventive strike against the U.S. although no U.S. carrier was in port at the time, serves as a reminder) may lead to a military escalation. Furthermore, given the possible escalation through the gamut of weapons systems, this would represent a risk that neither partner/opponent would want to take at the present time. Therefore, the old concept of deterrence remains a defining factor in this situation.

The USN's answer: air–sea battle[18]

Since A2/AD represents a serious obstacle to maritime joint operations, the U.S. Department of Defense has instructed both the USN and the USAF (U.S. Air Force) to develop an air–sea battle concept in response. The determining factor is the recognition that current U.S. strength is based on the cornerstones of global presence and unhampered projection capability. In turn, projection capability is based on a CSG's deployment rationale of an autonomous fighting group that, in NTG form, is capable of carrying out limited operations near and inside the opponent's coastal regions. Security guarantees and American alliances within the region, in particular in the region of the Chinese coast along the East and South China Seas facing Taiwan, South Korea and Japan, principally rest on this capability. It is complemented by the need to react quickly to the permanent threat posed by North Korea. Which primarily non-maritime components (with the exception of a submarine) can be used to keep a potential opponent with strong maritime forces away from extended coastal regions? Rockets – ballistic and cruise missiles – and aircraft may naturally be utilized as primary A2/AD systems. Currently, the ASBM and ASCM are being promoted within the framework of the Chinese armament programme. With its D-21 family, China seems to possess an effective arms system, assuming that the acclaimed technical, electronic and navigational systems really are proven and "safe." From the plethora of specialist articles and studies on this subject – almost all from American sources – attention is drawn to Loren Thompson's article in *Forbes* magazine[19] that examines the fundamental question of A2/AD capability, namely its capacity to sink an American carrier. Thompson concludes that, "If military commanders avoid taking unnecessary risks, U.S. aircraft carriers should retain their relevance to the balance of power in the Western Pacific through mid-century." And how could a radical change in American strategic and operational direction be possible, if the main elements of their global strategic objectives (sea power) and their operational implementation (power projection) are indeed very likely to remain in place to some extent?

For these reasons, the JCS, represented by their chairman (General Martin E. Dempsey), published the Joint Operational Access Concept in January 2012 (JOAC). It is the foundation for the measures to be taken in order to implement the air–sea battle concept in response to reinforced A2/AD capabilities (in particular, those of China). The aim is the capability for forcible entry operations, i.e. maintenance of full power-projection capacity to the point of assured access to any area of operation. Assured access signifies the unhampered national use of the global commons[20] achieved through the projection of all elements of national force. The deciding factor is that the credibility of the United States (particularly in respect of security alliances) is defined via power projection. It is the *sine qua non* for the protection of its global interests. Here, however, attention is drawn to two important historical and military factors regarding supplies and manpower. Firstly, the declaration made by General Douglas MacArthur in the 1950s "to avoid land wars in Asia" is equally valid today. He drew the right conclusions from the Korean War and wanted to underline that neither technical nor arms superiority can compensate for inferiority in numbers of personnel and in tactical intelligence. And in a blog commentary about the doctrine, Professor James Holmes of the U.S. Naval War College remarks that the "JOAC acknowledges the new, yet ancient reality that external powers can encounter resistance from local forces that boast sizeable advantages when fighting in their own backyard."[21]

It is also important to recognize the financial aspects of implementing the air–sea battle concept. It is even stated at JOAC that the concept "is in its fullest expression very resource-intensive." Its successful implementation is tied to the capacity to strike from great distances, employing newest generation long-distance bombers (which field stealth capability) and sea-based options, such as naval drones (UCLASS).[22]

The integration of air, land, sea, space and cyberspace is to be improved in order to give combatant commanders the necessary means to deter or defeat an opponent who possesses highly developed A2/AD capacities. Nevertheless, air–sea battle remains a limited operational concept that aims to form integrated air and sea combat forces (joint) to counter intense A2/AD threats.

The key is enhanced cooperation between USN and USAF that, in turn, rests on three pillars: the institutional development of organizational models into formal cooperation in order to meet the challenges of A2/AD in the long term; an agreement on the concept in order to ensure that the capabilities of military branch forces are sensibly integrated; and, finally to develop the best possible interplay of doctrine, organization, training, material, instruction, leadership and personnel in consideration of balance, redundancy, inter-operability and efficiency, wherever necessary. It involves a significant level of American preparation and planning in these areas.

In addition to the conceptual measures against A2/AD at these levels, the USN's arms- and systems-specific responses should also be briefly introduced. From the USN's point of view, the greatest threat for a CSG/NTG, especially relevant for the carrier, are two components of A2/AD: submarines and ASBM/ASCM. In the United States, there is a controversial and, to some extent, bitter discussion regarding the possible effect on a relatively cumbersome carrier which, in addition, offers a large target area. Proponents of a naval future without these "very vulnerable carriers" are bringing up numerous arguments against carrying on with the USN concept of power projection – in particular, economic, technological, increased capability in the A2/AD area and continuing technological development with an increasing threat to the carrier through ASBM/ASCM. As an example, mention can be made of an interesting contribution from a U.S. Coast Guard captain in active service (USCG R. B. Watts).[23] His main arguments (against the concept of carriers in relation to power projection, and the latter *per se*) are:

The changed world situation, the huge cost of large units, the replacement of the "Soviet Navy Syndrome" used in the Cold War by the "Chinese PLAN Syndrome" and the age-old question regarding the correct evaluation of the nature and kind of threat. Given that sea power remains vital for the United States, he demands a new strategic and operational orientation, in accordance with the classical model: analysis of the threat, establishing the means, new approaches, especially the absolute precedence of the War against Terror (an only extremely limited task for the navy) and the correct deployment of means. However, Watts does not offer concrete approaches as to how all this can be achieved in the light of the United States current (global on account of interests) strategic objectives. The suggestion that the battle-ship theory, which had, until that time, been valid, was no longer applicable after the attack on Pearl Harbour in December 1941 is too narrow an argument.[24]

The previously mentioned role of submarines both in terms of deployment within the framework of A2/AD and also as an integrated part of air–sea battle requires further explanation. The American and the Chinese naval forces have strategic and tactical submarine components at their disposal. The strategic component is mentioned here only for the sake of completeness. The five permanent members of the UN Security Council – the official nuclear powers – base their deterrence primarily on strategic nuclear submarines (SSBN);[25] such deterrence is conceived as a last resort. These submarines are difficult to locate, a certain number of them are permanently on patrol and their weapon systems are thus deployable at any time. They guarantee a potential of retaliation or, at a minimum, an equally powerful response (even after a nuclear first strike, at least according to the concept) that the attacker would also be destroyed. It is only the nuclear propulsion that permits the great distances and speeds (in particular under water) and extremely long deployment cycles on which the concept depends. In addition, all the components of this concept must be available nationally: the ship, the engine, the entire communication and combat electronics and above all the complex inter-continental missiles (ICBM)[26] – propulsion system, under water start, MRV and MIRV technology.[27] Key components that are technologically dependent naturally reduce the politically unlimited deterrence capability.[28] At a tactical level, however, diesel-electric hunter submarines (SSK)[29] are predominantly deployed world-wide; at the present time only the United States exclusively deploys nuclear-driven hunter submarines (SSN).[30] With reference to the USN's power projection concept, the CSG/NTG – together with the defending hunter submarines – must be able to travel great distances rapidly. Diesel boats make ideal A2/AD components with advantages over the nuclear-driven boats:

- quiet engine, more difficult to locate than relatively noisy nuclear-driven boats;
- compact construction, much more economic to purchase (1,500–3,500 t as against up to 20,000 t for nuclear-driven boats); and
- modern engine technologies (AIP[31]).

While submarine components within an A2/AD concept have the primary function of tracking down and destroying enemy targets above water (with consideration for self-defence), the primary function of submarine components of a USN-CSG/NGT is the defense of the former:

- escorting their own CSG/NTG;
- tracking down enemy CSG;
- tracking down enemy submarines (SS/SSK/SSN/ SSBN).

There is a general consensus of opinion that the best means of tracking down and destroying a submarine is through another submarine. In the same way as the hunter submarine is an essential part of the A2/AD concept, so power projection cannot be executed without powerful (nuclear, from a U.S. point of view) submarine forces.

The central component of the air–sea battle concept is the nuclear aircraft carrier. It is optimally protected for battle on, under and over the surface by the carrier's air wing as well as resources controlled by the AEGIS combat system and detached submarines.[32] The idea that an ASBM or even a submarine (SSK) could, in case of emergency and "without hindrance," put the carrier out of action is, to put it mildly, more of a romantic rather than an objectively analyzed and founded expectation.[33] Nevertheless, ASBM/ASCM and submarines pose a serious threat to the CSG and to the CVN in particular. As shown in Figure 13.1, the generic term CEC – Cooperative Engagement Capability (AEGIS) (and ESSM, ECM and ECCM[34]) – is given beside the unit. These are the principal means of a modern carrier unit in combat against A2/AD threats; CEC is the joint concept of the unit and is defined as a network of military sensor and weapons control systems. CEC controls the following systems in the unit:

- ACS (AEGIS Combat System);
- Ship Self Defense System;
- Advanced Combat Direction System;
- Naval Tactical Data System.

Contrary views regarding the role of the carrier are staunchly upheld. According to a study by the RAND Institute,[35] a modern equipped and tactically trained Carrier Air Wing can be selectively deployed with high efficiency at any time (except in exceptional weather conditions) as an intervention force for gradual, appropriate response to the political and military situation as it unfolds. This is not possible to the same extent with less sophisticated and less expensive weaponry (e.g. drones and other unmanned types of warfare). In the future, the air umbrella could come from unmanned, longer-range drones or from space, but power projection for strategic ends requires the capability to quickly send units to the area of operations. These units must represent a credible intervention capability (from a deterrence point of view) which may be deployed to several hot spots on the globe simultaneously; no current or projected manned or unmanned, sea- or land-based platform provides the capabilities needed in the most severe crises examined. There is nothing to add to this statement.

Evaluation/conclusions

From a Chinese point of view, A2/AD represents an absolutely essential operational and defensive concept against the offensive forces of the USN. Nevertheless, it does not even tentatively make up for the PLAN's present capabilities in relation to the ambition of securing sea routes and the protection capability that is necessary in light of the future role it aspires to play on the world stage.

Furthermore, we must always remind ourselves of the reality that hardware alone does not produce a robust unit that is ready for engagement. The PLAN's current lag is such that it must be judged extremely unlikely that they could quickly catch up, let alone equal the USN in the medium term. If one looks at Figure 13.2, the PLAN cannot (with the exception of supply ships) demonstrate the elements necessary for a comprehensive global functionality in any military branch at the present time.

Comparing the possibilities from a purely weaponry and operational point of view, the indications are that the position of the USN will remain globally dominant and unchallenged in the coming two decades. But naturally, operational capabilities always have an effect on political negotiations. Leaving aside China's occasional threats to neighboring states (Taiwan and Japan)

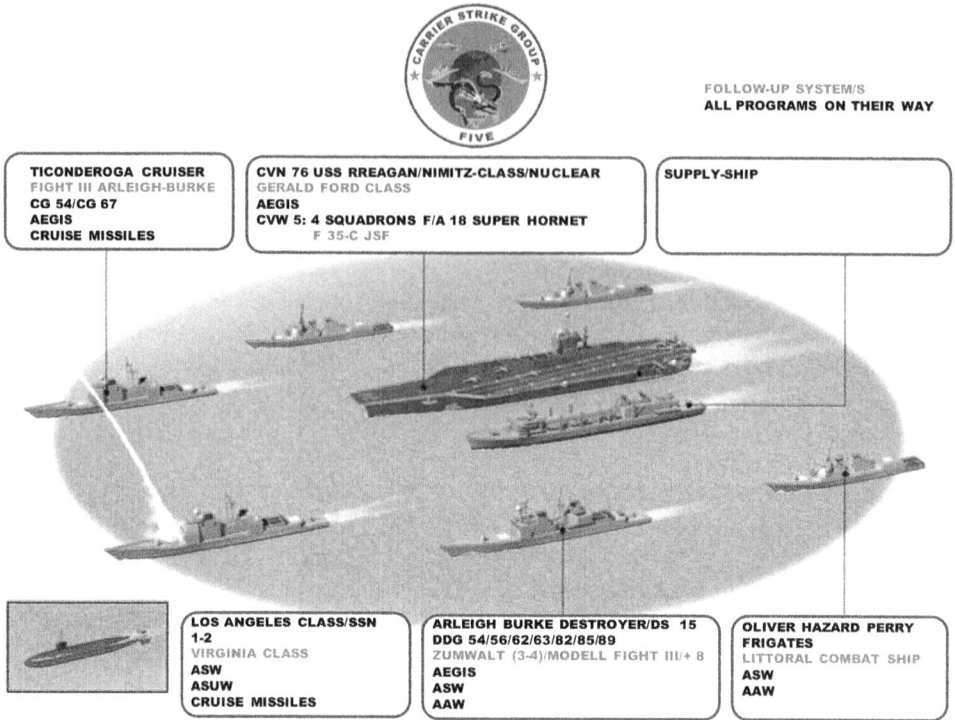

Figure 13.2 U.S. Navy carrier strike group/naval task group sample composition
Sources
U.S. Navy and U.S. Naval Institute.

and looking at Chinese foreign policy over the last two decades, we come to the conclusion that the political leadership is quite aware of its weaknesses in the maritime sphere. However, we should not forget that the USN, less so than the Army and Air Force, due to increasing global and economic difficulties, will have to accept budget cuts, delays and the postponement of arms programs, indeed even forgoing planned renewals, and, as time passes, this on a more frequent basis. China, on the other hand, regardless of domestic problems and increasing economic concerns about its future growth and targeted export markets, continues to upgrade and arm its armed forces, with particular emphasis on the PLAN. The recently publicized increases of 12.2 percent on Chinese military spending in the coming fiscal year are a clear indication of this trend (People's Congress, February 2014).

The future will show how quickly China will catch up, how it plans to move from being a defensive to being an offensive maritime force and how rapidly it can become a world power with global power projection capability.

Notes

1 Alfred Thayer Mahan, 1840–1914: U.S. Navy officer, historian, marine strategist. Major work: *The Influence of Sea Power upon History*, 1890.
2 Sir Julian Stafford Corbett, 1854–1922: British marine historian and strategist. Major work: *Some Principles in Naval Strategy*, 1911.

3 "Cyber," from Ancient Greek κυβέρνησις (kybérnesis) = control, term applied to "data room" and conflicts in this room (data security, hacking [paralyzing opponents' computers/networks through the internet] used in the expression cyber war.

4 Admiral Sergej Gorshkov, who shaped Soviet naval strategy during his tenure from 1956 to 1985, attempted to develop a powerful Soviet blue-water navy. This attempt was only partially successful, and came at tremendous economic and financial costs. Soviet sea power, still ranked No. 2 behind the United States at the time, became an important tool of Soviet statecraft and Moscow's foreign policy. In terms of aircraft carriers, the most important power projection tool, the USSR never came close to parity with the West. Only in the submarine area was some success palpable. Soviet power projection was always dominated by a strategic emphasis on air and ground forces, not naval or maritime thinking. This is most visible again under the current President of Russia, Vladimir Putin, who also focuses strongly on air and ground forces.

5 2013: exports from China to United States: 16.72 percent of total export volume of 2.21 billion USD; imports to China from United States: 7.8 percent of total volumes, 1.772 billion USD. Currently China holds approx. 1.27 billion USD Treasury bonds. The United States is China's most important export market.

6 The term "string of pearls" refers to a network of Chinese military and merchant bases and designations along its sea lines of communication (SLOC) that stretch from the ports of the Chinese Pacific coast to Sudan. The network line runs through several choke points (Straits of Bab el-Mandeb, Hormus, Malacca and Lomboc) and also important coastal states such as Pakistan, Sri Lanka, Bangladesh, the Maldives and Somalia. The term was used for the first time as a geo-political concept in an internal report ("Energy Futures in Asia") by the MoD. China does not use this term officially.

7 "Blue-water navy" refers to maritime powers that can operate on the world's oceans. The opposite would be a navy that principally operates in and around coastal waters.

8 "Joint" in a military sense means mutual cooperation and inter-operability of military branches.

9 PLAAF and PLAG: Chinese air and ground combat forces.

10 In English (and French) an area, in particular an area of deployment or interest is referred to as a theater (French: *théâtre*).

11 Distance from Shanghai to Los Angeles: 6,480 nautical miles or 10,428 km. One nautical mile corresponds to 1.852 km and is usually abbreviated to nm.

12 A CSG (Carrier Strike Group) is an independently operating unit around a nuclear carrier together with convoying and function boats. An NTG (Naval Task Group) is roughly the same as a CSG but, since the introduction of the JOE2010 Doctrine (Joint Operating Environment 2010) represents a CSG supplemented by marine infantry forces of the USMC (U.S. Marine Corps). The NGT represents the USN's new orientation towards joint.

13 CVW is a wing of a carrier-supported fighter and reconnaissance aircraft of the USN. Normally four attack squadrons, one submarine hunter squadron, two early warning squadrons and one anti-submarine helicopter squadron. In ground combat forces, a wing corresponds to approximately one regiment commanded by a colonel. The squadron corresponds to the company.

14 Kusnezow class Soviet carrier/steam turbine propulsion, approximately 55,000 tons, defined as flight deck carrier by the Russians in order to be able to pass through the Dardanelles, since, according to the Treaty of Montreux (July 20, 1936), international law forbids the passage of aircraft carriers.

15 ACS: Aegis Combat System.

16 EEZ: Exclusive Economic Zone (according to UNCLOS, with economic rights, however, not abrogating the 12 nm zone).

17 Avery Goldstein, "China's Real and Present Danger," *Foreign Affairs* (September/October 2013), 136–44.

18 Re-named on January 8, 2015 by the Joint Staff as "Joint Concept for Access and Maneuver in the Global Commons" (JAM-GC).

19 Loren Thompson, "Can China Sink a US Aircraft Carrier?" *Forbes*, January 23, 2012.

20 The high seas that are not subject to national sovereignty (12 nm limit).

21 James Holmes, "From Mahan to Corbett? The New U.S. Joint Operational Access Concept Implies a Shift in Navy Strategy in Contested Parts of the World," *The Diplomat* 11 (December 2011).

22 UCLASS (Unmanned Carrier-Launched Airborne Surveillance and Strike) aircraft is a current USN program to provide an unmanned intelligence and strike asset to the fleet.

23 R. B. Watts, "The End of Sea Power," *Naval Institute Proceedings* 135, 9/1,279 (September 2009): "Memo to Navy Leaders still hanging on the coattails of Alfred Thayer Mahan's century-old world view: Wake Up!"

24 Nikolaus Scholik, "The Geo-Political and Geo-Strategic Signification of Sea Routes: The Straits of Hormuz, Malacca and the Northwest Passage," unpublished doctoral dissertation, University of Vienna (2011).
25 SSBN: Ship Submersible Ballistic Nuclear.
26 ICBM: Inter-Continental Ballistic Missile.
27 MRV: Multiple/Missile Reentry Vehicle; multiple nuclear warheads on a carrier rocket. MIRV: Multiple Independently Targetable Reentry Vehicle; multiple nuclear warheads selecting independent targets on a carrier rocket.
28 Of the five states (UK, United States, China, Russia and France), only the UK is "dependent": the Trident ICBM of the British SSBN is of American provenance.
29 SSK: ship submersible conventional.
30 SSN: Ship Submersible Nuclear; nuclear-hunter submarine.
31 AIP: Air-Independent Propulsion.
32 ACS (Aegis Combat System) is a USN electronically controlled weapons system for combat under (ASW: Anti-Submarine Warfare), on (ASuW: Anti-Surface Warfare) and above the water (AAW: Anti-Air Warfare), plus strike capacity.
33 However, during an exercise (JTFEX 01.2) in the year 2001, a German submarine (U-24) with fuel cell drive (hydrogen and liquid oxygen) managed to approach a USN carrier unnoticed (as far as the deployment distance of the torpedoes). This exercise will certainly have influenced the USN to improve the ASW-capacities of their CSG.
34 ESSM: code for the RIM-162 Evolved Sea Sparrow Missile, a medium-range ground-to-air missile for combating ASM (Anti-Ship Missiles) and aircraft. ECM (Electronic Countermeasures) and ECCM (Electronic Counter-Countermeasures) are part of the electronic warfare (EloKa) that aim to destroy the opponent's weapon sensors. The deployment area encompasses the engagement over and under water (aircraft/sub-marines).
35 RAND, National Defense and Research Institute, *Leveraging America's Carrier Capabilities*, Santa Monica, CA: RAND Corporation, 2006.

14

THE IMPLICATIONS OF CYBERSPACE FOR NAVAL STRATEGY AND SECURITY

Alison Lawlor Russell

Introduction

Cyberspace is critical to modern naval strategy and security because it underpins the essential communications networks and capabilities of naval forces. Information-based capabilities are integrated throughout fleets and enhanced by cyberspace, thus enabling robust command and control, battlespace awareness, intelligence gathering, and precision targeting, which are at the core of mission success. In the modern era, navies must defend and maintain the freedom to operate within cyberspace in order to be effective forces at sea. As U.S. Secretary of Defense Leon Panetta said, "modern armed forces cannot conduct high-tempo, effective operations without reliable information and communication networks and assured access to space and cyberspace."[1]

Understanding the role that cyber plays in the maritime environment is fundamental to understanding the evolving responsibilities of naval forces in the twenty-first century. In order to understand the implications of cyberspace for navies, this chapter will examine the implications of cyberspace through the lens of the strategic, operational, and tactical levels of warfare. Then it will analyze the structure (or layers) of cyberspace to identity additional areas where naval forces rely on cyberspace. Finally, this chapter will present the potential opportunities and challenges of cyberspace for scholars and policy-makers interested in naval security and strategy.

Cyberspace is a global domain of interconnected and interdependent networks that use electronics and the electromagnetic spectrum to create, store, modify, exchange, and exploit information.[2] It is composed of four layers of operations that work together to provide the capabilities that are known collectively as "cyberspace." Its physical elements include computers, servers, cell towers, fiber-optic cables, satellites, and the electromagnetic spectrum. The logic-based layer of cyberspace, which is in charge of routing information from its source to destination, relies upon the physical layer to actually transmit the information. The information layer is where the content (such as photos, videos, and text documents) is created, stored, transmitted, and transformed. The final layer of cyberspace is the user layer, in which people and communities interact and shape the experience of cyberspace through communication, planning, and decision-making.[3]

Roles and responsibilities of naval forces in cyberspace

The core capabilities that navies seek to provide are the "blue water" capabilities of forward presence, deterrence, sea control, and power projection, as well as maritime security and humanitarian assistance/disaster response. All of these core capabilities are supported and enhanced by cyber capabilities. Thus, the full spectrum of naval operations, and the corresponding naval strategy, involves cyber capabilities. For more technologically advanced navies, these cyber capabilities are so integrated into weapons systems and platforms that they have become essential to full spectrum warfighting and operations. For less technologically advanced navies, cyber capabilities can still play an important role in augmenting other capabilities by improving command and control and acting as a force multiplier in certain situations.

Naval forces are responsible for providing cyberspace operations capabilities to support combatant commanders' objectives, in defense of national information networks, and for fleet deployment.[4] They are force providers to joint operations, supporters of the national mission, and blue-water warriors all at the same time.

Navies are one of several instruments of national power and just one branch of the armed services. In addition to their naval/maritime duties, naval forces have a responsibility to provide support to joint and interagency operations. Navies' role in national security is not limited to blue-water activities, but includes supporting strategy, policy, and planning for all elements of national security, including cyberspace. This is a significant responsibility for navy and other forces, thus there is some discussion and debate about potential alternative force models. For example, Admiral James Stavridis (USN, ret.), former Supreme Allied Commander of NATO (2009–13), argues that Cyber Command should not draw upon the traditional military services for manpower, but instead should create an entirely separate force dedicated to cyber security and recruit and train accordingly.[5]

Implications of cyberspace for naval strategies

Naval strategies are in a period of transition with regards to cyberspace. Most navies acknowledge the importance of cyberspace as a critical enabler, but there is emerging recognition that cyberspace is also much more than that. Ultimately, cyberspace is a "game-changer" for naval forces and security forces in general. All phases of conflict now have a cyber dimension, from Phase 0/Planning through Phase 5/Stabilization and Reconstruction. Cyberspace affects all levels of war, from the strategic, to the operational, to the tactical. All types of conflict are affected by cyberspace, including conflicts in the other four domains (land, sea, air, and space).[6] For naval forces in particular, cyberspace enables new kinds of fires, improves situational awareness, and enhances command and control (C2). It has also opened the door to new threats: anti-access/area-denial operations, improved targeting capabilities by adversaries, and presenting more targets for attacks – cyber attacks.

National policies for cyberspace provide naval commanders with the goals and objectives of operations in cyberspace and link them to overarching national security objectives. National strategies provide guidance on the types of cyber capabilities to be developed and employed by forces, and link this guidance to extant national legal frameworks for defensive operations and warfare.

U.S. Navy strategy for cyberspace

At the time of writing, the United States has the most robust, publicly available strategy for cyber and maritime security. This strategy explains how the U.S. Navy views the implications of cyberspace for naval security, and it is useful as a potential tell-tale for the direction that other navies may take for their own naval strategies.

The U.S. Department of Defense and U.S. Navy have released several documents in recent years dealing with cyberspace, cyber strategy, and cyber operations. Most significant of these for naval strategy are *U.S. Navy Information Dominance Roadmap 2013–2028*, *Navy Cyber Power 2020*, *Navy Strategy for Achieving Information Dominance 2013–2017*, and *Navy Information Dominance Corps Human Capital Strategy 2012–2017*. At the time of writing, an updated version of the U.S. maritime strategy, *A Cooperative Strategy for 21st Century Seapower*, has not been released, but it is anticipated that it will build upon the groundwork of the prior strategic documents. These strategic documents revolve around a core theme of three major opportunities presented by cyberspace to achieve what it calls "Information Dominance."[7]

The U.S. Navy's strategy revolves around three objectives:

1.) assuring access to cyberspace and confident C2 for deployed forces, regardless of the threat environment; 2.) enhancing battlespace awareness to better understand the maritime operating environment and prevent strategic surprise; and 3.) delivering decisive cyber effects and integrated kinetic and non-kinetic fires to expand warfighting options to both Navy and Joint commanders.[8]

The first objective, assured C2, means that naval forces have the ability to retain access to cyberspace for all mission-critical functions and provide commanders with resilient C2 capabilities. It seeks to maintain the Navy's ability to exercise C2 in a contested or denied operational environment, particularly in the presence of an informational or cyber blockade employed by adversaries. Assured C2 is necessary for commanders to coordinate action across sea, land, air, space, and cyberspace systems to support a range of military operations. Assured C2 entails the ability to command forces in any environment – permissive, contested, or highly contested/denied – regardless of the threat. In addition to commanding forces, it must be able to coordinate fires in all domains to achieve desired effects. Finally, naval forces rely on assured C2 to receive timely assessments of the mission and forces status, particularly during combat operations.[9]

The second objective, battlespace awareness, is the Navy's ability to understand the characteristics and conditions of the operational environment. Inherent in this is knowledge of the potential adversary location, activities, intent, and capabilities; knowledge of Navy's own force capabilities, capacity, and status; and knowledge of the physical and virtual environments and their potential impact on mission execution.[10] These elements of intelligence are timeless – Sun Tzu addressed this 2,500 years ago when he said "all warfare is based on deception" – but cyberspace capabilities allow for a much more complex, detailed, and integrated view of the modern battlespace that can mitigate the chance of unwelcome surprises. Preventing strategic surprise means using dedicated cyber intelligence collections and analysis and fully integrating timely cyber information and threat warnings into the commander's operational picture.[11]

The third objective, delivering decisive cyber effects and integrated fires, is the culmination of the previous two objectives and enables the delivery of accurate and timely information to commanders, deployed units, and weapons systems. Delivering decisive cyber effects means using cyber capabilities at the time and place of the commander's choosing across the full range of military operations.[12] The EM spectrum can be used to enable traditional kinetic fires, as well as non-kinetic fires including offensive cyberspace operations, jamming, and directed energy weapons. Integrated fires can be used to enhance navy forces' own or friendly fires and disrupt, deny, and defeat enemy fires. They can be coordinated and synchronized across multiple domains to overwhelm the adversary and achieve desired effects.[13] An example of synchronized integrated fires is the attacks on Georgia during the Georgia–Russia War of 2008, during which Russian forces assaulted Georgia on land, in the air, and from the sea, while at the same time Georgia was subjected to a disruptive Distributed Denial of Service (DDoS) attack on the websites of government offices, financial services, and news agencies.[14]

International naval strategies for cyberspace

Other countries with strategies that address cyberspace reinforce some of these themes. Australia, the United Kingdom, and Russia all have maritime strategies that deal with cyberspace in some way. They will briefly be discussed in the following section.

Australia

The Australian maritime defense strategy focuses on cyber capabilities as enabling operations and as a joint capability.

> In a future conflict or escalation to conflict, an adversary could use a cyber attack against Australia to deter, delay or prevent Australia's response or the [Australian Defense Force's] deployment of forces. This would probably include the targeting of information systems, networks and broader support infrastructure perceived to be integral to the ADF's decision-making and war-fighting capabilities. Once deployed, our forces will need to operate as a networked force in a contested environment.[15]

Australia established a Cyber Security Operations Center within the Defence Signals Directorate to detect cyber threats and respond to events in cyberspace. Network and systems management, along with personnel and physical security, is a part of Australian cyber strategy. In January 2013, the Australian government created a new Australian Cyber Security Center to improve relationships between and among government agencies and private industry.[16]

The United Kingdom

The *UK National Strategy for Maritime Security* identifies cyber attacks on UK maritime shipping or infrastructure as one of the "most pressing risks" that is "likely to cause significant harm and disruption to the UK."[17] As the strategy states, over 95 percent of intercontinental data travels through underwater cables, therefore it is important to "protect this essential flow of information, on which the global economy relies, from physical or cyber attack, as well as to ensure compliance by coastal States with the freedom to lay cables conferred by UNCLOS."[18]

Russia

Russia has advanced cyberspace capabilities, but there is very little information available about how cyberspace affects Russian naval or maritime strategy. Russian maritime strategy does not directly address cyberspace and cyber security as a maritime or naval responsibility, but it does recognize the importance of what it calls "information support of maritime activities" for the maintenance and development of global information systems, including systems for navigation, hydrographic, and "other" forms of security.[19]

Implications for the operational level of warfare

Cyberspace has clear implications for naval security at the operational level of warfare. Commander of U.S. Fleet Cyber Command/Commander, U.S. 10th Fleet, asserts that "defense of Navy and DoD networks and information is essential and cannot be separated from the overall maritime operational level of war."[20] Cyber has been such an integral part of Navy operations for the past two decades that its importance risks being taken for granted, but it is essential to Navy operations.

All parts of naval and maritime operations rely on cyber capabilities. Cyberspace enables assured command and control (C2), integrated fires, battlespace awareness, intelligence, protection, and sustainment. It also enables naval maneuvers with positioning, navigation, and timing support.[21] For sea-based power projection, in a landscape that is often devoid of signposts and landmarks, the ability to have precise navigational information and over-the-horizon situational awareness is particularly critical. Cyber and satellite-based global positioning systems and navigational systems provide this capability.

Cyberspace operations can be categorized three ways: offensive action, defensive action, and network operations. Offensive cyberspace operations are designed to project power through the application of force in or through cyberspace. Defensive cyberspace operations are intended to defend national (or friendly) cyberspace systems or infrastructure. Network operations design, build, configure, secure, operate, and maintain information networks and communications systems to ensure availability of data, integrity of the system, and confidentiality.[22]

Commercial and academic institutions that provide support to the fleet or the military in the form of design, manufacturing, research, and other products and services are also part of the broader environment for naval security. Thus, naval security and warfighting advantage depends, in part, upon thwarting attacks on military or government sites, as well as securing sensitive information from theft or espionage. Sensitive information in the wrong hands can undermine the operational effectiveness of the fleet by improving targeting of naval forces and platforms and increasing adversaries' knowledge of how forces man, train, and equip for warfighting.[23]

Implications for the tactical level of warfare

At the tactical level, naval commanders must incorporate the use of cyber technology into their battlefield tactics. In practical terms, this means that defensive and offensive cyber capabilities will be integrated alongside kinetic action. Cyberspace can increase the effectiveness of traditional kinetic means through improved intelligence and targeting. It also presents new challenges for defensive operations to protect systems from cyber attacks, as well as kinetic fires. Cyberspace and cyber capabilities play a particularly important role in supporting network-centric weapons systems, such as the Tactical Tomahawk missile, which receives in-flight targeting data from operational command centers.[24] Similarly, carrier aviation maintenance programs rely on cyberspace to enable them to provide mission-ready aircraft.[25] Alternatives exist for overcoming systems failures, but access to reliable cyberspace is critical to the successful employment of these systems. Dependency on cyberspace is increasing, thus increasing the need for assured access.[26]

Naval security also depends upon the protection of critical information in cyberspace. Because of its ubiquity and interconnectedness, the opportunities to gain illicit access or information abound. It is the responsibility of naval forces to ensure that they minimize their vulnerabilities. Information assurance manages the risks associated with use, processing, storage, and transmission of data and the systems and processes used in that process. It is designed to protect the availability, integrity, authenticity, and confidentiality of data. As a next-generation of operations security, it protects important information, whether it is classified or not. For naval forces, this process of protecting critical information means educating and training sailors in good cyber hygiene habits and having cyber security integrated into systems life cycles.[27]

Within the structure of cyberspace

Another way to understand the implications of cyber for naval strategy and security is to examine the structure of cyberspace and look for opportunities for naval strategy and security to play a role. The four layers of cyberspace are: the physical, the logical, the informational, and the user.[28]

Physical layer

The physical layer of cyberspace comprises the computers, servers, fiber-optic cables, cell towers, satellites, and other parts of the physical infrastructure that underpin the global domain, as well as the electromagnetic spectrum itself. These physical elements are vulnerable to tampering, damage, and destruction. Undersea cables traverse the ocean floor, sometimes buried but often not, and they come ashore in groups at designated landing sites. Most of the damage that has come to these cables has been accidental, such as a ship dropping anchor in the wrong place and damaging the cables as they run through shallower waters. However, tampering with fiber-optic cables can be intentional as well. As far back as the Spanish–American War, undersea telegraph cables were destroyed as part of the campaign to sever trans-Atlantic communications links.[29] During the Cold War, the United States famously tapped into Soviet cables to listen to conversations behind the Iron Curtain.[30] More recently, three men were arrested for trying to cut through an undersea cable off the coast of Alexandria, Egypt in 2013.[31] Whether subjected to tampering or destruction, these cables can suffer from unintentional damage as well as sabotage, which threaten to undermine the efficiency, reliability, and security of the global network.

There is no force tasked with protecting these cables, but as operators in the maritime domain, naval forces have a responsibility, at least, to do no harm, and potentially even protect this critical infrastructure from adversaries' tampering or destruction. Coast guards and navies focused on littoral operations have an increased responsibility to protect this critical infrastructure because these cables are most vulnerable as they come ashore on the beach head, where they ultimately meet pipes that protect them as they run inland. Thus, maritime forces – navies and coast guards – have a role to play in monitoring and protecting critical infrastructure for cyberspace.

The electromagnetic (EM) spectrum is a constituent element of cyberspace and critical for naval operations.[32] For decades, naval forces have operated in the electromagnetic spectrum and employed electronic warfare (EW) tactics in support of naval operations. Given that cyberspace constitutes a large portion of the information environment, and the electromagnetic spectrum is a constituent element of cyberspace, EW is a part of cyberspace. The purpose of EW is "to deny an opponent an advantage in the EM spectrum and ensure friendly and unimpeded access to the EM portion of the information environment."[33] EW uses offensive and defensive tactics to ensure unimpeded access through detection, denial, deception, disruption, degradation, protection, and destruction.[34] Traditional EW activities include jamming and spoofing radars and communication links. An example of a naval platform that engages in EW activities is the U.S. Navy's EA-6B Prowler, an airplane that interrupts enemy electronic activity and obtains tactical electronic intelligence within the combat area.[35]

According to CNO of the U.S. Navy, "In the next two decades, the [electromagnetic] environment may become our most critical warfighting arena. Control of information – much of it through the EM spectrum – is already growing more important than control of territory in modern warfare."[36] Electronic warfare, and now electromagnetic maneuver warfare, focuses on managing and controlling the EM spectrum. Capabilities within the EM spectrum are of critical importance to the mission of achieving optimal maritime domain awareness and battlespace awareness. Flexible operations and maneuverability to different frequencies within the EM spectrum allows naval forces to assure access and operations within the EW environment.[37]

Logic layer

The logic layer is the central nervous system of cyberspace; it is responsible for routing data packages to their final destinations, primarily via domain name systems (DNS), internet protocols, browsers, websites and software, all of which rely on the aforementioned fiber-optic cables and physical foundations. Targeted cyber attacks can manipulate the logic layer of cyberspace in a number of ways to cause it to malfunction or shut down completely in order to inhibit the flow of data. An example of an attack at this layer is the Stuxnet attack. The Stuxnet attack on Iranian nuclear facilities was executed by a computer worm that manipulated the inner workings of advanced technology equipment while simultaneously masking its effects to the system's operator.

Naval forces have a role in the logic layer of cyberspace through the use of offensive and defensive cyber weapons. Most cyber weapons involve the manipulation of the "logic" structure of cyberspace. Alterations in this layer can lead to malfunctions and misdirection to obfuscate operators, create barriers, install hidden entrance or exit points, and create new effects, potentially without the consent of the targeted party. Thus, the logical layer is where cyber fires often take place, cyber walls are constructed (i.e. the Great Firewall of China), and the popularly defined "cyber warfare" between machines takes place.

Information Warfare (IW) straddles the physical and logic layers of cyberspace.[38] IW is directly involved in every aspect of naval operations, as it delivers information to decision-makers by attacking, defending and exploiting networks to capitalize on vulnerabilities in the information domain.[39] IW involves the full spectrum of cyber, cryptology and signals intelligence; information operations; computer network operations; and electronic warfare missions across the cyber, electromagnetic and space domains.[40] IW operations such as computer network operations occur within this layer of cyberspace.

Information layer

The information layer consists of codes, text, photos, and other materials that are stored or transmitted through cyberspace. In this layer, information is shared and received by users, affecting their perceptions and knowledge. For military forces, the information environment consists of the physical world, information and data, and the human-centric cognitive dimension.[41] Information operations (IO) are characterized as "the integrated employment, during military operations, of [information-related capabilities] in concert with other lines of operations to influence, disrupt, corrupt, or usurp the decision-making of adversaries and potential adversaries while protecting our own."[42] The information-related capabilities are the tools, techniques, and activities that use data, knowledge, and information to create effects within the informational environment.[43] Types of information operations may include deception or psychological operations through the dissemination of disinformation to affect the cognitive understandings of the target actors.

User layer

Lastly, the user layer of cyberspace consists of the people, the individuals who engage with the technology in order to create communities and experiences through cyberspace. Clearly, information operations are designed to target the users, so those operations affect both layers. However, from the perspective of naval forces, operations security (OPSEC) is critical at the user layer. Operations security is the process of protecting data that may be useful to adversaries, essentially keeping information from unfriendly eyes. Military operations involving cyberspace require a high level of OPSEC because the cyber environment is ubiquitous and it is home to so much information on systems, even unclassified systems, which could be potentially beneficial to adversaries.

Opportunities and challenges for naval security and strategy in cyberspace

Cyberspace presents an array of opportunities and challenges for naval forces, policy-makers, and academics.

Opportunities

Cyberspace presents several opportunities for naval strategy and security. While they can be stated briefly here, their importance should not be underrated. First, the technological capabilities derived from cyberspace allows for enhanced C2, which increases the overall effectiveness of naval forces. Second, improved battlespace awareness will allow naval forces to have a better understanding of the environment in which they are operating. Third, cyber and integrated fires present new opportunities for offensive action against adversaries. Fourth, cyberspace presents new opportunities for modeling and simulations to help naval forces prepare and train for warfighting. Fifth, as a new domain, cyberspace presents opportunities for cooperation with partner nations for developing, maintaining, and protecting the domain to ensure reliable access for allies and partners, while limiting adversaries' maneuverability in the domain.

Challenges

The challenges that cyberspace presents are many. First, anti-access and area-denial (A2/AD) operations in cyberspace are the most significant challenge to the basic goals of naval forces to retain freedom of maneuver in cyberspace and deny freedom of action to adversaries. In order to use any capabilities in cyberspace, you must first have access to the domain. One of the primary objectives of naval forces in cyberspace is to maintain assured access and freedom of operations. If access to cyberspace can be controlled by an adversary through a cyber blockade or other means, then naval forces will face serious challenges executing across the spectrum of operations, not just cyber operations.[44]

Second, a significant challenge for naval forces – or any other forces – operating in cyberspace is that offense has the advantage. Threats in cyberspace develop faster than forces can protect against them. The domain is constantly evolving and innovation is creating new systems, platforms, and tools at a rapid pace. With the creation of new applications, comes the opportunity for new vulnerabilities within the systems. Adversaries are constantly seeking new ways of attack or penetration of networks, while defensive cyber operations struggle to keep up with the onslaught of attacks. Advanced Persistent Threats (APTs) – stealthy, persistent attacks on a targeted computer system in order to continuously monitor and extract data – are particularly problematic because they are so difficult to detect and can render significant damage. In addition, the speed at which some cyber attacks can take place, the relatively low barriers to entry into cyberspace, and the potential impact of an attack provide incentives for attackers to keep trying. It is difficult for defensive operations to keep up with them and innovate to protect against future attacks.

Third, while naval forces have had cyber-dependent systems for many years, the number of cyber-dependent systems and the degree to which they are dependent are expanding. This is a challenge because the more systems and platforms are linked to the domain, the more they are potentially vulnerable to cyber attacks. These systems typically have built-in resiliency capabilities, but these are not necessarily fail-safe and they may not allow for precisely the same capabilities or effects. In addition, known vulnerabilities within existing systems are not easy to fix. Upgrades and conversions must continually be worked into life-cycle plans and updated whenever vulnerability becomes known.

Fourth, the defense of national networks within cyberspace and the protection of critical national infrastructure invariably require resources. Time, money, expertise, and manpower must be diverted from other endeavors and assigned to cyberspace operations. While this is certainly true at the national level, naval forces are not exempt from sharing the burden of the costs associated with defending their networks and national networks. As for critical cyber infrastructure, in many cases the naval forces find themselves in a unique position to protect infrastructure located in the maritime domain and/or dissuade an adversary from tampering with it. For example, a foreign submarine covertly patrolling the coast of a northeastern European country could tamper with and tap into fiber-optic cables in order to gather intelligence that could be used to threaten that country or a neighboring country.

Fifth, because cyberspace is a partially man-made environment, its topography is subject to change and the capabilities of adversaries are constantly evolving. This makes it extraordinarily difficult to maintain optimal situational awareness at all times, since the domain is always evolving and new threats can take a variety of forms. Thus, a big challenge will be to prevent strategic surprise in cyberspace.[45]

Sixth, naval forces also face major challenges in relation to proximity. No longer do adversaries need to be within a relatively close distance to launch attacks; now they can be on the other side of the world launching cyber attacks against networks and systems afloat and ashore. Advanced targeting and improved situational awareness make this possible. This makes it particularly challenging for naval forces to be assured of their ability to conduct effective operations. Even if they do not face threats within the local environment, operations may be compromised by forces not just over the horizon, but around the world.[46]

Seventh, another significant challenge for naval forces is attribution. Attribution in cyberspace can be very difficult, and sometimes nearly impossible to connect an actor in cyberspace to an actual person.[47] Even when it is possible, in most cases it takes time to ascertain where a particular attack came from (country or region), who launched the attack (civilian hacker, criminal organization, non-state actor, military or other state agency), and under whose authority (an individual acting on their own or the agent of a state). Without these basic facts, naval forces will have a difficult time determining the appropriate response and applying appropriate rules of engagement and proportionality principles.

Eighth, naval forces face challenges in relation to the precision of cyber weapons. Cyber weapons can be more precise than any other type of weapons, as they can be programmed to activate only within certain networks and certain computers under specified conditions. This is a challenge for naval forces in that "precision in targeting is no longer constrained to line-of-sight, blue water, or over-the-horizon military capabilities. Cyber-enabled attackers can vary the precision of their targeting from a single person to cities, regions, or entire nations."[48]

Historically, precision in warfare has been very expensive and thus not available to all states, let alone non-state groups or individual actors. Precision is beneficial in weapons because it increases the effectiveness of the weapon while theoretically reducing the cost.[49] More accurate weapons mean that fewer need to be deployed in order to create the desired effect, which drives down the overall cost of operations (manpower, power projection, sorties flown, etc.). Precise weaponry also reduces the likelihood of unintentional collateral damage to civilians, thereby diminishing the risk of accidentally crossing "red lines" that widen the conflict.[50]

Ninth, the scale of cyber attacks and cyber weapons is unlike conventional weapons and attacks in other domains. Because the barriers to entry in cyberspace are low, cyber attackers can do a significant amount of damage with only limited investments. Not all cyber attacks are inexpensive – very sophisticated, high-end attacks are quite expensive to develop, test, and execute – but there are many options available to states, non-state actors, or individuals that do not require huge financial investments or significant resources devoted to research and development. Even advanced hacking skills are not required to launch some cyber attacks. Some criminal organizations have business models that involve cyber attacks for hire. Botnets can be rented out to launch attacks against targets for a set period of time, and then turned off. Because of this, small organizations such as terrorist groups, criminal enterprises, and individuals can have a disproportionate effect in cyberspace. These asymmetric advantages available in cyberspace empower smaller actors in an unprecedented way. The implications of this for naval forces are that they have a greater spectrum of threats to consider – adversaries no longer need to be able to build ships and go afloat, nor are missiles even necessary, rather cyber attacks can allow groups with the appropriate cyber tools, skills, and/or resources to threaten naval forces directly.[51]

Tenth, national boundaries exist within cyberspace, but the global nature of cyberspace and near-instantaneous transmission of information can seem to transcend them, or at least reduce their relevance for this domain. Ownership of the information that passes through cyberspace in a fraction of a second presents a challenge for governing authorities. Should the state where the information was sent from be responsible for it or the state where it was received? What are the responsibilities, if any, of the states through which information traverses? The boundaries of the modern state system are unhelpful with regard to legal jurisdiction for information that is passed through cyberspace at near-instantaneous speeds.

Eleventh, issues of jurisdiction and control are unclear in cyberspace, which is problematic for naval and maritime forces, as well as other national security and law-enforcement agencies. It is not always apparent which events in cyberspace are criminal actions and which are more than that, potentially acts of war. While there is growing concern by some over the perceived militarization of cyberspace and the hype of cyber warfare, there is also a real need to delineate between law-enforcement responsibilities and national defense responsibilities.[52] In some situations this difference will be obvious based on the scale and nature of the attack, but legal clarity to determine appropriate authorities and rules of engagement is necessary.

Twelfth, cyberspace presents many challenges in relation to cooperation among states and with the private sector. Amongst them, naval forces have different mission sets and legal authorities (in general and with regard to cyberspace), which can make cooperation difficult among willing partners. Additionally, not all naval forces consider cyber security a high priority, potentially making coordination and cooperation more difficult.

Cyberspace operations require private sector cooperation too. Insofar as it is a warfighting domain, cyberspace has private sector owners who have interests in its security; most of the physical infrastructure of cyberspace is owned and operated by private companies.

Innovation also comes from the private sector, which presents opportunities for naval forces to take advantages of new technologies, but challenges too in that naval forces are responding to innovations in the domain, not directing them. Thus, naval security relies upon cooperation with the private sector to protect the existing networks and create new products and technologies.

Thirteenth, traditional defense acquisition cycles struggle to keep pace with Moore's Law and the rapid advancement of cyber capabilities. New capabilities are created that must be leveraged and new vulnerabilities are discovered that must be defended against. The traditional defense acquisition cycle is better suited to planning for longer-term acquisitions, such as ships and aircraft, than responding to the constant evolution of cyber technologies.

Fourteenth, navies face challenges at the user layer of cyberspace. Leaving aside the issue of deliberate sabotage or espionage, most of the vulnerabilities at the user layer can be mitigated or eliminated with vigilance and rigorous security measures. Training and education to promote good cyber "hygiene" habits will go a long way, but mistakes and occasional lapses in judgment are inevitable in any large organization. This is a challenge that all navies will face; no matter how good the systems and technologies are, they can still be undone by human error.

Conclusion

The implications of cyberspace for naval strategy and security are profound. An indication of the importance of cyberspace for naval forces is reflected in newly developed naval strategies. While many navies have not yet released strategies that deal explicitly with the full spectrum of cyberspace and cyber capabilities as an integral part of their responsibilities, those that do provide a glimpse into what the future of navy-cyber strategy may look like.

Cyberspace is critical to modern geopolitical and economic security and it is essential for national security as well as naval security. Cyberspace is vital for modern naval operations and modern warfare because it underpins command and control of naval forces, which is essential for all operations. Technical and information-based systems that enable battlespace awareness, intelligence gathering, targeting, and other capabilities are at the core of mission success. Maneuverability and freedom of action, as well as the ability to deny freedom of action to adversaries in cyberspace, is fundamental to the success of naval operations and warfighting strategies. Thus, the goal of navies in the future will be to retain freedom of maneuver and deny freedom of action to adversaries at sea – and in cyberspace.

Protection of national and naval information networks requires defensive cyber operations to prevent attacks from penetrating the targeted systems. For some countries, cyber security may include offensive cyber operations to deter aggression by adversaries and respond in-kind to cyber attacks on naval or national systems. Cyber attacks and cyber-enhanced capabilities of adversaries, such as precision targeting or long-range attacks on systems, mean that navies are and will be more connected and vulnerable at sea than ever before. The traditional balance of power among navies and adversaries has been upset by the proliferation of cyber-based capabilities, which creates asymmetry and makes smaller navies and non-state actors disproportionately powerful.

Notes

1 U.S. Secretary of Defense Leon E Panetta, January 2012, as quoted in *Navy Cyber Power 2020: Sustaining U.S. Global Leadership – Priorities for 21st Century Defense*, Deputy Chief of Naval Operations for Information Dominance/Fleet Cyber Command/Tenth Fleet, Washington, DC, November 2012. Available at: www.defenseinnovationmarketplace.mil/resources/NavyCyberPlan2012.pdf, accessed August 28, 2015.

2 Nazli Choucri and David D. Clark, "Integrating Cyberspace and International Relations: The Co-Evolution Dilemma," in Explorations in Cyber International Relations: ECIR Workshop on Who Controls Cyberspace?, Harvard University and Massachusetts Institute for Technology, November 6–7, 2012.

3 Daniel T. Kuehl, "From Cyberspace to Cyberpower: Defining the Problem," in *Cyberpower and National Security*, ed. Franklin D. Kramer, Stuart H. Starr, and Larry K. Wentz, Washington, DC: National Defense University Press and Potomac Books, Inc., p. 28.

4 *Cyberspace Operations*, Joint Publication 3-12, U.S. Department of Defense, February 5, 2013, p. ix. Available at: www.dtic.mil/doctrine/new_pubs/jp3_12R.pdf, accessed August 28, 2015.

5 James Stavridis, "Time for a U.S. Cyber Force," *Proceedings Magazine* 140, 1/1331, January 2014. Available at: www.usni.org/magazines/proceedings/2014-01/time-us-cyber-force. For U.S. Navy strategy for an optimized cyber workforce, see *Navy Cyber Power 2020*.

6 Peter Dombrowski and Chris C. Demchak, "Cyber War, Cybered Conflict, and the Maritime Domain," *Naval War College Review* 67, 2 (Spring 2014), pp. 73–6.

7 The Information Dominance mission is to develop and deliver dominant information capabilities in support of U.S. Navy, Joint, and national warfighting requirements. Operationalizing Information Dominance involves Navy Cyber Forces and Fleet Cyber Command/Tenth Fleet. For more information, see "Information Dominance Corps Overview." Available at: www.usna.edu/Cyber/_files/documents/idc/IDC_Overview.pdf, accessed August 28, 2015.

8 *Navy Cyber Power 2020; U.S. Navy Information Dominance Roadmap 2013–2028*, Deputy Chief of Naval Operations for Information Dominance, Director of Warfare Integration for Information Dominance, March 2013, p. ii. Available at: www.defenseinnovationmarketplace.mil/resources/Information_Dominance_Roadmap_March_2013.pdf, accessed August 28, 2015.

9 *U.S. Navy Information Dominance Roadmap 2013–2028*, pp. 7–8; *Navy Cyber Power 2020*, p. 1.

10 *U.S. Navy Information Dominance Roadmap 2013–2028*, p. 15.

11 *Navy Cyber Power 2020*, p. 1.

12 *Ibid.*

13 *U.S. Navy Information Dominance Roadmap 2013–2028*, p. 24.

14 Alison Lawlor Russell, *Cyber Blockades*, Washington, DC: Georgetown University Press, 2014.

15 *Defence White Paper 2013: Defending Australia and its National Interests*, Department of Defence, Government of Australia, 2013, p. 20. Available at: www.defence.gov.au/whitepaper2013/docs/WP_2013_web.pdf, accessed August 28, 2015.

16 *Ibid.*, pp. 21, 75–6.

17 *The UK National Strategy for Maritime Security*, HM Government, May 2014, p. 19. Available at: www.gov.uk/government/publication, accessed August 28, 2015.

18 *Ibid.*, p. 33.

19 *Maritime Doctrine of the Russian Federation 2020*, July 2001, Ocean Policy 2020, p. 16. Available at: www.oceanlaw.org/downloads/arctic/Russian_Maritime_Policy_2020.pdf, accessed August 28, 2015.

20 VADM Jan E. Tighe, "The Impact of Cyber on the Maritime Operational Level of War," *MOC Warfighter* 3 (May 2014). Available at: www.usnwc.edu/mocwarfighter/Article.aspx?ArticleID=23, accessed August 28, 2015.

21 *Ibid.*

22 *Cyberspace Operations*, p. vii.

23 Tighe, "The Impact of Cyber."

24 *Navy Cyber Power 2020*, p. 1.

25 *Ibid.*

26 *Ibid.*

27 Department of Defense Instruction 8500.01, "Cyber Security," Department of Defense Chief Information Officer, 14 March 2014, p. 3. Available at: www.dtic.mil/whs/directives/corres/pdf/850001_2014.pdf, accessed August 28, 2015.

28 Gregory J. Rattray, *Strategic Warfare in Cyberspace*, Cambridge, MA: MIT Press, 2001; Choucri and Clark, "Integrating Cyberspace and International Relations."

29 Charles Cheney Hyde, *International Law, Chiefly as Interpreted and Applied by the United States*, 2nd rev. edn., 3 vols. Boston, MA: Little, Brown, 1945, p. 1956.

30 Sherry Sontag and Christopher Drew, *Blind Man's Bluff*, New York: HarperCollins, 1998.

31 "Egypt Arrests as Undersea Internet Cable Cut Off Alexandria," BBC News, March 27, 2013. Available at: www.bbc.com/news/world-middle-east-21963100, accessed August 28, 2015.

32 The electromagnetic spectrum is the range of all types of EM radiation, which is the energy that travels and spreads as it goes out. For more information on the EM spectrum, see "Electromagnetic Spectrum" article on NASA's website, available at: http://imagine.gsfc.nasa.gov/docs/science/know_l1/emspectrum.html, accessed August 28, 2015.

33 *Electronic Warfare*, Joint Publication 3-13.1, U.S. Department of Defense, Chairman of the Joint Chiefs of Staff, January 25, 2007, p. v. Available at: http://fas.org/irp/doddir/dod/jp3-13-1.pdf, accessed August 28, 2015.

34 *Ibid.*, pp. v–vi.

35 "EA-6B Prowler," Aircraft and Weapons, U.S. Naval Air Systems Command. Available at: www.navair.navy.mil/index.cfm?fuseaction=home.display&key=C8B54023-C006-4699-BD20-9A45FBA02B9A, accessed August 28, 2015.

36 ADM Jonathan Greenert, CNO, October 10, 2011 quoted in "Networks and EMS (NES) Roadmap – Navy EW and Cyber Convergence," briefing at 2011 DoD Spectrum Workshop, December 16, 2011. Available at: https://acc.dau.mil/adl/en-US/540243/file/66819/NavyEW.ppt, accessed August 28, 2015.

37 "Electromagnetic Spectrum Maneuver Warfare," Navy Live, October 30, 2013. Available at: http://navylive.dodlive.mil/2013/10/30/electromagnetic-spectrum-maneuver-warfare/, accessed August 28, 2015.

38 Traditional warfare areas do not align perfectly with the newer cyberspace environment, resulting in many different types of operations relying on cyberspace to generate at least some effects. Examples of these warfare areas include Information Warfare (IW), Electronic Warfare (EW), Information Operations (IO), and Psychological Operations (PSYOPS).

39 "Attacking and Exploiting Communications Networks: Information Warfare," Careers and Jobs, Navy.com. Available at: www.navy.com/careers/information-and-technology/information-warfare.html, accessed August 28, 2015.

40 *Ibid.*

41 *Information Operations*, Joint Publication 3.13, U.S. Department of Defense, Chairman of the Joint Chiefs of Staff, November 27, 2012, p. I-2.

42 *Ibid.*, p. vii.

43 *Ibid.*, p. 1-4.

44 Russell, *Cyber Blockades.*

45 *Navy Cyber Power 2020.*

46 Dombrowski and Demchak, "Cyber War," pp. 84–5.

47 *Cyberspace Operations*, p. vi.

48 Dombrowski and Demchak, "Cyber War," p. 83.

49 Reduced cost is theoretical because it may not actually be reduced once you factor in research and development expenses.

50 Dombrowski and Demchak, "Cyber War," pp. 85–7. For a discussion of precision and imprecision in targeting, see *ibid.*

51 *Ibid.*, p. 83.

52 Susan Brenner, *Cyberthreats: The Emerging Fault Lines of the Nation State*, New York: Oxford University Press, 2009.

15

(NO) PRINCES OF THE SEA

Reflections on maritime terrorism

Peter Lehr

Introduction: Al Qaeda's 'future works'

Two events in May 2011 presented us with a treasure trove of information on Al Qaeda's strategic and operational future plans. The first one was the now famous raid on Osama bin Laden's hide-out in Abbottabad, Pakistan, on 2 May 2011 that also resulted in a wealth of information found on laptops, memory sticks, CDs and other devices. The second one was the less widely reported arrest of Maqsood Lodin, an Austrian of Pakistani origin, by German police in Berlin on 16 May 2011. In his possession were digital storage devices containing more than a hundred documents, amongst them one titled *Future Works*, which also revealed an interesting Al Qaeda 'twin track' strategy consisting of a series of 'low cost, low tech attacks' on the one hand, and the planning for a large-scale attack comparable to 9/11 on the other.[1]

The information found in both incidents does not leave any doubt that Al Qaeda still has an interest in terrorist strikes at sea or against port facilities, with a special focus on attacking oil tankers at maritime choke points.[2] Likewise, an increasing incidence of 'rhetoric and threat'[3] in the shape of blogs and e-jihadist forum chatter related to maritime terrorism or 'sea terrorism', in addition to reported plans of Al Qaeda in the Arabian Peninsula (AQAP)[4] and other parts of the now rather dysfunctional Al Qaeda universe, point at a renewed interest in operations at the maritime front, after a lacuna of a couple of years. Amongst the plans were several ones revolving around so-called 'water-borne improvised explosive devices' (WBIED) in the shape of suicide boats steered into a vessel of choice, plus one featuring the hijack of a cruise liner which also involved putting the hostages into orange boiler suits like those worn by the inmates of the detention centre at Guantanamo Bay and shooting them one by one until the political demands had been met. Both types of plan are variations of tried-and-tested 'low impact, high probability' tactics used before, the WBIED one for example in the cases of the US Navy's guided-missile destroyer USS *Cole* (DDG-67) and the French-flagged tanker M/V *Limburg* attacks in 2000 and 2002, and the hijack one in the case of the Italian cruise ship *Achille Lauro* in 1984 on the political front and numerous vessels of all sizes on the (Somali) pirate side of things. Notably absent were more ambitious maritime terrorism scenarios of the 'high impact' or 'mega terrorism' nature that had been predicted by many observers in the immediate aftermath of 9/11.

Until very recently, all these plans could easily have been dismissed as mere mental exercises of some Al Qaeda members suffering from too much imagination. However, on 6 September

2014, the newly established Al Qaeda in the Indian Subcontinent (AQIS)[5] demonstrated that there might be, after all, some substance behind these plans. On that day, several AQIS members unsuccessfully attempted to take over the Pakistani Navy frigate PNS *Zulfiqar* (FFG-251) docked in the naval base of Karachi, with the aim of attacking nearby US warships with the eight C-802 anti-ship missiles of the frigate.[6] Had this audacious plan come to fruition, AQIS would have entered the (maritime) terrorist scene with quite a bang. But then again, it should still not be overlooked that the last attempt at a maritime terrorist 'spectacular' prior to this incident was the WBIED attack on the Japanese super-tanker M/V *M-Star* on 27 July 2010 – which again was the first major maritime terrorist attack since the 19 August 2005 Port of Aqaba rocket attack on the dock-landing ship USS *Ashland* (LSD-48) and amphibious assault ship USS *Kearsarge* (LHD-3). This naturally raises the question of why acts of maritime terrorism are such a rare, sporadic phenomenon: depending on the database one uses, they only constitute 1–2 per cent of all terrorist attacks. So, why do acts of maritime terrorism not happen – at least not nearly as often as was predicted?

This contribution aims to shed some light on this 'why not' issue by contrasting maritime terrorism with aviation terrorism and acts of terrorism against railways and underground systems – here simply called 'land transportation terrorism' for facility's sake. Due to the word limit, the focus of this investigation will be on possible entry barriers on the one hand, and the utility of maritime terrorism for Al Qaeda on the other.[7] It will be argued that future acts of maritime terrorism in the shape of a highly symbolic act of terror in the 'propaganda of the deed' tradition will be far less likely (although the probability is not exactly nil) to occur than less spectacular attacks of more strategic terrorism intended as asymmetric economic warfare.

Points of departure: the issue of entry barriers

Comments on 'imagined' versus 'real' maritime terrorism have been provided in some detail elsewhere,[8] so there is no need to repeat the history of maritime terrorism here at length. However, it should be noted that all of those rather rare attacks on the maritime front firmly belong to the category of 'low impact, high probability', with WBIED attacks being the most frequent method used so far, followed by conventional non-suicide IED attacks, followed by sub-surface attacks, stand-off weapon attacks and the hijacking of ships for political reasons. Some of those attacks, for example that on the Japanese tanker M/V *M-Star* in July 2010, do reveal a growing sophistication with regard to the terrorists' use of weapon systems: the tanker was the first vessel attacked during night time and while underway. Interestingly though, and despite the dire warning that terrorists are always on the look-out for new ideas, none of the imagined mega-terrorism scenarios developed by various specialists, all of them very innovative and creative indeed, were taken up by Al Qaeda terrorists as the presumed interested parties – which also explains why such scenarios are called 'high impact, low probability'. Some tentative explanations focusing on potential entry barriers have been offered to explain the absence of the predicted wave of maritime terrorism. Amongst the most frequently mentioned are issues such as the lack of mariner skills, the lack of cover at sea or the lack of soft targets. Taken together, these entry barriers seem to leave no doubt that even a superficial cost–benefit equation on the side of the terrorists basically militates against maritime terrorism. Alas, at the second glance those seemingly convincing arguments start falling apart, leading to more questions than answers.

With regard to targeting, there are basically two approaches a terrorist group can adopt, depending on their own strength and sophistication: either the group selects a suitable target on the basis of their current capabilities or the group selects a tempting target to then develop the capability needed to successfully attack it. It is the latter that drives the innovation cycle, with the 'underwear bombing' and 'liquid bomb' plots of aviation terrorism being perfect examples: here, the innovation cycle is driven by the intention to keep attacking hard targets despite additional layers of defences. The former is more suitable for attacks on unprotected soft targets: existing capabilities, even rather crude ones, are sufficient here, as the already mentioned 7/7 bombing or the WBIED attack on the M/V *Limburg* demonstrated. The case of the M/V *Limburg* attack as well as that on the M/V *M-Star* also serve to refute the argument that there are not too many soft targets in the maritime domain: statistics for the major sea lines of communication and for our ports and harbours prove beyond any doubt that the maritime domain is a target-rich one full of soft 'large lucrative targets',[9] despite all efforts to improve our defences and to harden our ships. Thus, this argument is not convincing at all, and should be discarded.

A lack of cover and concealment at sea should also not be taken as a given. Depending on the chosen location and tactic, maritime terrorists could easily blend in with the many small crafts dotting the littoral and confined waters through which many of our sea lines of communication lead. Ships on international voyage through the Strait of Malacca, for example, have to run a veritable gauntlet of fishing vessels of various sizes, criss-crossing and fishing in the sea lanes with utter disregard for procedures and 'right of way' rules. This means that for interested parties, such as pirates for instance, it is relatively easy to 'blend in'. If pirates can manage to close in unobserved in those waters to launch surprise attacks on unsuspecting vessels, it is unreasonable to assume that maritime terrorists cannot. And if the planned attack involves a suicide attack, the question of 'how to get away' undetected is a moot one in any case. Pelkofski is probably right to argue that tactics dependent on concealment and cover do indeed 'compress the theatre of operations covering more than three-fourths of the world into the littoral regions',[10] but the density of maritime traffic in these littorals or along major shipping straits more than makes up for this disadvantage. The expression 'shooting fish in a barrel' comes to mind if one observes the sheer number of vessels navigating the Malacca Straits, the Strait of Hormuz, the Bab el-Mandeb, the Suez Canal, the Strait of Gibraltar, the Bosporus or the Panama Canal. Furthermore, and although it sounds counter-intuitive at first, a lack of cover and concealment does not seem to always be an issue even with regard to penetrating the defences of naval installations as supposedly hard targets: in the case of a certain nuclear submarine base, for example, swimmers from certain protest groups successfully gained access to the base undetected, daubing graffiti on the hulls of nuclear submarines.[11] Again, if they can do so, there is no reason to believe that terrorists cannot. Thus, this argument is a rather weak one as well: it could be upheld in very special circumstances such as closely guarded naval installations but should be discarded as a general explanation for the near complete absence of maritime terrorism. But, as the case of PNS *Zulfiqar* demonstrates, even closely guarded installations can be infiltrated by terrorists via the use of either sleepers or personnel who have converted to their respective cause.

The lack of mariner skills seems to be a much stronger argument against maritime terrorism since these are indeed 'neither easily nor quickly acquired'.[12] We have already alluded to the fact that enthusiasm is not the same as capability, which means that if somebody intends to strike a maritime target, some mariner skills, at least some basic ones, would greatly facilitate the planned operation. Even in the case of just smuggling a bomb on board a vessel, it would be good to know where in the ship it would have the most devastating effect in terms of casualties or structural damage. For example, one remembers that Cain Redondo Dellosa, acting on behalf of the Abu Sayyaf Group, hid a television set filled with 8 pounds of TNT under a seat in the Philippine passenger vessel *SuperFerry 14*'s third class in order to maximize casualties – which indicates he had at least some knowledge of the ship's internal configuration.

Compared to such an IED attack, a WBIED attack is far more complicated. The level of complexity depends on a series of variables such as the nature of the target selected, whether it is stationary or underway, the distance to the target, weather conditions, visibility, sea state, currents and tides. An otherwise rather basic WBIED attack can fail if the actors ignore important details – such as the load capacity of the chosen vehicle, as an Al Qaeda cell attempting to attack the USS *The Sullivans* (DDG-68) had to learn the hard way in January 2000: as soon as they put their boat to sea, it went under since the cargo of about 800 kilograms of explosives was simply too much for it. With regard to more challenging attacks against offshore targets or vessels moored at more distant anchor points, actors might find it impossible to approach the chosen target before being intercepted if they fail to take tides and currents into consideration. And when it finally comes to carrying out a WBIED attack against moving targets, e.g. tankers underway, such as the M/V *M-Star,* the attackers need to do a quick relative motion calculus with regard to their vessel's speed, the targeted vessel's speed and the targeted vessel's course while factoring in things such as potential drift due to wind or currents, in order to hit the target at the best possible spot with the best possible angle to achieve maximum effect.[13] A suboptimal relative motion calculus may be the explanation for the botched attack on the M/V *M-Star* – although a not optimally rigged explosive charge could also have been responsible for the fact that the hull of the vessel was only dented and not breached.

However, the case of the guided-missile destroyer USS *The Sullivans* when seen in combination with the attack on the sister ship USS *Cole* nine months later in October 2000 demonstrates very clearly that Al Qaeda is indeed capable of learning from mistakes: the boat was salvaged, new explosives acquired, and the operation was successfully repeated with exactly the same operators. A repeat of the more challenging WBIED attack on a vessel underway as attempted against the M/V *M-Star* would require a new boat plus new operators as well, which reminds us of Pelkofski's argument that 'no campaign is sustainable if the expertise developed explodes along with the delivery vehicle and target in suicide attacks'.[14] Hence, training a number of operatives with the mariner skills needed to strike at sea may indeed take some time, but if one takes the botched January 2000 attack on *The Sullivans* as the starting point, such skills could have been acquired by now.

The *SuperFerry 14* case already hinted at yet another problem: obviously, there are actors who know what they are doing when it comes to maritime attacks, be it for political or criminal reasons. Which means, even if we accept that the majority of current Al Qaeda terrorists are 'landlubbers', there are groups with a high percentage of members familiar with the maritime domain. For example, the majority of the Moro Islamic Liberation Front (MILF) and Abu Sayyaf Group (ASG) members hail from communities with long-standing seafaring and fishing traditions. Hence, the availability of Al Qaeda-affiliated operators in possession of mariner skills plus the undeniable fact that the decade that passed after the USS *The Sullivans* and USS *Cole* attacks would and should have allowed Al Qaeda to develop mariner skills from scratch turns the 'absence of mariner skills' argument into a rather weak one as well. Instead, rather than satisfactorily explaining the absence of maritime terrorist attacks, it raises the question of why these capabilities still do not seem to exist.

In sum, the at-first-glance so formidable entry barriers barring Al Qaeda operatives from striking in the maritime domain as well do not look as nearly as formidable after closer inspection: they are formidable only if compared to the virtually absent entry barriers[15] in the field of land transport terrorism, where the sheer number of commuters on trains and buses generally precludes any meaningful security measures. However, they are most definitely not that formidable when compared to the entry barriers Al Qaeda encounters in the field of aviation terrorism. Al Qaeda did not hesitate to send many of its core operatives to flying schools in order to acquire the skills necessary to carry out the 9/11 attacks. Before that, in 1995, an Al Qaeda key operative Ramzi Yousef personally oversaw the development of a 'liquid bomb' that could be smuggled on board an airliner in seemingly innocuous contact lense fluid bottles, and even tested one himself, in order to launch the ambitious Bojinka plot aiming at bringing down 12 to 14 airliners on trans-Pacific routes. This plan was taken up again a decade later to strike at trans-Atlantic airliners, using a more sophisticated variant of this liquid bomb. Furthermore, Abdulmutallab's 'underwear bomb' was followed by a 'mark two' version, while 'mark threes' might well be invisible bomb implants.

Very obviously, Al Qaeda operatives went to great lengths to continue striking at the aviation sector, even though the flurry of new security measures passed after every botched attempt made it a fast-moving target. For some reason, they were really keen to attack in the air, and still keen enough to attack on land, while they seem to have been only rhetorically keen with regard to launching attacks at sea. Since it is obviously not really about entry barriers, could it then be the case that maritime terrorism is of no tactical or strategic utility for Al Qaeda?

Conceptualizing sea, air and land terrorism: tactical and strategic utilities

Following Wilkinson, we argue that terrorism should be seen as a method that can be used for tactical and for strategic purposes.[16] In its 'classic'[17] tactical usage, terrorist acts intend to draw the attention of a wider audience on a real or perceived grievance in order

> to try to influence political behaviour in some way, for example … to provoke an over-reaction, to serve as a catalyst for a more general conflict or to publicise a political or religious cause, to inspire followers to emulate violent attacks, to give vent to deep hatred and the thirst for revenge.[18]

This tactical use of terrorism is what Pisacane, Bakunin and Brousse called the 'propaganda of the deed', and Jenkins 'terrorism as theatre'.[19] As such, tactical terrorism usually consists of highly visible and spectacular 'shocking acts of violence … designed to produce a general sense of insecurity and fear, but also sympathy and support'.[20] The 9/11 attacks, London 7/7 or the Madrid train bombings of March 2004 are well-known examples.

In its strategic function, terrorism intends to weaken an adversary (be it a government, an ethnic, functional or religious group) over time by gradually whittling away the adversary's capacity to react and its resolve in a 'strategy of a thousand cuts'.[21] Strategic terrorism may well fall short of the criteria of 'shocking acts of violence'. It may also not necessarily tick the boxes of 'highly visible' and 'spectacular'. Rather, strategic terrorism could be seen as 'a process that is apt to change discourses, everyday life and public order in a society … [by] placing people in a permanent state of fear so that they must expect an attack at any time'.[22] The process character of strategic terrorism implies that it is not sporadic like tactical terrorism but of a sustained nature, thus nearer to guerrilla warfare than to 'classic' terrorism. This also implies the existence of secure bases or areas under control from which to launch such attacks.[23] In a sense, strategic terrorism could be called an asymmetric war of political, military or economic attrition aimed at 'haemorrhaging' the adversary. Examples for that would be sustained attacks of Al Qaeda in Iraq (AQI) between 2003 and 2007 on residential areas of the Shiite minority in a religio-political war of attrition, or the attacks on oil refineries and pipelines in Saudi Arabia in an economic war of attrition. With regard to maritime terrorism, we have already noted that the widely anticipated and feared 'high impact, low probability' incidents failed to make the crucial leap from imagination to reality, while even the far more pedestrian acts of a 'low impact, high probability' nature are few and far between. Pointing out that acts of maritime terrorism, depending on the database used, constitute a paltry 1–2 per cent of terrorism in general should not, however, stop us from realizing that both tactical and strategic terrorism is possible in this sub-field of terrorism – in theory and in practice.

First of all, when it comes to tactical terrorism, passenger vessels such as cruise liners or ferries can be, and have been, used as platforms for hostage crises just as airliners, trains and buses have. The best-known hostage crises on the maritime terrorism front are undoubtedly the hijacking of the Portuguese cruise liner *Santa Maria* in January 1961 and of the Italian cruise liner *Achille Lauro* in October 1985.[24] Although it is questionable whether the Al Qaeda–related cruise liner hijacking plan described in the introduction would ever have been acted upon, it indicates that Al Qaeda is aware of this variant of tactical terrorism. Furthermore, as the cases of the ferries *Scandinavian Star* of April 1990[25] and *SuperFerry 14* of February 2004 demonstrate, passenger vessels can also be targeted with conventional bombing/IED attacks for the purpose of creating mass casualties which fit more into the profile of Al Qaeda than hostage situations – as long as the perpetrators can credibly prove that they had been behind the attack, which was not the case in the *SuperFerry 14* incident.[26] The problem of credibility is of less relevance when it comes to suicide boat or WBIED attacks, although the exclusion zones around cruise liners in some ports and their speed when at sea would greatly complicate such operations – but not necessarily rule them out.

For both variants of tactical terrorism, we can state that the most modern, top-of-the-line ocean and cruise liners, as iconic symbols of Western affluence, would be perfect settings for 'terrorism as theatre': world-wide media attention would be guaranteed, and even the comparatively short-term rescue operations in the aftermath of a bombing attack would generate the same kind of vicarious horror as the airliner or train bombings. While these more iconic targets are usually protected by layers of security measures not unlike those in civil aviation (with the added protection of exclusion zones when in port), a wide range of 'softer' targets is still available even in the times of the International Ship and Port Facilities Security (ISPS) code. Ferries, for example, have tight sailing schedules that render strict security measures unenforceable or at least impracticable, and many parts of our sprawling port facilities are still poorly guarded, making it comparatively easy for an Al Qaeda commando to get inside or ashore unnoticed, as was the case in the November 2008 Mumbai shootings.[27] Hence, one is still tempted to agree with Peter Haydon that '[a] major maritime terror incident is inevitable; it is merely a matter of where and when'.[28]

The highest utility of maritime terrorism, however, as seen from an Al Qaeda-centric or a 'red teaming' perspective, lies in its strategic use in the shape of an economic jihad in order to 'destabilize the Western economy',[29] using the coastal areas of the Arabian Peninsula as launch pads. The reasons are similar to those for a strategic use of land terrorism in this region: AQAP enjoys the support of at least pockets of the population, and also seems to be well entrenched in some coastal areas, including the areas of the Strait of Hormuz and the Bab el-Mandeb – and here including the Somali side of the strait. Hence, the economic jihad we referred to above already has manifested itself in a series of attacks targeting oil supplies – correctly identified by Osama bin Laden as the 'lifelines of our economies' – in the Persian Gulf and Gulf of Aden regions. Among the better known of such attempts are the M/V *Limburg* attack of October 2002 (successful), the ABOT/KAAOT[30] attacks of April 2004 (unsuccessful) and, after a lull of six years, the M/V *M-Star* attack in July 2010 (unsuccessful). More recently but largely unreported by Western media, Yemeni naval forces foiled a terrorist attack on 20 November 2013 by engaging and sinking a small vessel approaching the country's only LNG export terminal at Balhaf, while on 11 August 2014 the same terminal came under attack from Al Qaeda again, this time from its land side. In this incident, four Yemeni soldiers were killed. The Yemeni government later claimed that the unnamed Al Qaeda cell also planned to take over the oil terminal of Mina al-Dhaba.

Although these attacks were of no more than nuisance value, with only a limited and temporary effect on oil prices and insurance costs, one cannot escape the impression that Al Qaeda is acutely aware of the damage they could inflict with sustained attacks in an asymmetric war of attrition at sea.[31] For example, in February 2010, then deputy leader of AQAP Said Ali al-Shihri[32] suggested that

> controlling the Bab al-Mandeb and bringing it 'back under the protection of Islam' would 'create a great victory and international power for us…. Then the strait will be closed and the grip will be tightened around the throat of the Jews, because the U.S. supports them through [the strait], by means of the Red Sea in particular.'[33]

And although interdicting traffic through the Bab el-Mandeb, and possibly even the Strait of Hormuz, 'might not be easy, especially as [AQAP] does not possess heavy weapons and modern boats that can be used for this purpose',[34] it is correct to point out that 'this does not mean it does not possess the logistical capabilities that can disrupt navigation in this vital international passageway'.[35]

In this context, it needs to be emphasized that following the unsuccessful attack on the Saudi Arabian Abqaiq refinery in February 2006, senior religious cleric Shaykh Abd-al-Aziz bin Rashid al-Anzi published a lengthy treatment titled *Hukm Esthdaf al-Masalih al-Nftiah* (The Religious Rule on Targeting Oil Interests) that 'legitimized the targeting of oil pipelines and oil workers who facilitate the looting of the ummah's wealth, but forbade the targeting of oil wells and fields, as they belong to the ummah'.[36] This 63-page document also contains chapters drawing on Islamic law to justify what al-Anzi calls 'economic jihad'.[37] According to this document, acts of maritime terrorism targeting oil terminals, port installations and oil or gas tankers thus would be allowed.

Regarding the documents found in the Abbottabad raid, spokespersons for the US government claimed that the documents 'reveal that al-Qaida considered hijacking and blowing up oil tankers to provoke an "extreme economic crisis"' in the West.[38] The *Guardian* article quoting them continues that '[according] to the documents, al-Qaida sought information on the size and construction of oil tankers in non-Muslim seas'[39], concluding that 'it would be easier to destroy the vessels by taking bombs on board, due to the strength of the hulls'.[40] Interestingly, the *Guardian* article also points at the learning effect the activities of the Somali pirates had on Al Qaeda/AQAP terrorists, arguing that '[the] threat to oil tankers suggests that al-Qaida was adopting the strategy of Somali pirates, who have had remarkable success in recent years using small boats to race alongside and board large commercial ships off the East African coast. They hold the cargo and crew for economic ransom.'[41] This is quite an interesting case of information sharing and institutional learning revolving around a possible switch of tactics from complicated and failure-prone WBIED attacks towards tried-and-tested (by Somali pirates) hijackings, in the not-unrealistic expectation that these tactics can be adapted to Al Qaeda's sabotage bombing purposes. Whatever the chosen tactic, it is also interesting to note that in October 2014 the theme of economic asymmetrical warfare at sea was taken up again by Al Qaeda's new online magazine *Resurgence*. The article titled 'On Targeting the Achilles' Heel of Western Economies' emphasized that '[simultaneous] attacks on western shipping or western oil tankers (a sea-based version of the cargo plane bomb plot) in more than one chokepoint would bring international shipping to a halt and create a crisis in the energy market'.[42] Once again, and whether or not these suggestions will ever be acted upon by interested terrorists, it is evident that Al Qaeda is acutely aware of the utility of maritime terrorism as part of an asymmetric economic war of attrition.

To conclude this part, we can well argue that maritime terrorism fits Al Qaeda's utility bill both with regard to tactical and strategic forms of terrorism. The entry barriers are not as formidable as they may look at first glance, and Al Qaeda's *Future Works* reveal that there is at least some residual interest in maritime terrorism. This again throws us back to the question of why, then, is maritime terrorism such a rare event?

Comparing sea, air, land terrorism: some observations

To finally answer this question, we need to compare maritime terrorism with aviation and land transport terrorism as the two other ways to strike at transportation systems. In this regard, the following observations can be made on the basis of our findings. First, when it comes to tactical terrorism or 'terrorism as theatre', plans such as the 'Transatlantic Airliner' plot, shoe bombs, liquid bombs and even 'underwear bombs' demonstrate that Al Qaeda has a manifest interest in striking airliners as the most iconic part of modern transport systems. These plans also demonstrate Al Qaeda's ability for terrorist innovation in order to circumvent the rising entry barrier of ever more effective security controls, which means that even failed attempts can still be 'sold' as successes later on. For example, in the case of underwear bomber Abdulmutallab, AQAP highlighted the fact that he passed through all security layers undetected. Terrorist innovation, however, depends on the availability of creative terrorist minds, such as those behind the shoe bombing and the underwear bombing plots. If such masterminds are not available, the default target for tactical terrorism seems to be land transportation systems such as trains, underground systems and buses or public spaces. Since land transportation systems and public spaces are largely unprotected and, thus, soft targets, existing capabilities are sufficient to attack them with a certain chance of success even for self-starters – which explains the tactical conservatism of land terrorism. When it comes to maritime terrorism, there is no pressing need for terrorist innovation either. This is especially true for WBIED attacks such as those on the USS *Cole*, the M/V *Limburg* and the M/V *M-Star*: although they have not always been successful, it is very difficult to counter them. Nevertheless, the mere fact that the maritime environment does indeed require at least some basic (and relatively easy to acquire) mariner skills goes a long way to explain why maritime terrorism seems to play second fiddle even when compared with terrorism against land transportation systems: if terrorists content themselves with attacking soft targets, they will find plenty of them on land; if they want to go the extra mile and innovate in order to strike the most iconic targets, they will opt to attack airliners. In a nutshell, maritime terrorism seems to fall between two stools: on the one hand, ships are somewhat less iconic targets than airliners; while on the other hand, they are more difficult to attack than trains and buses.

This leads us to our second observation: it is actually quite difficult for groups behind a maritime terrorist attack to credibly claim responsibility for them. For example, in the cases of the M/V *Limburg* and M/V *M-Star* WBIED attacks, authorities initially denied that the cause of the explosions were terrorist strikes, thus keeping media interest in these incidents rather low. When the authorities finally acknowledged the terrorist attacks three days after the events, they were already 'old news' in the fast-paced world of global media. The same can be said for the *SuperFerry 14* incident: ferry accidents resulting in a large loss of lives are a disturbingly frequent occurrence in some regions of the world – which is why the Abu Sayyaf Group found it difficult to convince the Philippine government and global media that it was them who were behind the *SuperFerry 14* disaster, and not just a boiler explosion. The Philippine government conceded that it was a terrorist attack only when Philippine Navy divers found traces of explosives in the hull of the capsized vessel – but since that was months after the event, global media interest was already elsewhere. The credibility issue would be even worse were such maritime terrorist attacks to occur on the high seas. After all, even today, approximately two large ships sink every week due to accidents or the forces of nature.[43] As a consequence, as a result of the relatively large number of deaths at sea per year, media interest in maritime disasters is, generally speaking, relatively low in any case.

Third, the lack of credibility also implies that the all-important 'it could have been me' effect of such attacks would be greatly reduced when compared to the psychological impact of a much less complicated bombing attack on a train or a bus on the one hand, or the admittedly much more complicated airliner bombings on the other. Here, the vicarious 'it could have been me' horror is amplified for much of the audience by the atavistic fear of flying: the prospect of having to face a suicide bomber on board a flight at an altitude of 30,000 feet with no way to escape is not a pleasant thought at all. Witness statements and photos from botched plots like the original underwear bombing attempt, or the mobile phone conversations of the passengers on board the doomed United Airlines flight 93 provide enough lurid details for our fantasies to latch on to. Even if similar eyewitness reports were to emerge after a maritime terrorist attack (as they did in the cases of the M/V *Costa Concordia* and M/V *Sewol* accidents[44]), the simple fact that in most countries far more people travel by train or by plane than by ferry or cruise liner also tends to mitigate the psychological impact of maritime terrorist attacks meant as propaganda of the deed: for most of the audience, it simply 'couldn't have been me'.

Related to this is our fourth observation: even when it comes to strategic terrorism, attacking oil and gas terminals so far has not inflicted costs as high as those incurred by an attack on aviation, be they successful or not. For example, the unsuccessful attack on the Northern Arabian Gulf oil terminals ABOT and KAAOT resulted in some superficial damage and approximately US $28 million worth of crude oil that could not be exported in the 24 hours the terminals were shut down. Compare this to the staggering costs inflicted by AQAP's printer cartridge bomb plot of 2010, appropriately nicknamed Operation Haemorrhage. Hence, despite the failure of the plot, AQAP still celebrated it as a success, devoting a whole issue of its *Inspire* magazine to it to highlight the economic damage:

> Two Nokia mobiles, $150 each, two HP printers, $300 each, plus shipping, transportation and other miscellaneous expenses add up to a total bill of $4,200. That is all what Operation Hemorrhage cost us.... This supposedly 'foiled plot' ... will without a doubt cost America and other Western countries billions of dollars in new security measures. That is what we call leverage.[45]

Arguably, the pinprick-like attacks on the maritime terrorist front don't offer the same degree of leverage – at least not as long as these attacks are not part of a sustained campaign, as suggested by some Al Qaeda members quoted above.

This leads us to our final observations: the role of terrorist entrepreneurs, or 'evil masterminds'. The interesting case of the *Fenian Ram*[46] illustrates that sometimes a terrorist mastermind or entrepreneur comes up with a plan for a terrorist attack that simply is breathtaking with regard to scope and ambition. This terrorist entrepreneur also espouses a 'yes, we can' and 'come on, let's do it' attitude, cajoling a probably initially rather reluctant group into doing something they have never done before. After all, even the most formidable capabilities remain latent and dormant as long as nobody is aware (a) that they exist, and (b) that they allow a terrorist group to do something they have never done before. In our opinion, the most notable one in the fields of aviation and land terrorism is Ramzi Yousef, who masterminded the 1993 World Trade Center bombing as well as the ambitious Bojinka plot, for which the first version of liquid bombs were developed in an exemplary case of terrorist innovation. Another terrorist entrepreneur about to make terrorist history comparable to Ramzi Yousef before his career was cut short by his arrest in November 2002 was Abd al-Rahim al-Nashiri. He was the mastermind behind the successful WBIED attacks on the USS *The Sullivans*, the USS *Cole*, and the M/V *Limburg*, which earned him the nickname 'Prince of the Sea'. At the time of his arrest, he plotted a range of other maritime terrorist strikes involving IED, WBIED and stand-off weapons attacks on the more tactically conservative side of things, and scuba diving attacks plus some airborne attacks revolving around light planes piloted into the bridges of warships or commercial vessels on the more innovative side.[47] His rather advanced plans for waging a 'scuba jihad'[48] – for which operators allegedly had been sent to various recreational diving schools – for example prompted the Department of Homeland Security and the FBI to release a bulletin in 2003 advising 'the maritime industry and owners and operators of maritime facilities of a number of incidents of suspicious activity and possible surveillance of maritime facilities around the U.S. over the past few months'.[49]

Interestingly, after his arrest in early 2002, none of al-Nashiri's ambitious and innovative plans ever came to fruition. Even the more tactically conservative attacks such as the WBIED attacks on the ABOT and KAAOT oil terminals in April 2004 and the M/V *M-Star* in July 2010 or the stand-off weapons attack on the USS *Ashland* and USS *Kearsarge* in August 2005 have been few and far between. Although the absence of open-source data makes it difficult to do more at the moment than speculate, it can be argued that the most important explanation for the absence of maritime terrorism is the Prince of the Sea's arrest: so far, he was the only terrorist entrepreneur with a keen interest in maritime affairs, espousing the same 'can do' approach as Ramzi Yousef had with regard to air and land terrorism, and obviously imbued with a deep conviction that (a) the entry barriers could be overcome, and (b) that the results would be worth the efforts. This also means that contrary to widespread belief, even a decentralized terrorist network such as Al Qaeda can be greatly weakened by removing one of the key players from the scene: as the case of al-Nashiri shows, there may not always be a suitable successor who could fill the sudden and unexpected vacancy.

Conclusion: not 'sea, air, land' but 'air, land, sea'

In conclusion, this chapter has demonstrated that neither the presence of allegedly formidable entry barriers nor a questionable tactical or strategic utility can sufficiently explain the lack of maritime terrorist attacks. Rather, it has shown that these formidable entry barriers are much less formidable when compared to those that have to be overcome in the field of aviation terrorism, and that the skill sets needed could have been developed in the meantime in any case. And when examining tactical and strategic manifestations of terrorism, it was found that maritime terrorism would indeed be possible as both in a tactical and a strategic variant. However, for a variety of reasons, tactical maritime terrorism seems to fall between two stools: on the one hand, ships are somewhat less iconic targets than airliners, while on the other hand, they are more difficult to attack than trains and buses. This explains sufficiently (a) the persistence in aviation attacks, (b) the continuation of land attacks as the default option, especially for inexperienced self-starters, and (c) the near-complete absence of tactical maritime terrorism – which means, with regard to tactical terrorism, there is an air ('really keen'), land ('sufficiently keen') and sea ('rhetorically keen') targeting hierarchy.

This is not necessarily the case with regard to a strategic use of maritime terrorism, for example targeting oil tankers voyaging through the Bab el-Mandeb. Here, the proper targeting hierarchy would be assaults on targets on land, followed by attacks on targets at sea, followed by attacks on air targets, for example cargo planes. The fact that such attacks still do not happen more frequently can be explained by the lack of a terrorist mastermind following in the footsteps of al-Nashiri. The attempted takeover of the Pakistani Navy frigate PNS *Zulfiqar* on 6 September 2014 by a cell of the newly established AQIS plus the increasing chatter on e-jihad forums and the recent *Resurgence* article 'On Targeting the Achilles' Heel of Western Economies' could be seen as indicators that this vacancy might be filled, and that future strategic maritime strikes are likely to occur in the foreseeable future.

This finally brings us to the risk of a 'black swan' event at sea, for example the capture of a major cruise liner in the Mediterranean, the Caribbean or the Far East by a well-trained and well-equipped Al Qaeda cell. Such an assault would result in a prolonged high-profile terrorist event in the shape of a Mumbai shooting or a Nairobi Westgate Mall siege at sea. As unlikely as that may sound, the risk of such an incident occurring is admittedly low but not zero – hence, remaining vigilant is the order of the day even for such rather well-protected assets, and by extension for port facilities, too. In sum, when it comes to maritime terrorism as compared to aviation terrorism and land transportation terrorism, the motto should be: 'be scared, be moderately scared …'.

Notes

1 Nic Robertson, Paul Cruickshank and Tim Lister, 'Documents reveal al Qaeda's plans for seizing cruise ships, carnage in Europe', CNN World, 1 May 2012, at http://edition.cnn.com/2012/04/30/world/al-qaeda-documents-future/index.html, accessed 28 August 2015.

2 See Damien Pearse, 'Al-Qaida hoped to blow up oil tankers, Bin Laden documents reveal', *Guardian*, 20 May 2011, at www.guardian.co.uk/world/2011/may/20/al-qaida-oil-tankers-bin-laden, accessed 28 August 2015.

3 'Maritime Update October/November 2010', *Triton Intelligence Report TIR-53* (Swindon: Allen Vanguard, 2010).

4 'Al-Qaeda vows to block strategic Al-Mandab Strait', *Terrorism Monitor* 8.7, 19 February 2010.

5 Other sources blame Thereek e-Taliban Pakistan (TTP), but an AQIS spokesperson claimed the attack for his group.

6 See Thomas Joscelyn, 'Al Qaeda in the Indian Subcontinent Claims Two Attacks in Pakistan', *Long War Journal*, 13 September 2014, at www.longwarjournal.org/archives/2014/09/al_qaeda_in_the_indi.php, accessed 28 August 2015.

7 The author acknowledges that there might be other terrorist groups with an interest in maritime terrorism, but since at the moment Al Qaeda and affiliated groups pose what in US parlance is called a 'clear and present danger', this chapter will exclusively deal with them. However, most of the observations made can be generalized.

8 In Peter Lehr, 'Maritime Terrorism: Locations, Actors, and Capabilities', in *Lloyd's Maritime Intelligence Unit Handbook of Maritime Security*, ed. Rupert Herbert-Burns, Sam Bateman and Peter Lehr (Boca Raton, London and New York: CRC Press, 2009), pp. 55–72.

9 James Pelkofski, 'Al Qaeda's maritime campaign', Military.com Forum, 27 December 2005, at www.military.com/forums/0,15240,83909,00.html, accessed 28 August 2015.

10 *Ibid.*

11 This issue was the topic of a thesis that this author supervised. For obvious reasons, the thesis is embargoed.

12 Pelkofski, 'Al Qaeda's maritime campaign'.

13 This argument was also made by James Pelkofski. See *ibid.*

14 *Ibid.*

15 Apart from preparing the explosives, that is – which is a formidable entry barrier in itself if there is no access to experienced bomb-makers for advice.

16 We should add that while these two forms may be clearly distinguishable in theory, in practice they tend to overlap.

17 Ekaterina Stepanova, *Terrorism in Asymmetrical Conflict. Ideological and Structural Aspects*. SIPRI Research Report 23 (Oxford: Oxford University Press, 2008), p. 9.

18 Paul Wilkinson, 'The Strategic Implications of Terrorism', in *Terrorism and Political Violence. A Sourcebook*, ed. M. L. Sondhi. (New Delhi: Har-anand Publications, 2000), at www.comw.org/rma/fulltext/00sondhi.pdf, accessed 28 August 2015.

19 On terrorism as theatre, see Brian Jenkins, *International Terrorism: A New Mode of Conflict* (Santa Monica, CA: RAND, 1974), pp. 1–15.

20 Peter Waldmann, 'Terrorismus als weltweites Phänomen: Eine Einführung', in *Die weltweite Gefahr. Terrorismus als internationale Herausforderung*, ed. Hans Frank and Kai Hirschmann (Berlin: Verlag Arno Spitz, 2002), pp. 11–26 (p. 11) (translation PL).

21 B. Raman, 'Al Qaeda's Operation Haemorrhage', *Geopolitical and Economic News and Analysis*, 22 November 2010, at http://globalgeopolitics.net/wordpress/2010/11/22/al-qaedas-operation-haemorrhage/, accessed 28 August 2015.

22 Wilhelm Heitmeyer, 'Right-Wing Terrorism', in *Root Causes of Terrorism. Myths, Reality and Ways Forward*, ed. Tore Bjørgo (London and New York: Routledge, 2005), pp. 141–53 (p. 144).

23 Stepanova prefers to call it 'conflict-related terrorism', arguing that it 'is practised by groups that enjoy at least some local support and tend to use more than one form of terrorism'; see Stepanova, *Terrorism in Asymmetrical Conflict*, p. 10.

24 See, for example, Michael K. Bohn, *The Achille Lauro Hijacking. Lessons in the Politics and Prejudice of Terrorism* (Washington, DC: Brassey's, 2004).

25 As a result of deliberately set fires, started by a pyromaniac, 158 passenger and crew died. See the report 'Scandinavian Star fire kills 159 cruise passengers, April 7, 1990', at www.cruisebruise.com/SCANDINAVIAN_STAR.html, accessed 28 August 2015.

26 Initially, the ASG claim of responsibility was dismissed as grandstanding, and an accident deemed to be more likely.

27 See, for example, BBC, 'UK "at risk of sea-borne attack"', BBC News, 18 May 2009, at http://news.bbc.co.uk/1/hi/uk_politics/8054491.stm, accessed 28 August 2015.

28 Peter Haydon, 'Terrorism and its Maritime Dimension', *Canadian Naval Review*, 22 July 2007, at http://naval.review.cfps.dal.ca/forum/view.php?topic=58, accessed 28 August 2015.

29 *Ibid*.

30 ABOT = Al Basra Oil Terminal; KAAOT = Khor al-Amaya Oil Terminal.

31 It should also be noted that the WBIED attack on the USS *Cole* cost only around US$50,000, while the repair costs amounted to approximately US$350,000. However, we would rather see this attack as a tactical one because of the symbolic character of this vessel.

32 Al-Shihri was allegedly killed in an airstrike on 12 February 2011 together with Anwar al-Awlaki.

33 'Al-Qaeda vows to block strategic Al-Mandab Strait'.

34 Al Quds al-Arabi, February 2010, as quoted *ibid*. See also Peter Lehr, 'Asymmetric Threats in the Indian Ocean: What Kind of Threat from Which Kind of Actor?', in *Maritime Security in the Indian Ocean Region: Critical Issues in Debate*, ed. V. R. Raghavan and Lawrence W. Prabhakar (New Delhi: Tata McGraw-Hill, 2008), pp. 165–85.

35 Al Quds al-Arabi, as quoted in 'Al-Qaeda vows to block strategic Al-Mandab Strait'.

36 Murad Batal al-Shishani, 'Al-Qaeda and Oil Facilities in the Shadow of the Global Economic Crisis', *Terrorism Focus* 6, 6 (25 February 2009), at www.jamestown.org/programs/gta/single-tf-rss-only/?tx_ttnews[tt_news]=34551&cHash=5afd3e6cf1, accessed 28 August 2015.

37 See Jack Williams, 'Al-Qaida Threats and Strategies: The Religious Justification for Targeting the International Energy Economy', Critical Energy Infrastructure Protection Policy Research Series, Canadian Centre of Intelligence and Security Studies at Carleton University, 2007, and IDC Herzliya, 'Oil installations as an attractive target for terrorism', *Insights*, November 2009, at www.ict.org.il/Article.aspx?ID=146, accessed 28 August 2015.

38 Pearse, 'Al-Qaida hoped to blow up oil tankers'.

39 *Ibid*.

40 *Ibid*.

41 *Ibid*.

42 As quoted in Patrick Goodenough, 'Al-Qaeda urges attacks on Achilles' Heel of Western economies', CNS News, 20 October 2014, at http://cnsnews.com/news/article/patrick-goodenough/al-qaeda-urges-attacks-achilles-heel-western-economies, accessed 28 August 2015.

43 Wolfgang Rosenthal, 'Rogue Waves: Forecast and Impact on Marine Structures', GKSS Research Centre, Geesthacht, Germany, 2004, at www.hzg.de/science_and_industrie/eu_projects/fp5/ earth/004170/index_0004170.html.en, accessed 28 August 2015.

44 Both incidents were the results of human error. In the case of the M/V *Costa Concordia*, this Italian cruise liner capsized on 13 January 2012 after hitting a submerged rock as a result of captain Francesco Schettino's decision to steer too near to the coast of Isola del Giglio (off Tuscany, Italy). During the belated evacuation of the vessel, 32 passengers and crew lost their lives. Captain Schettino, who was one of the first to abandon ship, was later charged with multiple manslaughter and sentenced to 16 years in prison on 10 February 2015. See, for example, 'Captain on trial: Costa Concordia's Francesco Schettino', BBC Europe, 11 February 2015, at www.bbc.co.uk/news/ world-europe-16584591, accessed 28 August 2015. On 16 April 2014, the South Korean ferry M/V *Sewol* capsized and sank under way from Incheon to Jeju after a sharp turn that resulted in flooding of the cargo bay. Of its 476 passengers, 304 lost their lives – many of them drowning in their cabins after being ordered to stay there for safety and security reasons. As in the case of the *Costa Concordia*, the *Sewol*'s captain, Lee Joon-Seok, was amongst the first to abandon ship. He was later charged with murder. See 'Four crew members of sunken South Korean ship charged with murder', *Asia Bulletin*, 16 May 2014, at www.asiabulletin.com/index.php/sid/222031775, accessed 28 August 2015.

45 As quoted in Scott Shane, 'Qaeda branch aimed for broad damage at low cost', *New York Times*, 20 November 2010, at www.nytimes.com/2010/11/21/world/middleeast/21parcel.html?_r=1, accessed 28 August 2015.

46 See, for example, 'John Holland: Father of the Modern Submarine', *Undersea Warfare*, Summer 2003, at www.navy.mil/navydata/cno/n87/usw/issue_19/holland2.htm, accessed 28 August 2015.

47 Scuba-diving attacks have been conducted by the Liberation Tigers of Tamil Eelam (LTTE) Sea Tigers, and could have been emulated by Al Qaeda commandos.

48 Jihad Watch, 'Scuba jihad', 28 June 2007, at www.jihadwatch.org/2007/06/scuba-jihad.html, accessed 28 August 2015.

49 As quoted in Charles R. Smith, 'Al Qaeda plans underwater attack', Newsmax.com, 26 August 2003, at http://archive.newsmax.com/archives/articles/2003/8/26/160951.shtml, accessed 28 August 2015.

16

PIRACY OFF THE SOMALI COAST

Is there light at the end of the tunnel?

Martin N. Murphy

Introduction

Piracy and Somalia have had a remarkably synergistic effect on each other. Piracy has helped Somalia gain world-wide recognition for its problems. Somalia has made the world aware of the threat piracy presents to international trade. Piracy off Somalia now appears to be over, which has allowed international attention to shift to other crises elsewhere in the world. The question is whether the measures taken to contain the piracy off Somalia, including interventions by states and international bodies, will have a lasting effect? Have they, moreover, contributed to social stability and improved economic prospects on land? If not then the social turmoil that allowed piracy to flourish in the first place may return.

A brief history of Somali piracy

The origins of Somali piracy are disputed. Many accounts fail to recognize that piracy started in the Gulf of Aden in 1989 two years before the fall of the Barre dictatorship in 1991; that is to say well over a decade before it attracted significant international attention. Targets included freighters as well as fishing vessels, giving the lie to the assumption made by many commentators that fishery disputes – and the attendant narrative of international exploitation – were the single cause of piracy. Nor were these early incidents devoid of sophistication. The MV *Bonsella*, for example, hijacked in September 1994, was a dhow that was used as a mother ship to attack other vessels for five days before being released.[1] Many of the characteristics that were said later to define Somali piracy were evident from the beginning.

However, in trying to restore some balance to the record it would be wrong not to acknowledge the role of unregulated fishing, including depredations by foreign fishing fleets, and the stimulus this gave Somalis to defend their fishing grounds. However, much of the violence was Somali-against-Somali, including the employment of warlord-backed guards placed on board some foreign vessels to drive artisanal Somali fishermen away from the foreign boats they were contracted to protect. There was also an organized Somali-managed fishing operation that relocated to Yemen following Barre's fall in 1991, which, using vessels that were originally state-owned, continued to operate in Somali waters where it preyed on local boats and stole their catches.

In 2000 many of the confrontations between local and distant water fishery fleets took place off the northeast region of Puntland. One UN official described the waters there as approximating to a "war zone." The Puntland administration, which had been established unilaterally in 1998, contracted the newly established, UK-owned Hart Security company to establish a coast guard to protect its self-declared Exclusive Economic Zone (EEZ). The coast guard was to be paid out of money raised from fishing licences. Political turmoil led to the company's departure in 2001, unfortunately leaving behind between 70 and 80 men trained in boat handling, navigation, small arms and ship boarding. Subsequent reports suggest that many of these men became the nucleus of the sophisticated pirate gangs that emerged in 2004.

This was when a new group started operating out of Haradhere, a village lying close to the coast in central Somalia. It announced its arrival by attacking a small gas-carrier in 2005, the *Feisty Gas*, for which it received a ransom of $300,000. Although this region where it was based lies south of Puntland, the driving force behind the group – a member of the local Suleiman clan named Mohamed Abdi Hassan, otherwise known as "Afweyne" – had close ties to Puntland and to Abdullahi Yusuf in particular. Yusuf was Puntland president until 2003 before he assumed the presidency of the new national government. The evidence remains circumstantial but it seems unlikely the group could have been launched without strong political protection considering it was based in the remote Mudug, far from any form of governmental control, and yet was able to recruit freely among the Majateen clan that dominate Puntland and of which Yusuf was a member.

According to "Boyah" (another pirate leader), Afweyne originated the business model that made Somali piracy so successful. He recruited experienced pirates, including Boyah, and others who became equally notorious, and moved them south to Haradhere. The model exploited the fact that Somalia was a largely "failed" state dominated by clan interests. Afweyne brokered deals with necessary clan leaders and then exploited the resulting sanctuary to hold ships and their crews for as long as it took to extract substantial ransoms for their release. Although piracy disrupted international shipping, drawing the attention of several states and their navies, it never threatened these states' interests enough for any one of them, let alone a coalition, to violate Somalia's largely nominal state sovereignty. No state, moreover, was prepared to risk repeating the United States' experience in Mogadishu in 1993, which was marked by a violent battle known popularly as "Black Hawk Down."[2]

Operating from a secure base, Fawn's operation was able to use men whose familiarity with the sea had either been gained as smugglers and part-time pirates in the Gulf of Aden, or from the training they had received as members of the short-lived, Hart-organized, Puntland Coast Guard (Hart is a maritime risk management company headquartered in Dubai). Later, as international shipping began to move away from the Somali coast in an effort to stay out of range of the small skiffs the pirates used initially, the idea of the "mother ship" was revived, eventually giving pirates the capability of operating as far north as the Gulf of Oman, as far east as the Laccadive Sea and almost as far south as the Mozambique Channel. The final element in the business model was to combine negotiators, whose skills were well honed in Somalia's deal-based society, with modern high-speed voice and data communications to barter seafarers' lives for cash. Ransom delivery was at first a risky business, but once cash began to be air-dropped directly to the groups in Somalia – literally out of the sky – then that too became relatively routine.

The International Maritime Bureau (IMB) counts 448 actual and attempted hijackings off Somalia between 2005 and 2012. The income from ransoms is hard to estimate. Government agencies may know – the U.S. Treasury Department in particular – but no reliable figures are in the public domain. It was not until early 2007 when the *Danica White* was ransomed for

$1 million that pirate groups began to make substantial money. The pirates proved themselves to be quick learners and adaptive opponents both at sea and on land, and they quickly learned how to exploit the advantage of sanctuary to achieve the highest ransoms. In 2011 they were estimated to have taken in around $140 million. Even in 2013, when ship self-protection measures and naval pressure had reduced drastically the number of ships been captured and held, pirates were still able to extract a ransom of around $13.5 million for a fully-loaded crude oil tanker – the MT *Smyrni* – captured in 2012.

The factors that make piracy possible

Seven factors encourage piracy.[3] All of them were present in Somalia:

1. *The opportunity for reward disproportionate to risk.* Pirates do not put to sea without the expectation that they will be both rewarded and survive. In Somalia they measured that expectation relatively against their prospects of achieving either on land.
2. *Inadequate security.* Inadequate state funding and training for law enforcement allows pirates freedom to operate. This is arguably the most salient factor pirates take into account anywhere when assessing risk. In much of Somalia, especially along the coasts of Puntland and Mudug, the area just to the south, they had virtually a free hand.
3. *Permissive politics.* Inadequate security is usually the result of underfunding or corruption, which is in turn usually the consequence of political choices. Both factors put down deep roots in post-independence Somalia, which has survived for many years thanks in large part to international aid, much of which has been diverted for political purposes.
4. *Favorable geography.* Piracy occurs along coasts that offer safe anchorages within range of valuable targets. Important trade routes run close to both of Somalia's coasts; almost all sea traffic between Europe and Asia, and all energy shipments from the Persian Gulf to Europe, pass through the Gulf of Aden. Pirates elsewhere, in Southeast Asia for example, need to hide, but lack of local law enforcement, and the unwillingness of the international naval forces to pursue them onto land, meant that in Somalia pirates could operate largely in plain sight.
5. *Legal and jurisdictional openings.* States with naval vessels operating off Somalia were for a long time reluctant to detain and prosecute pirates either because of problems with their own domestic laws on piracy or because the cost of repatriation to Western jurisdictions was deemed to be too great. The lack of judicial capacity in the region operating according to standards deemed acceptable by Western human rights bodies deterred local prosecutions initially but was eventually overcome following agreements with the governments of Kenya, the Seychelles and finally Mauritius. Steps were also taken to create judicial capacity within Somalia itself.
6. *Conflict and disorder.* The worst disorder in Somalia took place in Mogadishu and in the region to the south. In the center and north where the pirates were based, policing was largely absent but because clan-based sanctions continued to apply the environment was sufficiently stable for them to operate without the need to invest heavily in self-protection.
7. *Maritime tradition/cultural acceptability.* Somalia had little or no established maritime tradition yet the breakdown in government authority and the subsequent intensification of clan rivalry meant pirates found sufficient support for their actions.

The international response

The international response to piracy off Somalia was sparked by the 2005 attack on a cruise ship the *Seabourn Spirit*, with American passengers on board. Pirates from Afweyne's group fired at it using rocket-propelled grenades (RPGs) but it managed to escape without casualties. The incident gave the International Maritime Organization (IMO), the UN body responsible for all maritime matters, the opportunity to raise the problem of piracy at the UN Security Council (UNSC), although it took no action. The U.S. government, however, was more concerned. Along with its partners in Coalition Task Force (CTF) 150, which were operating in the Gulf of Aden and Arabian Sea under a UN mandate to intercept possible terrorist movements between Afghanistan and Yemen, it mounted a robust response.[4]

The UNSC was drawn into the problem more deeply in 2008 when it passed two substantive resolutions in response to the hijacking of a French cruise ship, *Le Ponant*, which had prompted a French Special Forces raid into Somali to apprehend the pirates responsible and retrieve some of the ransom. The passage of Security Council Resolution (UNSCR) 1816 extended the piracy provisions of UNCLOS into Somali territorial waters. The tone of the resolution and the measures it authorized were largely military in character.

However, while the international law on piracy is clear it was written in an era when piracy was seen as a problem of the past, and new states, just emerging from the colonial empires then in retreat, were eager to protect their sovereignty. Consequently, the age-old problem of pirate bases was left to individual states to deal with without acknowledging that some states, such as Somalia, would be unwilling or unable to fulfill their obligations.

The UN Security Council rectified this lacuna by passing UNSCR 1851, also in 2008, which authorized appropriate force to be used on land in Somalia. Moreover the language of the resolution, which emphasized a law enforcement rather than a military-based approach, paved the way for more broadly based international cooperation.[5] The U.S. government led the formation of the Contact Group on Piracy off the Coast of Somalia (CGPCS) in January 2009, basing it on an arrangement that had first proved its worth during the Balkan Wars of the 1990s. This was an informal discussion and negotiating forum without a permanent staff that operated outside the context of the UN and which consequently was free of that organization's consensus-driven rigidity. It set itself the objective of resolving four (later five) tasks under the direction of nationally led working groups (WG1-5):

- more effective naval operational cooperation and regional state capacity-building;
- improved guidance on legal aspects of counter-piracy, especially strengthening national judicial frameworks to ensure necessary legislation was in place to try pirates once caught;
- ship self-protection measures;
- improved public diplomacy and communications; and
- disruption of pirate financial operations and support networks.[6]

In an effort to replicate a counter-piracy agreement that was viewed as having yielded results in Southeast Asia, the IMO, also operating under the umbrella of UNSCR 1851, sponsored a series of meetings in the Horn of Africa region starting in 2005 that in 2009 resulted in agreement on the "Code of Conduct concerning the Repression of Piracy and Armed Robbery against Ships in the Western Indian Ocean and the Gulf of Aden," a mouthful that is generally referred to as the Djibouti Code of Conduct.[7] The 17 signatories, which included all the states in the region plus interested outside powers, agreed to review national legislation to ensure effective piracy prosecutions, improve domestic law enforcement capability, cooperate in capacity-building and coordinate communications through information centers. Achievements included the establishment of an information exchange in Sana'a, Yemen, and sub-regional search-and-rescue (SAR) centers in Dar-es-Salaam, Tanzania and Mombasa, Kenya, all three of which were important if local navies and coast guards were to make an effective contribution to maritime security regionally. It also laid the groundwork for updating national counter-piracy legislation; training including ship boarding techniques provided by NATO and command-and-control methods provided by Saudi Arabia, plus training in legal aspects of counter-piracy conducted with legislators, members of the judiciary and law enforcement officers from various states; and, finally, improved situational awareness through the provision of coastal radars and Automatic Identification System (AIS) access.

Naval contribution

UNSCR 1816 made it easier for nations to justify sending warships to the region on counter-piracy missions. Provided they cooperated with the UN-mandated TFG, the resolution allowed warships to pursue pirates right up to the Somali coast. States including the U.S., the U.K. and France sent vessels. Cooperation between them was rudimentary at first but improved quickly following the formation of three multinational task forces: the NATO mission, which became "Ocean Shield," the European Union NAVFOR mission "Operation Atalanta" (which drew its members from the EU member states plus Norway), both in 2008, and the U.S.-led Combined Maritime Forces CTF-151 mission that took over the counter-piracy role from CTF-150 in January 2009 and eventually attracted 27 national members. The NATO and EU missions, which co-located their headquarters in the Northwood Headquarters compound outside London, England, were authorized through to December 2014, and extended again to December 2016. EU NAVFOR offered specific protection to World Food Program (WFP) and African Union Mission in Somalia (AMISOM) ships sailing into Mogadishu. These task forces were supplemented by naval vessels from other states such as China, Russia, Japan, India and South Korea that remained under national control.

Two reporting centers were established to feed information to these naval elements. The UK Maritime Trade Organization (UKMTO), located in Dubai, became the first point of contact for all vessels in case of attack or suspicious approach. It set up the Voluntary Reporting System tracking ships in a region bounded by Suez to the West, 78 degrees east and 10 degrees south. The EU Maritime Security Center, Horn of Africa (MSCHOA), monitored vessels passing through the Gulf of Aden 24 hours a day, provided information and guidance and arranged for the protection of vulnerable merchant vessels, communicated the latest anti-piracy guidance to industry and enabled shipping companies and operators to register their vessels' transits through the region.

There were usually fewer than 30 naval vessels operating against Somali piracy at any one time. Consequently, the navies were most effective in the relatively restricted waters of the Gulf of Aden (205,000 square miles) compared to almost 2 million square miles (1.5 times the size of Europe) of the operating area as a whole. In July 2008 the U.S. Navy, working with its (then) CTF-150 partners and the IMO, established a Maritime Security Patrol Area (MSPA) in the Gulf within which were two internationally recognized Transit Corridors (IRTC) that ships could follow. Warships were stationed at intervals along their length, the space between calculated to optimize response times. Ships were encouraged to transit the Gulf either in pre-arranged convoys or using the Group Transit alternative, which coordinated traffic such that it passed through at night when the likelihood of attack was much reduced.[8]

To make more effective use of the limited naval resources, a coordination mechanism known as Shared Awareness and Deconfliction (SHADE) was established in December 2008 to coordinate the activities of the coalition and national forces to minimize duplication of effort.[9] SHADE was a monthly (later tri-monthly) series of informal meetings at which all the navies involved, industry representatives and others could meet to discuss and agree on issues relating to operations and tactics. To overcome the fact that the navies that did not operate to NATO standards had different communications systems, and therefore could not talk to each other or the various information centers, EU NAVFOR set up the web-based MERCURY system to facilitate the transfer of operational information.[10]

As the measures taken inside the Gulf made it harder for pirates to capture ships, they migrated in increasing numbers to the Arabian Sea, where naval assistance was stretched by the enormous distances involved. Better information on the whereabouts of what the navies labelled Pirate Action Groups (PAGs) meant merchant ships could be advised to take avoiding action. In April 2001 EU NAVFOR mounted a strong show of force against known pirate bases along the Somali coast but at that stage did not take advantage of UNSCR 1851 allowing counter-piracy action on land. In fact most EU states argued that despite the UN resolution there was no legal mandate for an over-the-beach assault absent a "pattern-of-life" reconnaissance to determine if people were living in the skiffs hauled up on the beach or close to the large fuel dumps just behind.[11] These reservations appeared to have been overcome by May 2012 when a pirate base near Haradhere was subjected to a helicopter-borne attack. No other similar operation was attempted.

Naval action was an important part of the counter-piracy mix but was by no means a dominant part. Navies were unable to effect the release of any vessel held hostage. The lives of the crew members were always (and rightly) paramount and, as more than one rescue attempt demonstrated, hostage safety could not be guaranteed in a violent assault. The reluctance of states to authorize coastal incursions to destroy pirate bases and skiffs was understandable; at the time the political risks appeared to be high although in retrospect this may have been exaggerated. However, the navies, along with ship self-protection measures and armed guards, imposed costs on the pirates which over time contributed to their demise.

Law enforcement measures

Articles 100–7 of the United National Convention on the Law of the Sea (UNCLOS) limit "piracy" to the high seas, where no state has jurisdiction but where any state can – and is in fact under an obligation to – take suppressive action, and created a new category called "armed robbery at sea" to cover those generally more numerous occasions when the same offense takes place within territorial waters where a coastal state has exclusive jurisdiction. Somali pirates, however, operated outside Somali waters and therefore the applicability of international law to their activities was clear.

The issues that arose with regard to the exercise of that law were therefore political and practical. Under international law only governments can take action against pirates and must do so in vessels that are readily recognizable as government-owned. Given the scale of the Arabian Sea and Gulf of Aden this meant warships. Navies, acting on behalf of their governments, might have been keen and eager to capture pirates, and governments might have been equally keen to do something to curb the problem, but as Kraska and Wilson put it: "What does the dog do when it catches the cat? Once pirates are detained and become 'persons under control' (PUCs), there are no good options."[12] Attempts were made early on, by France particularly in 2008, to hand pirates over to Puntland but this was unworkable. The captives were therefore held on board warships that were thousands of miles away from their home ports. Even if they had a helicopter embarked this would need to wait until the ship was within 100 miles or so of a secure base before the captives could be put ashore. In most cases therefore pirates were disarmed, set back in the skiffs in which they had been caught and pointed towards Somalia with only enough fuel to reach the coast. This hardly amounted to a deterrent. Pirates were often able to pick up new arms and supplies and quickly return to sea.[13] The policy became known as "catch-and-release" and was widely disparaged, but in the absence of a judicial infrastructure to detain, hold and try pirate suspects and incarcerate those found guilty, there was little else navies could do. "On any view," as Guilfoyle put it, "it seems that no more than a third of suspects encountered between late 2008 and early 2011 were sent for trial."[14]

Prosecution, moreover, remained dependent, as it always had, upon states enacting anti-piracy legislation domestically. Some states found either that they did not have such legislation, or that whatever they had was inadequate for modern conditions, or that human rights legislation potentially left them exposed to an asylum claim once pirates had completed their sentence. They also discovered that the prospect of jail time induced no fear; compared to conditions on the ground in Somalia those in Western jails bordered on the attractive.[15]

Starting with two early and isolated cases, the first involving pirates captured by the American guided-missile destroyer *Winston Churchill* (DDG-81) in 2006 the second involving those detained by the Royal Navy's frigate *Cumberland* (F-85) in 2008, pirate suspects began to be transferred to regional states for trial and imprisonment. However, while all states have a duty to cooperate to suppress piracy they are under no duty to prosecute. Consequently transfers between naval powers and the regional states that were willing to accept them – Kenya, the Seychelles and Mauritius – were regularized by memoranda of understanding ("transfer agreements"). Jurisdictional questions rarely arose. The reluctance that was encountered was driven by administrative and implementation concerns. Reservations about the case load it was being asked to accept eventually promoted Kenya to terminate its transfer agreements in 2010, accepting cases thereafter on an *ad hoc* basis only.[16]

Working Group (WG2) of the CGPCS contributed to this process by drawing up guidelines and templates to guide naval forces in particular, but also by steering the debate in Western legal and diplomatic circles as to which prosecutorial option would prove the most workable and cost-effective. The choices were between a new single-purpose international court, a hybrid international/national court operating within a national legal system but with UN support, a regional court established by treaty between affected states, or prosecution before national courts supported by agreements governing the transfer of suspects.

Opinion solidified around the final option by November 2010, spurred by the recognition on the part of the naval and donor states that the countries that were opening their courts to piracy prosecutions needed to know that prison capacity would be increased in the region, and that a model for post-sentencing transfer would be developed to accommodate the increasing number of suspected pirates being presented for trial.[17] The United Nations Office on Drugs and Crime (UNODC), which became involved in Somalia in 2008, supported prosecutions in the three regional states, prisoner transfers and, through its Rule of Law and Security Program, worked to develop judicial capacity within Somalia in support of the long-term aim of holding trials there.[18]

Between 2008 and 2012 about 1,000 suspected pirates were arraigned before multiple jurisdictions but despite this the number of young men coming forward to take their places in the boats suggested that legal prosecutions against the low-level operatives had little deterrent effect.[19] Jonathan Bellish agrees, writing that deterrence "through the rule of law has not been a model for piracy suppression." He argues that because attempts to capture and confine pirate kingpins have not been pursed systematically they have yielded similarly disappointing results.[20] Overall, suggests the IMB, it has been "the key role of international navies, the hardening of vessels, the use of private armed security teams, and the stabilizing influence of Somalia's central government" that have been most effective.[21]

On-shore initiatives

Most on-shore initiatives have been linked to the counter-piracy effort. Few have been directed at improving the internal security situation enough to enable political or economic change to take place.[22] Although most pirates were drawn initially from the clans located around the first pirate bases, pirate numbers have grown because of the availability of large numbers of unemployed young men with weakened clan affiliations – sometimes referred to as *moryean* – who are vulnerable to the inducements of the piracy network leaders. Effective counter-piracy requires concerted and coordinated efforts on several fronts, most especially onshore initiatives able to offer alternative employment opportunities, the restoration of a lawful economy and the strength to crowd out the piracy network leaders by depriving them of human and capital resources. In Somalia this process of crowding out requires the building of institutions for physical and economic security and sustained deterrence that do not merely mirror international models, but work with the grain of its messy and decentralized politics.

This last point is fundamental to success: Over the past decade, efforts in Somalia have been fragmentary and generally ineffective. Somalia has been a failed state for a quarter of a century. Throughout this time the international community has approached the problem through the prism of the statist paradigm, supporting multiple failed attempts to bring about its preferred solution of a single government to address what are clearly problems of inter-clan competition arising out of a climate of fear and violence. This history of repeated failure suggests that a new approach is needed, one which is opportunistic but also holistic, where the stakeholders – i.e. civil society, private sector, clan elders, local government – are geared to stabilizing those parts of Somalia where development measures can be implemented effectively and which have a reasonable hope of returning it to orderly growth. This means targeting those areas and groups where incentives capable of crowding out the piracy networks can be built and sustained. One approach would be to create zones of stability around ports and work out from there to develop Somalia's pastoral economy and inshore fishing, improve the availability of clean water and begin the exploitation of the country's energy and mineral wealth.[23]

All these developments require stability, which can only come about through domestic law enforcement arising out of political settlements and cooperation between the UN-mandated central government and the various regional political entities such as Puntland and Galmudug. This still appears to be a distant prospect. AMISOM, which operated first against the Islamic Courts Union and subsequently the Islamist group al-Shabaab under UNSCR 1744, is bringing a degree of stability to the area around the national capital, Mogadishu, and the area south towards the frontier with Kenya; certainly stability enough for the Kenyan government to sign a major deal with a Chinese construction company to develop a large port at Lamu just over the border.[24] Meanwhile in Somalia the CGPCS Trust Fund and EUCAP Nestor, the EU agency tasked with the implementation of the European Union's Strategic Framework for the Horn of Africa, have funded a small number of relatively minor, aid-related and training projects.[25] The United Nations Development Program (UNDP), which began working in Somalia in 1991, runs a number of other projects amongst which are four programs intended to strengthen the rule of law and internal security, and one (with the smallest budget) looking to encourage private sector growth.[26]

Ship self-defense

Success against Somali piracy has been achieved by an inter-locking series of measures: naval protection, improved law enforcement measures and greater political engagement on land are amongst them but the essential change has been ship self-protection including the use of armed guards.

Seafarers have an inherent right of self-defense. Because merchant shipping cannot rely on navies to protect it, the owners and crews of vulnerable vessels have had to adopt protective measures of their own. Passive means, including enhanced watch-keeping, maintaining best possible speed and installation of upper-deck lighting through to the construction of citadels to which the crew can retreat if these prove inadequate, were codified in a document. Entitled "Best Management Practice" (BMP) and written by UKMTO it was quickly taken up and extended by IMO and industry bodies.[27] Complying with BMP attracted lower maritime insurance rates. Despite this vessels continued to transit the so-called "at risk" zone without following its advice. These vessels appeared more likely to be hijacked. Protective measures deterred pirates, who always looked for the most vulnerable targets. Nonetheless, each of the individual measures recommended in BMP was overcome in one incident or another, although never all of them together. Despite this, states made it clear they were neither going to provide the level of naval protection that the industry believed it was entitled to nor would any more than a very few agree to embark Vessel Protection Detachments (VPDs) consisting of regular service personnel. Consequently, ship-owners began to employ what were termed "privately contracted armed security personnel" (PCASP).

Owners effectively had to abandon their long-held view that firearms had no place on civilian merchant vessels and accede to the use of privatized naval force to protect their ships militarily. American vessels were the first to do so in 2009 in response to U.S. Coast Guard directives. Experience gained from the small number of U.S.-flagged vessels was used to make the argument that no ship with an armed private maritime security company (PMSC) detachment on board had been hijacked. The industry reluctantly agreed. Most observers, including the more thoughtful private security providers, believed that it was only a matter of time before a ship was taken down but fortunately time ran out for the pirates before the harsh economics of international shipping reduced the level of protection the armed teams could provide.[28]

Conclusions: is there light at the end of the tunnel?

Somali piracy was always a matter of economics. Economic opportunity in a barren land wracked by war was intimately related to the exploitation of violence. Although the modalities of that exploitation changed over time, it was instigated under the Barre regime after the end of the Cold War, when the foreign assistance which had sustained him in power dried up.[29]

Civil society did not, despite outward appearances, break down. The basic Somali clan structure asserted itself as people looked to their kinsmen for protection and support. Powerful clans subordinated weaker clans as they had always done. The competition for resources that ensued spilled over onto the sea not, primarily, to extract profit from fishing directly but largely indirectly through the provision of protection to foreign deep-water fishing fleets. Indigenous large-scale fishing enterprises were mooted but were never sustained. Artisanal fishermen found it hard to survive.

The combination of seafaring skills acquired by fishermen at sea and fighting skills learnt by militiamen on land – and the training some men had received from the short-lived Puntland Coast Guard – were exploited by an insightful entrepreneur. For him and for those who followed and emulated his methods, the proposition was always economic: the application of Somali rent-seeking methods to ship-owners and their crews. For as long as the model remained profitable it survived. Cost control was always at the heart of the operation, because while – it became apparent – super-size profits could be wrested from the world's insurance companies and their shipping clients, the risks were also high, none more so than from political and clan groups on land. While the cost of physical protection was low, the cost of buying off politicians, clan leaders, local communities and suppliers was high and spiraled upwards as the size of ransom payments increased.

What the layered international response to piracy succeeded in doing – although there is no evidence that it thought this through in any coherent fashion – was to impose external costs on the pirate groups that ultimately proved to be crushing. While even as late as 2013 the return on an individual capture could be as good as it had been since 2007, the number of captures yielding these returns dropped dramatically as the number of ships taking self-protection measures grew. Increasingly the ships that were captured were not worth the effort expended. Many were uninsured, and it was insurance money – driven by obligations both contractual and moral which some politicians and bureaucrats argued should be put to one side for the greater good – that paid the ransoms without which seafarers would have been left to rot on shore. Fewer poorly defended ships meant pirates spent longer at sea and the already high attrition rate amongst pirate crews, who in many cases lacked basic seafaring skills, climbed to 30 percent or more causing consternation among communities that depended on young men to fulfill basic economic tasks. Coastal communities that had once paid host to pirates, willingly or reluctantly is still not clear, began to find their presence oppressive and offensive. The port of Eyl was the first to drive them out in 2012.

Falling returns at sea crossed with rising potential returns on land consequent to an improved security situation, in Mogadishu particularly. Although three of the most high-profile pirate bosses were apprehended this still left just short of 50 organizers free to pursue their new business interests within Somalia; nonetheless capital, leadership and the necessary pirate infrastructure remained in place. However, so long as the opportunity at sea remains unprofitable and the opportunities on land continue to improve then Somali piracy – certainly the large-scale piracy that affected international shipping – is likely to remain dormant.

Notes

1 Martin N. Murphy, *Somalia: The New Barbary? Piracy and Islam in the Horn of Africa*. New York: Columbia University Press; London: Hurst, 2011, pp. 12–13.
2 *Ibid.*, p. 47.
3 Martin N. Murphy, *Small Boats, Weak States, Dirty Money: Piracy and Maritime Terrorism in the Modern World*. New York: Columbia University Press; London: Hurst, 2009, pp. 28–9.
4 Murphy, *Somalia*, pp. 37–8.
5 Murphy, *Somalia*, p. 125; James Kraska, *Contemporary Maritime Piracy: International Law, Strategy, and Diplomacy at Sea*. Westport, CT: Praeger, 2011, pp. 155–7; Douglas Guilfoyle, "Piracy off Somalia and Counter-piracy Efforts," in Douglas Guilfoyle (ed.), *Modern Piracy: Legal Challenges and Responses*. Cheltenham, UK and Northampton, MA: Edward Elgar, 2013, p. 50.
6 Murphy, *Somalia*, p. 125; Kraska, *Contemporary Maritime Piracy*, pp. 159–61; Christian Bueger, "Responses to Contemporary Piracy: Disentangling the Organizational Field," in Guilfoyle (ed.), *Modern Piracy*, pp. 97–8.
7 Murphy, *Somalia*, p. 127; Kraska, *Contemporary Maritime Piracy*, p. 161.
8 Murphy, *Somalia*, p. 134; Bibi Van Ginkel and Lennart Landman, "In Search of a Sustainable and Coherent Strategy: Assessing the Kaleidoscope of Counter-Piracy Activities in Somalia." *Journal of International Criminal Justice* 10, 4, September 2012, p. 740.
9 Murphy, *Somalia*, p. 134.

10 Van Ginkel and Landman, "In Search," pp. 737–8.

11 Martin Murphy, interview with EU officials, 2013.

12 James Kraska and Brian Wilson, "Fighting Pirates: The Pen and the Sword." *World Policy Journal* 25, 4, Winter 2008/9, p. 45.

13 Van Ginkel and Landman, "In Search," p. 742.

14 Douglas Guilfoyle, "Prosecuting Somali Pirates: A Critical Evaluation of the Options." *Journal of International Criminal Justice* 10, 4, September 2012, p. 770.

15 Murphy, *Somalia*, pp. 123–5.

16 Douglas Guilfoyle, "Prosecuting Pirates: The Contact Group on Piracy off the Coast of Somalia, Governance and International Law." *Global Policy* 4, 1, February 2013, pp. 74–5.

17 *Ibid.*, pp. 75–6; Guilfoyle, "Prosecuting Somali Pirates," p. 779.

18 Van Ginkel and Landman, "In Search," p. 743; Guilfoyle, "Prosecuting Somali Pirates," pp. 779 and 791.

19 Guilfoyle, "Prosecuting Somali Pirates," p. 769.

20 Jonathan Bellish, "The Systematic Prosecution of Somali Leadership and the Primacy of Multi-Level Cooperation." One Earth Future and University of Denver Sturm School of Law, June 2014, pp. 1 and 4, at https://oneearthfuture.org/sites/oneearthfuture.org/files/documents/publications/systemat-icprosecutionpaperdu_0.pdf, accessed August 28, 2015.

21 Joshua Keating, "The Decline and Fall of Somali Piracy." *Slate*, January 16, 2014, at www.slate.com/blogs/the_world_/2014/01/16/the_decline_and_fall_of_somali_piracy.html, accessed August 28, 2015.

22 Van Ginkel and Landman, "In Search," p. 743.

23 Martin N. Murphy and Joe Saba, "Countering Piracy: The Potential of Onshore Development," in *Global Challenge, Regional Responses: Forging a Common Approach to Maritime Piracy.* Selected Briefing Papers. Dubai: Dubai School of Government, 2011, p. 47.

24 George Mwangi, "Chinese Firm Signs $478.9 Million Kenya Lamu Port Deal." *Wall Street Journal*, Frontiers Blog, August 3, 2014, at http://blogs.wsj.com/frontiers/2014/08/03/chinese-firm-si gns-478-9-million-kenya-lamu-port-deal/, accessed August 28, 2015; Van Ginkel and Landman, "In Search," p. 744.

25 Christian Bueger, "Drops in the Bucket? A Review of Onshore Responses to Somali Piracy." *WMU Journal of Maritime Affairs* 11, 1, April 2012, p. 25; European Union External Action, "EUCAP Nestor (Regional Maritime Capacity Building Mission in the Horn of Africa and Western Indian Ocean)," Mission Description, at www.eeas.europa.eu/csdp/missions-and-operations/eucap-nestor/mission-description/index_en.htm, accessed August 28, 2015.

26 United Nations Development Program, "UNDP in Somalia," March 2013, at www.us.undp.org/content/dam/washington/docs/CountryPapers/CountryPapersrevised/UNDP_DC_Somalia.pdf, accessed August 28, 2015.

27 *Best Management Practices for Protection against Somalia Based Piracy: Suggested Planning and Operational Practices for Ship Operators, and Masters of Ships Transiting the High Risk Area, version 4.* Edinburgh: Witherby Publishing Group, 2011.

28 Martin N. Murphy, "Somali Piracy: Why Should We Care?" *RUSI Journal* 156, 6, December 2011, p. 8.

29 Murphy, *Somalia*, pp. 43–8. There is a rich literature on the economic exploitation on civil conflict. See, for example, David Keen, *The Economic Functions of Violence in Civil Wars.* Adelphi Paper 320. Oxford and New York: Oxford University Press for the International Institute of Strategic Studies, 1998.

PART IV

Actor perspectives and policy options

17

AMERICAN NAVAL POLICY, STRATEGY, PLANS, AND OPERATIONS IN THE SECOND DECADE OF THE TWENTY-FIRST CENTURY

Peter M. Swartz[1]

Overview

This chapter seeks to explain broadly U.S. Navy policy, strategy, plans, and operations in the second decade of the twenty-first century.[2] It does so by discussing some basic fundamentals, and then the Navy's three major operational activities: peacetime engagement, crisis response, and wartime combat. For each activity, it describes the Navy's ends, ways, and means.[3]

The approach taken is deliberately specific, that is, it tries to present the actual application of concepts rather than just discussing the concepts themselves. While concepts are important, true understanding of the uses of naval power requires some explanation of actual operations, organizations, and systems.

Fundamentals

Some important underlying propositions must be understood first, in contemplating and analyzing American naval power today and its relationship to that of other nations and non-state actors:

- The United States is a nation of laws, and the Navy and its uses are deeply rooted in – and subordinate to – American law. The Constitution of the United States of America – the supreme law of the country – designates the U.S. President as the "Commander in Chief of the Army and Navy of the United States," and gives the power to the U.S. Congress to "provide and maintain a Navy," as well as to "make Rules for the Government and regulation of the land and naval Forces." It is important to remember that, at the end of the day, the U.S. Navy is not an independent actor, but clearly subject to the direction of the President.[4]
- The United States has used its Navy as an important tool of national security policy since the very earliest days of the Republic. The Navy has participated significantly in all the

nation's wars, since the American Revolution through Operation Enduring Freedom. It has also served as a significant tool of American diplomacy and international economic policy during times of prolonged peace. America is used to thinking of its Navy as one of its leading institutions, and calling upon it to carry out a wide range of diplomatic, information, military, and economic policies. These are fundamental bases of the American use of naval power – and while not unique in the world, they differ markedly from the experience of many other nations.

- The U.S. Navy seldom operates alone. America has many other such institutions with related mandates, and expects the Navy to coordinate and cooperate with them in its activities and operations. In the nineteenth century, U.S. Navy commanders coordinated their peacetime operations closely with the U.S. Consular Service, and in wartime with U.S. Army commanders. In the twentieth century, the Navy became increasingly integrated into a joint U.S. military system, evolving from the creation before World War I of the Joint Board of the Army and the Navy, through establishment during World War II of the Joint Chiefs of Staff and joint theaters of operation, through the passage of the National Security Act of 1947, the creation of the Office of the Secretary of Defense, and the passage of the Goldwater-Nichols Department of Defense Reorganization Act in 1986 and subsequent related legislation. U.S. naval operations today are typically embedded in inter-agency and joint operations – the culmination of decades of increasing U.S. national security agency and inter-service integration – directed by the President and the Secretary of Defense through the Joint Chiefs of Staff, and under the command of a designated joint Combatant Commander (supported by the forces of other appropriate combatant commanders).[5] Meanwhile, the organizing, manning, training, equipping, and maintaining of U.S. naval forces is the responsibility – under the President and Secretary of Defense – of the civilian Secretary of the Navy, the Chief of Naval Operations (the uniformed head of the Navy), and the bureaus, offices, and commands of the Department of the Navy, the Navy Shore establishment, and the Fleet – all with funds authorized and appropriated (in some detail) by the U.S. Congress each year.

- The U.S. Navy seldom operates without allies and/or partners. U.S. naval forces relied on forward French, Spanish, and Dutch bases and assistance in the American Revolutionary War against Great Britain; and on British and Neapolitan bases in the Republic's early wars with France, Tripoli, and Algiers. The U.S. Navy used British Hong Kong as a base in America's war with Spain, fought as part of an international force during the Chinese "Boxer" Uprising, and integrated into Royal Navy and other allied naval formations in the North Atlantic and Mediterranean during World War I. During World War II, the United States and Royal Navies achieved probably the most intimate naval alliance ever known, with numerous other allied navies integrated with them to varying degrees. During the Cold War, the Free World's alliance system provided the backdrop for a system of close U.S. Navy relationships with the navies of NATO and Rio Pact nations, as well as Japan, South Korea, Taiwan, the Philippines, Thailand, Australia, and others. Since the end of the Cold War, many of those relationships have, if anything, been enhanced – at sea, on planning staffs, in classrooms, and in laboratories.[6]

- By virtue of its geographical and geo-political situation in the world, America has mostly used its naval power forward, across the seas, far from its own shores. This has been as true in times of peace as in times of war. Whether protecting American merchants, missionaries, and diplomats in the nineteenth century or storming European and South Pacific beaches in the mid-twentieth century, the U.S. Navy – in conjunction with other elements of American power and influence – has been called upon to operate at a great distance from the North American continent, and for long periods of time. America's leaders and populace have come to expect that forward and sustained operations are central to its naval posture.[7] Again, while America is not unique in this regard, this experience is different from that of many other countries.

- Since the very beginnings of the nation and its Navy, that forward presence has been global, reflecting the global interests of the United States. America's very earliest wars were fought in the North and South Atlantic, the Mediterranean, the Southeast Pacific, and the waters of Indonesia. The American Civil War saw both "American" navies deployed in the Atlantic and the Far East, and Confederate raiders operating throughout the globe – from the Cape of Good Hope to the Bering Sea. The Spanish–American War was fought in the Caribbean and the Far East; World War I throughout the world but especially in the North Atlantic and Mediterranean; and World War II famously throughout the Atlantic, Pacific, and Mediterranean. The Cold War saw the creation of vast U.S. Navy fleets designed to contest, control, and use the North Atlantic, the Caribbean and Mediterranean, the North Pacific and even the Indian and Arctic Oceans. The United States sees the post-Cold War environment as necessitating a continuation of that global deployment pattern, albeit with far fewer individual warships in the force.[8]
- Within that global pattern, however, the U.S. Navy has often had to focus on one or more specific theaters of the world, as directed by the President. These focal seas have often shifted, reflecting and demonstrating a vital deployment flexibility that has always characterized the force. Before and during World War I, the preponderance of U.S. naval power shifted to the North Atlantic. After that war – and throughout World War II – the bulk of U.S. fleet strength was deployed forward in the Western Pacific. After that war, the fleet was again weighted in favor of the North Atlantic and Mediterranean, and today we are seeing yet another "rebalance" toward the Pacific. It should be pointed out that as all of these shifts occurred, one constant for almost 200 years has been the necessity for a permanent U.S. Navy force far forward in the Pacific, due to the political, diplomatic, economic, and societal interests of the United States in that region since its earliest days – well before it had even acquired its own Pacific seacoast. Before modern Imperial Japanese or Qing Dynasty Chinese fleets existed, an American East India Squadron was operating in the Western Pacific.
- The U.S. Navy is – and usually has been – a "full-service navy," capable of conducting a wide range of peacetime, crisis, and wartime tasks – from humanitarian assistance through combating piracy through anti-submarine warfare to strategic nuclear deterrence – and using a wide variety of specialized warship and aircraft types and weapon systems. There are few areas of naval endeavor or naval ship types that the U.S. Navy has not been proficient in at one time or another. At various times in its history, however, the Navy neglected one or more areas: battle-line war at sea and sealift for the Army during most of the nineteenth century, for example, and riverine warfare during most of its history (except for the American Civil War, the Vietnam War, and the decade since the 9/11 Al Qaeda terrorist attacks on New York and Washington). Nevertheless, the Navy normally seeks to provide a wide range of options to the President. A key debate throughout its history has been what is the optimum balance among the wide variety of tasks and ship, aircraft and weapon system types, given available resources. This debate is quite active today, both within and outside the Navy.
- America has been a rich, technologically advanced, and innovative country – especially at sea – from its very beginnings.[9] Since its origins as 13 British colonies, America has always had a reservoir of highly competent seafarers to officer its warships, and – somewhat more recently – to man them. American warships were sufficiently well constructed and equipped to battle and defeat Royal Navy warships during the American Revolution. The "super-frigates" of the early American republic were a technological marvel. The American Civil War saw innovative use – by both sides – of revolutionary new technologies: iron

armor, gun turrets, submarines, mines, and more. That technological prowess – indeed, super-iority – has continued through the present day, with American naval architects, engineers, and operators leading the world in naval technologies as diverse as aircraft carrier design, nuclear propulsion, cruise missiles, high-performance jet aircraft, sonar, electronic warfare, and ballistic missile defense. The U.S. government and American defense industry maintain a massive naval industrial base, concentrated heavily in the shipyards, factories, and laboratories of the Lockheed Martin, Northrop Grumman, Boeing, Raytheon and other corporations, and the U.S. Navy itself.[10]

- Above all, the U.S. Navy has been an operational Navy: a ready, sea-going, and tactically pro-ficient professional Navy.[11] Peacetime forward deployments, responses to crises, and foreign wars have always necessitated long periods forward at sea on station, and long transit times at sea to and from home port. Centuries of constant national direction to the Navy to be ready to conduct global deployments, combat operations, diplomatic visits, and engagement with foreign armed forces have driven intense schedules of at-sea exercises, training evolutions, and experiments across the whole gamut of naval missions and activities.[12] From the cruise of the "Squadron of Evolution" to Europe in 1891 to the circumnavigation of the globe by the Great White Fleet in 1907–9 to the immense "Fleet Problems" of the interwar period to the great NATO and other multinational at-sea exercises of the Cold War, the U.S. Navy has pushed itself (and its allies and partners) hard, at sea, to hone the skills necessary to carry out national and alliance tasking should the successful application of naval force be required.[13]

Peacetime, crises, and war

With a firm understanding of the foundations and characteristics of U.S. naval power, we can now turn to its uses: Just what is it that this forward-deploying, sea-going, global, technologic-ally advanced force is supposed to do?

An easy way to consider this is to discuss it in terms of three major conditions and activ-ities: peacetime readiness and engagement, crisis response, and wartime combat.[14] And for each of those, to describe the Navy's ends, ways, and means.[15]

Peacetime readiness and engagement

Ends

The role of the U.S. Navy in peacetime is to help preserve the security, freedom, commerce, and economic well-being of America and its people, at home and abroad, and of its friends and allies.

Ways and means

To help achieve these ends, the President and Secretary of Defense use the U.S. Navy for a var-iety of peacetime tasks, heavily focused on deterrence, reassurance of friends and partners, and readiness for possible future combat. In joint U.S. military parlance, many of these operations fall under the first and second phases ("Phase 0," or "shaping"; and "Phase I" or "deterring") of an often useful joint six-phase planning model.[16]

There are eight main ways in which the Navy serves the nation and the broader inter-national community during times of peace: through strategic nuclear deterrence, ballistic missile defense, deterrence of conventional crises and war (through naval readiness and engagement), maritime safety operations, maritime security operations, humanitarian assistance operation, naval diplomacy, and support to science. The Navy's capabilities in all these areas provide the President, the Secretary of Defense, and the U.S. joint combatant commanders with a wide range of options to implement national policy.

The United States government believes that purposeful global forward deployment of its naval forces, in various regions, with tailored forces capable of accomplishing relevant tasks, helps underpin world political, economic, and social stability, to the great benefit of the United States and, indeed, all of the world's nations.[17] The United States also believes that its naval forces cannot – and should not – be the only naval forces directed to carry out such activities; and seeks to coordinate and cooperate with naval partners – and especially with its highly capable European and East Asian allies – wherever possible, to share in providing a level of maritime security that benefits them as well.

Strategic nuclear deterrence

The nation's strategic nuclear policies and posture are designed specifically to help deter possible Russian and Chinese strategic nuclear attack on the United States and its allies and partners.[18] The U.S. Navy's contributions to the nation's strategic nuclear triad has two main elements: 14 treaty-limited Ohio-class nuclear-powered ballistic missile submarines (SSBNs) capable of launching Trident II D-5 sea-launched ballistic missiles (SLBMs); and a small fleet of land-based Boeing E-6B Mercury airborne command post and relay aircraft.[19] Several of these submarines are on patrol at any one time, in both the Atlantic and Pacific Oceans. These submarines are undetectable while on patrol, and are therefore the most survivable leg of the triad. American SSBN and SLBM plans and programs are carried out in close cooperation with those of the United Kingdom and its four Royal Navy Vanguard-class SSBNs. Planning is currently under way for 12 U.S. *Ohio* follow-on replacement SSBNs, including close coordination and cooperation with the Royal Navy's own SSBN replacement program.[20]

Ballistic missile defense (BMD)

U.S. combatant commanders routinely request and deploy U.S. Navy cruisers and destroyers capable of ballistic missile defense forward in the Northwest Pacific, Persian Gulf, and Eastern Mediterranean, as components of the U.S. 5th, 6th, and 7th Fleets, to help deter ballistic missile attacks and to defend if necessary against a short-warning North Korean or Iranian ballistic missile attack on U.S. or allied and friendly nations or forward U.S. forces in the theater.[21] Some BMD-capable warships are homeported forward in Japan and Spain, while those in the Persian Gulf rotate routinely forward from bases in the continental United States.[22] Several allied and friendly navies deploy similar sea-based ABM systems, including Spain, the United Kingdom, Australia, the Netherlands, Germany, Japan, and South Korea. U.S. Navy cooperative engagement with these allies on ballistic missile defense systems interoperability and operations is close and frequent.[23] Since 2014, the U.S. Navy has also manned a forward Aegis Ashore facility in Romania, as part of the European Phased Adaptive Approach (EPAA) to ballistic missile defense.[24]

Deterrence of conventional crises and war, through naval readiness and engagement

Readiness

A central and continuous role of the U.S. Navy in peacetime is deterrence of possible conventional crises and wars.[25] That role is exercised through a program of personnel, material, and operational readiness, to provide combat-ready forward-deployed and surge forces in response to Presidential direction.[26] The operational elements include constant at-sea work-ups and exercises, as well as global intelligence, surveillance, and reconnaissance operations (ISR). All of these at-sea operations are conducted in accordance with longstanding international law.

The central ways and means by which the U.S. Navy contributes to peacetime deterrence of crisis and war are through the permanent forward deployment of the U.S. 5th and 7th Fleets, in the Indian Ocean and the Western Pacific.[27] These are the most combat-ready, balanced, and capable conventional forces in the U.S. Navy. In the absence of crisis or war tasking – which has actually been the norm – their powerful forward deterrent presence is seen by the United States as an important contributor to the peace and stability of those regions.[28] Ships of these fleets are maintained forward through a variety of methods: *Rotation* of ships and crews from the United States; *forward basing* of ships and crews; *hull swaps* in which crews remain forward and ships are rotated for them to serve on; and *crew swaps*, in which ships remain forward and crews are rotated to serve on them.[29]

Carrier Strike Groups (CSGs), ships on BMD patrols, Amphibious Ready Groups/Marine Expeditionary units (ARG/MEUs), and attack and conventional cruise missile submarines (SSNs and SSGNs) all routinely rotate forward from the continental United States (CONUS) to the 5th Fleet to maintain a powerful permanent and ready in-theater forward presence. An Afloat Forward Staging Base (AFSB) and smaller units are permanently forward-based in-theater, with crews rotating in and out to serve on them. 5th Fleet ship maintenance capabilities are also available at the U.S. Navy facility on the British Indian Ocean Territory island of Diego Garcia.[30]

Meanwhile, the CSG, ARG/MEU, submarines, and mine warfare ships of the US 7th Fleet are largely forward-based in Japan and Guam, and new U.S. Navy Littoral Combat Ships (LCS) have been operating out of forward facilities at Singapore, with four planned to do so in the future.[31]

In European and African waters, the U.S. Navy permanently deploys the U.S. 6th Fleet, including a forward fleet flagship and land-based maritime patrol aircraft; as well as the above-mentioned permanent forward afloat BMD capability in the Eastern Mediterranean. The fleet periodically swells with intermittent warships transiting the Mediterranean to and from Arabian Sea, available to exercise with European and North African navies and to respond to crises or war requirements.[32]

Rebalancing

Since the end of the Cold War, the geographic focus of U.S. Navy forward presence readiness has shifted. And it continues to shift. The Western Pacific has remained as important as it did during the Cold War. Perhaps more so.[33] But presence – including combat operations – in the Arabian and adjacent seas became even more important than previously, with increasing demands on U.S. naval resources, especially due to Operations Enduring Freedom (OEF) and Iraqi Freedom (OIF), and later Inherent Resolve. Meanwhile, U.S. naval presence has already declined considerably in Atlantic and European waters and littorals, since the Soviet threat disappeared. The contemporary 6th Fleet is much smaller than its Cold War antecedent, despite a greatly expanded area of responsibility, beyond the Mediterranean. U.S. Navy bases in Maine, Newfoundland, Bermuda, Iceland, the Azores, the United Kingdom, Sardinia, and elsewhere have closed.

Much of the American (and western European) draw-down from European and Atlantic waters had already taken place in the decades preceding the Obama Administration announcement of a rebalancing of U.S. defense posture toward the Western Pacific.[34] The current rebalancing is more a rebalancing to the Western Pacific from the continental United States and Southwest Asia, than from Atlantic and European waters.[35] The U.S. naval presence in European waters and at European bases has been stable for years, and in fact has been increasing with the forward homeporting of U.S. Navy Ballistic Missile Defense destroyers at Rota, Spain in 2014.

Should a future President decide on a different rebalance of U.S. forces globally, U.S. naval forces should be able to respond quickly and with relative ease, given their inherent flexibility and mobility.

Force protection

Even in times of peace, real threats exist to U.S. naval forces. These include crime, terrorism, intelligence gathering, and cyber attack.[36] The 2000 Al Qaeda terrorist suicide attack on the guided missile destroyer USS *Cole* (DDG-67) while she was refueling in the port of Aden, Yemen, demonstrated the importance of peacetime protection to the nation's warships as they patrol the seven seas. The Navy subsequently instituted a range of force protection measures surrounding U.S. Navy port calls and ship visits – domestic and forward – including port vulnerability assessments, changed rules of engagement (ROE), the use of floating barriers and small boat patrols, and close coordination between the Navy's Naval Criminal Investigative Service (NCIS) agents and local police and harbor security authorities. The U.S. Navy also maintains U.S. 10th Fleet network defense units, a Coastal Riverine Force, and other elements to protect itself from these threats.[37]

Experimentation

Ongoing U.S. Navy experimentation at sea is also a part of fleet readiness, but geared more to the future than the present. As ideas for new systems to deter or wage war occur to naval planners and designers, the Navy tries to put them to sea during peacetime, to experiment with them and foster their development, if the experiment proves successful.[38] The *Sea Shadow* (IX-529) experimental stealth ship that operated from the 1980s through the first decade of the twenty-first century is one of the more striking examples of this.

Engagement

Many of these operations involve intense engagement with foreign navies and other military forces. The U.S. Navy needs to – and does – collaborate with a broad spectrum of partners, many of which have very limited naval means, while remaining committed to longstanding U.S. allies – most of which have deployed more robust naval forces.[39] Naval engagement can help improve international relationships and build international trust and confidence, while enabling the exchange of skills and information that could prove vital should the navies have to operate alongside each other during a crisis or war.[40] Bilateral and multilateral exercises at sea have been a principle means to engage positively with allied and friendly navies, to practice cooperation, transfer skills, and establish and maintain professional personal relationships. Many multilateral and bilateral exercises have become major recurring events, such as:

- NATO exercises in European waters, such as Noble Justification, Proud Manta, and Brilliant Mariner;[41]
- exercises with European navies, such as the United Kingdom's multinational Joint Warrior;[42]
- BALTOPS in the Baltic Sea;

- Sea Breeze and other exercises with Black Sea navies;
- Noble Dina, in the Mediterranean, with the Greek and Israeli navies;
- Phoenix Express with North African navies;
- Cutlass Express with East African navies;
- Obangame Express with West African and European navies (and the Brazilian Navy);
- International Mine Countermeasures Exercise (IMCMEX) in the Persian Gulf region;[43]
- Cooperation Afloat Readiness and Training (CARAT) and Southeast Asia Cooperation Against Terrorism (SEACAT) in Southeast Asia;
- Balikatan and PHIBLEX in the Philippines;
- Malabar with the Indian Navy in the Indian Ocean (in 2014 and 2015 with the Japanese Maritime Self Defense Force (JMSDF) also);
- Talisman Saber in the Southwest Pacific;
- Cobra Gold off Thailand;
- Naval Engagement Activities (NEA) with Vietnam;
- Foal Eagle and Ulchi Freedom Guardian in Korea;
- Keen Edge with Japan;
- Pacific Bond with Australia and Japan;
- Chilemar with the Chilean Navy;
- PANAMAX to practice protection of safe passage through the Panama Canal;
- Southern Partnership Station with Latin American and European navies;
- Trident Fury in the Pacific with Canada;
- Rim of the Pacific (RIMPAC) off Hawaii;[44]
- Bold Alligator;[45]
- Proliferation Security Initiative (PSI) exercises.[46]

Other engagement means include port visits, personnel exchanges, staff talks, and war games with close U.S. allies and partners, as well as various bilateral and multilateral material acquisition and research programs.[47] The U.S. Navy routinely hosts officers and enlisted students from allied and friendly nations at its schools and training events.[48] Since 1969, the Chief of Naval Operations (CNO) has hosted an International Seapower Symposium (ISS) at the Naval War College in Newport every two years: 155 heads of the world's navies or their representatives participated in the last event, in 2011, and the next meeting is scheduled for September 2016. The CNO also hosts bilateral visits to Washington from selected counterparts, and reciprocates in foreign capitals and naval headquarters as well.

In the case of NATO allies and Korea, longstanding integrated naval command structures have been evolving since the end of the Cold War. Common NATO doctrine, tactics, techniques, and procedures – in the development of which the U.S. Navy has participated – are widely and routinely practiced and used, including by several non-NATO navies, improving global naval interoperability.

Longstanding NATO institutions provide a framework for continuing multilateral approaches at sea by the U.S., Canadian, and European navies, and have allowed the navies of post-Cold War NATO members in the Baltic and the Balkans to integrate their operations and practices with those of older alliance members.[49] The U.S. Navy encourages this multinational activity, seeing it as a force-multiplier when future international naval coalitions need to be deployed at sea.[50] Prior to the Ukrainian Crisis of 2014, the U.S. regarded the NATO area as a zone of relative peace, and its NATO allies as potential "exporters" of security – alongside U.S. forces – to areas beyond the North Atlantic Treaty area, especially Middle Eastern and African waters, where both the interests and capabilities of most NATO nations often converge.[51]

No such multinational alliance framework exists, however, in the Middle East or the Indo-Pacific, and the U.S. Navy – within the limits set by U.S. foreign policy – actively encourages increased multi-nationalism at sea among its allied, partner, and friendly navies in those regions. For example, U.S. Navy engagement activity tries to help make the Indian, Australian, Japanese, and South Korean navies more interoperable, as well as the navies of the Gulf Cooperation Council (GCC) in Southwest Asia. The U.S. Navy has been especially active in fostering trilateral naval approaches among the U.S., Japanese, and South Korean navies; and among the U.S., Japanese, and Australian navies. The U.S. Navy also has routinely engaged in exercises with Ukrainian and Georgian naval forces in the Black Sea.

Brazil has been a traditional American naval partner. The navies were co-belligerents during the two World Wars, and allies during the Cold War. That partnership continues, as a sub-set of the overall relationship between the two large sovereign American nations. The U.S. Navy hopes that the naval partnership will deepen, as Brazil becomes a major world power. Recently, a Brazilian Navy diesel-electric submarine helped a U.S. Navy carrier strike group work up before deploying overseas. Likewise, the highly capable Chilean Navy also has provided diesel-electric submarine training services to U.S. Navy fleet units.

In the Eastern Mediterranean, the U.S. Navy continues its traditional but low-key engagement with the Israeli Navy.[52] This includes the annual Noble Melinda exercise, focusing on explosive ordnance disposal, diving, and salvage operations.

More dynamic has been the growing peacetime partnership between the U.S. Navy and the Indian Navy, manifested through the Malabar exercise program, increased sales of American naval equipment to the Indian Navy, research and development cooperation, and other activities.[53]

During the Cold War, the Soviet Navy was the chief potential wartime opponent of the U.S. Navy, and U.S. Navy policy, strategy, tactics, and equipment all had a heavy anti-Soviet Navy focus. This is no longer the case. While U.S. relationships with Russia – the main successor state to the Soviet Union – are hardly as warm as those with America's various allies, partners, and friends, U.S. Navy peacetime relationships with the Russian Navy had been cordial and often cooperative (until the Ukrainian Crisis of 2014). The Russian Navy participated in annual post-Cold War FRUKUS exercises with the navies of the United States, Britain, and France; in many of the annual U.S. Navy-sponsored multilateral Baltic Operations (BALTOPS) exercises; and in bilateral Incidents at Sea (INCSEA) talks with the U.S. Navy and several other navies since the middle of the Cold War. The Russian Navy was represented at the U.S. Navy-sponsored International Seapower Symposium (ISS) in Newport in 2011, participated in BALTOPS 2012, and engaged with the U.S. Navy and other navies in the U.S.-sponsored RIMPAC 2012 exercise off Hawaii – the world's largest multinational naval exercise.[54] The Russian and U.S. Navies – along with many others – have operated with each other closely at sea in the multinational anti-piracy offensive in the Arabian Sea. U.S. Navy ship visits to Vladivostok and other Russian ports before 2014 were routine. There have been worrisome disagreements, however, between the Russian and Western governments – exacerbated recently over Russia's 2014 actions in Ukraine. In any event, the U.S. Navy stands ready as a tool of U.S. national security, to engage or deter as required.

The U.S. Navy likewise engages the Chinese People's Liberation Army Navy (PLAN) in peacetime cooperative efforts. As discussed above, the U.S. Navy has been no stranger to the China Seas. Indeed, the U.S. 7th Fleet used Tsingtao as its main forward operating base from 1945 to 1949. Mutual port visits between U.S. Navy and PLAN warships took place throughout the 1980s, and sporadically ever since. PLAN warships have operated with U.S. Navy and other Western warships as part of the anti-piracy efforts in the Arabian Sea, and recently exercised closely with U.S. Navy warships, including surface combatant helicopter cross-decking operations. In September 2013, the U.S. Pacific Fleet hosted three PLAN warships at Pearl Harbor, Hawaii and exercised with them in Hawaiian waters.[55] The PLAN commander visited the United States in October 2013, and the U.S. Navy Chief of Naval Operations visited China in 2014. The PLAN participated for the first time in 2014 in the long-running U.S.-led RIMPAC exercise. U.S. naval engagement with the PLAN is constrained, however by Section 1201 of the U.S. 2000 Defense Authorization Act, which restricts certain forms of U.S. military-to-military cooperation with the Chinese.[56]

As with the Russian Navy, the U.S. Navy aspires to a cordial and mutually beneficial relationship with the PLAN, in East Asia and throughout the world. The Navy has made efforts to demonstrate its respect for the emerging Chinese power, while maintaining its traditional strong views on the benefits that accrue to all to respect customary international law.

There are only a handful of nations with which the U.S. Navy does not engage, North Korea being the main example. While formal U.S. Navy engagement with the various naval forces of Iran does not exist, the two sides normally avoid confrontations in the Persian Gulf (although as recently as 2008, Iran engaged in aggressive maneuvers toward transiting U.S. Navy warships in international waters near the Strait of Hormuz). A former U.S. Navy 5th Fleet commander has floated the possibility of an agreement to improve Iranian–American ship-to-ship communications in the Gulf, as a confidence-building measure and to avoid unwanted crises.[57]

Maritime safety

This is an area that is primarily the domain of the world's coast guards, but here too the U.S. Navy has certain important roles to play, engaging international partners. One key aspect of this issue area, for navies, is submarine escape and rescue. The U.S. Navy has been a strong participant in and supporter of the International Submarine Escape and Rescue Liaison Office (ISMERLO), established in 2003 at Norfolk, Virginia by NATO's Submarine Escape and Rescue Working Group (SMERG) to assist in the global coordination of international rescue operations. Inspired in part by the tragic sinking of the Russian submarine *Kursk* (K-141) in 2000, ISMERLO has evolved into a world-wide network within which navies engage to share equipment and procedural standards, to better come to the rescue of each other's stricken submarines.[58] In a related initiative, the U.S. Navy participates (alongside the Russian, Chinese, Indian, Pakistani, and 17 other navies) in the Asia Pacific Submarine Conference (APSC), in which submariners from every navy in that region engage each other, to share submarine rescue technologies, procedures and lessons learned.[59]

Maritime security operations

Since the end of the Cold War, U.S. Presidents and Secretaries of Defense have demanded more from the U.S. Navy than preparation for global or regional wars at sea. Responding to national direction, the U.S. Navy has become increasingly involved – and adept – in conducting a wide range of peacetime maritime security operations, including counter-drug operations (especially in the Caribbean), counter-piracy operations (especially in the Arabian Sea), and counter-terrorist operations (globally, but especially in the Arabian Sea and the Mediterranean).[60] These operations are often conducted in cooperation with the U.S. Coast Guard and/or foreign naval forces and coast guards.[61] Of particular note have been the Proliferation Security Initiative (PSI) operations, to counter the shipment by sea of weapons of mass destruction (WMD).[62] U.S. Navy units operating in the Caribbean and other Latin American waters are organized as the U.S. 4th Fleet.[63] Typically, maritime security operations utilize surface combatants and/

or amphibious ships (which operate sea-based small craft, helicopters, and unmanned aerial vehicles (UAVs) vital to these missions, and land-based maritime patrol and surveillance aircraft (MPSA) and UAVs. New U.S. Navy Littoral Combat Ships (LCS) and Expeditionary Fast Transports (EPF) are being integrated into these operations as they join the fleet.

A critical skill set – largely introduced since the end of the Cold War and required for many of these operations – is Visit, Board, Search, and Seizure (VBSS), using U.S. Navy sailors, naval special warfare teams (SEALS), Coast Guardsmen or Marines, depending on the situation, deploying directly from ships, small craft, or helicopters.

Mature navies with similar skill sets to those of the U.S. Navy often complement U.S. Navy vessels and aircraft in these operations, with command of the entire operation often vested in a non-U.S. Navy commander.[64] Developing navies are often involved as complementary forces, ship-riders, and trainees, to help enhance their own indigenous capabilities, especially in maritime law enforcement.[65]

In 2006, the U.S. Navy formed a Navy Expeditionary Combat Command (NECC), in large part to focus and expand its existing capabilities in certain maritime security operations, including combat construction, mobile dive and salvage, riverine, coastal, and harbor patrol and combat operations afloat; explosive ordnance demolition, force protection operations, expeditionary logistics support, and theater security cooperation. This effort has been aimed largely at less developed regions of the world, where indigenous naval capabilities might be low or lacking, and in need of engagement and assistance. New skill sets in maritime civil affairs and security force assistance were added as well. NECC commands routinely deploy small teams of specialists forward to engage and train local navies and others – often alongside colleagues from the U.S. Coast Guard, other U.S. services, civilian agencies and non-governmental organizations (NGOs) and other mature navies in Europe, North America, Asia and elsewhere.

Examples of recent U.S. Navy Maritime Security Operations, usually with allied and partner navies, include: NATO's Operation Active Endeavor in the Mediterranean (counter-terrorism since 2001); Straits of Malacca ship protection operations (in 2002); Africa Partnership Station (APS) (since 2007); Southern Partnership Station (SPS) in Latin American waters and ports (since 2008); and Operation Martillo in the Caribbean and Eastern Pacific (counter-drug operations since 2012).[66] The 2013 APS deployment to West African ports was on board a Royal Netherlands Navy ship, and included U.S., British, Dutch, and Spanish marines.[67] Certainly the most widely publicized U.S. Navy maritime security operation has been its participation in the intensive and extensive multinational cooperative counter-piracy operations in the Arabian Sea (since 2009).[68]

Counter-piracy operations in the Arabian Sea

This remarkable multinational Maritime Security Operation merits special mention. It shows the international naval community at its finest. Not only has the United States sent its ships, aircraft, sailors, and Marines to carry out United Nations resolutions and help the world's shippers and merchant seamen against the depredations of Somali pirates, but so too have NATO (in Operation Ocean Shield), the European Union (in Operation Atalanta), Russia, India, China, and numerous other countries. Many have joined in a multinational combined task force (CTF 151), the command of which has rotated among participating nations. Others – including the NATO and EU squadrons – have cooperated with CTF 151 under the auspices of the Shared Awareness and De-confliction (SHADE) initiative – an *ad hoc* mechanism of informal meetings in-theater aimed at coordinating and de-conflicting naval operations to the benefit of all. As with other maritime security operations in the area, the command organization is loose, based more on cooperation than direction. The effort has had a host of salutary spin-offs: providing much-needed operational and leadership experience at sea for the world's navies; introducing the Chinese to the concepts and issues of international maritime endeavor; and providing a venue for European contributions to Middle Eastern security and East Asian experience in multinational military constructs.[69]

Humanitarian assistance operations

Naval humanitarian assistance operations have attracted a great deal of international attention lately, but they are not particularly new. U.S. Navy – and especially U.S. Coast Guard – vessels and aircraft have been conducting these operations for years, in the wake of natural and man-made disasters.[70] These operations provide assistance to populations in dire need, in part due to simple concern for fellow human beings in distress and to help ensure that detrimental political instability does not result from the misfortune that had just befallen them.[71] U.S. Navy sailors on port visits have routinely sought out opportunities for humanitarian assistance, from painting schoolhouses to providing medical aid. Following the Cold War, the Navy's two hospital ships and large amphibious ships – although originally designed for national defense purposes – have proven particularly useful in that regard, with entire operations structured around their humanitarian assistance capabilities.[72]

Naval diplomacy

Navies have long been tools of their nations' peacetime foreign policies, and the U.S. Navy has been no exception.[73] Peacetime U.S. Navy ship movements are routinely directed to "show the flag," at sea or in port, to demonstrate diplomatic friendship or – in some instances – displeasure. Navy ships at sea are also routinely used to assert and maintain the rights granted to U.S. warships under international law, including the right of innocent passage. U.S. Secretaries of Defense and State frequently find afloat U.S. Navy commanders to be useful participants in forward U.S. diplomacy.

Support to science

Warships, airplanes, and weapons systems are all applications of the findings of scientists, engineers, and other technologists. Consequently, the U.S. Navy has had a long history of fostering scientific endeavors that have potential naval applications – from metallurgy to ballistics to aeronautics to nuclear engineering to meteorology and oceanography.[74] The Navy can and does, however, periodically use its capabilities and highly trained people to aid in scientific endeavor that does not have an obvious direct naval link. The Navy has a long history of supporting scientific exploration in the Antarctic, and Navy ships have been used to recover astronauts for years. The Navy has also supported scientific research in the Arctic, in support of U.S. policy.[75] In 2014, after a break of almost 40 years, a U.S. Navy warship was once again employed to recover a space capsule – an unmanned NASA Orion crew module – from the oceans.[76]

"A global force for good"[77]

In sum, the U.S. government believes that the global forward presence at sea of the U.S. Navy – carrying out all of the above activities and more – helps foster a climate of free and unimpeded transit of goods and services on the high seas that benefits all the nations of the world. It is one of the pillars of the global Bretton Woods world economic system from which all have benefited, despite financial crises and the recessions.

Crisis response

Ends

Should peacetime operations fail to help stem international crises from occurring, Presidents, Secretaries of Defense, and joint Combatant Commanders expect the Navy to be ready to respond to crises as they occur, to provide them with a wide range of options, to help dampen or resolve them, as the American national interest requires, and cooperate when necessary with the navies of like-minded allied and partner nations in so doing.[78] The inherent flexibility, scalability, mobility, and multiple capabilities of U.S. naval forces provide the President with a wide range of useful options during a crisis, to use as he calculates is warranted.[79]

Ways and means

As crises loom or unfold, the United States and like-minded nations typically gather together in "coalitions of the willing," normally under the auspices of a United Nations mandate and often by invoking alliance or other ties. If peacetime naval engagement has been productive, the U.S. Navy and other navies will be ready to operate together effectively at sea under crisis conditions, should the political leaders of coalition members so direct. They will understand each other's capabilities and capacities, and know how to communicate with each other quickly and securely, divide maritime tasks among themselves, formulate options for the political leadership to consider, and then combine to carry out coalition directives under stressful conditions.

Positioning and shows of force

Political leaders have used naval force movements to try to help defuse, stabilize, and resolve crises for centuries. Recent examples of U.S. presidential use of the U.S. Navy in this fashion include the movement of two American carrier battle groups to the Taiwan Straits area in 1996 and the deployment of U.S. Navy warships into the Black Sea in the wake of the Russo–Georgian War of 2008, and during the Ukrainian crisis of 2014.

Forward naval presence and crisis response

Some regions are more prone to crises of direct U.S. concern than others. In addition to contributing to regional stability and enabling engagement with allies and partners, permanent forward-deployed U.S. naval forces ensure that ready U.S. forces can be on scene to help dampen or resolve crises on terms favorable to the United States and its allies. During the Cold War, the forward deployed and ready U.S. 6th and 7th Fleets were able to respond quickly to crises in the Eastern Mediterranean and Black Sea, the Western Pacific, and adjacent waters. In the post-Cold War environment, the same is true for the 5th and 7th Fleets in the Arabian and China Seas.[80] The 6th Fleet as well, although greatly reduced in ship numbers, nevertheless retains this function in the Eastern Mediterranean today, as evidenced by its role in the 2013 Syrian chemical weapons crisis and the 2014 Ukrainian crisis. For quick response to Caribbean crises, the U.S. Navy can easily surge from its home bases on the American coasts.

Avoidance of unintended incidents at sea

While U.S. naval forces are often used to dampen and defuse crises, they must also ensure that they do not inadvertently (or willfully) exacerbate a crisis – or cause one to occur. To this end U.S. Navy commanders and their crews are trained in the rights and responsibilities of warships under the Laws of War and the Law of the Sea.[81] In 1972, the United Sates Navy and the Soviet Navy signed an "Incidents at Sea" (INCSEA) agreement that has served as an example for other similar agreements between other countries (and which is still in force between the U.S. and Russian navies).[82] In April 2014, the U.S. Navy Chief of Naval Operations was a party to the signing of a "Code for Unplanned Encounters at Sea" (CUES) in Qingdao, China, at a meeting of the Western Pacific Naval Symposium (WPNS).

Non-combatant evacuations (NEO)

U.S. Navy–U.S. Marine Corps amphibious forces are particularly suited to conduct NEOs from countries experiencing crisis conditions, as was demonstrated in Liberia in 2003 (Operation Shining Express) and Lebanon in 2006, especially in situations where air or road evacuation is too impractical or dangerous.

Disaster response operations

U.S. Navy – and especially U.S. Coast Guard – vessels and aircraft have responded to crises triggered by natural and man-made disasters for years, providing rapid assistance to populations in dire need. Recent disasters such as the 2004 tsunami in Asia, the 2007 cyclone in Bangladesh, the 2010 earthquake in Haiti, the 2011 tsunami in Japan, the 2013 typhoon in the Philippines, and the 2014 Korean ferry disaster occasioned rapid surges of U.S. Navy ships and aircraft to the affected regions, bringing badly needed medical, transportation. and security forces.[83]

Forward deployed and easily surged U.S. Navy aircraft carriers and amphibious ships have proven especially valuable during disaster response operations, due to their availability and high state of readiness, capacity to conduct significant helicopter operations, ability to transport large quantities of materials, and organic medical facilities on board.[84]

Special crisis responses

The roll-on/roll-off container ship MV *Cape Ray* was put under U.S. Navy command in 2014 to neutralize Syrian chemical weapons, illustrating the utility of imaginative sea-basing in certain crisis situations.[85]

U.S. Navy crisis response attributes

Attributes that enable the U.S. Navy to respond effectively to crises, when tasked, include:

- on-scene combat readiness, and repositioning and surge capability, globally;
- modulated combat capabilities, up and down the ladder of possible appropriate force responses;
- man-made and natural disaster response capabilities;
- well-established, inter-operable relationships with allied and friendly navies and their commanders, both in the region in question and available to deploy there as coalition forces from outside the region;

- command structures adaptable to joint direction, participation by U.S. sister services, and rapid situation changes;
- flexible, experienced, educated, and well-trained leaders capable of leading on-scene in fast-moving, complex, high-stakes crisis environments, and supporting American diplomacy.

Combat

Ends

The President and the American people expect that U.S. naval forces will fight skillfully and prevail in combat, to prevent and resist military attacks on the United States and its friends and allies, and their forces and populations. The U.S. Navy is a combat force. "Warfighting First" was the very first of a recent Chief of Naval Operations' three basic tenets (the others being "Operate Forward" and "Be Ready").[86]

Peacetime engagement and coalition combat

As in crises, the United States and like-minded nations also often gather together for war in "coalitions of the willing," normally under the auspices of a United Nations mandate and often by invoking alliance or other ties. If peacetime naval engagement has been productive, the U.S. Navy and other navies will be ready to operate together effectively at sea in combat, should the political leaders of coalition members so direct. As in crises, they will understand each other's capabilities and capacities, and know how to communicate with each other quickly and securely, divide maritime tasks among themselves, formulate options for the political leadership to consider, and then combine to carry out coalition directives under wartime conditions.

Ways and means

In discussing the U.S. Navy's ways and means of achieving the nation's ends through combat at sea, it is useful to lay out the warfare areas that comprise modern naval combat (and the capabilities that enable operations in each), as well as the phases of such combat.

Warfare areas

If directed to fight and win in combat, the U.S. Navy has developed a wide array of complementary capabilities necessary to prevail in 13 necessary warfare areas.[87] The spread of these areas ensures that no enemy will be able to identify and exploit a glaring vulnerability, and provides a complete range of options for war at sea and from the sea to the President as commander-in-chief of the U.S. armed forces and to joint and combined operational commanders.

Those warfare areas include strike warfare, amphibious warfare, naval special warfare, anti-submarine warfare, anti-air warfare, ballistic missile defense, anti-surface warfare, blockade, mine warfare, navy expeditionary combat, naval electronic warfare, ship protection, and strategic sealift – all supported by naval combat logistics and information dominance operations. With the exception of blockade, the U.S. Navy exercises continuously at sea to establish, maintain, and improve war-winning proficiency in all of these warfare areas.

Strike warfare

In strike warfare, Navy sea-based strike aircraft, land-attack missiles, and naval gunfire attack and destroy targets ashore. Precision is a principal attribute. The primary sea-based strike aircraft is the F/A-18 Hornet (which comes in a half-dozen variants: A through F), attacking from one or more of the Navy's nuclear-powered aircraft carriers (CVNs).[88] The reach of Navy strike aviation is greatly enhanced through use of long-range U.S. Air Force tanker aircraft. The principal land-attack weapon is the Tomahawk Land-Attack Missile (TLAM), a precise, long-range, all-weather cruise missile launched from nuclear-powered attack submarines (SSN) and guided missile submarines (SSGN), cruisers (CG), and destroyers (DDG).[89] Navy cruisers and destroyers mount guns that provide Naval Surface Fire Support (NSFS) against targets ashore. U.S. Navy long-range carrier strike operations from the Arabian Sea into Afghanistan and Iraq were ongoing in 2015 in support of U.S., Afghan, and Iraqi forces.[90] Land-based U.S. Air Force, U.S. Army, U.S. Marine Corps, and allied and friendly forces also can and do conduct strike operations, in coordination with the Navy, under joint and allied command.

Amphibious warfare

In amphibious warfare, the U.S. Navy combat loads U.S. Marines, gets them to their objective area, lands them on hostile shores, and continues to support them from the sea in order to assault and seize a beachhead, raid, divert attention, evacuate troops or civilians, or any of a host of other amphibious tasks.[91] The Navy provides three specialized types of large amphibious warships: amphibious assault ships (LHD), amphibious transport docks (LPD), and amphibious landing docks (LSD). Naval close air and gunfire support from Navy carriers, cruisers, and destroyers provides fire support to Marines ashore during the operation as necessary. Depending on the scope and scale of the operations, Marines organize into one of several possible forms of a Marine Air–Ground Task Force (MAGTF), landing with their own infantry, armor, artillery, helicopters and fixed-wing aircraft, and utilizing a mix of Navy and Marine Corps landing craft and connectors.[92]

The U.S. Marine Corps has also prepositioned equipment forward on two squadrons of U.S. Navy Maritime Prepositioning Ships (MPS) in the Western Pacific and at Diego Garcia, and ashore in Norway. The MPS ships deploy to a port near the scene of intended action, and the Marines fly in to meet their prepositioned equipment at those ports. The Marine Corps also deploys combat-ready Special Marine Air–Ground Task forces (SPMAGTFs) by air in situations where U.S. amphibious ships may be unavailable, and is considering other deployment options.

The U.S. Navy also supports the US Army in loading and unloading Army cargoes from ships in friendly or non-defended areas where there are no fixed port facilities. The two services annually exercise this capability, known as Joint Logistics Over the Shore (JLOTS).

Naval special warfare

The U.S. Navy's Naval Special Warfare Command (NSWC) can insert US Navy SEAL Teams ashore from U.S. Navy warships, especially from specially configured guided missile submarines (SSGN). NSWC also operates a variety of small Special Warfare Combatant Craft (SWCC), especially SEAL Delivery Vehicles (SDVs) and Mark V Special Operations Craft (SOC). Navy SEALS and special warfare craft are totally integrated into joint U.S. Special Operations Command (USSOCOM) operations.

Anti-submarine warfare (ASW)

Anti-submarine warfare is a highly complex, technologically sophisticated form of naval warfare.[93] To find and kill enemy submarines, Navy commanders orchestrate the coordinated operations of a wide array of platforms and systems, including attack submarines (SSN), ASW helicopters deployed on aircraft carriers, guided missile cruisers and destroyers (CG and DDG), land-based maritime patrol aircraft (P-3C and new P-8A aircraft), and fixed and mobile undersea surveillance systems. Submarines, surface ships, and aircraft deploy various types of sonar and other listening devices to find and identify hostile submarines and torpedoes to destroy them. An ASW module is under development as one of three inter-changeable modules for new U.S. Navy Littoral Combat Ship (LCS) "seaframes."[94]

Anti-air warfare (AAW)

In anti-air warfare, U.S. Navy commanders use missile-firing F/A-18 strike fighter aircraft to engage enemy aircraft, as well as a variety of surface-to-air missiles launched from guided missile cruisers (CG) and destroyers (DDG).[95] Some of these missile systems are designed to kill at a great distance; others are to destroy close-in air threats. The centerpiece of cruiser-destroyer anti-air warfare capabilities is the Aegis combat system, with its radar tracking, missile, and other elements.[96] The U.S. Air Force, U.S. Army and U.S. Marine Corps have significant complementary land-based aircraft and missile AAW capabilities.

Ballistic missile defense (BMD)

BMD is a relatively new naval warfare area, established to destroy or neutralize incoming enemy ballistic missiles from the sea. Many of the U.S. Navy's inventory of guided missile cruisers (CG) and destroyers (DDG) have a ballistic missile defense capability, capable of protecting themselves, other warships at sea, and adjacent land areas. Their systems represent an expansion of the Aegis anti-air warfare combat system, using enhanced radar and missile technologies. As discussed earlier, the U.S. Navy routinely deploys BMD ships forward in peacetime (and operates an Aegis Ashore facility in Romania) to deter ballistic missile attacks "out of the blue" on forward U.S. forces and U.S. allies, but BMD is also an important and integrated component of the U.S. Navy's arsenal in case of fuller, wider war.[97]

Anti-surface warfare (ASUW)

This classic naval warfare area seeks to neutralize or destroy enemy surface combatants, using missiles and gunfire from Navy strike-fighter aircraft, cruisers, destroyers, and patrol coastals (PCs); and torpedoes from aircraft, surface ships, and submarines. An ASUW module has been developed and deployed on the new LCS seaframes. U.S. Air Force aircraft have a certain ASUW capability as well.[98] Anti-surface warfare can also be conducted against civilian merchant ships, and includes blockade and anti-commerce warfare on the high seas.[99]

Blockade

In blockade operations, naval commanders seek to close down an enemy's ports and at-sea commercial shipping activity through the threatened and actual use of force at sea.[100] Against small hostile nations with few ports and little merchant shipping, mounting these operations do not present an onerous problem. For enemy nations with extensive coastlines, large merchant fleets, and powerful naval forces of their own, the problem is much more difficult and complex. The U.S. Navy participated in a "quarantine" – a form of blockade – around Cuba during the Cuban Missile Crisis with the Soviet Union in 1962. During the Vietnam War, U.S. Navy carrier aircraft sowed thousands of sea mines to blockade North Vietnamese ports in 1972. Blockade to enforce international sanctions was also an element in Operations Odyssey Dawn and Unified Protector against the Ghaddafi regime in Libya in 2011. There is a now a burgeoning open literature debating the virtues of blockade in a hypothetical future U.S. war with China.[101]

Mine warfare

Mine warfare includes the laying of mines in the sea, as well as detecting and neutralizing, sweeping, or destroying them (i.e. mine countermeasures). The U.S. Navy has the capability of sowing mines from its aircraft, surface ships, and submarines, and the U.S. Air Force can use its bomber aircraft for this purpose as well. Mine countermeasures are conducted by specialized Avenger-class mine countermeasures (MCM) ships. A mine warfare module is under development for the new LCS seaframes, and the U.S. Navy's large fleet of sea-based MH-60S helicopters has an airborne MCM capability.[102] Because America's allies often have superb mine countermeasures capabilities, in coalition operations the U.S. Navy often cedes much of the responsibility for this warfare area to them.[103]

Navy expeditionary combat

Navy expeditionary combat – as discussed earlier – comprises a variety of naval capabilities, including combat construction, mobile dive and salvage, riverine, coastal, and harbor patrol and combat operations afloat; explosive ordnance demolition; force protection operations, expeditionary logistics support, and theater security cooperation.[104] These capabilities are routinely applied in peacetime during forward Maritime Security Operations to enhance theater security cooperation and stability. They can also be, however, of great utility in wartime, especially where the combat area includes major coastal or riverine geography – as was the case historically during the American Civil War in the West, the Philippine Insurrection, and the Vietnam War. It can be expected that Navy expeditionary combat capabilities would be deployed and sent into battle as ancillary naval forces, should the situation call for them.[105]

Naval electronic warfare

Naval electronic warfare is used to jam, deceive, blind, or spoof enemy electronic systems, rendering ineffective any weapons they control.[106] Virtually every ship and aircraft in the U.S. Navy deploys with some form of electronic warfare capability. Without it, offensive strike warfare and other warfare areas would be difficult or impossible to implement, given the sophistication of current and expected hostile weapons systems.[107] In particular, the U.S. Navy deploys new EA-18G Growler airborne electronic attack (AEA) aircraft as integral components of its carrier air wings.[108] As the EA-18Gs enter the fleet, the Navy is retiring its venerable EA-6B Prowler AEA aircraft. Joint U.S. commanders used the EA-6B heavily in U.S. operations over Iraq and Afghanistan throughout the past decade.[109]

Ship protection

Sea control and power projection cannot be achieved if warships cannot protect themselves from hostile action. U.S. Navy warships are built to demanding naval architectural standards and incorporate numerous features to enable damage control in the event they are hit. U.S. Navy damage control training is demanding, frequent, and sophisticated.[110] Numerous combat systems are installed on board Navy warships to protect against incoming torpedoes, cruise missiles, fast-attack craft, and other threats.[111] The U.S. Army and U.S. Navy periodically experiment with using U.S. Army attack helicopters to protect U.S. Navy ships from enemy fast-attack craft.[112] The Navy has also begun to protect its ships against cyber attack.[113]

Strategic sealift

Through its Military Sealift Command (MSC), the Navy maintains, contracts for, and deploys the nation's strategic sealift and forward maritime prepositioning forces, to help support the rapid and effective projection of U.S. ground and land-based air power in a combat theater. Army and other services' combat equipment can be rapidly transported forward from the U.S. on government-owned, civilian-manned Large Medium-Speed Roll-on/Roll-off ships (LMSR), other Roll-on/Roll-off ships (RO/RO, and container ships, as well as domestic and foreign commercial ships chartered for the purpose. The MSC also maintains the nation's fleet of Maritime Prepositioning Ships, which store U.S. Marine Corps, Army, Air Force, and some Navy cargoes in far forward locations in the Western Pacific and at Diego Garcia. The U.S. Air Force provides a similar service for U.S. all-service military airlift, through its Air Mobility Command (AMC). American troops fly to forward theaters from the United States on military or civilian-chartered aircraft to meet up with equipment that has been prepositioned or transported there by sea.

Combat logistics support

Operating routinely tens of thousands of miles from North America, for months on end under demanding conditions, in peacetime and combat, has been a hallmark of the U.S. Navy. This is accomplished through building robust sustainability into American warships, as well as provision of a naval logistics support system capable of providing routine supply, maintenance, repair services, as well as surges for crises and wars. The U.S. Navy is also well served by a large and sophisticated private and public naval industrial base at home, and a network of vital forward bases and "places," as well as the transportation services of the Military Sealift and Air Mobility Commands.[114]

Underway replenishment (UNREP)

Particularly important is the Navy's large fleet of government-owned, civilian-crewed Combat Logistics Force (CLF) ships, capable of underway replenishment of U.S. Navy warships alongside, at sea. This fleet includes Dry Cargo/Ammunition Ships (T-AKE), Fast Combat Support Ships (T-AOE), and Fleet Replenishment Oilers (T-AO). It provides the fuel, food, ordnance, spare parts, mail, and other critical supplies that keep U.S. Navy warships combat-ready – or in combat – for extended periods of time.

The Navy also forward deploys two submarine tenders (AS), normally based in peacetime at Guam and Diego Garcia, but periodically deploying to ports in the Philippines, Malaysia, the United Arab Emirates (UAE), Bahrain, India, and elsewhere to provide resupply, maintenance, and repair services to forward-deployed U.S. Navy submarines and sometimes other types of warships.[115] They too would have wartime support roles.

"Navy information dominance" support

This is a new U.S. Navy term that includes Intelligence, Surveillance, Reconnaissance (ISR), as well as the rapidly expanding area of cyber warfare.[116] Classically, often the hardest part of naval combat was finding the enemy, and prowess (and luck) in "scouting" was as important as firepower in determining the outcome of sea battles. The Navy has recently created an "Information Dominance Corps," comprising its specialists in naval intelligence, cryptology, cyber warfare, information systems, information operations, and related specialties, to try to improve the synergies among them and deliver their outputs faster and clearer to naval combat commanders.[117]

Combat phases

It is useful to discuss U.S. naval forces engaged in combat at the behest of the President and under joint and combined operational commanders as proceeding through three phases: "Transition to War," "Seizing the Initiative," and "Carrying the Fight to the Enemy."[118]

During the Transition to War, naval forces already forward in the potential combat theater(s) maneuver into advantageous positions and increase their combat readiness. Ready naval forces in or near U.S. ports will surge forward to join them, as may other U.S. forward forces from unaffected theaters. Foreign governments that have joined in the military effort with the United States may surge their forces forward as well, usually in close consultation with other governments, any multinational command structures that may be involved (e.g. NATO), and U.S. and other naval commanders. Consultations to de-conflict Rules of Engagement (ROE) will be intense. Forward Intelligence, Surveillance and Reconnaissance (ISR) operations – especially in the affected theater – will intensify, including forward repositioning of land-based Navy maritime patrol aircraft. U.S. Navy Military Sealift Command maritime prepositioning and strategic sealift ships in support of U.S. Marine Corps, Army, and Air Force forward deployments would also move toward the affected theater. Navy demands on U.S. Air Force satellite, strategic airlift, and tanker aircraft support are bound to increase, as well as inter-service coordination on anti-air warfare and missile defense.

To Seize the Initiative, U.S. naval forces – in conjunction with other joint and allied forces – will strive to establish sea control as quickly as possible, seeking to identify and neutralize or destroy enemy aircraft, surface ships, submarines, and land-based anti-access/area denial (A2/AD) systems – at the direction of higher U.S. political and military authority, within any constraints that those authorities might set, using kinetic and non-kinetic means.[119] Naval electronic warfare systems will play a vital enabling role during this phase. Joint tactics and systems developed to implement the Air–Sea Battle concept – especially in conjunction with the U.S. Air Force – will be used during this phase as necessary.[120]

Anti-ballistic missile ships will maneuver into optimum intercept position and seek to destroy any incoming hostile missiles. Surge forces will continue to flow into the theater, bolstering the forces already present and engaged in combat. Should circumstances so dictate, a blockade against enemy ports and shipping may be instituted. Information dominance operations – including cyber operations – will play an important role.

In Carrying the Fight to the Enemy, U.S. naval forces – under joint or combined direction and alongside other U.S. services and the forces of allied nations – will seek to carry out the ultimate neutralization and destruction of enemy forces in all domains – on land, at sea, in the air, and in space and cyberspace – so as to achieve the goals of the war as set by the President and political allied leaders. Sea control operations will continue as necessary. U.S. naval forces will assist in the success of the ground campaign primarily through powerful power projection operations, including carrier air strikes, surface combatant and submarine missile strikes, off-shore naval gunfire, and landings of potent amphibious and special operations ground forces. If these operations are successful, all hostile forces will be defeated and war termination will be achieved on terms favorable to the United States and its allies.

Note that the sequencing of these notional phases, while useful to deconstruct and explain the thinking behind U.S. naval combat operations, is not etched in stone. In some cases they might even need to be executed simultaneously.

Post-combat

When war is terminated, U.S. naval forces typically are reduced in strength and return to some variant of their pre-war peacetime posture and activities.[121] But this seldom happens cleanly and without unanticipated significant post-war follow-on operations. In short, "when it's over, it's not over."[122] It can be anticipated that following any future combat operations, the same phenomenon will hold, and that the Navy will have to be ready to flex in unanticipated ways before regaining any semblance of a peacetime posture.[123] The Navy's recently organized Navy Expeditionary Warfare Forces – adept at riverine, coastal, and harbor patrol; civil affairs; construction; psychological operations; and related skills – should prove useful in this phase.

Future combat: why and where

The U.S. Navy is prepared to apply these ways and means globally, wherever tasked by the President, under joint or combined operational command, in furtherance of United Nations resolutions and/or U.S. defense commitments to its allies and partners, as well as in defense of its own national interests.[124] But in particular, the Navy is poised to help defeat any North Korean aggression on South Korea; to ensure that the Strait of Hormuz remains open to commerce, especially oil shipments, in the face of potential hostile Iranian actions; and to defend its forces and allied and partner nations from North Korean or Iranian ballistic missile attack.[125] Should the President so direct, in accordance with the U.S. Taiwan Relations Act (TRA) of 1979, the Navy must also be able to provide him with options to help resist should China attempt to use force to take over Taiwan.[126] The Navy also must plan to participate in operations against terrorists hostile to the United States and its friends and allies – state-supported and non-state actors – and to conduct armed NEOs and counter-piracy operations.

These contingencies differ from those of the Cold War and prior decades, and may well differ from those of the future. The inherent range of capabilities, flexibility, mobility, and scalability of U.S. naval forces enable them to adapt to changing national requirements as they evolve.

The Navy has no particular desire to participate in war, and expends a great deal of effort in engagement, deterrence, crisis response, and other activities designed to reduce the likelihood of war. But should the President decide the country must go to war, the U.S. Navy has a responsibility to be ready – a responsibility it takes most seriously.

The political leaders of the United States do not hunger for war. Neither do most men and women of the U.S. Navy – officers and enlisted. What they do hunger for is a world at peace, with increasing political freedom, economic prosperity, and social stability for all. They are grateful that they have been joined in this quest for decades by the nations and navies of their allies and partners, in Europe, the Americas, and the Indo-Pacific. They hope this partnership at sea will continue, even during the inevitable stresses of war.

Since the end of the Cold War, the U.S. Navy's combat capabilities have been honed in battle. Recent significant combat operations have included the ongoing Operations Enduring Freedom against Al Qaeda and the Taliban in Afghanistan (since 2001); Iraqi Freedom and New Dawn against the Saddam Hussein regime and insurgents in Iraq (2003–11); Operation Odyssey Dawn against the Gaddafi regime's attacks on its own people in Libya (2011); participation in the follow-on NATO operation Unified Protector (March–October 2011); and Operation Inherent Resolve against the Islamic State of Iraq and the Levant (ISIL) (since 2014). In all of these instances, the U.S. Navy has fought alongside its sister U.S. services under joint command, and alongside coalition forces with which it had previously closely engaged and trained. Should those coalitions fray and should those forces dissipate, both America and the international order that most nations depend on for their security and prosperity will be the losers.

More on the means: U.S. naval forces[127]

Ship numbers

The U.S. Navy fleet includes ships assigned to and not assigned to the Ship Battle Force, both civilian and military-manned. The number of ships in the Ship Battle Force is often used in discussing the size and composition of the fleet, and in comparing it to foreign fleets and those of past U.S. Navy eras. The Ship Battle Force, however, represents only a portion of U.S. naval power.[128] In November 2014, the Ship Battle Force stood at some 289 ships, including 10 aircraft carriers, 94 surface combatants, 73 submarines, 31 amphibious warfare ships, 8 mine warfare ships, 30 civilian-manned combat logistics ships, 26 fleet support ships, 3 auxiliary support ships, 10 combatant craft, and 4 Naval Reserve Force frigates.[129]

The number of Battle Force ships has been greatly reduced from Cold War force levels, although the capabilities of the individual warships have been markedly improved.[130]

U.S. Navy ships not assigned to the Ship Battle Force include dozens of civilian-manned Military Sealift Command ships for service support, special missions, sealift, and afloat forward prepositioning of military equipment.

The Navy forms only one part, however, of the U.S. "National Fleet," which also includes some 90 or so U.S. Coast Guard cutters, as well as ships in the U.S. Maritime Administration's National Defense Reserve Fleet (NDRF).[131]

The U.S. Navy also comprises more than 3,700 manned aircraft, with capabilities across all the Navy's warfare areas. These aircraft include F/A-18 sea-based strike fighters, a large number of various types of helicopters, land-based P-3C and new P-8A maritime patrol aircraft, and other aircraft types. Recently, a variety of new types of unmanned aircraft have also been introduced into the fleet, including the X-47B Unmanned Aircraft demonstrator.[132]

Aggregation and disaggregation

Many types of U.S. Navy warships routinely combine to form task forces comprising more than one ship and more than one ship type, the better to achieve synergies necessary to conduct combat operations forward at sea. Should combat operations not occur, those task forces can disaggregate, to enable joint force commanders to conduct peacetime forward presence operations in more than one place at a time, albeit with reduced combat capability.

Numbered Fleets exist in the Eastern Pacific (3rd Fleet); Latin American waters (4th Fleet); the Arabian and Red Seas and the Gulf (5th Fleet); European and African waters (6th Fleet); and the Western Pacific and Indian Oceans (7th Fleet). The commander of the U.S. 10th Fleet conducts global cyber operations. Geographic numbered fleet commanders command naval forces in peacetime, crises and war as part of a joint regional command structure, utilizing Maritime Operations Centers (MOCs), and responsive to geographical combatant commanders.[133] Fleet units are allocated to the numbered fleet commanders by various management mechanisms in the Pentagon, at the direction of the Secretary of Defense and with the advice of the Joint Chiefs of Staff and the joint combatant commanders.

Carrier Strike Groups (CSG) typically consist of a nuclear-powered aircraft carrier (CVN), a carrier air wing (CVW), a guided missile cruiser (CG), and three or four guided missile destroyers (DDG).[134] The air wing includes squadrons of strike fighter, electronic warfare, airborne early warning and logistics airplanes, as well as anti-submarine, anti-surface, and mine warfare helicopters. Amphibious Ready Groups and Marine Expeditionary Units (ARG/MEUs) typically consist of three U.S. Navy amphibious warships in the ARG (an amphibious assault ship (LHD), an amphibious transport dock (LPD), and a landing ship dock (LSD); and about 2,200 Marines in the MEU, including command, ground combat, air, and logistics elements armed with combat airplanes, helicopters, tanks, artillery, and small arms. Surface combatants (cruisers and destroyers) can also be aggregated as Surface Action Groups (SAGs). CSGs, ARG/MEUs, and SAGs work up off the east and west coasts of the United States to acquire the capability of operating as cohesive combat units. Then they deploy forward to joint theaters of operations where they are often disaggregated, but retain the capability to coalesce again if required to do so.[135]

When CSGs coalesce, they can simultaneously conduct combat strike, AAW, ASUW, ASW, EW, and other operations using a command and control construct called the Composite Warfare Concept (CWC).[136] When ARG/MEUs coalesce, they conduct combat and other amphibious operations using a different command and control construct.[137]

In the calendar year 2013, the Navy worked up and deployed five CSGs and three ARG/MEUs to the Western Pacific, Arabian Gulf, North Arabian Sea, and Mediterranean Sea.[138] For most of the year, the Navy kept two or three of those CSGs deployed forward, and one or two ARG/MEUs. The calendar year 2012 deployment pattern had involved an additional CVBG and an additional ARG/MEU.

Since 1995, U.S. Navy CSGs occasionally have included allied surface combatants, which have worked up and deployed as integral units of the CSG. Canada, Spain, Argentina, the United Kingdom, Germany, and Australia have each provided surface combatants to CSGs at various times. In the spring and summer of 2013, the German frigate *Hamburg* (F220) fully integrated and deployed with the USS *Dwight D. Eisenhower* (CVN69) carrier strike group, primarily providing important air defense capabilities.[139]

Submarines typically work up and deploy forward alone, but nuclear-powered attack and cruise missile submarines (SSNs and SSGNs) can operate to complement or supplement CSGs or SAGs.[140] Some destroyers deploy forward alone as well.

The Navy also deploys rotating detachments of its land-based Maritime Patrol and Surveillance Aircraft squadrons (VP) forward. In 2013, detachments rotated through airfields in Italy, Spain, Djibouti, Qatar, Bahrain, Japan, El Salvador, and elsewhere.[141]

Platform and force package issues

The forces and force packages just discussed are the product of a considered U.S. Navy predilection for building large, robust, multi-capable ships and deploying them forward in even larger and more robust force packages.[142] Several critics, however, have questioned this focus on "big ships" and instead have advocated "flotilla" concepts of forward-deployed warships that might prove – in varying degrees – lighter, faster, cheaper, more expendable, and less vulnerable – with their lethal power distributed among many very small ships rather than a small number of large, robust vessels.[143]

Ongoing and anticipated introduction of new platforms within the next decade or less[144]

These include:

- beginning to replace the Ohio-class Trident strategic nuclear SSBN force;[145]
- F-35 Joint Strike fighter "Lightning II" variants (F-35B US Marine Corps LHD- and shore-based short takeoff and landing (STOL) variant; and F-35C U.S. Navy and U.S. Marine Corps carrier-based variant);[146]
- EA-18G "Growler" electronic warfare aircraft;
- E-2D advanced "Hawkeye" early warning aircraft;[147]
- P-8A "Poseidon" land-based maritime patrol and surveillance aircraft;[148]
- CVN-78 Ford-class carriers;[149]
- DDG-1000 Zumwalt-class destroyers;[150]
- unmanned systems:[151]
  - airborne
  - surface
  - sub-surface;[152]
- Independence- and Freedom-class Littoral Combat Ship (LCS) seaframes, with mine countermeasures, ASW, ASUW modules;[153]
- Spearhead-class Expeditionary Fast Transports (EPF);[154]
- new LX(R) amphibious ships;[155]
- Expeditionary Transfer Docks (ESD) and Expeditionary Mobile Bases (ESB);[156]
- Mark VI patrol boats;
- Ship to Shore Connectors: the next generation landing craft;[157]
- T-AO(X) fleet oilers and other combat logistics ships;[158]
- V-22 "Osprey" Carrier On-board Delivery aircraft;[159]
- laser weapons;[160]
- rail guns;[161]
- continued procurement of Virginia-class attack submarines and Arleigh Burke-class destroyers, and modernization of existing ships and aircraft;[162]
- Small Surface Combatants (SSC), based on upgraded variants of the LCS.[163]

Funding

The U.S. Navy's budget has been robust, in both absolute and relative terms.[164] It could not have been otherwise, in order to deploy the ships, aircraft weapons systems, and personnel enumerated and discussed above.

Due to U.S. government funding constraints imposed in 2011, however, the service had to temper its future plans. In September 2013, the Chief of Naval Operations, Admiral John Greenert, noted that the Navy's Fiscal Year (FY) 2013 budget reduction had been $11 billion, causing cancellations of five ship forward deployments and a reduction in surge capacity by about two-thirds.[165] In March 2014, he noted that his budget submission for FY 2015 was $31 billion dollars less than he had earlier anticipated asking for.[166] Nevertheless, the U.S. naval arsenal will remain formidable for the foreseeable future.

Force design and balance

Given all the U.S. Navy has to do in peacetime, crises and war, the nation and the Navy struggle with the issue of balance: given finite resources and a changing global environment, what is the proper balance to be achieved among the Navy's various warfare tasks, platforms, and systems? Where should emphasis be placed? Where can more risk be accepted? The Navy's programming and budgeting processes – embedded in the larger Defense Department Planning, Programming, Budgeting and Execution (PPBE) system are the mechanisms whereby the Navy Department seeks to achieve appropriate balance and trade-offs in its acquisition programs and deployment policies.[167]

Conclusion

Again, to remind, this prodigious inventory of naval forces does not exist in a vacuum. It has been bought and deployed by the American government, on behalf of the American people, to ensure the country's economic prosperity, military security, and political freedom – and that of its friends and allies – through maintenance and defense of a mutually beneficial global system.

Notes

1 The opinions expressed here are those of the author and should not be construed as those of CNA, the Department of the Navy, Department of Defense, or of the United States government.

2 This chapter is an informed but personal interpretation of U.S. Navy policy, strategy, and operations. The Navy's official strategy was published in March 2015 and signed by Commandant of the Marine Corps General Joseph Dunford USMC, Chief of Naval Operations ADM Jonathan Greenert USN, and Commandant of the Coast Guard Admiral Paul Zukunft USCG. It updated Commandant of the Marine Corps General James T. Conway USMC, Chief of Naval Operations ADM Gary Roughead USN, and Commandant of the Coast Guard Admiral Thad W. Allen USCG, *A Cooperative Strategy for 21st Century Seapower (CS21)* (Washington, DC, October 2007). More detail on recent official Navy strategy, policy, concepts, and doctrine is in *Naval Operations Concept 2010* (NOC 2010) (Washington, DC, 2010); and *Naval Doctrine Publication 1: Naval Warfare* (NDP 1) (March 1, 2010), signed by the same three service leaders. During his tenure as Chief of Naval Operations (CNO) from 2011 to 2015, Admiral Greenert published undated short pieces of authoritative guidance and explanation, the latest editions of which are: *CNO's Sailing Directions, CNO's Position Report: 2014*, and *CNO's Navigation Plan 2015–2019*. Current high-level joint U.S. maritime doctrine is in Director, Joint Staff LTG Curtis M. Scaparrotti USA, *Joint Publication 3-32: Command and Control for Joint Maritime Operations* (Washington, DC: The Joint Staff, August 7, 2013). As he was leaving office, ADM Greenert also signed out *How We Fight: Handbook for the Naval Warfighter* (Washington DC: U.S. Government Printing Office, 2015). See also Secretary of the Navy Ray Mabus, *Department of the Navy Transformation Plan: FY 2014–2016* (Washington, DC: Department of the Navy, July 2, 2014).

3 For a recent brief treatment of U.S. maritime and naval strategy, policy, plans, and operations, see CAPT Bernard D. Cole USN (Ret), *Asian Maritime Strategies: Navigating Troubled Waters* (Annapolis, MD: Naval Institute Press, 2013), ch. 2, "The United States," 38–60.

4 Guidance to the Navy from the President can take many forms. For the latest public U.S. presidential national security guidance, see President Barack Obama, *National Security Strategy* (Washington, DC: The White House, February 2015). An example of informed congressional naval concerns is Rep. Randy Forbes (Republican, Virginia), "Revitalize American Sea Power," U.S. Naval Institute *Proceedings* 140 (March 2014), 16–21; "The Conservative Case for American Seapower," *Real Clear Defense* (July 24, 2013); and "What Congress Can Do to Restore the Balance of Power with China," *DefenseOne* (November 9, 2014). Congressman Forbes is a Republican from Virginia and serves currently as the chairman of the House Armed Services Seapower and Projection Forces Subcommittee and Co-Chairman of the Navy-Marine Corps Caucus.

5 The Chief of Naval Operations – the senior uniformed military officer in the U.S. Navy chain of command – is a member of the Joint Chiefs of Staff, and as such renders naval operational advice to his colleagues, to the Chairman of the Joint Chiefs of Staff, to the Secretary of Defense, and to the President. For a survey and analysis of recent guidance that the Navy has received from higher authority, see Catherine Dale, *National Security Strategy: Mandates, Execution to Date, and Issues for Congress*, R43174 (Washington, DC: Congressional Research Service (CRS), August 6, 2013 and subsequent editions). The most recent public guidance from the Secretary of Defense is in Leon Panetta, *Sustaining U.S. Global Leadership: Priorities for 21st Century Defense* (Washington, DC: Department of Defense, January 2012). For an analysis, see Catherine Dale and Pat Towell, *In Brief: Assessing the January 2012 Defense Strategic Guidance (DSG)*, R42146 (Washington, DC: Congressional Research Service (CRS), August 13, 2013 and subsequent editions). Additional guidance can be gleaned from Charles Hagel, *Quadrennial Defense Review 2014* (Washington, DC: Department of Defense, March 4, 2014). For informed commentary, see National Defense Panel, *Ensuring a Strong U.S. Defense for the Future* (Washington, DC: United States Institute of Peace, July 31, 2014). The standard work on the U.S. joint operational commands and their commanders is Cynthia Watson, *Combatant Commands; Origins, Structure, and Engagements* (Santa Barbara, CA: Praeger, 2011). For an argument in Congressional testimony that the Goldwater–Nichols Act and previous legislation has adversely constrained U.S. seapower, see Bryan McGrath, *Revisiting the Roles and Missions of the Armed Forces* (Washington DC: Hudson Institute, November 5, 2015).

6 For an example of the post-Cold War evolution of allied relationships at sea, see "NATO and Japan Conduct First Ever Joint Counter-Piracy Drill," *NATO News* (October 3, 2014). For an example of contemporary U.S. Navy–Royal Navy planning, see Chief of Naval Operations Admiral Jonathan Greenert USN and First Sea Lord Admiral Sir George Zambellas RN, "Combined Seapower: A Shared Vision for Royal Navy–United States Navy Cooperation" (December 10, 2014).

7 For a view that a forward force posture may no longer be sustainable, under certain budget conditions, see "Deputy Secretary of Defense Robert Work on the Asia-Pacific Rebalance" (New York: Council on Foreign Relations, September 30, 2014).

8 For an argument that the United States should continue such a policy, see Stephen Brooks, John Ikenberry, and William Wohlforth, "Don't Come Home, America: The Case against Retrenchment," *International Security* 37 (Winter 2012/13), 7–51. See also Rebecca Edelston, *Persistent Engagement in the Era of Minimal Footprint* (Alexandria, VA: CNA, April 2014). For the variety of alternative views, see Elbridge Colby, *Grand Strategy: Contending Contemporary Analyst Views and Implications for the U.S. Navy*, CRM D0025423.A2/Final (Alexandria, VA: CNA, November 2011); and Michael Gerson and Alison Lawler Russell, *American Grand Strategy and Seapower: Conference Report*, CRM D0025988.A2/Final (Alexandria, VA: CNA, November 2011). A recent analysis of this issue is in Evan Montgomery, "Contested Primacy in the Western Pacific: China's Rise and the Future of U.S. Power Projection," *International Security* 38 (Spring 2014), 115–49.

9 There is a large contemporary literature asserting that the fundamentals of American power – and the bases for American naval power – are in decline. For a carefully argued counter-argument, see Robert Lieber, *Power and Willpower in the American Future: Why the United States is Not Destined to Decline* (Cambridge: Cambridge University Press, 2012).

10 For current trends in the U.S. military industrial base, see Ben Fitzgerald and Kelley Sayler, *Creative Disruption: Technology, Strategy and the Future of the Global Defense Industry* (Washington, DC: Center for a New American Security (CNAS), June 5, 2014). For Defense Department views, see Under Secretary of Defense for Acquisition, Technology and Logistics, *Annual Industrial Capabilities Report to Congress* (Washington, DC: Office of the Deputy Assistant Secretary of Defense for Manufacturing and Industrial Base Policy, U.S. Department of Defense, October 2013). For a description and analysis of a key portion of that industrial base, see *The Economic Importance of the U.S. Shipbuilding and Repairing Industry* (Washington, DC: U.S. Maritime Administration (MARAD), November 2015).

11 For a characterization of the U.S. Navy's "operators," see CAPT Gerald G. O'Rourke USN (Ret), "Great Operators, Good Administrators, Lousy Planners," U.S. Naval Institute *Proceedings* 110 (August 1984), 75–8.

12 The focus of this chapter is therefore on U.S. Navy deployment and employment strategy, not on its – usually congruent – declaratory strategy. For studies of recent U.S. Navy declaratory strategy, see the 17 volumes of the *U.S. Navy Capstone Strategies* series by Peter Swartz with Karin Duggan (Alexandria, VA: CNA, 2009–12) and available on line at www.cna.org/research/capstone-strategy-series; the three edited volumes by John Hattendorf on U.S. naval strategies of the 1970s, 1980s, and 1990s, published by the Naval War College Press in their "Newport Papers" series; CAPT Peter D. Haynes USN,

"Toward a New Maritime Strategy: American Naval Thinking in the Post-Cold War Era" (Annapolis MD: Naval Institute Press, 2015); and "American Naval Thinking in the Post-Cold War Era: The U.S. Navy and the Emergence of a Maritime Strategy, 1989–2007" (PhD diss., U.S. Naval Postgraduate School, Monterey, CA, June 2013); Sebastian Bruns, *U.S. Navy Strategy & American Sea Power from 'The Maritime Strategy' (1982–1986) to 'A Cooperative Strategy for 21st Century Seapower* (2007) (Ph.D. diss.: University of Kiel, 28 July 2014), and Amund Lundesgaard, *U.S. Navy Strategy and Force Structure after the Cold War*, IFS Insights 4 (Oslo: Institutt for Forsvarsstudier (IFS), November 2011).

13 On the beginnings of the modern era of U.S. Navy operations, see James C. Rentfrow, *Home Squadron: The U.S. Navy on the North Atlantic Station* (Annapolis, MD: Naval Institute Press, 2014). On the Great White Fleet deployment, see James R. Reckner, *Teddy Roosevelt's Great White Fleet* (Annapolis, MD: Naval Institute Press, 2001); on the interwar Fleet problems, see Albert A. Nofi, *To Train the Fleet for War: The U.S. Navy Fleet Problems, 1923–1940* (Newport, RI: Naval War College Press, 2001).

14 While parsing naval actions by "peace, crises, and war" is a useful explanatory device, the real world is often far messier. In an era with a total global war being conducted – like today's global war on terror – the U.S. Navy may well be simultaneously conducting wartime operations in one theater, responding to a crisis in another theater, and conducting peacetime operations in two or three other theaters.

15 This chapter recognizes the difference between "ends," "ways," and "means" and the importance of distinguishing among them. Discussions of "ways" and "means" are combined throughout, however, so as to improve the flow of the narrative, which would otherwise be too stilted, choppy, and repetitious – as are many such papers that seek to rigidly apply the "ends-ways-means" construct. In particular, discussions of Navy "ways" without immediate discussion of the "means" to implement those ways are often at an impenetrable level of abstraction. This chapter's listing of "ways" and "means" – organized by "peacetime," "crises," and "war" – reflects the author's judgment and experience. *Joint Publication 3-32: Command and Control for Joint Maritime Operations* lists some 20 "specific maritime operations," but does not organize them in a "peacetime, crises, and war" (or any other) typology.

16 See *Joint Publication 5-0: Joint Operation Planning* (Washington, DC: Joint Chiefs of Staff, August 11, 2011), xxiii–xxiv and III-38–III-41.

17 For a critique of U.S. Navy peacetime operations, see CAPT Ivan T. Luke USCG (Ret), "Let's Get Serious About Peacetime Ops," U.S. Naval Institute *Proceedings* 139 (October 2013), 54–8.

18 For U.S. nuclear weapons employment strategy, see *Report on Nuclear Employment Strategy of the United States: Specified in Section 5491 of 10 U.S.C.* (Washington, DC: Department of Defense, June 12, 2013). For overall U.S. nuclear defense policy, see Secretary of Defense Robert Gates, *Nuclear Posture Review Report* (Washington, DC: U.S. Department of Defense, April 2010). For recent views of the Commander, U.S. Strategic Command, see ADM Cecil D. Haney USN, "Remarks on Strategic Deterrence in the 21st Century" (Washington, DC: Atlantic Council, January 15, 2015). A recent U.S. non-governmental expert policy consensus is in *An Agreement in Support of a Sustainable U.S. Nuclear Posture* (Washington, DC: Center for Strategic and International Studies (CSIS): January 18, 2013). See also Keith Payne and John S. Foster, Jr., *Nuclear Force Adaptability for Deterrence and Assurance: A Prudent Alternative to Minimum Deterrence* (Fairfax, VA: National Institute Press, 2014).

19 Other elements of the U.S. strategic triad include U.S. Air Force long-range nuclear bomber aircraft, land-based at U.S. airfields, and intercontinental ballistic missiles (ICBMs), capable of being launched from silos in the United States. For inter-relationships among these elements (and arms control issues), see Amy F. Woolf, *U.S. Strategic Nuclear Forces: Background, Developments, and Issues*, RL 33640 (Washington, DC: Library of Congress Congressional Research Service (CRS), July 14, 2013 and subsequent editions).

20 For an argument that the United States should cancel replacement of its SSBNs, and rely instead on anti-ballistic missile defense as a strategic deterrent, see Maxwell Cooper, "The Future of Deterrence? Ballistic Missile Defense," U.S. Naval Institute *Proceedings* 139 (September 2013), 52–7. See also Peter Dombrowski, "Strategic Stability and SSBNs: Arms Control May be the Answer," *The Interpreter*, October 2, 2014.

21 The most recent comprehensive public statement of U.S. ballistic missile defense policy is Secretary of Defense Robert Gates, *Ballistic Missile Defense Review Report* (Washington, DC: U.S. Department of Defense, February 2010). See also John F. Morton, "Modernize Aegis for Naval Dominance," U.S. Naval Institute *Proceedings* 140 (May 2014), 60–5; and Richard Weitz, "US Missile Defense," *World Affairs* 176 (July/August 2013), 80–7.

22 The U.S. Army also deploys ground-based ballistic missile defense systems – radars and/or missiles – forward in Japan, South Korea, Israel, Kuwait, and the United Arab Emirates, Turkey. Several U.S. allies

in Europe, the Middle East, and Asia also deploy Patriot missiles, including a NATO deployment to Turkey.

23 See especially Ronald O'Rourke, *Navy Aegis Ballistic Missile Defense (BMD) Program: Background and Issues for Congress*, RL 33745 (Washington, DC: Library of Congress Congressional Research Service (CRS), November 7, 2014 and subsequent editions); Ian E. Rinehart, Steven A. Hildreth, and Susan V. Lawrence, *Ballistic Missile Defense in the Asia-Pacific Region: Cooperation and Opposition*, R43116 (Washington, DC: Congressional Research Service (CRS), June 24, 2013 and subsequent editions); RADM Brad Hicks USN (Ret), CAPT George Galdorisi USN (Ret), and Scott C. Truver, "The Aegis BMD Global Enterprise: A 'High-End' Maritime Partnership," *Naval War College Review* 65 (Summer 2012), 65–80; and Steven J. Whitmore and John R. Deni, *NATO Missile Defense and the European Phased Adaptive Approach: The Implications of Burden Sharing and the Underappreciated Role of the U.S. Army* (Carlisle Barracks, PA: U.S. Army War College Strategic Studies Institute (SSI), October 2013). For an assessment of global missile forces, see *Ballistic & Cruise Missile Threat*, NASIC-1031-0985-13 (Wright-Patterson Air Force Base, OH: National Air and Space Intelligence Center (NASIC), 2013). On upgrading current U.S. Navy BMD systems, see Edward J. Walsh, "Cruisers, Destroyers Move Toward Integrated Air Defense," *U.S. Naval Institute Proceedings* 141 (February 2015), 88. See also Lance M. Bacon, "Missile Defense Ships Face Arms Race, High Op Tempo," *Navy Times* (February 9, 2015), 20.

24 On the EPAA, see Karen Kaya, "NATO Missile Defense and the View from the Front Line," *JFQ* 71 (4th quarter 2013), 84–9.

25 See especially Jonathan Solomon, "Conventional Deterrence Requires Forward Presence," Information Dissemination Blog (October 14, 2014), www.informationdissemination.net/2014/10/conventional-deterrence-requires.html, accessed August 28, 2015. For a thorough treatment of U.S. naval deterrence, see Michael Gerson and Daniel Whiteneck, *Deterrence and Influence: The Navy's Role in Preventing War*, CRM D0019315.A4/1Rev (Alexandria, VA: CNA, 2009). For the wide range of current national and trans-national threats that U.S. leaders must assess as requiring deterrence, see Director, Defense Intelligence Agency, LTG Michael T. Flynn USA, *Annual Threat Assessment: Statement before the Senate Armed Services Committee* (Washington, DC: Defense Intelligence Agency, April 18, 2013).

26 The current U.S. Navy approach to fleet readiness is discussed in Commander, U.S. Fleet Forces ADM Bill Gortney USN and Commander, U.S. Pacific Fleet ADM Harry Harris USN, "Applied Readiness," *U.S. Naval Institute Proceedings* 140 (October 2014), 40–5.

27 For the origins and development of these fleets, see Robert J. Schneller, Jr., *Anchor of Resolve: A History of U.S. Naval Forces Central Command/Fifth Fleet* (Washington, DC: Naval Historical Center, Department of the Navy, 2007); and Edward J. Marolda, *Ready Seapower: A History of the U.S. Seventh Fleet* (Washington, DC: Department of the Navy, Naval History and Heritage Command, 2012).

28 This "two forward hub" posture has characterized U.S. Navy deployment strategy more or less for over 60 years. For a discussion of its future tenability (and other options) in the face of declining U.S. defense budgets and changing world conditions, see Daniel Whiteneck, Michael Price, Neil Jenkins, and Peter Swartz, *The Navy at a Tipping Point: Maritime Dominance at Stake?* CAB D0022262. A3/1REV (Alexandria, VA: CNA, March 2010).

29 On forward basing, see Richard R. Burgess, "Force Multiplier," *Seapower* (December 2014), 24–6. For an illustration of a hull swap, see MC3 Mackenzie P. Adams, "USS Tortuga, USS Ashland Hold Hull-Swap Ceremony," NNS130823-01, Navy News Service, August 28, 2013.

30 On the importance of Diego Garcia, see Andrew Erickson, Walter Ladwig, and Justin Mikolay, "Diego Garcia: Anchoring America's Future Presence in the Indo-Pacific," *Harvard Asia Quarterly* 15, 2 (2013), 20–28.

31 For a good update on the LCS deployments to date, see 7th Fleet Public Affairs, "USS Fort Worth Arrives in US 7th Fleet," NNS 141204-01, Navy News Service (December 4, 2014). On the naval development of Guam, see Lea Eclavea, "Wharf Extension on Guam Improves Support for Navy Mission," NNS141218-10, Navy News Service (December 18, 2014). On the important role of the American Pacific island of Guam in the rebalance, see Shirley A. Kan, *Guam: U.S. Defense Deployments*, RS 22570 (Washington DC: Library of Congress Congressional Research Service (CRS), September 12, 2013 and subsequent editions).

32 On emerging requirements for more U.S. Navy warships in European waters, see David Larter, "NAVEUR: Ships Needed in 6th Fleet for High-End Training," *Navy Times* (January 13, 2015). See also Seth Cropsey, "Restore the U.S. Sixth Fleet," *National Review* (November 2, 2015).

33 On current security issues in the Indian Ocean and Western Pacific regions, see RADM Michael A. McDevitt USN (Ret), *The Long Littoral Project: Summary Report: A Maritime Perspective on Indo-Pacific Security*, IRP-2013-U-004654-Final (Alexandria, VA: CNA, June 23, 2013). See also his "America's New Defense Strategy and its Military Dimension," *Global Asia: A Journal of the East Asia Foundation* 7 (Winter 2012), www.globalasia.org/Issue/ArticleDetail/61/americas-new-security-strategy-and-itsmilitary-dimension.html, accessed August 28, 2015.

34 On the U.S. Navy's current rebalancing to the Asia-Pacific, see RDML Michael Smith USN's authoritative, "Roadmap to the Rebalance," U.S. Naval Institute *Proceedings* 139 (August 2013), 44–9. See also Phillip C. Saunders, *The Rebalance to Asia: U.S.–China Relations and Regional Security*, Strategic Forum 281 (Washington, DC: National Defense University Institute for National Strategic Studies (INSS), August 2013); Robert G. Sutter, Michael E. Brown, and Timothy J. A. Adamson, *Balancing Acts: The U.S. Rebalance and Asia-Pacific Stability* (Washington, DC: The George Washington University Elliott School of International Affairs and Sigur Center for Asian Studies, August 2013); and Patrick Cronin, *Achieving Strategic Rebalance in the Asia-Pacific Region: Testimony Before the House Armed Services Committee* (Washington, DC: Center for a New American Security (CNAS), July 24, 2013). Chief of Naval Operations Admiral Jonathan Greenert provided an update on the status of the U.S. Navy's rebalancing efforts in "Remarks at the Center for Strategic and International Studies (CSIS), 19 May 2014" (Washington, DC: Office of the Chief of Naval Information, 2014).

35 For a run-down of specific U.S. military elements being "rebalanced," see Ronald O'Rourke, *China Naval Modernization: Implications for U.S. Navy Capabilities – Background and Issues for Congress*, RL 33153 (Washington, DC: Congressional Research Service (CRS), September 8, 2014 and subsequent editions); and Karen Parrish, "U.S., Japan Agree to Expand Security, Defense Cooperation," Armed Forces Press News Service, October 3, 2013.

36 In the fall of 2013, the U.S. Navy's 10th Fleet successfully defended the unclassified Navy–Marine Corps Intranet (NMCI) against a foreign hostile hacking attack. For a press report of the incident, see Julian Barnes and Siobhan Gorman, "U.S. Says Iran Hacked Navy Computers," *Wall Street Journal* (September 27, 2013).

37 On NCIS, see Meghann Myers, "Exclusive: NCIS Director Focusing on Economic Crimes, Special Response Teams," *Navy Times* (December 1, 2014); and Director Mark Clookie, *The Naval Criminal Investigative Service Strategic Vision: Global Support to Global Challenges* (Washington, DC: NCIS, 2010).

38 On contemporary U.S. naval experimentation, see *Experimentation Planning Guide* (Norfolk, VA: Navy Warfare Development Command, 2010) and The Naval Studies Board, *The Role of Experimentation in Building Future Naval Forces* (Washington, DC: The National Academies Press, 2004). For some insights from history, see Brian McCue, *Wotan's Workshop: Military Experiments before World War II* (Alexandria, VA: CNA and Quantico. VA: Marine Corps University Press, 2013).

39 For current U.S. Navy engagement policy, see RDML Michael E. Smith USN, "Strategic Cooperation: Everybody Wins," U.S. Naval Institute *Proceedings* 139 (March 2013), 56–61. U.S. Navy engagement has long included a robust European component, and this continues. See RDML Michael E. Smith USN, "Navy's Continued Commitment to Europe," Information Dissemination Blog (April 17, 2013), www.eucom.mil/media-library/blog%20post/24852/navys-continued-commitment-to-europe, accessed August 28, 2015. See also Sam J. Tangredi (ed.), *The U.S. Naval Institute on Naval Cooperation* (Annapolis MD: Naval Institute Press, 2015).

40 For a rigorous analysis of the effect of such engagement on a U.S. ally's sovereignty, see CDRE Eric Lehre RCN (Ret) PhD, *At What Cost Sovereignty? Canada–US Military Interoperability in the War on Terror* (Halifax, NS: Dalhousie University Centre for Foreign Policy Studies, 2013).

41 Exercise Noble Justification was a recent significant NATO maritime exercise, taking place in the Mediterranean and Atlantic Ocean in October 2014. It involved more than 20 warships and several submarines and aircraft from the United States and 13 other NATO nations, plus two NATO partners – Sweden and Finland. It was under the command of VADM Peter Hudson RN, NATO's Maritime Commander. See "NATO Naval Drills Begin in Mediterranean Sea, Atlantic Ocean," *NATO News* (October 16, 2014).

42 The 2014 Sea Breeze exercise – in the wake of the Ukraine crisis – included warships from Ukraine, Georgia, Romania, Turkey, Canada, Spain, and the United States See "NATO Ships Take Part in Multinational 'Sea Breeze' Exercise in Black Sea," *NATO News* (September 9, 2014).

43 IMCMEX 2014 was a massive exercise involving 40 nations, 38 ships, and 19 unmanned underwater vehicles – the largest of its kind in the world. See VADM John Miller USN, "More Than 40 Nations

Unite to Protect the Global Commons from Mines," Navy Live Blog (November 2, 2014), http://navylive.dodlive.mil/2014/11/02/more-than-40-nations-unite-to-protect-global-commons-from-mines/, accessed August 28, 2015.

44 RIMPAC is the world's largest multinational naval warfare exercise. Sponsored by the U.S. 3rd Fleet, RIMPAC exercises began in 1971 and included naval forces from Australia, Canada, New Zealand, the United Kingdom, and the United States (the "AUSCANZUKUS" nations). Twenty-three nations participated in RIMPAC 2014, including the original five, Norway, and the People's Republic of China (for the first time). See Daniel P. Taylor, "The Main Event," *Seapower* 57 (December 2014), 34–6.

45 Bold Alligator 14, off the coasts of Virginia and North Carolina, was a major U.S. Navy–U.S. Marine Corps amphibious exercise, with participation by ships from the Netherlands, Denmark, Mexico, and Peru. See Megan Eckstein, "Exercise Bold Alligator," *Defense Daily* (October 30, 2014).

46 See Tony Bertuca, "PACOM Launches New Asia Pacific Proliferation Security Exercise," *Inside the Navy* (August 4, 2014), 13.

47 The U.S. Navy has, naturally, particularly close ties to the navies and other military forces of America's formal allies, including the navies of all the NATO maritime nations, Japan, South Korea, the Philippines, Australia, New Zealand, and Thailand. Very cooperative naval relations also exist with the navies of close U.S. military partners in the Middle East, especially Israel, Jordan, Bahrain, Kuwait, Morocco, and others. For an example of international participation in U.S. Navy war games, see *U.S. Naval War College Global 2013 Game Report* (Newport, RI: U.S. Naval War College, March 11, 2011).

48 A good example of such classroom engagement is the U.S. Navy's long-running International law of Military Operations (ILOMO) course, attended by legal advisors from dozens of nations. See Bob Krekorian, "International Military and Civilian Legal Advisors Graduate from DIILS," NNS130619-5, Navy News Service, June 19, 2013). See also David F. Manning, *Global Arms of Seapower: The Newport Connection: The International Officer Programs of the United States Naval War College* (October 29, 2014).

49 For NATO's current official post-Cold War maritime strategy, see NATO, *Alliance Maritime Strategy*, June 17, 2011. See also VADM Peter Hudson RN, "The Renaissance at Sea: A New Era for Maritime NATO," *RUSI Journal* (June–July 2014), 24–8. A U.S. Navy officer – ADM James Stavridis – recently served in the top operational military position in NATO – SACEUR: a first. See ADM James Stavridis, *The Accidental Admiral* (Annapolis, MD: Naval Institute Press, 2014).

50 A recent example of this policy has been the assignment of an American admiral to lead NATO's Standing NATO Maritime Group 2 and a U.S. Navy cruiser as the force command ship. See LTJG Timothy Dover USN, "USS Vicksburg Deploys to Support NATO," NNS141204-10, Navy News Service (December 4, 2014).

51 For an in-depth study of such convergences, see Gary E. Weir and Sandra J. Doyle (eds.), *You Cannot Surge Trust: Combined Naval Operations of the Royal Australian Navy, Canadian Navy, Royal Navy, and the United States Navy, 1991–2003* (Washington, DC: Naval History and Heritage Command, 2013). For recommendations for the future, see LCDR Mark Lawrence USN, "NATO's Maritime Future," *U.S. Naval Institute News* (October 7, 2014).

52 ON U.S. Navy–Israeli Navy engagement, see Dov S. Zakheim, *The United States Navy and Israeli Navy: Background, Current Issues, Scenarios, and Prospects*, COP D0026727.A1/Final (Alexandria, VA: CNA, February 2012).

53 For an important analysis of trends in U.S. Navy–Indian Navy relationships, see Nilanthi Samaranayake, Satu Limaye, Dmitry Gorenburg, Catherine Lea, and Thomas A. Bowditch, *U.S.–India Security Burden-Sharing? The Potential for Coordinated Capacity-Building in the Indian Ocean*, DRM-2012-U-001121-Final2 (Alexandria, VA: CNA, April 2013).

54 The Russian Navy, however, declined an invitation to participate in RIMPAC 2014.

55 See William Cole, "Chinese Navy Warships Will Arrive at Pearl Harbor Friday," *Honolulu Star-Advertiser* (September 4, 2013). For a discussion of USN–PLAN engagement by U.S. Navy commanders, see VADM Robert Thomas USN, "Here's What Has Been Done to Improve Military Relations with China," *Defense One*, November 9 2014; and CNO ADM Jonathan Greenert, "Charting the Navy's Future in a Changing Maritime Domain" (Washington, DC: Brookings Institution, November 4, 2014).

56 For opposing domestic U.S. policy expert views on the efficacy of engaging the PLAN, see Christopher J. Castelli, "Analysts: For China's Defense Proposals, Implementation is Everything," *Inside the Pentagon* (August 29, 2013), 4–5.

57 See VADM Kevin Cosgriff USN (Ret) and Ellen Laipson, "Testing the Waters for Normalizing U.S.–Iran Relations" (posted on *Defense One*, September 9, 2013).

58 On ISMERLO, see Journalist Seaman Andrew Zask, "New International Submarine Rescue Coordination Center Opens," NNS040929-08, Navy News Service (September 9, 2004).

59 On APSC and the related annual multi-national exercise Pacific Reach (PACREACH), see RDML Phillip G. Sawyer, "Working with our Asia-Pacific Partners," *Undersea Warfare* (Spring 2013), 4.

60 For trends in international lawlessness and international disorder, and the means to counter them, see Michael Miklaucic and Jacqueline Brewer, *Convergence: Illicit Networks and National Security in the Age of Globalization* (Washington, DC: National Defense University (NDU) Press, 2013). On U.S. government counter-drug strategy at sea in the Caribbean, see *Caribbean Border Counternarcotics Strategy* (Washington, DC: Executive Office of the President of the United States, January 2015).

61 On the U.S. Coast Guard, see *Safety, Security and Stewardship: 2011 DHS White Paper on the U.S. Coast Guard* (Washington, DC: Department of Homeland Security, 2011); *America's 21st Century Coast Guard: Resourcing for Safety, Security and Stewardship: 2013 White Paper on Resourcing the U.S. Coast Guard* (Washington, DC: Department of Homeland Security, 2013); and *United States Coast Guard Arctic Strategy* (Washington, DC: U.S. Coast Guard Headquarters, May 2013). On Navy–Coast Guard relationships, see Department of the Navy Office of the Chief of Naval Operations and United States Coast Guard Office of the Commandant "The National Fleet Plan," (Washington DC: August 2015).

62 Recent analyses of the implementation of the Proliferation Security Initiative include Aaron Dunne, *The Proliferation Security Initiative: Legal Considerations and Operational Realities* (Stockholm: Stockholm International Peace Research Institute (SIPRI), May 2013); Mary Beth Nikitin, *Proliferation Security Initiative (PSI)*, RL 34327 (Washington, DC: Congressional Research Service (CRS), June 15, 2012 and subsequent editions); and *Proliferation Security Initiative*, GAO-12–441 (Washington, DC: U.S. Government Accountability Office (GAO), March 2012).

63 For an argument that the U.S. Navy should pay more attention to Latin American waters, see RADM Sinclair Harris USN, "South is Forward," U.S. Naval Institute *Proceedings* 141 (February 2015), 18–23.

64 For a European view on maritime security operations, see VADM Lutz Feldt FGN (Ret), Dr. Peter Roell, and Ralph D. Theile, *Maritime Security – Perspectives for a Comprehensive Approach* (Berlin: Institut für Strategie- Politik- Sicherheits- und Wirtschatsberatung (ISPSW), April 2013).

65 U.S. Navy policy on maritime security cooperation is in Commandant of the Marine Corps General James F. Amos, Chief of Naval Operations Admiral Jonathan Greenert, and Commandant of the Coast Guard Admiral Robert J. Papp, *Maritime Security Cooperation: An Integrated Navy–Marine Corps–Coast Guard Approach* (Washington, DC, January 2013).

66 For an argument that NATO's considerable naval activities are all but unknown in the United States, even among policy elites, see Jacob Stokes and Nora Bensahel, *NATO Matters: Ensuring the Value of the Alliance for the United States* (Washington, DC: Center for a New American Security, October 2013). On Operation Martillo, see John C. Marcario, "Pooling Resources," *Seapower* 57 (December 2014), 50–1.

67 For more detail on the multinational 2013 APS deployment, see Donna Miles, "Partnership Station Promotes Security, Capacity in West Africa," U.S. Department of Defense: American Forces Press Service, September 3, 2013.

68 There is a large literature on the multinational counter-piracy operations in the Arabian Gulf. See especially RDML Terence McKnight USN (Ret) and Michael Hirsch, *Pirate Alley: Commanding Task Force 151 off Somalia* (Annapolis, MD: Naval Institute Press, 2012). On the effect of those operations and remaining global challenges, see the most recent *Reports on Acts of Piracy and Armed Robbery against Ships* published by the International Maritime Organization (IMO) (London). For historical context, see Bruce A. Elleman, Andrew Forbes, and David Rosenberg (eds.), *Piracy and Maritime Crime: Historical and Modern Case Studies*, Newport Paper 35 (Newport, RI: Naval War College Press, January 2010). A recent analysis of Somali piracy is in Sarah Percy and Anja Shortland, "The Business of Piracy in Somalia," *Journal of Strategic Studies* 36 (August 2013), 541–78.

69 A significant first was an August 2013 helicopter cross-decking exercise conducted by two U.S. Navy and PLAN destroyers in the Gulf of Aden. See MCS2 Rob Aylward, "US, China Conduct Counter Piracy Exercise," NNS 130825-01, Navy News Service (August 25, 2013); and Hendrick Simoes, "U.S. Navy Seeks More Cooperation with China in Counter-Piracy Exercise," *Stars and Stripes* (26 August 2013).

70 For a broad overview, see James J. Wirtz and Jeffrey A. Larsen (eds.), *Naval Peacekeeping and Humanitarian Operations: Stability from the Sea.* (London and New York: Routledge, 2008).

71 On U.S. Navy humanitarian assistance and disaster response policy, see RDML Michael Smith USN, "Humanitarian Assistance, Disaster Response Missions Strengthen Navy," Navy Live Blog, June 12, 2013), http://navylive.dodlive.mil/2013/06/12/humanitarian-assistance-disaster-response-mission s-strengthen-navy/, accessed August 28, 2015. See also ADM Gary Roughead USN (Ret), J. Stephen Morrison, RADM Thomas Cullison USN (Ret), and Seth Gannon, *U.S. Navy Humanitarian Assistance in an Era of Austerity* (Washington, DC: Center for Strategic and International Studies (CSIS), March 2013). For a critique of U.S. Navy policy on these operations, see Robert J. Carr, "The Mission is Warfighting, Not Relief," U.S. Naval Institute *Proceedings* 136 (December 2010), 10. For a recent instance of U.S humanitarian assistance in a coalition context, see Matthew Grund and Catherine Lea, *Japan–U.S. Alliance Management: Natural Disaster Response Cooperation with the U.S. Forces in Japan* (Arlington, VA: CNA, September 2014).

72 For example, annual Pacific Partnership (since 2006) and Southern (i.e. Caribbean) Partnership Station deployments.

73 For a recent commentary on naval diplomacy, see CDR Kevin Rowlands RN, "Decided Preponderance at Sea: Naval Diplomacy in Strategic Thought," *Naval War College Review* 65 (Autumn 2012), 89–105.

74 A current salient issue area is climate change and energy. See Ralph Espach, Duncan Depledge, and Tobias Feakin, *The Climate and Energy Nexus: Challenges and Opportunities for Transatlantic Security*, ICP-2013-U-004986-Final (Alexandria, VA: CNA and RUSI, June 2013); and CNA Military Advisory Board (MAB), *National Security and the Accelerating Risks of Climate Change* (Alexandria, VA: CNA, May 2014).

75 On the scientific thrust of U.S. and U.S. Navy Arctic policy, see President Barack Obama, *National Strategy for the Arctic Region* (Washington, DC: The White House, May 2013); *Implementation Plan for the National Strategy for the Arctic Region* (January 2014); and Chief of Naval Operations Admiral Jonathan Greenert, *U.S. Navy Arctic Roadmap 2014–2030* (Washington, DC: U.S. Navy Task Force Climate Change, February 2014). For an argument that maritime security issues are becoming more salient in the Arctic, necessitating increased international naval engagement there, see Lee Willett, "Frozen Over: Maritime Security Challenges in the 'High North'," *Jane's Navy International* (December 2012), 21–4. See also Ronald O'Rourke, *Changes in the Arctic: Background and Issues for Congress*, R41153 (Washington, DC: Congressional Research Service (CRS), August 4, 2014 and subsequent editions); and VADM Lutz Feldt FGN (Ret), *The Importance of the Arctic Region: Implications for Europe and Asia* (Berlin: Institut für Strategie- Politik- Sicherheits- und Wirtschaftsberatung (ISPSW), May 2013). For a recent U.S. Navy exercise in the Arctic that included support to science, see Ryan Hopper, "ICEX 2014," *Undersea Warfare* (Summer 2014), 10–15.

76 See Mass Communication Specialist Seaman Christopher A. Veloicaza, "Anchorage Completes NASA Orion Mission," NNS 141208-04, Navy News Service (December 8, 2014); and "Anchorage Departs on NASA's Orion Mission," NNS141202-01, Navy News Service (December 2, 2014).

77 "A Global Force for Good" was the U.S. Navy's recruiting slogan since 2009. On the validity of this assertion, see LCDR Matthew Krull USN, "We Really Are a Global Force for Good," U.S. Naval Institute *Proceedings* 140 (January 2014), 12. The Navy has been recently phasing out the phrase, however. See Mark D. Faram, "Forcing Out 'Force for Good'," *Navy Times* (December 29, 2014–January 5, 2015), 4.

78 There is a large literature on U.S. naval crisis response. See especially Eugene Cobble, Hank Gaffney, and Dmitry Gorenburg, *For the Record: All U.S. Forces' Responses to Situations, 1970–2000 (with Additions Covering 2000–2003)* (Alexandria, VA: CNA, 2005). A more recent analysis is Larissa Forster, *Influence without Boots on the Ground: Seaborne Crisis Response*, Newport Paper 39 (Newport, RI: Naval War College Press, January 2013).

79 For an argument that naval crisis response has become far more complex and diverse than heretofore, see CAPT Robert B. Watts USCG, "The New Normalcy: Sea Power and Contingency Operations in the Twenty-First Century," *Naval War College Review* 65 (Summer 2012), 47–64.

80 There is a large literature on potential South China Sea crises and the role of U.S. and other naval forces. See especially RADM Michael McDevitt USN (Ret), "The South China Sea and U.S. Policy Options," *American Foreign Policy Interests* 35 (July–August 2013), 175–87; and Carlyle A. Thayer, "Chinese Assertiveness and U.S. Rebalancing: Confrontation in the South China Sea?" Paper delivered at Annual Conference of the Association for Asian Studies, San Diego, CA, March 22, 2013.

81 On the Law of the Sea, see especially CAPT (Ret) Mark Rosen USN (JAGC), *Challenges to Public Order and the Seas* (Alexandria, VA: CNA, March 2014).

82 On the INCSEA agreement, see David Winkler, *Cold War at Sea: High-Seas Confrontation between the United States and the Soviet Union* (Annapolis, MD: Naval Institute Press, 2000).

83 These joint U.S. operations, including significant U.S. Navy participation, were termed Unified Assistance, Sea Angel II, Unified Response, and Tomadachi. For an excellent case study of Unified Assistance, see Bruce A. Elleman, *Waves of Hope: The U.S. Navy's Response to the Tsunami in Northern Indonesia*, Newport Paper 28 (Newport, RI: Naval War College Press, February 2007). An important earlier example is in Charles R. Smith, *Angels from the Sea: Relief Operations in Bangladesh, 1991* (Washington, DC: Headquarters, U.S. Marine Corps, 1995).

84 On the operational and tactical aspects of these operations, see CAPT Cathal O'Connor USN, "Foreign Humanitarian Assistance and Disaster-Relief Operations: Lessons Learned and Best Practices," *Naval War College Review* 65 (Winter 2012), 153–60.

85 See "Hagel Congratulates Cape Ray for Syria Mission," American Forces Press Service, August 18, 2014.

86 Chief of Naval Operations (CNO) Admiral Jonathan Greenert USN, *CNO's Sailing Directions* (Washington, DC, undated (but 2011)).

87 The listing is the author's. Other lists exist. See, for example, Allied Joint Publication (AJP) 3.1, *Allied Joint Maritime Operations* (April 2004), section V. For a view of the future of what he terms undersea, strike, air and electromagnetic spectrum warfare, see Bryan Clark, "Statement Before the Senate Armed Services Committee on the Future of Warfare," (Washington DC: CSBA, November 3, 2015).

88 On the F/A-18E/F, see Richard R. Burgess, "Advancing the Super Hornet," *Seapower* (November 2013), 32–6.

89 On use of the Tomahawk missile as a strike weapon, see William Matthews, "The Weapon of Choice," *Seapower* (November 2013), 38–40.

90 For an appreciation of the role of Navy strike/fighter aircraft in Afghanistan counter-insurgency (COIN) operations, see LT Jeff McLean USN, "A Junior Officer's Perspective on Close Air support and Counterinsurgency," U.S. Naval Institute Blog, August 22, 2013, http://blog.usni.org/201 3/08/22/a-junior-officers-perspective-on-close-air-support-and-counterinsurgency, accessed August 28, 2015. On SSGN capabilities, see Kelvin Wong, "USN Showcases SSGN Capabilities with USS *Michigan* in Latest Asia-Pacific Deployment," *IHS Jane's Defence Weekly* (September 8, 2014).

91 The U.S. Marine Corps is a large and powerful naval armed service unlike any other in the world. Like the U.S. Navy, it is a separate service within the U.S. Department of the Navy – one of the three service departments of the U.S. Department of Defense. Navy–Marine Corps relationships are close – especially in entry-level officer education and amphibious warfare. On Navy–Marine Corps relations, see Chief of Naval Operations Admiral Jonathan W. Greenert USN and Commandant of the Marine Corps General James F. Amos USMC, "A New Naval Era," U.S. Naval Institute *Proceedings* 139 (June 2013), 16–20. On recent exercises designed to re-invigorate the capabilities of the two services to conduct amphibious warfare operations, see Otto Kreisher, "Crisis Response: Amphibious Exercise Showcases Navy–Marine Teamwork, Engages International Coalition," *Seapower* 56 (September 2013), 16–18; and Lance M. Bacon, "Bold Alligator is Back," *Navy Times* (October 18, 2014). For a discussion of ways to bring the services even closer, see Col. Bradley E. Weisz USMC, "Optimizing the Blue-Green Team," *Marine Corps Gazette* 97 (September 2013), 50–4.

92 On the U.S. Marine Corps' vision of the future application of U.S. amphibious power, see Commandant of the Marine Corps General James E. Amos, *Expeditionary Force 21* (Washington, DC: Headquarters, U.S. Marine Corps, March 4, 2014).

93 See CAPT William J. Toti USN (Ret), "The Hunt for Full-Spectrum ASW," U.S. Naval Institute *Proceedings* 140 (June 2014), 38–43.

94 On the outlook for U.S. Navy ASW, see ADM Jonathan Greenert, "How the U.S. Can Maintain the Undersea Advantage," *Defense One* (October 12, 2013). See also Bryan Clark, *The Emerging Era in Undersea Warfare* (Washington, DC: Center for Strategic and Budgetary Assessments (CSBA), 2015).

95 For a classic discussion of naval anti-air warfare, see Michael W. Smith, *Antiair Warfare Defense of Ships at Sea* (Alexandria, VA: Center for Naval Analyses, September 1981).

96 For a recommended new approach to U.S. Navy anti-air warfare, see Bryan Clark, *Commanding the Seas: A Plan to Reinvigorate U.S. Navy Surface Warfare* (Washington, DC: Center for Strategic and Budgetary Assessments (CSBA), November 2014).

97 On naval Ballistic Missile Defense, see CAPT George Galdorisi USN (Ret) and Dr. Scott Truver, "Leading the Way in Ballistic Missile Defense," U.S. Naval Institute *Proceedings* 139 (December 2013), 32–8. On the future of U.S. naval Ballistic Missile Defense see, for example, U.S. 7th Fleet Public

Affairs, "7th Fleet Tests Innovative Missile Defense System," NNS 140626-30, Navy News Service (July 1, 2014).

98 For an example of a recent forward Navy–Air Force anti-surface exercise involving Air Force F-15 and JSTARS aircraft, see MC3 Billy Ho USN, "Monterey Conducts Exercise with US Air Force," NNS130801-09, Navy News Service (August 1, 2013).

99 Anti-commerce warfare was once a central feature of naval warfare. For an argument that its importance may well return, see Douglas C. Peifer, "Maritime Commerce Warfare: The Coercive Response of the Weak?" *Naval War College Review* 66 (Spring 2013), 83–109.

100 On the efficacy of blockades, especially nine post–World War II examples, see Bruce A. Elleman and S. C. M. Paine, *Naval Blockades and Seapower: Strategies and Counter-Strategies, 1805–2005* (London and New York: Routledge, 2006).

101 See, for example, Gabriel B. Collins and William S. Murray, "No Oil for the Lamps of China," *Naval War College Review* 61 (Spring 2008), 79–95; Sean Mirski, "Stranglehold: The Context, Conduct and Consequences of an American Naval Blockade of China," *Journal of Strategic Studies* 36 (June 2013), 385–421; Evan Braden Montgomery, "Reconsidering a Naval Blockade of China; A Response to Mirski," *Journal of Strategic Studies* 36 (August 2013), 615–23; Col. T. X. Hammes USMC (Ret), *Offshore Control: A Proposed Strategy for an Unlikely Conflict* (Washington, DC: National Defense University (NDU) Institute for Strategic Studies (ISS) (June 28, 2012); and Michael Haas, "Shipping as a Repository of Strategic Vulnerability" (Center for International Maritime Security (CIMSEC), August 16, 2013).

102 See Joshua J. Edwards and CAPT Dennis M. Gallagher USN, "Mine and Undersea Warfare for the Future," U.S. Naval Institute *Proceedings* 140 (August 2014), 70–5.

103 For a critique of U.S. Navy mine warfare policy, strategy, and acquisition, see Scott C. Truver, "Wanted: U.S. Navy Mine Warfare Champion," *Naval War College Review* 68 (Spring 2015), 116–27.

104 For one of the few analyses in the open literature, see Ronald O'Rourke, *Navy Irregular Warfare and Counterterrorism Operations: Background and Issues for Congress*, RS22373 (Washington, DC: Congressional Research Service (CRS), July 31, 2014 and subsequent editions).

105 For an analysis and recommendations on U.S. Navy riverine operations, see LT J. A. Cummings, Jr., "A Riverine Approach to Irregular Warfare," U.S. Naval Institute *Proceedings* 140 (January 2014), 52–7.

106 For recent developments in this warfare area, see Sidney J. Freedberg, "Navy Forges New EW Strategy: Electronic Maneuver Warfare," *Breaking Defense* (October 10, 2014).

107 See Jonathan F. Solomon, "Maritime Deception and Concealment: Concepts for Defeating Wide-Area Oceanic Surveillance-Reconnaissance-Strike Networks," *Naval War College Review* 66 (Autumn 2013), 87–116.

108 On air electronic warfare, see M. Thomas Davis, David Barno, and Nora Bensahel, *The Enduring Need for Electronic Attack in Air Operations* (Washington, DC: Center for a New American Security, January 2014).

109 On EA18G Growler operations, see CDR Dave Kurtz USN, "Dawn of the Expeditionary Growler," U.S. Naval Institute *Proceedings* 139 (September 2013), 22–6.

110 For an example of the successful application of U.S. Navy damage control techniques and procedures in a modern combat environment, see Bradley Peniston, *No Higher Honor: Saving the USS "Samuel B. Roberts" in the Persian Gulf* (Annapolis, MD: Naval Institute Press, 2006). For the Imperial German Navy roots of modern U.S. Navy damage control practices, see LCDR Jeremy P. Schaub USN, *U.S. Navy Shipboard Damage Control: Innovation and Implementation During the Interwar Period* (MA Thesis: U.S. Army Command and General Staff College, Fort Leavenworth KS: 2014).

111 See, for example, RADM Edward Masso USN (Ret), "Our Aircraft Carriers are not Sitting Ducks," *Forbes* (August 4, 2014).

112 See, for example, "Army Aviators, Sailors Team up in 5th Fleet," *Navy Times* (September 9, 2013).

113 See Sandra Erwin, "Navy to Begin Preparations for Cyber Warfare," *National Defense* (November 1, 2014).

114 For a discussion of the effect that fuel constraints may have on future U.S. naval operations, see CDR Gregory Knepper USN, *Access Assured: Addressing Air Power Reach, Persistence and Fueling Limitations for Contested and Permissive Air Operations* (Washington, DC: Brookings Institution, September 2014).

115 On the U.S. Navy's forward operational use of its tenders, see MC2(SW) Carey Hensley, "Submarine Tenders Continue to support Critical Operations in Pacific Fleet," *Undersea Warfare* (Spring 2013), 14–19; and LTJG Heather Hutchinson USN, "USS *Frank Cable* (AS 40): Ready and Able … Supporting Mission Readiness," *Navy Supply Corps Newsletter* (July/August 2013), 15–17.

116 On the Navy's vision for Information Dominance, see *U.S. Navy Information Dominance Roadmap, 2013–2028* (Washington, DC: U.S. Navy, 2013). See also Peter Dombrowski and Chris C. Demchak, "Cyber War, Cybered Conflict, and the Maritime Domain," *Naval War College Review* 67 (Spring 2014), 71–96.

117 On the Information Dominance corps, see VADM Ted N. Branch, "'A New Era' in Naval Warfare," U.S. Naval Institute *Proceedings* 140 (July 2014), 18–23. On the competence of U.S. Naval Intelligence, see RADM Paul Becker USN, "What Are We Doing Right?" U.S. Naval Institute *Proceedings* 141 (February 2015), 80–1. For a discussion of the role open-source literature can play in U.S. naval intelligence, see Peter M. Swartz with Michael Connell, *Understanding an Adversary's Strategic and Operational Calculus: A Late Cold War Case Study with 21st Century Applicability*, COP-2013-U-005622-Final (Alexandria, VA: CNA, August 2013).

118 This construct was used to great positive effect in explaining the U.S. Navy's "Maritime Strategy" of the 1980s. It also corresponds well to the three central phases of the current U.S. joint operational phasing model: "Deter" (Phase I), "Seize Initiative" (Phase II), and "Dominate" (Phase III). See John B. Hattendorf and Peter M. Swartz (eds.), *U.S. Naval Strategy in the 1980s: Selected Documents* (Newport, RI: Naval War College Press, Newport Paper 33, December 2008) and *Joint Publication 5-0: Joint Operation Planning*, II-42–III-43. For how naval operations map to contemporary joint U.S. military phases, see *Naval Doctrine Publication 1: Naval Warfare* (NDP 1), 49–57.

119 For a comprehensive discussion of anti-access warfare operations and ways to overcome them, see CAPT Samuel Tangredi USN (Ret), *Anti-Access Warfare: Countering A2/AD Strategies* (Annapolis, MD: Naval Institute Press, 2013).

120 The Air–Sea Battle concept has been the subject of enormous public discussion, much of it uninformed and inaccurate. Authoritative public statements include Terry S. Morris, Martha VanDriel, Bill Dries, Jason C. Perdew, Richard H. Schulz, and Kristen E. Jacobsen, "Securing Operational Access: Evolving the Air–Sea Battle Concept," *National Interest* (March–April 2015); and (U.S. Department of Defense) Air–Sea Battle Office, *Air–Sea Battle: Service Collaboration to Address Anti-Access and Area Denial Challenges* (Washington, DC, May 2013). For a recent debate on some of the issues involved, see Col. T. X. Hammes USMC (Ret), "Offshore Control vs. AirSea Battle: Who Wins?" *National Interest* website, August 21, 2013) and previous articles by Col. Hammes and Elbridge Colby cited therein. See CNO ADM Jonathan Greenert's remarks in "Charting the Navy's Future."

121 For example, following World War II, the great forward fleets that had helped defeat Germany, Italy, and Japan were called home, and reconstituted in American ports and waters as (greatly reduced) surge fleets akin to the Navy's pre-war deployment posture. Small forward stations were kept on in the Mediterranean, Northern Europe, and Northeast Asia, akin to the pre-war U.S. Asiatic Fleet and Squadron 40-T. Following the Vietnam War, the Navy stripped the 7th Fleet of much of its wartime strength, and rebalanced its global force again in favor of the Mediterranean and North Atlantic, as had been the case before the Vietnam War.

122 Examples abound. Immediately following the American Civil War, in 1865, U.S naval combat forces had to immediately but briefly deploy off Texas in the face of the Imperial French attempt to sustain the Emperor Maximilian on his Mexican throne against the wishes of the vast majority of the Mexican people. No sooner was the Spanish–American War ended in 1898 – and the Spanish Philippines ceded to the United States – than the Navy was directed to support the U.S. Army in counter-insurgency operations quashing the Philippine Insurrection. Following the end of World War I, U.S. Navy commanders found themselves conducting operations in the Adriatic in support of the newly constituted Yugoslav government; in the Eastern Mediterranean and the Black Sea as the Russian and Turkish revolutions and the Greco–Turkish War unfolded; and in Murmansk and Vladivostok in support of short American interventions in the Russian Civil War. Following Japan's surrender and the ending of hostilities after World War II, the U.S. Navy was directed to use its warships to repatriate thousands of U.S. and allied prisoners of war; to bring home millions of forward U.S. Army troops; to repatriate thousands of Japanese troops from all over Asia and the Pacific (and German and Italian prisoners from the United States); to transport hundreds of thousands of Nationalist Chinese troops to North China to fight the Communist Chinese; and to provide naval combat support for two divisions of U.S. Marines assigned ashore in northern China. U.S. military withdrawal from Vietnam in 1973 was followed two years later by operations to evacuate U.S. embassy personnel and others from South Vietnam and Cambodia.

123 The current U.S. joint operational phasing construct recognizes the existence of post-combat phases as well, including a "Stabilize" (Phase IV) and "Enable Civil Authority" (Phase V), but the discussion

is informed largely by the American experience in ground warfare and counter-insurgency during the past decade, and not by many of the types of post-combat naval operations cited above. See *Joint Publication 5-0: Joint Operation Planning*, III-43–III-44.

124 For an argument that the United States is actually threatened by very little, see Christopher Preble and John Mueller (eds.), *A Dangerous World? Threat Perception and National Security* (Washington, DC: Cato Institute, 2014).

125 On potential combat operations in the Gulf, see Daniel Whiteneck, "Conducting Naval Operations in the Arabian Gulf: An Essential Mission Capability," Information Dissemination Blog (January 7, 2015), www.informationdissemination.net/2015/01/conducting-naval-operations-in-arabian. html, accessed August 28, 2015. For recent analysis of the North Korean and Iranian threats, see Ken E. Gause, *North Korean Calculus in the Maritime Environment: Covert Versus Overt Provocations*, COP-2013-U-005210-Final (Alexandria, VA: CNA, July 16, 2013); *Military and Security Developments Involving the Democratic People's Republic of Korea 2012: A Report to Congress* (Washington, DC: Office of the Secretary of Defense, 2013); Michael Connell, *Iranian Operational Decision Making*, COP-2013-U-00529-1-Final (Alexandria, VA: CNA, July 12, 2013); Christopher Harmer, *Iranian Naval and Maritime Strategy*, Middle East Security Report 12 (Washington, DC: Institute for the Study of War, June 2013); and Michael Connell, "Iran's Power at Sea: What You Need to Know about Iran's Navy," Real Clear World (Washington, DC: U.S. Institute of Peace, March 28, 2013), www.realclearworld.com/articles/2013/03/28/irans_power_at_sea_what_you_need_to_know_about_irans_navy_105036.html, accessed 28 August, 2015.

126 On interpreting the Taiwan Relations Act, see Shirley A. Kan, *China/Taiwan: Evolution of the 'One China' Policy – Key Statements from Washington, Beijing, and Taipei*, RL 30341 (Washington, DC: Congressional Research Service (CRS), August 26, 2013 and subsequent editions). On U.S.–Taiwan relations, see Shirley A. Kan and Wayne M. Morrison, *U.S.–Taiwan Relationship: Overview of Policy Issues*, R 41952 (Washington, DC: Congressional Research Service (CRS), August 21, 2013). For views on how the U.S. might combat China at sea, should the situation arise, see CAPT Jeffrey E. Kline USN (Ret) and CAPT Wayne P. Hughes Jr. USN (Ret), "Between Peace and the Air–Sea Battle: A War at Sea Strategy," *Naval War College Review* 65 (Autumn 2012), 34–40. See also the notes to the section on "blockade" above.

127 The basic unofficial but comprehensive reference on the composition of the U.S. Navy is Norman Polmar, *Ships and Aircraft of the U.S. Fleet*, 19th edn. (Annapolis MD: Naval Institute Press, 2013).

128 The U.S. Navy modified its battle force counting rules slightly in March 2014, making comparisons of fleet size before and after that date somewhat difficult (under the new rules, the future Battle Force will be larger by five to ten ships. See SECNAVINST 5030.8B of 7 March 2014, "General Guidance for the Classification of Naval Vessels and Battle Force Ship Counting Procedures" (Washington, DC: Office of the Secretary of the Navy, posted March 26, 2014). In 2015, however, Congress intervened and changed the Navy's counting rules yet again. See Christopher P. Cavas, "Over a Weekend, US Navy 'Shrinks' by 9 Ships." *Defense News* (March 9, 2015).

129 On any given day, the size of the U.S. Navy's Ship Battle Forces can be found on the website of the Naval Vessel Register (NVR), published by the U.S. Navy's Naval Sea Systems Command.

130 For an analysis of the negative implications of the decline in U.S. Navy ship numbers, see Seth Cropsey, *Mayday: The Decline of American Naval Supremacy* (New York: Overlook: 2013). For an analysis of the ameliorating effects of the improvement in individual ship capabilities, see Robert Work, *The Challenge of Maritime Transformation: Is Bigger Better?* (Washington, DC: Center for Strategic and Budgetary Assessments, 2002).

131 For a discussion of the National Fleet concept, and further references, see Bryan Clark, *Commanding the Seas: A Plan to Reinvigorate U.S. Navy Surface Warfare* (Washington, DC: Center for Strategic and Budgetary Assessments (CSBA), November 2014), 39.

132 The Navy deployed the RQ-2A *Pioneer*, its first modern unmanned aircraft, for reconnaissance and surveillance operation in the 1980s.

133 For an example of how this U.S. naval command structure functions in wartime, see RADM James G. Foggo III USN and LT Michael Beer USN, "The New Operational Paradigm: Operation *Odyssey Dawn* and the Maritime Operations Center," *JFQ* (3rd quarter 2013), 91–3; and RDML James G. Foggo USN, LT Michael Beer USN, and CDR Patrick Moynihan USN, "Operating Forward at the Ready: The 6^F MOC in Action during Operation Odyssey Dawn," *MOC Warfighter*, 1 (April 2013), www.usnwc.edu/MOCwarfighter/Article.aspx?ArticleID=3, accessed August 28, 2015. For a history of the development of the MOC concept, see CAPT William Lawler USN and CAPT

Jonathan Will USN (Ret), "Moving Forward: Evolution of the Maritime Operations Center," *MOC Warfighter*, 1 (April 2013), www.usnwc.edu/MOCwarfighter/Article.aspx?ArticleID=4, accessed August 28, 2015. See also OPNAV Instruction 3500.42 Maritime Operations Center Standardization (Washington, DC: Office of the Chief of Naval Operations, December 16, 2014).

134 For a short useful summary analysis of past Carrier Strike Group (CSG) operations, see Christine H. Fox, *Carrier Operations: Looking toward the Future – Learning from the Past*, D0020669.A1/Final (Alexandria, VA: CNA, May 27, 2009). For differing views on the future efficacy of the Carrier Strike Group (CSG) and its centerpiece, the nuclear-powered aircraft carrier, see VADM David H. Buss USN, RADM William F. Moran USN, and RADM Thomas J. Moore USN, "Why America Still Needs Aircraft Carriers" (posted on *Foreign Policy*, April 26, 2013); Scott Truver, "Why America Needs Aircraft Carriers" (posted on *Breaking Defense*, October 2, 2013); and Col. T. X. Hammes USMC (Ret), "Beyond Carriers: Rapid Technological Change Sinks the Case for Big, Costly Platforms," *Armed Forces Journal* (August 1, 2013).

135 For the most recent U.S. Navy policy on the composition and capabilities of CSGs, ARG/MEUs, ESGs, and SAGs, see OPNAVINST 3501.316B "Policy of Baseline Composition and Basic Mission Capabilities of Major Afloat Navy and Naval Groups" (Washington, DC: Office of the Chief of Naval Operations, October 21, 2010).

136 For the Composite Warfare Commander concept, see *Joint Publication 3-32: Command and Control for Joint Maritime Operations* (Washington, DC: Joint Chiefs of Staff, August 7, 2013).

137 For U.S. doctrine on amphibious operations, including command and control, see *Joint Publication 3-02: Amphibious Operations* (Washington, DC: Joint Chiefs of Staff, July 18, 2014).

138 *Naval Aviation News* 96 (Summer 2014) 26, 32–3.

139 See LT Timothy Gorman, "Hamburg First German Ship to Deploy in U.S. Carrier Strike Group," NNS130403-06, Navy News Service (April 3, 2013).

140 On SSGN forward operations and logistic support, see "*Trident* Support: The Guided Missile Submarine Fleet," *Navy Supply Corps Newsletter* (July/August 2013), 7–8.

141 "Major Land-Based Deployments," *Naval Aviation News* 96 (Summer 2014), 28–9.

142 For a defense of the traditional approach, see CDR Steve "Lazarus" Wills USN (Ret), "Naval Supremacy Cannot be 'Piggybacked' on Small Ships," posted on Information Dissemination Blog (September 30, 2013), www.informationdissemination.net/2013/09/naval-supremacy-cannot-be-piggybacked.html, accessed August 28, 2015.

143 For arguments favoring a change to a "flotilla" approach, see the September 2013 issue of the U.S. Naval Institute *Proceedings*; and CAPT Jeffrey E. Kline USN (Ret) and CAPT Wayne P. Hughes, Jr. USN (Ret), "Between Peace and the Air–Sea Battle," *Naval War College Review* 65 (Autumn 2012), 36–40. See also CAPT Wayne P. Hughes, Jr., USN (Ret), "A Business Strategy for Shipbuilders," *Seapower* (November 2014), 6–7.

144 For the U.S. Navy's most recent detailed annual explanations to the U.S. Congress of its current status and near-term plans, see *U.S. Navy Program Guide 2015* (Washington, DC: Department of the Navy, 2015); and *Highlights of the Department of the Navy FY 2016 Budget* (Washington, DC: Department of the Navy Office of Budget, 2015). For an analysis of those plans, and much else, see Ronald O'Rourke, *Navy Force Structure and Shipbuilding Plans: Background and Issues for Congress*, 7-5700 (Washington, DC: Congressional Research Service (CRS), August 1, 2014 and subsequent editions). For a brief update of the Navy's goals, see Chief of Naval Operations Admiral Jonathan Greenert USN, *CNO's Navigation Plan, 2015–2019* (Washington, DC, 2014). For the Navy's current longer-range vision, see Deputy Chief of Naval Operations (Integration of Capabilities and Resources) (N8), *Report to Congress on the Annual Long-Range Plan for Construction of Naval Vessels for FY 2016* (Washington, DC: Office of the Chief of Naval Operations, March 2015). For an alternative analysis of the plan, see Eric J. Labs, *An Analysis of the Navy's Fiscal Year 2016 Shipbuilding Plan* (Washington, DC: Congressional Budget Office, October 2015). For current Navy interest in future technologies, see CNO ADM Jonathan Greenert USN, "Remarks at the Naval Future Force Science and Technology Expo" (Washington, DC: Office of the Chief of Naval Operations, February 4, 2015); and *Naval Science and Technology Strategy*, 4th edn. (Arlington, VA: Office of Naval Research, 2015).

145 On plans to replace the U.S. Navy SSBN force, see RADM Richard Breckenridge USN, "A History of Sea-Based Strategic Deterrence Optimization, Platform Versatility, Cost Efficiency" (posted on Navy Live Blog, August 26, 2013), http://navylive.dodlive.mil/2013/08/26/a-history-of-sea-based-strategic-deterrence-optimization-platform-versatility-and-cost-efficiency/, accessed August

28, 2015; and Ronald O'Rourke, *Navy Ohio Replacement (SSBN(X) Ballistic Missile Submarine Program: Background and Issues for Congress*, RL 33640 (Washington, DC: Library of Congress Congressional Research Service (CRS), July 31, 2014 and subsequent editions). See also Eric J. Labs, "Finding Funding for the New Boomer," U.S. Naval Institute *Proceedings* 141 (February 2015), 63.

146 For the status of the F-35C in November 2014, see Commander, Naval Air Forces Public Affairs, "F-35C Completes Initial Sea Trials aboard Aircraft Carrier," NNS141117-13, Navy News Service (November 17, 2014). The Navy is just beginning to examine the possibilities of a "sixth-generation" tactical aircraft, to follow the F-35 and replace the F/A-18. See Aaron Mehta, "Strategy to Acquire Sixth-Gen Fighter Set," *Navy Times* (February 16, 2015), 18.

147 On the E-2D, see Sidney J. Freedberg, "E-2D Hits IOC: Navy Hawkeye gets Larger, Lethal Role," *Breaking Defense* (October 17, 2014).

148 See "Poseidon's First Adventure," *Seapower* (May/June 2014), 40–2.

149 For analyses, see CAPT (Ret) J. Talbot Manvel, Jr. and David Perin, "Christened by Champagne, Challenged by Cost," U.S. Naval Institute *Proceedings* 140 (May 2014), 42–7; and Ronald O'Rourke, *Navy Ford (CVN-78) Class Aircraft Carrier Program: Background and Issues for Congress*, RS20643 (Washington, DC: Congressional Research Service (CRS), September 16, 2014 and subsequent editions). On U.S. Navy carrier employment, force structure, and acquisition, see Statement of the Honorable Sean J. Stackley, Vice Admiral John C. Aquilino, Rear Admiral Thomas J. Moore, and Rear Admiral Michael C. Manazir before the Readiness Subcommittee and Seapower and Projection Forces Subcommittee of the House Armed Services Committee on *The Navy's Aircraft Carrier Program*, (Washington DC: November 3, 2015). See also Seth Cropsey, Bryan G. McGrath and Timothy A. Walton, *Sharpening the Spear: The Carrier, the Joint Force, and High-End Conflict* (Washington DC: Hudson Institute, October 2015); and Dr. Henry Hendrix, "*Retreat from Range: The Rise and Fall of Carrier Aviation*," (Washington DC: Center for a New American Security, October 2015).

150 Ronald O'Rourke, *Navy DDG-51 and DDG-1000 Destroyer Programs: Background and Issues for Congress*, RL 32109 (Washington, DC: Library of Congress Congressional Research Service (CRS), July 31, 2014 and subsequent editions). Also Richard R. Burgess, "Big Ship, Small Complement," *Seapower* 57 (December 2014), 30–3.

151 On unmanned vehicles, see CAPT George Galdorisi USN (Ret), "Keeping Humans in the Loop," U.S. Naval Institute *Proceedings* 141 (February 2015), 36–41.

152 See MC2 Justin Johndro USN, "Development Squadron 5 Receives First Unmanned Undersea Vehicle," NNS140828-17, Navy News Service (August 29, 2014).

153 For an analysis, see Ronald O'Rourke, *Navy Littoral Combat Ship (LCS) Program: Background and Issues for Congress*, RL33741 (Washington, DC: Congressional Research Service (CRS), August 4, 2014 and subsequent editions). See also Gregory V. Cox, "Lessons Learned from the LCS," U.S. Naval Institute *Proceedings* 141 (January 2015), 36–40. For an argument that the U.S. Navy requires a dedicated mine countermeasures ship, see Peter von Bleichart, "It's Time for the MCM (X)," U.S. Naval Institute *Proceedings* 141 (February 2015), 1. Note that the Navy has recently announced that it will redesignate its Littoral Combat Ships (LCS) as Frigates (FF). See Leigh Munsil, "Mabus: LCS to be Re-designated a Frigate," *Politico* (January 15, 2015). For a view of what these frigates might look like, see Kris Osborn, "Frigate is a More Survivable and Lethal Variant of the Littoral Combat Ship" (SCOUT.COM: November 3, 2015).

154 For a discussion of the EPF (formerly designated the Joint High Speed Vessel (JHSV), see Daniel P. Taylor, "New Ship on the Block," *Seapower* 56 (August 2013), 38–9.

155 Ronald O'Rourke, *Navy LX(R) Amphibious Ship Program: Program: Background and Issues for Congress*, R43543 (Washington, DC: Library of Congress Congressional Research Service (CRS), October 22, 2014 and subsequent editions).

156 On the ESD, formerly designated the Mobile Landing Platform (MLP), see Gidget Fuentes, "Proof of Concept," *Seapower* 57 (December 2014), 42–4.

157 See Team Ships Public Affairs, "Fabrication Begins on the Navy's First Ship to Shore Connector," NNS14117-14, Navy News Service (November 17, 2014); and Otto Kreisher, "Moving Ship to Shore," *Seapower* (May/June 2014), 12–14.

158 See Hunter Keeter, "'Gas, Guns and Groceries': Shaping the 21st-Century Combat Logistics Force," *Seapower* (May/June 2014), 16–18; and Ronald O'Rourke, *Navy TAO(X) Oiler Shipbuilding Program: Background and Issues for Congress*, R43546 (Washington, DC: Library of Congress Congressional Research Service (CRS), August 1, 2014 and subsequent editions).

159 See Richard Whittle, "Navy Decides to Buy V-22 Ospreys for Carrier Delivery," *Breaking Defense* (January 13, 2015). See also Daniel Goure, "The Great COD Debate," U.S. Naval Institute *Proceedings* 140 (September 2014), 36–41.

160 See Ronald O'Rourke, *Navy Shipboard Lasers for Surface, Air, and Missile Defense: Background and Issues for Congress* (Washington, DC: Congressional Research Service (CRS), July 31, 2014 and subsequent editions). See also David Smalley, "Historic Leap: Navy Shipboard Laser Operates in Arabian Gulf," NNS141210-02, Navy News Service (December 10, 2014).

161 On the rail gun, see Dan Goure, *U.S. Navy Pursuing its Own Offset Strategy led by the Rail Gun* (Washington, DC: Lexington Institute, February 9, 2015).

162 See Ronald O'Rourke, *Virginia (SSN-774) Class Attack Submarine Procurement: Background and Issues for Congress*, RL 32418 (Washington, DC: Congressional Research Service (CRS), July 31, 2014 and subsequent editions); and Ronald O'Rourke, *Navy DDG-51 and DDG-1000 Destroyer Programs: Background and Issues for Congress*, RL 32109 (Washington, DC: Congressional Research Service (CRS), July 31, 2014 and subsequent editions). For concern that the future submarine program is nowhere near robust enough, See Seth Cropsey, "A Naval Disaster in the Making: The Misbegotten Plan to Shrink the U.S. Submarine Fleet," *Weekly Standard* (October 6, 2014). For a study of U.S. Navy amphibious warfare ships and alternatives, see Maren Leed, *Amphibious Shipping Shortfalls: Risks and Opportunities to Bridge the Gap* (Washington, DC: Center for Strategic and International Studies (CSIS), September 8, 2014).

163 On the SSC, see "Statement by Secretary Hagel on the Littoral Combat ship" (Washington, DC: Department of Defense, December 11, 2014).

164 For recent scholarship on American defense spending, see Rebecca U. Thorpe, *The American Warfare State: The Domestic Politics of Military Spending* (Chicago: University of Chicago Press, 2014).

165 See Jim Garamone, "Greenert Details Navy's Fiscal 2014 Budget Realities" (Washington, DC: American Forces Press Service, September 5, 2013).

166 Admiral Greenert described the U.S. Navy's budget submission for Fiscal Year (FY) 2015, as well as the Navy's situation following the budget uncertainly in FY 2013, the Bipartisan Budget Act of 2013 (BBA) and the National Defense Authorization Act (NDAA) for FY 2014 in *Statement of Admiral Jonathan Greenert, U.S. Navy, Chief of Naval Operations before the House Armed Services Committee, on FY 2015 Department of the Navy Posture, 12 March 2014* (Washington, DC: Office of the Chief of Naval Information, March 12, 2014). He discussed the budget several months later in "Charting the Navy's Future." For subsequent Department of Defense views on the state of the U.S. defense budget, see Deputy Secretary of Defense Robert O. Work, "Remarks Delivered at the CSIS Global Security Forum 2014 "(Washington, DC: Center for Strategic and International Studies (CSIS), November 12, 2014). For the concerns of several retired U.S. Navy admirals and two retired U.S. Marine Corps generals that the U.S. Navy is now underfunded and over-extended, see "Letter from Flag/General Officers to Congress from 'NavyNow'," Information Dissemination Blog (November 12, 2014), www.informationdissemination.net/2014/11/letter-from-flaggeneral-officers-to.html, accessed August 28, 2015. A dispassionate analysis is in *Long-Term Implications of the 2015 Future Years Defense Program* (Washington, DC: Congressional Budget Office, November 2014). See also *Growth in DoD's Budget from 2000 to 2014* (Washington, DC: Congressional Budget Office, November 2014).

167 For an argument that the U.S. Navy must reconsider its over-arching design strategy for new ships and aircraft – or risk drastic reduction in both – see CAPT Arthur H. Barber III (Ret), "Rethinking the Future Fleet," U.S. Naval Institute *Proceedings* 140 (May 2014), 48–53.

18

HAVING TO "MAKE DO"

U.S. Navy and Marine Corps strategic options in the twenty-first century

Sarandis ('Randy') Papadopoulos[1]

The second decade of the century confronts American military and naval forces with a different set of challenges than those of the previous ten years. Public support to confront terrorism, on the scale that followed the 9/11 attacks, has receded. Instead, that challenge is now the province of intelligence agencies and the U.S. military's potent, but numerically small, Special Operations Forces. Conversely, the potential for national rivalry, even warfare, seems to be increasing, with challenges to America spanning the heart and east coasts of Asia.[2] That the oceans adjoining those regions include a main artery of world trade makes the challenge only more difficult, with analyst Daniel Gouré's words best capturing their magnitude: "the end of history is over."[3]

This chapter's frame is rooted in historical works, balanced against U.S. government finances. It draws from the writing of Carl von Clausewitz to portray the Navy and Marine Corps as the maritime means needed to fulfill U.S. presidents' political ends. Fundamentally, it attempts to show how the devil truly is in the details, for any current discussion must be rooted in the specifics of twenty-first-century U.S. federal politics, especially finances. That condition stems from how government resources shape what forces and equipment the Navy and Marine Corps can create.[4] These problems are not new, having been confronted by the sea services after the end of the Vietnam War in 1975.[5] But the chapter's bias, to favor the "with what?" question of strategy, that is force structure and equipment, as opposed to questions of where and why American force will be used, is here because the country's present-day politics demands such an awareness.

America and seapower theory

As a guide to maritime strategy more focused than Clausewitz's *On War*, in this author's opinion the *Cooperative Strategy for 21st Century Seapower* best explains the foreseeable roles of American sea services.[6] Its durability stems from including a complete list of missions to deter or counter threats and emphasis on the human parts of strategy, specifically trust and cooperation. The 2007 document is also unconstrained by the need to address a specific opponent, to manage short-term fiscal limits, or balance specific concerns raised by the two wars taking place during its 2006–7 composition. In turn, it conforms to the words of naval theorist Julian Corbett:

> History shows that the actual functions of the fleet (except in purely maritime wars) have been threefold:–

1. The furtherance or hindrance of military operations ashore.
2. The protection or destruction of commerce.
3. The prevention or securing of alliances (i.e., deterring or persuading neutrals as to participating in the war).[7]

Such ideas had already entered American maritime thinking before the September 11, 2001 attacks in New York, Pennsylvania, and Virginia. Earlier U.S. writings such as … *From the Sea* and *Forward … From the Sea* had echoed Corbett, admittedly with variations and sometimes contradicting one another, in relating how to manage or deter conflict and wage war.[8]

Given that durable context, short of America withdrawing from the world in a manner not seen since the 1930s, and arguably before 1898, the future U.S. Navy and Marine Corps will continue to play the roles listed in the *Cooperative Strategy for 21st Century Seapower*. Readers will note that document emphasizes the peacetime commitments of the sea services. For most of their history, the United States Marine Corps and Navy have deployed globally in peace to protect American interests and citizens, emphasize diplomacy by deterring opponents, shape regional politics, and support allies.[9] Of acute importance, current-day Navy and Marine Corps forces take part in multinational exercises which build skills as well as trust between different national forces.[10] Drawing again from Clausewitz, these acts serve political ends, using military power as a means. But deploying naval forces *en masse* also taxes resources, people, equipment and money, which must be considered.[11]

Money and naval strategy

Managing strategy is bluntly complex today due to the state of American political economy. In the parlance of military planners, money has become *the* "forcing function." The central problem facing the two services is that their commitments seem slated to grow, even as available money falls. The much-discussed 2012 "rebalance" to Asia reflects making a choice to deal with challenges, yet itself opens demands for resources.[12] As context for how hard such choices are, when the Cold War ended professionals in the United States and other Western militaries had difficulty adjusting to "low-intensity" post-1989 conflicts, in the former Yugoslavia, Somalia, Rwanda, Afghanistan, and Iraq.[13] The current world is arguably more threatening, making today's military challenges harder to surmount.

Despite the supporting context of theory, then, scholars – and military planners – are compelled to respect U.S. government fiscal politics. In 2015, the American federal government no longer holds the bipartisan consensus on international affairs it did in the half-century of the Cold War. Political redefinition since 1980, with each American region typically bound to just one political party, makes compromise harder to achieve.[14] This divisiveness stands in sharp contrast to U.S. military leaders, who for example readily *and unanimously* accepted the Obama administration's 2012 "rebalance" to Asia. Instead, American conservatives and liberals share few political reasons to differentiate between defense spending and money for other programs, a condition making the crafting of strategy harder.

Fundamentally, U.S. military choices are shown by government dollar flows.[15] All Navy and Marine Corps equipment purchases, maintenance, and deployments overseas shape what is termed their "force structure." Force structure therefore provides the medium through which strategic choices, at the national level, most clearly appear. Parenthetically, it is also why Congress mandates the Department of the Defense submit 30-year plans for both shipbuilding and aircraft purchases.[16] Broadly, today's choices mean the future U.S. Marine Corps and Navy will cover the same regional responsibilities as they do today, but using slimmer resources. In terms of classical strategic thinking, the ends which the sea services of the United States seek to match will not change, but the means available to fulfill them will decline.

This condition results from continuous political trade-offs, and represents more than preserving American social welfare programs (for example, national health care) instead of defense, or exchanging guns for butter.[17] Rather, the American political process biases compensation for service members of the "All-Volunteer Force," as well as keeping bases in Congressional districts, rather building force size, funding maintenance, or buying equipment.[18] Not choosing to maintain a larger Navy and Marine Corps by holding down pay, the U.S. government indirectly pressures the services to shrink, yet without altering their missions. The same limit prevents the services from spending money on maintaining equipment.[19] Those constraints compel a different type of cost cutting, because they keep the Defense Department spending money on overhead. In that light, the most straightforward way to balance the ledger is for the U.S. Defense Department to cut forces evenly across each part of the globe.

These provisos mean high-priority arenas, such as the Arabian Gulf, face cuts at the same time as less-threatening regions, including Latin America and Africa. The cuts also reduce every armed service, so that the fewer Navy ships match a smaller Air Force as well as lower-strength Marine Corps and Army. Chopping money arbitrarily prevents prioritizing more central missions, builds in less flexibility to the force, and risks under-resourcing the most dangerous global regions to preserve balance.[20] The Defense Department has increased deployment times overseas to increase the capacity of the armed services, but at the expense of straining its people and their equipment.

Cutting money evenly also makes staffing of military units harder, undercuts battle-worthiness and limits the quantity and safety of the equipment used.[21] The sea services face rigid expenses which shape strategic choices, for warships and aircraft cost much to buy, need long times to create, and require constant maintenance. Past experience in the 1970s shows how pay and benefits for the Navy and Marine Corps can consume a large portion of their budget.[22] At that time, matching the Soviet Union demanded a national shift in investment, one made only after 1978. Similarly, over the decade between now and the year 2025, and including health care, personnel costs seem poised to compel cuts in force structure and equipment. Even so, such reductions would be best met within the theoretical framework of the *Cooperative Strategy for 21st Century Seapower*.

The final pressure on resources for the sea services stems from the past 13 years of war. In terms of measuring U.S. government choices, it is clear that lower investment in ships paid many of the bills for the Navy and Marine Corps' shares of wars in Afghanistan and Iraq. The historic budget levels for the post-9/11 Department of the Navy show that wartime money went to operations, maintenance and pay (see Table 18.1).

Despite higher wartime spending, the money went for ammunition, fuel, ground vehicles, equipment repairs, civilian pay, and contractors.[23] Over a decade of war, Navy procurement grew by over 50 percent in constant dollars, but shipbuilding money fell, even though sorely needed after the relatively lean 1990s, and just recovered value by the decade's end. Military pay cost one quarter more, despite the Navy cutting its number of uniformed personnel by 15 percent.[24] More grimly, warship costs always rise faster than the general inflation rate, meaning that over time the smaller dollars bought still fewer hulls.[25] Aircraft spending, including helicopters and unmanned systems used in the two conflicts did rise steeply in the 2000s, but on a smaller base. One should note that the total funding included so-called "Overseas Contingency Operations" money, non-renewable appropriations.[26] Operating globally against a diffuse enemy, while equipping and paying the Marine Corps and Navy, demanded more money than did buying major weapon systems.

Table 18.1 DON Total Obligational Authority by account and fiscal year (in constant FY 2012 $million)

	2001	2002	2003	2004	2005	2006	2007	2008	2009	2010	2011	2012
Shipbuilding	15,114	11,466	10,987	13,462	11,977	12,893	11,257	14,376	13,993	14,561	15,879	15,178
Aircraft	10,213	9,913	10,737	10,878	10,505	11,598	13,215	17,191	15,899	20,848	17,841	18,469
Procurement (including above)	28,916	30,718	31,537	33,562	33,535	34,907	37,330	41,646	43,351	45,832	45,430	43,779
Operations and maintenance	41,096	43,950	50,553	50,453	48,270	50,344	50,480	53,863	55,800	57,001	58,859	59,196
Active pay	37,982	41,228	47,378	47,170	49,449	48,192	46,686	48,780	48,961	49,655	50,787	46,551

Source
Department of the Navy, FY 2013 Budget Estimates Budget Data Book (Washington, DC: May 2012), at www.finance.hq.navy.mil/FMB/13pres/FY13_
DataBook.pdf, p. 4.6, accessed July 3, 2014.

Ultimately, the wartime costs since 2001 have built a significant problem for today's Navy and Marine Corps as the Iraq and Afghanistan wars wind down: how to recapitalize their most capable and expensive systems when the U.S. government lacks the money to do so. Adding yet more pressure, the U.S. Navy is about to start buying 12 ballistic missile submarines (SSBNs). Needed for strategic deterrence, these ships will demand half the shipbuilding budget for a decade. High-end forces are in shortest supply, aging, and hardest to obtain, yet are the most needed.

Again, amidst these declining resources, the present and near-future will see the U.S. shift to confronting more muscular challengers, meaning potentially deadlier ones. Moreover, military spending among the closest allies of the United States, in NATO and the Pacific, is falling, even as the rest of the world continues a decade-long rise.[27] In large measure this explains Chief of Naval Operations Jonathan Greenert's emphasis since taking office in 2011 on "warfighting first."[28] In the professional mindset of naval officers, combat against a similar opponent, a peer competitor, is the most dangerous scenario they can imagine. Focusing on warfighting allows the Navy's top admiral to get as much capability out of his force as possible.

The missed peer competitor

China's prospective rise to become the world's largest economy by the end of this decade broadens the challenge. "Soft power," economic and social influence, and a key American strength in the past, will now partly rest in a rival's hands, one also possessing considerable "hard power" military force.[29] Economic influence in a highly globalized world marked by rapid trade flows may make military action more difficult, even when central national interests are challenged. Worse still, the military hardware of China and other rising states is sophisticated and widely available for sale. This development compels "resetting" to higher-end military equipment and methods, as well as other changes in naval behavior.[30] The pending transition thus prompts a sense of crisis, although some scholars argue U.S. interpretations of the ambitions of China are overblown.[31] Now, dealing with a "near-peer competitor," a nation able to challenge American power on its own terms, or with its sophisticated weapons sold to other states or even non-state actors to create "anti-access/area-denial" (A2/AD) networks, demands ruthless focus on sophisticated capabilities.[32]

How did prospects of a rising peer get overlooked? The answer, it seems, lies in the obscure post-Cold War security environment. On one hand the early 1990s saw predictions of a non-Clausewitzian era, marked by decentralization of armed forces akin to the Palestinian *intifada*'s challenge to Israel.[33] In the absence of a state opponent, this argument went, non-state actors, even corporations, would employ force at levels hitherto reserved for governments. Indeed pre-1991 history suggested that path had been chosen by non-state groups in the Arab world, in the aftermath of national armies failing to defeat both Israel and the United States.[34] Before the 9/11 attacks, strategy discussions spoke of the U.S. maintaining military dominance with allies or coalitions supporting American goals to maintain global order.[35]

Post-Cold War popular culture deflected attention, giving a resurgent Japan the role as successor threat to America in novels and films such as Michael Crichton's 1992 *Rising Sun*. That story became only the first positing an earnest yet corrupt East Asian economic, technology, and security power threatening a weak America, with other cultural artifacts such as *Johnny Mnemonic* and *RoboCop III* echoing the message.[36] Together, they heightened perceptions that only peer competitors employing a type of American-style capitalism would challenge it. Only Tom Clancy chose to add a naval dimension to these fictional excursions, in 1994 positing a somewhat bizarre war between the United States and Japan in his novel *Debt of Honor*.[37]

Reality proved different, however, as the People's Republic of China created continuous economic growth after 1991. From the perspective of the early 1990s, China seemed destined for economic expansion, but within strict limits of global resources, especially of food and energy.[38] The scale, duration, and success of its economic revolution were therefore not broadly foreseen, at least before 1996.[39] In retrospect, the growth's cause was no accident: it had relied upon oceanic trade. As collective portions of the East Asian and Pacific economies, international trade – most of it carried by sea – nearly doubled in value to become 87 percent of those countries' Gross Domestic Products.[40] Militarily, the potential of the People's Republic of China to tackle the U.S. Navy remained likewise unanticipated until 1996's Third Taiwan Strait Crisis.[41]

The setting's consequences for naval operations

In maritime terms, these changes mean the U.S. Navy and Marine Corps must prepare to face challenges up to and including a continental peer state integrated into the global economy.[42] This nature suggests that an easy solution, relying on maritime force to create a low-cost and simple isolation of enemies, is misleading.[43] Twentieth-century history shows how difficult such efforts were, and the twenty-first century has accelerated the importance of globalized flows of trade and money.[44] Land-based opponents and neutral nations have too many ways to work around embargoes. Historically, Britain's Royal Navy briefly attempted "economic warfare" in the initial days of the First World War, but its linking of naval and economic (especially financial) power almost ruined the global economy.[45] Any future military effort to restrain major powers economically will require so much multinational coordination that such measures alone are unlikely to halt a peer-competitor's actions, or could prove globally ruinous.

Recent history has shown naval blockades working best when facing relatively weaker powers, a product of several factors emergent since 1991. Pre-eminently, late in the century international finance expanded more than trade in goods, and stopping the movement of money is difficult. The global economy has also made trade in raw materials more fungible. In particular, petroleum cargoes often shift ownership more than once during their voyage on board a tanker. When matched by a new prevalence of just-in-time delivery of manufactured goods, trade controls became complex. Consequently, maritime embargoes just were effective against non-maritime powers such as Iraq and the former Yugoslavia during the 1990s.[46]

Operating with a smaller U.S. Navy and Marine Corps, or losing global influence?

What, then, will the smaller U.S. Marine Corps and Navy look like in 10 or 15 years? After the Afghanistan war the Marine Corps plans to shed 20,000 personnel, to total 182,000 Marines, but may drop to 174,000 or even 155,000 members.[47] Those goals will be met by lower recruiting, or by early retirements. As a result of the Benghazi consulate attack of 2012, Marines will more often serve as diplomatic guards, pulling some strength away from forces afloat. Such cuts might compel deploying smaller groups than Marine Expeditionary Units (MEUs). Instead of deploying all 2,200 MEU personnel – an infantry battalion, vehicles, aircraft and headquarters, and carried on three Navy amphibious ships – the Marine Corps could deploy individual companies.[48] Smaller forces would fulfill more discreet missions than those needing a full MEU, yet larger than those performed by Navy SEALs or Marine Corps Force Reconnaissance units. The Navy's Joint High Speed Vessels are useful to deliver forces in such numbers.

Employing smaller units will compel tighter integration with the U.S. Navy, and after more than 12 years of land wars the Marine Corps wants to cleave more closely to its maritime roots. It has also proposed to deal with challenges through a joint Navy–Marine Corps concept called "Single Naval Battle."[49] The exploitation of more than one "domain," air, sea and land environments, especially in a littoral context, highlights maneuvering to counter complex operational problems. Rather than hit opposing strength head on, this reasoning goes, exploiting other domains allows flanking moves. The idea is not wholly new to Corps thinking, as shown in its "Operational Maneuver from the Sea" in the late twentieth century.[50] But under Single Naval Battle the Marine Corps has developed methods to play a unique role during future medium- and large-scale operations.[51]

Discussions regarding the Marine Corps admit that high-end wars are not the sole mission for which it must prepare. Given their lengthy service waging counterinsurgency campaigns (over one third of the period since 1900), the Marine Corps could customize its force structure for the "small wars" mission.[52] Or, if the world's politics fragment, the Marine Corps could reinforce its capabilities to meet the need for missions as diplomatic guards, for humanitarian assistance, non-combatant evacuations, and managing the threat of weapons of mass destruction inside the United States.[53] These moves make disaggregation the centerpiece of the Marine Corps. Admittedly, they would move the Marine Corps farther away from the Navy and the amphibious warfare mission, but they could be performed by roughly 160,000 personnel.

For the U.S. Navy disaggregation is different. Since 1990 its ships have more often operated independently, lacking reason to mass in the absence of a blue-water competitor, while covering more locations. For example, and despite being attached to the *George Washington* (CVN-73) carrier battle group, in October 2000 the destroyer *Cole* (DDG-67) made the entire voyage from the American east coast to the port of Aden, Yemen on its own.[54] The aircraft carrier and other ships had arrived in the region earlier, then rushed to help the destroyer after the suicidal terrorist attack had killed 17 of its crew. The twenty-first-century need to cover all parts of the globe spreads U.S. naval power more thinly, while driving the navy to build smaller vessels, most notably its frigates, formerly referred to as Littoral Combat Ships.[55]

In parallel, Navy combat power is decentralizing. While the striking power of its 1980s fleet lay in aircraft carriers, sometimes grouped, other systems now complement them. Each of the 2014 Navy's 88 cruisers and destroyers, and nuclear attack submarines, carry Tomahawk Land Attack Missiles, able to deliver accurate firepower up to 650 nautical miles away.[56] They mean the service's 10 aircraft carriers are supplemented by over 140 other ships which can hit targets ashore. The cruisers' and destroyers' Aegis systems are also the core of the Navy's defense against air and missile threats.[57] To redistribute its airborne reconnaissance and combat capacity, the Navy plans to spread manned aircraft and, significantly, unmanned platforms to ships across the fleet.[58] While dependent upon sensors and data networks, these changes promise to make the fleet operate as an entity even if geographically dispersed.[59]

For the Navy, changing how it deploys also reflects the threat accurate weapons pose to the survival of its ships and planes. Accurate missiles, when integrated with radar and other sensors, become anti-access/area denial complexes, limiting the entry and maneuver of naval and air forces.[60] Such threats are illustrated by the 2006 damage inflicted on the Israeli Navy corvette *Hanit*, hit off the Lebanese coast by a missile fired from shore by the Hezbollah organization.[61] Diffusion of such accurate weapons, even in small numbers, forces the Navy to use its ships differently, dispersing and operating at greater distances for their own protection. These systems, grouped together, pose such difficult threats to American military power that all U.S. services are bundling their efforts through the operational concept known as Air–Sea Battle.[62]

Table 18.2 Declining navies in history

How they were created/sustained	How achieved	Global navy example of achievement	How lost	Global navy example of loss
National economic base	Develop symbiotic relationship with national commerce/industry	United States: steel industry, late nineteenth century	Navy no longer seen as essential for commerce or industry	Holland: attempted commercial dominance without maintaining navy, 1700s
Adequate national financial structure	Perceived efficient steward of funds in period of responsible national fiscal policy	Great Britain: balance of affordable ship readiness during the eighteenth century	Inefficient use of funding overshadows routine budget process	Spain: misdirected spending depleted treasury, ruined credit, 1580s–1600s
Support of national leadership	Establish naval strategy/policy to support political goals/national interests	United States: Maritime Strategy, 1980s	Unable to provide relevance rationale in national global strategy and policy	United Kingdom, post-1945: RN unable to argue relevance in decolonization
Able naval leadership with strategic vision and operational expertise	Strong emphasis on education at all levels, training for global operations	United States: post-Second World War	Low education/process investment, retrenchment in overseas operations	France: eliminates naval leadership, 1790s
Technology adequate to create effective naval systems	Investment in technology suitable to achieve operational goals	Great Britain pre-1815: shipbuilding adequate, not innovative	Unneeded technology bought at cost of systems needed that meet operational goals	France, 1800: better ships, unable to produce/sustain/train adequate navy

Source
Table courtesy of U.S. Naval History and Heritage Command.

The foregoing suggests the sea services are prone to particular stresses not seen in land or air forces. Five important nodes are key to creating a worldwide naval power: the industrial base needed to build one, the national financial base, commitment of national politicians, a strategic vision to commit the force effectively, and appropriate technology. These are all fragile characteristics, readily lost if inapt choices are made. Table 18.2 illustrates cases where naval services enjoyed success in gaining these inputs, and other examples where they were lost. Without effectively managing these characteristics, the U.S. Navy and Marine Corps will decline in the same manner as earlier sea services.

Since 1948 the U.S. Navy has mainly deployed to two regional hubs, one always off East Asia. The other cruised the Mediterranean, until the 1990s; since then an Indian Ocean commitment has replaced it. Marine Corps units have continuously remained afloat with these forces. These pairs of locations remained consistent, even during the Korean, Vietnam, 1991 Gulf and post-2001 wars. During them, the U.S. Marine Corps sent one third of its total forces to combat in specific areas, but their sea-borne deployments remained forward in the Navy's two regional hubs. Smaller crises have, exceptionally, made forces swing between regions, but the centerpiece Navy and Marine Corps mission, "forward presence" chiefly for deterrence and reassurance, has remained.[63] Given the very high cost of sustaining these fleets – one third of the Navy ships at all times – couldn't a change in naval strategy repair the fiscal challenge confronting the sea services?

In 2009, the staff of the Chief of Naval Operations asked the Center for Naval Analyses (CNA) to measure the effect of overstretching the U.S. Navy, either regionally or by number of missions. The timing was key: the U.S. was in its ninth year of the war against terrorism, fighting in Afghanistan, Iraq, and elsewhere, for which the Navy had contributed thousands of sailors each year for shore duty. These demands drew heavily upon Navy readiness. In its report *The Navy at a Tipping Point: Maritime Dominance at Stake?*, CNA also suggested what alternative deployment patterns to the two forward presence hubs might exist, and what improvement, if any, such changes might make to the future condition of the Navy.[64]

The CNA analysts highlighted five patterns to balance the demand for Navy forces (the Marine Corps was not included) with numbers and their readiness. They used three measures of the Navy – its potential to dominate opponents, readiness for operations, and ability to influence in peace and war – to assess the longer-term viability of the service.[65] The five Navy options, strategic choices which could be made by the U.S. government, are summarized as follows:

1 It could continue operating the Navy in two hubs with combat-credible forces, performing its past roles, but ultimately ruining its readiness and ending its engagement of allies.
2 The U.S. could reduce the Navy's commitment to support just one combat-credible hub, preserving readiness but writing off a combat commitment to either East Asia or the Arabian Gulf.
3 The Navy could become a "shaping" force, working to engage with allies but solely to support maritime constabulary missions, and not creating a combat-credible force fit for war.
4 The U.S. could bring home the Navy, reserving its use to "surging" to crises, but limiting the service's ability to engage with allies or partners and robbing it of influence in peacetime.
5 The Navy could gradually reduce its strength everywhere, stretching its readiness, perhaps breaking its units, and forcing it to accept higher risk to its smaller forces if they entered combat.[66]

It is worth noting that the *Navy at a Tipping Point* considers the last option the worst, as it creates a Navy unsuited to war, lacking readiness, and without ability to shape peacetime events. Consonant with the beliefs of serving members of the U.S. Navy, the fleet reduced by "salami-slicing" fails to meet all three tests for a global navy.[67] It is also the result if no other strategic choice is made.

Between the Scylla of high operational demands and Charybdis of resource shortfalls, could these Navy options be combined? Can any move lower risk, allowing the sea services to bridge needed peacetime capabilities with maintaining their forces' readiness? To this author there are parallel approaches, most notably the "Forward Partnering" coined by Frank Hoffman.[68] And while beyond the ability of U.S. military services to compel their government to rely on its allies, the Marine Corps and Navy can show what friendly services can offer.

Lest critics assume American allies bring little of consequence to the naval equation, consider Table 18.3, relating to the historic sizes of such fleets. Clearly, most allied fleets have shrunk in

Table 18.3 Destroyers and frigates in allied navies: Cold War to 2009

	1988/1989	1998/1999	2008/2009	Projected Aegis ships 2020 (includes USN cruisers)
USA	164	99	73	88
UK	49	35	25	–
France	41	39	31	–
Canada	23	17	15	–
Germany	24	15	15	–
Denmark	18	8	7	–
Netherlands	16	16	7	–
Italy	20	22	14	–
Norway	5	4	4	5
Spain	21	17	11	5
Australia	12	11	12	3
Japan	61	57	53	8
South Korea	29	34	44	9

Sources

U.S. Naval History and Heritage Command www.history.navy.mil/branches/org9-4.htm#1993, accessed May 22, 2014, and IISS *Military Balance*, various years.

the past generation, but they also continue to share sizeable portions of the globe's naval power, much of it suited to the most stressful scenario, combat. Drawing from the table, allies have double the number of surface combatants of the U.S. fleet. At the high end of naval capabilities, the Aegis sensor and battle management tool – so good it is being deployed ashore as well as at sea – is shared, and five allied navies' systems will soon match one third the numbers available on U.S. Navy ships. More broadly, all these navies can automatically exchange data with one another through the Link 11 system, and use the CENTRIXS network to share classified information.[69] Crucially, their professionals understand one another, sharing tactics and logistics standards, created under NATO sponsorship, to operate together at sea. Allowing ships from most of these navies to deploy with a U.S. aircraft carrier strike group regularly, these capabilities are far in advance of what allied armies can swap. They are backed by a community of practice reflecting professional trust built over decades.

As added evidence of this trust, four navies (the Royal Australian, Royal Canadian, Royal Netherlands and U.S.) employ the same submarine torpedo (the Mark 48), while all 13 of them use the same family of surface- and helicopter-launched undersea weapons (the Mark 46/50/54). Almost every one of them also operates the RGM-84 Harpoon surface-to-surface missile or variants of Standard (the SM-series) surface-to-air missiles. And these weapons are sold by the United States to friendly navies in fully capable form, not down-rated "export versions" of some land and air systems, meaning that they are the world's best guided weapons of their type. Their routine deployment by different nationalities, without difficulty, represents a minor triumph of negotiation and the interaction of two generations of naval officers and their political leaders.

Conclusion

Managing the contemporary world's oceanic and littoral trials pushes the U.S. Marine Corps and Navy into navigating through a complex universe, problems which are intimately linked to America's emergence from 13 years of land wars. But for the sea services, future failure in peacetime to commit their forces overseas could build regional instabilities. Conversely, deploy too many of their units, or for too long, and their ships and planes cease to function, and personnel will quit serving. Yet if they are sent overseas in times of crisis in too small numbers, war might result because they constitute an adequate deterrent or might even be defeated in combat. These corollaries are not easy to reconcile, yet absent their settlement the services could break or war could result.

To this author the resources to manage the globe's oceans and littoral regions by the U.S. Navy and Marine Corps are going to be scarce for the foreseeable future. American political leaders are unable to pay for the force levels needed to accomplish unilaterally such a goal. But the attributes the sea services offer – persistent engagement, scalable response, operational maneuver, and strong relations with allied navies – could be turned into the capital needed to balance the strategy–resources equation. The alternative they offer is preferable to any other defense structure choice currently on the table. It remains to be seen whether these elements are seized upon to help create a durable good order at sea and ashore.

Notes

1   The opinions expressed here are those of the author and should not be construed as those of the Department of the Navy, Department of Defense, or of the United States government.
2   This chapter was begun before the 2014 crisis in Ukraine, although those events had been partly presaged by the 2008 Russia–Georgia War.
3   Daniel Gouré, "Robert Work's Really Big Challenge," *Real Clear Defense* (February 8, 2014), at www.realcleardefense.com/articles/2014/02/08/robert_works_really_big_challenge_107078.html, accessed July 8, 2014.
4   Mark Mandeles, *The Future of War: Organizations as Weapons* (Washington, DC, 2005). As the two services submit their budgets together, this discussion necessarily includes the U.S. Marine Corps.
5   See Steven Miller and Stephan Van Evera (eds.), *Naval Strategy and National Security* (Princeton, 1988), Keith Dunn and William Staudenmaier, *Strategic Implications of the Continental–Maritime Debate* (New York, 1984), and Andrew Krepinevich, Simon Chin, and Todd Harrison, *Strategy in Austerity* (Washington, DC, 2012), at www.csbaonline.org/publications/2012/06/strategy-in-austerity/, accessed August 14, 2014.
6   The 2007 version is at www.navy.mil/maritime/maritimestrategy.pdf, accessed February 24, 2014. For discussion and critique of it see Robert Rubel, "The New Maritime Strategy: The Rest of the Story," *Naval War College Review* (Spring 2008), 69–78, Karl Walling, "Why a Conversation with the Country? A Backward Look at Some Forward-Thinking Maritime Strategists," *JFQ* (Summer 2008), 130–9, and Robert Work and Jan van Tol, *A Cooperative Strategy for 21st Century Seapower: An Assessment* (Washington, DC, March 26, 2008).
7   Taken from the "Green Pamphlet" in Julian Corbett, *Some Principles of Maritime Strategy*, Eric Grove (ed.) (Annapolis, MD, 1988), 336.
8   These documents are respectively at www.navy.mil/navydata/policy/fromsea/fromsea.txt and www.dtic.mil/jv2010/navy/b014.pdf, both accessed April 11, 2014. They echo analyst Samuel Huntington's 1954 essay "National Policy and the Transoceanic Navy," USNI *Proceedings* 80:5 (May 1954), especially 489–91. In the author's experience, Huntington's essay is the most-cited theoretical source cited within U.S. Navy circles.
9   See the forthcoming work by Peter Swartz, *Sea Changes: Transforming U.S. Naval Deployment Strategy* (Alexandria, VA, 2016), Stephen Brooks, G. John Ikenberry, and William Wohlforth, "Don't Come Home America: The Case against Retrenchment," *International Security* (Winter 2012), 7–51, and Andrew Krepinevich and Robert Work, *A New US Global Defense Posture for the Second Transoceanic Era* (Washington, DC, 2007).
10   See S. Papadopoulos, "The Combined Framework: How Naval Powers Deal with Military Operations Other than War," in Gary E. Weir and Sandra Doyle (eds.), *You Cannot Surge Trust: Combined Naval Operations of the Royal Australian Navy, Canadian Navy, Royal Navy, and the United States Navy, 1991–2003* (Washington, DC, 2013), 8–10.

11 Several contrary views inform the following. See Commander Salamander, "When Your Buzzword Becomes Your Punchline," at http://cdrsalamander.blogspot.com/2014/07/when-your-buzzword-becomes-punchline.html and Claude Berube, "A Rose by Any Other Name Still has Thorns: A Global Network of Navies," at http://warontherocks.com/2014/07/a-rose-by-any-other-name-still-has-thorns-a-global-network-of-navies/, both accessed July 17, 2014. For a counterpoint see Robert Farley, "Managing the United States' Global Naval Partnerships," July 10, 2014 at http://thediplomat.com/2014/07/managing-the-united-states-global-naval-partnerships/, accessed July 23, 2014.

12 Department of Defense, *Sustaining U.S. Global Leadership: Priorities for 21st Century Defense* (Washington, DC, January 2012), 2, at www.defense.gov/news/defense_strategic_guidance.pdf, accessed July 28, 2014, Admiral Jonathan Greenert, "Sea Change: The Navy Pivots to Asia," *Foreign Policy*, November 15, 2012, at www.foreignpolicy.com/articles.2012/11/14/sea_change, accessed July 14, 2014, and Council on Foreign Relations, "Deputy Secretary of Defense Robert Work on the Asia-Pacific Rebalance," September 30, 2014, at www.cfr.org/defense-and-security/deputy-secretary-defense-robert-work-asia-pacific-rebalance/p33538, accessed December 5, 2014.

13 Weir and Doyle, *You Cannot Surge Trust*, 295. On the U.S. military in Somalia see, U.S. Army Center of Military History, *United States Forces, Somalia After-Action Report and Historical Overview: The United States Army in Somalia, 1992–1994* (Washington DC, 2003); for the Canadian-led United Nations mission see Romeo Dallaire, *Shake Hands with the Devil: The Failure of Humanity in Rwanda* (Toronto, 2003).

14 Austin Wright, Jeremy Herb, Philip Ewing *et al.*, "Confronting Cuts, Hawks Say 'Not It'," *Politico*, May 4, 2014, Peter Beinart, "Reminder: Not All Republican Opposition to Obama Is Racist," *The Atlantic*, May 2, 2014, at www.theatlantic.com/politics/archive/2014/05/radical-republican-opposition-is-not-new/361536/, accessed May 5, 2014, Thomas Parker, "Is America a Declining Power?" *Israel Journal of Foreign Affairs* 38, 2 (2014), 40–1, and Pew Research Center for the People and the Press, "Political Polarization in the American Public," June 12, 2014, at www.people-press.org/files/2014/06/6-12-2014-Political-Polarization-Release.pdf, accessed September 2, 2014.

15 See the financial explanation of the "rebalance" to Asia, "Major Budget Decisions Briefing from the Pentagon," January 26, 2012, at www.defense.gov/transcripts/transcript.aspx?transcriptid=4962, accessed February 28, 2014.

16 Deputy Chief of Naval Operations (Integration of Capabilities and Resources), "Report to Congress on the Annual Long-Range Plan for Construction of Naval Vessels for FY2015" (Washington, DC, June 2014), at http://news.usni.org/2014/07/07/document-navys-30-year-shipbuilding-plan-fiscal-year-2015, and Department of Defense, "Annual Aviation Inventory and Funding Plan Fiscal Years (FY)2014–2043" (Washington, DC, May 2013), at http://breakingdefense.com/wp-content/uploads/sites/3/2013/06/DoD-Aircraft-Report-to-Congress-.pdf, both accessed July 8, 2014.

17 See Congressional Budget Office, *The 2013 Long-Term Budget Outlook* (Washington, DC, September 17, 2013), 22 and 58–9, at www.cbo.gov/sites/default/files/cbofiles/attachments/44521-LTBO2013_0. pdf, accessed April 28, 2014, and Clark Murdoch, Ryan Crotty, and Angela Weaver, *Building the 2021 Affordable Military* (Washington, DC, June 2014), 2–5, at http://csis.org/files/publication/140625_Murdock_Building2021Military_Web.pdf, accessed September 11, 2014.

18 Confirmation Hearings for Deputy Secretary of Defense Robert O. Work *et al.*, at www.armed-services.senate.gov/hearings/watch?hearingid=1b6a40cf-5056-a032-5230-f7e0c2122a8a, with Advance Policy Questions' responses, at www.armed-services.senate.gov/imo/media/doc/Work_02-25-14.pdf, 58–9. See also U.S. Congressional Budget Office, *Costs of Military Pay and Benefits* (Washington, DC, November 2012), 12–13, at www.cbo.gov/sites/default/files/cbofiles/attachments/11-14-12-MilitaryComp_0.pdf, all accessed February 25, 2014, Tom Philpott "Allow Pay Curbs or Harm Readiness, Joint Chiefs Expected to Tell Congress," *Military Update*, April 17, 2014, at www.stripes.com/news/us/allow-pay-curbs-or-harm-readiness-joint-chiefs-expected-to-tell-congress-1.278490, accessed April 19, 2014, and Anna Mulrine, "Military Budget: Four Ways U.S. Lawmakers Are Blocking Pentagon Cost-Cutting," *Christian Science Monitor*, May 20, 2014, at www.csmonitor.com/USA/Military/2014/0520/Military-budget-Four-ways-US-lawmakers-are-blocking-Pentagon-cost-cutting, accessed May 21, 2014.

19 Philip Ewing, Jeremy Herb, and Austin Wright, "DoD Struggles with Readiness Spending," *Politico*, June 10, 2014, at www.politicopro.com/story/defense/?id=34924, accessed June 11, 2014. For the 2013 Budget Control Act choices on force size, readiness, and pay, see Todd Harrison and Mark Gunzinger, *Strategic Choices: Navigating Austerity* (Washington, DC, 2012), at www.csbaonline.org/publications/2012/11/strategic-choices-navigating-austerity/, accessed June 11, 2014.

20 See video of work questions from Senator Jack Reed (Democrat, Rhode Island) in Confirmation Hearings, See also "Remarks by Secretary Hagel and Gen. Dempsey on the fiscal year 2015 budget preview in the Pentagon Briefing Room," February 24, 2014.

21 Best reflected in the term "Hollow Force." For an Army-focused study, see Andrew Feickert and Stephen Daggett, *A Historical Perspective on 'Hollow Forces'* (Washington, DC, January 31, 2012), especially 5 and 11, at www.fas.org/sgp/crs/natsec/R42334.pdf, accessed April 11, 2014.

22 See Peter Huessy, "The Four Great Waves of Defense Neglect: The Dangers of a Hollow Military," at www.gatestoneinstitute.org/4125/defense-neglect-hollow-military, accessed January 15, 2014. See also Dinah Walker, "Trends in U.S. Military Spending," July 15, 2014, at www.cfr.org/defense-budget/trends-us-military-spending/p28855, accessed July 18, 2014.

23 On the cost of services provided by contractors see Leigh Munsil, "Services Could Pose Challenge to Acquisition Reform," *Politico*, June 16, 2014, at www.politicopro.com/story/defense/?id=35177, accessed June 17, 2014. Payments for such services came out of the operations and maintenance accounts.

24 For the period 2001–10; see www.history.navy.mil/faqs/faq65-1.htm. The U.S. Marine Corps did grow by 20 percent in the same period, but from a smaller base. See www.marines.com/history-heritage/timeline, both accessed July 7, 2014. On the 80 percent increase in personnel costs see Walker, "Trends in U.S. Military Spending."

25 Walker, "Trends in U.S. Military Spending," notes that between 1950 and 2000 aircraft carrier prices annually rose more than 3 percent faster than general inflation, attack submarine costs climbed 5 percent faster, and both surface combatants and amphibious ships rose by more than 6 percent above general inflation. See also "Report to Congress on the Annual Long-Range Plan for Construction of Naval Vessels for FY2015," 8 and Appendix 1, for the annual costs of the 30-Year Shipbuilding Plan.

26 Office of the Under Secretary of Defense (Comptroller), *National Defense Budget Estimates for FY 2014* (Washington, DC, May 2013), 237–43, at http://comptroller.defense.gov/Portals/45/Documents/defbudget/fy2014/FY14_Green_Book.pdf, accessed May 6, 2014.

27 Sam Perlo-Freeman and Carina Solmirano, "Trends in World Military Expenditure, 2013" (SIPRI Fact Sheet, April 2014), Figure 3, at http://books.sipri.org/files/FS/SIPRIFS1404.pdf accessed May 9, 2014; Walker, "Trends in U.S. Military Spending." On allies, James Sheehan, *Where Have All the Soldiers Gone: The Transformation of Modern Europe* (New York, 2008), Patrick Balbierz, "Remilitarizing Japan: An Enticing Prospect," World Policy Blog, March 19, 2014, at www.worldpolicy.org/blog/2014/03/19/remilitarizing-japan-enticing-prospect, Walter Russell Mead, "PM Abe Leads Japan on the Road to Remilitarization," *American Interest*, May 15, 2014, at www.the-american-interest.com/blog/2014/05/15/pm-abe-leads-japan-on-the-road-to-remilitarization/, accessed July 29, 2014.

28 In his September 27, 2011 "CNO's Sailing Directions," at www.navy.mil/cno/cno_sailing_direction_final-lowres.pdf, accessed May 20, 2014. Its other elements, "Operate Forward" and "Be Ready," both resonate for U.S. Navy and Marine Corps thought explained here.

29 Joseph Nye, "The Decline of America's Soft Power," *Foreign Affairs* (May–June 2004), John Mearsheimer, "Can China Rise Peacefully?" *National Interest*, April 8, 2014, and J. Randy Forbes, "We're Losing Our Military Edge Over China. Here's How to Get It Back," *National Interest*, March 27, 2014. On the cost of U.S. focus on East Asia, see Parker, "Is America a Declining Power?" On soft power needing force, Admiral James Stavridis, USN (Ret), "Rethinking U.S. Enduring Strengths, Challenges and Opportunities," Johns Hopkins University APL talk, minute 47:00, April 19, 2014, at https://dnnpro.outer.jhuapl.edu/rethinking/VideoArchives/Stavridis2014PresentationVideo.aspx, accessed July 29, 2014. For contrary views see David Ignatius, "Claims of U.S. Weakness and Retreat of U.S. Power Are Unfounded," *Washington Post*, June 5, 2014, at www.washingtonpost.com/opinions/david-ignatius-our-cycles-of-national-worry/2014/06/04/a175425a-ec0c-11e3-9f5c-9075d5508f0a_story.html, accessed June 10, 2014, and Charles Kenny, "America's Slipping to No.2. Don't Freak Out," *Washington Post*, January 19, 2014, B4.

30 Gordon Adams and Matthew Leatherman, "A Leaner and Meaner Defense: How to Cut the Pentagon's Budget While Improving Its Performance," *Foreign Affairs* (January/February 2011), at www.foreignaffairs.com/articles/67145/gordon-adams-and-matthew-leatherman/a-leaner-and-meaner-defense/, accessed April 13, 2014.

31 See M. Taylor Fravel and Christopher Twomey, "Projecting Strategy: The Myth of Chinese Counter-intervention," *Washington Quarterly* (Winter 2015), 171–87.

32 As enunciated by Secretary of Defense Robert Gates in a September 16, 2009 speech, at www.defense.gov/speeches/speech.aspx?speechid=1379, accessed August 7, 2014. See also Sam J. Tangredi,

Anti-Access Warfare: Countering A2/AD Strategies (Annapolis, MD, 2013) and Christopher McCarthy, "Anti-Access/Area Denial: The Evolution of Modern Warfare," at www.usnwc.edu/Lucent/OpenPdf. aspx?id=95, accessed April 28, 2014. The July 17, 2014 destruction of Malaysia Airlines Flight 17 over eastern Ukraine reflects the challenge posed by precision weapons and their proliferation, in this case an anti-aircraft missile being used by non-state actors.

33 Martin van Creveld, *The Transformation of War: The Most Radical Reinterpretation of Armed Conflict since Clausewitz* (New York, 1991).

34 Kenneth Pollack, *Arabs at War: Military Effectiveness, 1948–1991* (Lincoln, NE, 2002).

35 Steven Kosiak, Andrew F. Krepinevich, and Michael Vickers, *A Strategy for a Long Peace* (Washington, DC, January 2001), i.

36 Michael Crichton, *Rising Sun* (New York, 1992), *RoboCop 3* (Orion, 1993), *Johnnie Mnemonic* (Tristar, 1995).

37 Tom Clancy, *Debt of Honor* (New York, 1994).

38 See Paul Krugman, "The Myth of Asia's Miracle," *Foreign Policy* (November/December 1994), especially 75–6, at http://econ.sciences-po.fr/sites/default/files/file/myth_of_asias-miracle.pdf, accessed July 21, 2014, and H. P. Willmott, *When Men Lost Faith in Reason: Reflections on War and Society in the Twentieth Century* (Westport and London, 2002), 182.

39 Zuliu Hu and Mohsin S. Khan, "Why is China Growing so Fast?" *IMF Economic Issues* (June 1997) at www.imf.org/EXTERNAL/PUBS/FT/ISSUES8/INDEX.HTM, accessed July 8, 2014.

40 The World Bank, *World Development Indicators 2008* (Washington, DC, 2008), 317.

41 Frank Borik, "Sub Tzu and the Art of Submarine Warfare," in Mary Somerville (ed.), *Essays on Strategy XIII* (Washington, DC, 1996), 3–42. Commander Borik's essay, positing China's fictional asymmetric naval victory over the United States in 2007, won First Place in the Chairman of the Joint Chiefs of Staff essay competition for 1995. See also Hon Lee, "China in the 21st Century: America's Greatest Strategic Challenge," in Somerville, *Essays on Strategy*, 81–115. That year saw the publication of Samuel Huntington's *The Clash of Civilizations and the Remaking of World Order* (New York, 1996), which drew attention to the South China Sea as a potential flashpoint. See also Joseph Gagliano, *Congressional Policymaking in Sino-U.S. Relations during the Post-Cold War Era* (London and New York, 2015), ch. 4, for a highly nuanced view of the consequences for U.S. politics of the crisis.

42 Peter Apps, "West Ponders How to Stop – or Fight – A New Great War," *Reuters*, June 3, 2014, at www.reuters.com/article/2014/06/03/us-security-war-idUSKBN0EE13L20140603, accessed June 4, 2014.

43 Michael Mandelbaum, *The Frugal Superpower: America's Global Leadership in a Cash-Strapped Era* (New York, 2010). Without explicit reference, Mandelbaum's work echoes French Admiral Castex's "strategic *manoeuvre*," in Raoul Castex, *Strategic Theories* (Eugenia Kiesling, ed. & trans.) (Annapolis, MD, 1994), 101–26.

44 One third of global goods, services, and finance. James Manyika, Jacques Bughin, Susan Lund, Olivia Nottebohm, David Poulter, Sebastian Jauch, and Sree Ramaswamy, "Global Flows in a Digital Age" (San Francisco, April 2014), at www.mckinsey.com/insights/globalization/global_flows_in_a_digital_age, accessed August 18, 2014, and Sean Mirski, "Stranglehold: The Context, Conduct and Consequences of an American Naval Blockade of China," *Journal of Strategic Studies* (Winter 2013), 385–421.

45 See Nicholas Lambert, *Planning Armageddon: British Economic Warfare and the First World War* (Cambridge, 2012), echoed by James Goldrick, "Mahan and Corbett: Concepts of Economic Warfare," in Peter Dennis (ed.), *Armies and Maritime Strategy* (Newport, NSW, 2014), 19–24, and Stephen Carmel, "Globalization, Security, and Economic Well-Being," *Naval War College Review* (Winter 2013), 41–55, especially 48–9.

46 Weir and Doyle, *You Cannot Surge Trust*, chs. 1–3, 6, and 7. See also James Cable, *The Political Influence of Naval Force in History* (London, 1998), Nicholas Tracy, *Attack on Maritime Trade* (London and Toronto, 1991), Gary Hufbauer, Jeffrey J. Schott, Kimberly Anne Elliott, and Barbara Oegg, *Economic Sanctions Reconsidered* (Washington, DC, 3rd edn., 2008), and CDRE Eric Lerhe (Ret), *At What Cost Sovereignty: Canada–US Military Interoperability in the Age of Terror* (Halifax, NS, 2013).

47 Andrew Feikert, *Marine Corps Drawdown, Force Structure Initiatives, and Roles and Missions: Background and Issues for Congress* (Washington, DC, January 9, 2014), 5–9.

48 *Ibid.*, 13. Feikert presents the opportunities for the Marine Corps by extending the Marine Air-Ground Task Force (MAGTF) concept to include smaller-scale missions. Historically preferred, the MEU is the smallest version of the MAGTF; see Aaron B. O'Connell, *Underdogs: The Making of the Modern Marine Corps* (Cambridge, 2012), especially ch. 6.

49 Marine Corps Ellis Group, "U.S. Amphibious Forces: Indispensible Elements of American Seapower" (August 2012), at http://smallwarsjournal.com/jrnl/art/us-amphibious-forces-indispensible-elements-of-american-seapower, accessed April 22, 2014. Admiral Jonathan Greenert, "CNO's Position Report 2012" (Washington, DC, 2012), at www.navy.mil/cno/121031_PositionReport.pdf, accessed April 22, 2014, endorsed this idea, briefly, but the Navy has not mentioned it since.

50 Wayne Hughes, "Naval Maneuver Warfare," *Naval War College Review* (Summer 1997), 44, at www.usnwc.edu/NavalWarCollegeReviewArchives/1990s/1997%20Summer.pdf. For an alternative view, see US Army, Marine Corps and Special Operations Command White Paper, *Strategic Landpower: Winning the Clash of Wills*, at www.tradoc.army.mil/FrontPageContent/Docs/Strategic%20 Landpower%20White%20Paper.pdf. Both accessed April 21, 2014.

51 Frank G. Hoffman and G. P. Garrett, *Envisioning Strategic Options: Comparing Alternative Marine Corps Structures* (Washington, DC, March 2014), at: www.cnas.org/sites/default/files/publications-pdf/CNAS_MarineCorps_HoffmanGarrett.pdf, accessed January 30, 2015.

52 *Ibid.*, 11.

53 *Ibid.*, 14.

54 Kirk Lippold, *Front Burner: Al Qaeda's Attack on the USS Cole* (New York, 2012), ch. 2.

55 CAPT Arthur H. Barber III (Ret), "Rethinking the Future Fleet," *Proceedings* (May 2014), 48–52.

56 Robert O. Work, *Strategy for the Long Haul. The U.S. Navy: Charting a Course for Tomorrow's Fleet* (Washington, DC, 2009), 10, at www.csbaonline.org/4Publications/PubLibrary/R.20090217.The_US_Navy_Charti/R.20090217.The_US_Navy_Charti.pdf. See also, Owen Cote, *Precision Strike from the Sea: New Missions for a New Navy* (Cambridge, MA, 1997), at http://web.mit.edu/ssp/publications/conf_series/strike/strike_report.html, both accessed June 30, 2014.

57 Wayne Hughes, *Fleet Tactics and Coastal Combat* (Annapolis, MD, 2000), 307.

58 Thomas Grund, "Distributed Air Wing Concept," *Naval Warfare Development Command's NEXT* 2, 1 (Spring 2014), 12–15.

59 On shared information building an operational picture, see Norman Friedman, *Network-Centric Warfare: How Navies Learned to Fight Smarter through Three World Wars* (Annapolis, MD, 2009), especially ch. 17.

60 Again, see Secretary of Defense Gates speech of September 16, 2009, and the other works cited in note 33, above.

61 See http://en.wikipedia.org/wiki/INS_Hanit, accessed April 11, 2014.

62 See "Air–Sea Battle: Service Collaboration to Address Anti-Access and Area Denial Challenges," May 2013, at http://navylive.dodlive.mil/2013/06/03/overview-of-the-air-sea-battle-concept/, and Hon. Robert O. Work, Undersecretary of the Navy, "The Importance of Integrated Air and Missile Defense to the Department of the Navy (and the Joint Force)," presentation to the Johns Hopkins University Applied Physics Laboratory, July 12, 2012, at www.dtic.mil/ndia/2012IAMD/RobertOWork.pdf, both accessed October 21, 2014.

63 Michael Gerson and Daniel Whiteneck, *Deterrence and Influence: The Navy's Role in Preventing War* (Alexandria, VA, March 2009). "Presence" is described by Secretary of the Navy Ray Mabus in a September 25, 2014 speech at the University of Pennsylvania, at https://vimeo.com/107630651, accessed February 12, 2015.

64 Daniel Whiteneck, Michael Price, Neil Jenkins, and Peter Swartz, *The Navy at a Tipping Point: Maritime Dominance at Stake?* (Alexandria, VA, 2010), at www.cna.org/sites/default/files/research/The%20Navy%20at%20a%20Tipping%20Point%20D0022262.A3.pdf, accessed January 27, 2015.

65 *Ibid.*, 6–9.

66 *Ibid.*, 23–40. See the summary tables on the first and last of those pages for CNA's measures of risk.

67 See Richard Burgess, "Greenert, Dunford: Sequestration Hurts Personnel, Modernization, Readiness," *Seapower* (January 28, 2015), at www.seapowermagazine.org/stories/20150128-sasc.html, accessed January 29, 2015.

68 Frank Hoffman, "The Case for Forward Partnership," *Proceedings* 139:1 (January 2013), at www.usni.org/magazines/proceedings/2013-01/case-forward-partnership, and Hoffman, "No Strategic Success without 21st Century Seapower: Forward Partnering," *War on the Rocks*, at http://warontherocks.com/2014/07/no-strategic-success-without-21st-century-seapower-forward-partnering/, both accessed July 1, 2014.

69 Weir and Doyle, *You Cannot Surge Trust*, 12–13.

19

ELEMENTS OF TWENTY-FIRST-CENTURY GERMAN NAVAL STRATEGY

Sebastian Bruns[1]

Introduction

2015 marked the sixtieth anniversary of the establishment of armed forces in post–World War Germany. It is also the silver jubilee of German reunification and thus of an all-German Navy.[2] For much of the twenty-first century, German defense policy discourse and its accompanying strategic narrative had largely been dominated by the combat operations in Afghanistan (2001–14) and the threat of international terrorism,[3] even if the Navy had already carried a substantial burden in various maritime security operations in and around Europe since 1990.[4] In a country still struggling with the "coming of age" in a multipolar, violent world order (and clearly uneasy regarding the military aspects of international relations), the German Navy's roles and missions beyond broad sea control objectives were poorly articulated in Berlin, harly reflected in capstone documents, and inadequately reflected in fleet design. As Bryan McGrath, the primary author of the U.S. "Cooperative Strategy for 21st Century Seapower" (2007), has pointed out:

> Germany lacks a history and culture (since World War II) of a 'balanced' fleet capable of the full range of modern naval operations. With no carrier or amphibious fleet to speak of, and without a sea-based nuclear deterrent, the German Navy has historically focused on sea-control missions centered around ASW, ASuW, and maritime security.[5]

Amidst recently risen tensions over the Russo-Ukrainian war in the Black Sea littorals (accompanied by a deep souring of relations between the West and Moscow), an increasingly chaotic international order, the brutal ascent of the Islamic State (IS) in the Levant, a disintegrating Middle East and claims to regional hegemony in Southwest Asia and the Indo-Pacific, as well as continuing deep fiscal troubles in the European Union, Germany intends to partially reorganize its security policy – once again.

However, years of neglect when it comes to strategic conceptual thinking and, more importantly, standing empurpled hopes for a post-Cold War peace dividend have led to a rather regrettable state in many of the constituents of successful maritime strategy: machinery, men, manufacturing, management, money, and mentality.[6] Germany is still very much uneasy about using its military as a tool of statecraft and in assertion of its national interests. In addition, post-Cold War Germany has groomed its aversion to capstone documents. For only the third time since 1990, the government is currently underway in creating a defense policy White Book (due to be published in 2016). So-called defense-policy guidelines, the last of which was published in 2011, have served as a stand-in for the national defense establishment. The Navy has been no exception and has largely committed itself to managing its own ever-shrinking posture[7] and handling ongoing naval operations.

This chapter will discuss some history-driven factors which govern how Germany thinks about naval power. Furthermore, a survey of maritime focus areas outlines the current and assumed future operating areas, and a look at the major naval assets will inform about capabilities. Subsequently, this study will delineate how a strategic contribution of the German Navy should be viewed. Thus, this investigation seeks to provide a fresh intellectual prism for an analysis and the strategic and effective employment of German naval power in the maritime twenty-first century.

Conceptual and intellectual frameworks as governing factors for German strategy

The roles and missions of any navy are fundamentally a function of geography (or, more precisely, a country's sea-strategic position) and the articulated political and economic interests of a government – often denoted as national interests. In Germany, a third central factor comes into play: its recent twentieth-century history. Kaiser Wilhelm's Empire and Adolf Hitler's Third Reich are forever linked to the monstrosities of two World Wars and, in the latter case, also the Holocaust.[8] The total defeat of 1945 ensured, at least in West Germany, a modest and cautious intellectual and strategic restart, which was naturally subject to the will of the four allied powers and the emerging bipolar world of the Cold War. It should come as no surprise that sea power (indeed the very notion of Machiavellian *Machtpolitik*, or "power politics") as a concept was quickly laid to rest after 1945.[9] Even if the legacy of the *Kriegsmarine* remained, in part, an intellectual burden to reckon with,[10] naturally there is no line of tradition in post-war strategic naval thinking to these previous German navies and the sea-strategic concepts they embodied.

During the Cold War, both German states – from the start – were firmly integrated in military alliances in the emerging and quickly consolidating bipolar world order.[11] East Germany's armed forces were part of the Warsaw Pact. West Germany was integrated into the North Atlantic Treaty Organization (NATO) and the Western European Union (WEU). The central difference between both German naval services in their respective alliances was not so much their operations: both focused on homeland defense and alliance operations by means of coastal combat and escort roles for a coming war, but rather in the strategic grand design.

While the integration of West Germany into NATO naval strategy was a political gambit to alleviate allied concerns about a resurgent and renegade Germany under Cold War terms, East Germany's integration into the Warsaw Pact was a result of direct Soviet pressure. Whereas the *Volksmarine* in the East had limited roles to play and would have been under strict Red Fleet command in the case of hostilities, the *Bundesmarine* in the West had some room for maneuver (both figuratively as well as operationally). NATO simply provided the conventional and nuclear umbrella as well as a strategic ceiling called "flexible response." The German constitution, adopted in 1949, restricted the use of military force to solely serve national (and, by implication, territorial) defense (Art. 87a), although the Federation may enter into a system of mutual collective security (Art. 24) if necessary.

The flipside of this firm grip was an atrophy of strategic thinking about the role of naval power on both sides of the Iron Curtain (complemented by the fundamentally nuclear-, air-, and land-dominated expectations about a coming war in and over Germany). Both Germanys were not expected to formulate true naval strategic thought, and both were reasonably content in not having to think about anything other than their insular position, let alone anything that insinuated larger geopolitical aspirations. The absence of a naval strategy, which would deserve such a name today, needs to be viewed in light of the lack of fertilization of strategic thought during the Cold War.[12]

Operationally, the East Germans were confined to the Baltic Sea and were generally subordinate to the Soviet armed forces. For West Germany, in accordance with NATO partners, naval objectives included securing the Baltic Sea approaches, defense of the sea lines of communication into its territorial waters, attacks on enemy shipping in the Baltic Sea in the event of war, and support of the Army in amphibious operations (the latter task was abandoned in the 1960s).[13] The fleet inventory reflected these tasks accordingly.[14] The *Bundesmarine* expanded its focus in the 1980s, once again in close coordination with its NATO allies, to include areas of the North Atlantic.[15] It was the era of a new U.S. "Maritime Strategy," a forward-leaning strategy that emphasized the Northern (European) flank and focused on sea control, power projection, and the conventional (and nuclear) value of naval forces.[16] Since the end of the Cold War, crisis response and conflict prevention objectives took center stage in naval roles for Germany. Still, this snapshot of past German naval history must be considered when assessing contemporary foreign and security policy in the maritime and naval realm. Germany's history explains the changed role of German naval power and its application since the 1950s.

The absence of a true naval strategy (or a strategic community, for that matter) well into the twenty-first century has its roots in the experiences of the twentieth century. Germany was simply not required to think about the effects of maritime power due to its recent history, its geographically as well as politically limited tasks, and the low but very firm strategic ceiling which NATO provided. Often cautious of a wayward country, many allies hold little reservation against the tight grip which NATO strategy exercises have on any strategic evolvement by Germany. In such an environment, the development of a strategic community at universities, think tanks, or within the Navy was neither necessary nor encouraged. Germany's marked anti-expeditionary strategic mindset has only gradually changed in recent years, in part due to the various rounds of reform which the German Navy underwent in the 1990s and the emerging pragmatic generation of maritime strategists and practitioners. This transformation was characterized by a changed security environment in Europe, a shrinking force, a diffusion of maritime risks, and technological innovation.[17]

Maritime focus areas since 1990

The evolution of the escort navy of Cold War days to the expeditionary navy of the era of globalization occurred neither in a vacuum nor overnight. Instead, normative developments of the 1990s in a unipolar world mandated naval action. Germany was increasingly expected to play a more responsible and assertive role internationally, one which would not principally rule out military means. In the eyes of many, the German government could be expected to step up to such responsibilities because as one of the leading industrial nations of the globe and a champion in exporting processed goods it was very much dependent on a functioning system of international trade.[18] Since the 1990s, rapid globalization – buttressed by containerized shipping – underscores the importance of safe and secure maritime trade routes. Stable littoral states along the modern sea-lines of communication which span from Asia to Europe and to North America are integral to the defense of the system as a whole. Accordingly, a responsibility can be deduced that falls on those countries which benefit from economic integration and globalization.[19]

However, such conceptual causal links emerged only very slowly. Germany evolved from an importer of security – under the conditions of the Cold War – to an exporter of security, but it had neither the mindset nor the structures in place to formulate a strategic approach to security policy. The German government, deeply aware that the days of simple checkbook diplomacy were quickly disposed of, increasingly sought to fend off calls for more robust international engagement by citing the economic consequences of its reunification and by focusing on deeper European integration. In addition and in line with the perceived or actual post-heroic character of the electorate, the government framed its contributions to international security increasingly at the lower end of the spectrum, emphasizing the civilian aspects of conflict prevention and crisis response over the military dimensions.[20] This national security consensus in Germany always crossed party lines. Politically, the "primacy of politics" put ministries, such as the Federal Foreign Office and the Federal Ministry for Economic Cooperation and Development, into the driver's seat of international security policy. The Ministry of Defense was often sidelined and the German government – regardless of its political background and domestic coalition dynamics – often happily delegated more robust military action to its allies.

Only very slowly did stakeholders in Germany acquaint themselves with the use of military force, such as the controversial decision to engage militarily in the Kosovo War in 1999. In this respect, the Navy increasingly turned into a preferred tool for national security issues, as it allowed measured engagement without committing ground troops or bombing runs to crisis areas. The continuing contributions to the Standing NATO Maritime Groups (SNMG 1/2) and the Standing NATO Mine-Countermeasures Groups (SNMG 1/2) speaks volumes to the relentless operating tempo of the German Navy. In the absence of a national maritime capstone document, however, the *Deutsche Marine* practiced naval strategy by default, while managing the fallout from consolidating defense budgets and ever-recurring reforms at the same time.

The first post-Cold War naval mission came along quickly and was related to the Persian Gulf War: German naval assets operated in the Mediterranean and the Persian Gulf in support of the UN-mandated allied military effort to expel Iraqi troops from Kuwait (1990/91). It was not until 1994 that the Federal Constitutional Court ruled such "out-of-area" operations of German military forces constitutional with the Basic Law. As the Balkans erupted in a violent civil war in 1993, the German Navy was once again called to action in the Mediterranean in support of allied operations against Serbia. It needed to venture even further – to the Horn of Africa – in 1994 to evacuate German UN peacekeeping troops from war-torn Somalia, which was rapidly disintegrating at the time. After the terrorist attacks on the United States on September 11, 2001, the German Navy supported the "Global War on Terrorism" by participating in the naval leg of Operation Enduring Freedom (OEF) off the Horn of Africa as well as in Operation Active Endeavor (OAE) in the Mediterranean. Capacity-building off Lebanon and counter-piracy operations in the Western Indian Ocean added to the spectrum of naval tasks. Recently, the overwhelming stream of refugees from Africa to Europe has drawn the German Navy to participate in EU NAVFOR MED ("Operation Sophia"), a European Union maritime security operation centered on SAR, intelligence collection, and counter-traffikking. In the words of one author, Germany assumed "a reduced 'asymmetric' role focus [on] counter-piracy, peacemaking and peacekeeping operations, rather than full-scale, high intensity operations."[21] Table 19.1 offers a quick recap of major German naval operations since 1990.

None of these naval operations was laid down in a capstone document deserving such a name. In fact, Germany, to this day, does not have an official national security strategy or a formal national military strategy. The last German defense-policy review of 2006 mentioned the security of sea lines only in passing. It is otherwise silent on maritime security.[22] Paradoxically, the German Navy since 1990 has been tasked to use the sea for military roles (such as sea control, [limited] power projection ashore, and sea denial), diplomatic functions (such as showing of the flag), and constabulary roles (such as peacekeeping and maintenance of good order) – without ever stating the obvious.[23] It also actively and repeatedly integrated with partner navies in bilateral exercises,[24] standing and special naval groups and task forces, and conducted coalition

Table 19.1 Major naval operations of the Germany Navy, 1990–2015

Date	Name	Objectives
August 1990–September 1991	Operation Southern Flank	MCM units in the Mediterranean Sea and the Northern Persian Gulf
June 1993–October 1996	Operation Sharp Guard	Enforcement of economic sanctions and a weapons embargo against Yugoslavia in the Adriatic Sea
January 1994–April 1994	UNOSOM II/ Operation Southern Cross	Evacuation of German United Nations contingent from Mogadishu (Somalia)
1999/2000	Allied Harvest I+II	Recovery of ammunition from the Adriatic Sea after the Kosovo War (1999)
November 2001–June 2010	Operation Enduring Freedom (Task Force 150)	Fight against al-Qaida and affiliates, combat piracy off the Horn of Africa (under the umbrella of the "Global War on Terrorism")
Since November 2001	Operation Active Endeavour	Enhance Maritime Domain Awareness (MDA) in the Mediterranean, deter terrorist attacks (under the umbrella of the "Global War on Terrorism"); Art. 5 (NATO Treaty) operation
Since September 2006	UNIFIL	Prevention of smuggling of arms and illegal goods into Lebanon, training of Lebanese naval component
Since December 2008	EU NAVFOR Atalanta	Protection of World Food Program (WFP) cargo vessels off Somalia, defense of commercial shipping against piracy Column 1: since June 2015 Column 2: EU NAVFOR MED Operation Sophia Column 3: surveillance of human traffikking routes, intelligence gathering, SAR, search for/diversion of suspicious vessels in the Central Mediterranean between North Africa and Southern Europe
Since June 2015	EU NAVFOR MED Operation Sophia	surveillance of human trafficking routes, intelligence gathering, SAR, search for/diversion of suspicious vessels in the Central Mediterranean between North Africa and Southern Europe

naval operations under NATO, EU, or UN mandate. Furthermore, the country has continuously groomed its maritime industry: Many German-flagged, -owned, or -operated cargo vessels plow the maritime highways across the globe. German yards build some of the world's premier specialty ships. By all estimates, the air-independent submarines built in Kiel (Type 212-A ff.) are among the world's most capable, conventionally powered submarines. Many countries have procured German-designed U-boats, MEKO-class multipurpose surface warships, offshore patrol vessels (OPV), or engines for naval vessels, and many more have expressed interests. The major policy shortfall has been that these elements of a strategic concept are yet to be verbalized.[25]

Towards a new prism: German naval missions and maritime areas of responsibility

This chapter suggests a fourfold approach to frame, understand, explain, and ultimately to better utilize German naval strategic contributions. This paradigm should not be construed as developing something entirely new; instead, such a verbalization helps to frame naval and broader maritime contributions. In fact, the prism binds together existing requirements and objectives as well as operational and political experiences in order to develop a model which intends to put an end to a rather erratic security policy. It seeks to lay the groundwork for a ways-means-ends relationship – a strategy.[26]

A suitable point of departure is the set of missions that Stansfield Turner conceived in 1974.[27] Turner's article is significant not because the German Navy should aspire to emulate the U.S. Navy of the 1970s – it clearly shouldn't – but because it succeeds in framing naval missions consistently. In fact, this mission set can well be considered the foundation of modern sea power. According to the then-President of the U.S. Naval War College, naval missions include strategic deterrence, maritime power projection, sea control, and naval presence. Whereas these independent missions had been devised against the backdrop of the Cold War and a Soviet Union that aspired to challenge American maritime predominance at the time, its vocabulary survived the end of the bipolar world order and even transferred into the twenty-first century. It has since transcended the exclusive focus on the U.S. Navy, and should rather be understood as the principle organizing factors for contemporary naval strategy. Geoffrey Till has conceptualized and further developed it into characterizations of modern and post-modern navies. Whereas the modern navy's priorities include sea control, nuclear deterrence and ballistic missile defense, maritime power projection, exclusive good order at sea, and competitive gunboat diplomacy, the five missions of the post-modern (evolved) navy are sea control, expeditionary operations, stability operations and humanitarian assistance (as well as disaster relief), a more inclusive good order at sea, and a cooperative naval diplomacy.[28]

This mission set is something that the German Navy has been designed for, at least implicitly. It is time to embrace and market these roles – and to develop a strategic narrative. This narrative's underlying motif could be "responsibility," which includes accountability for Germany's own territorial integrity (naturally), for collective defense, and for systemic defense of the global maritime commons.

To frame these three objectives in geographic terms, it is instructive to consider the maritime focus areas of interest for Germany. Naturally, the "home waters" form the inner layer. The North Sea and the Baltic Sea, connected by the Kiel Canal (incidentally the world's busiest artificial shipping channel), are consequently the most important maritime focus areas.[29] The port of Hamburg, one of the world's largest and most hectic harbors, is located some 70 nm inland on the river Elbe.[30] Other major ports with substantial international traffic on the German coasts include Emden, Wilhelmshaven, Bremerhaven, Kiel, Lübeck, and Rostock.[31] The second layer could include the Central and Eastern Mediterranean, as well as the High North.[32] As a somewhat outer layer, one should consider the Gulf of Guinea region in West Africa,[33] the Horn of Africa in East Africa, and the Western Indian Ocean.[34]

With the exception of the "home waters," the German Navy would, as a principle, always seek to operate in close conjunction and even in temporary integration with allied and partner navies. From a supranational perspective, NATO's Alliance Maritime Strategy (2011) and the EU Maritime Security Strategy (2014) frame a host of institutional expectations towards the German Navy. These hard issues are often too easy to ignore. Whereas these overarching documents have clear implications for a German national capstone document, there is also something less tangible at play: Germany's desire to further the value-based system which could be understood as freedom of the seas and a broader responsibility (even aspiration) for the global commons must be taken into account. It holds true that even in maritime and strategic terms, one cannot have one's cake and eat it too: In order to shoulder more international responsibility, Germany (and its Navy) must consider the hard- and soft-power demands that stem from idealist and realist politics, and articulate maritime security policy options accordingly.

Naval assets

Since 1990, Germany ventured into shouldering more maritime responsibility in the Mediterranean and the Western Indian Ocean with the fleet from the days of the late Cold War. This resulted in frigates, optimized for ASW in the North Atlantic, to conduct maritime security operations in the Indian Ocean. Fast patrol boats designed for the colder climate of Northern European shallow waters operated in the hot and humid climate of the Eastern Mediterranean. Planning cycles, traditionally measured in decades rather than in years, reduced budgets, and a permissive international security environment that envisioned stabilizing forces instead of power projection, contributed to strategic disorientation (and the resulting hands-off mentality when it came to formulating a ship-building and naval operations strategy). Instead, in an effort to shrink and modernize the fleet, organizational changes became a primer.

Since 2006, the German Navy has been grouped into two flotillas.[35] *Einsatzflottille 1* is headquartered in Kiel and envelops the smaller units such as submarines, corvettes, MCM units of various classes, and the smaller tenders. *Einsatzflottille 2* calls Wilhelmshaven its home and envelops all frigates as well as the larger tenders of the *Berlin*-class. Still under the impression of substantial 2010 defense cuts and an ambitious *Bundeswehr*-wide reform agenda of 2011 (which included the suspension of conscription), the German Navy today has about 16,000 personnel. It is the smallest of the three branches of the German military, and disproportionally suffers from low recruitment rates and overall cuts. The financial investment bottleneck in material and infrastructure is substantial. Still, the German Navy today fields six domestically built submarines (Type 212-A) which are considered among the most capable conventionally powered boats worldwide, and have triggered a number of exports of these submarines. In turn, the older Type 206-A boats have all been retired early. There are merely 12 principal surface combatants in service (as of December 2015). The larger ones are four frigates of the *Brandenburg*-class (Type F123) which joined the fleet between 1994 and 1996 and three frigates of the *Sachsen*-class (Type F124) that entered the scene between 2004 and 2006.[36] In addition, the German Navy operates five corvettes of the *Braunschweig*-class (Type K130), in service since 2008. In contrast, the workhorse frigates of the *Bremen*-class (Type F122), eight of which were procured for Cold War tasks between 1979 and 1987 (and which truly achieved an economies-of-scale effect), are now being retired. The aging fast-patrol boats of the *Gepard*-class are also being phased out. In turn, the German Navy expects four new large frigates (Type F125) of the *Baden-Württemberg*-class to join the fleet from 2017 on.[37] To sustain expeditionary operations, there are also three large combat support ships (Type 702) in the inventory.[38] Of note is Germany's large fleet of MCM units of various classes and types. Three *Oste*-class reconnaissance ships typically plow the waves in areas of strategic interest to obtain and process various forms of intelligence. These SIGINT ships and the MCM units are quickly approaching the end of their lifespan, but a replacement is not in clear sight yet.

The naval air arm has in recent years been drastically reduced, in part reflecting the changing objectives of German sea power in its shift to expeditionary operations.[39] Naval jet aircraft were assigned to the *Luftwaffe* after the end of the Cold War. Today, there is but one base remaining (Nordholz Naval Airbase, near Cuxhaven). It is the home of the Naval Air Command.[40] It envelops two air wings fielding 8 maritime patrol aircraft (Type P-3C *Orion*) in addition to 22 *Sea Lynx* (Type Mk88A) and 21 *Sea King* (Type Mk41) helicopters. These particular aircraft are dramatically aging and need to be replaced soon. Further future additions to the fleet will likely include new double-hull tankers to replace the aging *Spessart*-class vessels, and six multi-role frigates (Type MKS180) for the 2020s. Procurement of a future joint support ship for the German Navy – a type of command ship and helicopter carrier for joint operations from the sea against the shore – periodically surfaces in the public and professional debate.[41]

For much of its existence, the German Navy has planned its fleet around various ship (and aircraft) classes, and it has often favored indigenous designs and developments over readily available allied platforms. This luxury is likely to end, even if slowly consolidating defense budgets and a reassessment of international security risks should materialize. It will be interesting to see whether new models for procurement can be established soon, i.e. a standardized frigate-size platform which could be adapted to various mission packages.[42] The price could likely include a further consolidation of Germany's own naval defense industry. Here, as much as in other areas of security policy, a national shipbuilding and defense industry strategy would be highly desirable.

Conclusion

It is not hard to imagine the value of a Navy capstone document that provides top-level explanations on what the Navy does, and how it can help support Germany's interests in terms of both its people and its allies. After all, more than 400,000 people are employed in the maritime industry sector in Germany, with an aggregate value of no less than €85 billion.[43] Firmly embedded in a maritime and a more comprehensive national security strategy, aligned with stating the obvious aspects of a German grand strategy, and infused by the careful collaborative spirit of twenty-first-century sea power, a genuine maritime strategy would better inform and educate the public. It would also provide Germany's allies (and its antagonists) with a better documentation about the degree of responsibility that Berlin is willing to bring to the table. Planners, programmers, and procurement professionals would benefit from this as well. Germany must verbalize its security interests much better, and make the connection to the larger national narrative of a country with in fact a rich maritime history, a dependence on unhindered sea-borne trade, and significant interests in littoral good governance as well as in the well-being and security of the global commons. In other words, maritime domain awareness is not just a technical term for the operator, but also, in a global strategic meaning, a requirement for German strategists and military-political planners alike.

It holds true that navies are certainly not the solution to every given security problem, but sea power can provide scalable and flexible support of Germany's specific national and international cooperative interests. Given the challenges of such a medium-sized navy which has to cope with adverse political dynamics, and considering Germany's past, this is hardly an easy feat. Conceptualizing and verbalizing naval strategy that honors the term, however, is a timely undertaking in an era of resurgent appreciation for security problems. Such a capstone document can emphasize that sea power is the right fit for conscious political leaders in Berlin who seek not to entangle themselves in costly military operations ashore. In addition, chances are that through outside pressure from overarching strategic developments, Germany will be pressed to provide policy-makers, the electorate, and its partners in Europe and beyond a capstone document rather sooner than later. Quite disturbingly, until this very day the Navy (or the government) has neither a dedicated academic strategic studies branch, an established strategy-writing office, nor a maritime-focused think tank that could sustainably make the larger maritime case. Here, as much as in some other areas, much is to be gained for Germany and the allies alike.

Notes

1 The author wishes to thank Torsten Albrecht, David Helmbold, Jan C. Kaack, Dirk Peters, and Konstatinos Tsetsos for helping to frame the debate on future German maritime and naval strategy methodologically. Tom Niepage supported data collection for this chapter in his capacity as an intern of the Institute for Security Policy at the University of Kiel in 2014.

2 The *Bundesmarine* (Federal German Navy) of West Germany was formally commissioned in 1956. For a review, see Hajo Lippke, *Die Zukunft der Deutschen Marine*, Frankfurt/Main: Peter Lang (2009), pp. 26–69. The *Volksmarine* (People's Navy), as the *Bundesmarine*'s German Democratic Republic counterpart, was established in 1960. It ceased to exist on the eve of Germany's Unification on October 3, 1990 with only a fraction of its men and machinery absorbed by the new all-German *Deutsche Marine* (German Navy). The merging of the two navies under rather one-sided terms is subject of a 2007 volume by Stephan Huck and Hartmut Klüver, *Die Wende. Die Deutsche Marine auf dem Weg in die Einheit* (= Kleine Schriftenreihe zur Militär- und Marinegeschichte, 13), Bochum: Dieter Winkler. It must be noted that the tradition of today's German Navy is fundamentally centered on the West German Navy. This perspective also governs the view of the chapter at hand.

3 Robin Schroeder and Martin Zapfe, "'War-Like Circumstances': Germany's Unforeseen Combat Mission in Afghanistan and Its Strategic Narratives," in: Beatrice de Graaf, George Dimitriu, and Jens Ringsmose (eds.), *Strategic Narratives, Public Opinion and War: Winning Support for Foreign Military Missions*, London/New York: Routledge (2015), pp. 177–98. The Balkan wars of the 1990s, which also rested on the Army as far as the public is concerned, served to deepen the land-forces focus when it comes to how military power is framed in Germany.

4 Autorenteam Flottenkommando, "Die Deutsche Marine ist eine Marine im Einsatz," in: *MarineForum* 11/2012, pp. 8–13. See also Illustration 1 there.

5 Bryan McGrath, *NATO at Sea. Trends in Allied Naval Power*, Washington DC, American Enterprise Institute, National Security Outlook 3, September 2013, p. 5.

6 Jon Sumida and David Rosenberg, "Machines, Men, Manufacturing, Management and Money. The Study of Navies as Complex Organizations and the Transformation of Twentieth Century Naval History," in: J. Hattendorf (ed.), *Doing Naval History. Essays towards Improvement*, Newport, RI: Naval War College Press (1995), pp. 25–40, and Wilfried Stallmann, "Die maritime Strategie der USA nach 1945: Entwicklung, Einflußgrößen und Auswirkungen auf das atlantische Bündnis." Dissertation zur Erlangung des Doktorgrades der Philosophischen Fakultät der Christian-Albrechts-Universität zu Kiel, 2000, microfiche, p. 259.

7 As of May 2015, the German Navy had 16,135 sailors (of 180,676 men and women in uniform for the whole *Bundeswehr* – less than 9 percent). Bundesministerium der Verteidigung, Presse- und Informationsstab, "Die Stärke der Streitkräfte." http://goo.gl/rj6o9Z, May 5, 2015 (last retrieved May 17, 2015). By comparison, the Himmenrod Memo (1950) that established the force levels for the young *Bundeswehr* estimated 15,000–19,000 sailors, whereas planning for 1955 already consisted of 35,000 soldiers. In October 1973, the German Navy numbered 38,000 men (cited in Lippke, *Die Zukunft*, p. 29).

8 World War I and World War II involved substantial naval and maritime dimensions, although Germany fought primarily on land. Its respective political and military decision-makers saw the *Reichsmarine* of the 1910s, as well as the *Kriegsmarine* of the 1930s and 1940s, as rather costly diversions from the real objectives in war, regardless of how meaningful naval contributions in keeping sea lines of communication open and wrestling with its enemies through battle at sea or submarine warfare could be. See Werner Rahn, "Strategische Optionen und Erfahrungen der deutschen Marineführung 1914–1944. Zu den Chancen und Grenzen einer mitteleuropäischen Kontinentalmacht gegen Seemächte," in: Werner Rahn (ed.), *Deutsche Marinen im Wandel. Vom Symbol nationaler Einheit zum Instrument internationaler Sicherheit*, Munich: Oldenbourg (2004), pp. 197–234. The naval staff war diaries were edited by Werner Rahn and Gerhard Schreiber (by order of the German Armed Forces Military History Research Office, together with the Federal Military Archives and the German Naval Officers' Association), as *Kriegstagebuch der Seekriegsleitung 1939–1945*, Berlin/Bonn/Hamburg: Mittler, between 1988 and 1997 (68 volumes). See also Michael Salewski (ed.), *Die deutsche Seekriegsleitung 1935–1945*, 3 vols (vol. I: *1935–1941*; vol. II: *1942–1945*; vol. III: *Denkschriften und Lagebetrachtungen 1938–1944*), Frankfurt: Bernard & Graefe Verlag (1970–).

9 The German political scientist Herfried Münkler has described modern German society as "postheroic" – unable to think in military terms and unwilling to accept casualties.

10 Admirals Karl Dönitz (1890–1981) and Erich Raeder (1876–1960) were among the most high-ranking war criminals that stood trial in Nuremberg after World War II. It was Raeder and Dönitz who, after their release from the Berlin-Spandau prison, busied themselves fashioning the navy of the Third Reich as detached and uninvolved in Nazi war crimes (see VADM (Ret) Wolfgang Wegener, *The Naval Strategy of the World War*, ed. and trans. Holger Herwig, Annapolis, MD: U.S. Naval Institute Press [1989]). For the leadership of the young *Bundesmarine*, this spelled the uneasy challenge in answering the "mythical Grand Admiral question," as the magazine *Der Spiegel* called it ("Rüstzeit für Offiziere,"

Der Spiegel 49, December 3, 1958). A more honest discussion of the role of the *Kriegsmarine* in the Third Reich, at least in German political, military, and academic circles, was long avoided until the 1980s – and thus in line with the general feeling in German society which sought to "move on" (the student revolts of 1968 had caused some stir, although that debate was largely driven by left-wing and Marxist ideas). The landmark anti-war movie *Das Boot* (1980) and, more importantly, President Richard von Weizsäcker's speech in the German parliament on May 8, 1985 (on the occasion of the fortieth anniversary of the capitulation) finally spurred on a more honest debate about the legacy of the war for Germany, even in the central and conservative circles of society. However, the collective military memory in Germany of the wars is fundamentally land- and air-power-driven, not maritime in nature.

11 The key study of the transition years between 1945 and 1960 is Douglas Peifer's book, *The Three German Navies: Dissolution, Transition, and New Beginnings, 1945–1960*, Gainesville, FL: University of Florida Press (2002).

12 This should not be construed as the total absence of strategic thinking on German naval contributions to defense. See, for example, works by Vice Admiral Friedrich Ruge, first Chief of Staff of the *Bundesmarine*, in *"Erleben – Lernen – Weitergeben," Friedrich Ruge (1894–1985)*, ed. Jörg Hillmann (= Kleine Schriftenreihe zur Militär- und Marinegeschichte 10), Bochum: Dieter Winkler (2007). In 1974, Hans-Peter Schwartz and Dieter Mahnke published the first, and for a long time only, compendium which analyzed the political role of naval power: *Seemacht und Außenpolitik*, Frankfurt/Main: Metzner. That book, perhaps along with the expanded German version of the voluminous historiography *Seemacht. Eine Seekriegsgeschichte von der Antike bis zur Gegenwart*, ed. E. B. Potter and Chester Nimitz, Herrsching: Pawlak (1986), remained the go-to source until the end of the Cold War. In the absence of the need to think about strategy and the political role of German sea power, thinking about technological developments took comparatively more room, and were subsequently subject to deeper study. For example, see Sigurd Hess, "Der Übergang der Marine in das Zeitalter der Führungs-, Waffeneinsatzsystemen und Flugkörpern. Die Phase der Innovation 1963 bis 1976," in: Frank Nägler (ed.), *Die Bundeswehr 1955 bis 2005. Rückblenden, Einsichten, Perspektiven*, Munich: Oldenbourg (2005), pp. 417–36, and the visionary study by Heinz Dieter Jopp, *Marine 2000. Neue wehrtechnische Entwicklungen und ihr Einfluss auf die Seekriegführung*, SWP Study S-346, Ebenhausen, April 1988 (also published as a book, with an introduction by Lothar Rühl, Baden-Baden: Nomos [1989]). It took until 2013 and 2014, respectively, for a changing of the guard to take place. The volumes *Maritime Sicherheit*, Wiesbaden: VS (2013), edited by Sebastian Bruns, Kerstin Petretto, and David Petrovic, as well as *Maritime Sicherheit im 21. Jahrhundert* (= Democracy, Security, Peace 215), Baden-Baden: Nomos, edited by Heinz Dieter Jopp, are the first German-language handbooks which consider issues of maritime security and naval power since at least 1990.

13 For an authoritative discussion on the inner development of the *Bundesmarine* in its formative years, see the study by Johannes Berthold Sander-Nagashima, *Die Bundesmarine 1955 bis 1972: Konzeption und Aufbau*, Munich: Oldenbourg (2006), and its condensed version by the same author, "Konzeptionelle Probleme der Bundesmarine 1955 bis 1972," in: Eckardt Opitz (ed.), *Seestrategische Konzepte vom kaiserlichen Weltmachtstreben zu Out-of-Area-Einsätzen der Deutschen Marine*, Bremen: Edition Temmen (2004), pp. 109–33. For a view from the 1970s, see Klaus-Jürgen Bühring, "Strategie und Aufbau der Flotte der Bundesrepublik Deutschland," in: Dieter Mahnke and Hans-Peter Schwarz (eds.), *Seemacht und Außenpolitik*, Frankfurt/Main: Metzner (1974), pp. 289–98.

14 For illustrated handbooks of the major units of both German navies during the Cold War, see Ulf Kaack, *Typenatlas Bundeswehr. Die Schiffe der Bundesmarine 1956–1990*, and *Typenatlas NVA. Die Schiffe der Volksmarine 1960–1990*, Munich: GeraMond (2013).

15 The Federal Minister of Defence, *White Paper 1985. The Situation and the Development of the Federal Armed Forces*, Bonn: Bundesministerium der Verteidigung (1985), pp. 211–20.

16 For a small sample of European and German views on "The Maritime Strategy," see: Robert Wood and John Hanley, "The Maritime Role in the North Atlantic," *Naval War College Review* 38, 6, pp. 5–18; M. P. Gretton, "The American Maritime Strategy. European Perspectives and Implication," *Royal United Services Institute for Defence Studies* 134, 1, pp. 19–26; Ulrich Weisser, *Strategie im Umbruch. Europas Sicherheit und die Supermächte*, Herford: Busse + Seewald (1987), pp. 102–14; Joachim Schmidt-Skipiol, "Die Maritime Strategy der Vereinigten Staaten von Amerika nach 1945." Unpublished conference paper, 32. Historisch-Taktische Tagung der Flotte (HiTaTa), n.p., 1992.

17 See Gottfried Hoch, "Einsätze am Horn von Afrika. Die Flotte im neuen Einsatzspektrum 1994–2002," in: Werner Rahn (ed.), *Deutsche Marinen im Wandel. Vom Symbol nationaler Einheit zum Instrument internationaler Sicherheit* (= Beiträge zur Militärgeschichte 63), Munich: Oldenbourg (2004), pp. 675–704; Hans

Frank, "Von der Landesverteidigung zum Kampf gegen den Terror," in: Werner Rahn (ed.), *Deutsche Marinen im Wandel. Vom Symbol nationaler Einheit zum Instrument internationaler Sicherheit* (= Beiträge zur Militärgeschichte 63), Munich: Oldenbourg (2004), pp. 705–28; Bernhard Chiari, "Von der Escort Navy zur Expeditionary Navy: Der deutsche Marineeinsatz am Horn von Afrika," in: Dieter Kollmer and Andreas Mükusch (eds.), *Wegweiser zur Geschichte Horn von Afrika*, Paderborn: Schöningh (2007), pp. 126–39; and Rüdiger Schiel, "Operation Sharp Guard: Die Deutsche Marine auf dem Weg von der Escort Navy zur Expeditionary Navy," in: Bernhard Chiari (ed.), *Auftrag Auslandseinsatz. Neueste Militärgeschichte an der Schnittstelle von Geschichtswissenschaft, Politik, Öffentlichkeit und Streitkräften* (= Neueste Militärgeschichte, Analysen und Studien 1), Freiburg i.Br./Berlin/Vienna: Rombach (2012), pp. 161–73.

18 Since 1986, the Naval Command (*Marinekommando*) has published an annual survey of Germany's maritime relations and interests. What began as a small photocopied pamphlet has meanwhile developed into a glossy, saturated brochure ("Facts and Figures on Germany's Maritime Dependence") issued by the Chief of Staff, Navy (currently VADM Andreas Krause).

19 Geoffrey Till, *Seapower. A Guide for the 21st Century*, London: Routledge (2013), pp. 27–44; Robert Rubel, "Navies and Economic Prosperity – The New Logic of Sea Power," Corbett Paper No. 11, King's College University of London (2012).

20 For introductions to German foreign and security policy in the post-Cold War era, see Stephan Böckenförde and Sven Bernhard Gareis, *Deutsche Sicherheitspolitik. Herausforderungen, Akteure und Prozesse*, Opladen: Budrich (2014); Stephan Bierling, *Vormacht wider Willen. Deutsche Außenpolitik von der Wiedervereinigung bis zur Gegenwart*, Munich: C. H. Beck (2014).

21 Peter Hartley, "The German Navy – The Way Forward?" Defense-Update.com, November 29, 2011.

22 Federal Ministry of Defence, *White Paper 2006 on German Security Policy and the Future of the Bundeswehr*, Bundesministerium der Verteidigung.

23 The uses of the sea were first developed by Ken Booth, *Navies and Foreign Policy*, London: Routledge (1977), p. 16, and Eric Grove, *The Future of Seapower*, London: Routledge (1990), p. 234.

24 The integration of German frigates into U.S. Navy carrier strike groups (CSG) for air-defense purposes is one of the more prominent examples. The German-led exercises "Northern Coasts" and "Baltic Operations" reflect German Navy leadership in formulating operational and geographic naval objectives – and practicing these with allied and friendly navies.

25 The calls for a more self-confident and responsible foreign policy for Germany, one that better reflects the economic power of the country and its international responsibilities, have become louder since the economic crisis in Europe and dramatically increasing crisis management tasks. Notably, the addresses by Foreign Minister Frank-Walter Steinmeier, Secretary of Defense Ursula von der Leyen, and Federal President Joachim Gauck on the occasion of the 2014 Munich Security Conference all included calls for more robust international German engagement, not excluding military means. For relevant samples from the accompanying academic and policy debates in Germany, see Stiftung Wissenschaft und Politik (SWP) and German Marshall Fund of the United States (GMFUS) (eds.), *Neue Macht. Neue Verantwortung. Elemente einer deutschen Außen- und Sicherheitspolitik für eine Welt im Umbruch*, Berlin: Stiftung Wissenschaft und Politik/German Marshall Fund (2013); Gunther Hellmann, Daniel Jacobi, and Ursula Stark Urrestarazu (eds.), *"Früher, entschiedener und substantieller"? Die neue Debatte über Deutschlands Außenpolitik*. Special Issue, *Zeitschrift für Außen- und Sicherheitspolitik* (*ZfAS*) 8, 1, Supplement, January 2015.

26 This is in line with a stern warning of the acclaimed political scientist Samuel Huntington, who noted that "a military service may be viewed as consisting of [1] a *strategic concept* which defines the role of the service in national policy, [2] *public support* which furnishes it with the resources to perform this role, and [3] *organizational structure* which groups the resources so as to implement most effectively the strategic concept" (Samuel Huntington, "National Policy and the Trans-Oceanic Navy," *U.S. Naval Institute Proceedings* 80, 5 (May 1954), pp. 483–93; author's emphasis) – or otherwise risk irrelevancy.

27 Stansfield Turner, "Missions of the U.S. Navy," *Naval War College Review* 26, 5 (March/April 1974), pp. 2–17.

28 Cf. Till, *Seapower*, pp. 32–41.

29 Since 1990, the North Sea and the Baltic Sea have largely been devoid of larger military and defense issues (with the exception of massive amounts of unexploded ordnance – reminders of two World Wars – in the Baltic Sea). Their geopolitical value seemed to decline rapidly. Instead, Germany drove to develop these maritime areas economically and politically, such as through the installment of large offshore wind farms to support Germany's ambitious energy supply reform. In addition, since 2011, the Nord Stream seabed pipeline has supplied Russian gas to Germany while bypassing transit countries

like Poland and the Baltic countries. The Baltic Sea, in particular, was turned into an area of increasing multilateral cooperation. This somewhat relaxed security situation allowed policy-makers and operators well into the twenty-first century to focus on maritime security and safety issues by way of forums such as SUCBAS (Sea-Surveillance Cooperation Baltic Sea) and international agreements like HELCOM (Baltic Marine Environment Protection Commission). With the return of geopolitics in the Baltic Sea region in the wake of a resurgent Russia, long-standing convictions on the role of naval force by NATO navies in the region ought to be reconsidered – with potentially lasting consequences for naval operations and procurement as well, and once again outlining the need to better network the strategic community in Germany.

30 Due to complex, historically reasoned jurisdiction, the military (on the national level) and the police (federal/state/municipal level) have strictly divided powers and responsibilities, which leads the Navy to support inner security (inside the territorial waters and the EEZ) only in very limited instances during peacetime. Domestic maritime constabulary organizations, as well as such players as the Federal Ministry of the Interior, the Federal Ministry of Finance, and the Federal Ministry for Transport and Digital Infrastructure, share the responsibility for maritime safety and security, but often lack the capabilities. Germany does not have a dedicated national Coast Guard.

31 In addition, the port of Duisburg on the river Rhine constitutes the world's largest inland shipping port.

32 For the High North, Germany traditionally maintains close ties with the Scandinavian countries, which includes combined training, exercises, and planning. Major naval operations with German contributions in the Mediterranean during the past ten years include Operation Active Endeavour, the United Nations' UNIFIL maritime task force, the support of the sea-based destruction of Syrian chemical weapons, and, very recently, aiding refugees drifting from North Africa towards Southern Europe. For a German review of OAE, see Felix Seidler, "Enduring Freedom und Active Endeavour: Wie effektiv kann maritime Terrorismusbekämpfung sein?" in: *Jahrbuch Terrorismus 2013/2014*, ed. Joachim Krause and Stefan Hansen, Opladen: Budrich (2014), pp. 379–400. For a German view on UNIFIL, see Sebastian Bruns, "UNIFIL's Maritime Task Force and Germany's Contribution," in: Bernhard Chiari (ed.), *Auftrag Auslandseinsatz. Neuste Militärgeschichte an der Schnittstelle von Geschichtswissenschaft, Politik, Öffentlichkeit und Streitkräften* (= Neueste Militärgeschichte, Analysen und Studien 1), Freiburg i.Br./ Berlin/Vienna: Rombach (2012), pp. 151–9.

33 The complex maritime security situation in the Gulf of Guinea region is a subject of increasing political and military planning, not least because of massive economic dependencies at stake. The participation of the German Navy in the Obangame Express exercises in 2014 and 2015 serves as an illustration for the rising importance of the region to Germany.

34 The German Navy actively participated in Operation Enduring Freedom's Task Force 150 (counter-terrorism effort) and is still engaged in the European Union's Operation Atalanta (counter-piracy). For a German perspective on OEF, see also Seidler, "Enduring Freedom and Active Endeavour." For a review of Operation Atalanta, consider Sebastian Bruns, "Operation ATALANTA at Three – A Success or Failure?" *Strategic Insights. Global Maritime Security Analysis* 36 (November 2011), pp. 8–12.

35 See Hannes Ewerth and Peter Neumann, *The German Navy. Deutsche Marine*, Hamburg: Mittler (2006).

36 The German Navy designated these vessels as frigates, although international works of reference, such as the International Institute for Strategic Studies' annual assessments, more appropriately consider these large ships as guided-missile destroyers (DDG). For the most recent work to date, see International Institute for Strategic Studies, *The Military Balance 2015. The Annual Assessment of Global Military Capabilities and Defence Economics*, London: Routledge (2015).

37 Cf. Albrecht Müller, "New Frigate Underscores Germany's Shift from Cold War Naval Combat," *Defense News*, January 13, 2014.

38 A procurement of two additional such vessels – in lieu of specialized fleet tankers – would offer an economics-of-scale effect and provide the German Navy with a significantly wider operational range.

39 For an overview of the history of naval aviation in Germany, see Ulf Kaack, *Die Flugzeuge und Hubschrauber der Marine: 100 Jahre Marineflieger im Jahr 2013*, Munich: GeraMond (2013), and Heinrich Walle, *100 Jahre Marineflieger, 1913–2013*, Hamburg: Mittler (2013).

40 Like the two flotillas in Kiel and Wilhelmshaven, the command in Nordholz is subordinated to the Naval Command (*Marinekommando*) in Rostock.

41 For a sample discussion, see Dieter Stockfisch, "Joint Support Ship. Ein Schiffstyp für streitkräftegemeinsame (joint) Operationen," *MarineForum* 12 (2013), pp. 10–12. Many European allies – such as Spain, Italy,

and France – have already built and procured such larger vessels. It has even been insinuated that Germany could obtain one of the *Mistral*-class amphibious assault/helicopter carrier ships which France built for the Russian Navy. Delivery of the planned two units was halted in 2014 due to the Ukraine crisis.

42 See "Linien statt Klassen," presentation by Christian Peters, Planning Office of the German Armed Forces, held at the Symposium Ausrüstung und Technologie See, Mannheim, January 22, 2015.

43 Lutz Feldt, Carlo Masala, Hans-Joachim Stricker, and Konstantinos Tsetsos, "Kein Land in Sicht?" *Frankfurter Allgemeine Zeitung*, April 1, 2013. The authors provide much further food for thought, such as the pitch to create a dedicated maritime ministry, a national coast guard, and a better coordination of European maritime interests, not simply from the economic point of view, but from a strategic perspective.

20

UNITED KINGDOM NAVAL STRATEGY AND INTERNATIONAL SECURITY IN THE TWENTY-FIRST CENTURY

Eric Grove

In concluding my book on the Royal Navy since 1815 at the beginning of this century I ended on an optimistic note about the future.[1] The Cold War, and the necessary preoccupation with a continental commitment of ground and air forces to mainland Europe that it entailed, had ended. Although the Royal Navy suffered very serious cuts in the 1990s as part of the 'peace dividend' and the other two services, the Army in particular, fought a considerable rearguard action that almost saw the *Ocean*-class amphibious helicopter transports (LPH) cancelled, the Navy had been able to prove its vital utility in the confused 1990s. Cold War anti-submarine carriers emerged as very useful providers of mobile and responsive air power not subject to the vagaries of host nation support. This was proved both in the Adriatic and in the Gulf. As a 'sweetener' in the final 'Front Line First' phase of the Major Government's rather tentative and extended 'Options for Change' defence review, British nuclear powered submarines obtained Tomahawk land-attack cruise missiles, a major expansion of their capabilities and a role that was soon to be proved in action in the Kosovo intervention in 1999.

The 1990s also saw the replacement of Polaris by Trident D-5 as the primary British nuclear delivery system with an operational flexibility that allowed Trident also to replace the RAF's air-delivered 'sub-strategic' WE177 lay-down bombs (in both their low-yield nuclear and high-yield thermonuclear versions). Although conventionally powered submarines were abandoned, a new nuclear-powered attack submarine better configured for cruise missile operations was ordered. The long-delayed replacement of the amphibious transport docks (LPDs) was also begun and the important role played by British mine countermeasures (MCM) vessels in the Gulf provided a rationale for a substantial flotilla of 25 mine hunters and minesweepers.

In 1997 Prime Minister Tony Blair's New Labour Party had a landslide victory over the hopelessly split Conservatives and began a 'Strategic Defence Review' (SDR) that was in many ways a major triumph for the Royal Navy. The new government's desire to pursue a more global interventionist policy was even greater than that of its predecessor and was reflected in the 1998 Strategic Defence Review The role of expeditionary force projection in a more littoral context was stressed with a substantial naval component of a planned Rapid Reaction

Force. The explicit move away from confronting the former Soviet Union allowed marginal reductions in force levels to 32 frigates and destroyers, 10 submarines (but all to be fitted with Tomahawks) and 22 MCM vessels. The amphibious force would remain untouched, however, and receive replacement, more capable landing ships logistics (LSLs) better adjusted to force projection operations.[2]

The main victory for the Navy was, however, the decision to build two much larger aircraft carriers to replace the existing fleet of three CVS (only two of which were ever operational). This had been a controversial part of the Review and was only settled shortly before the final document appeared. The Navy had, however, fought a skilful bureaucratic campaign, having learned the lessons of previous serious Whitehall defeats in 1966 and 1982. The carrier was defended in scenarios even including defending East European states from aggressive neighbours, where, much to the surprise of the civil servants, carrier-based air was proved by operational analysis to be more cost-effective than land-based (a scenario with a certain contemporary relevance).

The main factor in the favourable carrier replacement decision was the perceived requirement to deploy responsive air power on a more global basis. The carrier was indeed the only project mentioned specifically by Secretary of State George Robertson in his introduction to the Review. In the new strategic world, he argued, one had to go to the crisis rather than expect the crisis to come from afar. This required mobile airfields, i.e. the future carrier (CVF). As the twenty-first century started, the carrier project was maturing into a large, 65,000-ton ship capable of carrying 36 high-performance STOVL (short take-off vertical landing) F-35B stealthy fast jets, a sufficient capability to make any Joint Forces Air Component Commander (JFACC) take British views into account. The Royal Navy's main concession to get the carrier was the merging of the Fleet Air Arm Sea Harriers with the RAF's Harriers in a Joint Force Harrier. That would be the prototype of the air groups that would operate from the CVFs.

In 2000, the new expeditionary strategy was proved by operations in Sierra Leone that helped stabilise the country. The Navy, including a carrier and the LPH, played a major role in this activity. Then things began to go terribly wrong. The September 11 2001 attacks on the United States, which provided the 'Pearl Harbor Event' for which the American neo-conservatives had been yearning, led to the re-emergence of a continental strategy. This time the continent was Asia, rather than Europe. The invasions of Afghanistan and Iraq (although maritime forces played important roles, especially in the former) gave the Army a new priority in UK defence planning. British defence policy began to lose whatever balance it had had. Misjudgements about the true cost of the SDR posture led to further marginal cuts in maritime capability in 2003, but the true nature of the resulting strategic distortion would only become clear after the General Election in 2010.

The resulting Conservative–Liberal Democrat coalition began a hurried 'Strategic Defence and Security Review' (SDSR) to address the problems posed by both the contemporary economic crisis and the Ministry of Defence's overspending. The armed services circled their wagons to defend what they regarded as core capabilities, all in the context of an Afghan commitment that had been deliberately created by the Army, to safeguard its inflated force structure.[3]

In addition, the coalition set up a National Security Council to coordinate security policy. Hence the SDSR was notionally based on a 'National Security Strategy' produced at the same time to provide a context for the resulting defence posture. This expected the UK to be able to 'help resolve conflicts and contribute to stability' as well as being able 'where necessary (to) intervene overseas in support of the UK's vital interests, and to protect our overseas territories and people'.[4]

The companion SDSR set out a set of 'military tasks' (MT) congruent with the above strategy. As slightly amended and reordered into the 2011 *Defence Planning Assumptions* these were:

MT1 – Providing strategic intelligence;

MT2 – Providing nuclear deterrence;

MT3 – Defending the UK and its overseas territories;

MT4 – Supporting civil emergency organisations in times of crisis;

MT5 – Providing a defence contribution to UK influence;

MT6 – Defending our interests by projecting power strategically and through expeditionary interventions; and

MT7 – Providing security for stabilisation.[5]

The commitment to power projection was clear and explicit, but the paradox was that the review cut precisely those forces best fitted to project power. Static Army formations were saved because of the Afghan war and the Navy and RAF suffered serious surgery. The latter was not entirely guiltless in this regard, as it was able to put into effect plans to delete Joint Force Harrier. The Air Force had never been happy with the STOVL aircraft that required it to operate from uncomfortable temporary ground facilities or RN warships. The Harrier's success as a close support aircraft was ignored especially by the 'Tornado mafia' of long-range bomber crews, who were in influential positions in the defence establishment at this time, not least as the Chief of Defence Staff (CDS), Sir Jock Stirrup. The RAF, in fact, had developed an effective long-term strategy, first of all achieving the demise of the Sea Harriers and reducing RN influence in the Joint Force and then treating Harrier deployment to ships as just one of a number of possible options. This culminated in the 'rationalisation' of the RAF on two fast jet types, Typhoon and Tornado (both, of course, land-based), a decision taken at the last minute in the review process with the Prime Minister apparently not fully aware of the effect of carrier abandonment on the future of the UK's carrier strike capability.

The UK's maritime capabilities suffered devastating cuts in the SDSR. Carrier strike was to be abandoned, in the short term at least, with the immediate – and unexpected – withdrawal from service of both the Harrier and the carrier *Ark Royal* (R-07). Her sister ship *Illustrious* (R-06) was to be retained as an LPH to cover for *Ocean* (L-12) in refit. One of the LPDs was to be placed in reserve as part of reductions in amphibious capability that included the sale of one of the new LSLs. As for the new large future carriers, the decision was to complete one to a revised design with catapults and arrester gear to carry the F-35C variant of the Joint Strike Fighter. The other might be placed in reserve. Cancellation of the second ship had been seriously considered, but BAE, the main partner in the Alliance building the ships, pointed out that such a decision would produce a hiatus in warship building that would effectively mark the end of the industry. It was therefore decided to complete both *Queen Elizabeth* and *Prince of Wales*, as the two ships had been named. This would leave a gap of at least a decade in carrier capability, which the Government claimed was a reflection of the expected level of risk in that period.

Another blow to maritime capability was the abandonment of maritime patrol aircraft (MPA) with the cancellation of the Nimrod MRA4 programme that had, admittedly, proved overly expensive, but which was approaching operational capability. Caught between the RAF 'Tornado mafia' and a Navy with no institutional commitment (and which was able to offer frigates and helicopters to 'replace' the aircraft in its roles), it had no chance of survival. With submariners in influential positions in the Navy, it was not surprising that the Navy maintained a mildly cut fleet of seven SSNs (to maintain about five running in service) and replacement of the Trident submarines, the only realistic way that the National Security Policy priority of the maintenance of nuclear deterrence could be achieved. The price paid was the carrier and amphibious cuts already mentioned and the reduction of the destroyer and frigate force to an unprecedentedly low 19 units, 50 per cent of the 'about 40' in service at the end of the Cold

War. Although the six new Type 45 destroyers entering service had a capability in the anti-air warfare role many times that of the old Type 42s they were replacing, they could not be in two places at once for the wider roles expected of a surface combatant.

What those roles were expected to be was set out shortly afterwards in the new 2011 edition of *British Maritime Doctrine* (JDP 0-10). The Navy had first issued a public doctrine publication in the mid-1990s. It had evolved over the years and this fourth edition was a significant rewrite in a more overtly joint tri-service context. In many ways this was a natural evolution, as ever since the days of Sir Julian Corbett British thinking had always emphasised the role of navies in affecting what happened ashore. The first edition of *Maritime Doctrine* had indeed had considerable influence on the initial drafting of the joint *British Defence Doctrine*.

Maritime power as defined in the new doctrine iteration is the 'ability to project power at sea and from the sea to influence the behaviour of people and the course of events'.[6] The document went on to put this ability in a UK context. As 'a maritime nation dependent on the sea for prosperity, stability and security and access to the international system of law and free trade', the UK, it argued is a 'global player' whose maritime capacity 'contributes significantly' to protecting and promoting British interests 'across the world at sea and from the sea'. A high proportion of future conflict was likely to occur in or adjacent to 'a zone of maritime influence', while Britain's overseas territories, most of which were islands, were subject to external territorial claims.[7]

A paragraph taken from the 2007 *Future Maritime Concept* set out the role of maritime power in a joint context:

> The maritime environment provides critical access for joint assets allowing influence in support of political objectives, the conduct of a wide range of maritime security and international engagement and, when necessary, the means to assemble and apply decisive combat power at a time and place of political choice.[8]

JDP 0-10 went on to analyse the three 'roles of British maritime power' developed from the triangle set out in this author's 1990 book *The Future of Sea Power*.[9] There, the functions of navies were defined as military, constabulary and diplomatic. The new official iteration argued that these had 'evolved' into three inter-related 'doctrinal roles': war fighting, maritime security and international engagement. These three roles 'collectively or individually, depending on the specific circumstances, seek to stabilise the strategic maritime environment as well as help ensure a secure and resilient UK'.[10]

British maritime war fighting doctrine, as set out in JDP 010, continued to emphasise sea control as 'a necessary condition to allow use of the sea for further purposes, including protection of sea lines of communication and to enable maritime manoeuvre'.[11] The latter was deemed to be of particular importance as 'predictions of the future strategic environment indicate that our national interests will continue to be located around the periphery of land masses, where centres of population, resources, industrial production, political control and trade are concentrated'. A capacity to operate in the littoral was therefore 'of crucial importance, either as the main effort or as the staging area for deploying and sustaining ground forces'. The ability 'to control events *at* sea' had to be complemented by a capability to influence event '*from* the sea'.[12] The sea is 'a three dimensional space in which and from which maritime forces can manoeuvre at a time of choosing to demonstrate political will, apply influence or, if required, use force'.[13]

JDO 0-10 defined the British approach to maritime power projection as:

> [T]he threat or use, of national power at range from the UK to influence events *from* the sea. It exploits sea control and maritime manoeuvre to achieve access in order to threaten,

or project, force ashore, using a combination of amphibious forces, embarked aircraft, land attack weapons and special forces.[14]

This could be used in a number of ways to shape, reassure, deter, coerce, disrupt, project, support, limit and/or recover.[15]

Next to be analysed was the second role, maritime security, which was to be provided on a global basis where UK interests needed protection. Maritime security was defined as a 'wide range of operations from defence (short of war fighting) through to security to development and relieving human suffering by utilising the full spectrum of maritime forces and their attributes'.[16] Maritime security operations were carried out in a legal framework, international, national or the laws of a partner state with its approval. The activities to be curbed were defined as 'piracy, slavery, people smuggling, illegal immigration, drug smuggling, arms smuggling, terrorism and the proliferation of weapons of mass destruction; as well as the protection of the maritime environment, including fisheries'.[17]

In the post-Cold War environment, the Royal Navy had tended to emphasise such maritime security roles, with frigates deployed to the West Indies with US Coast Guard enforcement teams on board, successfully capturing drugs in the Caribbean. The rise of piracy off Somalia led to deployments of surface combatants in the Indian Ocean. A small number of offshore patrol vessels was maintained, although their commitments were reduced with Scottish devolution, the Scots' own vessels policing northern waters. Three 'River' class vessels were built for use in home waters, plus a fourth with helicopter facilities for use in Falklands waters. After the SDSR, it was decided to build a third batch of three vessels to a modified design similar to those built for Brazil and Thailand to substitute for the dwindling numbers of frigates and destroyers in global maritime security operations. Another major purpose of this order was to keep BAE's surface shipbuilding facilities occupied until the first new Type 26 'global combat ship' orders.

The latter ships are due to enter service in the 2020s to replace the Type 23 frigates, eight of which have full anti-submarine capability, with the remaining five effectively ocean-going gunboats. Despite studies into 'future surface combatants' that had recommended a range of ships, C1 (fully combatant anti-submarine warfare (ASW) frigate), C2 (a similar-sized ship but less well equipped) and C3 (a smaller offshore patrol vessel/corvette), current plans seem to call for an initial class of at least eight Type 26s fully equipped for high-level anti-submarine warfare and a range of modular options including capabilities for maritime security operations. C3 has been transformed into a combined mine countermeasures and patrol vessel, but its future may be affected by plans to re-engine existing MCM vessels and adopt uninhabited underwater vehicles (UUVs) operated from larger ships, such as the Type 26. It remains unclear what the final solution to this dilemma will be.[18]

An important part of maritime security operations is what previous doctrine had defined as 'benign' operations, humanitarian assistance and disaster relief. As the 2011 document said:

> Maritime forces can provide a comprehensive logistics base and refuge onshore for humanitarian assistance with maritime helicopters providing a valuable means of transport. The flexibility of maritime forces makes them particularly effective in disaster relief, especially in the early stages, when they may well be the only means available to provide emergency assistance. A maritime force can provide a wide range of assistance such as fresh water, food, medical assistance … temporary shelter, fuel and electric power, while other agencies and non-governmental organisations mobilise more long term assistance.[19]

The point was illustrated by the role played by the frigate *Chatham* (F-87) and repair ship *Diligence* (A-132) and fleet auxiliary *Bayleaf* (A-109) in providing disaster relief for the Indian Ocean tsunami in 2004.[20]

The third 'International Engagement' role was defined as follows:

> British maritime forces, working with partners, exert power and influence in support of national political objectives with the aim to prevent conflict by deterring, coercing, stabilising and reassuring others in time of crisis.[21]

A major aim of such engagement was 'conflict prevention'. 'Maritime power', it argued,

> contributes significantly to international engagement encompassing outreach, confidence and security building measures and the promotion of UK interest and influence abroad. Such diplomacy is designed to influence the will and decision-making apparatus of a state or group of states in peacetime and all situations short of full hostilities. It is a powerful tool that provides political choice. It can be used to support or reassure and can be a significant contributor to coalition building. It can sway the uncommitted and it can be used to deter and coerce trouble makers.[22]

Much was made in this section of deterrence whose 'purpose is to dissuade a potential opponent from adopting a course of action that threatens national interests'. A primary function here was 'strategic deterrence' through the Trident submarines. The emphasis here was on 'continuous at sea deterrence' recently entitled 'Operation Relentless'. The capability of a Vanguard class Trident submarine constantly on patrol and the Trident D5 missiles armed with British warheads were 'the ultimate military safeguard for our national security and what underscores the communication of a deterrent message by the UK Government'.[23]

Complementary to strategic deterrence was 'conventional deterrence', a once taboo subject that – rather controversially – had become respectable in the 1990s, as symbolised in the decision to arm some, later all, the nuclear-powered attack submarines with Tomahawk land-attack missiles. As *Marine Doctrine* now put it:

> The purpose of conventional deterrence is to persuade an adversary not to do something by demonstrating that the likely costs will outweigh the benefits. It is based on potential rather than the actual use of force and is essentially preventative.[24]

The document went on to claim that maritime forces were 'particularly well suited to the delivery of conventional deterrence' because of their eight attributes: access, mobility, lift capacity, sustained reach, versatility (flexibility in response, adaptability, joint and multinational attributes), poise, resilience and leverage. 'Poise' is a distinctively British concept. It was developed in the 1990s, with operations in the Adriatic by carrier-based forces held in theatre to provide contingency support for troops ashore. It was now defined thus:

> Once in theatre, maritime forces can remain on station for prolonged periods either overtly or covertly, as long as required and are able rapidly to adapt to the tempo of the operation. They can signal political resolve and act as a force for deterrence or coercion. The ability of maritime forces to poise in international waters allows the *footprint* ashore to be minimised or avoided altogether, that is to say that the political complications and military risks of committing forces and their logistic support on land can be minimised,

if required or desirable. Poise exploits mobility, sustained reach, lift capacity and versatility to enable both military and political choice.[25]

JDP 0-10 concluded its 'conventional deterrence' section, with the assertion that maritime forces were 'one of the UK Government's most versatile military means of increasing political pressures as a crisis develops. Unimpeded use of the high seas allows a maritime force directly to deliver either support to allies and partners, or military deterrence, coercion and containment.' An example of conventional deterrence was offered in the use of the previous conventional carrier *Ark Royal* (R-09) in 1972, to demonstrate British resolve with her Buccaneer aircraft to show a capacity to intervene if Guatemala invaded British Honduras.[26] The Guatemalans seem to have been deterred. The use of a large carrier to make this point was perhaps related to the navy's fight to retain as capable a carrier force as it could after the ten-year SDSR hiatus.

The last major asset maritime forces provided according to JDP 0-10 was 'Presence', providing a defence contribution to UK influence. As the last First Sea Lord Sir Mark Stanhope had put it: 'Our presence in the first place: engagement without entanglement, may a sufficient demonstration of intent and deterrence to prevent the need for final engagement.'[27] JDP 0-10 enlarged on this:

> Maritime forces can alter the tempo of a crisis by their presence alone, creating opportunities for non-military solutions to be developed (such as may occur with other capabilities if deployed into a sensitive region). They can provide a clear demonstration of commitment to an ally and, at the same time, deter or coerce an adversary. Critically, maritime forces offer choice as events unfold and, with minimal or no change to their personnel or equipment, can provide decision makers with options at the tactical, operational or strategic levels.[28]

The example of presence used was Sierra Leone in March 2003, when even though the invasion of Iraq

> was in full swing, Operation Keeling was mounted to provide visible support to the Sierra Leone Government and prevent interference with the UN's indictment and arrest of suspected war criminals. The deployment of a Company Group of Royal Marines, the frigate *Iron Duke* (F-234), a Royal Fleet Auxiliary and two Royal Marine protection teams was later assessed by the FCO (Foreign and Commonwealth Office) as having been highly effective in stabilising the situation and preventing further loss of life.

The document went on to describe presence operations when there is no threat of force (showing the flag, as it used to be known) as a means of 'projecting influence'. 'In sum', it concluded, 'the key tenet of forward presence is to shape and influence a situation to prevent conflict, projecting hard and soft power concurrently, the presence alone of maritime forces provides a potent expression of national commitment and resolve.'[29]

The mismatch of this doctrine as a context with the realities of capabilities was demonstrated in 'Operation Ellamy', carried out in the year the latest BMD came out, to provide air support to the rebels in Libya. This was just the operation where the British carrier strike capabilities would have been most useful, but *Ark Royal* had been decommissioned and the LPH *Ocean* was used with Army Apache attack helicopters as a kind of ersatz replacement. Naval forces did what they could in blockade and gunfire support roles, but it was a serious lesson in the inadequacy of the Whitehall expectations that had advised SDSR.

In the run-up to the next SDSR, due after the 2015 general election, the Royal Navy has developed a new bureaucratic strategy in the attempt to achieve the restoration of a more pro-maritime balance in the UK's defence posture. In 2014, the Naval Staff, under the dynamic leadership of First Sea Lord Admiral Sir George Zembellas, developed a tripod of roles to support the size, shape and capabilities of the future fleet. First of these is 'continuous at sea deterrence'. This came out of the debate over the future of the UK's nuclear forces and whether a ballistic missile submarine (SSBN) should be on station at all times. The current aim is to build a 'successor' class of SSBNs to enter service in the late 2020s, with a reduced armament of 8 tubes carrying 40 warheads. The new design of reactor might allow three boats to replace four and maintain continuous at sea deterrence. It would also maintain vital nuclear construction capabilities as the 'Astute' class programme runs down; the last of the seven 'Astute' class, *Ajax*, is due to complete in 2024.

These boats are a second, conventional branch of 'continuous at sea deterrence'. With their large weapon capacity, they are admirably placed to contribute to an extra dimension of this concept. Currently, there is a Tomahawk-equipped submarine East of Suez within range of a number of potential Middle Eastern targets. This capacity can be maintained under this concept that will retain a requirement for nuclear missile submarines (SSNs) greater than that required just to support the SSBNs. As JDP 0-10 argued, SSNs have 'a power projection capability of considerable range and penetrability, with important uses for deterrence and coercion'.[30]

The second leg of the new strategic tripod is 'continuous carrier strike'. Since the 2014 Cardiff NATO Summit and Prime Minister Cameron's speech in the context of Russian aggression in Europe, policy now seems to operate both *Queen Elizabeth* and *Prince of Wales* side by side, as far as can be done (the original aim was to have two ships so one could always be operational). The problem is numbers of aircraft, with only 48 F35Bs expected. The SDSR's reversion to a catapult arrester gear was happily abandoned on grounds of cost and delays. *Queen Elizabeth* will therefore begin to have trials with F35Bs in 2018 and on present plans the number of aircraft procured for the future Joint Force will be 48, which will allow a front line of 16 aircraft for the carrier. This is not enough for the minimum necessary strike of 24 aircraft on deck from a total force of 36 embarked jets. The plan at the moment is to supplement the British air group in the carrier strike role with a balance of US Marine Corps jets to deploy enough striking power. This can be developed from a force of 36 jets, unlike in an American carrier, which for various reasons requires 44. Of course, the carrier has a number of other potential roles such as LPH, Special Forces insertion or a combination under the heading of 'carrier-enabled power projection' (CEPP). It can also be used in more benign roles such as a floating hospital. The arrival of the two carriers will see a step change in the restoration of the Royal Navy's global reach.

The third leg of this strategic tripod is 'continuous amphibious readiness'. This capability was the key to the Royal Navy's major interim post-SDSR power projection capability, the 'Response Force Task Group' that is holding the ring as a proper carrier strike is resurrected over the next five years. Depending on circumstances, the carrier strike capability could swing to a more amphibious role, with either the first or second carrier configured as an LPH, together with one or both of the LPDs plus the remaining LSD(A)s. and part or all of the Third Commando Brigade.

To support these core capabilities, as well as to engage in international engagement and constabulary roles, a new generation of surface combatants is required. As discussed above, this will be the Type 26 'Global Combat Ship' that is intended to replace the old Type 23s from about 2022. How far these will be supplemented by new Mine Countermeasures and Hydrography Capability (MHPC) assets is unclear. One option is putting new engines in some existing MCM vessels which will also keep Portsmouth Dockyard in work.

Whatever the actual shape of the future fleet, the maritime strategic emphasis for the UK will remain on power projection via submarines, carriers and amphibious ships supported by flexible surface combatants. This fleet will allow the UK to maintain the necessary capabilities to exploit its position as a maritime power to protect its interests in terms of war fighting, international engagement and the always vital constabulary role. Despite recent vicissitudes, logic should drag the UK back to its maritime strategic realities to maintain security in a world where Russia, the Islamic State and China each pose their own challenges to Western interests. Only by maintaining a capability to contribute significantly to sea control and maritime power projection can the UK remain secure in this context. There are encouraging signs that British decision-makers may at last be waking up to this reality.

Notes

1 E. J. Grove, *The Royal Navy since 1815*. Basingstoke: Palgrave, 2005, p. 263.
2 HM Government, *Strategic Defence Review: Modern Forces for the Modern World* Webarchive, National Archives, Kew, 1998.
3 'UK troops deployed to Afghanistan "to avoid cuts"', BBC News, 13 January 2011, www.bbc.co.uk/news/uk-12186888, accessed 28 August 2015. Sir Richard Dannatt's denial of this assertion by Ambassador Cowper-Coles is unconvincing.
4 'Military Tasks', in HM Government, *A Strong Britain in an Age of Uncertainty: The National Security Strategy*, Cm 7963, 2010, p. 33.
5 Quoted in Ministry of Defence, *Joint Doctrine Publication 0-10: British Maritime Doctrine*. Shrivenham: UK Development, Concepts and Doctrine Centre, pp. 1–13 (hereafter JDP 0-10).
6 *Ibid.*, p. v.
7 *Ibid.*
8 Development, Concepts and Doctrine Centre, *Future Maritime Operating Concept*, 2007, para. 123, quoted JDP 0-10, p. vi.
9 E. J. Grove, *The Future of Sea Power*. Annapolis, MD: Naval Institute Press, 1990.
10 JDP 0-10, pp. 2–7.
11 *Ibid.*, pp. 2–10.
12 *Ibid.*, pp. 2–13.
13 *Ibid.*
14 *Ibid.*, pp. 2–14.
15 Explained more fully *ibid.*, pp. 2–14, 15.
16 *Ibid.*, pp. 2–16.
17 *Ibid.*
18 This is a highly sensitive issue. There were two attempts to bring forward a C3 type ship as 'Global Corvette' and 'Black Swan'. The Naval Staff successfully saw off the challenge as it wished to defend its frigate programme.
19 JDP 0-10, pp. 2–19.
20 *Ibid.*, pp. 2–20.
21 *Ibid.*, pp. 2–21.
22 *Ibid.*, pp. 2–22.
23 *Ibid.*, pp. 2–23.
24 *Ibid.*
25 *Ibid.*, pp. 2–5.
26 *Ibid.*, pp. 2–25.
27 At the Institute for Strategic Studies, 24 February 2010, quoted *ibid.*, pp. 2–25.
28 *Ibid.*
29 *Ibid.*
30 *Ibid.*, pp. 3–14.

21

THE RUSSIAN NAVY

"Russia's pride, strength, and asset"[1]

Klaus A. R. Mommsen

One may well argue whether Russia fulfills the criteria of a sea power. According to Alfred Thayer Mahan, natural factors more than politics furthered "maritime thinking." First of all, the geography of a coastal state would prompt a government to have a "maritime-political understanding" which in turn affected its foreign, security, and economic policy. To Mahan, sea power built on a "national character" saw the priority of its economic interests in overseas trade (including colonies). That, in turn, would require a sizable own merchant navy which in turn needed protection by naval forces which, for their part, required bases abroad.

Sea power?

When in the early eighteenth century Tsar Peter I ruled the Russian Empire, the European colonial powers already had divided the world outside Eurasia into spheres of influence. Russia was a pure land power; it had no overseas colonies, although the external frontiers of its huge empire were often only accessible by sea. The only viable sea port at that time had been Arkhangelsk, at the White Sea, which due to ice could be reached only a few months a year. Since little developed with inland trade routes, sea trade with a direct, unhindered (clear of ice) connection to sea channels of trade became indispensable. Peter I had a large commercial fleet and a new Baltic Sea port (St. Petersburg) built and – to protect these new assets – established a Russian navy.

While Peter I remained focused on the Baltic area, 50 years later Catherine II also pursued interests in the southern flank. During her reign, Russia conquered Crimea, where the port city of Sevastopol was founded (1793). The empire now had a maritime gate to the south, although control of the Turkish Straits and consequently free access to and from the Mediterranean has been denied until today. In 1860, the town of Vladivostok was founded at the Pacific coast. Initially a mere naval outpost, it quickly became Russia's main port in the Far East and with completion of the Trans-Siberian Railway it developed into a commercial hub, linking the Far East with the Moscow center. In 1916, Murmansk was established on the Kola Peninsula; offsets of the Gulf Stream kept that Arctic port free of ice even during winter.

At the external frontiers of the vast empire, the naval fleets fulfilled merely regional missions. The huge distances between them forbade any combined operations. Apart from a (failed) attempt during the Russo-Japanese War to relieve the Pacific Fleet by deploying the Baltic Fleet, there were no operational ventures outside the fleets' respective home waters.

Soviet military power

Only very little changed in the Soviet Union. During World War II, the "Red Fleet" had a simple supporting function for the Soviet land forces, securing sea supply routes (near home waters), and protecting the seaside flank.

In the early years of the Cold War, the Soviet Navy retained its primarily defensive mission. U.S. Navy aircraft carriers and amphibious task forces were regarded as the main threat, which was to be countered with layered defensive lines. With the creation of a sea-based nuclear second-strike capability (i.e. submarines of Northern Fleet and the Pacific Fleet) and systematic courting of bloc-free nations outside the immediate "satellite" region, the Red Fleet gradually became an instrument for a more offensive foreign policy. Ocean-capable warships such as cruisers and eventually also (small) aircraft carriers became a tool in displaying the alleged power and superiority of the Soviet system.

Still, the Soviet Navy did not intervene in any major conflict with a maritime dimension. During the Arab–Israeli Wars of 1967 and 1973, although the Soviet Union was formally allied with Syria and Egypt, the Black Sea Fleet and its Mediterranean Eskadra (squadron) anxiously avoided being drawn into any combat action; their mission remained limited to presence.

Under Admiral Sergey Gorshkov (chief of the Soviet Navy from 1956 to 1985), the Soviet Navy saw a massive build-up of its surface and submarine forces. Eventually, the Northern Fleet's area of operations grew to span the entire North Atlantic, where a strong submarine component and long-range naval bombers were to disrupt Europe-bound NATO reinforcements. Nevertheless, the overall military doctrine of the Soviet Union remained predominantly land-oriented. The Navy's concept of operations basically continued to be limited to defensive and supportive functions. The Soviet Navy was not to conduct expeditionary warfare from the sea; its main task was creating favorable conditions for land operations. It had to prevent the U.S. Navy and NATO navies from attacking Soviet territory and reinforcing their (European) land forces by sea. In addition, it sought to protect the "Motherland's" coasts, ports, and naval bases. It also needed to safeguard the nuclear-strategic submarines' second-strike capability by shielding deployed ballistic missile submarines from any attacks by U.S. or NATO forces.

Strong amphibious forces were not meant to conduct global deployments but rather to provide flank protection to land operations. The concept included capturing the Danish and Turkish Straits, still, the overall aim was not to expand operations to the world's oceans, but to guarantee access to ports, shipyards, and repair facilities in the Baltic Sea and the Black Sea.

Protection of merchant shipping or securing global sea-lines of communication – for Tsar Peter I predominant motives for creating the Russian Navy, and later a central criterion for Mahan – played a lesser role in the Soviet Navy's concept of operations. Notwithstanding, the Soviet Union was widely regarded as a sea power. In fact, responses to perceived and actual Soviet naval power, in many parts of the world, dominated naval shipbuilding as well as naval strategy and operational and tactical thinking for decades.

Post-Soviet Navy: from Cold War to international cooperation

The demise of the Soviet Union was an obvious watershed. Now once again the Russian Navy, it invoked old Tsarist traditions, though the renaming of ships or the adoption of the blue and white flag with the cross of St. Andrew were little more than symbolic acts. With the independence of former Soviet Republics in the Baltic Sea (Estonia, Latvia, and Lithuania) and the Black Sea (Ukraine and Georgia), and the loss of basing rights at the ports of former Warsaw Pact allies and abroad (with the exception of Tartus, Syria), the navy had lost core elements of its operational and logistic basis. It was literally stripped of one of its key sea-strategic points of reference.

On the Baltic Sea, it retained only the bases at St. Petersburg-Kronstadt (not permanently free of ice) and Baltiysk (in the enclave of the Kaliningrad Oblast). On the Black Sea, under a basing agreement it had to share Sevastopol and other facilities on the Crimean Peninsula with Ukraine. Admittedly, except for some repair yards in the Baltic States, the important naval ship-yards at St. Petersburg and Kaliningrad remained in Russian territory. In the Black Sea, how-ever, nearly the entire shipbuilding and repair capacity was now concentrated on the Ukrainian mainland.[2]

The Russian Navy inherited the bulk of the Soviet Navy, but Russia's economy could not support such a large fleet. Bases now situated in "foreign countries" on the Baltic Sea and the Black Sea had to be dissolved, but the combat ships, submarines, and support vessels stationed there for decades could not be accommodated at the remaining Russian bases – there just was not enough berthing space. Large numbers of ships, planes, and submarines were cast aside, or simply tied up at the dock to rust. Images of derelict, rusty, and half-submerged hulls became a symbol for the sorry state of the Russian Navy. The Northern Fleet and the Pacific Fleet were also affected. Due to a lack of money, a number of projects to build or repair naval vessels had to be frozen – and, of course, the head count had to be significantly reduced, with grave conse-quences for the fleet's social structure.

The Navy was dilapidated; hundreds of vessels were paid off, but there was neither room nor money for their orderly utilization. At nearly all naval bases, ship graveyards sprang up. Officially, the role as a global sea power was still conjured, but the Russian Navy desperately strove to at least retain a small combat core of operational units. Inadequate supply of fuel and spare parts and above all an outflow of qualified personnel (not least due to missed wage payments) made regular training nearly impossible.

Conceptually, under such conditions the only option remaining was to place emphasis on the defense of Russia's own coastal waters. Therefore, the Russian Navy retreated by and large to the marginal seas. More than half of the submarines were retired for good, and large surface combatants – optimized for ocean warfare – were laid up.

There was no longer room to continue a confrontational policy toward the West. In fact, the Russian Navy also sought rapprochement with the former enemy navies. As early as 1992, the destroyer *Admiral Vinogradov*[3] participated in embargo operations against Iraq in the Persian Gulf; one year later, a Baltic Fleet *Krivak*-class frigate was a welcome guest at the U.S.-led multinational exercise "Baltops" in the Baltic Sea. In 1994, Northern Fleet units exercised with NATO ships in exercise "Pomor"[4] off the North Cape. 1998 saw a first joint exercise of the Pacific Fleet with the Japanese Navy, and in 2001, the Black Sea Fleet joined the BlackSeaForce established by all Black Sea littoral states. The sinking of the *Oscar*-II class submarine *Kursk* (in August 2000) served as an incentive to worldwide cooperation in developing submarine rescue technologies and procedures. The Russian Navy joined these efforts and since has participated in a number of submarine rescue exercises.

Biannual exercises were kicked off with the Indian Navy, and the Russian Navy joined the fleets of France, the U.K., and the U.S. in alternatingly hosted annual exercises denoted as "FRUKUS." The Black Sea Fleet began annual bilateral exercises off Sicily with the Italian Navy; that same year, the Baltic Fleet participated in a multinational mine-countermeasures exercise clearing mines laid in the two World Wars off the coasts of the Baltic States. Black Sea Fleet ships even joined NATO's Mediterranean anti-terror operation "Active Endeavour." There also were an increasing number of trips abroad, albeit with some restrictions: The fleet should only sail where it was "strategically reasoned – and financially viable."[5]

Such increasing international cooperation was reflected in the 2010 "Military Doctrine of the Russian Federation." The main tasks of the armed forces now included multilateral cooperation with partner states, combating piracy, participating in international peacekeeping activities, and combating international terrorism. In this conceptual way at least, the Russian Navy eventually returned to the seven seas, where it had been trying to maintain a small presence with very limited operational activities since the end of the Soviet Union.

Strategic reconsideration: back to the oceans

Not least because national interests as formulated in the key policy directive dictated a "vital necessity to protect and secure maritime transport routes for energy resources," a requirement for more presence outside the immediate operational areas of the various fleets gradually developed. In 2013, the current chief of the Russian Navy, Admiral Viktor Chirkov, spoke of plans to establish a number of "flotillas" for more or less permanent presence far from the home bases. These were to be stationed and to operate in the Pacific, the Indian Ocean, and the Mediterranean. Initially, the focus was on the Pacific – in line with the rise of Asia as the focal point of geostrategic interests and events. Contrary to the western theatre of war with its three fleets (Northern Fleet, Baltic Fleet, and Black Sea Fleet), there were no crisis management instruments based on bilateral political agreements with other Pacific nations; at the same time, new threats were recognized to be evolving in the Pacific region.

Notwithstanding this, the Mediterranean moved to the center of planning. In 2007, Admiral Vladimir Masorin, the then-chief of the Russian Navy, demanded that Russia's foreign policy goals in this strategically important region be underlined with routine naval presence. In 2013, a new permanent Mediterranean Squadron was set up, basically following in the footsteps of the Soviet Navy's former Mediterranean Eskadra. Its staff was established at the Black Sea Fleet headquarters in Sevastopol.

Warships and auxiliary vessels not only of the Black Sea Fleet but also the Northern Fleet and the Baltic Fleet have regularly contributed to this new task force. The participation of all three fleets was intended to give an impression of overarching command and control – actually, it rather shows how stretched the Black Sea Fleet really is. Logistic support has been provided by Black Sea Fleet bases but also at the Syrian port of Tartus – the only former Soviet naval base in a foreign country which has remained active to date. During peacetime, there has been no problem replenishing at regional civilian ports such as Limassol (Cyprus), Valetta (Malta), or the Spanish enclave of Ceuta.

Until now, however, plans for establishing a "Standing Task Force for out-of-Area Operations" – beyond the Mediterranean – have proved unrealizable. All extended deployments abroad pose the problem of resupplying ships and conducting maintenance work or even repairs far from home. This dilemma is also reflected in the Russian Navy's standing procedure to have nearly all out-of-area deployments joined by a salvage tug. Time and again, Russian media outlets have reported on plans to create logistic bases in foreign countries. Allegedly there were negotiations with Cuba, Cyprus, Egypt, Libya, Montenegro, Nicaragua, the Seychelles, Singapore, Venezuela, Vietnam, and Yemen. They all would not mind Russian Navy ships berthing and resupplying at their ports if need be. Yet, they have remained hesitant or outright opposed to the idea of having a permanent Russian naval base on their territory. Only Vietnam is said to be "in principle" prepared to re-establish the former Soviet naval base at Cam Ranh, a base that was initially set up by the United States during the Vietnam War.

The Georgian conflict (2008) in some aspects constituted a turning point in Russia's relations with the West. On the one hand, it strained Western trust in Russia. After 15 years of gradual rapprochement, there were now misgivings on the reliability and true willingness for security/political cooperation of the Russian "partner." On the other hand, mere protests and some faltering sanctions (such as temporary suspension of military contacts), which ultimately amounted to Western acquiescence with the post-conflict situation, appeared to have considerably strengthened the self-conception of the Russian military. To them, there could be no doubt they might "conduct such military campaigns with near impunity."

In the following years, the Russian Navy demonstratively increased its presence on the seven seas. For the first time in many years, Northern Fleet submarines operated off the U.S. Atlantic coast. At the same time, an increasing number of exercises spanning all military services and the geographic fleets signaled significant changes to strategic structures and the naval concept of operations. For instance, the bilateral (with Belarus) joint exercise "Zapad 2009"[6] saw Northern Fleet and Black Sea Fleet combat ships joining the Baltic Fleet off Kaliningrad. One year later, a Northern Fleet task group (with the *Kirov*-class missile cruiser *Petr Velikiy*), a Black Sea Fleet task group (with the *Slava*-class missile cruiser *Moskva*), and Baltic Fleet naval infantry deployed to Vladivostok for the Far East joint strategic exercise "Vostok 2010."[7]

The Russian Navy – with good publicity – demonstrated a capability for global all-fleet operations – although aside from the mere transit of task groups there were no open-ocean activities. In addition, aspects of homeland defense were firmly stressed. Since the "Vostok 2010" exercise, the Russian armed forces have also increased their focus on readiness, with snap drills becoming routine. Exercises are designed more closely to reality by preceding them with "unannounced" alerts, ordered from the "very top."[8]

During "Vostok 2010," plans for the restructuring of the Russian armed forces were publicly announced for the first time. The exercise was to prove in practice whether new operational-strategic commands could replace the military districts in command and control of large operations by joint and combined forces. Effective as of December 1, 2010, the six military districts were rearranged into four new strategic commands, centrally responsible for command and control of all military forces in their region, including naval, air, and air defense forces. Only the nuclear-strategic forces have remained directly subordinate to the General Staff.

The borders of these new strategic commands follow existing strategic zones. Both the Northern Fleet and Baltic Fleet are allocated to the Western Strategic Command (St. Petersburg); the Black Sea Fleet and Caspian Flotilla find themselves under the Southern Strategic Command (Rostov-na-Donu), and the Pacific Fleet is subordinate to the Eastern Strategic Command (Khabarosvsk). The Central Strategic Command has no naval forces assigned. The new structure is to facilitate improved, more efficient and above all joint (all-service) reaction to regional crises and other developments. Moreover, it is relevant during peace, crisis, and war, thus eliminating interface problems with shifting of command responsibilities.

Only recently, another modification to this new structure was announced. With the ongoing global climate change, the Northern Sea Route following Russia's coastline through Arctic waters between the Barents Sea and the Bering Strait has become increasingly navigable. At the same time, prospects for mining raw materials in the Arctic regions have significantly improved. This needed to be reflected in Russian naval thinking and organizational structures.

For a number of years, Russia has been striving to stake out claims in the Arctic, reaching far beyond its Exclusive Economic Zone (EEZ) – and has shown a willingness to also militarily secure and protect its "interests and strategic resources" in the region if need be. In 2012 and 2013, Northern Fleet task groups with the missile cruiser *Petr Velikiy* navigated the Northern

Sea Route as far east as the New Siberian Islands to conduct coastal defense and even missile defense exercises. Meanwhile, restoration of military infrastructure in the Arctic has begun, with former Soviet bases being reactivated and some new facilities being built.

Since the end of December 2014, this new focus of interest is also reflected in the Russian armed forces' structure. The new "Northern Fleet-Unified Strategic Command" is to safeguard Russia's interests in the Arctic region. It comprises Arctic Warfare Brigades (including naval infantry), Air Force, Air Defense Forces, and the Northern Fleet, which has separated from the Western Strategic Command.

Fleet renewal: plans vs. reality[9]

Since the demise of the Soviet Union, resources have remained scarce for the Russian Navy. In 2001, nearly 90 percent of the budget was spent on personnel and operations; just 10 percent remained for investments, and only part of it for shipbuilding. At the same time, however, it became increasingly apparent that the fleet no longer could live off its ever-shrinking substance. Not surprisingly, in 2001 a state-sponsored shipbuilding program "appropriate to Russia's defense requirements and national interests"[10] was announced; by 2020, the fleet was to be "substantially renewed."

A large blue-water ocean-capable fleet, with new aircraft carriers and cruisers, initially did not play any role in the concept of naval operations. In fact, aircraft carriers were primarily regarded as a geopolitical tool rather than as a military requirement. In the long term, however, new Russian aircraft carriers should become the core of complex task forces with the Northern Fleet and the Pacific Fleet. To bridge a gap, the only remaining aircraft carrier, *Admiral Kuznetsov*, and its Su-33 Flanker combat aircraft were to remain in active service.

Priority was given to nuclear-powered submarines and small to medium multi-purpose surface combatants optimized for anti-submarine warfare (ASW) and surface warfare in coastal waters, offshore economic zones, and marginal seas. Subsequently, in a second step, larger, high-sea- (and land-attack-) capable multi-purpose frigates were to follow. For the first time in 20 years, a new class of larger landing ships was also planned.

This renewal of the Russian fleet and its rebuilding into a combat-capable instrument for Russian foreign and security policy started ten years ago, but has progressed very slowly. Hardly a single project has adhered to its timetable. Extremely long actual construction times have frequently required readjustments to state-of-the-art technology – more often with time-consuming design changes. With the introduction of new ships regularly delayed by years, lifetime-extending overhauls of older ships have become an unplanned and unpleasant necessity. In June 2014, Admiral Viktor Chirkov openly described major parts of his fleets as obsolete beyond reason.

The reasons are manifold and range from ministerial bureaucracy and state authorities failing to pay for what they ordered, to material flaws, outdated shipyard infrastructure, botched-up work, and low quality of parts/systems provided by subcontractors. On top of everything, fraud, embezzlement, bribery, and misappropriation are said to swallow up as much as 20 percent of the Navy's procurement budget.

President Vladimir Putin and his Defense Minister Sergey Shoigu have vowed to clamp down on corruption. The budget has markedly increased (2013/14 by nearly 50 percent), and the President has tasked the Defense Ministry with compiling a new Plan for the Development of the Armed Forces by the end of 2016. In the medium or long term, this may look promising; currently, however, it seems that Russia's shipbuilding industry is in no condition to deliver the quantity nor the quality of the necessary weapons and equipment.

Construction of the new *Borej*-class ballistic missile submarines (SSBN) has lagged several years behind schedule. Construction of the type boat *Yuri Dolgorukiy* started in 1996, but only shortly afterwards had to be temporarily suspended due to a "lack of steel." Problems with the new submarine-launched ballistic missile (SLBM) Bulava added to delays. After ten years of test launches (with 7 out of 20 failing), it is still unclear whether Bulava will be apt for safeguarding a reliable maritime second-strike capability. A final series of test launches is to conclusively clarify this, but the current *Borej* design would not allow for any other SLBM to make good for Bulava.[11]

Not knowing whether Bulava would be available, the construction of further *Borej* had to be delayed time and again – while older *Delta-IV*-class boats have been upgraded for a prolonged in-service life. Meanwhile, it has been decided to go along with the *Borej/Bulava* combination.[12] In December, 2015, manufacturer Sevmash planned to lay the keel for the seventh *Borej*-class boat; a total of eight is planned. Due to the year-long delays in the program, new boats receive more modern equipment and are officially called *Borej-A* class.

Development of new *Yasen*-class nuclear-powered attack submarines (SSN) has followed a similar path. The *Severodvinsk*, type boat of these "next-generation" submarines, was commissioned into service only in 2014, more than 20 years after construction had started – and media reports allege the Russian Navy accepted delivery only after considerable political pressure. Delays were attributed to deficiencies with the propulsion system, problems with system integration, and a much too high noise level. Not surprisingly, after 20 years a larger part of the original equipment and gear has become outdated; *Severodvinsk* has remained more or less a prototype, and further boats are being built after a modified design as *Yasen-M*-class. By 2020, eight *Yasen/Yasen-M* are planned to join the Russian Navy; at the same time, older SSNs are being overhauled and upgraded.

Conventional diesel-electric-powered new *Lada*-class submarines, also meant for export, fell considerably short of expectations. Problems with a self-acclaimed "revolutionary" new propulsion system delayed commissioning of the type boat *Sankt Peterburg* by more than five years – and led to a building freeze for two sister boats. One of these boats is now tentatively planned to have a newly developed air-independent propulsion system installed, hopefully available by 2017. Most certainly also as a stopgap, submarines of an improved *Kilo-II*-class were ordered. The first of these *Kilo-III* has entered service with the Black Sea Fleet; a total of at least eight are planned by 2020.

New aircraft carriers or large missile cruisers have not been included in the current ship-building plan (until 2019), but according to official statements construction of new aircraft carriers may start after 2020. A draft design already presented by the shipbuilding industry has, however, been outright rejected as cleaving to the past; most probably it was just an updated variant of the former Soviet aircraft carrier *Ulyanovsk* (begun in the 1980s but not completed and then scrapped). As to cruisers, the Russian Navy will have to make do with overhauling and modernizing its three *Slava*-class ships for the remainder of this decade – and reconstructing the nuclear-powered *Kirov*-class missile cruiser *Admiral Nakhimov*, laid up for some 15 years. Work is planned to be completed in 2018.

New large missile destroyers, tentatively dubbed *Lider*-class, are scheduled to be built from 2018 to replace the *Sovremenniy*-class destroyers. Design work reportedly has followed two tracks, with both a conventional and a nuclear power plant. Regarding the current status of the shipbuilding industry, the first ship is unlikely to be delivered before 2023. Not surprisingly, the *Udaloy* class destroyers, current workhorses in overseas deployments, are to get a service-life extension and upgrade.

Grigorovich- and *Gorshkov-*class frigates are being built as follow-ons to the *Krivak-*class. Both projects are years behind their original schedule. First sea trials of the *Admiral Gorshkov*, type ship of the *Gorshkov-*class, had to be delayed by two years because a subcontractor proved incapable of delivering a functional main gun. Meanwhile, the first *Steregushchiy-*class corvettes have joined the Baltic Fleet, but ten years after the project started the basic design obviously no longer reflects the Navy's original requirements.

Only a few more *Steregushchiy* will be built – with a modified design; then the program will be abandoned in favor of new patrol ships, the construction of which has begun. The Russian Navy expects a greater autonomy, flexibility, and – with higher sea endurance – better suitability for out-of-area operations. They also will be the first Russian warships built in a modular fashion from ready-made blocks, making production cheaper. A total of at least 12 ships are planned for all fleets. Other new construction projects such as *Buyan* and *Buyan-M* corvettes and small "anti-terror boats" aim at strengthening capabilities in home littoral waters (e.g. protecting resources).

For the first time in decades, new high-seas capable mine hunters (*Alexandrit-*class) and large landing ships are being built. Eight years after keel-laying, landing ship *Ivan Gren* was launched in 2012 – well behind its original time table. A second ship will follow, after which the program is to end. *Ivan Gren* sticks to the conversant Soviet/Russian practice of disembarking troops and vehicles directly at a beach, over a bow ramp – contrary to the international trend, which has dock landing ships or helicopter carriers operate from a (safe) distance off the coast.

This stance clearly has changed in recent years, but Russian shipyards seem to have been incapable of quickly producing a viable contemporary design. In late 2010, in a thus far unique move, two *Mistral-*class helicopter carriers were ordered from French DCNS, with an option for having another two built at Russian shipyards after their deliveries in 2014/15.[13] In line with European Union sanctions imposed as a consequence to the Ukrainian conflict the two French-built ships were, however, not delivered. Russia is looking at an indigenous replacement program. Until their arrival, the Russian Navy will have to make do with extended use of veteran *Ropucha-* and *Alligator-*class landing ships. Other, smaller amphibious vessels currently under construction are only suitable for operations in marginal seas but hardly for the open oceans.

Procurement of new auxiliary vessels is focused on Arctic-capable research/survey ships, new replenishment ships, and larger search and rescue vessels (submarine rescue); new intelligence collectors are under construction as well. Many of the small vessels supporting the navy in port or at the roadsteads (tugs, diving tenders, etc.) are currently being replaced with new boats. Russian naval aviation can look forward to the new variants of carrier-capable fighter aircraft Su-33 and Mig-29, combat helicopters Ka-52 (destined for the *Mistral-*class helicopter carriers), and even new amphibious aircraft. The maritime patrol aircraft Ilyushin-38 are being modernized.

The way ahead: from cooperation back to confrontation?

If it is up to President Vladimir Putin, the Russian Navy will be equal to the Soviet Navy of the 1970s and 1980s in its size and strength by 2020. He envisions an inventory with some 300 combat ships, including major combatants optimized for global open-ocean operations.

The Northern Fleet and Pacific Fleet are to operate up to three aircraft carrier groups each. Otherwise, priority will be given to the Black Sea Fleet, which – consequentially to the annexation of Crimea – will receive the bulk of new frigates/corvettes and conventional-powered submarines. Another emphasis will be on safeguarding the northern Arctic region and its strategic resources. In addition to more than ten ice-capable support ships to be built by 2016, the Russian Navy plans to start construction of new warships optimized for operations under Arctic conditions by 2020.

Foreign analysts, however, have been consistent in their assessment that the Russian Navy is not on a trajectory to reach the goals set for 2020. It still has major problems with readiness and quality of both personnel and equipment, and the industrial base is expected to remain a source of substantial weakness. That view had been taken even before the current conflict with the Ukraine – which certainly will exacerbate the situation even further.

From its perspective, Russia may have had no choice but to annex Crimea. The overthrow of Ukrainian President Viktor Yanukovich certainly triggered fears of a looming cancellation of the (already heavily disputed) extension of the Black Sea Fleet leasing agreement. With Novorossiysk far from being an alternative, Sevastopol and its bases have been and will be of paramount importance to Russia's Southern Strategic Direction (Mediterranean, Middle East). The "lukewarm" Western response to Russia's Georgian campaign (2008) may well have been a factor in determining Moscow's course of action.

The ongoing conflict has led Russia, its economy, its armed forces – and with these also its Navy – in dire straits. In March 2014, Defence Minister Sergey Shoigu ordered all services to look for money-saving options. In July, President Putin, with a view to impending EU sanctions on Russia's arms sectors, urged the defense industry to expedite efforts in order to reduce dependence on foreign suppliers. Such dependence, for example, has existed with gas turbines for warships, which have not been manufactured in Russia at all but exclusively imported from Ukraine; the Ministry of Defense hopes to have a domestic alternative working by 2017. In October 2014, Finance Minister Anton Siluanov bluntly stated, that Russia "cannot afford to carry out the 2016–25 armament plan … the current level of military spending is unsustainable due to economic slowdown amid declining oil prices and Western sanctions."[14]

For the time being, it remains unclear whether a political solution to the Ukraine conflict will have Russia and the West return to a more or less harmonious relationship (with some mistrust remaining), or whether failing to reach a mutual accord will lead to a renewed (but somewhat diminished) Cold War. Whatever the outcome, the Russian Navy will to a certain extent be capable of sea control and area denial off its home coasts, in the marginal seas, and in the Arctic region. Prospects for global naval presence, much less global naval operations, however, will remain meager.[15] Notwithstanding the launching of long-range cruise missiles from the Caspian Sea at targets in Syria, for the foreseeable time, there will be no capability for real "power projection" beyond home waters. Quite clearly, the Russian Navy will have to lower its sights.

Notes

1 Russia's President Vladimir Putin, on the occasion of Russian Navy Day, July 27, 2014.

2 Russia has not ordered any new warships from shipyards on the Ukrainian mainland; construction of partly completed ships, such as the nuclear-powered aircraft carrier *Ulyanovsk*, the aircraft carrier *Varyag*, and a fourth *Slava*-class missile cruiser, was suspended; Ukraine eventually sold the *Varyag* to China.

3 This chapter will forgo any hull/pennant numbers, as the Soviet/Russian Navy had/has a tradition of changing these once in a while.

4 Pomors had been Russian settlers living on the Arctic White Sea coasts who discovered the Northern Sea Route.

5 Admiral Vladimir Masorin, shortly after taking over as Russian Navy chief in September 2005.

6 Zapad: Russian for "West."

7 Vostok: Russian for "East."

8 In September 2014, President Vladimir Putin himself set off the alarm preceding exercise "Vostok 2014."

9 For a comprehensive review of Russian fleet renewal plans, see Dimitry Gorenburg, "Russian naval shipbuilding plans: Rebuilding a blue water navy," January 23, 2015, https://russiamil.word-press.com/2015/01/23/russian-naval-shipbuilding-plans-rebuilding-a-blue-water-navy/ and "Russian naval capabilities and procurement plans," January 14, 2015, https://russiamil.wordpress.com/2015/01/14/russian-naval-capabilities-and-procurement-plans/, both accessed August 28, 2015.

10 Chief of the Russian Navy, Admiral Vladimir Kurojedov.

11 SS-N-23 Sineva missiles (launching tubes), deployed on board the *Delta*-IV-class ballistic missile submarine, are much too large for *Borej*. Their installation would require major changes to the basic design of the *Borej*-class submarines.

12 Two successful test launches by the *Borej*-class submarines *Vladimir Monomakh* (in September 2014) and *Yuri Dolgorukiy* (in late October 2014) supported this decision.

13 Against the backdrop of the Ukraine crisis, the delivery of the two French-built *Mistral*-class helicopter carriers *Vladivostok* and *Sevastopol* has remained in limbo. Optional domestic construction of two more ships of this class is not included in current ship-building plans and may have been forgone.

14 See also *Moscow Times*, October 20, 2014.

15 There will be the usual long-distance cruises and also continued Mediterranean presence, but participation in anti-piracy operations already seems to have been scaled down, and fallout from the Ukraine crisis most likely will continue to affect participation in international exercises.

22

MARITIME SECURITY ORDER IN ASIA

A perspective from India

Vijay Sakhuja

The sea is an important medium for conduct of international relations and has shaped the historical and contemporary maritime discourse based on two drivers, i.e. economics and security. In former times, the seas linked the different trading systems of the Greeks, Romans, Egyptians, Jews, Arabs, Indians, and Chinese. In contemporary times, the seas have connected the economies in the Asia-Pacific, Europe, and North and South America through a complex network of free trading arrangements and agreement. In the security domain, there is historical evidence of states dispatching ships to distant waters to protect trade and to dominate regional affairs, an objective that continues to date. Likewise, the significance of the oceans in the strategic calculus of states is growing and navies are engaged across the globe to protect sea lanes that serve as the umbilical cord of the respective economies. Further, these forces safeguard national interests and support alliance and partnership commitments. The naval and maritime forces are usually forward-deployed through a multitude of bilateral and multilateral access and basing agreements, over-flight rights, naval engagements that pivot around military exercises, logistical support, and infrastructure developments. This analysis begins by defining maritime security order and examines the likely challenges for the U.S.-led maritime security order from states, non-state actors, stakeholders, multilateral structures and the responses from the Asian powers.

What is maritime security order?

There are several ways to define maritime security order. It can be understood as the state of affairs wherein the stakeholders exploit the seas and the oceans as a medium of transport, source of livelihood, or any such other uses for peaceful purposes. It can also be expressed as a state of affairs in which the sea is considered safe and free of disorders resulting from asymmetric threats and challenges such as piracy, terrorism, drug running, gun smuggling, human trafficking, and other illegal activities. These are all generally transnational in nature and act as impediments to the growth of maritime enterprise and challenge the peaceful uses of the seas. Maritime security order is also shaped by the nature of relationships among the states who transact their politico-diplomatic businesses through alliances, partnerships, multilateral engagements, and bilateral relations. The individual navies, their respective areas of operation, the degree of technological sophistication, and the ability to be interoperable also shape the maritime security order. Maritime security order can be viewed from the perspective of laws and conventions that regulate maritime affairs on the seas. This order is built on the foundation of an internationally accepted established legal system that prevents lawlessness at sea, safeguards national interests, and precludes falling prey to the devious that could visit, board, search, and seize vessels at sea. At another level, maritime security order is significant for upholding international treaties, conventions, and laws such as Convention on the International Maritime Organization, United Nations Convention on the Law of the Sea, 1982, International Convention for the Safety of Life at Sea, 1974, Convention for the Suppression of Unlawful Acts against the Safety of Maritime Navigation, 1988, etc.

Maritime security order is also determined by the nature of physical geography, which dictates the conduct of maritime enterprise for economic growth and development. At another level, maritime order could very well be defined as the state of affairs and situations prevalent in any regional maritime space. It connotes the patterns of relations that exist among the littoral, archipelagic, and the extra-regional powers that characterize the region.

The ongoing trends in globalization shape the emergent maritime security order of the twenty-first century wherein a number of stakeholders are engaged in the smooth conduct of transactions across a wide spectrum of maritime activities. Interestingly, the rapid advancements and application of information and communication technologies to support maritime infrastructure and its use as a destructive force through cyber attacks has furthermore shaped the maritime security order. Maritime security order is driven by the increasing awareness of environment with special focus on ecology and climate change which has attracted the attention of the global maritime community.

Some of the above aspects of maritime security order have been prevalent since ancient times, exhibiting a strong element of continuity. It is plausible that newer elements will be added in the future and would be significant in shaping the coming maritime security order. Given that there are a number of ways[1] to understand and define maritime security order, for the purpose of this analysis "maritime security order" is understood as the broad trends that characterize and shape the contemporary maritime security environment based on the politico-diplomatic and strategic engagements among states.

U.S.-led maritime security order

In the twenty-first century, the U.S. is the dominant power and enjoys a global footprint. Its power is perceived as coercive but also as a security provider. In this context, an independent assessment of the American force posture and its underlying strategy in the Asia-Pacific region notes that:

> The United States has enjoyed a comprehensive set of diplomatic, information, military, and economic instruments of power to advance national interests and shape the strategic environment in the Asia Pacific region. Despite a relative decline in overall American military and economic power when measured against increased influence of other nations (e.g. China), the United States will retain distinct advantages over potential state adversaries for decades to come. Diplomatically, the United States will benefit from the desire of major maritime states on China's periphery – particularly Japan, Australia, South Korea, and India – to align more closely in a beneficial strategic equilibrium as Chinese power grows.[2]

The U.S.-led maritime security order reflects a strong proclivity towards dominance, display of power, and at times it engages in sabre rattling. It is not surprising that regional countries engage the U.S. to correct power imbalances, challenge the hegemony of the dominant power, and develop strategies to create legitimate space for the U.S. military presence. The U.S. has security treaties with Japan and Korea, commitment towards Taiwan under the Taiwan Relations Act, and it has also nurtured several bilateral strategic relationships with Singapore, Thailand, and the Philippines. Some members of the Association of South East Asian Nations (ASEAN) look towards the United States for security and stability in the region against the rising military profile of China.[3] In June 2013, at the Shangri-La Dialogue in Singapore, then-U.S. Secretary of Defense Chuck Hagel assured the Southeast Asian countries that the U.S. stood firmly against "any coercive attempts to alter the status quo" and "incidents and disputes should be settled in a manner that maintains peace and security, adheres to international law, and protects unimpeded lawful commerce, as well as freedom of navigation and over flight."[4] The U.S. has supplied military hardware to its regional allies and friends through transfers leading to military transformation.[5] For instance, India received P-8I maritime surveillance aircraft and the Pakistan Navy was supplied with P3C Orion aircraft and Harpoon missiles. This has contributed to regional deterrence and reduced the direct use of force against its allies and partners. The U.S. has military access arrangements in the region – Japan and South Korea – for rapid surge during crises and the new access and basing agreements with Singapore and Australia support its "rebalancing strategy."[6] In essence, the U.S. has adopted a proactive posture in Asia with significant offensive capabilities, causing anxiety in Beijing, which is increasingly devising a strategy to challenge the American hegemony in the Asia-Pacific region. In the naval construct, the U.S. and its alliance partner navies engage the U.S. Navy to balance the regional hegemonic designs of the dominant rising challenger, i.e. China. In its operational construct, the navies conduct joint and multilateral naval exercises, antisubmarine warfare training, Ballistic Missile Defence (BMD) operations, and exchange intelligence which assures the alliance partners of American political and diplomatic commitment.

In Asia, some countries are embroiled in territorial disputes with their neighbors (China and Japan over the Senkaku Islands, Japan and Korea over the Dokdo Islands, China and some Southeast Asian countries over the South China Sea) arising from historical divisions that have, in some cases, resulted in wars, tensions in interstate relations, contested sovereignties, and nationalistic interpretations of the 1982 Law of the Sea (LoS). Given the nature of conflicts and contestations in the maritime domain, particularly in East Asia, the regional countries look towards the United States as a stabilizing force and remain engaged in the region. This aspect became more pronounced after China announced the South China Sea as its "core national interest."[7] Further, a number of initiatives by China such as the China National Offshore Oil Corporation (CNOOC) offer of nine blocks (drilling areas) in the South China Sea for joint exploration with foreign companies,[8] the Hainan Province announcement to designate four areas around the Xisha Islands as a cultural relics protection area,[9] the newly established city administration of Sansha,[10] and the recent positioning of the oil drilling rig 981 in waters claimed by Vietnam[11] have been interpreted by the Southeast Asian countries as "new Chinese moves to reinforce its sovereignty over the South China Sea."[12] In that context, the Chinese Foreign Minister Yang Jiechi had clarified that China remains committed to world peace and development, does not support "aggression by any means," and cautioned that it is "unfair to misrepresent actions taken to safeguard one's own core interests as an aggressive stance."[13] In July 2010, then-U.S. Secretary of State Hillary Clinton observed that the United States encouraged adherence to customary international law for the resolution of territorial disputes and rejected use of force by the contending parties.[14] It was also noted that the U.S. had a "national interest" in the South China Sea and "could facilitate talks, worrying China that it was going to step into the territorial rivalry."[15] This was in response to China declaring the South China Sea its "core interest."

The evolving maritime security order in Asia

In the twenty-first century, Asian countries appear to exhibit a newfound confidence largely driven by economic growth and technological development, which is shaping the growth of their strategic profile. As far as conventional military capabilities are concerned, Asian powers are attempting to achieve, if not parity, at least deterrence to safeguard sovereignty, as protection against external threats, and to uphold their national interests. Further, nuclear and missile developments in China, India, North Korea, and Pakistan drive the region into a competitive pattern that can potentially invite extra-regional politico-military intervention. These developments have necessitated responses such as land- and sea-based missile defence systems.

At another level, the Asian maritime security order rests on a variety of treaties and alliances among regional and extra-regional powers to prevent escalation of prevalent tensions or outbreak of new crisis in the region and provide stability.[16] These treaties and alliances are significant tools for access and basing and to exercise strategic influence. However, the implications of these alliances can undermine regional stability.[17]

Asia continues to be crisis-prone for a number of reasons, such as China's rise, Chinese–U.S. relations, and Chinese assertiveness, particularly over boundary disputes in the East China Sea and South China Sea. China's rise to power pivots on its extraordinary economic growth and unprecedented foreign exchange reserves (US$3.95 trillion in April 2014).[18] This has propelled the People's Republic to the status of a global economic power. The Chinese economy has grown at nearly 10 percent in the last decade[19] and has provided the critical ballast for its strategic and military modernization. China's leveraging of its economic power for military modernization has alarmed the region[20] and raised concerns about the nature of its "rising power." Further, China has aggressively invested and has nurtured strong economic bilateral relations with several countries in South Asia, Southeast Asia, Africa, and Latin America[21] that have facilitated trade and also resulted in strategic partnerships for military access. China would like to play a leading role in Asia and dominate regional affairs, but it must contend with the U.S., whom it considers as a "hegemonic power" with huge military capability that can quite easily overwhelm it. It has been noted that the

> United States spends nearly as much money on defense as all the other countries in world combined. Moreover, because the American military is designed to fight all around the globe, it has abundant power projection assets. Much of that capability is either located in the Asia-Pacific region or can be moved there quickly should the need arise. China cannot help but see that the United States has formidable military forces in its neighborhood that are designed in good part for offensive purposes.[22]

China believes that the Sino-U.S. relationship requires a "new historical starting point" and there is a need to craft a "new model" and "draw a new path" for the relationship. President Xi Jinping has observed that China and the U.S. need to "think creatively and act energetically" to examine three major issues for enhancing bilateral ties, i.e. (1) what type of Sino-U.S. relationship both countries hope for; (2) how can they cooperate for mutual benefit; and (3) what joint efforts can be devised to promote world peace and development.[23]

China is also concerned about the U.S.–Taiwan security cooperation and for Beijing the fears arise from the belief that

> the greatest challenge to its [China] state sovereignty and authority comes from Western powers, particularly from the United States. Washington has maintained its military commitment to Taiwan, an island that China regards as its territory, by selling advanced weapons and sharing military-related intelligence.[24] It is feared in Beijing that should the Chinese mainland have to use military means to prevent Taiwan from achieving de jure independence, the United States would invoke the Taiwan Relations Act to protect the island, which would result in a major war between China and the United States.[25]

Further, China is conscious of the fact that it is unable to compete with the U.S. and the latter would be unwilling to accept China's rise.[26] It is concerned about the U.S. military presence in its periphery

> in Afghanistan, which borders China, since 2001, and the United States has strengthened its military ties with Japan, South Korea, the Philippines, Singapore, Australia, and other regional players. More recently, the United States has enhanced security cooperation with India and Vietnam, neighbors of China that once fought border wars with Beijing, and territorial disputes between the countries are ongoing.[27]

China's concerns also emerge from India's rise and its evolving close relationship with the U.S.,[28] the primary challenger to China's rise as a global power. It has been noted that "Beijing is particularly sensitive to any security and military relationship established between Washington and Delhi, as many in China's defense establishment view U.S. actions as designed to strategically encircle China in the Asia-Pacific region."[29] China would also like to erode any possible India–U.S.–Japan partnership and limit cooperative ventures between India and the United States, as it perceives such cooperation would be inimical to its interests.[30]

China remains cognizant of the fact that Japan is fast turning into a "normal" state and the Japanese military is technologically superior and has far-ranging capabilities that could challenge the Chinese People's Liberation Army (PLA) in conventional military terms.[31] In such a context, North Korea and Pakistan serve as significant brinkmanship actors for China's strategy against India, Japan, and the U.S. China's policy towards India has been to use Pakistan as a challenger to India[32] through supplying naval hardware such as ships and missile technology and keeping it "boxed" in the region and exploiting North Korea to keep Japan and the U.S. constantly puzzled by the leadership in Pyongyang.[33]

India's strategic interests have undergone a profound transformation and this has been possible partly due to India's choices of globalization resulting in strong economic growth. The new economic strength has resulted in significant opportunities for increased economic engagements with major economies of the world such as China, Japan, the European Union, ASEAN, and the United States. In strategic terms, the economic strengths have also spawned defence-technology relations which have accrued immense dividends thus fostering a series of new defense-technological collaborative enterprises.

Indian–U.S. strategic cooperation includes sale of military hardware, training, naval exercises involving aircraft carriers and submarines, has reached new heights, and could even compete with the Indo-Russian strategic partnership that has been in existence for more than four decades and featured military sales and equipment training. Although their pathways and approaches are different, these strategic partnerships have resulted in the augmentation of India's military prowess and added to India's growing strategic strengths.[34] At their recent meeting in Washington, President Barack Obama and the then-Prime Minister Manmohan Singh endorsed a Joint Declaration on Defence Cooperation to enhance their partnership in defense technology transfer, research, co-development and co-production, and identify "specific opportunities for cooperative and collaborative projects in advanced defence technologies and systems."[35]

India and China are the two rising powers in Asia and the former perceives the latter as a threat. Though India acknowledges that it is not in any economic competition with China, in the security domain the two sides have a long-standing border dispute in the Himalayas. Both sides have attempted to use diplomacy to lower tensions. Further, China's skilful use of Pakistan, Bangladesh, and Myanmar has resulted in India being boxed-in in South Asia. In response, India has projected its navy as a tool to caution China of the vulnerability of its sea lanes through the Indian Ocean.

There are several issues that plague China–Japan relations and range from historical mistrust, contentious issues such as war crimes, territorial disputes in the East China Sea, and foreign policy choices. Further, Japan is concerned about the growing military and nuclear capabilities of China and is responding in its own ways, keeping in mind the self-imposed limitations under Article 9 of the Japanese constitution. It is attempting to be a "normal power" and the current leadership is keen to formulate a defense policy that would help Japan move out of its overtly pacifist role.[36] It has supported the U.S.-led war on terror and deployed the Maritime Self-Defence Force (MSDF) in the Indian Ocean and engaged in anti-piracy operations in the Gulf of Aden. In a historic move, the Self-Defence Force is forward-deployed in Djibouti. Its force posturing and defence transformation aim at developing significant capabilities, which, when combined with the American forces in the region, would have the capability to challenge any military adventurism by China.

At another level, Japanese investments in China had been increasing, hence supporting the Chinese economic miracle. However, in recent times, Japanese investments in China are falling amid political tensions and anti-Japanese sentiments and are shifting to Southeast Asia. For instance, the Japan External Trade Organization has noted that the Japanese investment in Southeast Asia increased by 55 percent in the first six months of 2013 to US$10.29 billion, while outlays in China dropped 31 percent to US$4.93 billion.[37]

ASEAN had been concerned about the U.S. interest in the region after its absence in the 2005 and 2007 ASEAN Regional Forum meetings and the U.S. had refused to accede to the protocol of the ASEAN Treaty of Amity and Cooperation (TAC) in Southeast Asia.[38] However, ASEAN states have generally welcomed the U.S. rebalance to Asia[39] but are also closely watching the evolving U.S.–China equation. They are careful not to take sides and prefer to engage both U.S. and China through a host of multilateral structures such as the East Asia Summit and the ASEAN Defence Ministers Meeting (ADMM) Plus, which pave the way for cooperative engagements.[40]

Nuclear and missile developments in Asia

There has been a significant growth in nuclear weapons capability and their delivery systems in Asia. In 1964, China conducted its first nuclear test and India followed in 1974. In 1998, India and Pakistan conducted nuclear tests and North Korea conducted its first nuclear test in 2006. The drivers for nuclear weaponization among these countries have varied and are based on a number of factors, including distrust and deterrence. The Chinese nuclear capability was built with generous technology transfers by the USSR and was subsequently used to develop an indigenous capability.[41] For North Korea the motivations range from "an attempt to engage the United States in bilateral talks, to ensure the security of the regime, and to satisfy hard-line elements within the Pyongyang government, as well as technical motivations for carrying out a nuclear test."[42] India's nuclear weapons program (largely indigenous and evolved from its civil nuclear program) was in response to China's nuclear and missile capability,[43] and for Pakistan, nuclear tests (with assistance from China) helped it to build deterrence against India.[44]

The Chinese inventory includes a variety of intercontinental, cruise, and ballistic missiles capable of hosting nuclear warheads including Multiple Independently Targetable Re-entry Vehicle (MIRV) capability. In April 2014, China released its white paper on defense, *The Diversified Employment of China's Armed Forces*, which noted that the PLA Second Artillery Force (PLASAF) was the core of China's strategic deterrence and responsible for "deterring other countries from using nuclear weapons against China, and carrying out nuclear counterattacks and precision strikes with conventional missiles." The PLASAF is equipped with the "Dong Feng" series of ballistic missiles and "Chang Jian" cruise missiles.[45] The long-range missile inventory of the DF-31 and DF-41 Inter-Continental Ballistic Missiles (ICBM) can hit targets at 6,000–10,000 km. The DF 21 appears to have attracted greater attention due to its ability to attack mobile targets such as aircraft carriers.[46] In addition, there are a variety of short-range missiles deployed along China's coastal provinces and those deployed in the Tibet Autonomous Region (TAR) can hit targets in South Asia.[47] The Indian inventory is built around Agni I (700 km range) and Agni II (over 2,000 km range), Agni III (3,000 to 3,500 km) and the tests for Agni V (5,000 km range) are in progress, which would result in India possessing ICBM capability.[48] The latter are likely to be targeted against China.

Pakistan's inventory includes an assortment of missiles which are capable of carrying nuclear weapons, cruise missiles, and sea-based attack-capable missiles. These have been classified as "Hatf" series, "Abdali," "Ghaznvi," and "Shaheen" series "Babur" and "Raad."[49] It is important to note that these were assembled or developed with outright purchase and technology transfer from China and North Korea.

The North Korean inventory includes Scud-type road-mobile missiles and Nodong missiles capable of delivering a variety of warheads such as high explosive, chemical, and perhaps biological weapons.[50] Given their ranges, these missiles can strike Japan and South Korea. In addition, North Korea is known to have exported missile technology to Iran and Syria. Interestingly, there has been significant nuclear cooperation among Beijing, Islamabad, and Pyongyang, which includes transfer of technology and joint development of military equipment.

China and India have also developed a survivable and assured retaliatory second-strike capability built around the sea-based nuclear deterrent. The Type 094 Jin class SSBN fitted with 12 × JL-2 ballistic missile (8,000 km range) with MIRV capability of smaller yield is a potent platform. India has two nuclear submarines: *Chakra* (S71) is on lease from Russia and *Arihant* (S73) is being built in India. This has prompted Pakistan to explore the possibility of equipping its nuclear-capable missiles to be fitted onboard warships and submarines.

The nuclear threat from China and North Korea led Japan and the Republic of Korea to develop ballistic missile defense systems. In the past, Japanese ships have successfully engaged a ballistic missile target, including two successful intercepts, with the sea-based midcourse engagement. Similarly, the Navy of the Republic of Korea (ROK) has the Aegis BMD system, which is fitted onboard the *Sejong the Great*-class destroyers.

Southeast Asian countries have understood the nuclear dynamics in the region. In 1995, ASEAN declared the South East Asian Nuclear Weapon Free Zone (SEANWFZ). The multinational treaty entered into force after two years. ASEAN has called on Nuclear Weapon States (NWS) to sign the SEANWFZ Treaty but these states have objected to the contents of the treaty on a number of grounds, including "inclusion of continental shelves and exclusive economic zone (EEZ)"; "restriction not to use nuclear weapons within the zone"; and "restriction on the passage of nuclear-powered ships through the zone *vis-à-vis* the issue of the high seas as embodied in the UN Convention on the Law of the Sea (UNCLOS)." Further, they aver that "the continental shelves and EEZ are not clearly defined in the South China Sea, which creates uncertainty over the scope of the treaty, as well as the treaty's protocol obligations."[51] The naval nuclear developments in India are also a matter of concern for the ASEAN countries.

The American pivot

The U.S. rebalance to Asia is a significant development for the maritime security order in the Asia-Pacific region. The January 2012 strategic guidance for the Department of Defense titled "Sustaining US Global Leadership: Priorities for 21st Century Defense" notes that "The United States is investing in a long-term strategic partnership with India to support its ability to serve as a regional economic anchor and provider of security in the broader Indian Ocean region."[52] It has given India the status of a "security provider" and Washington expects New Delhi to play a major role in Indian Ocean affairs.[53] The U.S. also hopes to draw it to be more proactive in the region and support its strategy. As far as China is concerned, the strategic guidance emphasizes its importance in "peace and stability in East Asia" and seeks a "cooperative bilateral relationship." Although it does not point overtly towards China as the primary challenger in the Asia-Pacific, it seeks greater transparency and "greater clarity of its strategic intentions in order to avoid causing friction in the region."[54]

The document received mixed reactions in India.[55] There is a view, though a minority one, that both India and China enjoy civilization contacts built on culture, trade, and Buddhism. They argue that the two Asian giants have extensive economic engagements and that bilateral trade is growing and is expected to touch US$100 billion by 2015 compared to US$74 billion in 2011.[56] Both are members of the BRICS and have common views on a number of issues such as climate change, piracy in the Gulf of Aden, etc. Although the boundary dispute is a lingering issue, both sides have committed to maintaining peace and tranquility in the border areas. There is another school of thought which argues that Asia is big enough for both China and India and can accommodate their ambitions, aspirations, and interests and there is no place for outsiders. It has also been argued that external powers such as the United States have "long-established interests" in the region and are therefore integral to the rise of Asia, particularly given that there are ongoing trends in the "globalization of economics, security and technology," and ignoring the interests of other stakeholders would be a folly.

The new U.S. posture is seen as potentially keeping China busy in the Pacific region. It could also prevent it from openly influencing India's neighbors such as Pakistan, Nepal, Bangladesh, Sri Lanka, and Myanmar who have been overtly leaning towards China and supporting it against India and thus threatening Indian interests in South Asia. Further, there is also an opportunity for India to play a major role in the rapidly changing Asian maritime security order, and India's support for the U.S. rebalancing strategy could propel it to new strategic position in the region. Also, this could help India profit from the U.S. security guarantee particularly in the South China Sea, without committing resources for the safety of its trade and other economic interests. This would also prevent China containing India in South Asia to some extent. Further, it would enable India to dominate the Indian Ocean. In essence, the Indian strategic community is divided and expects India to follow a middle path and stay out of any American–Chinese rivalry. China appears to have welcomed the Indian approach to the U.S. rebalancing strategy and the view from Beijing is that "There is enough space in the world for India and China to achieve common development of both countries."[57]

Indo-Pacific: the new formulation

An attempt is made to combine the Indian Ocean and the Pacific Ocean to create a new maritime strategic space called the Indo-Pacific. Interestingly, the concept has become popular in Asia among a few countries. The Indo-Pacific formulation combines two oceanic spaces, i.e. the Indian Ocean and the Pacific Ocean, and its genesis lies in at least two important articulations. First, Karl Haushofer coined the term *Indopazifischen Raum* and observed that "dense Indo-Pacific concentration of humanity and cultural empire of India and China, which … are geographically sheltered behind the protective veil of the offshore island arcs."[58] The second is the statement by the Japanese Prime Minister Shinzo Abe in the Indian Parliament in 2007 where he announced his vision of the "confluence of the seas."[59]

The Australian Defence White Paper 2013 is the first official document that defines the space encompassing the Indo-Pacific. The concept has been interpreted differently as "encompassing both the Pacific and Indian Oceans, defined in part by the geographically expanding interests and reach of China and India, and the continued strategic role and presence of the United States in both." The Australian Defence Minister Stephen Smith refers to it as "as an amalgam of the Asia-Pacific and the Indian Ocean Rim, and the Australian Department of Foreign Affairs and Trade (DFAT) see it as an "expanded East Asia Summit" that extends "from India, through Southeast Asia to Northeast Asia."[60]

The Indo-Pacific formulation has a predominant maritime dimension and is significant for India. There are a number of reasons for defining this sea space for analysis and at least five of these merit attention: (1) Asia's economic power potential; (2) bridging the Indian and the Pacific Oceans through the concept of "confluence of the seas"; (3) competing political priorities and changing security perspectives of regional as well as extra-regional powers; (4) U.S. "rebalance" to play a bigger role in the Asia-Pacific region; and (5) U.S. strategic shift has forced its alliance partners to restructure their strategic orientations towards the Indo-Pacific.[61] The Indo-Pacific as a spatial formulation has found place in the strategic literature originating in Europe as well. It has been contended that "the rise of large countries around the Indo-Pacific region – such as China and India, but also South Korea, Japan and Russia – and the corresponding shift in the United States' geostrategic focus, away from Europe, and towards the Asian zone, compromises both the Atlantic Alliance, and, by implication, the European Union."[62]

Some EU member countries appear to be worried about the shift in the U.S. "pivot" and its focus on the Asia Pacific. Apparently they may not be ready to take more responsibilities for the security of the European continent; while others see the shift in the U.S. "pivot" as an opportunity for a greater role in the Indo-Pacific region. In fact a case is being made under which the European Union flag should be visible to demonstrate its willingness to remain active in the Indo-Pacific by dividing responsibilities. Those European nations who do not possess large navies may be tasked to remain active in the Indian Ocean; while the British and French forces which possess good power projection capability be deployed in the Pacific waters so that there is substantive European presence in the Indo-Pacific region.

It is true that EU member states are geographically far from Asia or for that matter away from the Asian hot spots such as the South China Sea (Spratly Island) and East China Sea (Senkaku Islands) involving a number of ASEAN and East Asian countries. However, EU states have enormous economic stakes involving investments and businesses in several East Asian countries[63] and a large volume of trade passes through hot-spot areas. If the safety and security of neutral shipping were jeopardized, EU states could be drawn into territorial disputes that have witnessed high pitch nationalism. However, the presence of extra-regional navies can potentially cause concern among the regional powers.

There are now calls for an Indo-Pacific treaty which would preclude conflict in the region, offering a pre-emptive mechanism for conflict prevention and resolution. This call is led by Indonesia, whose government believes that the country is strategically located and suitably poised to take the lead because of its "size, the neutrality and track record as well as the diplomatic brains to convince major powers to accept its proposal."[64] Apparently, Indonesia's fears arise from the changing nature of power equations among the major Asian powers such as China, the U.S., India, and Japan, which reflect a "Cold War type of mentality" in which "one country [is] becoming more prominent and there must be some kind of a balance of power, or a coalition of power rallied against it." The Indo-Pacific treaty could "create and introduce a new kind of perspective paradigm" which has "equilibrium through the promotion of common security, prosperity, and stability."[65]

Maritime multilateralism

The Asia-Pacific region has a number of security structures and bilateral and multilateral arrangements which have spawned political, diplomatic, economic, and security dialogue among the regional countries. ASEAN has been in the driver's seat and is constantly engaged in newer initiatives to integrate the region through multilateral structures. Significantly, a number of Asian countries appear to be quite comfortable with the ASEAN-led processes. Within the regional structure, the East Asia Summit (EAS) includes Russia and the United States. In November 2012, after the second EAS meeting in Phnom Penh, Cambodia, the White House statement noted that "President Obama used the summit to explore with other Asia-Pacific leaders ways to enhance cooperation on the region's most pressing challenges, including energy, maritime security, non-proliferation and humanitarian assistance and disaster response."[66] Further, the "President made clear that full and active U.S. engagement in the region's multilateral architecture helps to reinforce the system of rules, norms and responsibilities, including respect for universal human rights and fundamental freedoms, that are essential to regional peace, stability, and prosperity."[67] Likewise, the ADMM Plus includes all EAS members and provides a platform for security cooperation among the partners particularly in the five priority areas: (1) maritime security; (2) counter-terrorism; (3) disaster management; (4) peacekeeping operations; and (5) military medicine.[68] The Council for Security cooperation in the Asia-Pacific (CSCAP) is an offshoot of the ASEAN Regional Forum (ARF) and is a Track II initiative to "discuss political and security issues and challenges facing the region"[69] and has been in existence since 1993. These are proving useful and are contributing towards a favorable and an amicable balance of power in a region which remains plagued with competition, rivalries, and a strong proclivity to use force.

Concluding remarks

The Cold War had established well-defined geopolitical divides and the United States–USSR rivalry had shaped the security dynamics. In the post-Cold War period, more actors and stakeholders have emerged on the scene. Significantly, the evolving Asian maritime security order is no longer divided along geopolitical and ideological lines. Asian countries wish to actively engage in regional affairs without being forced to choose between contending powers. In fact, they do not wish to play second fiddle and are yearning to exercise strategic autonomy. At another level, these states are also building up maritime and naval capability to serve as a deterrent and preclude dominance by regional and extra-regional powers. There are visible signs of states acquiring modern aircraft, ships, and submarines which also facilitate interoperability with the alliance partners. At the same time these acquisitions can potentially result in an arms race. The Asian states also have to contend with asymmetric threats and challenges that are transnational in nature and shape the regional security agenda. These have in fact generated a new synergy of networking among states that are developing among themselves new capacities for cooperative and convergent security. It is apparent that such an approach is a potential source of regional stability.

In the evolving Asian maritime security order, the nature of engagement is based on economic cooperation reinforced by security cooperation, which serves as the primary artery of economic vitality of the region. However, maritime access for trade and transit remains fundamental to the economic vitality of Asian states and any assertive attempt to challenge this by regional and extra-regional powers can potentially disrupt the existing maritime security order.

Notes

1 A typological discussion on "Maritime Order" and its contexts in the Indian Ocean is Lawrence W. Prabhakar, "The Emergent Maritime Security and Maritime Order in the Indian Ocean Region," in V. R. Raghavan and Lawrence W. Prabhakar (eds.), *Maritime Security in the Indian Ocean Region: Critical Issues in Debate* (New Delhi: McGraw-Hill, 2006).

2 *U.S. Force Posture Strategy in the Asia Pacific Region: An Independent Assessment* (Washington, DC: Center for Strategic and International Studies), p. 15.

3 Donald E. Weatherbee, "China, the Philippines and the US Security Guarantee," PacNet No. 28, Pacific Forum CSIS, April 26, 2012.

4 Karen Parrish, "U.S. Following Through on Pacific Rebalance, Hagel Says," American Forces Press Service. www.defense.gov/news/newsarticle.aspx?id=120186 (accessed September 13, 2013).

5 "Empowering Partners: A Strategy for Helping Allies Share the Security Burden." www.lexington-institute.org/library/resources/documents/Defense/EmpoweringPartners.pdf (accessed September 17, 2013).

6 Ely Ratner, "Rebalancing to Asia with an Insecure China." http://csis.org/files/publication/TWQ_13Spring_Ratner.pdf (accessed September 13, 2013).

7 "The term 'core interests' is defined by China to identify the issues considered to be critically important and in defense of which China is ready to use force and go to war. The phrase was at first restricted to Taiwan, and as China's 'core interest' and always considered to be a Chinese province, China is ready to use force to 'liberate' when necessary." See "Highlighting 'Core Interests', China's New Trick in Monopolizing the East Sea." www.southchinasea.com/analysis/474-highlighting-core-interests-chinas-new-trick-in-monopolizing-the-east-sea.html (accessed September 26, 2013).

8 "CNOOC to offer 9 blocks in S. China Sea for joint exploration," *Global Times*, June 27, 2012.

9 Wang Qi, "Xisha Islands to see four cultural heritage protection areas," *Sina* [English], June 25, 2012.

10 "China's new-established Sansha seeks investment," *Xinhua*, September 21, 2012.

11 "China urges against Vietnamese interference in territorial water exploration," *Global Times*, May 7, 2014.

12 "China patient, not reckless over islands," *Global Times*, July 1, 2012.

13 "China's declaration of key interests misinterpreted," *Beijing Review*, August 26, 2013.

14 "Remarks at Press Availability." www.state.gov/secretary/rm/2010/07/145095.htm (accessed June 17, 2013).

15 Edward Wong, "Beijing warns U.S. about South China Sea disputes," *New York Times*, June 22, 2011.

16 Xenia Dormandy, "Prepared for Future Threats? US Defence Partnerships in the Asia-Pacific Region." Royal Institute of International Affairs, London, June 2012.

17 Evans J. R. Revere, "The United States and Japan in East Asia: Challenges and Prospects for the Alliance," *American Foreign Policy Interests* 35 (2013), pp. 1–10.

18 Josh Noble, "China's foreign exchange reserves near record $4tn," *Financial Times*, April 15, 2014.

19 Zhu Ningzhu, "Chinese economy enters phase of medium to high rate growth: Premier Li," *Xinhua*, September 11, 2013.

20 "The dragon's new teeth," *The Economist*, April 7, 2012.

21 Zhao Kejin, "China Turns to Southeast Asia." http://carnegietsinghua.org/2014/03/28/china-turns-to-southeast-asia/h621 (accessed May 21, 2014); Matt Ferchen, "China's Latin American Interests." http://carnegieendowment.org/2012/04/06/china-s-latin-american-interests/a7av (accessed January 25, 2014); Christopher Alessi and Stephanie Hanson, "Expanding China–Africa Oil Ties." www.cfr.org/china/expanding-china-africa-oil-ties/p9557 (accessed January 25, 2014).

22 John J. Mearsheimer, "The Gathering Storm: China's Challenge to US Power in Asia," *Chinese Journal of International Politics* 3, 4, pp. 381–96.

23 Teddy Ng, "China and US vow to build a new model for ties at summit in California," *South China Morning Post*, June 9, 2013.

24 "Taiwan Receives First US Anti-Submarine Aircraft," Agence France-Presse, September 25, 2013.

25 Wang Jisi, "Changing Global Order," in Ahley J. Tellis and Sean Mirski (eds.), *Crux of Asia: China, India and Global Order* (Washington, DC: Carnegie Endowment for International Peace, 2013), p. 47.

26 Jeff Faux, "Complacent consensus on China," *Huffington Post*, August 13, 2013.

27 Wang Jisi, "Changing Global Order," pp. 51–2.

28 "China worried over US-India military cooperation." www.globalresearch.ca/china-worried-over-us-india-military-cooperation/15389 (accessed June 13, 2013).

29 Wang Jisi, "Changing Global Order," pp. 51–2.

30 Yang Jinglie, "Trilateral talks 'Target China'," *Global Times*, October 30, 2012.

31 "Defense paper shows Tokyo's hysteria," *Global Times*, July 10, 2013.

32 Robert Farley, "China's 'all-weather' threat to India," *The Diplomat*, August 8, 2013.

33 Roger Baker, "China and North Korea: A Tangled Partnership." www.stratfor.com/weekly/china-and-north-korea-tangled-partnership (accessed June 13, 2013).

34 Pranab Dhal Samant, "Defence cooperation deal makes India 'closest partner' of the US," *Indian Express*, September 29, 2013.

35 "India, US agree to identify joint defence projects in a year," *Times of India*, September 27, 2013.

36 Noriyuki Suzuki, "Abe's Article 9 blitz alarms Asia," *Japan Times*, May 17, 2014.

37 Yuka Hayashi and Mayumi Negishi, "Japan's companies shun China for Southeast Asia," *Wall Street Journal*, September 12, 2013.

38 Dewi Fortuna Anwar, "An Indonesian Perspective on the U.S. Rebalancing Effort toward Asia." The National Bureau of Asian Research, Seattle, WA, February 26, 2013.

39 *Ibid.*

40 ADMM Plus is the ASEAN's Defense Minister Meeting plus the Defense Ministers of its eight cooperation partners.

41 For a concise history of the Chinese nuclear weapons development program, see www.fas.org/nuke/guide/china/nuke/index.html (accessed April 22, 2010).

42 Emma Chanlett-Avery and Sharon Squassoni, "North Korea's Nuclear Test: Motivations. Implications, and U.S. Options," CRS Report for Congress, Congressional Research Service, Washington, DC, October 24, 2006, pp. 9–11.

43 John W. Garver, "Asymmetrical Indian and Chinese Treat Perceptions," in Sumit Ganguly (ed.), *India as an Emerging Power* (London: Frank Cass, 2002), p. 109.

44 Michael Krepon, "Looking Back: The 1998 Indian and Pakistani Nuclear Tests." www.armscontrol.org/act/2008_05/lookingback (accessed July 14, 2013). Report to Congress on "Status of China, India and Pakistan Nuclear and Ballistic Missile Programs. [I] People's Republic of China," National Security Council, Washington, DC, August 4, 2000. www.fas.org/irp/threat/930728-wmd.htm (accessed April 15, 2010).

45 "The Diversified Employment of China's Armed Forces," Information Office of the State Council, The People's Republic of China, Beijing, April 2013.

46 Harry Kazianis, "Chinese missiles pose serious threat," *Taipei Times*, May 21, 2013.

47 "China's Strategic Posture in Tibet Autonomous Region and India's Response," Vivekananda International Foundation, New Delhi, 2012.

48 "Agni-V boosts India's defence, morale," *Deccan Chronicle*, September 18, 2013.

49 For more on "Pakistan's Missile Inventory" see Ajey Lele and Parveen Bhardwaj, *India's Nuclear Triad: A Net Assessment*, IDSA Occasional Paper 31, Institute for Defence Studies and Analyses, New Delhi, April 2013, p. 14.

50 Duyeon Kim, "Fact Sheet: North Korea's Nuclear and Ballistic Missile Programs," Center for Arms Control and Non-Proliferation, Washington, DC. http://armscontrolcenter.org/publications/factsheets/fact_sheet_north_korea_nuclear_and_missile_programs/ (accessed September 14, 2013).

51 "Southeast Asian Nuclear-Weapon-Free-Zone (SEANWFZ) Treaty (Bangkok Treaty)," www.nti. org/treaties-and-regimes/southeast-asian-nuclear-weapon-free-zone-seanwfz-treaty-bangkok-treaty/ (accessed May 17, 2014).

52 "Sustaining US Global Leadership: Priorities for 21st Century Defence," U.S. Department of Defense, 2012, p. 2.

53 *Ibid.*

54 *Ibid.*

55 For a detailed discussion of the Indian perspective of the US rebalancing, see Vijay Sakhuja, "Mixed Reactions from India," *Strategic Vision for Taiwan Security* 1, 2, March 2012, pp. 14–17.

56 J. Michael Cole, "Navigating the Pivot," *Strategic Vision for Taiwan Security* 1, 2, March 2012, p. 9.

57 Zhu Ningzhu, "China, India pledge closer cooperation in joint statement," *Xinhua*, May 20, 2013. Ernst Haushofer, *An English Translation and Analysis of Major Karl Ernst Haushofer's Geopolitics of the Pacific Ocean*, trans. Lewis Tambs and Ernst Brehm (Lampeter: Edwin Mellen, 2002), p. 141. Cited in Lawrence W. Prabhakar, "The Emergent Vistas of the Indo-Pacific," Paper presented at Geopolitics of the Indo-Pacific Region: Asian Perspectives conference, New Delhi, March 21–22, 2013.

58 Haushofer, *Geopolitics of the Pacific Ocean*, p. 141.

59 "Confluence of the Two Seas," Speech by H. E. Mr. Shinzo Abe, Prime Minister of Japan at the Parliament of the Republic of India, August 22, 2007. www.mofa.go.jp/region/asia-paci/ pmv0708/speech-2.html (accessed June 7, 2013). In 2013, Abe reiterated the idea of Indo-Pacific and noted, "You [Mr Manmohan Singh, the Prime Minister of India] remember that I spoke of the Confluence of the Two Seas in 2007 at the Indian Parliament. I am of a belief that it is the task for the maritime democracies to safeguard our vast oceans. India from the west, Japan from the east, the confluence of the two most deep-rooted democracies is already one important part of international common goods for the 21st Century. I am of a belief that it is the important task that Japan and India should shoulder to ensure that Asia remain in peace and prosperity." "Prime Minister Shinzo Abe's Dinner Remarks," May 29, 2013. http://japan.kantei.go.jp/96_abe/ statement/201305/29india_e.html (accessed June 7, 2013).

60 Brendan Taylor, "The Indo-Pacific Places Australia at the Centre of the Action." www.aspistrategist. org.au/the-indo-pacific-places-australia-at-the-centre-of-the-action/ (accessed August 17, 2013).

61 For a detailed view on the issue see the Concept paper for the ICWA–AAS IV Annual Asian Relations Conference, New Delhi, India on "Geopolitics of the Indo-Pacific Region: Asian Perspectives," March 21–22, 2013.

62 James Rogers, "The Atlantic Alliance's New Strategic Concept: Implications for the European Union," Documento de Trabajo 65/2012, Fundación Alternativas, Observatorio de Política Exterior Española, Madrid, 2012, p. 4.

63 James Rogers, "From Suez to Shanghai: The European Union and Eurasian Maritime Security," Occasional Paper 77, EUISS, Paris, March 2009.

64 Abdul Khalik and Dessy Aswim, "Marty urges treaty to ward off Indo-Pacific conflict," *Jakarta Globe*, August 2, 2013.

65 *Ibid.*

66 Fact Sheet: East Asia Summit Outcomes. www.whitehouse.gov/the-press-office/2012/11/20/fact- sheet-east-asia-summit-outcomes (accessed August 7, 2013).

67 *Ibid.*

68 Vijay Sakhuja, "IBSA Navies: Strengthening Maritime Multilateralism." www.defstrat.com/exec/ frmArticleDetails.aspx?DID=191 (accessed August 23, 2013).

69 Council for Security Cooperation in the Asia Pacific. www.cscap.org/ (accessed June 5, 23, 2013).

23

MAJOR MARITIME POWERS AND THEIR CHANGING RELATIONSHIP

The United States, Europe, China, India, and others

Brahma Chellaney

Maritime challenges have been fundamentally transformed by new technological and geopolitical realities and the rise of unconventional threats. It is important to view these challenges in the broader context of global power dynamics, including the ongoing power shifts, which are altering basic power equations and maritime realities. When political power becomes widely dispersed, it creates the conditions for healthy inter-country competition, broadly shared prosperity, and inclusive international institutions.[1] It also changes the international order on which the leading states so far have agreed upon. The current international order is clearly in transition. The ongoing power shifts make fundamental reforms in the existing global institutional structure inevitable. On the positive side, the spread of prosperity in the world will create more stakeholders in international peace and stability. At the same time, it will make wide-ranging institutional reforms unavoidable in order to effectively manage the new maritime challenges, some of which are unique in nature. Even as a systemic shift in the global distribution of power is under way, the international institutional structure has remained static since the mid-twentieth century. It has to be adjusted to the changed economic and societal environment.

The pace of technological change has been revolutionary since the 1980s, opening the path to the rise of the post-industrial, information-based economies and facilitating the ascent of the so-called emerging economies. The growing tide of new innovations has also contributed to the accelerated weaponization of science, even as the pace of innovations has shrunk the shelf-life of most technologies. Today, technological forces are playing a greater role in shaping geopolitics and maritime power equations than at any other time in history.

Economically, the fast pace of change in technology, transportation costs, and regulatory environment has acted as a spur to the ascent of the emerging economies. Since 1991, the annual exports of developing economies have continued to grow faster than those of developed ones. Consequently, the share of world trade of the advanced economies in the same period has sunk from 75 percent to just below 50 percent. Developing economies are also attracting increasing amounts of foreign direct investments, with such inflows jumping from 20 percent to 50 percent just between 2002 and 2012. The global shifts in relative economic weight promise to only accentuate. The pace of geopolitical change has been no less extraordinary. Since the late 1980s, the world has been dramatically transformed geopolitically. In fact, the world has changed fundamentally since the fall of the Berlin Wall, the most momentous event in post-World War II history that heralded the end of the Cold War and spurred the collapse of the Soviet Union. Given the pace of political, economic, and technological transformation that has been witnessed, one can assume that the next two decades will bring about equally dramatic geopolitical change.

But just as no one predicted the sudden collapse of the Soviet Union or the dramatic rise of Asia since the 1990s, reliable predictions on major geopolitical changes in the next two decades will be hard to come by. That is why it is important to focus on the emerging geopolitical fault lines, because they tell us what the risks are and, more importantly, what the direction of future geopolitical change and maritime challenges may look like.

The changing maritime security environment

The rise and fall of maritime powers and other great powers has been a recurring phenomenon since ancient times.[2] The global power structure, far from being static, continually evolves. Although the focus currently is on the post-Cold War power changes, the Cold War era itself witnessed important power shifts. For example, it was only after the Cold War began that the Soviet Union rose as a global military power, although it failed to become a true economic power. By the second half of the Cold War, Japan and Germany had emerged from the ruins of World War II as formidable economic giants. In keeping with the profound technological and geopolitical changes since the late 1980s, power shifts have become even more pronounced, as underscored by the gradual rise of the East since the 1990s.

The United States emerged as the sole superpower due to a quirk of history – the sudden, unexpected collapse of the Soviet Union. Indeed, when viewed against history, the existence of a single superpower is highly unusual. The normal pattern in history is one of uneasy coexistence among several great powers. So, the emergence of a single superpower was an anomalous development. Although the United States remains the world's preeminent maritime and political power, it is no longer able to play the global guardian or set the international agenda on its own. To secure issue-based support, it has to reach out to states outside its traditional alliance system. By 2030, according to the U.S. National Intelligence Council, there will be no global hegemon.[3]

The post-World War II transatlantic order, meanwhile, is slowly giving way to a more global international order. With just 12 percent of the world's population living in the West, the transatlantic order had to give way to an international order with global reach. Rudyard Kipling once said, "East is East and West is West, and never the twain shall meet." But now they do in an increasingly interdependent world. In fact, Western economies are increasingly dependent on capital inflows from the cash-laden economies of the East.

The world is becoming more interdependent not just in trade and capital flows; the interdependencies indeed extend to technological, public-health, environmental, and climate spheres. According to former World Trade Organization Director-General Pascal Lamy:

> Globalization first denationalized consumption, allowing consumers to buy goods and services from places where they are produced more efficiently. More recently, we have also witnessed a new phenomenon: the denationalization of production. The advent of new technologies and reduced trade costs makes it feasible to separate stages of production geographically, leading to the formation of value chains that span across borders.

World trade in parts and components of manufactured goods, a rough measure of the importance of cross-border value chains, has doubled between 2000 and 2010, rising from 1.4 to 2.7 trillion dollars. But economics is hardly the only domain where interdependence across countries has increased. Migration is a powerful vector of social interaction across diverse cultures. In the past ten years, the total number of international migrants has increased by over 40%, reaching 214 million people worldwide. This means that migrants today would constitute the 5th most populous country in the world.[4]

The rise of new regional or subregional powers from South America to Asia with increasing maritime capabilities poses tricky challenges centered on power stability and equilibrium. There is no new global hegemon, however, in the making or on the horizon. The United States will have the distinction of being the world's first and last global hegemon.

Let alone in the wider world, even in Asia, China, despite its growing maritime ambitions and capabilities, will be in no position for the foreseeable future to match the United States in power-projection force capabilities, including the range of overseas military bases and the number of security allies and partners. The United States is set to stay more powerful than any other single state. According to the quadrennial report of the U.S. National Intelligence Council – the senior analytic body within the Office of the Director of National Intelligence – America will remain the most powerful state for the foreseeable future but its standing will diminish to being "one of a number" of important players in the world, as a "global multipolar system" emerges.[5] That report, which represents the U.S. intelligence community's most comprehensive examination of long-term security issues, predicted that the outcome of the power shifts will leave "less room for the U.S. to call the shots" and that the international alliances and networks that have dominated global affairs since the end of World War II "will be almost unrecognizable by 2025." A world characterized by greater distribution of power thus faces new uncertainties. After all, once the international economic power structure changes fundamentally, shifts in military power will inevitably follow, even if gradually.

The implications of the power shifts for maritime peace and security indeed seem ominous, even though the changes may symbolize a return to the more normal conditions of human history, in which Asia was the international center of gravity for two millennia before the advent of the industrial revolution. If, as liberal theorists have argued, hegemonic restraint demands a rules-based international system that can, through creative and durable multilateral institutions, compel hegemons to eschew arbitrary exercise of power in their own interest,[6] some developments at present are not conducive to encouraging such hegemonic self-restraint.

One is the rise or return of authoritarian great powers, which implies that the new order, far from being liberal or rules-based, will be centered on classical balance-of-power strategies of the major powers. The union between autocratic politics and state-guided capitalism indeed has emerged as the leading challenge to the international spread of democratic values. In a reflection of the changing balance of financial power, autocracies increasingly are financing democracies, with Western economies dependent on capital inflows from the cash-laden Chinese and Persian Gulf economies. As a result, the foreign assets of the world's undemocratic governments are on the rise while those of the deeply rooted democracies are on the decline.

This raises the specter of a global divide centered on political values. Such a divide, if it materializes, will carry important geopolitical and maritime implications because, as modern history attests, regime character can come in the way of observing norms and rules. Ordinarily, the readiness to play by international rules ought to matter more than regime form. But regime character often makes playing by the rules difficult. Even if authoritarian capitalism does not pit an axis of autocracies against a constellation of democracies – with pragmatism, rather than political values, guiding the foreign-policy strategies of important players – building international rules that all major powers respect and adhere to may prove difficult. Democratic governments may not be more wedded to peace than autocracies, yet it is well established that democracies rarely go to war with each other.

Another maritime security-related development, also linked to the rise of new powers, is the recrudescence of territorial and maritime disputes, often tied to the competition over natural resources. The increasing competition for natural resources has fueled territorial and maritime disputes in the East and South China Seas, raised maritime security concerns in the Indian Ocean region, and prompted a scramble for resources in Africa. Those coveting resources in distant lands have employed aid and arms exports as a diplomatic instrument for commodity outreach. As resource competition has sharpened, the contours of a twenty-first-century version of the Great Game have emerged in resource-rich lands – a Great Game with major maritime dimensions.

The energy-related equations between the maritime powers, however, are being transformed by an emerging development: The center of gravity in the hydrocarbon world is beginning to quietly shift from the oil sheikhdoms of the Persian Gulf to the Americas, thanks to the shale boom. Gas and oil reserves that geologists and analysts previously thought were unrecoverable or uneconomical to exploit have, with new technologies like "fracking" and horizontal drilling, become newly available and profitable. Gas and oil extracted from shale and other "tight rock" fields has proved a game changer, with the United States surpassing Russia as the world's largest gas producer and the U.S. industry now even initiating moves to export gas.

By relying on production from Canadian tar sands – a black, gooey mixture of sand, oil, and water that lies just below Alberta province's boreal forest – and stepping up its domestic shale liquids production, the United States has also become less dependent on oil supplies from an unstable Middle East. It is projected to become self-sufficient in oil by 2024, and even a net exporter. (Canada's economically recoverable oil sands are estimated to be about 170 billion barrels, or reserves second in size only to Saudi Arabia. The Canadian Association of Petroleum Producers estimates that production, currently at 1.7 million barrels a day, could nearly double by 2020, enough to supply nearly 20 percent of U.S. oil consumption. With that, the oil sands would be producing more oil than Venezuela, Nigeria, Iraq, or Kuwait.[7]) By contrast, Asia remains heavily dependent on oil imports by sea from the Persian Gulf countries, notably Saudi Arabia, Iran, the United Arab Emirates, Kuwait, and Iraq.

The Arab world plus Iran sit astride one of the world's most active maritime fault lines – a fault line that could trigger major geopolitical earthquakes with far-reaching effects extending beyond this region. The Arab Spring came to symbolize the ascent of people's power, yet hope has given way to a bleak sequel. The post-Gaddafi Libya has sunk into lawlessness; Egypt's future political direction remains uncertain; a once-peaceful and secular Syria has been engulfed by a civil war with increasingly jihadist overtones; Yemen remains a sanctuary for transnational terrorists; Iraq and Lebanon continue to be battered by sectarian strife; and the political future of Saudi Arabia and the other oil sheikhdoms appears uncertain.

One of the more positive signs to emerge in this region is the thaw in relations between Iran and the United States, which had waged an indirect war to financially throttle Tehran by imposing an oil-export embargo. History attests to the linkage between an oil embargo and military hostilities. Although the 1941 Pearl Harbor attack took the United States by surprise, the attack was triggered in some measure by a U.S.–British–Dutch oil-import embargo against Japan as part of a larger economic squeeze of that country that began in 1939. Those states that spearheaded the oil embargo against Iran (including the U.S., Britain, France, and Germany) buy little or no oil from that country, while those countries advising caution (such as India, Japan, South Korea, and China) are important importers of Iranian oil.

These four Asian economies account for 60 percent of Iran's oil sales. The United States, in fact, stopped importing Iranian oil way back in 1987. A thaw in U.S.–Iranian relations after the election of Hassan Rouhani as Iran's president and the nuclear deal thus holds geopolitical and maritime implications extending beyond the Persian Gulf region. The negotiations over Iran's nuclear program, which started in late 2013, yielded a framework agreement in 2015 after a series of meetings held in Lausanne, Switzerland between late March and early April. Then in July 2015 in Vienna the Joint Comprehensive Plan of Action (the nuclear deal) was unveiled. The deal's successful implementation[10] would ease concerns that missteps could trigger military hostilities with the potential to shut down the world's most important oil-export route, the Strait of Hormuz.

Another development that impinges on the equations among the maritime powers is the phenomenon of failing states, which continues to trouble international and regional security. This development is a direct consequence of the end of the Cold War. While the Cold War raged, weak states were propped up by one bloc or the other. After the Soviet Union's disintegration, the United States got out of that game. That is one of the reasons why dysfunctional or failing states began to emerge from the 1990s in a significant way. The phenomenon of failing states has contributed to making such nations a threat to regional and international security, either because they are home to transnational pirates (like Somalia) or transnational terrorists (the Afghanistan–Pakistan belt), or because of their defiance of global norms (North Korea) or their internal conflicts (Syria, Iraq, Yemen, and Libya).

Compounding this phenomenon is the sanctity the world attaches to existing borders. Sanctity of borders has become a powerful norm in world politics. Border fixity is seen as essential for peace and stability. Yet, paradoxically, this norm has allowed the emergence of weak states, whose internal wars spill over and create wider regional tensions and insecurities.[8] In other words, a norm intended to build peace and stability may be creating conditions for greater regional conflict and instability. This norm is likely to come under challenge in the Afghanistan–Pakistan belt, Iraq, Syria, Libya, Somalia, and elsewhere where the dangers of political fragmentation can no longer be dismissed.

These various developments have sharpened maritime competition and spurred greater maritime ambitions on the part of some key players. They have also contributed to new geopolitical fault lines.

It is not an accident that the Asia-Pacific region is becoming the center of global maritime competition. After all, the era of West European and North American domination is not even two centuries old, while Asia for millennia was the global center of gravity, dominating the world in economy, knowledge, and culture. In the period up to 1820, China and India were the world's largest economies. In the year AD 1, according to the British economic historian Angus Maddison, India's economy made up 33 percent of the world GDP compared with China's 26 percent. But by the sixteenth century, China's economy matched India's, before vaulting into a significant lead.[9] Today, Asia's re-emergence is only resulting in the world moving toward the "normal" power conditions. In fact, given Asia's size (it is home to three-fifths of the global population), it is only natural that it is gaining in global prominence and economic power.

By 2030, according to International Monetary Fund projections, Asia's GDP will surpass that of the Group of Seven major industrial economies.[10] In fact, the international shifts in the basic-commodity, energy, and metal markets, with the East making up the largest growth in demand, mirror the way the center of gravity in international relations is moving toward the Asia-Pacific. On the supply side, "Asia's strong demand environment for energy and basic materials, coupled with its low labor costs, means that the region will increasingly become a global producer of aluminum, chemicals, paper, and steel."[11] The ongoing structural shifts in the global energy markets, for example, carry important long-term political, economic, and maritime implications, in addition to challenging the stability of these markets.

Changing equations among major maritime powers

The power shifts and new maritime security challenges actually symbolize the birth-pangs of a new world order. Although the world is clearly in transition, with the age of Atlantic dominance in retreat and the East re-emerging as a major player on the global stage, the contours of the new order are still not visible. That has only helped promote greater international divisiveness. The divisiveness, in turn, has hindered effective action on international challenges, including rooting out transnational terrorist nests, curbing resource competition, discouraging mercantilist policies aimed at locking up long-term supplies of raw materials, and stemming anthropogenic climate change.

The ascent of new powers has ignited much debate on the larger implications for maritime security and regional and international peace. In history, whenever the rise of an aggressive power disturbed the power equilibrium, it led to war, as was exemplified by the Napoleonic Wars and the two World Wars. However, it is important to remember that conflict is not built into the rise of any new power. The United States, for example, rose as a great power without triggering conflict with the then leading powers. Nor is conflict inherent in a rising power's attempt to alter the international order so as to gain a greater say in various matters. Any rising power is a revisionist power, even if a discreet one. The risks of conflict, however, grow when a new power accepts norms and rules selectively, pursues an aggressive maritime strategy, seeks unremittingly to alter the territorial and maritime status quo, and secures unfair advantages in trade, resource, security, currency, intellectual property, investment, and other issues.

For the foreseeable future, the United States will remain the dominant sea power and Europe will be a significant maritime player; yet the international maritime order will change fundamentally as new powers acquire greater economic and naval heft. According to one projection, as the global GDP doubles by 2030, China will come to own a quarter of the world's merchant fleet.[12] The other maritime states in Asia, including Japan, South Korea, India, and Vietnam, are also set to enlarge their maritime footprints significantly. Asia's insatiable appetite for natural resources from distant lands will spur increased production of huge container ships. LNG tonnage is expected to double by 2030 to meet increasing gas demand in Asia and Europe; bulker tonnage is also projected to double in response to the fast-rising imports of coal, iron ore and other commodities by the emerging economies.

The Asia-Pacific region will influence, and help reshape, maritime equations. The Indo-Pacific region, because of its centrality to international trade and energy shipments, will, in particular, become increasingly critical to international maritime security. Against this background, Asian security issues will gain international salience because of their extra-regional implications. Asia's remarkable economic rise has been accompanied by a new cold war over political and maritime disputes. Not only does Asia's political integration lag behind its economic integration, Asia has no security framework of any kind. Regional consultation mechanisms remain weak. Differences persist over whether a security architecture or community should extend across Asia, or be confined to an ill-defined "East Asia." At the same time, Asia must cope with entrenched territorial and maritime disputes, such as in the South and East China Seas and between China and India; harmful historical legacies that weigh down its most important inter-country relationships; increasingly fervent nationalism; growing political or religious extremism; and sharpening competition over natural resources, especially water and energy.

One central concern arises from the legacy of wars. Unlike Europe's bloody wars of the first half of the twentieth century, which have made war there unthinkable today, the wars in Asia in the second half of the twentieth century only accentuated bitter rivalries. The role of war in peace-making hinges on decisive outcome. Peace could be built in Europe in large part because the outcome of World War II was decisive. In Asia, the outcome of World War II was also decisive but the main combatants were U.S. and Japan. The wars fought in Asia in the second half of the twentieth century were either not decisive or, if decisive, they were limited in scale.

Several inter-country wars have been fought in Asia since 1950, when both the Korean War and the annexation of Tibet started, without resolving the underlying disputes. To take the most significant example, China staged military interventions even when it was poor and internally troubled. A 2010 Pentagon report cites Chinese military preemption in 1950, 1962, 1969, and 1979 in the name of strategic defense. According to the report, "The history of modern Chinese warfare provides numerous case studies in which China's leaders have claimed military preemption as a strategically defensive act."[13] There was also China's seizure of the Paracel Islands from Vietnam in 1974, its occupation of the disputed Johnson Reef in the Spratly Islands in 1988, its 1995 occupation of Mischief Reef in the Spratlys, and its 2012 control of the Scarborough Shoal. This history helps to explain why China's rapidly growing military power raises important concerns today in the Asia-Pacific region and beyond.

Indeed, not since Japan rose to world-power status during the reign of the Meiji Emperor (1867–1912) has another non–Western power emerged with such potential to reshape the global maritime and political order. But there is an important difference: Japan's rise was accompanied by the other Asian civilizations' decline. After all, by the nineteenth century, Europeans had colonized much of Asia, leaving no Asian power that could reign in Japan.

Today, China is rising alongside other important Asian countries, including South Korea, Vietnam, India, and Indonesia. Although China now has displaced Japan as the world's second largest economy, Japan will remain a strong maritime power for the foreseeable future. On a per-capita basis, Japan remains six times richer than China, and it possesses Asia's largest naval fleet and its most advanced high-tech industries. Japan is considered by many as an economic power in decline, yet one of the least-noticed developments in Asia in this century has been Japan's political resurgence. With its pride and assertiveness rising, the nationalist impulse has become conspicuous. Tokyo is intent on influencing Asia's power balance.

The balance of power in Asia, in fact, will be determined by events principally in two regions: the Indian Ocean and East Asia. This underscores the centrality of peace and stability, and the security of vital sea lanes, in the wider Indo-Pacific region, marked by the confluence of the Indian and Pacific Oceans. It is not an accident that the United States, as symbolized by its "pivot" to Asia, is increasingly focusing on this region. However, it is not clear whether the Obama administration's "pivot" toward Asia will acquire concrete strategic content or remain largely a rhetorical repackaging of policies begun over the past decade.

In recent years, the United States has made the most of regional security concerns in Asia by strengthening its military ties with existing Asian allies and forging security relationships with new friends. The heady glow of America's return to the Asian center-stage, however, has obscured the key challenges it faces to remain the region's principal security anchor in the face of China's relentless push to expand its sphere of influence. One challenge is connected with the imperative to arrest the erosion in America's relative power through comprehensive domestic renewal, including by reining in its mounting budget deficit. The need for spending cuts raises the specter that the United States, especially if its Congress cannot agree on a longer-term fiscal deal, might be unable to fund a military shift toward Asia or, worse, be forced to retrench on its assets in the Asia-Pacific. This could raise doubts about Washington's ability to provide strategic heft to its "pivot" policy by sustaining a higher level of commitment in the Asia-Pacific, where it already maintains 320,000 troops. The U.S. deployment of 2,500 Marines in Australia is largely symbolic.

In fact, Washington, after appearing to raise Asian expectations about a more robust U.S. response to Asian security concerns, has started to tamp down the military aspects of its "pivot" and instead lay emphasis on greater U.S. economic engagement with Asian countries. The renewed emphasis on the economic aspects has come as a relief to some regional states apprehensive about being caught in a situation where they might be forced to choose between the United States and China. But for the countries bearing the brunt of China's recidivist policies on territorial or maritime disputes, this emphasis raises new doubts about the U.S. commitment.

The U.S. economic reorientation actually signals a correction in a "pivot" policy that began overemphasizing the military component, putting Washington on an uncomfortable path of seeking to take on Beijing. It was Secretary of State Hillary Clinton who signaled a more hawkish U.S. stance on China by talking tough at the 2010 ASEAN Regional Forum meeting in Hanoi but who later began moderating that line by playing the role of a business promoter in visits to Asian countries. The correction in the U.S. policy actually extends even to terminology, with the original term "pivot" being dumped in favor of "rebalancing." U.S. diplomats now avoid using the "pivot" term because it is seen as having a military ring to it. The refocus on trade and economic issues has also prompted Washington to launch the Trans-Pacific Partnership initiative, which aims to create a new free-trade group in the Asia-Pacific that excludes China. Washington is also emphasizing the importance of the East Asia Summit (EAS) and the Association of Southeast Asian Nations (ASEAN), whose summits overlap. However, Barack Obama's historic visit to Myanmar – the first ever by a U.S. president – was as much about trade as it was about the geopolitical objective of weaning that strategically located, resource-rich country away from Chinese influence. Paradoxically, it was the U.S. sanctions policy that penalized Myanmar but condoned China for crushing pro-democracy protests in 1988 and 1989, respectively, that helped push the former into the latter's strategic lap. The Asia-Pacific region is looming larger in U.S. foreign policy, especially with the end of the majority of combat operations in Afghanistan in 2014. China, for its part, has not only weathered the international democratization push but also has emerged as a potential peer rival to America, with its economic growth still surging impressively and its military spending racing far ahead of its GDP growth.[14] Today there is talk of even a U.S.–China diarchy – a G-2 – ruling the world. Yet, China's spectacular rise as a global power in just one generation under authoritarian rule represents the first direct challenge to liberal democracy since the rise of Nazi Germany in the 1930s. Communism was never a credible alternative to liberal democracy, but authoritarian capitalism is. Through its remarkable success story, China advertises that authoritarianism is a more rapid and smoother path to prosperity and stability than the tumult of electoral politics and the constant tussle between the executive branch and the legislature, best illustrated by the recent U.S. government shutdown.

China's increasing emphasis on the oceans is evident from the key report to the 18th National Congress of the Chinese Communist Party in November 2012 that outlined the country's "maritime power" strategy. It called for assertively safeguarding China's maritime rights and interests, including by building improved capacity for exploiting marine resources and for asserting the country's larger rights. In 2012, China formally staked a claim under the United Nations Convention on the Law of the Sea to more than 80 percent of the South China Sea – a claim that could potentially crimp freedom of navigation and become a source of friction with other maritime powers.

In this context, the Chinese leadership's repeated calls for the People's Liberation Army to be prepared to plan, fight, and win wars is an ominous sign that can hardly be overlooked while examining future security scenarios. Indeed, such is the PLA's growing political clout that this institution, enjoying increasing autonomy and soaring budgets, appears ready at times to upstage even the Communist Party. In fact, the Party, ideologically adrift, is becoming dependent on the PLA – the ultimate arbiter of nationalism – for its political legitimacy and to ensure domestic order. China's expanding "core interests" and revanchist territorial claims, as well as its willingness to take on several neighbors simultaneously, point to how the PLA is beginning to call the shots in strategic policymaking.

China's new leader, Xi Jinping, since taking power, has manifested an increasing authoritarian lurch, using an anti-corruption drive to crack down on political dissent and criticism of the party and glorifying China's blood-soaked Communist past. No less significant is his championing of efforts to build China into a global maritime power, saying his government will do everything to safeguard China's "maritime rights and interests" and warning that "in no way will the country abandon its legitimate rights and interests." Xi has also called for building "the marine economy into a new growth engine of the country."

Even as equations between maritime powers change across the world, maritime tensions remain high in the Asian theater due to rival sovereignty claims, resource-related competition, naval build-ups, and rising nationalism. Indeed, the Indo-Pacific sea lanes are becoming "more crowded, contested and vulnerable to armed strife," with a growing risk of incidents escalating to confrontation.[15] This has underscored the importance of maritime military diplomacy and confidence-building measures, including opening direct channels of operational communication between the navies in the Asian-Pacific region and developing a comprehensive and binding code of conduct to govern economic and security activities on the seas.

More broadly, the changing global power equations are set to transform maritime relationships between and among the important players. The growing importance of maritime resources and sea lanes, as well as the concentration of economic boom zones along the coasts, has made maritime peace and security more critical than ever for international security. The oceans and seas have not only become pivotal to any power's security and engagement with the outside world, but they also constitute the strategic hub of the global political, economic, and military competition.

It has become imperative to deal with maritime security challenges in a holistic strategic framework. Nontraditional maritime security issues – from energy security and climate security to transnational terrorism and environmental degradation – are as important as traditional maritime security issues, like freedom of navigation, security of sea lanes, maritime boundary and domain security, proliferation of weapons of mass destruction, and challenges to law and order (including piracy and sea robbery, criminal activities like drug, people and arms smuggling, illicit, unreported and unregulated fishing, illegal immigration, and maritime terrorism). The nontraditional issues extend to the maritime aspects of economic security, food security, environmental security, and human security. Put simply, the oceans and seas have become closely linked with national and regional security and the building of broader environmental and climatic security.

Conclusions

The implications of the ongoing global power shifts for maritime peace and security remain unclear, even though the changes may symbolize a return to the more normal conditions of human history. The evolving architecture of global governance will determine how the world handles the pressing maritime challenges it confronts. The problem of political myopia – or looking at issues in a short-term framework – that afflicts leaders and institutions has been a principal handicap to developing a forward-looking approach. Compounding this is the Westphalian political order, which is pivoted on the notion of full sovereignty of nation-states. The assertive pursuit of national interest for relative gain in an increasingly interdependent world is hardly a recipe for more harmonious maritime relations. Yet another concern, in the absence of an integrated approach to addressing the maritime challenges, is the pursuit of a narrow, compartmentalized approach that seeks to deal with each issue separately, instead of in a holistic framework. The recrudescence of territorial and maritime disputes, largely tied to the competition over natural resources, will increasingly have a bearing on maritime peace and security, especially in the Asia-Pacific region. Given the transformed nature of international politics, economy and trade, including the new interdependencies, global governance or the maritime order can no longer by driven by one or a handful of powers. Rather, it must be anchored in international rules and regulations. When multiple powers vie for influence and relative advantage without being constrained by rules, balance-of-power politics becomes less a choice and more an inevitability. With the world at a defining moment in its history, it faces the task of building a stable power equilibrium while having to deal with major new maritime challenges.

Notes

1 Daron Acemoglu and James Robinson, *Why Nations Fail: The Origins of Power, Prosperity, and Poverty* (New York: Crown Publishers, 2012).

2 See the ancient manual on great-power attributes and statecraft by one of greatest minds India has ever produced, Kautilya, also known as Chanakya, who wrote the *Arthashastra* before AD 150. Kautilya, *The Arthashastra* (New Delhi: Penguin Classics, 1992). For accounts of the rise and fall of great powers in more recent centuries, see Paul Kennedy, *The Rise and Fall of the Great Powers: Economic Change and Military Conflict 1500–2000* (New York: Random House, 1987); Robert Gilpin, *War and Change in World Politics* (Cambridge: Cambridge University Press, 1981); and Geir Lundestad (ed.), *The Fall of Great Powers: Peace, Stability, and Legitimacy* (Oslo and New York: Scandinavian University Press and Oxford University Press, 1994).

3 U.S. National Intelligence Council, *Global Trends 2025: A Transformed World* (Washington, DC: National Intelligence Council, November 20, 2008).

4 World Trade Organization Director-General Pascal Lamy, Speech at the Singapore Global Dialogue at the Rajaratnam School of International Studies, September 21, 2012, www.wto.org/english/news_e/sppl_e/sppl248_e.htm, accessed August 28, 2015.

5 U.S. National Intelligence Council, *Global Trends 2030: Alternative Worlds* (Washington, DC: National Intelligence Council, December 10, 2012).

6 G. John Ikenberry, *After Victory: Institutions, Strategic Restraint, and the Rebuilding of Order after Major Wars* (Princeton, NJ: Princeton University Press, 2001), p. 36.

7 Steven Mufson, "Keystone XL Pipeline Expansion Driven by Oil-Rich Tar Sands in Alberta," *Washington Post*, July 1, 2012.

8 Boaz Atzili, *Good Fences, Bad Neighbors: Border Fixity and International Conflict* (Chicago: University of Chicago Press, 2012).

9 Angus Maddison, *The World Economy: A Millennial Perspective* (Paris: Organization for Economic Cooperation and Development, 2001).

10 Anoop Singh, "Asia Leading the Way," *Finance and Development* (June 2010), p. 6.

11 Ivo J. H. Bozon, Warren J. Campbell, and Mats Lindstrand, "Global Trends in Energy," *McKinsey Quarterly* 1 (2007), p. 48.

12 Lloyd's Register, QinetiQ, and the University of Strathclyde, Glasgow, *Global Marine Trends 2030* (2013), www.lr.org/sectors/marine/GTC/gmt2030.aspx, accessed August 28, 2015.

13 U.S. Department of Defense, *Military and Security Developments Involving the People's Republic of China 2010*, Report to Congress Pursuant to the National Defense Authorization Act for Fiscal Year 2010 (Washington, DC: Office of the Secretary of Defense, 2010), p. 24.

14 Niall Ferguson, *The War of the World: Twentieth-Century Conflict and the Descent of the West* (New York: Penguin Press, 2006); Aaron L. Friedberg, *A Contest for Supremacy: China, America, and the Struggle for Mastery in Asia* (New York: W. W. Norton, 2011); and Brahma Chellaney, *Asian Juggernaut: The Rise of China, India, and Japan* (New York: HarperCollins, 2010).

15 Rory Medcalf, Raoul Heinrichs, and Justin Jones, "Crisis and Confidence: Major Powers and Maritime Security in Indo-Pacific Area," Lowy Institute Paper, June 20, 2011.

24

A PERSPECTIVE ON CHINA'S MARITIME SECURITY STRATEGY

Xu Hui and Cao Xianyu[1]

Introduction

With the rapid development of China's maritime force, its maritime strategy has become the subject of many speculations. What is China's intention in developing a maritime force? How will China employ its growing maritime force and what implications will it have for global maritime security? Will it be a threat, challenge, or a constructive force? Especially in recent years, as tensions between China and some of its neighbors over maritime issues have grown, China's maritime security policy has been labeled as "aggressive," "assertive," "coercive," or "revisionist." Some experts even contend that China's maritime strategy reflects a fundamental shift in its foreign policy.[2] Other authors, however, have taken different views and have argued that the Chinese government pursues defensive interests in the region and that its maritime efforts have been a far cry away from presenting threats to anyone.

China has never released a definite maritime security strategy – a fact that might have contributed to uncertainty over the direction of its maritime strategy. Yet, there is a lively Chinese debate about strategic planning and guidance in the maritime domain. Particularly during the past few years, maritime strategy has become an increasingly prominent topic in China's economic, security, and diplomacy debates and has increasingly attracted the attention of decision-makers as well as scholars at home and abroad. This chapter provides a systematic overview of the available literature and attempts to draw some conclusions as to the main directions China is taking in the field of maritime strategy.

Evolution of China's maritime strategy

Maritime strategy is determined by a country's capabilities to understand and exploit the seas, whether coastal waters or the high seas. Since the founding of the People's Republic of China (PRC), China's maritime strategy has witnessed significant transformations. It started with a strong focus on military security, but it became increasingly comprehensive in focusing on the developing resources of the ocean and on global maritime commons. The new policy of "Building a Strong Maritime Country," put forward by the 18th Congress of the Communist Party of China (CPC) in November 2012, marked the beginning of China's new maritime strategy.

During the early decades of its existence, the People's Republic of China viewed maritime matters from the perspective of military security since China had been invaded by Western powers mainly from the sea in the nineteenth century. Later, after World War II, also owing to the Taiwan issue and the United States' maritime superiority, the maritime borders were considered to harbor many threats to the national security of the People's Republic of China. Defending the coastlines against any military aggression from the sea and maintaining national security were the main goals of maritime strategy. "To resist against imperialist aggression, we must build a strong navy," declared Chairman Mao Zedong.[3] The coastal defense strategy was implemented by the PLA Navy through coastal operational forces and coastal combat missions. China also successfully developed nuclear submarines.

After the economic reform and the opening up of China, its maritime trade rapidly grew in size and initiated a new era of looking at maritime issues. During the 3rd Plenary of the 11th Congress of the CPC, held in 1978, China fundamentally adjusted its assessment of the international and the domestic situation and put economic development at the top of its agenda. This shift brought about comprehensive and far-reaching implications for China's maritime strategy and policy:

- The significant growth in maritime trade put the security of sea lines of communication (SLOCs) at the center of attention.
- The Chinese government put forward an initiative on "Sovereignty Belonging to China, Shelving Disputes, Seeking Joint Development," the purpose of which was to provide guidance in handling and solving maritime disputes with neighbors.
- China prioritized its offshore defense strategy and, in line with the normalization of the political relationship to the U.S., transferred its naval capability from emergency combat readiness to peacetime status.

Since the turn of the twenty-first century, China's maritime economy has taken a major boost and maritime forces have grown accordingly. A first maritime economic development plan was introduced during the 16th Congress of the CPC held in 2002, and the subject continued to be on the agenda of all CPC congresses held since then. In February 2008, China released its first general maritime plan, the "National Planning Outline of Maritime Industry Development," which demonstrated how decidedly China attached importance to the development and exploitation of oceans and coastal waters. During this period, maritime force building was strengthened. Responding to challenges from separatism in Taiwan and new security threats, China strengthened its military preparations and accelerated maritime force building. Simultaneously, China put forward its vision of maritime security based on the concept of "Harmonious Ocean" to address concerns voiced by some countries over China's build-up of maritime forces.

Since 2008, China has embarked on a new path in making more contributions to the security of global maritime commons. In doing so, its maritime strategy is becoming increasingly systematic and comprehensive. Since December 2008, China's Navy has participated in escort missions in the Gulf of Aden and off the coast of Somalia, creating several precedents: it was the first time that military force was employed to safeguard national interests overseas, that maritime combat forces were used to participate in overseas international humanitarian relief operations, and that vital SLOCs were protected in waters distant from China.[4] China also expressed its maritime rights in a more effective way during the Huanyan Island dispute which had been provoked by the Philippines in 2012. During the 18th Congress of the CPC, held in November

2012, the Communist Party decided to build a strong maritime force. In line with this decision, President Xi Jinping called for "strengthening capabilities of resource development, protecting environment, developing science and technology and maintaining rights in maritime domain."[5] These elements marked the preliminary formation of China's maritime strategy.

To sum up, since the founding of the PRC, the Chinese focus on the sea has changed from being a topic of defensive military matters to encompassing a broad set of issues of economic, security, scientific, technological, and environmental protection relevance. Oceans and coastal waters are playing a growing role in China's national strategy, which makes China's future more closely connected with the maritime domain, and which provides China with a more powerful and lasting driving force to develop maritime forces to maintain national interests and to promote maritime security in the global commons.

China's maritime security interests

In order to understand China's maritime strategy, one has to start with a review on the national interest of China. As Hans-Joachim Morgenthau and other representatives of the Realist school of international relations have repeatedly stated, national interest is the fundamental basis and guiding principle of the formulation and implementation of strategy, and the sole criteria of judging and directing political behaviors. These interests can be listed as seen below:

1. *To cope with security threats from the sea and maintain national security, sovereignty and territorial integrity.* State sovereignty, national security, and territorial integrity are the basic conditions for any country's survival, and this also holds true for China. China has some core interests which include the protection of its political system established by the Constitution, overall social stability, and the basic preconditions for ensuring sustainable economic and social development.[6] Regarding the maritime dimension of security interest, one has to start from the notion that during the past centuries China's main security challenges have come from the seas. As a scholar of Chinese history wrote, "about 100 years after the Opium War in 1840, imperialist powers had invaded China from the sea as many as 470 times."[7] These and other lessons of history have beyond doubt influenced China in its strategic assessment. But geography and demography play an important role as well. Today, the coastal areas, which cover about 15 percent of China's total landmass, accommodate 40 percent of its population, 60 percent of its GDP, and 88–90 percent of its foreign investment,[8] which makes it vital for China to maintain security and deter threats from the sea. Additionally, reunification of the nation remains one of the predominant aspects.

China's interest in defending its national security against any threats coming from the seas does not mean that China needs to unilaterally expand its jurisdiction over its exclusive economic zones (EEZ). Since the 1990s, China and the U.S. have argued over reconnaissance flights by U.S. military aircraft and over maneuvers by naval craft in China's EEZ. In some cases, even a confrontation could not be excluded. To prevent maritime incidents, the two countries established a Maritime Military Consultative Agreement (MMCA) in 1998, but disputes are still lingering.[9] It is not only because of the ambiguity of the United Nations Convention on the Law of the Seas (UNCLOS) over this issue, but also because of U.S. hostility to China. In other words, it is a legal issue as well as a strategic issue. The U.S., however, criticizes China for "undermining navigational freedom." After the incident with the USNS *Impeccable* (T-AGOS 23) in 2009, Timothy J. Keating, then Commander of U.S. Pacific Fleet, said that China was unwilling to accept the current norms, and was becoming increasingly aggressive.[10] He was quoted as saying, "now, China not only shows muscles in regional waters, but also seeks to revise the rule of freedom of navigation."[11] In fact, navigational freedom in the East and the South China Sea has never been a problem. Rather, it is to be assumed that the U.S. is seeking legitimacy for naval maneuvers in China's EEZ in the name of navigational freedom.[12]

Another subject of contention has been the extension of the Chinese Air Defense Identification Zone (ADIZ) in the Eastern Chinese Sea. It has been common practice for many countries to establish an ADIZ in order to protect national interests and to avoid accidents. Prior to China, the U.S., Japan, and the ROK had already established an ADIZ as they saw fit. However, China's establishment of an ADIZ in the East China Sea in November 2013 triggered strong protests, mainly from the U.S. and Japan. On the same day, U.S. Secretary of Defense Chuck Hagel stated that this action would change the status quo in the region and, hence, increase the risk of miscalculation. U.S. Secretary of State John Kerry criticized China by saying that the action would raise tensions in the region.[13] The U.S. also challenged China's claim with B-52 bombers entering the ADIZ without notifying China in advance.

2. To safeguard island sovereignty and maritime rights. According to Chinese legislation, China's islands include coastal islands, Taiwan, and all islands appertaining thereto, including the Diaoyu Islands, Penghu Islands, Dongsha Islands, Xisha Islands, Zhongsha Islands, Nansha Islands as well as all the other islands belonging to the People's Republic of China.[14] By the same token, China's maritime rights include not only rights and interests provided by international and domestic law (such as waters under its jurisdiction, the sovereignty over inland waters and jurisdiction rights over a contiguous zone, sovereignty and jurisdiction rights within the EEZ and the continental shelf), it also claims historical rights as well as legitimate rights and requirements in waters outside of its jurisdiction, such as maritime rights and interests in the high seas, the international seabed, and the poles.[15]

Maritime economy is becoming the new engine of China's economy. In 2011, China's total maritime production volume has surpassed 4.5 trillion Renminbi (RMB), accounting for 9.7 percent of its GDP.[16] To achieve the goal of doubling the 2010 GDP per capita by the year 2020, the share of maritime industry at net production will have to grow, making it an important pillar of China's national economy.[17] In the future, shortages of resources will be one of the crucial bottlenecks for China's economic development. The sea areas claimed by China, however, hold potential for oil, natural gas, mineral, and biological resources. Thus, it is of strategic significance for China to safeguard the sovereignty of its islands and its broader maritime rights.

China safeguards its island sovereignty and maritime rights, but never pursues an expansionist maritime strategy. In 2010, some observers stated that China considered the South China Sea as its "strategic core interests," thus creating the impression of an expansionist scheme.[18] Some scholars argued that China was promoting its interests with salami-slicing tactics.[19] Some scholars, however, hold that China's maritime policy has not undertaken dramatic changes compared with the period before.[20] They argue that Beijing is displaying a greater capability to support its longstanding maritime claims while proactively responding to challenges from other states.[21]

During testimony before the U.S. congress on February 5, 2014, U.S. Assistant Secretary of State Daniel Russel asked China to clarify its "Nine-Dash Line" claims in the South China Sea. He said that "under international law, maritime claims in the South China sea must be derived from land features. Any use of the 'nine-dash line' by China to claim maritime rights not based on land features would be inconsistent with international law."[22] UNCLOS, however, does not deny the legitimacy of historical rights. Instead, it shows recognition of and respect for historical rights by use of terms such as "historical gulf" or "historical ownership" in Article 10, Article 15, and Article 298. Meanwhile, China makes it clear in the *Law on the Exclusive Economic Zone and the Continental Shelf of the People's Republic of China* that China will not give up its historical rights in peripheral waters which are being defined as EEZ or continental shelf.

3. *To safeguard SLOCs and overseas interests.* Since the economic reform of the late 1970s and after the general opening up of China, contacts and the exchange of persons, goods, and services between China and the outside world are on the rise. As a result, China's interests have been globalized and security issues are increasingly connected to the world. Access to overseas markets, security of persons, property and SLOCs have become major pillars of China's national maritime interests.

In particular, since China's entry into the World Trade Organization (WTO) in 2001, the country has witnessed a rapid rise in its foreign trade. In 2013, China became the world's largest trading country for goods, with a total volume of imports and exports of $4.16 trillion, of which 90 percent is traded by maritime transportation.[23] The dependence of China on secure foreign trade lines for strategic raw materials, such as oil, gas, and iron ore, is on the rise. Since 1993, when China became a net oil importing country, the dependence on foreign sources has grown at a speed of 3 percent annually. It reached 58 percent in 2012, with the net import volume of crude oil as high as 284 million tons.[24] Some experts predict that its dependence rate may surpass 80 percent by 2035, much higher than the international alarm line, which is set at 50 percent.[25] About 60 percent of China's energy import is transferred by maritime transportation, 90 percent of which is through the Indian Ocean and the Malacca Straits.[26] It is imaginable that the interruption of SLOCs will have serious implications for China's economic and social development.

In its report to the 18th Congress of CPC, the Chinese leadership has made it clear that China must "adopt a more proactive opening-up strategy."[27] This means that China's overseas interests will continue to expand and, accordingly, the influence of external players on China's security and development will also rise. Meanwhile, with the furthering of China's "Going Out" strategy, competition between China and other countries has grown. China's overseas interest will face more and intense competitions and challenges.

4. *To maintain a sound maritime security environment.* National security not only refers to national survival and development, but also to the capabilities that a nation possesses to effectively cope with threats and challenges. With the expansion of its armed forces, China seeks to maintain a secure and stable regional and international environment. This is more relevant than the danger of being invaded by other powers (which is quite remote). In 2010, China and the U.S. had a dispute over an American aircraft carrier's entry into the Yellow Sea. China opposed the presence of that aircraft carrier not because of the fear of an invasion, but because the carrier's entry could escalate the tensions in the Korean Peninsula where the situation already was quite tense.

China's commitment to maintaining a sound security environment does not necessarily mean that it is looking for a "Monroe Doctrine" in East Asia. In recent years, with China's rapid economic development and its friendly peripheral policy, Beijing's influence has grown rapidly in the region. China also pursues an open regional policy and welcomes the U.S. in playing a constructive role in regional efforts towards peace, stability, and prosperity. However, some American observers hold the opinion that "China sees the South China Sea as its backyard" and China intends to expand its sphere of influence at U.S. cost. If this trend continues, the U.S. is likely to be expelled from Asia.[28] To cope with the challenge posed by Taiwan, China builds anti-intervention operational capabilities. But in the eyes of the U.S., China is developing "Anti-Access" and "Area-Denial" capabilities with allegedly much broader ambitions. As a result, the U.S. has introduced the Air–Sea Battle Concept in the region and is pursuing the pivot-to-Asia policy, which so far has not contributed to stability in Asia. Through this, the U.S. has rather made the region more tense and conflict-prone.[29]

Challenges for China's maritime security

With the diversification and the expansion of China's maritime interests, the challenges and threats it faces are becoming more serious and increasingly complex. Traditional threats and non-traditional threats coexist, and sometimes they intertwine, which makes the situation even more uncertain. Among the main challenges for China's maritime security are the following:

1. *Taiwan separation forces and activities remain the biggest threat for China's maritime security.* Taiwan's reunification with the mainland remains China's core national interest and there is no room for compromise. For quite a long time, conflicts around the Taiwan Straits triggered by Taiwan separatist activities and aggravated by an extra-region power's involvement have been China's biggest maritime security concern. Since the Taiwan Straits Crisis in 1995–6, preparing for anti-secession operations has been the most important driving force of China's military build-up, especially the maritime naval build-up. With the improvement of political relations across the Straits since 2008, the risk of military conflict across the Straits has more or less decreased. However, there is still a long way to go before China will achieve its complete reunification. More than that, major changes might happen in domestic politics in Taiwan, and the current positive trend may be reversed. Thus, opposition to Taiwan's separation and maintaining the national sovereignty and the territorial integrity of the whole of China still remains the basic mission of China's maritime security strategy.

2. *Dramatic changes in the U.S. Asia-Pacific strategy and Japan's assertive revisionist approach make the regional security situation complicated and dangerous.* For decades, the Asia-Pacific region has been one of the most stable and peaceful in the world. The region has, since the end of the Cold War, enjoyed unprecedented economic and social development despite the fact that many historical disputes still remain. Due to the widely accepted regional consensus of shelving (or managing) differences for the sake of common economic development and due to the "ASEAN Way" of non-intervention, avoidance of force, and the resolution of territorial disputes in a step-by-step manner through peaceful negotiations, regional territorial disputes and differences have not escalated during the past three decades. However, these disputes have become a major international bone of contention since the Obama Administration embarked on its "rebalancing" strategy. This strategy implies that Washington is upgrading its bilateral and multilateral security alliances in East Asia, enhancing its military presence in the region, and openly meddling in regional disputes. In particular, the U.S. has actually abandoned its ambiguity and its neutral stance on maritime disputes in the region by declaring that "the South China Sea issue involves U.S. interests" and by declaring that Diaoyu Island is under the protection of its treaty with Japan, despite its claims of "taking no position" on sovereignty in regional disputes. In recent years, especially since Abe Shinzou came into power in 2012, the revisionist elements in Japan have been growing stronger and have made their imprint on the foreign policy agenda of Tokyo. If this trend continues, revision of the Peace Constitution of Japan and military expansion is just a matter of time. Meanwhile, unlike Germany, Japan has become a destabilizing factor in the region through assertively seeking a normal state identity without self-examination of its war crimes during World War II.

3. *Provocative actions by some regional countries raise the tensions in the region.* The twenty-first century has been called the Century of Seas, and it has been the common understanding of coastal countries that maritime resources should be made available for economic development. In an environment in which the U.S. is returning to Asia, some countries, which have disputes with China over the sovereignty of islands and maritime rights, are exploiting the situation by escalating local situations. In April 2012, Philippine warships violated the Declaration of Conduct

on the Sea and tried to arrest Chinese fishing boats near Huangyan Island. This triggered a confrontation between two countries at sea. In September 2012, the "purchase of an island" by the Japanese government led to the escalation of the dispute over Diaoyu Island between China and Japan. In June 2012, the National Congress of Vietnam included China's Xisha and Nansha Islands within its territory by approving a new Vietnamese Law of the Sea. These provocative actions raised tensions and changed the status quo in the region.

It is alarming to see that in this environment China is portrayed in the global media as aggressive, whereas the Philippines, Vietnam, and Japan do not attract any criticism. In fact, it is not China which has triggered tensions, be it on Huangyan Island and Diaoyu Island, or on the establishment of Sansha City. "China has not diverged from its peaceful development path and defensive deterrence strategy, but has rather reacted to foreign aggression."[30] From this perspective, China is passive and is responding to the challenges posed by other countries. Why is there so much focus on China, and why is so little attention being paid to the behavior of the other actors? One explanation might be that China's overall policy has changed from passivity to activity.[31] Another explanation might be that China's responses often came unexpectedly – at least for Western observers.[32]

4. *Rise of maritime non-traditional challenges that threaten SLOC security*. Since the start of the new century, non-traditional maritime threats, such as piracy, armed robbery, and natural disasters, have grown in importance dramatically. The Gulf of Aden could be taken as an example: about 200,000 ships sail across these waters annually. Somalia piracy has brought about the loss of as much as $15 billion annually to the international community. In 2008 alone, $120 million was given to Somalia pirates as ransom.[33] More than that, non-traditional maritime threats are difficult to eradicate fundamentally. Somalia piracy still exists, although the international community has been combating piracy for years with much success.

In addition, Japan seeks to enlarge its EEZ by artificially consolidating the Okinotorishima Reef. Some Arctic countries want to impose stricter supervision and control on ships sailing through this area. All these developments will have negative implications on the freedom of navigation globally. After the Cold War, the U.S. made positive contributions to the global maritime security order by securing many global sea lines of communication. In recent years, however, due to its reduced dependence on imports of oil, the U.S. contribution to the security of SLOCs has declined.[34] Also, cuts in U.S. military spending have raised questions about the will and strength of the U.S. to secure SLOCs on a global scale. As a result, the power pattern of maintaining the global maritime security order may face restructuring, with other maritime powers joining in. China's Prime Minister, Li Keqiang, has just recently pointed out that it was necessary to study the implications of the decline of U.S. energy dependence for foreign trade and for global economy and politics.[35] As a rising power, China should develop a more powerful maritime force and be ready to take more international responsibilities in maintaining maritime security in a Chinese way.

China's approaches in maintaining maritime security

The analysis of interests and threats forms the basis and is the prerequisite of any formulation of strategy. However, how to cope with threats and safeguard interests depends on the strategic choices of a country. History shows that, owing to different grand strategies, security concepts, and strategic cultures, different countries have devised different choices even when they are facing almost the same security challenges.

In order to understand China's approaches in maintaining maritime security, the following points should be noted. First, globalization has turned the world into a community of common destiny in which all members are closely interconnected. Overall confrontation between major powers would be disastrous for all. Thus, China does not identify the U.S. as an adversary although Washington is posing some serious challenges to China's security. Second, China considers economic development as its main objective, which requires a secure and stable regional and international environment. Third, Chinese tradition, culture, and its peculiar security concept have a preference for settling disputes through peaceful means. Fourth, today's maritime security challenges are beyond the capability of one country to control or cope with individually, no matter how strong the country is.

All these aspects have significant implications for China's choices with regard to its basic policy objectives and its approaches in the field of maritime security strategy. Its objectives mainly include maintaining national unity, defending the country against any threat coming from the sea, safeguarding island sovereignty and maritime rights, building a naval force which is commensurate with China's international standing, meeting the needs of broader security and development interests, and contributing to maritime security and stability in the region and the world at large. As to strategic approaches, China has neither the intention nor the capability to pursue its maritime interests through sea control or gunboat policy. Thus, international cooperation is the only viable option. Here, the policy of China rests on various instruments:

1. *Resolving maritime disputes through peaceful means.* China's policy of managing (or shelving) disputes for common development has not changed. China seeks to keep maritime disputes under control and intends to create conditions for the eventual settlement through promoting cooperation and expanding common interests. Maritime disputes are only a small part of relations between claiming countries. Hence, China will address maritime disputes with its neighbors within the broader framework of its relations with them. But China also tries to go the multilateral path: since 2013, China has made several proposals for improving its relations with ASEAN, such as the twenty-first-century Silk Road on the Sea initiative, the idea of an Asia Infrastructure Investment Bank, the concept of a new China–ASEAN Free Trade Zone, or the proposal for a Community of Common Destiny of China and ASEAN Countries. The Peripheral Diplomatic Meeting, held in October 2013 in Beijing, stated that China's priority in its regional diplomacy is to develop friendly and cooperative relations with ASEAN countries. It is a first sign of success that China could reach some understanding with countries such as Brunei and Indonesia on joint development and on the principle that regional disputes should not be internationalized and thus become complicated.

China handles maritime disputes according to the principle of "Sovereignty Belonging to China, Shelving Disputes, Seeking Joint Development." This principle involves four elements: (1) sovereignty belonging to China is the prerequisite; (2) disputes over sovereignty and ownership should be shelved until conditions become mature for the eventual settlement of disputes. However, it does not mean giving up the claim of sovereignty; (3) joint development of resources can be conducted in the disputed waters; (4) the purpose of joint development is to create conditions for the eventual consensual settlement of disputes through cooperation and promotion of mutual understanding.[36] Unfortunately, since it has been put forward, this principle has been misinterpreted. It has resulted in China's unilateral restraint and has failed to safeguard China's sovereignty and maritime rights in the South China Sea.[37] In fact, it is not a question of the principle itself, rather that the principle is not understood and implemented completely, systematically, and comprehensively. It will eventually be conducive to regional security and beneficial to all claimants to turn this principle into rules and regulations adhered to by all parties.

On the other hand, China should be prepared to safeguard its maritime rights. China seeks to settle disputes through negotiations, but it needs other parties to share this intention and proceed in the same spirit. Unfortunately, some countries have taken provocative actions in maritime disputes, seeking to profit by stirring up trouble. Against these countries, China is forced to adopt different policies and respond with firm resolve and effective measures. Therefore, China must make itself well prepared politically, economically, diplomatically, and militarily for unexpected scenarios.

2. *Promoting international cooperation and safeguarding security of the SLOC.* China has undertaken many efforts to study the risks for SLOCs and to devise solutions. At the beginning of the twenty-first century, with the rise of dependence on maritime trade, SLOC security has become a prime issue in China with particular reference to the Malacca Straits. About 80 percent of China's oil import goes through the Malacca Straits. China would be faced with the interruption of its oil supply if the Malacca Straits were to be blocked.[38] Some scholars even argued that the key threat of a "Malacca Dilemma" comes from the United States.[39] Yet, since the Malacca Straits is part of the global maritime commons in an interdependent world (Japan, ROK, and ASEAN members all heavily rely on the Straits), some scholars suggest that the possibility of the U.S. blocking the Malacca Straits is limited even if a conflict were to break out between the U.S. and China.[40] Most observers believe that the main challenges for China's energy security result from piracy, terrorism, and transportation accidents in peacetime rather than from energy blockade and containment by major powers during war.[41]

In line with this argumentation, non-traditional maritime challenges will improve the chances for international cooperation. These challenges have transnational features and are beyond the capabilities of any one country to cope with them. In 1999, China began its cooperation with Malaysia, the Philippines, and Vietnam in combating piracy. In 2002, China and ASEAN released the China–ASEAN Declaration of Cooperation on Non-Traditional Security. Since December 2008, China has been carrying out escort missions in the Gulf of Aden and in the waters off the Somalia coast. During these missions, the Chinese Navy has established communication mechanisms with its international counterparts for joint escort, information sharing, coordination, and liaison. Since December 2013, China has also been participating in escorting the mission of the American naval vessel *Cape Ray*, which had taken on the task of transporting Syrian chemical weapons. All these initiatives have enhanced cooperation and understanding with other powers.

3. *Strengthening maritime confidence-building measures (CBMs) and building a harmonious ocean.* Although some countries would like to take measures against or "balance" China's efforts at building a blue-water navy, China has chosen to strengthen maritime security confidence-building measures instead of responding with tit-for-tat measures. On April, 2009, Admiral Wu Shengli, Commander of PLA Navy, elaborated China's maritime security policy by putting forward the concept of "Harmonious Ocean."[42]

China attaches great importance to promoting maritime security CBMs with major powers, in particular with the U.S. Maritime confidence building is an important part of a new type of major power relations between the two countries and might play an overall special role in improving their bilateral political relations. For many years, China and the U.S. have exchanged frequent high-level visits and in 1998 both sides concluded an MMCA, whereby the navies of the two countries should face disputes and de-escalate them, control and avoid incidents. They should also expand practical cooperation and improve interaction mechanisms, thus contributing to the development of a new type of major power relations and also to peace and stability in the Asia-Pacific region. China has recently proposed two new mechanisms for confidence building between the U.S. and China. One is the establishment of a notification measure for major military activities; the other suggests setting up standards for air and naval operations in different maritime environments. Meanwhile, China will also look for maritime CBMs with regard to Russia, India, NATO, and the EU.

At the same time, China must initiate maritime CBMs with neighboring countries. In recent years, China has achieved progress in maritime confidence building with its neighboring countries bilaterally as well as multilaterally. Bilateral CBMs so far concluded are, for instance, the Agreement on Joint Patrols by the Navies of China and Vietnam in the Beibuwan, as well as the establishments of direct telephone links between China and ROK Naval and Air Force Troops. Currently there are consultations between China and Japan over the establishment of various maritime liaison mechanisms. Multilateral mechanisms have also been developed. China will continue to promote maritime exchange with neighboring countries, handle maritime disputes peacefully, and keep them under control. It will also promote the establishment of rules of maritime behavior and ensure the common security of the seas with its neighboring countries.

4. Developing comprehensive naval power and integrating resources so as to support the maritime security strategy. Naval power is the basis of maritime security strategy. Power is indispensable for cooperation as well as for safeguarding national interests. For China, comprehensive maritime power includes not only military power, such as naval forces and air forces, but also maritime law enforcement, maritime development force, and maritime science and technology force.

China should build a sea power which is commensurate with its international standing. It is a common practice that naval power building should meet the requirements of national interests. With the growth of China's overseas interests and the rising calls for China to take more international responsibility, building a blue-water navy has become a must for China. Some argue that China's building of a blue-water navy will unavoidably result in conflict with geopolitical interests of major maritime powers; however, overall confrontation is not predestined. Maintaining peace instead of seeking hegemony, developing limited sea power instead of gaining absolute advantage, respecting the current maritime order instead of undermining it, and promoting cooperation instead of monopolizing is the best way for China to safeguard its maritime interests and rights while avoiding fundamental confrontation with major maritime powers.[43]

China should also develop and integrate maritime law enforcement forces and maritime scientific and technological capabilities. In recent years, China's maritime law enforcement force has witnessed a rapid development. In 2011, China finished the construction of 7 1,000-ton maritime surveillance ships, 3 maritime surveillance planes, and 36 provincial law enforcement ships.[44] In March 2013, the National Oceanic Administration was re-established by integrating several separate law-enforcement agencies. This marked a "historic transformation of China's management system and working mechanism of the sea."[45] More than that, China has achieved breakthroughs in maritime developments and maritime technologies. In May 2012, Oceanic Petro 981, China's first self-designed, self-made deep-water semi-submarine oil rig achieved success in rigging, which marks a substantial step forward to deep-water access for China's oil and gas development.

Conclusion

The sea plays an increasingly important role in the economic and social development as well as in the maintenance of sovereignty and security of China. Hence, utilization of the sea is

China's indispensable choice. With the development of national power instruments, in particular maritime power instruments, China is now able to safeguard its maritime interests with a stronger will and more effective measures. Meanwhile, it neither gives up its maritime security policy, which is defensive and cooperative in nature, nor does it harbor expansionist goals. China will cooperate with neighboring countries in handling maritime disputes, work together with other countries in establishing and furthering a maritime security order, and it will contribute more to security in global maritime domains. At the same time, however, it is also necessary for countries concerned to view and handle the development of China's maritime power in an open, inclusive, and cooperative manner, and avoid brinkmanship and stirring up incidents. Thus, it is highly possible to ensure maritime security in the region and construct a harmonious ocean.

Notes

1 Xu Hui is a professor and Cao Xianyu is a research associate at the National Defense University (NDU), PLA, China. All views expressed in this chapter are those of the authors and do not necessarily represent the authority of NDU and PLA of China.

2 See Dan Twining, "Were U.S.–India Relations Oversold? Part XX," http://shadow.foreignpolicy.com, accessed August 28, 2015.

3 *Mao Zedong's Military Anthology*, vol. 6, Beijing: Military Science Press and CCCPC Literature Press, 1993, p. 343.

4 See "Escort in Aden Gulf: China Navy goes to Deep Blue," *People's Daily*, August 22, 2009.

5 "Relying on the ocean and building a strong and prosperous country," *People's Daily Overseas Edition*, August 1, 2013.

6 See Information Office of the State Council: *China's Peaceful Development*, Beijing, September 2011, www.politics.people.com.cn/GB/1026/15598619.html, accessed August 28, 2015.

7 Ma Zhirong, "Maritime strong country: China's strategic choice in the new century," *Ocean Development and Management*, June 2004, p. 4.

8 Zhang Wei and Feng Liang, *China's Maritime Security*, Beijing: Hai Chao Press, October 2008, p. 386.

9 See Zhai Wenzhong. "China–US maritime military consultative agreement: background, operations and prospect," *Defense Magazine*, October 2008.

10 Al Pessin, "US Admiral Calls for Renewed US-China Military Talks," VOANews.com, March 19, 2009, www.voanews.com/english/2009-03-19-voa63.cfm, accessed August 28, 2015.

11 See Peter Dutton, "China Undermines Maritime Law," *Far Eastern Economic Review (Hong Kong)* (April 2009).

12 "Do not stir up trouble by the name of navigational freedom in the South China Sea," *People's Daily*, March 16, 2012. "Who says 'no navigational freedom' in the South China Sea?" *National Defense Journal*, November 2, 2010; "Navigational freedom is never a problem," *China's Defense Daily*, July 12, 2011.

13 Bonnie Glaser and Jacqueline Vitello, "Biden visits China amid ADIZ fracas," *Comparative Connections: A Triannual E-Journal on East Asian Bilateral Relations* (January 2014), http://csis.org/files/publication/1303qus_china.pdf, p. 1, accessed August 28, 2015.

14 *Law of the PRC on the Territorial Sea and the Contiguous Zone*, Article 2, www.en8848.com.cn/hangye/law/chinaflfg/92442.html, accessed August 28, 2015.

15 China Institute for Marine Affairs, *China's Ocean Development Report 2013*, Beijing: China Ocean Press, 2013, p. 46.

16 Liu Xigui, "Speech of transmitting the spirit of 18th congress of CPC in the Oceanic administration system," *China Ocean News*, November 17, 2012.

17 "Relying on the ocean and building a strong and prosperous country," *People's Daily Overseas Edition*, August 1, 2013.

18 As quoted in Alastair Iain Johnston: "How New and Assertive Is China's New Assertiveness?" *International Security* 37, 4 (Spring 2013), pp. 7–48 (pp. 17–20).

19 Bonnie Glaser, "People's Republic of China Maritime Disputes," Testimony before the U.S. House Armed Services Subcommittee on Seapower and Projection Forces and the House Foreign Affairs Subcommittee on the Asia Pacific, January 14, 2014.

20 As quoted in Johnston, "How New and Assertive?"

21 Michael D. Swaine and M. Taylor Fravel, "China's Assertive Behavior, Part Two: The Maritime Periphery," *China Leadership Monitor*, no. 35, p. 7.

22 Daniel R. Russel, "Maritime Disputes in East Asia," www.state.gov/p/eap/rls/rm/2014/02/221293.htm, accessed August 28, 2015.

23 "Promoting transformation and upgrade of maritime industry," *Xiamen Daily*, May 11, 2011.

24 Guo Li, "The analysis of china's economic dependence on foreign trade and the related policy suggestions," *China Business and Market* (April 2013), p. 56.

25 "China's oil dependence rate on foreign trade almost doubles," *Oil Science and Technology Information* (April 2013), p. 18.

26 Cai Yi, "China's energy lifeline and strategic security," *Leader's Reference* (February 2014), p. 28.

27 Hu Jintao, *Firmly March on the Path of Socialism with Chinese Characteristics and Strive to Complete the Building of a Moderately Prosperous Society in All Respects*, Beijing: People's Publishing House, November 2012, p. 24.

28 U.S. scholars Toshi Yoshihara and James R. Holmes draw a parallel between how the Chinese view that body of water in the South China Sea and how the U.S. has traditionally viewed its own maritime backyard. See Toshi Yoshihara and James R. Holmes, "Can China Defend a 'Core Interest' in the South China Sea?" *Washington Quarterly* (Spring 2011), pp. 45–59.

29 See Robert S. Ross, "The Problem with the Pivot," *Foreign Affairs* (November/December 2012), p. 70.

30 Øystein Tunsjø, "China's maritime security policy in a bipolar international system," Paper presented at the SIPRI conference, Stockholm, April 18–19, 2013.

31 See Dave Finkelstein, "Is China getting assertive on territorial disputes?" The South China Sea and U.S.–China–ASEAN Relations, CSIS Roundtable, October 28, 2011.

32 Swaine, "China's assertive behavior," p. 9.

33 Sun Degang, "Study on Global Governance of Somalia Piracy," *Forum of World Economics & Politics* (April 2010), p. 152.

34 Guo Li, "The analysis of China's economic dependence on foreign trade and the related policy suggestions," *China Business and Market* (April 2013), p. 56.

35 *Ibid.*

36 "New China's basic proposals in settling border disputes," www.fmprc.gov.cn/chn/gxh/xsb/wjzs/wjs/2159/t8978.htm.2009-05-27, accessed August 28, 2015.

37 Zhong Feiteng, "Three Strategic Issues of South China Sea Studies," *Foreign Affairs Review* (April 2014), p. 33.

38 See Xue Li, "Argument of 'Malacca Dilemma''s Connotation and China's Response," *World Economy and Politics* (October 2010), p. 118.

39 Li Chenyang, "China's solutions to 'Malacca Dilemma'," *Reference News*, August 5, 2004.

40 Xue Li, "Argument of 'Malacca Dilemma''s Connotation," p. 137.

41 Zhao Hongtu, "Rethinking of 'Malacca Dilemma' and China's energy security," *Contemporary International Relations* (June 2007), p. 36.

42 "Harmonious ocean symposium held in Qingdao," *PLA Daily*, April 22, 2009.

43 Gu Dexin, "Six relations should be handled well in establishing China's maritime security strategy," *China's Foreign Affairs* (January 2012), p. 12.

44 "Managing the sea by law becomes guidance of National Oceanic Administration," *Law Daily*, March 27, 2013.

45 "Unprecedented importance attached to maritime affairs," *People's Daily*, April 1, 2013.

25

CHINESE VIEWS OF THE U.S.-LED MARITIME ORDER

Assessing the skeptics

Toshi Yoshihara

China's seaward turn has stimulated a lively internal debate among its elites. Over the past decade, Chinese researchers have published widely on China's maritime power, cracking open a window onto Beijing's strategic calculus. The writings address numerous topics, ranging from maritime strategy to naval operations. The literature is impressive for its candor and analytical rigor. Scholars routinely challenge each other, revealing a competitive intellectual environment. More recently, commentators have devoted their attention to the global maritime order and China's place in it, suggesting that the Chinese are starting to take the long view on seapower. This trend warrants attention because the future stability of maritime Asia hinges on how well – or how badly – China settles into the current order.

Among the many factions that have emerged in this discourse, the skeptics stand out for their misgivings about the oceanic order and America's role in it. They rail against the dark side of globalization and reject Western liberal internationalist assumptions about the world. They distrust U.S. stewardship of the seas and urge Beijing to revise the order in favor of China. Some want Beijing to lead instead. Contrary to Western expectations that Beijing will become a "responsible stakeholder," this growing body of work points China in a worrisome direction. If such an unhappy worldview takes hold within the policy-making process, then the latest maritime confrontations and crises involving China may be a harbinger of things to come in Asia. Indeed, the skeptics have egged on Chinese assertiveness at sea. That their views have gained traction in the wake of Chinese provocations in the East and South China Seas is perhaps no coincidence.

It is the contention of this study that this ambivalence about the current order offers insights into Beijing's recent intemperance. Western policy-makers would benefit from better understanding such Chinese reservations. To make sense of the writings, this study first examines the maritime order, likening it to a public good. The chapter then assesses the factors that have impelled the United States to defend the maritime system. This larger context provides a baseline for comparing against the views of the skeptics, underscoring just how far apart these Chinese perspectives are from Western views of order. Next, the chapter reviews the open-source literature. Words matter, for they convey the assumptions and convictions peculiar to these skeptics. This study thus lets the Chinese speak for themselves, quoting their works at length. The chapter concludes with an assessment of the Chinese writings and what they might mean for U.S. policy.

Maritime order as a public good

The current maritime order rests on the premise that the seas are a shared space, facilitating the unrestricted movement of goods and services across the world's oceans. This inclusive framework has been the centerpiece of the postwar international system of exchange. The freedom to use the seas – a legal tradition spanning 400 years – helped forge a global network of commerce that has in turn generated wealth for those participating in the system. To the export-oriented economies of Asia, like China, such accessibility has been essential to their prosperity.

The maritime order is best understood as a public good. Harvard scholar Joseph Nye elegantly defines a public good as "something everyone can consume without diminishing its availability to others."[1] The global maritime order, then, is an international public good that permits universal access to the seas without prejudice to any state. Ideally, the beneficiaries of this nautical public good should share a common interest in upholding – and avoiding actions that might undermine – its open character. In fact, self-restraint is vital to maintaining the public good's integrity. Critically, states may not carve out the seas for the purposes of asserting exclusive control.

But, spoilers may arise in such collective enterprises among states. Based on a host of calculations, countries may assert excessive jurisdictional claims over portions of the maritime commons, as China and others have already done. Exclusionary policies – and international acquiescence to them – could set an unwelcome precedent. Other states may follow suit, possibly encouraging wider defections. Such a cascading effect would reverse the logic of a public good. A more closed maritime order would diminish the availability of a shared good, leading to curtailed economic consumption for all.

Order, framed in terms of a public good, is fragile. Order is not necessarily self-regulating. While the incentives to uphold the integrity of a public good are substantial, they may not always override the value that some states attach to other national objectives. Consent to restraint can be withdrawn. At the same time, order is not indivisible. Countries cannot take exception to a public good without undermining its openness. As such, order is not immutable. Consensus about the public good's value could well break down, resulting in its collapse. Order, in short, cannot be left to its own devices.

The U.S.-led liberal maritime order

The maritime order's vulnerability thus demands its defense. For the past seven decades, the United States, the preponderant naval power, has safeguarded the maritime system. Major trends following the Cold War's end cemented America's postwar primacy at sea. Economic globalization, the prohibitive costs of building and maintaining a blue-water navy, and the absence of an existential threat to the international system disinclined states to challenge or replicate U.S. naval power. Instead, participants in the global economy looked to the United States to furnish maritime security.[2]

But the convergence of unique historical circumstances is insufficient to explain the U.S. Navy's role in guaranteeing the freedom to use the seas. The theory of public goods again supplies a useful framework for understanding why the United States enforces the rules of the maritime order. Nye reasons:

> If the largest beneficiary of a public good (for example, the United States) does not take the lead in directing disproportionate resources towards its provision, the smaller

beneficiaries are unlikely to be able to produce it, because of the difficulties of organizing collective action when large numbers are involved. While this responsibility of the largest often lets others become 'free riders', the alternative is that the collective bus does not move at all.[3]

Moreover, delivering a service that others are unable or unwilling to offer helps the United States earn legitimacy in the eyes of those that depend on the public good. By providing for maritime security in the postwar era, the U.S. Navy has legitimized American rule of the seas, much as the Royal Navy legitimized British supremacy before. A dominant naval power committed to an open maritime order can acquire the consent of weak and strong states alike to police the seas even as it accepts the bulk of the risks and costs associated with constabulary tasks. This was as true for Britain then as it is for the United States today.

American defense of the Asian maritime order

The idea that the maritime order is a public good has enjoyed something of a renaissance, gaining currency in U.S. policy and academic circles. Over the past decade, Washington has championed the defense of the "global commons," a quintessentially public goods concept. MIT professor Barry Posen was among the first to revive awareness of the global commons, namely the seas, skies, space, and cyberspace. While Posen is primarily concerned with explaining how U.S. command of these realms sustain American hegemony, his analysis also illustrates why such command prods others to acquiesce to U.S. military primacy.

Framing his proposition in terms of public goods, Posen observes, "Command of the commons," not only "gives the United States a tremendous capability to harm others," but also creates "collective goods for U.S. allies." Such command also helps:

> Connect U.S. military power to seemingly prosaic welfare concerns. U.S. military power underwrites world trade, travel, global communications, and commercial remote sensing, which all depend on peace and order in the commons. Those nations most involved in these activities, those who profit most from globalization, seem to understand that they benefit from the U.S. military position – which may help explain why the world's consequential powers have grudgingly supported U.S. hegemony.[4]

The concept of the commons has subsequently found its way into the Pentagon's lexicon. Successive strategy documents, from the 2005 National Defense Strategy to the 2012 Defense Strategic Guidance, have identified defense of – and access to – the global commons as a major strategic objective. They define access as a public good.[5]

American seapower defends Asia's maritime commons in three ways. First, U.S. naval power and forward presence in the region have been instrumental in preserving the maritime order. During the Cold War, the containment of communist expansion, aided by seapower, furnished the conditions for the Asian economies of the "free world" to flourish. Today, the U.S. Navy contributes to deterrence in the Taiwan Strait and on the Korean Peninsula while guaranteeing the free flow of goods along critical sea lanes. The pacifying effects of American naval prowess have thus enabled commerce.

Owing to the complex and often unstable relationships among Asian nations, the U.S. Navy is the only credible arbiter of regional maritime affairs.[6] Local actors were – and remain – unable or unwilling to defend Asia's maritime order. American naval power has been entrusted, although reluctantly by some, to keep the peace at sea.

Second, the United States has counted on a maritime coalition of like-minded states to uphold the existing system. The hub-and-spokes allied structure in East Asia not only permitted the forward basing of American military power, but it also brought together stakeholders deeply committed to an open order. Japan and Australia, the northern and southern anchors of U.S. forward strategy in Asia, have helped preserve maritime openness.

In 2011, the U.S.–Japan alliance reaffirmed its commitment to maritime security as a common strategic objective. A joint statement pledged that the partnership would "maintain safety and security of the maritime domain by defending the principle of freedom of navigation."[7] Similarly, the U.S.–Australia alliance declared in 2011, and reiterated in 2012, that it shared a "national interest in freedom of navigation … and unimpeded lawful commerce in the South China Sea."[8] Both alliances explicitly acknowledged the close linkage between universal access to the seas and prosperity for all.

The United States looks to other non-allied seafaring powers to keep the seas open. The 2007 U.S. Maritime Strategy sends the message that all nations are stakeholders in the maritime order and should help preserve it, jointly supplying the public good of free navigation.[9] In the process, combined action at sea will "build confidence and trust among nations through collective security efforts that focus on common threats and mutual interests in an open, multipolar world." Building the habits of trust and cooperation on functional matters, proclaims the Maritime Strategy, will foster a healthier world system.

Third, the United States defends the norms that underwrite access to the commons. While Washington has not ratified the UN Convention on the Law of the Sea (UNCLOS), it recognizes the bulk of the treaty's provisions as customary international law. The U.S. government regards the freedom of navigation as a widely accepted, centuries-old practice that has been codified and reaffirmed by UNCLOS. The United States abides by the navigational provisions of the Convention, which binds all nations on the basis of custom.

To defend high seas freedoms, the United States routinely exercises its naval power – dubbed "operational assertions" – to deny the legitimacy of certain practices that, left unchallenged, could undermine the norms of the maritime system.[10] The U.S. Navy regularly sends units into waters where coastal states have asserted excessive jurisdictional claims. Such freedom-of-navigation operations tangibly demonstrate the rights of seafaring nations while rejecting attempts to restrict access to certain bodies of water. In sum, hard power, maritime coalitions, and norms underwrite access to maritime Asia.

China's growing ambivalence

The maritime order draws its strength from a collective agreement, akin to a social contract, between the leading naval power and the states that depend on access to the maritime commons. The former assumes responsibilities for keeping the seas open while the latter accepts the former's primacy at sea, conferring an aura of legitimacy to the provision of public goods. Conversely, states may withdraw their acquiescence to such a bargain, undermining the leading power's stewardship of the seas. The more strategically consequential the dissenting state, the more stress the order undergoes.

China's views of the current order – and of America's centrality in it – are thus a policy concern of substantial import. At present, China neither endorses American naval supremacy nor opposes the stabilizing role that the U.S. Navy plays in Asia. On the one hand, China is among the greatest beneficiaries of the U.S. provision of public goods. China's economic rise over the past three decades owes in large measure to the global system's openness. Until recently, Beijing seemed comfortable to free ride on U.S. naval power.

On the other hand, China's strategic community has long exhibited ambivalence toward America's naval role in Asia. A contentious history informs this skepticism. President Harry Truman's decision to interpose the 7th Fleet between China and Taiwan shortly after the outbreak of the Korean War virtually guaranteed Sino-U.S. enmity during the first decades of the Cold War. Subsequently, the U.S. Navy engaged actively in escort and patrol missions in support of Nationalist forces during the 1954 and 1958 Taiwan Strait crises. At the height of the 1995–6 Taiwan Strait crisis President Bill Clinton dispatched two carrier battle groups near Taiwan in a major show of force. To many Chinese, the U.S. Navy has long stood in the way of reunification.

American reconnaissance and surveillance along the mainland coast are another major source of bilateral tensions. China has long regarded such intelligence-gathering activities as unfriendly, if not hostile. As Beijing modernizes its military, it has backed its rhetorical objections to U.S. naval and aerial operations with action, leading to dangerous encounters in international airspace and waters. Major incidents include the collision between a Chinese fighter and an American reconnaissance aircraft in April 2001, the harassment of a U.S. ocean surveillance vessel by Chinese fishing trawlers and government ships in March 2009, the near-collision between a U.S. destroyer and a Chinese amphibious dock ship in November 2013, and the dangerous Chinese aerial interception of a U.S. reconnaissance aircraft in August 2014.

China's push back against U.S. military operations in what Beijing considers its nautical backyard correlates with the ascent of Chinese seapower and a more outward-looking naval strategy. The People's Liberation Army Navy (PLAN or PLA Navy) has grown rapidly from a coastal defense force composed of largely obsolescent Soviet-era technologies into a modern naval service. Over the past two decades, multiple classes of China's major surface combatants – notably the Type 052D *Luyang III* destroyer, the Type 054A *Jiangkai II* frigate, and the Type 056 *Jiangdao* corvette – have all entered serial production, adding mass and balance to the fleet. The build-up of these warships has accelerated since 2008. Between 2000 and 2012, China's fleet of attack submarines, increased eightfold from 5 to 40 boats.[11] In the meantime, China's first aircraft carrier, *Liaoning*, joined the fleet in 2012. Only 20 years have elapsed since China began to construct and import modern frontline fighting ships. This is an impressive feat by any standard.

This force modernization has enabled China to more fully meet the operational demands of its "near-seas defense" strategy, which remains the bedrock directive for the Chinese Navy. Near-seas defense is a regionally oriented strategy that enlarges China's maritime defense perimeter, extending the Chinese Navy's area of operations beyond the mainland shores. Instead of fighting the enemy in China's coastal waters, the PLAN seeks to keep the opponent at arm's length while shielding important political and economic centers on the seaboard from attack. Near-seas defense would defeat and roll back the enemy offensive in a series of echeloned naval engagements with organized formations. Compared to its previous subordination to the army and its role as an adjunct to land operations, the PLAN would enjoy far greater scope for action as an independent, strategic service.

While the most recent defense white papers insist that the Chinese Navy's primary task remains near-seas defense, the 2009 and 2011 editions explicitly acknowledge the need for the PLA Navy to operate in the "far seas." The 2013 report calls on the Chinese navy to "enhance far seas mobile operations." While the geographic scope of the far seas has been subject to varying interpretations, actual Chinese naval operations in recent years suggest that it likely encompasses "a vast area that stretches from the northwest Pacific to the eastern Indian Ocean."[12] It has become commonplace for Chinese naval flotillas to sail through the narrow seas of the Ryukyu island chain and cruise on the open waters of the western Pacific. The PLAN has also dispatched naval escorts on the anti-piracy missions in the Gulf of Aden on an uninterrupted basis since December 2008. Chinese power and strategy will thus ensure that Sino-U.S. naval encounters will increase in frequency and in intensity over the coming years.

It is against this backdrop of a major power shift in maritime Asia that some elite commentaries in China have turned sharply critical. Chinese analysts have objected to all three prongs of the American-led maritime order in Asia, namely U.S. naval power, American-led coalitions, and the defense of norms. The literature, as sampled below, portrays American seapower in exclusively strategic terms, evidencing little consideration of the public goods that the U.S. Navy has provided for decades.

Objections to U.S. defense of the global commons

Chinese observers express doubts that American concerns about the commons have much to do with the welfare of others. Rather, they sense much harder-edged motives. Ma Jianying of Ocean University of China asserts that, "Ensuring America's hegemonic position and preventing the emergence of a new challenger in the global commons are the primary objectives of the U.S. global commons strategy."[13] To Ma, the emphasis on the global commons hands Washington an excuse to intervene in maritime disputes involving China and to hype China's potential threat to the commons.

For Wang Yiwei, a scholar at Tongji University, the United States has promoted the concept of the global commons to achieve six strategic aims: (1) "offer a new theoretical foundation for advancing the legitimacy of American hegemony," (2) "establish a new system during the globalization process," (3) "find new excuses to intervene abroad," (4) "identify a new driver behind military transformation," (5) "seek new missions for America's security alliance system," and (6) "provide a new laboratory for integrating new elements of national power to threaten potential adversaries."[14] The objective is to entrench American power.

Some perceive the U.S. defense of the global commons as a scheme to slow America's relative decline. Cao Shengsheng and Xia Yuqing contend:

> Under the strategic circumstances of America's declining power, [the theory of the global commons] leverages strong soft power, relies on multiple allied systems, unceasingly forms cliques, and maintains control behind proxies. It pursues self-interest in the name of global interests, seeking to minimize costs while maximizing benefits. It is the new thinking and new practice for upholding American hegemony.[15]

Sun Kai and Feng Liang, too, believe that Washington seeks to lure other regional powers into defending the commons. Such a ploy would reduce the burden on the United States, freeing up resources to sustain its primacy. They observe, "The proposed global commons theory is designed to let emerging countries share responsibilities while continuing America's leading role in constructing the international system and maintaining America's global leadership position."[16]

Still others point to a cynical use of the global commons concept to justify U.S. involvement in the South China Sea. As Wang Yiwei contends, "Especially on the question of the South China Sea, the United States views the South China Sea as a so-called 'global commons,' falsely claiming that China's sovereign claims threatens the passage rights and the freedom of navigation in the 'global commons' while the United States flaunts itself as the defender of the 'global commons.'"[17]

Zhang Ming, a researcher at the Shanghai Academy of Social Science, censures Western analysts for "hyping the so-called 'anti-access/area-denial' capabilities of China and the South

China Sea problem, claiming that China's development of maritime and air power, space power, and cyber power threatens the security of the 'global commons.' The fomenting of the South China Sea problem is a reflection of this larger 'global commons' security issue."[18]

These writings share the belief that the U.S. policy discourse about the global commons is driven by fears of decline and by anxieties about China. They dismiss Washington's concerns about contested access to the commons, deprecating the value of public goods.

Objections to U.S. naval power

Chinese analysts depict American naval power as a blunt instrument to achieve global hegemony. Senior Captains Zhang Wei and Feng Liang believe that the U.S. Navy's dominance of the high seas has enabled it to focus on projecting power ashore in the post-Cold War period. The two authors, affiliated with the Naval Military Art Studies Institute and the Naval Command College respectively, cite U.S. Navy documents of the early 1990s, including ... *From the Sea* and *Forward ... From the Sea*, as evidence of a forward-leaning posture that threatens coastal states.[19]

Other analysts recount a deterministic history of American naval power. According to these interpretations, the U.S. Navy progressed along an unbroken, upward trajectory that culminated in global supremacy after the Soviet Union collapsed.[20] These teleological views of American seapower as an inexorably expansive force border on caricature.

Even as the U.S. Navy struggled in the midst of fiscal austerity in recent years, Chinese commentators insist that the United States seeks to maintain hegemony. In an interview about the U.S. Navy's latest 30-year shipbuilding plan, which projects a net decline in the fleet size, Li Li of the National Defense University asserts that, "The core of the plan is still to maintain the U.S. Navy's globally unmatched position as the hegemon over the next 30 years."[21] This judgment ignores the growing concerns about the shrinking fleet among U.S. experts.

In a detailed study of U.S. naval strategy under the Obama administration, Zhang Yuan at Wuhan University discerns troubling signs that the United States would adopt policies harmful to China's security.[22] In the author's view, the two enervating wars in the Middle East and the 2008 financial crisis compelled the U.S. Navy to prioritize its missions, reallocate resources, and emphasize burden sharing with allies. This strategic readjustment has also spurred a renewed focus on China. Zhang foresees a naval service more inclined to intervene in Asian affairs, exaggerate Beijing's maritime challenge, and encircle China with coalition partners.

A study by the China Institute of Contemporary International Relations rejects the idea that the U.S. Navy has contributed to maritime security. Wei Zonglei, for example, asserts that, "American control of sea lanes is clearly not about protecting the security and unimpeded use of the global sea lanes, but it is about protecting American interests, including access to oil supplies and forward military bases designed to suppress other countries."[23] Given the author's affiliation with a leading Chinese think tank, such an interpretation of American naval power is by no means an outlier in China's strategic community.

Objections to U.S.-led maritime coalitions

Chinese skepticism about American naval power deepens doubts about Washington's calls for collective action at sea. They point to the 2007 U.S. Maritime Strategy – a document organized around multilateral cooperation – as evidence of mendacity. Indeed, many believe that the strategy disguises American ambitions. Despite the Maritime Strategy's emphasis on international cooperation, Cao Wenzhen believes that the document "does not completely discard maritime hegemonic thinking" and is designed "to serve the global dominance of the United States."[24]

Li Xiaodan and Wang Wei, hailing from the Naval Command College and the Jiangsu Academy of Social Science respectively, concur. To them, "The goals [of the Maritime Strategy] are to integrate the maritime power and other forms of power of the United States with other nations to maintain American superiority at sea, uphold maritime hegemony, thus achieving the goal of global hegemony."[25]

Others worry that the United States may be conscripting its democratic allies to form a maritime coalition that excludes China. Some are particularly worried about the U.S.–Japan alliance. Duan Tingzhi and Feng Liang, senior captains at the Naval Command College, warn:

> In recent years, Japan and the United States have used antipiracy, counterterrorism, and international sea lane security as rationales to extend their military feelers to the South China Sea and the Western Pacific sea area while seeking to meddle in the affairs of the Malacca Strait. It is conceivable that if this chokepoint is controlled by the United States and Japan, should the international situation or the South China Sea situation change, Japan will coordinate with the United States to pressure China, perhaps even blockade the strait to cut off China's oil supply route.[26]

This is a jarring description of the alliance's maritime purpose. Tellingly, Duan and Feng do not acknowledge the positive contributions that the partnership has made to regional maritime security.

Shu Biquan of Fudan University believes that the United States seeks to enlist Japan, South Korea, Australia, and India to secure sea lanes stretching between the Indian and Pacific Oceans. Shu expresses particular concern that the U.S.–Japan alliance may exploit the norm of openness to contain China. According to the author:

> Using the upholding of freedom of navigation in the South China Sea as a pretext and by interfering in the territorial disputes between China and some countries in Southeast Asia, the United States and Japan have gathered together related countries in the South China Sea region to construct a network to guard against and contain China.[27]

This view dovetails with widely shared suspicions of the U.S.-led alliance system in Asia.

Objections to foreign military activities in the EEZ

The dispute between China and the United States over freedom of navigation within the Chinese-claimed exclusive economic zone is about norms. Beijing asserts its right to regulate military activities within its EEZ while Washington insists that navigational freedoms apply equally to the EEZs as they do to the high seas. In other words, China believes that the EEZ confers sovereign jurisdiction to the coastal state while the United States contends that the coastal state's governing powers are limited to economic matters.

Chinese analysts attribute America's position to strategic motives rather than the broad principles of openness at sea. As Zhou Zhonghai and Zhang Xiaoyi of the China University of Political Science and Law observe, "In recent years, as the strategic scheme to return to Asia and contain China progressively advances, secret surveillance and military information-gathering in China's exclusive economic zone by American research and survey vessels have grown more intense."[28]

Zhang Xianglan and Zhang Zhifan concur that, "On the one hand, the ambiguities of UNCLOS have led states to interpret differently the concrete substance behind freedom of navigation. On the other hand, America's 'strategic move to the east' leverages the freedom of navigation issue to intervene in East Asian affairs while squeezing China's sea space."[29] The Chinese believe that the Obama administration's pivot to Asia explains the legal contest.

In recent years, Chinese scholars have hardened their position that Beijing's security should trump the principle of free navigation. Zhou Zhonghai and Zhang Xioayi insist that, "The freedom of navigation is not an absolute freedom…. In the system of modern oceanic laws, absolute freedom no longer exists, even on the high seas."[30] They believe that the navigational freedoms must bend to will of coastal states. Zhang Xianglan and Zhang Zhifan agree that coastal state interests should supersede the needs of the seafaring nations. They aver, "When the freedom of navigation of another country operating in the EEZ and the national security of the coastal state come into conflict, the coastal state's national security interest should take precedence over the right of freedom of navigation."[31]

Zhou Ligang, a law professor from Nanhai University, argues that coastal states are vulnerable to the long-range striking power of modern navies. Thus, foreign naval presence in China's EEZs is inextricably tied to national security. To Zhou, coastal states must employ their jurisdictional rights over the EEZ to erect a buffer against outside powers. Zhou concludes, "The coastal state's regulatory rights over foreign military activities in the EEZs not only favorably safeguard the national interests of the coastal state, but they also ensure world peace. These rights are thus absolutely necessary and justifiable."[32]

Zhang Tuosheng echoes the proposition that national security should override high seas freedom. The author finds the U.S. military's reconnaissance operations near China's coasts particularly objectionable. Zhang calls on the United States to "gradually reduce and finally halt its point-blank military reconnaissance against China."[33] Along a parallel track, Beijing and Washington would negotiate a separate deal on "the necessary norms for maritime conduct" outside of the existing legal framework governing the seas. To Zhang, not only does Beijing reserve the right to exempt itself from international law that it disagrees with, but it expects the custodian of the seas to concede such an exception.

A delicate balance prevails between the rights of coastal states – which can assert exclusive sovereignty, sovereign rights, and jurisdiction over waters as prescribed by international law – and the rights of seafaring nations. However, these Chinese legal arguments unhinge that balance of interests, undermining the equitable distribution of the rights and responsibilities among the users of the commons.

Assessing the Chinese literature

These sharply worded commentaries stand in stark contrast to the anodyne official statements on maritime issues. Under former President Hu Jintao, Chinese government mouthpieces frequently promoted "harmonious oceans."[34] President Xi Jinping has championed the construction of a "maritime silk road" as a signature initiative. The disparity between officialdom and the literature above raises questions about the Chinese writings. Some arguments may not reflect policy or a consensus view in the Chinese decision-making process. But, these voices do not represent fringes of China's chattering class. Most authors are affiliated with prominent think tanks, universities, and professional military education institutions. Rather, the deviations from Chinese government positions are the result of an emerging "military-intellectual complex" in China.

For over a decade, the leadership nurtured a freewheeling academic environment, encouraging scholars to debate China's seaborne future. This willingness to tolerate intellectual diversity reflects the belief that it takes a clash of ideas to yield creative thinking of sufficient quality to inform policy and strategy. And by grooming a cohort of (relative) freethinkers, China solidifies the elite consensus that seapower is a natural if not inevitable choice for the nation. Letting a hundred flowers bloom, then, has let intellectual curiosity flourish, to the benefit of China's nautical cause. The outcome of this new openness is an explosion in scholarly works, a small cross-section of which has informed this study.

And, there is little debate among China watchers today that competing academic factions vie for policy attention and influence. David Shambaugh, for example, detects the emergence of a "realist-nativist" school of thought that has gained substantial purchase in internal Chinese debates and in the policy-making process.[35] This intellectual nexus consists of nationalists and conservatives who advocate a singular focus on building up comprehensive national power and who voice deep skepticism about international institutions. Many of the arguments sampled above would fit in this policy orientation. Their views thus merit serious consideration.

There are several ways of thinking about these writings as they relate to Chinese strategy and policy. Some of the perspectives have been integral to Beijing's worldview and its public persona for decades. For instance, opposition to "hegemonism," a shorthand for U.S. policy, has been a staple of China's strategic narrative since the earliest days of the People's Republic. Many authors use politically correct language to frame their arguments about the United States. In this sense, the literature reflects more continuity than change in Chinese policy discourse.

Nevertheless, there *is* something new about these assessments. The writings engage the public goods aspects of the U.S.-led maritime order. Yet, they describe American policy pronouncements as empty rhetoric or, worse, a public relations ploy to fulfill narrow self-interests. They refuse to confer legitimacy to the U.S. provision of public goods at sea. What is perhaps most striking is the idea that certain norms could be renegotiated exclusively between China and the United States.

It is possible that these rejectionist perspectives merely capture a snapshot of an ongoing evolution in Chinese scholarship. As relative newcomers in the fields of international relations, strategic studies, military history, and international law, many of the analysts may still be grappling with various maritime theories and how they apply to a more powerful China. The Chinese may be playing intellectual catch-up. Perhaps the Chinese theory class is undergoing a gradual socialization process that will eventually deepen its acquaintance with such concepts as public goods. A flattening learning curve could lead to a convergence of views between China and the West, easing the potential for disagreements and confrontation.

But, it is equally persuasive that the Chinese writings reflect fully formed views informed by bedrock assumptions about the international system and how it ought to function. For example, recent Western scholarship shows that China holds a uniquely Sino-centric perspective of the Asian order that is sharply at odds with the Westphalian view of interstate relations.[36] Beijing's territorial and thus exclusionary approaches toward the maritime domain may be a reflection of this continental tradition. For example, numerous Chinese analysts refer to maritime areas under China's jurisdiction in explicitly terrestrial terms. As Major General Peng Guangqian states:

> China's "sea territory" includes its territorial waters, the contiguous zone, the exclusive economic zone, and the continental shelf … China's sea territory, or "blue-colored land," is an important part of its entire national territory. Although it is different from land territory, sea territory is important strategic space for the country in the same way as land territory. It is the second cradle of the nation.[37]

China's proprietary attitudes about the exclusive economic zone can thus be understood as an extension of Beijing's continental mentality. If such an orientation explains Chinese reservations about the maritime order, then China's refusal to acknowledge the U.S. Navy's provision of public goods may be less about a gap in understanding and more about a fundamental clash of worldviews.

It is worth reiterating that these writings neither determine Beijing's policies nor predict the future of Chinese behavior. Rather, the Chinese literature gives outside observers a sense of a policy debate's direction. It thus behooves Western analysts to monitor the energetic debates in China.

Implications for the United States

For Washington, it is important not to prejudge China's potential challenge to the current maritime system, even assuming that the leadership agrees with the views espoused above. The foundations of the prevailing order are still sound. In terms of hard power, the U.S. Navy remains unrivaled while China's naval forces are relatively weak. In normative terms, the vast majority of nations agree with the U.S. interpretation of the navigational rights in the EEZ. By contrast, only a decided minority, numbering between 17 and 26 states, assert restrictions on military activities in their EEZs similar to those of China. For now, China possesses neither the power nor the kind of international following necessary to offer credible alternatives to the U.S.-led liberal maritime order.

Nevertheless, the rise of conservative constituents in China's policy-making community suggests that Washington should not be complacent. Chinese analysts are clearly responding to Beijing's increased heft on the world stage and its willingness to throw that weight around. China's navy and the shore-based elements of its seapower, including missiles and aircraft, have vaulted ahead of their regional counterparts. The non-military implements of Chinese maritime power, such as the China Coast Guard, have bulked up. By the end of this decade, China will be better positioned materially to influence the course of events unfolding around its nautical periphery, giving it more leverage in (re)shaping the larger maritime order.

At the same time, the normative pillars of maritime order are only as durable as the prevailing international consensus and widespread state practice, both of which are subject to change. As Peter Dutton argues:

> We cannot take the current state for granted. Indeed, the Chinese perspective holds some attraction even among China's neighbors. Despite the fact that their governments remain among those that are on record as accepting traditional military freedoms in the EEZ, representatives from the Philippines, Indonesia, and other regional states sometimes quietly express general support for the Chinese perspective, if for no other reason than it could help them hold rising Chinese power at bay.[38]

Regional states hedging their bets on China's maritime ascent are not the only reasons that norms might shift. Beijing could coerce its weaker neighbors to conform to its worldview. Martin Murphy warns:

> Some states are nonetheless sympathetic to [China's] position, and while none assert it as vigorously as China, they may well be tempted to follow China's lead if it crushes the objections of its neighbors and gains the level of control over the South China Sea to

which it feels entitled. If China succeeds and its blue-water naval capability expands, it is likely that it will have the power to shift subtly in its favor the international rules governing the maritime domain.[39]

Maritime order and the norms that underwrite it are not immutable. It is likely that China will seek, at a minimum, to modify the prevailing order in ways that accommodate its interests. The question is whether such Chinese amendments might fracture the indivisibility of the existing order. By seeking exceptions to a rules-based system that is singularly inclusive, could China undermine the norms that sustain the international system? This is the question before the United States and other stakeholders of the maritime order.

Notes

1 Joseph S. Nye, Jr., "The American National Interest and Global Public Goods," *International Affairs* 78, 2 (April 2002), 239.

2 Sam J. Tangredi, "Globalization and Sea Power: Overview and Context," in *Globalization and Maritime Power*, ed. Sam J. Tangredi (Washington, DC: National Defense University, 2002), 6.

3 Nye, "The American National Interest," 239–40.

4 Barry Posen, "Command of the Commons: The Military Foundation of U.S. Hegemony," *International Security* 28, 1 (Summer 2003), 45–6.

5 See U.S. Department of Defense, *The National Defense Strategy of the United States of America: A Strategy for Today, A Vision for Tomorrow* (Washington, DC: Department of Defense, March 2005), 6; and U.S. Department of Defense, *Sustaining U.S. Global Leadership: Priorities for 21st Century Defense* (Washington, DC: Department of Defense, January 2012), 3.

6 Edward J. Marolda, *Ready Seapower: A History of the U.S. Seventh Fleet* (Washington, DC: Naval History and Heritage Command, 2012), 143.

7 Joint Statement of the Security Consultative Committee, "Toward a Deeper and Broader U.S.–Japan Alliance: Building on 50 Years of Partnership," June 21, 2011, 5.

8 Australia–United States Ministerial Consultations (AUSMIN), 2011 Joint Communiqué and 2012 Joint Communiqué.

9 U.S. Department of the Navy, *A Cooperative Strategy for 21st Century Seapower* (Washington, DC: U.S. Department of the Navy, October 2007), 2.

10 James Kraska, *Global Swing States and the Maritime Order* (Global Swing States Working Paper, Center for a New American Century, Washington, DC, November 2012), 2.

11 Ronald O'Rourke, *China Naval Modernization: Implications for U.S. Navy Capabilities* (Washington, DC: Congressional Research Service, September 8, 2014), 14.

12 Nan Li, "The Evolution of China's Naval Strategy and Capabilities: From 'Near Coast' and 'Near Seas' to 'Far Seas'," *Asian Security* 5, 2 (2009), 160.

13 Ma Jianying, "An Evaluation of the U.S. Global Commons Strategy," *Xiandai Guoji Guanxi* [Contemporary International Relations] 2 (2013), 9.

14 Wang Yiwei, "The Global Commons and U.S. Smart Power," *Tongji Daxue Xuebao* [Tongji University Journal of Social Sciences] 23, 2 (April 2012), 52–3.

15 Cao Shengsheng and Xia Yuqing, "'Global Commons' Becomes New-Type Theory for U.S. Hegemonism: Assessing the Center for New American Security and Its Strategy Design for Northeast Asia," *Taipingyang Xuebao* [Pacific Journal] 19, 9 (September 2011), 32.

16 Sun Kai and Feng Liang, "The Experiences and Lessons of U.S. Maritime Development," *Shijie Jinji yu Zhengzhi Luntan* [World Economics and Politics Forum] 1 (January 2013), 50.

17 Wang Yiwei, "Global Commons and U.S. Smart Power," 52.

18 Zhang Ming, "'Global Commons' Security Governance and China's Choices," *Xiandai Guoji Guanxi* [Contemporary International Relations] 5 (2012), 26.

19 Zhang Wei and Feng Liang, eds., *National Maritime Security* (Beijing: Hai Chao Press, 2008), 196.

20 Feng Liang, ed. *Research on Maritime Security Strategies of Major Asia-Pacific Nations* (Beijing: Shijie Zhishi Press, 2012), 6–32.

21 Shu Zhengjiang, "The Ideal and Reality of a 306-ship Fleet," *Jiefangjun Bao* [Liberation Army Daily], June 24, 2013, 3.

22 Zhang Yuan, "Assessing the Adjustment and Influence of U.S. Naval Strategy," *Xiandai Guoji Guanxi* [Contemporary International Relations] 3 (2012), 30.

23 Wei Zonglei, "America's Sea Lane Security Strategy," in *Sea Lane Security and International Cooperation*, ed. Yang Mingjie (Beijing: Shi Shi Press, 2005), 302–3.

24 Cao Wenzhen, "U.S.–China Maritime Geopolitics and Strategy in the Era of Globalization," *Taipingyang Xuebao* [Pacific Journal] (December 2010), 47.

25 Li Xiaodan and Wang Wei, "American Maritime Security Strategy: Historical Evolution and Development Features," *Shijie Jingji yu Zhengzhi Luntan* [World Economics and Politics Forum] 2 (February 2011), 81.

26 Duan Tingzhi and Feng Liang, "Japan's Maritime Security Strategy: Historical Evolution and Actual Influence," *Shijie Jingji yu Zhengzhi Luntan* [World Economics and Politics Forum] 1 (January 2011), 79–80.

27 Shu Biquan, "A Study of Japan's Maritime Strategy and Development Trends of the Japan-U.S. Alliance," *Taipingyang Xuebao* [Pacific Journal] (January 2011), 96.

28 Zhou Zhonghai and Zhang Xiaoyi, "On Military Research and Survey Activities in the Exclusive Economic Zone," *Faxue Zazhi* [Law Science Magazine] 10 (2012), 101.

29 Zhang Xianglan and Zhang Zhifan, "On the Border between Freedom of the Seas and the Freedom of Navigation Rights," *Faxue Pinglun* [Law Review] 2 (2013), 79.

30 Zhou and Zhang, "On Military Research and Survey Activities," 103.

31 Zhang and Zhang, "On the Border," 80.

32 Zou Ligang, "On a Nation's Regulatory Rights over Foreign Peacetime Military Activities in the Exclusive Economic Zone," *Zhongguo Faxue* [China Legal Science] 6 (2012), 54.

33 Zhang Tuosheng, "Five Maritime Security Challenges Facing China and Countermeasures," *Shijie Zhishi* [World Affairs] (December 2010), 27.

34 "China Advocates Building, Maintenance of Harmonious Maritime Order," *Xinhua*, December 12, 2012, 4.

35 David Shambaugh, "Coping with a Conflict China," *Washington Quarterly* 34, 1 (Winter 2011): 7–27.

36 See Christopher A. Ford, *The Mind of Empire: China's History and Modern Foreign Relations* (Lexington, KY: University of Kentucky Press, 2010).

37 Peng Guangqian, "China's Maritime Rights and Interests," in *Military Activities in the EEZ: A U.S.–China Dialogue on Security and International Law in the Maritime Commons*, ed. Peter Dutton (Newport, RI: Naval War College Press, December 2010), 15.

38 Maritime Disputes and Sovereignty Issues in East Asia, Hearing before the Committee on Foreign Relations, United States Senate, 111th Cong. (July 15, 2009) (statement of Peter Dutton, Professor, Naval War College, Newport, RI).

39 Martin Murphy, "Deep-Oil Rigs as Strategic Weapons," *Naval War College Review* 66, 2 (Spring 2013), 113.

26

A MARITIME RENAISSANCE
Naval power in NATO's future

Diego A. Ruiz Palmer

NATO: the world's maritime alliance

NATO is the world's foremost maritime alliance. The Alliance includes several member nations with extended coastlines, centuries-old seafaring traditions, global trade interests, and formidable maritime capabilities. In the globalized twenty-first century, Allies' welfare is, more than ever, tied to the security and safety of navigation and of maritime trade and travel. At the same time, their security is no less dependent today than in earlier decades on the contributions of an invulnerable undersea nuclear deterrent and of capable and versatile naval forces that can perform the full range of maritime missions and contribute to maritime security in its broadest conception.[1] At sea, NATO's legacy and destiny merge.

Paradoxically, the centrality of the maritime dimension in NATO's security calculus has often been overlooked. During the Cold War, the neglect of the maritime contribution to the Alliance's defense posture could be attributed to the priority that the Warsaw Pact and NATO gave to Central Europe, over the so-called "flank" regions, as the pivot of any general war in Europe.[2] Since the end of the Cold War, the side-lining of NATO's maritime dimension results, in part, from the land force orientation of stabilization operations in the Balkans and in Afghanistan, even though, in both instances, a maritime contribution, in the form of air support and logistical resupply, was an essential, if often overlooked, component of their execution. The neglect of the maritime domain – referred to by specialists as "sea blindness"[3] – also owes to the fact that maritime forces operate mostly beyond the horizon, out-of-sight, and, more generally, that the vast majority of global merchant shipping sails unhindered.

Yet, during the Cold War, NATO's strategy and overall military capacity were tightly linked to the maritime domain – whether in the form of a sea-based nuclear deterrence and retaliation capability; support from the sea to forward defense on land; or transatlantic and cross-Channel reinforcement and resupply. Following the end of the Cold War, for the next two decades from 1992 Allied navies were engaged in a succession of NATO operations underpinning wider crisis-management and conflict resolution efforts. These operations have extended NATO's horizon from the familiar waters of the Mediterranean Sea to those, less familiar for the Alliance, of the Red Sea and western Indian Ocean.[4]

As the Alliance's operational engagement in Afghanistan drew to a close – at the end of 2014, a follow-on training and assistance mission in support of the Afghan National Security

Forces succeeded the NATO-led International Security Assistance Force (ISAF) – NATO has initiated a process of transition from a "deployed posture" to a "prepared posture." With many forces repatriated home from overseas theaters, NATO now aims at maintaining a high level of readiness and responsiveness to help prevent emerging crises from escalating into open conflicts that could require the deployment of vast numbers of "boots-on-the-ground." In an environment characterized by growing strategic uncertainty along the Alliance's eastern and southern periphery, but also by enduring economic austerity and the expectation of a lower operational tempo, a greater emphasis is being placed on forward presence, early warning, and prompt conflict prevention. This new outlook is encapsulated in the *Connected Forces Initiative* that was launched at NATO's May 2012 Summit meeting in Chicago.[5]

The transition to a "prepared NATO" will challenge Allied navies to reflect on their distinct contribution to conflict prevention and de-escalation. It also represents for them a new opportunity to chart a successful path forward for the Alliance's maritime dimension that encompasses exercising "presence" in European waters, conducting "forward engagement" with non-NATO partner countries around and beyond Europe, and developing new, innovative approaches to contingency "force packaging." The approval of an Alliance Maritime Strategy in March 2011, to guide NATO's engagement on, and from the sea, constituted the political stepping stone for what can be rightly considered as a "maritime renaissance."[6] NATO's Wales Summit in September 2014 marked another milestone in the re-invigoration of the Alliance's maritime posture. Allies agreed, in particular, to a bolstering of NATO's Standing Naval Forces and the intensification of maritime education, training, and exercises.[7] At the same time, NATO will need to consider carefully several operational and institutional developments that have challenged its once uncontested naval pre-eminence. As aptly observed by Royal Navy Vice-Admiral Peter Hudson, the former commander of NATO's Maritime Command at Northwood, in the United Kingdom, "While the Alliance can call upon the finest collective maritime force in the world, this pre-eminence is neither invulnerable nor unquestioned."[8]

During the Cold War, NATO's maritime command structures stood at the core of operational arrangements among Western navies. Following the Islamic Revolution in Iran and the Soviet invasion of Afghanistan in 1979, and more decisively in the wake of the 9/11 terrorist attacks against the United States in 2001, the geographic extension of Western maritime operations to the Arabian Sea and the quickening tempo of operations in various *ad hoc* frameworks resulted in NATO losing part of its former naval pre-eminence. In the Middle East, the United States led the way in developing the Combined Maritime Forces (CMF) as the preferred collaborative framework for the planning and the conduct of coalition counter-terrorism, counter-piracy, and maritime security operations by a large number of like-minded nations, including most NATO Allies with a naval capability.[9] Likewise, multilateral maritime interdiction trials and exercises held in the framework of the U.S.-sponsored Proliferation Security Initiative (PSI) include many NATO Allies, but they are not conducted under NATO auspices.[10]

Furthermore, over the past decade, both the United Nations and the European Union initiated their first maritime operations ever. The United Nations activated a maritime task force in the Eastern Mediterranean Sea in October 2006, in support of the UN Interim Force in Lebanon, while the European Union established in December 2008 an EU Naval Force to conduct the counter-piracy operation Atalanta off the coast of Somalia.[11] In addressing new security challenges on, or from the sea, whether in the field of sea-based counter-proliferation, counter-terrorism or counter-piracy, NATO is neither the only, nor necessarily the pre-eminent, operational or institutional actor.

The completion of major operational engagements in Iraq and Afghanistan in 2011 and 2014, respectively, when combined with the steady decline of piracy incidents off the coast of Somalia since 2012, may result in a relative decline in the importance of non-NATO naval operations in the Arabian Sea and the western Indian Ocean. At the same time, Russia's illegal annexation of the Crimean Peninsula in March 2014 and the continuing coercion of Ukraine, as well as enduring uncertainty in North Africa and the Near East, will likely shift attention to Europe and its surrounding seas (Baltic, Black, and Mediterranean Seas) and to the maritime dimension of collective defense. Together with the greater salience assumed by the Allied Maritime Command at Northwood, UK, in the context of the implementation of the Alliance's Maritime Strategy, these developments could contribute powerfully to the restoration of NATO's once pre-eminent naval role. Already, the frequency and scale of NATO and other Allied maritime activity in European waters has grown. Willing and able partners, such as Finland and Sweden, are eager to make an expanded contribution.

NATO's maritime call, however, sits at a higher plane than operational expediency. Enduring resource constraints on both sides of the Atlantic, as well as declining ship inventories, will continue, in all likelihood, to call for bolder visions of enhanced mutual support, task-sharing, resource pooling, and armaments cooperation among the Allies, as well as with NATO's varied maritime partners, around Europe and beyond. If it is to reach its full potential, NATO's maritime *renaissance* must become, therefore, the stepping stone to a bolder, more ambitious maritime *transformation* that reaches across strategy, fleet composition, concept development, and operational employment, from the High North to the eastern littoral of the Indian Ocean. NATO's maritime renaissance could well be the vehicle for a broader transformation.

Set against this vision, this chapter aims to provide a panoramic view of NATO's maritime heritage, roles, and future. Accordingly, the chapter starts with NATO's formative maritime experience during the Cold War and its enduring influence. NATO's Cold War maritime record is relevant to NATO's maritime future in three ways: First, the four-decade-long experience of planning operations and conducting exercises against the Soviet Navy built a perishable but, if properly preserved, sustainable legacy of shared skills among Allied navies; second, since the end of the Cold War, this legacy has been attractive to an increasingly large number of navies from like-minded countries around the world with whom NATO has developed cooperative partnerships; and, last but not least, as the prospect of great power competition rises, reinvigorating the capacity to execute high-end maritime operations on a multinational basis assumes greater importance from a deterrence and defense standpoint.[12] Next, the chapter addresses the two decades of NATO operations that followed the end of the Cold War and the evolving impact of a changing strategic context on NATO's "role at sea." Last, in a final section, the chapter sets out the rationale for, and explores the scope of, a NATO "maritime renaissance" that would leverage NATO's enduring maritime strengths.

Cold War years

From NATO's early days and the build-up of the Alliance's integrated military structure, Allied maritime forces assumed important roles in supporting a forward defense of NATO territory, particularly in the protection of the Central Region's maritime flanks, and, once U.S. aircraft carriers were given an atomic delivery capability in the 1950s, in the execution of a nuclear counter-offensive aimed at defeating the Soviet Union's war-making capacity.[13] In the Cold

War's later decades, NATO's maritime forces kept dual nuclear and conventional roles, the former by means of ballistic missile submarines (SSBN), the latter through the contribution of specialized surface action, convoy escort, anti-submarine warfare, mine counter-measures, and amphibious assault assets at the cutting edge of technology and readiness.

The evolution of NATO's maritime strategy during the Cold War can be broken down essentially into three phases – from the early 1950s through the mid-1960s; from the mid-1960s through the late 1970s; and from the latter to the end of the Cold War in the late 1980s.[14]

(i) Forward and nuclear

From the early 1950s through the mid-1960s, concern over the resilience of NATO's forward defences in Norway and West Germany (at the time anchored on the Rhine River), and over NATO's transatlantic reinforcement capability, was driven by the growth of the Soviet attack submarine fleet and the requirement to keep it "bottled-up" in the Baltic and Barents Seas. In turn, control of the Norwegian, North, and Mediterranean Seas was seen as indispensable to prevent, in a war, the "out-flanking" of NATO's ground defenses by Soviet land and air forces. Last, exercising sea control successfully was seen as requiring attacking Soviet naval assets and shore installations by means of nuclear strikes launched from aircraft carriers.

(ii) Conventional and in-depth

From the mid-1960s through the late 1970s, the emphasis in NATO's maritime strategy shifted to a layered defense in-depth in the North Atlantic and the eastern Mediterranean Sea that conceded that, in wartime, the Allies might not be able to maintain sea control in the Norwegian and Black Seas. This reorientation reflected a steep decline in NATO's naval inventories on both sides of the Atlantic, as well as the rise of a diversified Soviet cruise missile strike capability that encompassed nuclear-powered submarines, surface vessels, and naval bombers.[15] As a result of this changing balance of maritime power, the Alliance would seek to deny Soviet access to the high seas by "closing down" passage through the Greenland–Iceland–United Kingdom (GIUK) "gap." This "mid-Atlantic" focus reflected the new emphasis on transatlantic reinforcement, in support of conventional defense, embedded in NATO's new "Flexible Response" strategy formally adopted in 1967.

(iii) Forward and conventional

The period from the late 1970s through the end of the Cold War marked a return to a more ambitious forward strategy aimed at keeping the Soviet Navy on the defensive and wresting the strategic initiative in a general war in Europe from the USSR. It also marked a "golden age" in NATO's maritime planning.

By the early 1980s, the United States had become aware of the emergence in Soviet planning of a definitive preference for conducting a theater-scale, conventional offensive operation below the nuclear threshold, including by preventing a first nuclear use by NATO through relentless conventional attack and, only if absolutely necessary, through the execution of a last-minute theater-wide nuclear strike.[16] This new strategy reflected a growing Soviet recognition of the scale of the devastation that nuclear warfare would inflict on Europe, from which the USSR would not escape. The USSR's strategic preference for employing its conventional

Table 26.1 NATO'S major maritime exercises, 1975–1990

CONMAROPS campaign	Exercise	Sponsoring command	Periodicity
Norwegian Sea	Team Work	SACLANT	Every four years (1976, 1980, 1984, 1988)
Shallow Seas	Northern Wedding	SACLANT/ CINCHAN	Every four years, alternating with Team Work (1978, 1982, 1986)
Atlantic lifelines	Ocean Safari	SACLANT	Every two years (1975, 1977, 1979, 1981, 1983, 1985, 1987)
Mediterranean lifelines	Dawn Patrol	SACEUR/ CINCSOUTH	Every year in the spring
Eastern Mediterranean	Display Determination	SACEUR/ CINCSOUTH	Every year in the autumn

forces massively early in a conflict and for withholding the use of nuclear weapons for nuclear intimidation and escalation dominance suggested, in turn, that deterrence and, if deterrence failed, defense would be strengthened by focusing NATO's maritime forces on the destruction of the Soviet Union's conventional capabilities and, concurrently, on denial of its nuclear option. This was accomplished by developing a concept of maritime operations that, in wartime, would have sought to threaten the survivability of Soviet SSBN bastions in the Barents Sea, while, at the same time, placing critical Soviet assets and installations located in and around the Kola Peninsula, as well as strategic-level army and air force reserves stationed in the southwestern USSR, at risk from air attack by aircraft launched from aircraft carriers positioned in the Norwegian and Aegean Seas, respectively.

The outcome of this conceptual revolution was an unprecedented Concept for Maritime Operations (CONMAROPS) approved by NATO in 1981, which set out five maritime campaigns that Allied forces would have been expected to conduct in wartime:

1 the Norwegian Sea campaign;
2 the Shallow Seas campaign in the North Sea;
3 the Atlantic lifelines campaign in support of the transatlantic reinforcement of NATO forces in Western Europe;
4 the Mediterranean lifelines campaign to protect reinforcement shipping to Italy, Greece, and Turkey;
5 the Eastern Mediterranean campaign.[17]

A distinct maritime exercise was devoted to training Allied navies for each of the campaigns envisaged in the CONMAROPS (see Table 26.1).

The completion of the CONMAROPS preceded by a few years the adoption by the U.S. Navy of its famed *Maritime Strategy*.[18] In effect, development of the CONMAROPS was a multinational laboratory for the formulation of the *Maritime Strategy*.[19]

The *Maritime Strategy* sparked considerable controversy.[20] Opponents claimed that by:

• diverting resources to fighting the USSR on the Alliance's "flank" regions, the *Maritime Strategy* would undermine NATO's military capacity to defend West Germany;

- expanding the geographic scope of a Central European conflict to the flanks, the *Maritime Strategy* risked converting it into a world war; and
- threatening the integrity to Soviet SSBN bastions, the *Maritime Strategy* could, unintentionally, provoke the Soviet Union into a premature and highly escalatory use of strategic nuclear weapons, before war termination at lower levels of violence could be explored and pursued. This implicit offensive nature of the *Maritime Strategy*, therefore, constituted a repudiation of the long-standing defensive nature of NATO strategy.

The *Maritime Strategy*'s proponents took the position that, in wartime, rather than divert resources from NATO's Central Region, the strategy would deny the Soviet Union the option of concentrating its forces in Central Europe and, instead, force Moscow to divert attention and important capabilities to other areas; would deny the USSR early access to NATO's vulnerable coastlines around the Jutland peninsula and the Turkish Straits, by exerting a countervailing influence from the sea; and would serve notice to the Soviet leadership that its sea-based, second strike, assured destruction capability, even if smaller than its growing mobile land-based ballistic missile force, would be vulnerable to attack and attrition, thereby playing on Soviet fears of uncontrolled nuclear escalation and devastation.[21]

By embedding the U.S. Navy's maritime operations in the North Atlantic and around Europe in a NATO framework, CONMAROPS sought to bridge these perceptual divergences over different, but, in the end, compatible, "maritime" and "continental" preferences in defending Europe. Because of its wide scope, CONMAROPS represented the high-water mark of NATO's Cold War maritime thinking and the 1980s marked the apex of what can be termed as the Cold War's "naval era."

The scale and depth of this Cold War operations planning, extending over a period of nearly four decades, had a profound and enduring influence on the Alliance's navies, large and small. Operational concepts and war plans translated NATO's grand strategy into maritime campaign strategies that brought together considerations related to Allied naval missions and tasks, geography, enemy employment concepts and capabilities, own operational and logistical capabilities, shore infrastructure, communications and information systems, and technological capacity. These various processes helped ensure that Allied naval assets, irrespective of nationality, could operate seamlessly as part of multinational task groups and task forces.

In this regard, the now defunct Striking Fleet, Atlantic, was NATO's maritime crown jewel. When assembled, typically once a year, for a major maritime exercise in the autumn, it brought together the cutting edge of NATO's navies centered on two to four attack aircraft carriers. In this unique multinational structure, with no equivalent in the world, before or since, carriers and other surface combatants, as well as submarines and amphibious ships, could exercise the full spectrum of maritime tasks and hone the entire range of naval skills. In between activations of the Striking Fleet, the Standing Naval Force, Atlantic, helped ensure in the 1970s and 1980s that familiarity with tactics, techniques and procedures, and communications interoperability was maintained.[22]

Many of the command and force structures that sustained NATO's deterrence and defense posture during the Cold War were disbanded following its end. What endures, however, is the legacy of common procedures and practices and the shared mindset of a "fraternity of the blue uniform" inherited from the Cold War and now extended to an ever larger group of Allied and like-minded naval services across the globe.[23]

Two decades of operations

The end of the Cold War marked the opening of a new maritime era. NATO naval planning was no longer geared to deterring and, if necessary, defending against a hostile super-power on land and at sea. Carrier operations in the upper Norwegian Sea and large amphibious landing exercises in Greece and Turkey became memories of a rapidly fading past. The Russian Navy of the 1990s was a shadow of its Soviet predecessor, and up to the war between Russia and Georgia in 2008, Russian Navy ships even sailed, from time to time, under the NATO flag. In this new era, attention focused increasingly on the protection of the "global commons" against emerging unconventional risks, and on the contributions of a growing number of maritime partners to a broad concept of maritime security.[24]

This change of strategic paradigm away from high-end, blue-water operations against a naval challenger, if not a fully-fledged peer competitor, prompted, particularly in the U.S. Navy, an unprecedented level of soul-searching regarding the strategic purpose of naval power and future fleet composition.[25] Opinion has ranged from declaration of the "end of the naval era"[26] to the questioning of the enduring relevance of large aircraft carriers,[27] against the background of successive "revolutions of military affairs" (and of maritime affairs), the rise of new powers and of new hybrid forms of warfare, and growing budgetary adversity. Hidden beyond the horizon lurks the question of what kind of new naval operational art will be required for these fundamentally changed circumstances.

In the meantime, the emergence of new kinds of ship design and of unmanned vessels, and the rise of wholesale automation and the decline in crew size, as well as the worldwide diffusion of state-of-the-art technologies, are transforming the maritime operational environment. Advances in precision location, targeting and strike, navigation, large data transmission and discrimination, and weapon-system range and maneuverability, as well as the growing importance of the outer space and cyber domains, are altering the spatial dimensions of naval warfare. The correlations between ship displacement and size, crew size, and ship technological capacity and operational effectiveness are being altered in novel and not always well-understood ways.

For NATO, adaptation to the new circumstances of the post-Cold War era has meant striking a delicate balance between competing realities. On the one hand, a rising operational tempo for Allied navies, particularly, following the 9/11 terrorist attacks, and a displacement of the center of gravity of Western maritime engagement from the North Atlantic Ocean and the Mediterranean Sea to the Arabian Sea, placed growing limitations on ship availability for NATO-led maritime exercising in European waters;[28] as a result, opportunities for combined exercising under NATO command and control declined steeply in all categories of maritime warfare. On the other hand, the relatively narrow focus of many maritime operations since the end of the Cold War has been a reminder that operations are not a satisfactory substitute for exercises, as a means to maintain fleet capability and multinational interoperability across a range of warfare skills, particularly for operations against a capable and determined adversary.

"NATO goes to sea": maritime support to stabilization operations in the Balkans, 1992–2000

In the 1990s, upholding that balance was facilitated by three factors:

1 The momentum that had been built during the previous decade under the auspices of the NATO CONMAROPS (with large maritime exercises like North Star and Sharp Spear succeeding Northern Wedding and Ocean Safari, but without their Cold War focus).

2   The adoption of a sea-based variant of the Combined Joint Task Force (CJTF) Concept agreed by the Alliance in 1994,[29] which gave maritime forces a distinct and important role in NATO's evolving crisis response roles (with the involvement of the U.S. Navy's command ship *Mount Whitney* [LCC-20], operating as flagship and embarking a sea-going CJTF battle staff).[30]
3   The initiation, for the first time ever, of NATO maritime operations, triggered by United Nations Security Council resolutions.

NATO's first ever real-world operation was Operation Maritime Monitor, launched in July 1992, with the objective of patrolling the waters of the Adriatic Sea and identifying violations of sanctions imposed by the United Nations Security Council on the Federal Republic of Yugoslavia. Maritime Monitor was succeeded by Operations Maritime Guard and Sharp Guard, with an expanded UN mandate, the latter resulting from its merger with a concurrent maritime operation, Sharp Fence, led by the Western European Union.

NATO's maritime operations in the Adriatic were seminal in many ways. They demonstrated the adaptability of NATO's capabilities and procedures to circumstances that were a world apart from Cold War scenarios. Gradually, successive UN Security Council Resolutions became more ambitious and the scope of NATO's operations in support of the UN in the Former Yugoslavia widened in the air and at sea. Maritime surveillance gave way to the shadowing, interception, compliant boarding, and diversion of merchant ships and smaller vessels suspected of violating a UN-mandated embargo on arms shipments to the belligerents. A by-product of these maritime operations was a new and greater understanding of the need for, and potential of, expanded situation awareness and all-source information-sharing between navies, coast guards, national and international border control and law-enforcement agencies, and judicial authorities, within the constraints imposed by constitutional and legal statutes. In many ways, the concepts of "comprehensive approach" and "whole-of-government" were born as much at sea as on land.

As soon as the international community's focus of attention shifted from Bosnia to Kosovo, Allied navies assumed again an important role in the generation of responsive, on-the-scene air power, this time in the form of four aircraft carrier task forces from France, Italy, the United Kingdom, and the United States. Of note, it is at this time that the French Navy and the Royal Navy started the practice of providing escort vessels to each others' carrier task forces, thereby setting the scene for closer bilateral cooperation between their armed forces under the Lancaster House Treaty of November 2010 and for the establishment of a British-French Combined Joint Expeditionary Force.[31]

NATO's maritime operations in the Adriatic Sea in the 1990s were stepping stones for the operations that followed: maritime counter-terrorism in the Mediterranean Sea in the framework of Operation Active Endeavor, initiated following the 9/11 terrorist attacks, and air support to ISAF in Afghanistan from Allied aircraft carriers sailing in the Arabian Sea; naval escort and counter-piracy operations in the western Indian Ocean (Operations Allied Provider; Allied Protector; and Ocean Shield); and embargo enforcement off Libya's shores, as well as air support from the sea, during Operation Unified Protector in April–September 2011 (see Table 26.2).[32]

NATO goes beyond Europe: the Indian Ocean as the Alliance's new "southern boundary"

The 2000–9 decade turned out to be much more challenging for Allied navies than the preceding decade, for a host of reasons. First, the defense spending cuts associated with the

Table 26.2 NATO'S maritime operations, 1992–2013

Location	Operation	Period
Adriatic Sea	Maritime Monitor	July–November 1992
Adriatic Sea	Maritime Guard	November 1992–June 1993
Adriatic Sea	Sharp Guard	June 1993–October 1996
Adriatic Sea	Allied Force	March–June 1999
Mediterranean Sea	Active Endeavor	October 2001–present
Arabian Sea	Enduring Freedom/ISAF[a]	October 2001/August 2003–present
Indian Ocean	Allied Provider	October–December 2008
Indian Ocean	Allied Protector	March–August 2009
Indian Ocean	Ocean Shield	August 2009–present
Mediterranean Sea	Unified Protector	March–September 2011

Note

a Under the operational control of the U.S. 5th Fleet and the U.S. Central Command's Combined Air Operations Center, with ISAF/NATO participation.

post-Cold War "peace dividend" forced the accelerated retirement of older naval vessels and the scaling-back of ship-building plans, resulting in declining ship inventories. Second, the rise of constabulary-like tasks associated with the emergence of new (and old) sources of risk at sea and from the sea, on a grander scale, such as human, narcotics and arms trafficking, as well as piracy, required Allied navies to reconsider the balance within their fleets between capable, blue-water, frigate-size vessels and less capable, brown-water, littoral ships, such as corvettes, better suited to these tasks. And, third, the Indian Ocean assumed an ever growing importance in Allied maritime planning and operations in relation to the Atlantic Ocean and the Mediterranean Seas, NATO's traditional areas of maritime presence.

Counter-piracy operations in the Indian Ocean were game-changers for NATO, strategically as well as operationally:

1 For the first time, Allied naval vessels started operating beyond the North Atlantic Treaty area, at a strategic distance from Europe, under NATO operational command.
2 Without an extensive shore infrastructure, as in Europe, sustaining such operations required new approaches to mutual logistical support, including through host nation support arrangements with Allies enjoying access to harbors in the region.
3 Sailing Allied ships placed under NATO operational command alongside other Allied naval vessels operating within other chains of command (such as under the authority of the European Union) required mutual awareness and the harmonization of operating concepts and Rules of Engagement, as well as the optimization of respective mandates, operating areas, and operational capabilities.

Counter-piracy operations in the Indian Ocean also moved the comprehensive approach at sea in new directions, notably by strengthening NATO's cooperation, particularly through NATO's Shipping Centre at Northwood, UK, with the International Maritime Organization and with shipping and insurance companies.

At the same time, the scale of the operational and logistical facilitation provided by the U.S. Navy to Allied navies sailing in the Indian Ocean as part of the Combined Maritime Forces, as well as the political impetus which Operation Atalanta has enjoyed among EU member states, have meant that NATO's Operation Ocean Shield has been under-resourced almost systematically, despite its distinct contribution to counter-piracy efforts and its value for European allies who are not members of the EU.[33] This pattern is regrettable, because, in addition to undermining the operation's effectiveness, it has complicated efforts to leverage Ocean Shield to build up formal and informal maritime partnerships with NATO's institutional partners in the region (Bahrain, Kuwait, Qatar, and the United Arab Emirates), as well as those operating at sea in the Indian Ocean (Australia, Japan, Republic of Korea, and New Zealand).[34]

Continuous combined maritime operations in the Arabian Sea and off the Horn of Africa have contributed in several important ways to the development, over more than a decade, of a new body of practices for the provision of air support from the sea, as well as the conduct of maritime surveillance and interdiction operations in a complex geopolitical environment. The shift of the geographical center of gravity of U.S. Navy carrier operations from the Mediterranean Sea to the Arabian Sea, following the 9/11 terrorist attacks, has meant that the U.S. 5th Fleet, rather than the U.S. 6th Fleet, has now become the hub for multinational, multi-carrier operations among the NATO allies with aircraft carrier capabilities (France, Italy, United Kingdom, and United States). Indeed, the last time that U.S. Navy aircraft carriers operated in the Mediterranean Sea, in a multinational context, under NATO operational control, was on the occasion of exercise Medshark 2004, over a decade ago.[35]

As NATO's operational engagement in Afghanistan transitions to a follow-on "train and assist" mission by the end of 2014, carrier operations in the Arabian Sea that have been supporting ISAF may well decline in scale, although continued uncertainty in Iraq and in Yemen may place this prospect in jeopardy. Already, the U.S. Navy, reportedly, has scaled back its carrier presence from two carriers to one, although it returns to two during relief periods. This transitional process may result, possibly, in the U.S. 6th Fleet assuming again a more salient role in the planning and exercising of carrier, as well as amphibious assault, operations in the Mediterranean Sea, particularly considering the increasingly troubled security environment around the southern and eastern rives of the Mediterranean basin in the wake of the start of the "Arab Spring." It is worth noting, in this regard, that the U.S. Navy's Chief of Naval Operations' most recent *Navigation Plan* gives forward presence in Europe more than passing mention, alongside naval deployments in the Asia-Pacific and Middle East theaters.[36]

Already before the crisis in Ukraine and Russia's illegal annexation of the Crimean Peninsula, the U.S. Navy had been taking steps to rebalance part of its assets east, as well as west, of the Indian Ocean, as the scale and tempo of operations in Southwest Asia was being scaled back. For the first time since the short-lived stationing of a destroyer squadron in Greece in the early 1970s, the U.S. Navy will homeport surface combatants in Europe – in the form of four *Arleigh Burke*-class guided missile destroyers at Rota, Spain – for ballistic missile defense duty in the Mediterranean Sea. This means that the U.S. 6th Fleet will have permanently assigned surface ships other than its flagship, the *Mount Whitney*. The U.S. Navy will also enhance its broad area maritime surveillance capability through the rotation to Sigonella, Sicily, of a mix of its new P-8 *Poseidon* maritime patrol aircraft and RQ-4 *Triton* unmanned aerial vehicles (UAV).[37] Because of its close relationship with the U.S. 6th Fleet, the STRIKFORNATO headquarters at Lisbon is ideally suited to leverage to the benefit of the Alliance as a whole this renewed U.S. naval presence in the Mediterranean Sea, in close cooperation with the MARCOM headquarters at Northwood. In this context, it is worth noting that, as part of the strengthening of the NATO Response Force, STRIKFORNATO was certified in spring 2014 as a deployable maritime expeditionary headquarters during the command post exercise Trident Jaguar 14.[38] Last, on the occasion of the United Kingdom-hosted Joint Warrior 14/1 live exercise in spring 2014, the U.S. Navy deployed no less than three destroyers, two cruisers and a frigate, as well as a fleet replenishment ship, in a welcome sign that it intends to preserve interoperability with Allies, in accordance with the aims of NATO's Connected Forces Initiative.[39]

NATO's maritime renaissance: the way ahead

The Atlantic alliance sits, today, atop the largest and most powerful maritime coalition of nations, both member nations and partners, in history. At its core, the U.S. Navy's surface fleet, while shrinking in numbers, is at its apex of military capability. It combines 10 *Nimitz*-class carriers, 9 helicopter carriers, and over 80 *Ticonderoga*-class cruisers and *Arleigh Burke*-class destroyers. *America*- and *San Antonio*-class large amphibious ships are joining the fleet, as well as *Zumwalt*-class destroyers and *Freedom*- and *Independence*-class Littoral Combat Ships. Naval aviation is being strengthened with the F-18E/F *Super Hornet* and EF-18G *Growler* fighters and the new F-35 *Lightning* II fighter, P-8 *Poseidon* maritime patrol aircraft and *Global Hawk* remotely piloted vehicle.

This unrivalled naval capacity notwithstanding, the U.S. Navy faces at least two important ship-building challenges over the next decade, taking into account resource constraints that are likely to persist. The first challenge is whether to build ten *Gerald R. Ford*-class aircraft carriers to replace an equal number of *Nimitz*-class carriers or opt for a yet-to-be designed carrier "high–low mix," in effect resurrecting the debate of the early 1970s around the merits of the "sea-control ship," but in a different era;[40] and, second, whether to complement the building of additional *Arleigh Burke*-class destroyers with a new multi-purpose frigate class that would be more capable than the Littoral Combat Ships.[41]

European allied navies, while also smaller in size than at any time since the rearmament of the 1950s, pack unprecedented punch. Together they combine several aircraft and helicopter carriers, such as the French *Charles de Gaulle* (R-91), the Italian Navy's *Cavour* (550), the Spanish *Juan Carlos I* (L-61), and the Royal Navy's *Ocean* (L-12), as well as large amphibious ships, such as the French Navy's three *Mistral*-class vessels and the Royal Navy's two *Albion*-class ships. These will be joined by the large Royal Navy aircraft carrier HMS *Queen Elizabeth* (R-08) in 2020. European navies also operate approximately 30 modern air defense destroyers and frigates.

Furthermore, NATO's partnerships with 40 non-NATO countries in Europe and across the globe contribute additional naval capability to the shared goal of securing the maritime global commons, by associating several countries with a similar outlook, proud maritime heritage and capable navies, such as Australia, Japan, and Sweden. Maritime tasks are a natural vehicle for strengthening cooperation among like-minded, but geographically dispersed, nations, and more should be done to this end.

These varied maritime capabilities are underpinned by the world's most comprehensive array of shore naval headquarters, afloat commands, and maritime training centers and research establishments – a dozen in all. This NATO constellation encompasses the MARCOM and STRIKFORNATO headquarters at Northwood and Lisbon, respectively; the four NATO High Readiness maritime staffs at Toulon (France), Taranto (Italy), Rota (Spain), and Portsmouth (Great Britain); the NMIOTC at Souda Bay; the three maritime-oriented Centres of Excellence at Norfolk, Kiel (Germany), and Ostend (Belgium); the NATO Shipping Centre at Northwood; and, lastly, the Maritime Research and Experimentation Centre at La Spezia (Italy). Together, they provide the Allies, as well as cooperating partner countries, with an unrivalled array of expertise and training skills, planning capacity, and command and control capabilities.

As the Alliance sets its sights on the medium-term horizon of "NATO Forces 2020" agreed at the NATO Summit meeting in Chicago in May 2012, there is a new opportunity for the Alliance's navies to seize the moment and pursue a bold and ambitious vision of "NATO's role at sea." The Alliance's Maritime Strategy provides the conceptual backdrop for this effort; without content and substantive contributions by the Allies, however, this strategy risks being an empty shell.

The Alliance's transition to a "readiness posture" represents an opportunity to single out and leverage the distinct contribution which maritime forces and naval headquarters "in-being" can make to achieving a high level of Allied preparedness, by means of "permanent presence" on the Alliance's periphery, "forward engagement" with interested partner countries, and "force packaging" and "mission tailoring" in support of contingency response. But it is also a challenge.

A prepared posture requires a mindset and practices geared towards versatility and responsiveness, which are different from, yet ostensibly compatible with, those associated with a deployed posture. A prepared posture might be logistically less challenging, because part of the pressure derived from a high operational tempo and a large footprint has been lowered, but the level of accessible human and financial resources will also, likely, be lower as a result.

At the same time, a prepared posture places an onus on optimizing available assets, not the least because the burden associated with maintaining forces on high readiness must be necessarily shared among the Allies, larger and smaller. To this end, NATO's Smart Defence and Connected Forces Initiatives provide attractive mechanisms to leverage cooperative impulses in the maritime domain, on the one hand, and new training and exercising opportunities, on the other. Collaboration and connectivity, however, do not happen naturally among sovereign nations, even if allied and like-minded. There must be a political impetus coming from above and single-minded resolve generated bottom-up. The two must intersect in an enduring way.

The notion of sharing must also extend beyond the military and encompass the civilian components of the broader maritime community, again because the military and civilian dimensions of maritime security, in its wider meaning, while distinct, overlap and are, often, mutually dependent. This complementarity is particularly obvious along Europe's coastlines, particularly on the northern shores of the Mediterranean Sea, in the fight against illegal immigration and various forms of trafficking, and militates for a concerted implementation of the Alliance's Maritime Strategy and the European Union Maritime Security Strategy that preserves the focus of each, while stimulating synergies between the two institutions. This aim could be accomplished by vesting in the national maritime operations centers of EU Member States that are also Allies the authority to fuse maritime-oriented law-enforcement and military information, derived from EU agencies, such as FRONTEX, and from NATO sources, such as Headquarters, MARCOM, subject to the applicable constitutional and legal restrictions on the protection of information.

Against this rich canvas, NATO's maritime community should continue on its path of addressing this spectrum of opportunities through the lens of a "maritime enterprise" paradigm, which promises to deliver substantial benefits. To be fully successful, however, such an undertaking should strive to integrate the following considerations:

1　The collective security and political influence that Allies derive from their combined maritime strength is predicated on the successful delivery of the maxim according to which NATO is more than the sum of its parts; hence a common sense of purpose lies at the core of the Alliance's maritime enterprise and naval ambition. In this context, while European allied navies need not aim to "copy" the U.S. Navy on a smaller scale, they should aim for a collective naval ambition that matches better their very significant collective maritime capability.

2   To that end, much greater effort should be placed on leveraging and combining existing multinational arrangements. Since the end of the Cold War, European allied navies
have entered into, or adapted, a myriad of bilateral and multilateral arrangements, including: Admiral BENELUX;[42] European Maritime Force (EUROMARFOR);[43] European
Amphibious Initiative;[44] European Carrier Group Interoperability Initiative;[45] United
Kingdom–Netherlands and Spanish–Italian Amphibious Forces;[46] etc. While many or all
may fulfill their individual aims satisfactorily, an opportunity is forfeited by not seeking
to bring greater coherence and achieve enhanced complementarity among these varied
arrangements.

3   Within the framework of their respective missions and terms of reference, MARCOM at
Northwood and STRIKFORNATO in Lisbon should strive to attain an optimized div-
ision of labor to assist European navies in achieving the desirable outcomes outlined above.
Such an endeavor should include strengthening their links and partnerships with European
national naval and fleet staffs, as well as with the U.S. Fleet Forces Command in Norfolk, VA,
U.S. Naval Forces Europe/Africa in Naples, and U.S. Naval Forces, Central Command, and
Combined Maritime Forces in Bahrain.

4   High-end capability and specialization need not be incompatible: while all Allies should strive
to continue to field high-end capabilities, not all Allies need to cluster around the medium
range of naval capabilities, leaving dangerous blind spots, gaps, and vulnerabilities across the
wider spectrum, particularly in anti-submarine warfare and mine counter-measures. Allied
navies should consider what having balanced maritime capabilities and naval forces on a
multinational basis means in terms of fleet composition and systems mix, as well as the contribution that the concept of competitive advantage can make to those ends.

5   Care should be exercised in not opposing blue-water and brown-water operations. Many
ocean-going naval capabilities are relevant to littoral operations, particularly against stealthy
attack submarines and difficult-to-detect sea mines, while the coastal defence assets of an
adversary, particularly if combined with space-based assets, can have an extended reach
against naval forces operating in the high seas up to 1,000 nautical miles.[47]

The considerations outlined above suggest a dual-track approach. In the shorter term,
achieving higher levels of maritime effectiveness and efficiency among Allies will require
that greater priority and urgency be given to broad-based multinationality, including pooling and sharing; force compatibility; joint and combined force packaging; and ship rotation. In particular, the navies of France, Italy, Spain, and the United Kingdom, which have
the largest and most powerful fleets, and which have stood-up a NATO-certified, deployable, high-readiness maritime battle staff, should endeavor to harmonize their doctrinal
approaches to maritime force packaging and the generation of national and multinational
task groups and task forces. Such follow-on maritime formations could include the Royal
Navy's Response Force Task Group[48] and the French Navy's *Groupe Aéronaval*, as well as
carrier strike and surface action groups built around the Italian Navy *Cavour* carrier, the
Spanish Navy *Juan Carlos I* amphibious ship, and other surface vessels contributed by other
European navies.[49] Wherever sensible, fleet integration training and full-spectrum warfare
exercising should be shared, making maximum use of mutual exercise opportunities and
ashore training establishments. These steps could lead, in due course, to harmonized and
synchronized task group/task force rotation, in order to optimize the availability at any
one time of individual surface vessels, submarines, and other assets. Although the Striking
Fleet, Atlantic, cannot be reclaimed, the concept of a "top-of-the-league" NATO Maritime
Contingency Force should be pursued actively.

In between the periodic activations of such a Maritime Contingency Force on the occasion of NATO exercises or real-world operations, the current Standing NATO Maritime Groups (SNMG/SNMCMG) would maintain currency with NATO tactics, techniques, and procedures among allied navies. To that end, the concept underpinning the Standing Maritime Groups should be revised to accommodate more flexible participation by various allied navies and ship types, in order to make Standing Maritime Group rotations more attractive to allied navies. Giving Standing NATO Maritime Groups a new salience should also lead to their relabeling as "Standing Naval Forces."

Looking at the longer term, larger Allied navies are confronted with the dual challenges of, on the one hand, balancing the preservation of a "full-spectrum" maritime capacity with the further development of a balanced expeditionary capability that they alone can afford, and, on the other, ensuring an optimized level of complementarity between their own capabilities and the naval contributions of smaller Allies. This applies as much between the U.S. Navy and the navies of the larger European Allies (France, Italy, United Kingdom), as between the latter and the navies of nations such as Germany, the Netherlands, and Spain. This balancing exercise will need to reconcile the competing demands of expeditionary strike and power projection from the sea; anti-air and missile defence; anti-submarine warfare; and constabulary operations, through innovative ship design decisions and astute division-of-labor schemes.

NATO represents a formidable enabling framework for member and partner navies. But its relevance is determined, ultimately, by its member nations' collective level of ambition. As the United States considers how best to balance means and ends on a global scale with diminishing resources, in the face of varied and significant security challenges, European allies and Canada have an opportunity, through NATO, to step in and agree, together with their American ally, a concerted strategy of maritime deterrence, through presence and engagement. In this way, Allied navies could contribute substantively to a rebalancing of the Alliance.

Otherwise, if neglected, NATO will atrophy operationally, gradually losing its sharp edge. Such an outcome would be at variance with the original ambition of the Alliance's founding fathers and with the sterling experience accumulated by allied naval forces over six decades. It would be in total contradiction with the emergence of a new maritime age.

Acknowledgments

The author is thankful to Professor Sten Rynning at the University of Southern Denmark for his helpful comments on an earlier version of this chapter, and to Captain Peter M. Swartz, United States Navy (Ret), for his untiring assistance and support in accessing maritime-related information and knowledge. The views expressed in this paper are the author's own and should not be taken to represent necessarily those of NATO or NATO member nations.

Notes

1 "Maritime security" should be understood as encompassing all maritime-oriented missions and not only constabulary-like naval tasks associated with law enforcement at sea. This wide-ranging definition is necessary to reflect the complexity of the contemporary security environment.
2 Joel J. Sokolsky, *Seapower in the Nuclear Age: The United States Navy and NATO, 1949–1980* (London: Routledge, 1991).
3 On contrasting perspectives on "sea blindness," see Jasper Gerard, "Ministers accused of 'sea blindness' by Britain's most senior Royal Navy figure," *Daily Telegraph*, June 12, 2009; Peter Haydon, "Maritime Blindness, You Say?" *Canadian Naval Review* 6, 3, Fall 2010, pp. 2–3; Tom Mahnken, "Avoiding sea

blindness: The decline of American naval power," *Foreign Policy*, September 13, 2012; and "Poll reveals UK's 'sea blindness'," *Mail Online*, June 24, 2014, accessed August 20, 2014.

4 Diego A. Ruiz Palmer, "New Operational Horizons: NATO and Maritime Security," *NATO Review* (Spring 2008), pp. 10–15.

5 *Chicago Summit Declaration on Defence Capabilities: Toward NATO Forces 2020* (Brussels: North Atlantic Treaty Organization, May 2012), paragraph 11.

6 *Alliance Maritime Strategy* (Brussels: North Atlantic Treaty Organization), March 18, 2011.

7 *Wales Summit Declaration* (Brussels: North Atlantic Treaty Organization, September 4, 2014).

8 Peter Hudson, "The Renaissance at Sea: A New Era for Maritime NATO," *RUSI Journal* 159, 3, June–July 2014, p. 26.

9 Combined Maritime Forces is a self-standing, multinational arrangement between the United States and some 30 other nations anchored on the U.S. 5th Fleet. See http://combinedmaritimeforces.com, accessed August 20, 2014.

10 On the Proliferation Security Initiative, see Mary Beth Nikitin, *Proliferation Security Initiative*, 7-5700 (Washington, DC: Congressional Research Service, June 15, 2012). Allied maritime forces taking part in PSI exercises benefit, however, from the training provided by the NATO Maritime Interdiction Operational Training Centre (NMIOTC) located at Souda Bay, on the island of Crete, in Greece. Captain (A) M. Kaltenbrunner, "WMD MIO Training in NMIOTC," *NMIOTC Journal* 1, February 2010, pp. 18–19. Exercise Phoenix Express 2012, led by the United States and involving several NATO Allies as well as non-NATO countries from the Mediterranean basin region, was conducted in May 2012 at Souda Bay with the support of the NMIOTC. Caitlin Conroy, "Phoenix Express 2012 begins in Souda Bay" (Stuttgart: United States European Command, May 7, 2012).

11 *UNIFIL Marine Operations*, audit report AP2008/672/09 (New York: United Nations Organization, April 16, 2009). On Operation Atalanta, see http://eunavfor.eu, accessed August 20, 2014.

12 Walter Russell Mead, "The Return of Geopolitics," *Foreign Policy* (May/June 2014).

13 Sean M. Maloney, *Securing Command at Sea: NATO Naval Planning, 1948–1954* (Annapolis, MD: Naval Institute Press, 1995).

14 This summary presentation of the evolution of NATO's maritime strategy through the Cold War relies, in part, on an unpublished, but comprehensive and authoritative, assessment of the subject by Peter M. Swartz of the U.S. Center for Naval Analyses. Peter M. Swartz, "Evolution of U.S. Navy Roles in NATO: Always an Important Part of a Larger Whole," dated October 2004 (unpublished).

15 The expanded scope of Soviet naval activities in the North Atlantic, from 1960 onwards, was tracked closely by NATO and was the subject of an unusually detailed article published in the September 1970 issue of NATO's official magazine at the time, *NATO News*.

16 This new understanding of Soviet military thought grew from the systematic cultivation and exploitation, from the mid-1970s onwards, of clandestine intelligence sources with access to the Soviet Union's and the Warsaw Pact's deepest defense secrets. Christopher A. Ford and David A. Rosenberg, "The Naval Intelligence Underpinnings of Reagan's Maritime Strategy," *Journal of Strategic Studies* 28, 2, April 2005, pp. 381–3. The virtually unprecedented quality of these sources was such that, for instance, the English translation of the highly sensitive critique of the Warsaw Pact's Zapad 77 command post exercise undertaken by Marshal of the Soviet Union Nikolai Ogarkov at the end of the exercise in June 1977 was available to the Central Intelligence Agency within 16 months of the event. *Critique of the Operational-Strategic Command Staff Exercise ZAPAD-77*, Intelligence Information Special Report TS no. 788301, dated October 13, 1978, classified Top Secret (Langley, VA: Central Intelligence Agency), CIA Freedom of Information Act Electronic Reading Room, declassified and approved for public release June 18, 2012. Diego A. Ruiz Palmer, "The NATO–Warsaw Pact Competition in the 1970s and 1980s: A Revolution in Military Affairs in the Making or the End of a Strategic Age?" *Cold War History* 14, 4, Autumn 2014, pp. 533–73.

17 Eric Grove (with Graham Thompson), *Battle for the Fiords: NATO's Forward Maritime Strategy in Action* (Annapolis, MD: United States Naval Institute Press, 1991), pp. 18–19.

18 Peter M. Swartz, *The Maritime Strategy Debates: A Guide to the Renaissance of U.S. Naval Strategic Thinking in the 1980s* (Monterey, CA: U.S. Naval Postgraduate School, February 24, 1988); and John B. Hattendorf, *The Evolution of the U.S. Navy's Maritime Strategy, 1977–1986*, Newport Paper 19 (Newport, RI: Naval War College Press, 2004).

19 Peter M. Swartz, *Preventing the Bear's Last Swim: The NATO Concept of Maritime Operations (CONMAROPS) of the Last Cold War Decade* (Athens, Greece: European Institute of Maritime Studies and Research, 2003), pp. 47–61.

20 The controversy is summarized in Ronald O'Rourke, *Nuclear Escalation, Strategic Anti-Submarine Warfare, and the Navy's Forward Maritime Strategy* (Washington, DC: Congressional Research Service, February 27, 1987). See also Peter M. Swartz, USN, "Contemporary U.S. Naval Strategy: A Bibliography," supplement to the January 1986 issue of the U.S. Naval Institute *Proceedings*, pp. 41–7; and Peter M. Swartz, USN, "The Maritime Strategy in Review," U.S. Naval Institute *Proceedings*, February 1987, pp. 113–16.

21 See, for instance, John A. Battilega, "Soviet Views of Nuclear Warfare: The Post-Cold War Interviews," in Henry D. Sokolsky (ed.), *Getting MAD: Nuclear Mutually Assured Destruction, Its Origins and Practice*, Strategic Studies Institute (Carlisle Barracks, PA: United States Army War College, November 2004), pp. 151–74.

22 NATO's Striking Fleet, Atlantic (STRIKFLTLANT) was built around the U.S. 2nd Fleet as its nucleus. STRIKFLTLANT was activated in 1952 and disbanded in 2005. The 2nd Fleet was deactivated in 2011. The Standing Naval Force, Atlantic (STANAVFORLANT) was activated in January 1968. STANAVFORLANT was the ancestor of the present-day Standing NATO Maritime Groups.

23 Joel J. Sokolsky, *The Fraternity of the Blue Uniform: Admiral Richard J. Colbert, U.S. Navy, and Allied Naval Cooperation*, Historical Monograph Series 8 (Newport, RI: U. S. Naval War College Press, 1991).

24 Initial steps are captured in Joel J. Sokolsky, *Projecting Stability: NATO and Multilateral Naval Cooperation in the Post Cold War Era* (Kingston, Ontario: Royal Military College of Canada, 1997).

25 Jan S. Breemer, "The End of Naval Strategy: Revolutionary Change and the Future of American Naval Power," *Strategic Review* (Winter 1994), pp. 40–53.

26 Barrett Tillman, "Fear and Loathing in the Post-Naval Era," U.S. Naval Institute *Proceedings*, June 2009, pp. 16–21; and Diego Ruiz Palmer, "The End of the 'Naval Era'?" *NATO Review*, 2010.

27 Captain Henry J. Hendrix, USN, *At What Cost a Carrier?* (Washington, DC: Center for a New American Security, March 2013); and Jon Harper, "Sunset for a Strong Fleet?" *Stars and Stripes* (European edition), June 10, 2014.

28 David Maddox, "Royal Navy pulls out of NATO commitments," *The Scotsman*, July 30, 2013; and Michael Byers, "Sorry, NATO – We're fresh out of warships," *National Post*, March 12, 2014.

29 Charles L. Barry, "NATO's Bold New Concept – CJTF," *JFQ* (Summer 1994), pp. 46–54.

30 This was the case, notably, during the CJTF exercises Strong Resolve in 1998 and 2002. See Lieutenant General Mario da Silva, "Implementing the Combined Joint Task Force Concept," *NATO Review* 46, 4, Winter 1998, pp. 16–19.

31 "Navy ship joins French carrier for Christmas," *The News*, December 23, 2010. The Combined Joint Expeditionary Force's maritime component's first live exercise was Corsican Lion 2012, off the island of Corsica in October 2012. Henri-Pierre Grolleau, "Corsican Lion 2012," *Air International* (February 2013), pp. 84–9.

32 For two rare and insightful assessments of the contribution of naval forces to NATO's Operation Unified Protector, Scott Bishop, "Libya and the Lessons of Naval Power," *Canadian Naval Review* 8, 4 (Winter 2013), pp. 14–18; and Brooke A. Smith-Windsor, *NATO's Maritime Strategy and the Libya Crisis as Seen from the Sea*, Research Paper N°90, NATO Defense College, Rome, March 2013.

33 "La stratégie maritime de l'OTAN: Interview de l'amiral Canova," *Mer et Marine*, July 18, 2014.

34 New Zealand contributed a frigate to Operation Ocean Shield in January 2014, in the framework of its partnership with NATO, marking the first time that a NATO partner nation from a the Asia-Pacific region contributed a ship to the operation. "New Zealand joins NATO's Counter-Piracy Mission Ocean Shield," *Observatory on European Defence* (Rome: Istituto Affari Internazionali, January 2014), p. 1.

35 News Release 627-04, "Allied countries join forces in maritime exercise" (Washington, DC: Department of Defense, July 1, 2004); and Scott Schonauer, "Medshark to Begin Soon," *Stars and Stripes* (European edition), July 4, 2004.

36 Admiral Jonathan Greenert, *CNO's Navigation Plan, 2015–2019* (Washington, DC: Office of the Chief of Naval Operations, August 19, 2014). The rationale for a "three hub Navy" is argued in Bryan McGrath and Mackenzie Eaglen, "America's Navy Needs 12 Carriers & Three Hubs" (Washington, DC: Hudson Institute, March 11, 2014).

37 The air station at Sigonella already hosts rotational deployments of the U.S. Air Force of the *Global Hawk* UAV, such as during Operations Odyssey Dawn and Unified Protector in 2011, and, later this decade, will also be the home base for NATO's own fleet of *Global Hawk* airborne ground surveillance unmanned aircraft. On the forward deployment of the Triton to Sigonella, see Joshua Stewart, "UAV squadron to stand-up Oct. 1; first since 2007," *Navy Times*, February 5, 2013.

38 Julian Halle, "NATO conducts exercise to respond to global crises at short notice," *Defense News*, May 9, 2014.

39 Ensign Zachary Keating, "SBR, HSM-46 Leave for Joint Warrior Exercise," *The Mirror* [Naval Station Mayport, FL] 56, 11, March 20, 2014.

40 On the "high–low mix" and Sea Control Ship controversy, see John Fass Morton, *Mustin: A Naval Family of the 20th Century* (Annapolis, MD: Naval Institute Press, 2003), pp. 336–9.

41 On the U.S. Navy's ship-building plans and challenges, see Ronald O'Rourke, *Navy Force Structure and Shipbuilding Plans: Background and Issues for Congress* (Washington, DC: Congressional Research Service, August 1, 2014).

42 Admiral Benelux is a bilateral arrangement between the navies of Belgium and the Netherlands, dating back to 1948, aimed at pooling assets, sharing training, and enhancing interoperability.

43 Established in 1995, EUROMARFOR is a rotational maritime force assembled periodically from assets contributed by France, Italy, Portugal, and Spain.

44 The European Amphibious Initiative, launched in May 2000, brings together the marine and naval infantry forces of France, Italy, the Netherlands, Spain, and the United Kingdom, with the aim of enhancing interoperability through shared practices and common training. A multinational amphibious exercise is held every five years, the first one of the kind – exercise Emerald Move – having been held off the coast of Senegal in November 2010.

45 The intent of the European Carrier Group Interoperability Initiative, launched in November 2008, is to enhance interoperability, common training, and mutual support among European allied navies around aircraft and helicopter carrier groups and their surface and sub-surface escorts. Participating nations are Belgium, France, Germany, Greece, Italy, the Netherlands, Portugal, Spain, and the United Kingdom. Exercise Levante held in the Mediterranean Sea in October 2012 between the French *Charles de Gaulle* and the Italian *Cavour* carrier task groups was carried out in the context of this initiative.

46 The United Kingdom–Netherlands Amphibious Force (UKNLAF) was established in 1973, the Spanish–Italian Amphibious Force in 1996. In each instance, these on-call formations bring together their marine and naval infantry forces. On the UKNLAF, see Major Marc Brenkman, "The Dutch Contribution to the UKNL Amphibious Force: Adapting to Changes in the Global Security Situation," *RUSI Defence Systems* (Summer 2006), pp. 70–1.

47 On coastal defences during the Cold War, see "Soviets Expand Coastal and Anti-Landing Defense," *International Defense Review* (July 1990), p. 731–4. On contemporary views of China's and Iran's offensive coastal defense capabilities, see Ron Christman, "China's Second Artillery Force: Capabilities and Missions for the Near Seas," in Peter Dutton, Andrew S. Erickson, and Ryan Martinson (eds.), *China's Near Seas Combat Capabilities*, China Maritime Study 11 (Newport: RI: U.S. Naval War College, February 2014); and Anthony H. Cordesman, *The Iranian Sea–Air-Missile Threat to Gulf Shipping* (Washington, DC: Center for Strategic and International Studies, August 14, 2014).

48 Hudson, "Renaissance at Sea," p. 28.

49 On the *Cavour* aircraft carrier, see Francesco Militello Mirto, "Le porte-aéronefs Cavour," *Marine et Forces Navales* 143, February–March 2013, pp. 57–63. On the amphibious ship *Juan Carlos I*, see Emmanuel Huberdean, "L'Armada navigue en eaux troubles," *Marines et Forces Navales* 149, February–March 2014, pp. 39–49.

27

THE EUROPEAN UNION'S APPROACH TO MARITIME SECURITY

Rudolf Roy

Context

Maritime security is an enabler of economic development, trade and regional stability. Freedom of navigation, unimpeded lawful commerce and the peaceful resolution of disputes are based on international law. Maritime piracy and armed robbery at sea, but also other threats to maritime security, can obstruct these rights and affect the international community, including the European Union.

Some 90 per cent of the European Union's external trade and 40 per cent of its internal trade is transported by sea. The European Union (EU) is the third largest importer and the fifth global producer of fisheries and aquaculture. More than 400 million passengers pass through EU ports each year. The EU's maritime regions are home to almost half of its population and account for almost half of its GDP. In terms of territorial surface area, there is more sea than land under the jurisdiction of EU countries.

Consequently, maritime security issues are a key topic for the EU and have been addressed in different frameworks such as the European Security Strategy (2003)[1] or the Integrated Maritime Policy of 2007.[2] The European Security Strategy addresses security in general terms and highlights maritime piracy as a new dimension of organized crime, but solely with a specific focus on the Horn of Africa. The Report on the Implementation of the European Security Strategy of 2008[3] includes a whole paragraph on piracy and makes reference to the first maritime Common Security and Defence Policy (CSDP) Operation – Atalanta. But neither document has a specific reference to the wider maritime security domain.

The 2007 Integrated Maritime Policy looks at the maritime domain in a holistic way, but with limited references to the external dimension and security. In the Commission's Communication of 15 October 2009 – 'Developing the international dimension of the Integrated Maritime Policy of the European Union' – security aspects are highlighted more by stressing the need to ensure maritime safety, maritime security and freedom of navigation.

It was against this background that on 26 April 2010 the Council invited the High Representative, together with the Commission, the European External Action Service (EEAS) and member states to undertake work on a Security Strategy for the global maritime domain.

Moreover, the European Parliament in its Resolution of 12 September 2013 had called on member states to actively engage with the EEAS and the Commission in elaborating the new

European Union Maritime Security Strategy (EUMSS), with the aim of making efficient use of all their varied assets, as well as bearing in mind the identification and creation of new capabilities through pooling and sharing; furthermore, the new strategy should also integrate joint bilateral or multilateral force creation initiatives.[4]

The post-Lisbon Treaty arrangement created a wider scope for action. Although the request initially focused only on one policy area (CSDP), the High Representative/Vice President was able to initiate a cross-sectoral approach involving a broad spectrum of stakeholders. The Joint Communication from the European Commission and the High Representative of the European Union 'For an open and secure global maritime domain: elements for a European Union maritime security strategy',[5] adopted on 6 March 2014, was a demonstration of how broad the approach could be. This joint communication was a proposal from the EU's services setting out a vision of the Union's maritime security interests and threats, and the areas in which cooperation between various maritime players could be enhanced.

Based on this document, the EUMSS[6] was prepared and approved by the General Affairs Council of the European Union on 24 June 2014. As one compares these various documents it becomes clear that the approach on how to address maritime security evolved over time. Initially, in 2010, this policy area was very much focused on maritime security in the context of the Common Foreign Security Policy (CFSP) or even more narrowly on the Common Security and Defence Policy (CSDP) angle. However, given the experience with the EU Naval Force (EUNAVFOR) Operation Atalanta, and the comprehensive approach in the Horn of Africa, a fundamental debate started about whether the EU should concentrate only on the external dimension of maritime security or whether an EU approach should endorse a wider, more integrated approach.

It appeared that in the maritime domain many different sectors and stakeholders come together such as defence policy and navies, law enforcement, customs, justice and home affairs, maritime transport, environmental protection, crisis management, economic activities, fisheries, tourism and the protection of critical maritime infrastructure. This led to the conclusion that any approach to maritime security inevitably had to take a holistic view of all these challenges and that an effective maritime security strategy requires a comprehensive or integrated approach. The term often used in this context is the 'cross-sectoral' approach to maritime security. Another aspect of this discussion was the nexus of internal and external security. Particularly in the maritime domain, the external dimension of the Commission's policies was already very advanced and well articulated. The work on an EU approach to maritime security was thus a good opportunity to create a shared strategic framework that would allow an increased joint approach to maritime security, including both the external and internal dimensions of security. As said, this new approach is a direct result of the Lisbon Treaty.

Approach of the European Union to maritime security

Virtually every major issue which the European Union faces may have a maritime dimension. This relates to global economy, security and stability of states and regions, global competitiveness and job creation, environment, etc. The Lisbon Treaty allows for the pursuit of coherent European external action, as it requires consistency between external action and other policies.

The Joint Communication was structured around three main issues. First, it set out the European interests in the maritime domain; second, it described maritime threats; and third, it formulated elements of response. The same approach was followed in the Maritime Strategy.

Pursuant to Article 22 of the Treaty on European Union (TEU) and on the basis of various existing Commission and Council documents (such as the Internal Security Strategy, the 3rd Maritime Safety Package, the Integrated Maritime Policy and the European Security Strategy), strategic 'interest areas' were identified and highlighted. Reading the two documents (Joint Communication and the EUMSS), it becomes clear that the European interests are wide-ranging, from the prevention of conflicts and the preservation of peace to the protection of the EU's global supply chain. The strategy sets out that its interests are built around the security of the EU, its member states and their citizens. It is also important to underline that the EU's security interests also include the promotion of international cooperation and the rule of law. To facilitate maritime trade and sustainable growth and development are other important elements in this respect.

On the threats side, the EU approach is equally far-reaching. The EUMSS underlined that acts of external aggression include those related to maritime disputes and economic interests at sea. In addition, other threats beyond piracy and armed robbery at sea such as terrorist attacks, organised crime or the proliferation of weapons of mass destruction, including chemical, biological, radiological and nuclear threats, have to be addressed. Threats related to illegal, unreported and unregulated fishing, environmental crimes and climate change make it clear that the perceived threat scenarios have evolved over time. As a consequence, response components have also become more complex and multifaceted. Cyber security and cyber crime should be considered as an additional cross-cutting factor.

Strengthening the EU response to maritime threats

Responding to maritime challenges at the EU level is the core element of the Union's approach on maritime security. Four key principles (cross-sectoral, functional integrity, multilateralism, rules/principles) guide this approach. Both the Joint Communication and the EUMSS advocate a *cross-sectoral* approach. This means that all relevant actors and partners on the civilian and military side (navies, law enforcement, customs, fishery authorities, etc.) ought to cooperate. Private sector and social partners are part of this cooperation.

Functional integrity is another guiding principle that implies that further work can build on existing achievements and that specific functions or tasks can be more efficiently achieved by working together, each party acting within their respective mandates and respecting their competences. Another element of this principle is to avoid creating new structures or legislation and not to create additional administrative burdens.

Maritime issues by their very nature cross borders. Consequently, when dealing with these issues international cooperation and *multilateralism* are required. The EU promotes respect for core values and international law. Full compliance with relevant *rules and principles*, in particular the provisions of the 1982 UN Convention on the Law of the Sea (UNCLOS), are major cornerstones of the EU approach.

Areas of response

The EU approach foresees five areas of response for enhanced cooperation: external action, awareness information sharing, capability development, risk management and research and training.

These areas must be understood as interconnected. For example, joint exercises in the maritime security arena are relevant both in an external action context and in an interagency training context. Similarly, the use of space-related capabilities, such as the Earth Observation programme (Copernicus) and GALILEO, contribute to awareness and surveillance and are part of the discussion on dual-use capabilities.

As described before, the EU approach is built upon existing policies or instruments and the best use of capabilities both at member state and EU level. In relation to external relations, such instruments range from political dialogues with international, regional and bilateral partners, to capacity-building and military or civilian CSDP missions.

Some examples of existing achievements should be mentioned: driven by increased piracy incidents in 2008 off Somalia's coast, the EUNAVFOR Operation Atalanta[7] was launched. It promoted naval cooperation at sea – cooperation with international partners such as NATO's Operation Ocean Shield, the US-led Combined Maritime Forces and the first EU–China naval exercise (held in March 2014). This process can also be seen as a contribution to a more comprehensive approach towards the Horn of Africa. Beyond the naval component, there are well-established development and capacity-building activities such as the regional Maritime Security Programme (MASE) under the European Development Fund (EDF) that support the implementation of the Eastern and Southern Africa–Indian Ocean Regional Strategy and Action Plan, which was adopted in October 2010 in Mauritius to fight piracy and promote maritime security by strengthening the capacity of the region. The Critical Maritime Routes Programme under the Instrument contributing to Stability and Peace (IcSP) contributes to regional maritime capacity-building in support of the Djibouti Code of Conduct since its adoption – assisting the setting up of the Djibouti Regional Training and Documentation Centre, as well the Regional Maritime Information Sharing Centre in Sana'a – the MARSIC project. Another capacity-building project is CRIMLEA (implemented by INTERPOL) that supports maritime law enforcement at a regional level, focusing on investigations. The programme started its activities in the Western Indian Ocean, but now has projects both in the Wider Indian Ocean (CRIMARIO) supporting maritime situational awareness, as well as in the Gulf of Guinea (CRIMGO). It covers activities in the area of law enforcement, information sharing, coast guard and maritime law. All these activities aim to enhance existing regional cooperation, as well as capacity-building, to support information sharing and maritime law enforcement. In addition, there are two CSDP missions: the training mission EUTM Somalia, which trains military security staff, and the EUCAP Nestor, which focuses on coast-guard training as well as expertise in fields such as legislative drafting and the development of organisational structures.

Another good example is the role of the EU as chair of the Contact Group on Piracy off the Coast of Somalia during 2014, which provides a key platform for international coordination and the exchange of information. In 2014, the EU also adopted the Gulf of Guinea strategy that supports the region in addressing maritime insecurity and maritime crime. Another activity is the SEACOP programme, which was set up under the Instrument contributing to Stability and Peace in order to strengthen cooperation against maritime trafficking and to support capacity-building in the fight against international criminal networks in West Africa. The activities within SEACOP aim to counter maritime related crime by building up maritime capabilities, such as the development of regional intelligence and maritime cooperation, the setting up of joint maritime control units or the support of maritime coordination centres.

With the EUMSS, the EU aims to develop these approaches further, in a more systematic way. Cooperation in external action means, in simplified terms, that the Union should be more successful in promoting its maritime security agenda if all member states act together and have a common position in international fora. How the EU common position is to be determined depends, in legal terms, on the respective rules of the concerned area. It is not intended that the EU, as such, will assume roles that it has not had until now, i.e. representing the EU in the respective fora; it means the development and usage of the same messages when engaging on the international scene.

An important aspect of external action is cooperation with international partners. The EUMSS confirms the need to develop partnerships with international organisations, highlighting the UN, NATO, regional partners, such as the African Union or ASEAN, as well as multilateral civil cooperation platforms, but this list is not exhaustive. The document particularly emphasises the dispute-settlement provisions of the 1982 UN Convention on the Law of the Sea (UNCLOS). Another important partner in this respect is NATO. The strategy underlines that in the area of crisis management engagement should be complementary and coordinated. It also cautiously emphasises that this engagement has to be realised in accordance with the agreed framework of partnership between the two organisations. Thus, the EUMSS manages to strike a very delicate balance between short-term and long-term priorities, combining the interests of coastal and non-coastal, as well as NATO and non-NATO member states.[8]

EU–NATO cooperation will be further developed on already existing examples of cooperation. The established dialogue through the Shared Awareness and Deconfliction (SHADE) mechanism in Bahrain is a good tactical tool as it includes the three prominent coalition forces operating in theatre (EU NAVFOR, Ocean Shield, and the Coalition Maritime Forces (CMF)). A similar mechanism exists for training and exercises – TRADE.[9] On the operational side, there has been exchange of information at the tactical level – through the EUNAVFOR Atalanta unclassified 'Mercury'[10] system. Additionally, it has to be noted that the OHQs (Operational Headquarters) of EUNAVFOR Atalanta and NATO's Ocean Shield are both located in the same compound at Northwood, UK, which facilitates communication at a tactical level.

The EU Maritime Security Action Plan

As the EUMSS needed to be translated into more concrete action, the EU adopted a rolling EU Maritime Security Action Plan on 16 December 2014.[11] The Action Plan comprises about 130 sub-actions, which will be implemented in the short to long term by EU institutions and member states. The Action Plan is structured around five thematic areas: (1) external relations and cooperation; (2) information sharing; (3) capability development; (4) risk management and (5) research and training. It covers both the internal and external aspects of the Union's maritime security. From the external action perspective, this includes measures such as engaging with third parties on maritime security matters, further promoting the existing international legal framework, particularly UNCLOS, and contributing to maritime capacity-building in third countries and builds on best practices, such as the Critical Maritime Routes Programme.

The Action Plan is a key tool to translate the objectives elaborated in the EUMSS into concrete actions and it is a 'living document' which will be regularly adapted and reviewed.

In terms of external action, the deepening of coordination on the international scene is one of the cornerstones. This encompasses the promotion of engagement with third partners and international stakeholders on maritime security in particular with NATO and the UN. In operational terms, exercises are envisaged. This may consist of not only exercises with third countries, such as the training exercise on counter-piracy that EUNAVFOR Atalanta conducted with the Chinese Navy in March 2014, but also possibly between other relevant authorities (for example law enforcement) involving military and civilian components. Another important aspect is the mainstreaming of maritime issues into bilateral and international meeting agendas.

In the field of search and rescue capabilities, the Action Plan foresees the support of third countries in establishing and upgrading capabilities related to maritime security. In this regard, specific training, exercises and support in close coordination with any pre-existing bilateral arrangements will be carried out, also through existing instruments, including those within the framework of the EU Civil Protection Mechanism.

Another important topic of the action plan is the strengthening of the ties between the EU external and internal security dimensions and the cross-sectoral cooperation in order to prevent cross-border and organised crime. Highly operational examples can illustrate how, in a cross-sectoral approach, internal/external aspects can be put into concrete action.

Examples of this approach are the Maritime Analysis and Operations Centre – Narcotics (MAOC-N), the Mediterranean Area Anti-Drug Enforcement Coordination Centre (CeCLAD-M) and the cooperation of the EU Naval Operation Atalanta with INTERPOL or the EUROSUR cooperation (European Border Surveillance System).[12]

Under the MAOC cooperation, naval and military assets have been brought together to intercept vessels trafficking bulk shipments of cocaine. There is a link with the EU law enforcement agency, EUROPOL, which participates in regular MAOC meetings.[13] The Mediterranean Area Anti-Drug Enforcement Coordination Centre (CeCLAD-M) carries out operations and intelligence collection in the Mediterranean Sea. The MAOC-N and CeCLAD-M cooperation include non-EU partner countries. In the Action Plan, EU member states are invited to ensure that by 2015 all civilian and military relevant authorities with responsibility for maritime border surveillance share information via the EUROSUR national situational pictures and cooperate via the EUROSUR national coordination centres on a regular basis. This is another example of civil military components working together.

EU NAVFOR Atalanta and INTERPOL bring together military and law-enforcement components, for instance, cooperation on information exchange on suspected pirates collected by members of Atalanta in order to check these data against INTERPOL's databases.[14] The Action Plan builds on such cooperation models and seeks to develop further best practice and cooperation models.

In terms of key capabilities, the EU approach also uses a consistent approach in supporting maritime surveillance and a coordinated use of available space and remote-sensing technologies. This concerns the important area of satellite applications where activities have already begun, for example, the Earth Observation programme (Copernicus) and GALILEO and their use for maritime security purposes. Moreover, the issue of remote-sensing technologies, such as the use of remote-piloted aircraft (RPAS), has been implemented in the Action Plan by highlighting that CSDP missions should be complemented by space-based technology with the applications of RPAS as well as ship reporting systems, *in situ* infrastructure (radar stations) and other surveillance tools, to ensure a global maritime awareness picture.

Conclusion

The Joint Communication on maritime security described the three main elements of a common EU maritime security approach: first, to identify and articulate the main strategic maritime interests of the EU; second, to identify and articulate the maritime threats, challenges and risks to the strategic maritime interests of the EU; and finally to organise the response. This response should provide common policy objectives, common principles and areas of common support as the backbone of a joint strategic framework in order to create coherence between the diverse and wide array of sector specific maritime policies and strategies. Measured against these requirements, the EU Maritime Security Strategy has produced excellent results as it has defined a more systematic approach by addressing the issues of internal and external dimension, finding synergies between military and civilian aspects and by promoting a cross–cutting approach. This conceptual approach has been translated into a more operational action plan. The implementation of this action plan will lead to more security in the maritime domain.

Note: The views expressed in this chapter are the sole responsibility of the author.

Notes

1 Council of the European Union, *European Security Strategy 'A Secure Europe in a better World'* (Brussels: European Union, 12 December 2003).

2 European Commission, *Communication from the Commission to the European Parliament, the Council, the European Economic and Social Committee and the Committee of the Regions of 10 October 2007 on an Integrated Maritime Policy for the European Union*, COM (2007) 575 (Brussels: European Union, 2007).

3 Council of the European Union, *Report on the Implementation of the European Security Strategy – Providing Security in a Changing World*, 407–408 (Brussels: European Union, 11 December 2008).

4 European Parliament, *Resolution of 12 September 2013 on the Maritime Dimension of the Common Security and Defence Policy*, 2012/2318 (INI).

5 European Commission, *Joint Communication to the European Parliament and the Council: For an open and secure global maritime domain: elements for a European Union maritime security strategy*, JOIN (2014) 9 (Brussels: European Union, 3 March 2013).

6 Council of the European Union, *European Union Maritime Security Strategy*, 11205/14 POLGEN 103 (Brussels: European Union, 24 June 2014).

7 Council of the European Union, *Joint Action 2008/851/CFSP of 10 November 2008 on a European Union Military Operation to Contribute to the Deterrence, Prevention and Repression of Acts of Piracy and Armed Robbery off the Somali Coast*, OJ L 301 (Brussels: European Union, 12 November 2008), 33.

8 Andrea Frontini, 'The European Union Maritime Security Strategy: Sailing Uncharted Waters?' European Policy Centre Commentary, 26 June 2014.

9 The 'Training Awareness and Deconfliction' mechanism (TRADE) is a voluntary coordination forum attended by governments and organizations involved in providing nations in the Western Indian Oceans region affected by piracy with maritime tactical training. The first TRADE meeting was held in March 2010 and TRADE has been held approximately every quarter since then. TRADE is co-chaired by NATO and EUNAVFOR, participants are: NATO, EU, CMF/NAVCENT, IMO and others.

10 The web-based Mercury network provides near-real-time chat between participants in any of the counter-piracy missions to share threat notifications and declare intentions. Mercury is operated by the Maritime Security Centre Horn of Africa (MSCHOA) of the European Union.

11 Council of the European Union, *EU Maritime Security Strategy Action Plan*, 17002/14 (Brussels: European Union, 16 December 2014).

12 European Parliament and Council of the European Union, *Regulation No 1052/2013 of the European Parliament and the Council Establishing the European Border Surveillance System (Eurosur)* (OJ L 295, 6 November 2013), 11.

13 The headquarters of MAOC is staffed by Country Liaison Officers (CLOs) representing the police, customs, military and maritime authorities. The European Commission, EUROPOL, the United Nations Office on Drugs and Crime (UNODC), the European Monitoring Centre for Drugs and Drug Addiction (EMCDDA), the European External Action Service (EEAS), the European Defence Agency (EDA), EUROJUST and FRONTEX are all observers of MAOC (N).

14 Council of the European Union, *Decision 2010/766/CFSP of 7 December 2010 amending Joint Action 2008/851/CFSP on a European Union Military Operation to Contribute to the Deterrence, Prevention and Repression of Acts of Piracy and Armed Robbery off the Somali Coast* (OJ L 327/49, 11 December 2010).

INDEX

Page numbers in *italics* are figures; with 't' are tables; with 'n' are notes.